INTRODUCTION TO ECONOMICS

SECOND EDITION

Marc Lieberman
Department of Economics
New York University

Robert E. Hall
Department of Economics
Stanford University

THOMSON
™
SOUTH-WESTERN

Australia · Canada · Mexico · Singapore · Spain · United Kingdom · United States

THOMSON
SOUTH-WESTERN

Introduction to Economics, 2e

Marc Lieberman and Robert E. Hall

Vice President / Editorial Director:
Jack W. Calhoun

Vice President / Editor-in-Chief:
Michael P. Roche

Publisher of Economics:
Michael B. Mercier

Acquisitions Editor:
Michael W. Worls

Sr. Developmental Editor:
Susanna C. Smart

Executive Marketing Manager:
Janet Hennies

Senior Marketing Manager:
John Carey

Sr. Marketing Coordinator:
Jenny Fruechtenicht

Production Editor:
Daniel C. Plofchan

Manufacturing Coordinators:
Sandee Milewski

Manager of Technology, Editorial:
Vicky True

Technology Project Manager:
Peggy Buskey

Media Editor:
Pam Wallace

Compositor:
Pre-Press Company, Inc.
East Bridgewater, MA

Sr. Design Project Manager:
Michelle Kunkler

Cover and Internal Designer:
Ramsdell Design, Cincinnati

Cover Image:
© Getty Images, Inc.

Printer:
QuebecorWorld
Versailles, KY

For more information
contact South-Western,
5191 Natorp Boulevard,
Mason, Ohio 45040.
Or you can visit our Internet site at:
hyyp://www.swlearning.com

Brief Contents

Preface

TO THE INSTRUCTOR

This book provides an introduction to economic *principles*—and how those principles are applied in the real world. It's based on our well-received one-year principles book (*Economics: Principles and Applications*, by Robert Hall and Marc Lieberman, now in its third edition), but substantially rewritten for a one-semester course in economic principles that combines both micro- and macroeconomics.

While this book covers fewer topics than a one-year course, we believe we've avoided frustrating and confusing gaps in coverage. In revising this book, we have tried to stick to a simple rule: If a topic can't be covered in a fully satisfying way, don't introduce it at all. The result is a book that provides a comprehensive introduction to economic principles and applications that can be read and absorbed in one semester.

The overall approach of Introduction to Economics can be summed up as follows:

- We avoid nonessential material. When we believed a topic was not essential to a basic understanding of economics, we left it out. The features your students will find in our book are there to help them understand basic economic theory itself, or to help them explore sources of information on their own, using the Internet.
- We explain difficult concepts patiently. Because we have avoided the encyclopedic approach, we can explain the topics we do cover thoroughly and patiently. We try to lead students, step-by-step, through each aspect of the theory, through each graph, and through each numerical example. Moreover, as we developed this book, we asked other experienced teachers to tell us which aspects of economic theory are hardest for their students to learn, and we've paid special attention to those trouble spots.
- We use concrete examples. Students learn best when they see how economics can explain the world around them. Whenever possible, we develop the theory using real-world examples. When we employ hypothetical examples because they illustrate the theory more clearly, we try to make them realistic. In addition, each chapter ends with a thorough, extended application of the material.

SPECIAL PEDAGOGICAL FEATURES

We've chosen features that reinforce the basic theory, rather than distract from it. Here is a list of the most important ones, and how we believe they help students focus on essentials.

The Eight Basic Principles of Economics

Economic theory makes repeated use of some fundamental ideas that appear again and again in many contexts. To truly understand what economics is all about, students need to learn what these central ideas are, and they need to see them in action in different contexts. We've identified and stressed eight basic principles of economics in this text. These are:

- Maximization Subject to Constraints
- Opportunity Cost
- Specialization and Exchange
- Markets and Equilibrium
- Policy Tradeoffs
- Marginal Decision Making
- Short-Run versus Long-Run Outcomes
- The Importance of Real Values

A full statement of these principles appears in Chapter 1 (pp. 13–14), and a full statement of each individual principle appears again later, when it is *used* for the *first* time. Thereafter, whenever the principle is used in a significant way, it is identified with a key symbol shown in the margin.

Dangerous Curves

Anyone who teaches economics for a while learns that, semester after semester, students tend to make the same familiar errors. In class, in office hours, and on exams, students seem pulled as if by gravity toward certain logical pitfalls in thinking about, and using, economic theory. We've discovered in our own classrooms that merely explaining the theory properly isn't enough; the most common errors need to be *confronted*, and the student needs to be shown *specifically* why a particular logical path is incorrect. This was the genesis of our *Dangerous Curves* feature, which anticipate the most common traps in economics and warn students just when they are most likely to fall victim to them. We've been delighted to hear from instructors how effective this feature has been in overcoming the most common points of confusion for their students.

Using the Theory

This text is full of applications that are woven throughout the narrative. In addition, virtually every chapter ends with an extended application—Using the Theory—that pulls together several of the tools learned in that chapter. These are step-by-step presentations that help students see how the tools of economics can explain things about the world—-things that would be difficult to explain without those tools.

WHAT'S DIFFERENT IN CONTENT, AND WHY

In addition to the special features just described, you will find some important differences in topical approach and arrangement. These, too, are designed to make the theory stand out more cleanly, and to make learning easier. The pedagogical differences in this text are the product of years of classroom experience.

A few of the differences may require minor adjustments in class lectures, and these are listed below. But we would be remiss if we merely listed them without also pointing out why we believe they are improvements.

Innovations in Microeconomics

- *Scarcity, Choice, and Economic Systems* (Chapter 2): This early chapter, while covering standard material like opportunity cost, also provides early coverage of comparative advantage, and the basic principle of specialization and exchange. We have placed them near the front of our book because we believe they provide important building blocks for much that comes later. For example, economies of scale (Chapter 5) can result from comparative advantage and specialization within the firm. International trade (Chapter 18) can be a special application of these principles to trade between nations.
- *The Theory of the Firm* (Chapter 6): Students quite naturally think of firms as facing *downward*-sloping demand curves—not horizontal ones. We have found that they have an easier time learning the theory of the firm with the more familiar, downward sloping demand curve than with the perfectly competitive model.

Further, by treating the theory of the firm in a separate chapter, *before* perfect competition, we can separate concepts that apply in *all* market structures from concepts that are unique to perfect competition. This avoids confusion later on.

- *Description vs. Assessment* (Chapters 7, 8, and 10): We treat the four basic market structures comprehensively as unified topics, and include descriptions of different markets and assessments of market outcomes (Chapters 7 and 8).

Our book covers economic efficiency in a single chapter (Chapter 10). The advantages of this are 1) it permits you to focus on description and prediction when teaching about the four market structures; 2) a chapter devoted to efficiency and market failure allows a more comprehensive treatment of the topic; and 3) our approach—in which students learn about efficiency after they have mastered the four market structures—allows students to study efficiency with the perspective needed to really understand it.

Innovations in Macroeconomics

- *Long-Run Macroeconomics* (Chapter 14): This text presents long-run growth before short-run fluctuations.

We believe this treatment is better for two reasons. First, the long-run model makes full use of the tools of supply and demand, providing for an easier transition from microeconomics to macroeconomics. Second, we believe that economic fluctuations are best understood by viewing them as deviations from a long-run trend. This requires a prior treatment of how that long-run trend is determined.

In addition, our treatment is analytical. We use a very simple supply and demand framework to explain the causes—and costs—of economic growth in both rich and poor countries.

- *Economic Fluctuations* (Chapter 15): Our discussion of the short-run macroeconomic model includes all of the *insights* of the Keynesian cross diagram without the diagram itself. Our view is that this diagram—which takes time for students to master—is best left out of a one-semester course. Nevertheless, an instructor who wants to present the diagram should find substantial support for it in the chapter.
- *Aggregate Demand and Aggregate Supply* (Chapter 17): Finally, in this text, the *AD* and *AS* curves do not appear until Chapter 17, where they are fully explained. Our treatment of aggregate supply is based on a very simple mark-up model that our students have found very accessible.

Building a Syllabus

We have arranged the contents of each chapter, and the table of contents as a whole, according to the order of presentation that we recommend. But we've also built in some flexibility. For example, Chapter 4 develops consumer theory with both marginal utility and (in an appendix) indifference curves, allowing you to present either method in class. If you wish to highlight international trade, you could assign Chapter 18 immediately after Chapter 3. And if you wish to teach the efficiency properties of perfect competition along with the chapter on perfect competition, you can assign the first parts of Chapter 14 immediately after Chapter 7.

Finally, we have included only those chapters that we thought were both essential and teachable in a one-semester course. But nothing in Chapter 9 (Labor Markets and Wages) or Chapter 10 (Economic Efficiency and the Role of Government) is required to understand the other chapters in the book. And the treatment of macroeconomics could end with Chapter 16, leaving out Chapter 17 (Aggregate Supply and Demand). Finally, an instructor could drop Chapter 18 (International Trade and Comparative Advantage), since comparative advantage as a general concept is fully treated earlier in Chapter 2.

NEW TO THE SECOND EDITION

For this second edition, we've incorporated many excellent suggestions from reviewers and adopters. While the overall approach and philosophy of the book remains unchanged, you'll find that every chapter has been affected by the revision.

For example, we've written eight entirely new end-of-chapter "Using the Theory" sections and done major rewrites on another four. Within each chapter, we've replaced examples and adjusted the narrative on every page, recognizing that often a more apt example or a slight change in phrasing can vastly improve clarity. We've worked hard to clarify and simplify figures, and increased the use of caption boxes that enable students to work their way through diagrams more easily. We've added a few dozen new Dangerous Curves boxes, in response to some great suggestions from instructors. And, of course, we've updated all tables and figures with new data, and adjusted content to reflect the rapid economic changes that have taken place over the past few years.

In addition, we've made some major changes that all instructors should know about in preparing their course.

- *Chapter 1 (What Is Economics?):* We've added entrepreneurship as a fourth resource. We've substantially rewritten the math appendix (to emphasize shifts vs. movements along curves, and used tangent lines to measure the slope of a curve), and moved it to the end of this chapter.
- *Chapter 2 (Scarcity, Choice and Economic Systems):* We've revised the discussion of opportunity and incorporated "the opportunity cost of college" as a running example. We've also added a new section on technological change and the PPF.

- *Chapter 4 (Consumer Choice):* This chapter has been extensively reorganized to allow a genuine choice between the marginal utility approach (in the body) and the indifference curve approach (in an expanded appendix). Instructors wishing to cover the indifference curve approach should assign all sections except "The Marginal Utility Approach," using the appendix instead. This substitution now results in a seamless fit with the rest of the chapter. We've also added a discussion of behavioral economics.
- *Chapter 5 (Production and Cost):* We've eliminated the section "Why Employees," and shortened the discussion of different types of business firms to make the chapter leaner. Also, to help motivate the chapter, we've brought forward material on *minimum efficient scale* and *natural monopoly.*
- *Chapter 6 (How Firms Make Decisions—Profit Maximization):* We've removed the material on the principal-agent problem from this chapter, paid more attention to the relationship between "totals" and "marginals," and revised the data in our running examples to bring out the cost concepts more clearly.
- *Chapter 8 (Monopoly and Imperfect Competition):* The section on price discrimination is moved to an appendix, and can be optional. A full discussion of *network externalities* has been added as an explanation for monopoly, replacing the older (and increasingly less-relevant) explanation of *controlling scarce inputs.*
- *Chapter 9 (The Labor Market and Wage Rates):* The chapter begins with a new table, providing more interesting and relevant data on wage inequality. We've also tried to write more balanced discussions of labor unions and the minimum wage.
- *Chapter 10 (Economic Efficiency and the Role of Government):* We've reorganized this chapter significantly, and enhanced the discussion of monopoly as a market failure and the regulation of natural monopoly. The material on externalities includes a fully-integrated discussion of the Coase Theorem. We added a section on tradable permits, and reframed the discussion of the free-rider problem (in the context of externalities, rather than public goods).
- *Chapter 12 (Production, Income, and Employment):* The chapter now uses the term "investment" (and the symbol "I" with no superscript) to indicate investment in GDP, and the term *planned investment* (and the symbol I^P) to indicate investment as a component of total spending. To help students see the relevance of this material, the chapter ends with a discussion of GDP after 9/11/01.
- *Chapter 14 (Economic Growth and Rising Living Standards):* The first half of the chapter has been entirely rewritten, and the rest substantially revised. The chapter is now organized around a simple framework separating the factors responsible for growth, and stressing the role of productivity.
- *Chapter 18 (Comparative Advantage and the Gains from Trade):* We've added the ideas behind Heckscher-Ohlin (without using the term) to explain how comparative advantage arises, and included a new section on "Attitudes and Influence on Trade Policy," including the role of the WTO, multilateral agreements, and industries as con-

sumers. Our development of the logic behind comparative advantage is reorganized with a new running example.

Finally, we have posted a more extensive list of chapter-by-chapter changes on our Web site, (http://lieberman.swlearning.com), indicating page numbers where significant changes have occurred.

TEACHING AND LEARNING AIDS

To help you to present the most interesting principles courses possible, we have created an extensive set of supplementary items. Many of them can be downloaded from the Lieberman/Hall Web site (http://lieberman.swlearning.com) Contact your Thomson Learning sales representative for more information on any of these products. The list includes:

For the Student

- The *Active Learning Guide,* by Geoffrey A. Jehle of Vassar College, provides numerous exercises and self-tests for problem-solving practice. It is a valuable tool to help students strengthen their knowledge of economics.
- The *Lieberman/Hall Xtra!* (http://liebermanxtra.swlearning.com) provides students with complimentary access to the robust set of additional online learning tools found at the site. Here is a tour through some of the study support features you will find there:
    - **Diagnostic Pretests** These innovative quizzes offer students diagnostic self-assessment of their comprehension of each chapter and an individualized plan for directed study.
    - **The Graphing Workshop** The Graphing Workshop is a one-stop learning resource for help in mastering the language of graphs.
    - **CNN Video Clips** CNN video segments bring the real world right to students' desktops.
    - **Ask the Instructor Video Clips** Via streaming video, difficult concepts from each chapter are explained and illustrated by an economics instructor, Dr. Peter Olson from Indiana University.
    - **Economic Applications (e-con @pps)** EconNews Online, EconDebate Online, EconData Online, and EconLinks Online features help students' with theoretical concepts through hands-on exploration and analysis of the latest economic news stories, policy debates, and data.

Xtra! is available as an optional package with the text.

- **NEW** to this edition—and in conjunction with these Xtra! features—are *Economic Applications exercises* at the end of every chapter. Prepared by Brian J. Peterson (Manchester College) and Hamid Azari-Rad (SUNY-New Paltz), the exercises direct students to one or more of the applications to solve problems through brief research.
- *Economics Alive!* CD-ROMs are interactive multimedia study aids that provide a high-tech, high-fun way to study economics. Through a combination of animated presentations, interactive graphing exercises, and simulations, the core principles of economics come to life in an upbeat and entertaining way. Available in macro and micro versions. http://econalive.swlearning.com.

- *The Wall Street Journal.* The Hall and Lieberman texts are available with a special fifteen-week *Wall Street Journal* subscription offer. Have your instructor contact your Thomson Learning sales representative for package pricing and ordering information.
- With *InfoTrac® College Edition* students can receive anytime, anywhere, online access to a database of full-text articles from hundreds of scholarly and popular periodicals such as *Newsweek, Fortune, American Economist,* and the *Quarterly Journal of Economics.* An InfoTrac® subscription card can be packaged with this text.
- *Hits on the Web: Economics.* This resource booklet supports students' research efforts on the Internet and covers materials such as: Browsing the Web, Finding Information, Email discussion Groups, Newsgroups, and Documenting Internet Sources for research.

For The Instructor:

- An *Instructor's Manual,* by Jane Himarios of The University of Texas, Arlington, provides chapter outlines, teaching ideas, Experiential Exercises for many chapters, and suggested answers to the end-of-chapter questions and problems and the Economic Applications exercises.
- The *Test Bank,* revised by Dennis Hanseman, University of Cincinnati, contains approximately 3,000 multiple-choice and true/false questions.
- *ExamView Computerized Testing Software* contains all of the questions in the Test Bank. ExamView is an easy-to-use test creation package compatible with both Microsoft Windows and Macintosh client software. You can select questions by previewing them on the screen, selecting them by number, or selecting them randomly. Questions, instructions, and answers can be edited, and new questions can easily be added. You can also administer quizzes online—over the Internet, through a local area network (LAN), or through a wide area network (WAN).
- *Full-Color Transparency Acetates* are available for many graphs and illustrations in the text.
- *PowerPoint Lecture and Figures Slides.* Available only on the Web site and the IRCD are two versions of the PowerPoint presentations: a comprehensive lecture outline presentation for use in the classroom and a set of key graphs from the text, many with animation.
- *Instructor's Resource CD-ROM* allows quick access to instructor ancillaries from your desktop. This easy-to-use CD allows you to review, edit, and copy exactly the material you need.
- *The Principles of Economics Videotape* is a 40-minute production that offers students an insightful overview of ten important economic concepts. The Principles of Economics video shows viewers how to apply economic principles to their daily lives. This video is filled with interviews from some of the country's leading economists, includes profiles of real students facing economic choices, and shows the economy's impact on U.S. and foreign companies.

- **CNN *Video with Integration Guide*** Professors can bring the real world into the classroom by using the CNN Principles of Economics Video Updates. This video provides current stories of economic interest, and the accompanying integration guide provides a summary and discussion questions for each clip. The video is produced in cooperation with Turner Learning Inc.

For Instructors and Students:

- The ***Lieberman/Hall Web site*** (http://lieberman. swlearning.com) contains a wealth of useful teaching and learning resources. Important features available at the Web site include:
  - Downloadable ancillary materials for instructors and students.
  - *Interactive Quizzes* with feedback on completed quizzes can be emailed to instructors.
- ***Favorite Ways to Learn Economics: Student* and *Instructor Edition*s** Authors David Anderson (Centre College) and Jim Chasey (Homewood Flossmoor High School) use experiments to bring economic education to life. Students are far more likely to retain new knowledge when it is reinforced with hands-on experiments. *Favorite Ways to Learn Economics* is a lab manual for the classroom or for individual study that contains experiments and problem sets to reinforce the key principles of economics covered in most college and AP courses.
- ***MarketSim.*** MarketSim, by Tod Porter at Youngstown State University, is an online simulation designed to help students in microeconomics classes better understand how markets work, by having students take on the roles of consumers and producers in a simulated economy. In the simulations, students "make" and "accept" offers to buy and sell labor and goods asynchronously via the Internet.
- ***TextChoice.*** TextChoice is a custom format of Thomson Learning's online digital content that provides the fastest, easiest way for you to create your own learning materials. You may select content from hundreds of best-selling titles, choose material from our numerous databases, and add your own material. http://thomsoncustom.com.
- ***eCoursepacks.*** Create a customizable, easy-to-use, online companion for any course with eCourse packs. eCourse packs give educators access to current content from thousands of popular, professional, and academic periodicals, including NACRA and Darden cases, and business and industry information from Gale. You can easily add your own material—even collecting a royalty if you choose. http:// ecoursepacks.swlearning.com.
- ***WebTutor Advantage.*** *WebTutor Advantage* is an interactive, Web-based, student supplement on WebCT and/or BlackBoard that harnesses the power of the Internet to deliver innovative learning aids to actively engage students. The instructor can incorporate WebTutor as an integral part of the course, or the students can use it on their own as a study guide. Benefits to students include automatic and immediate feedback from quizzes and exams; interactive, mul-

timedia-rich explanation of concepts; online exercises that reinforce what students have learned; flashcards that include audio support; and greater interaction and involvement through online discussion forums. Visit WebTutor to see a demo and for more information at http://webtutor. swlearning.com.

- ***WebTutor Toolbox.*** WebTutor ToolBox provides instructors with links to content from the book companion Web site, and communication tools to instructors and students that include a course calendar, chat, and email.

ACKNOWLEDGMENTS

Our greatest debt in this second edition is to the reviewers who carefully read the book and provided numerous suggestions for improvements. While we could not incorporate all their ideas, we did carefully evaluate each one of them. To these reviewers, and those of the previous edition, we are most grateful:

Steve Abid, *Grand Rapids Community College*
Ali Akarca, *University of Illinois, Chicago*
Donna Bueckman, *University of Tennessee, Knoxville*
James Burnell, *College of Wooster*
Barbara Craig, *Oberlin College*
Sherman Folland, *Oakland University*
Arthur Gibb, *U.S. Naval Academy*
David Jaeger, *Hunter College*
Geoffrey Jehle, *Vassar College*
Roger Little, *U.S. Naval Academy*
Diego Méndez-Carbajo, *Illinois Wesleyan University*
Stan Mitchell, *McLennan Community College*
Paul Munyon, *Grinnell College*
Oladele Omosegbon, *Indiana Wesleyan University*
Z. Edward O'Relley, *North Dakota State University*
Robert Schenk, *St. Joseph's College*
Lee J. VanScyoc, *University of Wisconsin, Oshkosh*

We also wish to acknowledge the talented and dedicated group of instructors who helped put together a supplementary package that is second to none. Geoffrey Jehle of Vassar College co-wrote the *Active Learning Guide* and created numerous improvements to this edition, making it even more user-friendly for active learning. Jane Himarios of the University of Texas, Arlington, revised the *Instructor's Manual*, and the Test Bank was carefully revised by Dennis Hanseman. We appreciate the contributions of Hamid Azari-Rad of SUNY-New Paltz and Brian J. Peterson of Manchester College, both of whom created the new Economic Applications exercises for this edition. And we are grateful to Mark Karscig of Central Missouri State University for his contributions to the *Using the Theory* exercises for the Web site. In addition, we appreciate the work of the three people who contributed to the Web site's Online

Quizzes: Brian Peterson, Jeff Johnson, and Doug Kinnear. Our thanks go also to John and Pamela Hall (Western Washington University) who thoroughly revised and improved the PowerPoint slides for this edition.

The beautiful book you are holding would not exist except for the hard work of a talented team of professionals. Book production was overseen by Dan Plofchan, Production Editor at Thomson Business and Professional Publishing, and undertaken by Pre-Press Company, Inc. At Pre-Press, all things are possible because of the dedicated work of Gordon Laws. Dan and Gordon showed remarkable patience, as well as an unflagging concern for quality throughout the process. We couldn't have asked for better production partners. Leslie Miller did an excellent job finding errors and omissions in early drafts.

The overall look of the book and cover was planned by Michelle Kunkler and executed by Craig Ramsdell of Ramsdell Design. John Hill managed the photo program, and Sandee Milewski made all the pieces come together in her role as Manufacturing Coordinator.

Finally, we are especially grateful for the hard work of the dedicated and professional Thomson Business and Professional Publishing editorial, marketing, and sales teams. Mike Worls, Acquisitions Editor, has once again shepherded this text through publication with remarkable skill and devotion. John Carey, Senior Marketing Manager, and Janet Hennies, Executive Marketing Manager, have done a first-rate job getting the message out to instructors and sales reps. Susan Smart, Senior Development Editor, did a great job keeping the text on track and managing the ancillaries, and her patience, flexibility, and skill went far beyond the call of duty. Peggy Buskey, Technology Project Manager, has put together a wonderful package of media tools, along with the help of Pam Wallace, Media Editor. And the Thomson Business and Professional Publishing sales representatives have been extremely persuasive advocates for the book. We sincerely appreciate all their efforts!

A REQUEST

Although we have worked hard on the second edition of this book, we know there is always room for further improvement. For that, our fellow users are indispensable. We invite your comments and suggestions wholeheartedly. We especially welcome your suggestions for additional "Using the Theory" sections and "Dangerous Curves." You may send your comments to either of us care of Thomson Business and Professional Publishing.

Marc Lieberman / Bob Hall

ABOUT THE AUTHORS

Marc Lieberman is Clinical Associate Professor of Economics at New York University. He received his Ph.D. from Princeton University. Lieberman has presented his extremely popular Principles of Economics course at Harvard, Vassar, the University of California, Santa Cruz, and the University of Hawaii, as well as at NYU, where he won the university's Golden Dozen teaching award and also the Economics Society Award for Excellence in Teaching. He is coeditor and contributor to *The Road to Capitalism: Economic Transformation in Eastern Europe and the Former Soviet Union.* Lieberman has consulted for the Bank of America and the Educational Testing Service. In his spare time, he is a professional screenwriter. He co-wrote the script for *Love Kills,* a thriller that aired on the USA Cable Network, and he teaches screenwriting at NYU's School of Continuing and Professional Studies.

Robert E. Hall is a prominent applied economist. He is the Robert and Carole McNeil Professor of Economics at Stanford University and Senior Fellow at Stanford's Hoover Institution where he conducts research on inflation, unemployment, taxation, monetary policy, and the economics of high technology. He received his Ph.D. from MIT and has taught there as well as at the University of California, Berkeley. Hall is Director of the research program on Economic Fluctuations of the National Bureau of Economic Research, and Chairman of the Bureau's Committee on Business Cycle Dating, which maintains the semiofficial chronology of the U.S. business cycle. He has published numerous monographs and articles in scholarly journals, and coauthored a popular intermediate text. Hall has advised the Treasury Department and the Federal Reserve Board on national economic policy, and has testified on numerous occasions before congressional committees.

Contents

PART IV: MACROECONOMICS: BASIC CONCEPTS

PART VI: INTERNATIONAL TRADE

What Is Economics?

Economics. The word conjures up all sorts of images: manic stock traders on Wall Street, an economic summit meeting in a European capital, a somber television news anchor announcing good or bad news about the economy. . . . You probably hear about economics several times each day. What exactly *is* economics?

First, economics is a *social science,* so it seeks to explain something about *society.* In this sense, it has something in common with psychology, sociology, and political science. But economics is different from these other social sciences, because of *what* economists study and *how* they study it. Economists ask fundamentally different questions, and they answer them using tools that other social scientists find rather exotic.

ECONOMICS, SCARCITY, AND CHOICE

A good definition of economics, which stresses the difference between economics and other social sciences, is the following:

> *Economics is the study of choice under conditions of scarcity.*

Economics The study of choice under conditions of scarcity.

1

This definition may appear strange to you. Where are the familiar words we ordinarily associate with economics: "money," "stocks and bonds," "prices," "budgets," . . . ? As you will soon see, economics deals with all of these things and more. But first, let's take a closer look at two important ideas in this definition: scarcity and choice.

Scarcity and Individual Choice

Think for a moment about your own life—your daily activities, the possessions you enjoy, the surroundings in which you live. Is there anything you don't have that you'd *like* to have? Anything you'd like *more* of? If your answer is "no," congratulations! You are well advanced on the path of Zen self-denial. The rest of us, however, feel the pinch of limits to our material standard of living. This simple truth is at the very core of economics. It can be restated this way: We all face the problem of **scarcity**.

At first glance, it may seem that you suffer from an infinite variety of scarcities. There are so many things you might like to have right now—a larger room or apartment, a new car, more clothes . . . the list is endless. But a little reflection suggests that your limited ability to satisfy these desires is based on two other, more basic limitations: scarce *time* and scarce *spending power*.

> As individuals, we face a scarcity of time and spending power. Given more of either, we could each have more of the goods and services that we desire.

The scarcity of spending power is no doubt familiar to you. We've all wished for higher incomes so that we could afford to buy more of the things we want. But the scarcity of time is equally important. So many of the activities we enjoy—seeing a movie, taking a vacation, making a phone call—require time as well as money. Just as we have limited spending power, we also have a limited number of hours in each day to satisfy our desires.

Because of the scarcities of time and spending power, each of us is forced to make *choices*. We must allocate our scarce *time* to different activities: work, play, education, sleep, shopping, and more. We must allocate our scarce *spending power* among different goods and services: housing, food, furniture, travel, and many others. And each time we choose to buy something or do something, we also choose *not* to buy or do something else.

Economists study the choices we make as individuals and also the *consequences* of those choices. For example, in 2002 and 2003, large numbers of consumers in the United States decided to spend less on air travel, due to concerns about safety and increased delays at airport security checkpoints. Many shifted their vacation spending toward home-improvement projects. Collectively, these decisions led to a contraction and layoffs in the airline industry, and in businesses associated with air travel (e.g., hotels and car rental firms). At the same time, businesses associated with home improvement (e.g., lumber mills, contractors, hardware stores) expanded, and hired additional workers.

Economists also study the more subtle and indirect effects of individual choice on our society. Will most Americans continue to live in houses or—like Europeans—will most of us end up in apartments? Will we have an educated and well-informed citizenry? Will traffic congestion in our cities continue to worsen or is there relief in sight? These questions hinge, in large part, on the separate decisions

Scarcity A situation in which the amount of something available is insufficient to satisfy the desire for it.

of millions of people. To answer them requires an understanding of how individuals make choices under conditions of scarcity.

Scarcity and Social Choice

Now let's think about scarcity and choice from *society*'s point of view. What are the goals of our society? We want a high standard of living for our citizens, clean air, safe streets, good schools, and more. What is holding us back from accomplishing all of these goals in a way that would satisfy everyone? You already know the answer: scarcity.

In society's case, the problem is a scarcity of **resources**—the things we use to make goods and services that help us achieve our goals. Economists classify resources into four categories:

1. **Labor** is the time human beings spend producing goods and services.
2. **Capital** is something produced that is long-lasting, and used to make *other* things that we value. Note the word *long-lasting*. If something is used up quickly in the production process—like the flour a baker uses to make bread—it is generally *not* considered capital. A good rule of thumb is that capital should last at least a year, although most types of capital last considerably longer.

   It's useful to distinguish two different types of capital. **Physical capital** consists of things like machinery and equipment, factory buildings, computers, and even hand tools like hammers and screwdrivers. These are all long-lasting *physical* goods that are used to make other things.

   Human capital consists of the skills and knowledge possessed by workers. These satisfy our definition of capital: They are *produced* (through education and training), they help us produce *other* things, and they last for many years, typically through an individual's working life.[1]

   The **capital stock** is the total amount of capital at a nation's disposal at any point in time. It consists of all the physical and human capital made in previous periods that is still productively useful.
3. **Land** is the physical space on which production takes place, as well as the natural resources found under it or on it, such as crude oil, iron, coal, or fertile soil.
4. **Entrepreneurship** is an individual's ability (and the willingness to *use* this ability) to combine the *other* resources into a productive enterprise. An entrepreneur may be an *innovator* who comes up with an original idea for a business or a *risk taker* who provides her own funds or time to nurture a project with uncertain rewards.

Anything *produced* in the economy comes, ultimately, from some combination of these resources. Think about the last lecture you attended at your college. You were consuming a service—a college lecture. What went into producing that service? Your instructor was supplying labor. Many types of capital were used as well. The physical capital included desks, chairs, a chalkboard or transparency projector, the classroom building itself, and the computer your instructor may have used to

Resources The labor, capital, land and natural resources, and entrepreneurship that are used to produce goods and services.

Labor The time human beings spend producing goods and services.

Capital Something produced that is long-lasting and used to produce other goods.

Physical capital The part of the capital stock consisting of physical goods, such as machinery, equipment, and factories.

Human capital The skills and training of the labor force.

Capital stock The total amount of capital in a nation that is productively useful at a particular point in time.

Land The physical space on which production takes place, as well as the naturally occurring materials that come with it.

Entrepreneurship The ability and willingness to combine the *other* resources—labor, capital, and natural resources—into a productive enterprise.

---

[1] An individual's human capital is ordinarily supplied along with her labor time. (When your instructor lectures or holds office hours, she is providing both labor time and her skills as an economist and teacher.) Still, it's often useful to distinguish the *time* a worker provides (her labor) from any skills or *knowledge* possessed (human capital).

compose lecture notes. In addition, there was human capital—your instructor's specialized knowledge and lecturing skills. There was land—the property on which your classroom building sits. And some individual or group had to play the role of innovator and risk taker in order to combine the labor, capital, and natural resources needed to create and guide your institution in its formative years. (If you attend a public college or university, this entrepreneurial role was largely filled by the state government and the risk takers were the state's taxpayers.)

The scarcity of resources like these causes the scarcity of all goods and services produced from them.

> As a society, our resources—land, labor, capital, and entrepreneurship—are insufficient to produce all the goods and services we might desire. In other words, society faces a scarcity of resources.

This stark fact about the world helps us understand the choices a society must make. Do we want a more educated citizenry? Of course. But that will require more labor—construction workers to build more classrooms and teachers to teach in them. It will require more land—space for classrooms and natural resources to build them. And it will require more capital—cement mixers, trucks, and more. These very same resources, however, could instead be used to produce *other* things that we find desirable, things such as new homes, hospitals, automobiles, or feature films. As a result, every society must have some method of *allocating* its scarce resources—choosing which of our many competing desires will be fulfilled and which will not be.

Input Anything (including a resource) used to produce a good or service.

Many of the big questions of our time center on the different ways in which resources can be allocated. The cataclysmic changes that rocked Eastern Europe and the former Soviet Union during the early 1990s arose from a very simple fact: The method these countries used for decades to allocate resources was not working. Closer to home, the never-ending debates between Democrats and Republicans in the United States about tax rates, government services, and even foreign policy reflect subtle but important differences of opinion about how to allocate resources. Often, these are disputes about whether the private sector can handle a particular issue of resource allocation on its own or whether the government should be involved.

DANGEROUS CURVES

Resources vs. Inputs The term *resources* is often confused with another, more general term—**inputs.** An input is *anything* used to make a good or service—including (but not limited to) a resource. *Resources,* by contrast, are the *special* inputs that fall into one of four categories: labor, land, capital, and entrepreneurship.

What's so special about resources? They are the ultimate source of everything that is produced. If you think about any good or service that you use—say, an automobile—it is made from the four resources and *other* inputs (such as steel). But any of these *other* inputs can be traced back to the resources used to produce it (steel is made from iron ore, labor, capital, etc.). Goods and services, and the inputs used to make them, are all made from resources. This is why a nation's capacity to produce goods and services is limited by the amounts of the four resources at its disposal.

Scarcity and Economics

The scarcity of resources—and the choices it forces us to make—is the source of all of the problems you will study in economics. Households have limited incomes for satisfying their desires, so they must choose carefully how they allocate their spending among different goods and services. Business firms want to make the highest possible profit, but they must pay for their resources; so they carefully choose *what* to produce, *how much* to produce, and *how* to produce it. Federal, state, and local government agencies work with limited budgets, so they must carefully choose which goals to pursue. Economists study these decisions made by households, firms, and governments to explain how our economic system operates, to forecast the future of our economy, and to suggest ways to make that future even better.

THE WORLD OF ECONOMICS

The field of economics is surprisingly broad. It extends from the mundane—why does a pound of steak cost more than a pound of chicken?—to the personal and profound—how do couples decide how many children to have? With a field this broad, it is useful to have some way of classifying the different types of problems economists study and the different methods they use to analyze them.

Microeconomics and Macroeconomics

The field of economics is divided into two major parts: microeconomics and macroeconomics. **Microeconomics** comes from the Greek word *mikros*, meaning "small." It takes a close-up view of the economy, as if looking through a microscope. Microeconomics is concerned with the behavior of *individual* actors on the economic scene—households, business firms, and governments. It looks at the choices they make and how they interact with each other when they come together to trade *specific* goods and services. What will happen to the cost of movie tickets over the next five years? How many management-trainee jobs will open up for college graduates? How would U.S. phone companies be affected by a tax on imported cell phones? These are all microeconomic questions because they analyze individual *parts* of an economy rather than the *whole*.

> **Microeconomics** The study of the behavior of individual households, firms, and governments; the choices they make; and their interaction in specific markets.

Macroeconomics—from the Greek word *makros*, meaning "large"—takes an *overall* view of the economy. Instead of focusing on the production of carrots or computers, macroeconomics lumps all goods and services together and looks at the economy's *total output*. Instead of focusing on employment of management trainees or manufacturing workers, it considers *total employment* in the economy. Instead of asking why credit card loans carry higher interest rates than home mortgage loans, it asks what makes interest rates *in general* rise or fall. In all of these cases, macroeconomics focuses on the big picture and ignores the fine details.

> **Macroeconomics** The study of the behavior of the overall economy.

Positive and Normative Economics

The micro versus macro distinction is based on the level of detail we want to consider. Another useful distinction has to do with our *purpose* in analyzing a problem. **Positive economics** deals with *how* the economy works, plain and simple. If someone says, "Recent increases in spending for domestic security have slowed the growth rate of the U.S. economy," she is making a positive economic statement. A statement need not be accurate or even sensible to be classified as positive. For example, "Government policy has no effect on our standard of living" is a false, but positive, statement. Whether true or not, it's a statement about how the economy works and its accuracy can be tested by looking at the facts—and just the facts.

> **Positive economics** The study of how the economy works.

Normative economics concerns itself with what *should be*. It is used to make judgments about the economy, identify problems, and prescribe solutions. Rather

> **Normative economics** The study of what *should be;* it is used to make value judgments, identify problems, and prescribe solutions.

DANGEROUS CURVES

Seemingly Positive Statements Be alert to statements that may *seem* positive but are actually normative. Here's an example: "If we want to reduce pollution, our society will have to use less gasoline." This may *sound* positive, because it seems to refer only to facts about the world. But it's actually normative. Why? Cutting back on gasoline is just *one* policy among many that could reduce pollution. To say that we *must* choose this method makes a value judgment about its superiority to other methods. A purely positive statement on this topic would be, "Using less gasoline—with no other change in living habits—would reduce pollution."

Similarly, be alert to statements that use vague terms with hidden value judgments. An example: "All else equal, the less gasoline we use, the better our quality of life." Whether you agree or disagree, this is *not* a positive statement. Two people who agree about the facts—in this case, the consequences of using less gasoline—might disagree over the meaning of the phrase "quality of life," how to measure it, and what would make it better. This disagreement could not be resolved just by looking at the facts.

than limiting its concerns to just "the facts," it goes on to say what we should *do* about them and therefore depends on our values.

If an economist says, "We should cut total government spending," she is engaging in normative economic analysis. Cutting government spending would benefit some citizens and harm others, so the statement rests on a value judgment. A normative statement—like the one about government spending above—cannot be proved or disproved by the facts alone.

Positive and normative economics are intimately related in practice. For one thing, we cannot properly argue about what we should or should not do unless we know certain facts about the world. Every normative analysis is therefore based on an underlying positive analysis. But while a positive analysis can, at least in principle, be conducted without value judgments, a normative analysis is always based, at least in part, on the values of the person conducting it.

Why Economists Disagree. The distinction between positive and normative economics can help us understand why economists sometimes disagree. Suppose you are watching a television interview in which two economists are asked whether the United States should eliminate all government-imposed barriers to trading with the rest of the world. The first economist says, "Yes, absolutely," but the other says, "No, definitely not." Why the sharp disagreement?

The difference of opinion may be *positive* in nature: The two economists may have different views about what would actually happen if trade barriers were eliminated. Differences like this sometimes arise because our knowledge of the economy is imperfect or because certain facts are in dispute.

More likely, however, the disagreement will be *normative*. Economists, like everyone else, have different values. In this case, both economists might agree that opening up international trade would benefit *most* Americans, but harm *some* of them. Yet they may still disagree about the policy move because they have different values. The first economist might put more emphasis on benefits to the overall economy, while the second might put more emphasis on preventing harm to a particular group. Here, the two economists have come to the same *positive* conclusion, but their *different values* lead them to different *normative* conclusions.

In the media, economists are rarely given enough time to express the basis for their opinions, so the public hears only the disagreement. People may then conclude that economists cannot agree about how the economy works, even when the *real* disagreement is over goals and values.

WHY STUDY ECONOMICS?

Students take economics courses for all kinds of reasons.

To Understand the World Better

Applying the tools of economics can help you understand global and catastrophic events such as wars, famines, epidemics, and depressions. But it can also help you understand much of what happens to you locally and personally—the worsening traffic conditions in your city, the raise you can expect at your job this year, or the long line of people waiting to buy tickets for a popular concert. Economics has the power to help us understand these phenomena because they result, in large part, from the choices we make under conditions of scarcity.

Economics has its limitations, of course. But it is hard to find any aspect of life about which economics does not have *something* important to say. Economics cannot explain why so many Americans like to watch television, but it *can* explain how TV networks decide which programs to offer. Economics cannot protect you from a robbery, but it *can* explain why some people choose to become thieves and why no society has chosen to eradicate crime completely. Economics will not improve your love life, resolve unconscious conflicts from your childhood, or help you overcome a fear of flying, but it *can* tell us how many skilled therapists, ministers, and counselors are available to help us solve these problems.

To Gain Self-Confidence

Those who have never studied economics often feel that mysterious, inexplicable forces are shaping their lives, buffeting them like the bumpers in a pinball machine, determining whether or not they'll be able to find a job, what their salary will be, whether they'll be able to afford a home, and in what kind of neighborhood. If you've been one of those people, all that is about to change. After you learn economics, you may be surprised to find that you no longer toss out the business page of your local newspaper because it appears to be written in a foreign language. You may no longer lunge for the remote and change the channel the instant you hear "And now for news about the economy. . . . " You may find yourself listening to economic reports with a critical ear, catching mistakes in logic, misleading statements, or out-and-out lies. When you master economics, you gain a sense of mastery over the world, and thus over your own life as well.

To Achieve Social Change

If you are interested in making the world a better place, economics is indispensable. There is no shortage of serious social problems worthy of our attention—unemployment, hunger, poverty, disease, child abuse, drug addiction, violent crime. Economics can help us understand the origins of these problems, explain why previous efforts to solve them have failed, and help us to design new, more effective solutions.

To Help Prepare for Other Careers

Economics has long been a popular college major for individuals intending to work in business. But it has also been popular among those planning careers in politics, international relations, law, medicine, engineering, psychology, and other professions. This is for good reason: Practitioners in each of these fields often find themselves confronting economic issues. For example, lawyers increasingly face judicial rulings based on the principles of economic efficiency. Doctors will need to understand how new technologies or changes in the structure of health insurance will affect their practices. Industrial psychologists need to understand the economic implications of workplace changes they may advocate, such as flexible scheduling or on-site child care.

To Become an Economist

HTTP://

The Federal Reserve Bank of Minneapolis asked some Nobel Prize winners how they became interested in economics. Their stories can be found at http://www.minneapolisfed.org/pubs/region/int.cfm.

Only a tiny minority of this book's readers will decide to become economists. This is welcome news to the authors, and after you have studied labor markets in your *microeconomics* course you will understand why. But if you do decide to become an economist—obtaining a master's degree or even a Ph.D.—you will find many possibilities for employment. Of 16,780 members of the American Economic Association who responded to a recent survey,[2] 62 percent were employed at colleges or universities. The rest were engaged in a variety of activities in the private sector (19 percent), government (8 percent), and international organizations (3 percent). Economists are hired by banks to assess the risk of investing abroad; by manufacturing companies, to help them determine new methods of producing, marketing, and pricing their products; by government agencies, to help design policies to fight crime, disease, poverty, and pollution; by international organizations, to help create aid programs for less developed countries; by the media, to help the public interpret global, national, and local events; and even by nonprofit organizations, to provide advice on controlling costs and raising funds more effectively.

THE METHODS OF ECONOMICS

One of the first things you will notice as you begin to study economics is the heavy reliance on *models*. Indeed, the discipline goes beyond any other social science in its insistence that every theory be represented by an explicit, carefully constructed *model*.

You've no doubt encountered many models in your life. As a child, you played with model trains, model planes, or model people—dolls. In a high school science course, you probably saw a model of an atom—one of those plastic and wire contraptions with red, blue, and green balls representing protons, neutrons, and electrons. You may have also seen architects' cardboard models of buildings. These are physical models, three-dimensional replicas that you can pick up and hold. Economic models, on the other hand, are built not with cardboard, plastic, or metal but with words, diagrams, and mathematical statements.

What, exactly, is a model?

Model An astract representation of reality.

> A **model** is an abstract representation of reality.

The two key words in this definition are *abstract* and *representation*. A model is not supposed to be exactly like reality. Rather, it *represents* the real world by *abstracting* or *taking from* the real world that which will help us understand it. In any model, many real-world details are left out.

---

[2] *American Economic Review,* Table of Employment, 2003 (*http://www.vanderbilt.edu/AEA/Tbl.Employ.htm*).

The Art of Building Economic Models

When you build a model, how do you know which details to include and which to leave out? There is no simple answer to this question. The right amount of detail depends on your purpose in building the model in the first place. There is, however, one guiding principle:

> *A model should be as simple as possible to accomplish its purpose.*

This means that a model should contain only the *necessary* details.

To understand this a little better, think about a map. A map is a model—it represents a part of the earth's surface. But it leaves out many details of the real world. First, maps are two-dimensional, so they leave out the third dimension—height—of the real world. Second, maps always ignore small details, such as trees and houses and potholes. Third, a map is much smaller than the area it represents. But when you buy a map, how much detail do you want it to have?

Let's say you are in Boston, and you need a map to find the best way to drive from Logan Airport to the downtown convention center (your *purpose*). In this case, you would want a very detailed city map, with every street, park, and plaza in Boston clearly illustrated and labeled. A highway map, which ignores these details, wouldn't do at all.

But now suppose your purpose is different: to select the best driving route from Boston to Cincinnati. Now you want a highway map. A map that shows every street between Boston and Cincinnati would have *too much* detail. All of that extraneous information would only obscure what you really need to see.

Although economic models are more abstract than road maps, the same principle applies in building them: The level of detail that would be just right for one purpose will usually be too much or too little for another. When you feel yourself objecting to a model in this text because something has been left out, keep in mind the purpose for which the model is built. In introductory economics, the purpose is entirely educational. The models are designed to help you understand some simple, but powerful, principles about how the economy operates. Keeping the models simple makes it easier to see these principles at work and remember them later.

Of course, economic models have other purposes besides education. They can help businesses make decisions about pricing and production, help households decide how and where to invest their savings, and help governments and international agencies formulate policies. Models built for these purposes will be much more detailed than the ones in this text, and you will learn about them if you take more advanced courses in economics. But even complex models are built around very simple frameworks—the same frameworks you will be learning here.

Assumptions and Conclusions

Every economic model begins with *assumptions* about the world. There are two types of assumptions in a model: simplifying assumptions and critical assumptions.

A **simplifying assumption** is just what it sounds like—a way of making a model simpler without affecting any of its important conclusions. The purpose of a simplifying assumption is to rid a model of extraneous detail so its essential features can stand out more clearly. A road map, for example, makes the simplifying assumption, "There are no trees," because trees on a map would only get in the way. Similarly, in

© SUSAN VAN ETTEN

These maps are models. *But each would be used for a different purpose.*

Simplifying assumption Any assumption that makes a model simpler without affecting any of its important conclusions.

an economic model, we might assume that there are only two goods that households can choose from or that there are only two nations in the world. We make such assumptions *not* because they are true, but because they make a model easier to follow and do not change any of the important insights we can get from it.

Critical assumption Any assumption that affects the conclusions of a model in an important way.

A **critical assumption**, by contrast, is an assumption that affects the conclusions of a model in important ways. When you use a road map, you make the critical assumption, "All of these roads are open." If that assumption is wrong, your conclusion—the best route to take—might be wrong as well.

In an economic model, there are always one or more critical assumptions. You don't have to look very hard to find them, because economists like to make these assumptions explicit right from the outset. For example, when we study the behavior of business firms, our model will assume that firms try to earn the highest possible profit for their owners. By stating this assumption up front, we can see immediately where the model's conclusions spring from.

Two Fundamental Assumptions

The economy is complex. In the twenty seconds or so that it takes you to read this sentence, America's 250 million people will produce about $5 million worth of goods and services, the U.S. government will collect about $1 million in taxes and spend about the same, and U.S. firms will buy about $600,000 worth of goods and services from foreign firms in more than a hundred different countries.

Economists make sense of all this activity—and more—in two steps. First, the decision makers in the economy are divided into four broad groups: households, business firms, government agencies, and foreigners. In *micro*economic models, the focus is on the behavior of *individual* households, firms, and government agencies and how they interact with each other. In *macro*economic models, we group these decision makers into sectors—the household sector, the business sector, the government sector, and the foreign sector—and study how each interacts with the others.

The next step in understanding the economy is to make two critical assumptions about decision makers. These two assumptions are so universal in economic models that we may fairly consider them part of the foundation of economic thought.

First Fundamental Assumption. The first assumption has to do with *what* it is that individual decision makers are trying to accomplish. It can be stated as follows:

Every economic decision maker tries to make the best out of any situation.

Typically, making the best out of a situation means *maximizing some quantity*. Business firms, for example, are usually assumed to maximize profit. Households maximize utility—their well-being or satisfaction. In some cases, however, we might want to recognize that firms or households are actually groups of individuals with different agendas. While a firm's owners might want the firm to maximize profits, the managers might want to consider their own power, prestige, and job security. These goals may conflict, and the behavior of the firm will depend on how the conflict is resolved.

While economists often have spirited disagreements about *what* is being maximized, there is virtually unanimous agreement that any economic model should begin with the assumption that *someone* is maximizing *something*. Even the behavior of groups—like the decision makers in a firm or officials of the federal govern-ment—is assumed to arise from the behavior of different maximizing individuals, each pursuing his or her own agenda.

The first fundamental assumption seems to imply that we are all engaged in a relentless, conscious pursuit of narrow goals—an implication contradicted by much of human behavior. As you read this paragraph, are you consciously trying to max-imize your own well-being? Perhaps. You may be fully aware that reading this will improve your grade in economics; that, in turn, will help you achieve other impor-tant goals. But most likely, you aren't thinking about any of this. In truth, we only rarely make decisions with conscious, hard calculations. Why, then, do economists assume that people make decisions consciously, when, in reality, they often don't?

This is an important question. Economists answer it this way: The ultimate pur-pose of building an economic model is to *understand and predict behavior*—the be-havior of households, firms, government, and the overall economy. As long as peo-ple behave *as if* they are maximizing something, then we can build a good model by *assuming that they are*. Whether they *actually, consciously* maximize anything is an interesting philosophical question, but the answer doesn't affect the usefulness of the model. Thus, the belief behind the first fundamental assumption is that people, for the most part, behave *as if* they are maximizing something.

One last thought about the assumption that people maximize something: It does not imply that people are selfish or that economists think they are. On the contrary, economists are very interested in cases where people take the interests of others into account. For example, much economic life takes place in the family, where people care a great deal about each other. Our first fundamental assumption would then be applied to the family as a whole. That is, we would assume that the entire family, rather than any one individual within it, is trying to make the best out of any situation.

Economics also recognizes that people often care about their friends, their neigh-bors, and the broader society in which they live. Useful economic models have been built to explore charitable giving by individuals and corporations, volunteer activity, and ethical behavior such as honesty, fairness, and respect for fellow citizens.

Second Fundamental Assumption. A second critical assumption underlying all eco-nomic models is a simple fact of life:

> *Every economic decision maker faces constraints.*

Society's overall scarcity of resources constrains each of us individually in much the same way as the overall scarcity of space in a crowded elevator limits each rider's freedom of movement. Because of the scarcity of resources, households are con-strained by limited incomes, business firms are constrained by requirements that they pay for all of the inputs they use, and government agencies are constrained by limited budgets.

Together, the two fundamental assumptions help define the approach econo-mists take in answering questions about the world. To explain why there is poverty, illiteracy, and crime, to explain the rise and fall of industries and the patterns of trade among nations, or to explain why some government policies succeed while others fail, economists always begin with the same three questions:

1. Who are the individual decision makers?
2. What are they maximizing?
3. What constraints do they face?

This approach is used so heavily by economists that it is one of the *basic principles of economics* you will learn in this book.

Math, Jargon, and Other Concerns . . .

HTTP://

An online inroduction to the use of graphs can be found at http://syllabus.syr.edu/cid/graph/book.html.

Economists often express their ideas using mathematical concepts and a special vocabulary. Why? Because these tools enable economists to express themselves more precisely than with ordinary language. For example, someone who has never studied economics might say, "When used textbooks are available, students won't buy new textbooks." That statement might not bother you right now. But once you've finished your first economics course, you'll be saying it something like this: "When the price of used textbooks falls, the demand curve for new textbooks shifts leftward."

Does the second statement sound strange to you? It should. First, it uses a special term—a *demand curve*—that you haven't yet learned. Second, it uses a mathematical concept—a *shifting curve*—with which you might not be familiar. But while the first statement might mean a number of different things, the second statement—as you will see in Chapter 3—can mean only *one* thing. By being precise, we can steer clear of unnecessary confusion.

If you are worried about the special vocabulary of economics, you can relax. All of the new terms will be defined and carefully explained as you encounter them. Indeed, this textbook does not assume you have any special knowledge of economics. It is truly meant for a "first course" in the field.

But what about the math? Here, too, you can relax. While professional economists often use sophisticated mathematics to solve problems, only a little math is needed to understand basic economic *principles*. And virtually all of this math comes from high school algebra and geometry.

Still, you may have forgotten some of your high school math. If so, a little brushing up might be in order. This is why we have included an appendix at the end of this chapter. It covers some of the most basic concepts—such as interpreting graphs, the equation for a straight line, and the concept of a slope—that you will need in this course. You may want to glance at this appendix now, just so you'll know what's there. Then, from time to time, you'll be reminded about it when you're most likely to need it.

THE BASIC PRINCIPLES OF ECONOMICS

As you learn economics, you will encounter a variety of different theories, ideas, and techniques, each suited to analyzing a particular problem. But a few of these ideas are so central that they are used again and again in a variety of different contexts. And these ideas are not only useful in their own right; they also form the foundation on which the rest of economic theory is built. In this book, we call these ideas *basic principles of economics:*

Basic Principles of Economics A small set of methods and conclusions that appear repeatedly in analyzing economic problems. They form the foundation of economic theory.

> The **basic principles of economics** *are methods or conclusions that appear again and again in analyzing economic problems. They form the foundation upon which economic theory is built.*

In this sense, the body of economic theory is like an upside-down pyramid, with a few basic principles at the narrow bottom and the many ideas that spring from them forming the wider top.

In this book, you will learn eight basic principles of economics. A "key" symbol will appear each time one of them is introduced for the first time. Then, each time the principle is *used* in the text—to analyze a problem or to help form a more specific theory—you'll be alerted with the same key symbol, in the margin.

For example, earlier in this chapter, you learned about the two *fundamental assumptions* that economists use when analyzing almost any problem. Together, these two assumptions form the first of the basic principles you will learn about. Let's now introduce this principle formally:

 Basic Principle #1: Maximization Subject to Constraints
The economic approach to understanding a problem is to identify the decision makers, and then determine what they are maximizing and the constraints that they face.

As you will see, the principle of *maximization subject to constraints* will be used again and again in this book.

What about the rest of the basic principles? Following is the complete list, in the order they are introduced in the text. You are welcome to read the list now, but don't expect to understand it . . . yet. By the time you've finished reading this book, however, you will understand what these principles mean, how they are used, and why they are so basic to economics.

The Eight Basic Principles of Economics

- **Basic Principle #1—Maximization Subject to Constraints:** *The economic approach to understanding a problem is to identify the decision makers, and then determine what they are maximizing and the constraints that they face.*

- **Basic Principle #2—Opportunity Cost:** *All economic decisions made by individuals or society are costly. The correct way to measure the cost of a choice is its opportunity cost—that which is given up to make the choice.*

- **Basic Principle #3—Specialization and Exchange:** *Specialization and exchange enable us to enjoy greater production and higher living standards than would otherwise be possible. As a result, all economies exhibit high degrees of specialization and exchange.*

- **Basic Principle #4—Markets and Equilibrium:** *To understand how the economy behaves, economists organize the world into separate markets and then examine the equilibrium in each of those markets.*

- **Basic Principle #5—Policy Tradeoffs:** *Government policy is constrained by the reactions of private decision makers. As a result, policy makers face tradeoffs: Making progress toward one goal often requires some sacrifice of another goal.*

- **Basic Principle #6—Marginal Decision Making:** *To understand and predict the behavior of individual decision makers, we focus on the incremental or marginal effects of their actions.*

- **Basic Principle #7—Short-Run versus Long-Run Outcomes:** *Markets behave differently in the short run than in the long run. In solving a problem, we must always know which of these time horizons we are analyzing.*

- **Basic Principle #8—The Importance of Real Values:** *Since our economic well-being depends, in part, on the goods and services we can buy, it is important to translate from nominal values (which are measured in current dollars) to real values (which adjust for the dollar's changing value).*

You may want to flip back to this list from time to time, especially when you see the "key" symbol in the margin and need to refresh your memory about the principle that it refers to.

HOW TO STUDY ECONOMICS

As you read this book or listen to your instructor, you may find yourself following along and thinking that everything makes perfect sense. Economics may even seem easy. Indeed, it *is* rather easy to *follow* economics, since it's based so heavily on simple logic. But *following* and *learning* are two different things. You will eventually discover (preferably *before* your first exam) that economics must be studied actively, not passively.

If you are reading these words lying back on a comfortable couch, a phone in one hand and a remote control in the other, you are going about it in the wrong way. Active studying means reading with a pencil in your hand and a blank sheet of paper in front of you. It means closing the book periodically and *reproducing* what you have learned. It means listing the steps in each logical argument, retracing the cause-and-effect steps in each model, and drawing the graphs that represent the model. It means *thinking* about the basic principles of economics and how they relate to what you are learning. It does require some work, but the payoff is a good understanding of economics and a better understanding of your own life and the world around you.

Summary

Economics is the study of choice under conditions of scarcity. As individuals, and as a society, we have unlimited desires for goods and services. Unfortunately, the *resources*—land, labor, capital, and entrepreneurship—needed to produce those goods and services are scarce. Therefore, we must choose which desires to satisfy and how to satisfy them. Economics provides the tools that explain those choices.

The field of economics is divided into two major areas. *Microeconomics* studies the behavior of individual households, firms, and governments as they interact in specific markets. *Macroeconomics,* by contrast, concerns itself with the behavior of the entire economy. It considers variables such as total output, total employment, and the overall price level.

Economics makes heavy use of *models*—abstract representations of reality. These models are words, diagrams, and mathematical statements that help us understand how the economy operates. All models are simplifications, but a good model will have just enough detail for the purpose at hand.

Most economic models are based on two fundamental assumptions. The first is that every decision maker tries to make the best out of any situation; the second is that every decision maker faces constraints. In every problem that economists analyze, the starting point is determining (1) Who are the decision makers, (2) what are they maximizing, and (3) what constraints do they face?

Key Terms

Basic principles of economics	Input	Normative economics
Capital	Labor	Physical capital
Capital stock	Land	Positive economics
Critical assumption	Macroeconomics	Resources
Economics	Microeconomics	Scarcity
Entrepreneurship	Model	Simplifying assumption
Human capital		

Review Questions

1. What is a *resource*? What are the four different types of resources?

2. What determines the level of detail that an economist builds into a model?

3. What is the difference between a simplifying assumption and a critical assumption?

4. Would each of the following be classified as microeconomics or macroeconomics? Why?
   a. Research into why the growth rate of total production increased during the 1990s.

   b. A theory of how consumers decide what to buy.
   c. An analysis of Dell Computer's share of the personal computer market.
   d. Research on why interest rates were unusually high in the late 1970s and early 1980s.

5. What is the difference between an input and a resource?

Problems

1. Come up with a list of critical assumptions that could lie behind each of the following statements. Discuss whether each assumption would be classified as normative or positive.
   a. The United States is a democratic society.
   b. European movies are better than American movies.
   c. The bigger the city, the higher the quality of the newspaper.

2. Discuss whether each statement is an example of positive economics or normative economics or if it contains elements of both:
   a. An increase in the personal income tax will slow the growth rate of the economy.
   b. The goal of any country's economic policy should be to increase the well-being of its poorest, most vulnerable citizens.
   c. Excess regulation of small business is stifling the economy. Small business has been responsible for most of the growth in employment over the last 10 years, but regulations are putting a severe damper on the ability of small businesses to survive and prosper.

   d. The 1990s were a disastrous decade for the U.S. economy. Income inequality increased to its highest level since before World War II.

3. For each of the following, state whether economists would consider it a *resource*, and if they would, identify which of the four types of resources the item is.
   a. A computer used by an FBI agent to track the whereabouts of suspected criminals.
   b. The office building in which the FBI agent works.
   c. The time that an FBI agent spends on a case.
   d. A farmer's tractor.
   e. The farmer's knowledge of how to operate the tractor.
   f. Crude oil.
   g. A package of frozen vegetables.
   h. A food scientist's knowledge of how to commercially freeze vegetables.
   i. The ability to bring together resources to start a frozen food company.
   j. Plastic bags used to buy a frozen food company to hold its product.

 *These exercises require access to Lieberman/Hall Xtra! If Xtra! did not come with your book, visit http://liebermanxtra.swlearning.com to purchase.*

1. Use your Xtra! password at the Hall and Lieberman Web site (http://liebermanxtra.swlearning.com), select Chapter 1, and under Economic Applications, click on EconDebates. Choose Economic Fundamentals; Scarcity, Choice and Opportunity Cost; and scroll down to find the debate, "Are Americans Overworked?" Read the debate, and use the information to answer the following questions.

   a. Is the question in the title of this debate an example of positive or normative economics? Why?
   b. Why is leisure time becoming scarcer over time?
   c. Identify three statements of positive economics in this debate.

APPENDIX

GRAPHS AND OTHER USEFUL TOOLS

TABLES AND GRAPHS

A brief glance at this text will tell you that graphs are important in economics. Graphs provide a convenient way to display information and enable us to immediately *see* relationships between different variables.

Suppose that you've just been hired at the advertising department of Len & Harry's—an up-and-coming manufacturer of high-end ice cream products, located in Texas. You've been asked to compile a report on how advertising affects the company's sales. It turns out that the company's spending on advertising has changed repeatedly in the past, so you have lots of data on monthly advertising outlays and monthly sales revenue, both measured in thousands of dollars.

Table A.1 shows a useful way of arranging this data. The company's advertising outlays in different months are listed in the left-hand column, while the right-hand column lists total sales revenue ("sales" for short) during the same month. Notice that the data here is organized so that spending on advertising increases as we move down the first column. Often, just looking at a table like this can reveal useful patterns. Here, it's clear that higher spending on advertising is associated with higher monthly sales. These two variables—advertising and sales—have a **positive relationship**.[3] A rise in one is associated with a rise in the other. If higher advertising had been associated with *lower* sales, the two variables would have a **negative** or **inverse relationship**: A rise in one would be associated with a fall in the other.

We can be even more specific about the positive relationship between advertising and sales: Logic tells us that the association is very likely *causal*. We'd expect that sales revenue *depends on* advertising outlays, so we call sales our **dependent variable** and advertising our **independent variable**. Changes in an independent variable cause changes in a dependent variable, but not the other way around.

To explore the relationship further, let's graph it. As a rule, the *independent* variable is measured on the *horizontal* axis and the *dependent* variable on the *vertical* axis. In economics, unfortunately, we do not always stick to this rule, but for now we will. In Figure A.1, monthly advertising outlays—our independent variable—are measured on the horizontal axis. If we start at the *origin*—the corner where the two axes intersect— and move rightward along the horizontal axis, monthly advertising outlays increase from $0 to $1,000 to $2,000 and so on. The vertical axis measures monthly sales—the dependent variable. Along this axis, as we move upward from the origin, sales rise.

The graph in Figure A.1 shows six labeled points, each representing a different pair of numbers from our table. For example, point *A*—which represents the

TABLE A.1 Advertising and Sales at Len & Harry's	Advertising ($1,000 per Month)	Sales ($1,000 per Month)
	2	46
	3	49
	6	58
	7	61
	11	73
	12	76

[3] Key Terms found in this appendix are defined at the end of the appendix and in the glossary.

numbers in the first row of the table—shows us that when the firm spends $2,000 on advertising, sales are $46,000 per month. Point *B* represents the *second* row of the table, and so on. Notice that all of these points lie along a *straight line*.

Straight-Line Graphs

You'll encounter straight-line graphs often in economics, so it's important to understand one special property they possess: The "rate of change" of one variable compared with the other is always the same. For example, look at what happens as we move from point *A* to point *B*: Advertising rises by $1,000 (from $2,000 to $3,000), while sales rise by $3,000 (from $46,000 to $49,000). If you study the graph closely, you'll see that anywhere along this line, whenever advertising increases by $1,000, sales increase by the same $3,000. Or, if we define a "unit" as "one thousand dollars," we can say that every time advertising increases by one unit, sales rise by three units. So the "rate of change" is three units of sales for every one unit of advertising.

The rate of change of the *vertically* measured variable for a one-unit change in the *horizontally* measured variable is also called the **slope** of the line. The slope of the line in Figure A.1 is three, and it remains three no matter where along the line we measure it. For example, make sure you can see that from point *C* to point *D*, advertising rises by one unit and sales rise by three units.

What if we had wanted to determine the slope of this line by comparing points *D* and *E*, which has ad-

vertising rising by four units instead of just one? In that case, we'd have to calculate the rise in one variable *per unit* rise in the other. To do this, we divide the change in the vertically measured variable by the change in the horizontally measured variable.

$$\text{Slope of a straight line} = \frac{\text{change in vertical variable}}{\text{change in horizontal variable}}.$$

We can make this formula even simpler by using two shortcuts. First, we can call the variable on the vertical axis "Y" and the variable on the horizontal axis "X." In our case, Y is sales, while X is advertising outlays. Second, we use the Greek letter Δ ("delta") to denote the words "change in." Then, our formula becomes:

$$\text{Slope of straight line} = \frac{\Delta Y}{\Delta X}.$$

Let's apply this formula to get the slope as we move from point *D* to point *E*, which causes advertising (X) to rise from 7 units to 11 units. This is an increase of 4, so $\Delta X = 4$. For this move, sales rise from 61 to 73, an increase of 12, so $\Delta Y = 12$. Applying our formula,

$$\text{Slope} = \frac{\Delta Y}{\Delta X} = \frac{12}{4} = 3.$$

This is the same value for the slope that we found earlier. Not surprising, since it's a straight line and a straight line has the same slope everywhere. The particular pair of points we choose for our calculation doesn't matter.

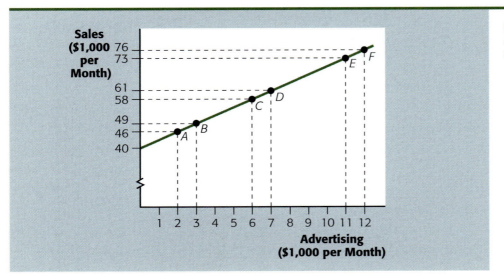

FIGURE A.1
A Graph of Advertising and Sales

FIGURE A.2
Measuring the Slope of a Curve

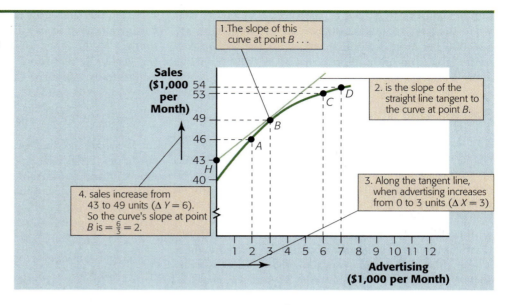

Curved Lines

Although many of the relationships you'll encounter in economics have straight-line graphs, many others do not. Figure A.2 shows *another* possible relationship between advertising and sales that we might have found from a different set of data. As you can see, the line is curved. But as advertising rises, the curve gets flatter and flatter. Here, as before, each time we spend another $1,000 on advertising, sales rise. But now, the rise in sales seems to get smaller and smaller. This means that the *slope* of the curve is *itself changing* as we move along this curve. In fact, the slope is getting smaller.

How can we measure the slope of a curve? First, note that since the slope is different at every point along the curve, we aren't really measuring the slope of "the curve" but the slope of the curve *at a specific point along it*. How can we do this? By drawing a **tangent line**—a straight line that touches the curve at just one point and that has the same slope as the curve at that point. For example, in the figure, a tangent line has been drawn for point *B*. To measure the slope of this tangent line, we can compare any two points on it, say, *H* and *B*, and calculate the slope as we would for any straight line. Moving from point *H* to point *B*, we are moving from 0 to 3 on the horizontal axis ($\Delta X = 3$) and from 43 to 49 on the vertical axis ($\Delta Y = 6$). Thus, the slope of the tangent line—which is the same as the slope of the curved line at point *B*—is:

$$\frac{\Delta Y}{\Delta X} = \frac{6}{3} = 2.$$

This says that, at point *B*, the rate of change is two units of sales for every one unit of advertising. Or, going back to dollars, the rate of change is $2,000 in sales for every $1,000 spent on advertising.

The curve in Figure A.2 slopes everywhere upward, reflecting a positive relationship between the variables. But a curved line can also slope downward to illustrate a negative relationship between variables, or slope first one direction and then the other. You'll see plenty of examples of each type of curve in later chapters and you'll learn how to interpret each one as it's presented.

LINEAR EQUATIONS

Let's go back to the straight-line relationship between advertising and sales, as shown in Table A.1. What if you need to know how much in sales the firm could expect if it spent $5,000 on advertising next month? What if it spent $8,000, or $9,000? It would be nice to be able to answer questions like this without having to pull out tables and graphs to do it. As it turns out, anytime the relationship you are studying has a straight-line graph, it is easy to figure out an equation for the entire relationship—a *linear equation*. You then can use the equation to answer any such question that might be put to you.

All straight lines have the same general form. If *Y* stands for the variable on the vertical axis and *X* for the variable on the horizontal axis, every straight line has an equation of the form

$$Y = a + bX,$$

where a stands for some number and b for another number. The number a is called the vertical *intercept,* because it marks the point where the graph of this equation hits (intercepts) the vertical axis; this occurs when X takes the value zero. (If you plug $X = 0$ into the equation, you will see that, indeed, $Y = a$.) The number b is the slope of the line, telling us how much Y will change every time X changes by one unit. To confirm this, note that as X increases from 0 to 1, Y goes from a to $a + b$. The number b is therefore the change in Y corresponding to a one-unit change in X—exactly what the slope of the graph should tell us.

If b is a positive number, a one-unit increase in X causes Y to *increase* by b units, so the graph of our line would slope upward, as illustrated by the red line in panel (a) of Figure A.3. If b is a negative number, then a one-unit increase in X will cause Y to *decrease* by b

units, so the graph would slope downward, as the blue line does in panel (a). Of course, b could equal zero. If it does, a one-unit increase in X causes no change in Y, so the graph of the line is flat, like the black line in panel (a).

The value of a has no effect on the slope of the graph. Instead, different values of a determine the graph's position. When a is a positive number, the graph will intercept the vertical Y-axis above the origin, as the red line does in panel (b) of Figure A.3. When a is negative, however, the graph will intercept the Y-axis *below* the origin, like the blue line in panel (b). When a is zero, the graph intercepts the Y-axis right at the origin, as the black line does in panel (b).

Let's see if we can figure out the equation for the relationship depicted in Figure A.1. There, X denotes advertising and Y denotes sales. Earlier, we calculated that

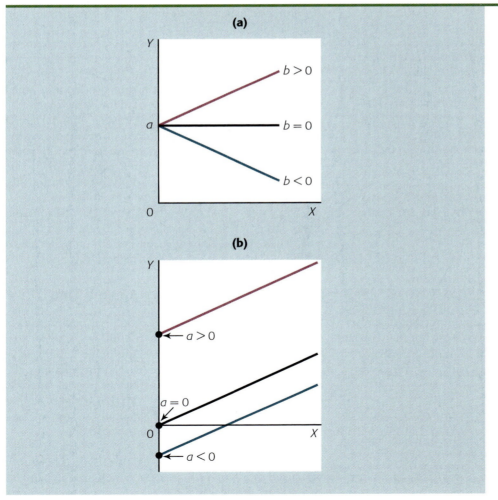

FIGURE A.3
**Straight Lines with Different
Slopes and Vertical Intercepts**

the slope of this line, *b*, is 3. But what is *a*, the vertical intercept? On the graph, you can see that when advertising outlays are zero, sales are $40,000. That tells us that $a = 40$.[4] Putting these two observations together, we find that the equation for the line in Figure A.1 is

$$Y = 40 + 3X.$$

Now if you need to know how much in sales to expect from a particular expenditure on advertising, you'd be able to come up with an answer: You'd simply multiply the amount spent on advertising by 3, add $40,000, and that would be your sales. To confirm this, plug in for *X* in this equation any amount of advertising in dollars from the left-hand column of Table A.1. You'll see that you get the corresponding amount of sales in the right-hand column.

HOW STRAIGHT LINES AND CURVES SHIFT

So far, we've focused on relationships where some variable *Y* depends on a single other variable, *X*. But in many of our theories, we recognize that some variable of interest to us is actually affected by more than just one other variable. When *Y* is affected by both *X* and some third variable, changes in that third variable will usually cause a *shift* in the graph of the relationship between *X* and *Y*. This is because whenever we draw the graph between *X* and *Y*, we are holding fixed every other variable that might possibly affect *Y*.

> *A graph between two variables X and Y is only a picture of their relationship when all other variables affecting Y are held constant.*

But suppose one of these other variables *does* change? What happens then?

Think back to the relationship between advertising and sales. Earlier, we supposed sales depend only on advertising. But suppose we make an important discovery: Ice cream sales are *also* affected by how hot the weather is. What's more, all of the data in Table A.1 on which we previously based our analysis turns out to have been

from the month of June in different years, when the average temperature in Texas is 80 degrees. What's going to happen in July, when the average temperature rises to 100 degrees?

In Figure A.4 we've redrawn the graph from Figure A.1, this time labeling the line "June." Often, a good way to determine how a graph will shift is to perform a simple experiment like this: Put your pencil tip anywhere on the graph labeled June—let's say at point *C*. Now ask the following question: If I hold advertising constant at $6,000, do I expect to sell more or less ice cream as temperature rises in July? If you expect to sell more, then the amount of sales corresponding to $6,000 of advertising will be *above* point *C*, at a point such as *C'* (pronounced "C prime"), representing sales of $64,000. From this, we can tell that the graph will *shift upward* as temperature rises. In September, however, when temperatures fall, the amount of sales corresponding to $6,000 in advertising would be less than it is at point *C*. It would be shown by a point such as *C''* (pronounced "C double-prime"). In that case, the graph would shift downward.

The same procedure works well whether the original graph slopes upward or downward and whether it is a straight line or a curved one. Figure A.5 sketches two examples. In panel (a), an increase in some third variable, *Z*, increases the value of *Y* for each value of *X*, so the graph of the relationship between *X* and *Y* shifts upward as *Z* increases. We often phrase it this way: "An increase in *Z* causes an increase in *Y*, *at any value of X*." In panel (b), an increase in *Z decreases* the value of *Y*, at any value of *X*, so the graph of the relationship between *X* and *Y* shifts *downward* as *Z* increases.

You'll notice that in Figures A.4 and A.5, the original line is darker, while the new line after the shift is drawn in a lighter shade. We'll use this convention—a lighter shade for the new line after a shift—throughout this book.

Shifts versus Movements Along a Line

If you look back at Figure A.1, you'll see that when advertising increases (say, from $2,000 to $3,000), we *move along* our line, from point *A* to point *B*. But you've just learned that when average temperature changes, the entire line *shifts*. This may seem strange to you. After all, in both cases, an independent variable changes (either advertising or temperature). Why should we move *along* the line in one case and *shift* it in the other?

The reason for the difference is that in one case (advertising), the independent variable is *in our graph*, measured along one of the axes. When an independent variable in the graph changes, we simply move along

---

[4] We could also use direct logic to find the vertical intercept. In the figure, locate any point—we'll use point *A* as our example, where $X = 2$ and $Y = 46$. From this point, to get to the vertical intercept, we'd have to decrease *X* by two units. But with a slope of 3, a two-unit decrease in *X* will cause a six-unit decrease in *Y*. Therefore, *Y* will decrease from 46 to 40. Summing up, we've found that when $X = 0$, $Y = 40$, so our vertical intercept is 40.

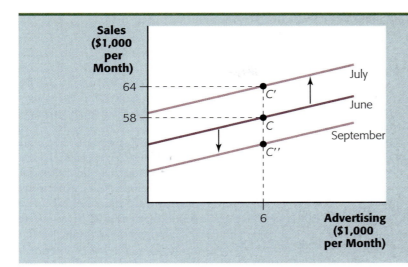

FIGURE A.4
Shifts in the Graph of Advertising and Sales

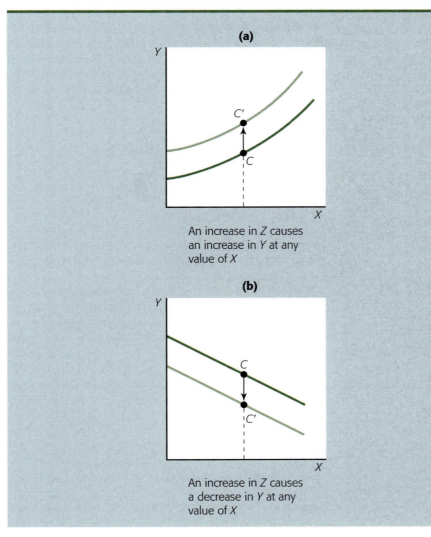

FIGURE A.5
Shifts of Curved Lines and Straight Lines

(a)

An increase in *Z* causes an increase in *Y* at any value of *X*

(b)

An increase in *Z* causes a decrease in *Y* at any value of *X*

the line. In the other case (temperature), the independent variable does *not* appear in our graph. Instead, it's been in the background, being held constant.

Here's a very simple—but crucial—rule:

> *Suppose Y is the **dependent** variable, which is measured on one of the axes in a graph. If the independent variable **measured on the other axis** changes, we **move along** the line. But if **any** other independent variable changes, the **entire line shifts**.*

Be sure you understand the phrase "any other independent variable." It refers to any variable that actually *affects Y* but is *not* measured on either axis in the graph.

This rule applies to straight lines as well as curved lines. And it applies even in more complicated situations, such as when *two different* lines are drawn in the same graph, and a shift of one causes a movement along the other. (You'll encounter this situation in Chapter 3.) But for now, make sure you can see how we've been applying this rule in our example, where the three variables are total sales, advertising, and temperature.

SOLVING EQUATIONS

When we first derived the equation for the relationship between advertising and sales, we wanted to know what level of sales to expect from different amounts of advertising. But what if we're asked a slightly different question? Suppose, this time, you are told that the sales committee has set an ambitious goal of $64,000 for next month's sales. The treasurer needs to know how much to budget for advertising, and you have to come up with the answer.

Since we know how advertising and sales are related, we ought to be able to answer this question. One way is just to look at the graph in Figure A.1. There, we could first locate sales of $64,000 on the vertical axis. Then, if

we read over to the line and then down, we find the amount of advertising that would be necessary to generate that level of sales. Yet even with that carefully drawn diagram, it is not always easy to see just exactly how much advertising would be required. If we need to be precise, we'd better use the equation for the graph instead.

According to the equation, sales (Y) and advertising (X) are related as follows:

$$Y = 40 + 3X.$$

In the problem before us, we know the value for sales, and we need to solve for the corresponding amount of advertising. Substituting the sales target of $64,000 for Y, we need to find that value of X for which

$$64 = 40 + 3X.$$

Here, X is the unknown value for which we want to solve.

Whenever we solve one equation for one unknown, say, X, we need to *isolate X* on one side of the equals sign and everything else on the other side of the equals sign. We do this by performing identical operations on both sides of the equals sign. Here, we can first subtract 40 from both sides, getting

$$24 = 3X.$$

We can then divide both sides by 3 and get

$$8 = X.$$

This is our answer. If we want to achieve sales of $64,000, we'll need to spend $8,000 on advertising.

Of course, not all relationships are linear, so this technique will not work in every situation. But no matter what the underlying relationship, the idea remains the same:

> *To solve for X in any equation, rearrange the equation, following the rules of algebra, so that X appears on one side of the equals sign and everything else in the equation appears on the other side.*

Key Terms

Dependent variable A variable whose value depends on the value of some other variable.

Independent variable A variable that causes changes in some other variable (the dependent variable).

Negative or inverse relationship A relationship between two variables that move in opposite directions to each other (when one increases the other decreases).

Positive relationship A relationship between two variables that move in the same direction (when one increases

so does the other; when one decreases so does the other).

Slope The rate of change of one variable with respect to another variable. In a graph, the change in the vertical-axis variable divided by the change in the horizontal-axis variable.

Tangent line A straight line that touches a curve at just one point, and has the same slope as the curve at that point.

Scarcity, Choice, and Economic Systems

What does it cost you to go to the movies? If you answered eight or nine dollars, because that is the price of a movie ticket, then you are leaving out a lot. Most of us are used to thinking of "cost" as the money we must pay for something. A Big Mac costs $2.70, a new Toyota Corolla costs $16,000, and the baby-sitter costs $8.00 an hour. Certainly, the money we pay for a good or service is a *part* of its cost. But economics takes a broader view of costs, recognizing monetary as well as nonmonetary components.

THE CONCEPT OF OPPORTUNITY COST

The total cost of any choice we make—buying a car, producing a computer, or even reading a book—is everything we must *give up* when we take that action. This cost is called the *opportunity cost* of the action, because we give up the opportunity to have other desirable things.

> The **opportunity cost** of any choice is what we must forego when we make that choice.

Opportunity cost What is given up when taking an action or making a choice.

Opportunity cost is the most accurate and complete concept of cost—the one we should use when making our own decisions or analyzing the decisions of others.

Opportunity Cost for Individuals

Virtually every action we take as individuals uses up scarce money, scarce time, or both. This money or time *could* have been used for other things that you value. Thus, the true cost of any choice you make—the *opportunity cost*—is everything you actually sacrifice in making the choice.

Suppose, for example, it's 8 P.M. on a weeknight and you're spending a couple of hours reading this chapter. As authors, that thought makes us very happy, especially because we know there are many other things you could be doing: going to a movie, having dinner with friends, playing ping pong, earning some extra money tutoring high school students, watching TV. . . . Some of these alternatives might be more fun than reading your economics text. But, assuming you're still reading—and you haven't just run out the door to do something else—let's relate this to opportunity cost.

What *is* the opportunity cost of reading this chapter? Is it *all* of those other possibilities we've listed? Not really, because if you weren't reading for these two hours, you'd probably have time to do only *one* of them. And you'd no doubt choose whichever one among these alternatives you regarded as best. So, by reading, you sacrifice the best choice among the alternatives that you could be doing instead.

> *The opportunity cost of a choice is the best among the available alternatives to that choice.*

For many choices, a large part of the opportunity cost is the money sacrificed. If you spend $15 on a new DVD, you have to part with $15, which is money you could have spent on something else (whatever the best choice among the alternatives turned out to be). But for other choices, money may be only a small part, or no part, of what is sacrificed. If you walk your dog a few blocks, it will cost you time but not money. Still, economists often like to attach a monetary value even to costs that *don't* involve money. By translating such sacrifices into a dollar value, we can express opportunity cost as a single number, albeit a roughly estimated one. That, in turn, enables us to compare the cost of a choice with its benefits, which are also often expressed in dollars.

An Example: The Opportunity Cost of College. Let's consider an important choice you've made for this year: to attend college. What is the opportunity cost of this choice? A good starting point is to look at the actual monetary costs—the annual out-of-pocket expenses borne by you or your family for a year of college. Table 1 shows the College Board's estimates of these expenses for the average student. For example, the third column of the table shows that the average in-state resident at a four-year state college pays $4,694 in tuition and fees, $817 for books and supplies, $5,942 for room and board, and $2,380 for transportation and other expenses, for a total of $13,833 per year.

So, is that dollar figure the opportunity cost of a year of college for the average student at a public institution? Not really. Even if the entries are what you or your family actually pays out for college, there are two problems with using these figures to calculate the opportunity cost.

First, the table includes some expenses that are *not* part of the opportunity cost of college. For example, room and board is something you'd need no matter *what* you choose to do. That's obvious if, as part of your best choice among the alterna-

Type of Institution	Two-year Public	Four-year Public	Four-year Private
Tuition and fees	$ 1,905	$ 4,694	$19,710
Books and supplies	$ 745	$ 817	$ 843
Room and board	$ 5,681	$ 5,942	$ 7,144
Transportation and other expenses	$ 2,650	$ 2,380	$ 1,844
Total out-of-pocket costs	$10,981	$13,833	$29,541

TABLE 1

Average Cost of a Year of College, 2003–2004

Source: Trends in College Pricing, The College Board, New York, NY, 2003.

Notes: Averages are enrollment-weighted by institution, to reflect the average experience among students across the United States. Average tuition and fees at public institutions are for in-state residents only. Room and board charges are for students living on campus at four-year institutions, and off-campus (but not with parents) at two-year institutions.

tives, you'd have lived in an apartment and paid rent. But even living in your old room at home doesn't eliminate this cost: Your family *could* have rented out the room to someone else, or used it for some other valuable purpose. Either way, something is sacrificed. Let's suppose, for simplicity, that if you weren't in college, you or your family would be paying the same amount for room and board as your college charges. Then, that room and board expense should be excluded from opportunity cost. And the same applies to transportation and other expenses, at least the part that you would have spent anyway even if not in college.

Now we're left with payments for tuition and fees, and for books and other school supplies. For an in-state resident going to a state college, this averages $5,511 per year. Since these dollars are paid only when you attend college, they represent something sacrificed for that choice and are part of its opportunity cost. Costs like these—for which dollars are sacrificed through actual payments—are called **explicit costs,** and they are *part* of the opportunity cost.

But college also has **implicit costs**—sacrifices for which no money changes hands. The biggest sacrifice in this category is *time.* But what is that time worth? That depends on what you *would* be doing if you weren't in school. For many students, the alternative would be working full-time at a job, something most students can't manage while attending college. If you are one of these students, attending college requires the sacrifice of the income you *could* have earned at a job—a sacrifice we call *foregone income.*

How much income is foregone when you go to college for a year? In 2003, the average total income of an 18- to 24-year-old high school graduate who worked full-time was about $23,000. If we assume that only nine months of work must be sacrificed to attend college, and that you could still work full-time in the summer, then foregone income is about 9/12 of $23,000, or $17,250.

Summing the explicit and implicit costs gives us a rough estimate of the opportunity cost of a year in college. For a public institution, we add $5,511 in explicit costs and $17,250 in implicit costs, giving us a total of $22,761 per year. Notice that this is significantly greater than the total charges estimated by the college board, which—in addition to including some expenses that are not part of opportunity cost—excludes the largest cost of all: foregone income. When you consider paying this opportunity cost for four years, its magnitude might surprise you. Without

Explicit cost The dollars sacrificed—and actually paid out—for a choice.

Implicit cost The value of something sacrificed when no direct payment is made.

financial aid in the form of tuition grants or other fee reductions, the average in-state resident will sacrifice about $91,000 to get a bachelor's degree at a state college and about $151,000 at a private one.

Our analysis of the opportunity cost of college is an example of a general, and important, principle:

> *The opportunity cost of a choice includes both* **explicit costs** *and* **implicit costs.**

A Brief Digression: Is College the Right Choice? Before you start questioning your choice to be in college, there are a few things to remember. First, in addition to its high cost, college has substantial *benefits*, including financial ones. In fact, over a 40-year work life, the average college graduate will make about $2.5 million, which is about a million dollars *more* than the average high school graduate.[1] So, even when we properly add the foregone income into our measure of opportunity cost, attending college appears to be one of the best *financial* investments you can make.

Second, remember that we've left out of our discussion many important aspects of this choice that would be harder to estimate in dollar terms, but could be very important to you. Do you *enjoy* being at college? If so, it would be difficult (although not impossible) to value that enjoyment in dollars. But your enjoyment should still be considered—along with the more easily measured financial rewards—as part of your benefits. (Of course, if you *hate* college and are only doing it for the financial rewards or to satisfy your parents, that's an implicit cost—which is part of your opportunity cost—that we haven't included.)

Time Is Money. Our analysis of the opportunity cost of college points out a general principle, one understood by economists and noneconomists alike. It can be summed up in the expression, "Time is money." Those three words contain a profound truth: The sacrifice of time often means the sacrifice of money—in particular, the money that *could* have been earned during that time.

As a rule, economists have a simple technique to estimate the dollar value of time. First, we assume that working additional hours for pay is the best among the alternatives to the choice being considered. Then, each hour sacrificed for the choice is multiplied by the individual's hourly wage. (Even someone paid a monthly salary has an implied hourly wage: their total monthly income divided by the total monthly hours of work.)

For example, suppose Jessica is a freelance writer who decides to see a movie. The ticket price is $8, and the entire activity—including getting there and back—will take three hours out of her evening. What is the opportunity cost of seeing this movie? Let's say Jessica earns an annual income of $40,000 by working 2,000

---

[1] Jennifer C. Day and Eric C. Newburger, "The Big Payoff: Educational Attainment and Synthetic Estimates of Work-Life Earnings," in *Current Population Reports* (U.S. Census Bureau), July 2002. There are two provisos. First, part of the additional earnings of college graduates may be due to the type of person that goes to college, rather than the degree itself. Second, remember that much of the additional income you'll earn with a college degree is postponed far into the future, which reduces its value to you right now. These two provisos reduce the benefits of attending college. But even when economists account for these reductions in benefits, a college degree still appears to be one of the best financial investments you can make.

hours per year, giving her an implied hourly wage of $40,000 / 2,000 hrs = $20 per hour. Then for Jessica, the opportunity cost is the sum of the explicit costs ($8 for the ticket) and the implicit costs ($20 × 3 hrs = $60 in foregone income), giving her a total opportunity cost of $68.

The idea that a movie "costs" $68 might seem absurd to you. But if you think about it, $68 is a much better estimate than $8 of what the movie costs for Jessica. After all, Jessica gives up three hours that *could* have been spent working on an article that, on average, would provide her with another $60. Thus, in a very real sense, Jessica sacrifices $68 for the movie.[2]

Our examples about the cost of college and the cost of a movie point out an important lesson about opportunity cost:

> *The explicit (direct money) cost of a choice may only be a part—and sometimes a small part—of the opportunity cost of a choice.*

Indeed, the higher an individual's income, the less important is the direct money cost, and the more important the time cost of an activity. For example, suppose that Samantha is an attorney who bills out her time at $100 per hour. For her, the opportunity cost of the same movie—which entails three hours and the ticket—would be $308 dollars!

You might wonder if Samantha would ever see a movie at such a high cost. The answer for Samantha is the same as for Jessica or anyone else: yes, as long as the benefits of the movie are greater than the explicit and implicit costs. It's easy to see why Samantha might decide to see a movie. Imagine that she begins taking on more and more clients, working longer and longer hours, and earning more and more income. At some point, she will realize that leisure activities like movies are very important, while earning more income will seem less important. And at some point, the enjoyment of taking time off to see a movie might be well worth sacrificing the $308 that she could have had.

Once you understand the concept of opportunity cost and how it can differ among individuals, you can understand some behavior that might otherwise appear strange. For example, why do high-income people rarely shop at discount stores like Kmart or Target and instead shop at full-service stores where the same items sell for much higher prices? It's not that high-income people *like* to pay more for their purchases. But discount stores are generally understaffed and crowded with customers, so shopping there takes more time. While discount stores have lower *money* cost, they impose a higher *time* cost. For high-income people, discount stores are actually more costly than stores with higher price tags.

---

[2] In using the wage rate to measure the opportunity cost of time, we are assuming (1) that Jessica *could* work three additional hours and earn an additional $20 per hour; and (2) that among all the alternatives to the movie, working for pay is the best. Any violations of these assumptions would make our measure of opportunity cost less accurate. For example, suppose Jessica would *like* to work longer hours for additional pay, but her job doesn't permit this. Then she may already be diverting her nonwork time into an alternative she values at *less* than $20 per hour—say, $15 per hour. In this case, when Jessica considers a new choice, any time sacrificed would be worth only $15 an hour to her, so using her $20 hourly wage would *overestimate* the opportunity cost of the new choice.

On the other hand, if Jessica *could* work more hours but has chosen *not* to, she must already be doing other things that she values *more highly* than $20 per hour—say, at $25. In this case, a new choice would require giving up time worth $25 per hour, and using her $20 wage would *underestimate* the opportunity cost of the new choice.

We can also understand why the most highly paid consultants, entrepreneurs, attorneys, and surgeons often lead such frenetic lives, doing several things at once and packing every spare minute with tasks. Since these people can earn several hundred dollars for an hour of work, every activity they undertake carries a correspondingly high opportunity cost. Brushing one's teeth can cost $10, and driving to work can cost hundreds! By combining activities—making phone calls while driving to work, thinking about and planning the day while in the shower, or reading the morning paper in the elevator—the opportunity cost of these routine activities is reduced.

And what about the rest of us? As our wages rise, we all try to cram more activities into little bits of free time. Millions of Americans now carry cell phones and use them while waiting for an elevator or walking their dogs. Books on tape are becoming more popular and are especially favored by runners. (Why just exercise when you can also "read" a book?) And for some, vacations have become more exhausting than work, as more and more activities are crammed into shorter and shorter vacation periods. These trends can be partly explained by the increasing opportunity cost of time.

Opportunity Cost and Society

For an individual, opportunity cost arises from the scarcity of time or money. But for society as a whole, opportunity cost arises from a different source: the scarcity of society's *resources*. Our desire for goods is limitless, but we have limited resources to produce them. Therefore,

> *virtually all production carries an opportunity cost: To produce more of one thing, society must shift resources away from producing something else.*

For example, we'd all agree that we'd like better health for our citizens. What would be needed to achieve this goal? Perhaps more frequent medical checkups for more people and greater access to top-flight medicine when necessary. These, in turn, would require more and better-trained doctors, more hospital buildings and laboratories, and more high-tech medical equipment such as positron emission tomography (PET) scanners and surgical lasers. In order for us to produce these goods and services, we would have to pull resources—land, labor, capital, and entrepreneurship—out of producing other things that we also enjoy. The opportunity cost of improved health care, then, consists of all the other goods and services we would have to do without.

The Principle of Opportunity Cost

Principle of Opportunity Cost All economic decisions made by individuals or society are costly. The correct way to measure the cost of a choice is its opportunity cost—that which is given up to make the choice.

Opportunity cost is one of the most important ideas you will encounter in economics. The concept sheds light on virtually every problem that economists study, whether it be explaining the behavior of consumers or business firms or understanding important social problems like poverty or racial discrimination. In all of these cases, economists apply the **principle of opportunity cost.**

> ⚷ *Basic Principle #2: Opportunity Cost*
> *All economic decisions made by individuals or society are costly. The correct way to measure the cost of a choice is its opportunity cost—that which is given up to make the choice.*

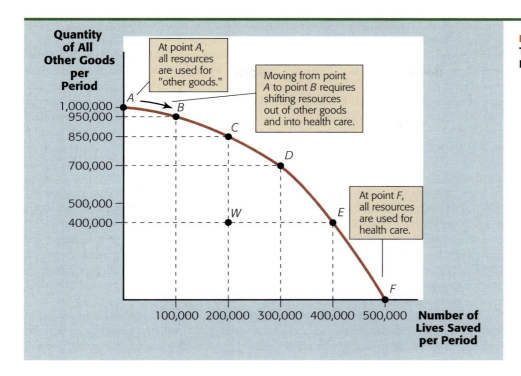

FIGURE 1
The Production Possibilities Frontier

Production Possibilities Frontiers

Let's build a simple model to help us understand the opportunity cost we must pay for improved health care. To be even more specific, we'll measure production of health care by the *number of lives saved*. This variable is plotted along the horizontal axis in Figure 1. To measure the opportunity cost of health care, we'll make a simplifying assumption: that all goods *other* than lifesaving health care can be lumped into a single category, and that we can measure how many units of these "other goods" we're producing. In Figure 1, the quantity of "other goods" is measured on the vertical axis.

Now look at the curve drawn in Figure 1. It is society's **production possibilities frontier (PPF)**, *giving the different combinations of goods that can be produced with the resources and technology currently available.* More specifically, this PPF tells us the *maximum quantity* of all other goods we can produce for each number of lives saved and the maximum number of lives saved for each different quantity of other goods. Positions outside the frontier are unattainable with the technology and resources at the economy's disposal. Society's choices are limited to points *on* or *inside* the PPF.

Let's take a closer look at the PPF in Figure 1. Point *A* represents one possible choice for our society: to devote all resources to the production of "other goods" and none to health care. In this case, we would have 1,000,000 units of other goods, but we would have to forego every opportunity to save lives. Point *F* represents the opposite extreme: all available resources devoted to lifesaving health care. In that case, we'd save 500,000 lives, but we'd have no other goods.

If points *A* and *F* seem absurd to you, remember that they represent two *possible* choices for society but choices we would be unlikely to make. We want lifesaving health care to be available to those who need it, but we also want housing,

Production possibilities frontier (PPF) A curve showing all combinations of two goods that can be produced with the resources and technology currently available.

clothing, entertainment, cars, and so on. So a realistic choice would include a *mix* of health care and other goods.

Suppose we desire such a mix, but the economy, for some reason, is currently operating at the undesirable point A—no health care but maximum production of everything else. Then we need to shift some resources from other goods to health care. For example, we could move from point A to point B, where we'd be saving 100,000 lives. But as a consequence, we'd have to cut back on other goods, producing 50,000 fewer units. The opportunity cost of saving 100,000 lives, then, would be 50,000 units of all other goods.

Increasing Opportunity Cost. Suppose we are at point B and now we want to save even more lives. Once again, we shift enough resources into health care to save an additional 100,000 lives, moving from point B to point C. This time, however, there is an even *greater* cost: Production of other goods falls from 950,000 units to 850,000 units, or a sacrifice of 100,000 units. The opportunity cost of saving lives has risen. You can see that as we continue to save more lives—by increments of 100,000, moving from point C to point D to point E to point F—the opportunity cost of producing other goods keeps right on rising, until saving the last 100,000 lives costs us 400,000 units of other goods.

The behavior of opportunity cost described here—the more health care we produce, the greater the opportunity cost of producing still more—applies to a wide range of choices facing society. It can be generalized as the *law of increasing opportunity cost*.

Law of increasing opportunity cost The more of something that is produced, the greater the opportunity cost of producing one more unit.

> According to the **law of increasing opportunity cost**, the more of something we produce, the greater the opportunity cost of producing even more of it.

The law of increasing opportunity cost causes the PPF to have a *concave* shape, becoming steeper as we move rightward and downward. To understand why, remember (from high school math) that the slope of a line or curve is just the change along the vertical axis divided by the change along the horizontal axis. Along the PPF, as we move rightward, the slope is the change in the quantity of other goods divided by the change in the number of lives saved. This is a negative number, because a positive change in lives saved means a negative change in other goods. The absolute value of this slope is the opportunity cost of saving another life. Now—as we've seen—this opportunity cost increases as we move rightward. Therefore, the absolute value of the PPF's slope must rise as well. The PPF gets steeper and steeper, giving us the concave shape we see in Figure 1.[3]

Why should there be a law of increasing opportunity cost? Why must it be that the more of something we produce, the greater the opportunity cost of producing still more?

Because most resources—*by their very nature*—are better suited to some purposes than to others. If the economy were operating at point A, for example, we'd be using all of our resources to produce other goods, including resources that are much better suited for health care. A hospital might be used as a food cannery, a surgical laser might be used for light shows, and a skilled surgeon might be driving a cab or trying desperately to make us laugh with his stand-up routine.

---

[3] You might be wondering if the law of increasing opportunity cost applies in both directions. That is, does the opportunity cost of producing "other goods" increase as we produce more of them? The answer is yes, as you'll see when you do Problem 1 at the end of this chapter.

As we begin to move rightward along the PPF, say from *A* to *B*, we shift resources out of other goods and into health care. But we would *first* shift those resources *best suited to health care*—and *least* suited for the production of other things. For example, the first group of workers we'd use to save lives would be those who already have training as doctors and nurses. A surgeon—who would probably not make the best comedian—could now go back to surgery, which he does very well. Similarly, the first buildings we would put to use in the health care industry would be those that were originally built as hospitals and medical offices, and weren't really doing so well as manufacturing plants, retail stores, or movie studios. This is why, at first, the PPF is very flat: We get a *large* increase in lives saved for only a *small* decrease in other goods.

As we continue moving rightward, however, we shift away from other goods to those resources that are less and less suited to lifesaving. As a result, the PPF becomes steeper. Finally, we arrive at point *F*, where all resources—no matter how well suited for other goods and services—are used to save lives. A factory building is converted into a hospital, your family car is used as an ambulance, and comedic actor Jim Carrey is in medical school, training to become a surgeon.

The principle of increasing opportunity cost applies to all of society's production choices, not just that between health care and other goods. If we look at society's choice between food and oil, we would find that some land is better suited to growing food and some land to drilling for oil. As we continue to produce more oil, we would find ourselves drilling on land that is less and less suited to producing oil, but better and better for producing food. The opportunity cost of producing additional oil will therefore increase. The same principle applies in choosing between civilian goods and military goods, between food and clothing, or between automobiles and public transportation: The more of something we produce, the greater the opportunity cost of producing still more.

The Search for a Free Lunch

This chapter has argued that every decision to produce *more* of something requires us to pay an opportunity cost by producing less of something else. Nobel Prize–winning economist Milton Friedman summarized this idea in his famous remark, "There is no such thing as a free lunch." Friedman was saying that, even if a meal is provided free of charge to someone, society still uses up resources to provide it. Therefore, a "free lunch" is not *really* free: Society pays an opportunity cost by not producing other things with those resources. Therefore, some members of society will have to make do with less.

The same logic applies to other supposedly "free" goods and services. From society's point of view, there is no such thing as free Internet service, free broadcast television, or free medical care, even if those who enjoy these things don't pay for them as individuals. Providing any of these things requires us to sacrifice *other* things, as illustrated by a movement along society's PPF.

But there are some situations that seem, at first glance, to violate Freidman's dictum. Let's explore them.

Operating Inside the PPF. What if an economy is not living up to its productive potential, but is instead operating *inside* its PPF? For example, in Figure 1, suppose we are currently operating at point *W*, where the health care system is saving 200,000 lives and we are producing 400,000 units of other goods. Then we can move from point *W* to point *E* and save 200,000 more lives with no sacrifice of other goods. Or, starting at point *W*, we could move to point *C* (more of other goods with no sacrifice in lives saved) or to a point like *D* (more of *both* health care *and* other goods).

But why would an economy ever be operating inside its PPF? There are two possibilities.

Productive Inefficiency. One reason an economy might be operating inside its PPF is that resources are being wasted. Suppose, for example, that many people who could be outstanding health care workers are instead producing other goods, and many who would be great at producing other things are instead stuck in the health care industry. Then switching people from one job to the other could enable us to have more of *both* health care *and* other goods. That is, because of the mismatch of workers and jobs, we would be *inside* the PPF at a point like *W*. Creating better job matches would then move us to a point *on* the PPF (such as point *E*).

Economists use the phrase *productive inefficiency* to describe the type of waste that puts us inside our PPF.

Productive inefficiency A situation in which more of at least one good can be produced without sacrificing the production of any other good.

> *A firm, an industry, or an entire economy is **productively inefficient** if it could produce more of at least one good without pulling resources from the production of any other good.*

The phrase *productive efficiency* means the absence of any productive *inefficiency*. For example, if the computer industry is producing the maximum possible number of computers with the resources it is currently using, we would describe the computer industry as productively efficient. In that case, there would be no way to produce any more computers except to use more resources and shift them from the production of some other good. For an entire *economy* to be productively efficient, there must be no way to produce more of *any* good except by pulling resources from the production of some other good.

Although no firm, industry, or economy is ever 100 percent productively efficient, cases of gross inefficiency are not as common as you might think. When you study microeconomics, you'll learn that business firms have strong incentives to identify and eliminate productive inefficiency, since any waste of resources increases their costs and decreases their profit. When one firm discovers a way to eliminate waste, others quickly follow.

For example, empty seats on an airline flight represent productive inefficiency. Since the plane is making the trip anyway, filling the empty seat would enable the airline to serve more people with the flight (produce more transportation services) without using any additional resources (other than the trivial resources of the in-flight meal). Therefore, more people could fly without sacrificing any other good or service. When American Airlines developed a computer model in the late 1980s to fill its empty seats by altering schedules and fares, the other airlines followed its example very rapidly. And when—in the late 1990s— Priceline.com enabled airlines to auction off empty seats on the Internet, several airlines jumped at the chance and others quickly followed. As a result of this—and similar efforts to eliminate waste in personnel, aircraft, and office space—many cases of productive inefficiency in the airline industry were eliminated.

The same sorts of efforts have eliminated some easy-to-identify cases of productive inefficiency in all types of industries: banking, telephone service, Internet service, book publishing, and so on. There are certainly instances of inefficiency that remain (a possible example appears at the end of this chapter). But on the whole, if

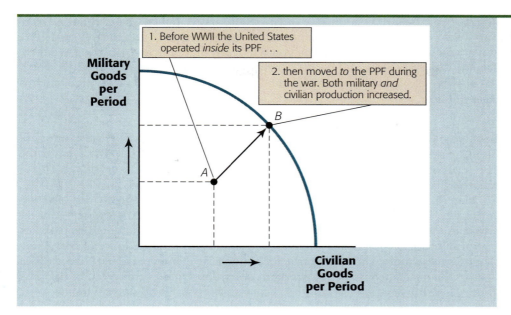

FIGURE 2
Production and Unemployment

1. Before WWII the United States operated *inside* its PPF . . .

2. then moved *to* the PPF during the war. Both military *and* civilian production increased.

Military Goods per Period

B

A

Civilian Goods per Period

you search the economy for a free lunch due to productive inefficiency, you won't find as many hearty meals as you might think.

Recessions. Another reason an economy might operate inside its PPF is a *recession*—a slowdown in overall economic activity. During recessions, many resources are idle. For one thing, there is widespread *unemployment*—people *want* to work but are unable to find jobs. In addition, factories shut down, so we are not using all of our available capital or land either. An end to the recession would move the economy from a point *inside* its PPF to a point *on* its PPF—using idle resources to produce more goods and services without sacrificing anything.

This simple observation can help us understand an otherwise confusing episode in U.S. economic history. During the early 1940s, after the United States entered World War II and began using massive amounts of resources to produce military goods and services, the standard of living in the United States did *not* decline as we might have expected but actually improved slightly. Why?

Figure 2 helps to solve this puzzle. The PPF in Figure 2 is like the PPF in Figure 1. But this time, instead of pitting "health care" against "all other goods," we look at society's choice between *military* goods and *civilian* goods. When the United States entered the war in 1941, it was still suffering from the Great Depression—the most serious and long-lasting economic downturn in modern history, which began in 1929 and hit most of the developed world. For reasons you will learn when you study macroeconomics, joining the allied war effort helped end the Depression in the United States and moved our economy from a point like *A, inside* the PPF, to a point like *B, on* the frontier. Military production increased, but so did the production of civilian goods. Although there were shortages of some consumer goods, the overall result was a rise in the material well-being of the average U.S. citizen.

An economic downturn, such as the Great Depression of the 1930s, does seem to offer the possibility of a free lunch. And a war is only one factor that can reverse a downturn. In fact, no rational nation would ever *choose* war as an economic policy designed to cure a recession, since there are alternative policies that virtually every-one would find preferable. Still, eliminating a recession is not *entirely* cost-free. When you study macroeconomics, you will learn that policies to cure or avoid re-cessions can have risks and costs of their own. Of course, we may feel it is worth the possible costs, but they are costs nonetheless. Once again, a truly free lunch is hard to find.

Economic Growth. If the economy is already operating *on* its PPF, we cannot ex-ploit the opportunity to have more of everything by moving *to* it. But what if the PPF itself were to change? Couldn't we then produce more of everything? This is exactly what happens when an economy's productive capacity grows.

Many factors contribute to economic growth, but they can be divided into two categories. First, the quantities of available *resources*—especially capital—can in-crease. An increase in physical capital—more factories, office buildings, tractors, or high-tech medical equipment—enables the economy to produce more of *everything* that uses these tools. The same is true for an increase in human capital—the skills of doctors, engineers, construction workers, software writers, and so on. In thinking about growth from greater resources, economists focus mostly on capital because, over time, increases in the capital stock have contributed more to higher living stan-dards than other resources.

The second main factor behind economic growth is *technological change,* which enables us to produce more from a *given* quantity of resources. For example, the de-velopment of the Internet has enabled people to retrieve information in a few seconds that used to require hours of searching in a library. As a result, teachers, writers, gov-ernment officials, attorneys, and physicians can produce more without working longer hours.

These two main causes of economic growth—increases in capital and techno-logical change—often go hand in hand. In order for the Internet (a technological change) to be widely used, the economy had to produce and install servers, Internet-capable computers, and fiber-optic cable (increases in capital). In any case, both technological change and increases in the capital stock have the same type of effect on the PPF.

Let's explore a specific example that affects the PPF: body scanners that use PET. This technology enables doctors to quickly view every organ system in the body, and diagnose tumors, brain anomalies, cancers, and even potential heart problems more rapidly and accurately than previous scanning systems like magnetic resonance imaging (MRI). As this is being written (late 2003), PET scanners are be-ing installed in hospitals around the country. Once they're widely distributed, we'll be able to save thousands more lives every year even if we use unchanged quantities of *other* resources (doctors, nurses, hospitals, lab technicians, etc.).

What is the impact on the economy's PPF, like the one in Figure 3? First look at point *F,* where we assume *all* of our resources are devoted to lifesaving, with 500,000 lives saved per period. Under this assumption, having PET scanners would enable us to save even *more* lives—say, a total of 600,000 per period. Thus, the hor-izontal intercept of the PPF moves rightward, from *F* to *F'*.

Now consider point *A,* where we assume *none* of our resources would be de-voted to lifesaving, and we'd produce 1,000,000 units of other goods. The new PET scanners have no productive use other than lifesaving, so having them would *not* change the vertical intercept, *A.*

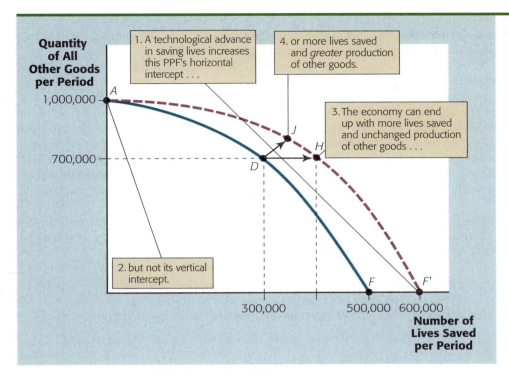

FIGURE 3
The Effect of a New Medical Technology

As you can see, the impact of PET scanners is to stretch the PPF outward along the horizontal axis. Our society can then choose any point along the *new* PPF. For example, we could move from point *D* on the original PPF to point *H* on the new one. For this move, we'd be using all of the benefits of the new technology to save lives, with *unchanged* production of other goods. Or we could choose to move from point *D* to point *J* where, as you can verify, we produce more of *both* things that we value: more lives saved *and* more of other goods.

You may be wondering: How can a technological change in lifesaving enable us to produce more goods in *other* areas of the economy? The answer is: Society can choose to use *some* of the increased lifesaving potential to shift other resources *out* of the medical care and into the production of other things. Because of the technological advance and the new capital, we can shift these resources without sacrificing lives.

We'd get a similar result from a technological change, or an increase in capital, that directly affected only *non*medical production. For example, the development and distribution of new assembly-line robots for the mass-production of automobiles, televisions, and home furniture would shift the *vertical* intercept of the PPF but leave its *horizontal* intercept unchanged. But once again, we could choose to save more lives *and* produce more of other goods. (You may want to draw the old and new PPFs for this case, and find a point that illustrates this choice.)

In general,

a technological change or an increase in the capital stock, even when the direct impact is to increase production of just one type of good, allows us to choose greater production of all types of goods.

This conclusion certainly *seems* like a free lunch. After all, if we can produce more of the things that we value, without having to produce less of anything else, haven't we escaped from paying an opportunity cost?

Yes . . . and no. Figure 3 tells only *part* of the story, because it leaves out the steps needed to *create* this shift in the PPF in the first place. For example, technological innovation doesn't just "happen." Rather, resources must be used to create it—mostly by the research and development (R&D) departments of large corporations. In 2002, these corporations used $300 billion worth of resources on R&D, resources that *could* have been used to produce other things that we'd like right now—cars, apartments, entertainment, or even more *unimproved* medical services that can save lives in the present. The same is true when we produce and install new capital equipment; this, too, uses resources that could have been used for some other purpose.

> In order to produce more goods and services **in the future**, we must shift resources toward R&D and capital production, and away from the production of things we'd enjoy right now.

We must conclude that although economic growth—at first glance—*appears* to be a free lunch, someone ends up paying the check. In this case, the bill is paid by those members of society who will have to make do with less in the present.

ECONOMIC SYSTEMS

As you read these words—perhaps sitting at home or in the library—you are experiencing a very private moment. It is just you and this book; the rest of the world might as well not exist. Or so it seems. . . .

Actually, even in this supposedly private moment, you are connected to the rest of the world in ways you may not have thought about. In order for you to be reading this book, the authors had to write it. Someone had to edit it, to help make sure that all necessary material was covered and explained as clearly as possible. Someone else had to prepare the graphics. Others had to run the printing presses and the binding machines, and still others had to pack the book, ship it, unpack it, put it on a store shelf, and then sell it to you.

And there's more. People had to manufacture all kinds of goods: paper and ink, the boxes used for shipping, the computers used to keep track of inventory, and so on. It is no exaggeration to say that thousands of people were involved in putting this book in your hands.

And there is still more. The chair or couch on which you are sitting, the light shining on the page, the heat or the air conditioning in the room, the clothes you are wearing—all these things that you are using right now were *produced by somebody else*. So even now, as you sit alone reading this book, you are economically linked to others in hundreds—even thousands—of different ways.

Take a walk in your town or city, and you will see even more evidence of our economic interdependence: People are collecting garbage, helping schoolchildren cross the street, transporting furniture across town, constructing buildings, repairing roads, painting houses. Everyone is producing goods and services for *other people*.

Why is it that so much of what we consume is produced by other people? Why are we all so heavily dependent on each other for our material well-being? Why doesn't each of us—like Robinson Crusoe on his island—produce our own food, clothing, housing, and anything else we desire? And how did it come about that *you*—who did not produce any of these things yourself—are able to consume them?

These are all questions about our *economic system*—the way our economy is organized. Ordinarily, we take our economic system for granted, like the water that runs out of our faucets. But now it's time to begin looking at the plumbing—to learn how our economy serves so many millions of people, enabling them to survive and prosper.

Specialization and Exchange

If we were forced to, many of us could become economically *self-sufficient*. We could stake out a plot of land, grow our own food, make our own clothing, and build our own homes. But in no society is there such extreme self-sufficiency. On the contrary, every economic system over the past 10,000 years has been characterized by two features: (1) **specialization,** in which each of us concentrates on a limited number of productive activities, and (2) **exchange,** in which most of what we desire is obtained by trading with others rather than producing for ourselves.

These two features are at the heart of a basic principle of economics:

Specialization A method of production in which each person concentrates on a limited number of activities.

Exchange The act of trading with others to obtain what we desire.

> *Basic Principle #3: Specialization and Exchange*
> *Specialization and exchange enable us to enjoy greater production, and higher living standards, than would otherwise be possible. As a result, all economies exhibit high degrees of specialization and exchange.*

There are three reasons why specialization and exchange enable us to enjoy greater production. The first has to do with human capabilities: Each of us can learn only so much in a lifetime. By limiting ourselves to a narrow set of tasks—fixing plumbing, managing workers, writing music, or designing Web pages—we are each able to hone our skills and become experts at one or two things instead of remaining amateurs at a lot of things. It is easy to see that an economy of experts will produce more than an economy of amateurs.

A second gain from specialization results from the time needed to switch from one activity to another. When people specialize, and thus spend more time doing one task, there is less unproductive "downtime" from switching activities.

Adam Smith first explained these gains from specialization in his book *An Inquiry into the Nature and Causes of the Wealth of Nations*, published in 1776. Smith explained how specialization within a pin factory dramatically increased the number of pins that could be produced there. In order to make a pin . . .

> *One man draws out the wire, another straightens it, a third cuts it, a fourth points it, a fifth grinds it at the top for receiving the head; to make the head requires three distinct operations; to put it on is a [separate] business, to whiten the pins is another; it is even a trade by itself to put them into the paper; and the important business of making a pin is, in this manner, divided into about eighteen distinct operations, which, in some manufactories, are all performed by distinct hands.*

Smith went on to observe that 10 men, each working separately, might make 200 pins in a day, but through specialization they were able to make 48,000! What is true for a pin factory can be generalized to the entire economy: Total production will increase when workers specialize.

HTTP://

Economics is a subject that has benefited from specialization and the division of labor. To get a feel for the many different subjects that economists investigate, take a look at the *Journal of Economic Literature*'s classification system at **http:// www.econlit.org/ subject_descriptors.html**.

Notice that the production gains from specialization we've been discussing—and that Adam Smith described so well—do *not* depend on any differences in individuals' capabilities. Even in a society where initially everyone is *identical* to everyone else, specialization would still yield gains for the two reasons we've discussed: People would develop expertise over time and there would be less downtime from switching tasks.

Of course, in the real world, workers are *not* identically suited to different kinds of work. Nor are all plots of land, all natural resources, or all types of capital equipment identically suited for different tasks. This observation brings us to the *third* source of gains from specialization—one based on individual differences.

Further Gains to Specialization: Comparative Advantage.

Imagine a shipwreck in which there are only two survivors—let's call them Maryanne and Gilligan—who wash up on opposite shores of a deserted island. Initially they are unaware of each other, so each is forced to become completely self-sufficient.

On one side of the island, Maryanne finds that it takes her half an hour to pick one cup of berries and an hour to catch one fish, as shown in the first row of Table 2. On the other side of the island, Gilligan—who is less adept at both tasks—requires two hours to pick a cup of berries and six hours to catch one fish, as listed in the second row of the table. Since both castaways would want some variety in their diets, we can assume that each would spend part of the week catching fish and part picking berries.

Suppose that, one day, Maryanne and Gilligan discover each other. After rejoicing at the prospect of human companionship, they decide to develop a system of production that will work to their mutual benefit. Let's rule out any of the gains from specialization that we discussed earlier (minimizing downtime or developing expertise). Will it still pay for these two to specialize? The answer is yes, as you will see after a small detour.

Absolute Advantage: A Detour.

When Gilligan and Maryanne sit down to figure out who should do what, they might fall victim to a common mistake: basing their decision on *absolute advantage*. An individual has an **absolute advantage** in the production of some good when he or she can produce it using *fewer resources* than another individual can. On the island, the only resource being used is labor time, so the reasoning might go as follows: Maryanne can pick a cup of berries more quickly than Gilligan (see Table 2), so she has an *absolute advantage* in berry picking. It seems logical, then, that Maryanne should be the one to pick the berries.

But wait! Maryanne can also catch *fish* more quickly than Gilligan, so she has an absolute advantage in fishing as well. If absolute advantage is the criterion for assigning work, then Maryanne should do *both* tasks. This, however, would leave Gilligan doing nothing, which is certainly *not* in the pair's best interests. What can

Absolute advantage The ability to produce a good or service, using fewer resources than other producers use.

TABLE 2
Labor Requirements for Berries and Fish

	Labor Required for:	
	1 Cup of Berries	**1 Fish**
Maryanne	½ hour	1 hour
Gilligan	2 hours	6 hours

we conclude from this example? That absolute advantage is an unreliable guide for allocating tasks to different workers.

Comparative Advantage. The correct principle to guide the division of labor on the island is comparative advantage:

> *A person has a **comparative advantage** in producing some good if he or she can produce it with a smaller opportunity cost than some other person can.*

🔑 Opportunity Cost

Comparative advantage The ability to produce a good or service at a lower opportunity cost than other producers.

Notice the important difference between absolute advantage and comparative advantage: You have an *absolute* advantage in producing a good if you can produce it using fewer *resources* than someone else can. But you have a *comparative* advantage if you can produce it with a smaller *opportunity cost*. As you'll see, these are not necessarily the same thing.

Let's see who has a *comparative* advantage in fishing, by calculating—for each of the castaways—the opportunity cost of catching one fish. For Maryanne, catching a fish takes an hour. This is time that could instead be used to pick *two* cups of berries. Thus, we can write

Maryanne: opportunity cost of 1 fish = 2 cups of berries

It takes Gilligan *six* hours to catch a fish, time with which he could pick *three* cups of berries. Thus,

Gilligan: opportunity cost of 1 fish = 3 cups of berries

Comparing the two results, we see that the opportunity cost of one fish is *lower* for Maryanne than it is for Gilligan. Therefore, *Maryanne has a comparative advantage in fishing.*

Now let's determine who has a comparative advantage in berries by determining the opportunity cost of one cup of berries for both castaways. For Maryanne, one cup of berries takes half an hour, time that could be used to catch half a fish. Thus, we can write

Maryanne: opportunity cost of 1 cup berries = ½ fish

Of course, no one would ever catch *half* a fish, unless they were fishing with a machete. But it's still useful to know the *rate* of trade-off of one good for the other. It tells us, for example, that Maryann's opportunity cost for *two* cups of berries would be *one* fish—which is easier to imagine.

It takes Gilligan *two* hours to pick a cup of berries, time that could get him ⅓ fish instead. Thus,

Gilligan: opportunity cost of 1 cup berries = ⅓ fish

Comparing these results, we see that for berries, it's *Gilligan* who has the lower opportunity cost. Therefore, Gilligan—who has an absolute advantage in nothing—has a *comparative* advantage in berry picking.

© COURTESY NEAL PETERS COLLECTION

Even castaways do better when they specialize and exchange with each other, instead of trying to be self-sufficient.

Let's see what happens as the two decide to move toward *specializing* according to their comparative advantage. Let's have Gilligan catch *three fewer fish* each week, freeing up 18 hours that he can use to pick *nine* more cups of berries:

Gilligan: Fish ↓ 3 ⇒ Berries ↑ 9

Since Maryanne has the comparative advantage in fish, let's have her catch *four more fish* each week. This requires that she shift eight hours out of berry picking, sacrificing eight cups of berries:

Maryanne: Fish ↑ 4 ⇒ Berries ↓ 8

Now, what happens to *total* production as a result of these moves? As you can see, Maryanne *more* than makes up for the fish that Gilligan is no longer catching, and Gilligan *more* than makes up for the berries that Maryanne isn't picking. Taken together, the pair is producing one more fish *and* one more cup of berries, without requiring either to work more hours.

Since—by producing according to comparative advantage—total production on the island increases, total *consumption* can increase, too. Gilligan and Maryanne can figure out some way of trading fish for berries that makes each of them come out ahead. In the end, each of the castaways can enjoy a higher standard of living when they specialize and exchange with each other, compared to the level they'd enjoy under self-sufficiency.

What is true for our shipwrecked island dwellers is also true for the entire economy:

Specialization and Exchange

> *Total production of every good or service will be greatest when individuals specialize according to their comparative advantage. This is another reason why specialization and exchange lead to higher living standards than does self-sufficiency.*

When we turn from our fictional island to the real world, is production, in fact, consistent with the principle of comparative advantage? Indeed, it is. A journalist may be able to paint her house more quickly than a housepainter, giving her an *absolute* advantage in painting her home. Will she paint her own home? Except in unusual circumstances, no, because the journalist has a *comparative* advantage in writing news articles. Indeed, most journalists—like most college professors, attorneys, architects, and other professionals—hire house painters, leaving themselves more time to practice the professions in which they enjoy a comparative advantage.

Even comic book superheroes seem to behave consistently with comparative advantage. Superman can no doubt cook a meal, fix a car, chop wood, and do virtually *anything* faster than anyone else on the earth. Using our new vocabulary, we'd say that Superman has an absolute advantage in everything. But he has a clear comparative advantage in catching criminals and saving the known universe from destruction, which is exactly what he spends his time doing.

Specialization in Perspective. The gains from specialization, whether they arise from developing expertise, minimizing downtime, or exploiting comparative advantage, can explain many features of our economy. For example, college students need to select a major and then, upon graduating, to decide on a specific career. Those who follow this path are often rewarded with higher incomes than those who dally. This is an encouragement to specialize. Society is better off if you specialize, since you will help the economy produce more, and society rewards you for this contribution with a higher income.

The gains from specialization can also explain why most of us end up working for business firms that employ dozens, or even hundreds or thousands, of other employees. Why do these business firms exist? Why isn't each of us a *self-employed* expert, exchanging our production with other self-employed experts? Part of the answer is that organizing production into business firms pushes the gains from specialization still further. Within a firm, some people can specialize in working with their hands, others in managing people, others in marketing, and still others in keeping the books. Each firm is a kind of minisociety within which specialization occurs. The result is greater production and a higher standard of living than we would achieve if we were all self-employed.

Specialization has enabled societies everywhere to achieve standards of living unimaginable to our ancestors. But, it can have a downside as well. Adam Smith himself—while lauding specialization for raising living standards—worried that it could be taken too far, narrowing the range on an individual's interests and abilities, and damaging his character.

Of course, maximizing our material standard of living is not our only goal. In some instances, we might be better off *increasing* the variety of tasks we do each day, even if this means some sacrifice in production and income. For example, in many societies, one sex specializes in work outside the home and the other specializes in running the home and taking care of the children. Might families be better off if children had more access to *both* parents, even if this meant a somewhat lower family income? This is an important question. While specialization gives us material gains, there may be *opportunity costs* to be paid in the loss of other things we care about. The right amount of specialization can be found only by balancing the gains against these costs.

Resource Allocation

It was only 10,000 years ago—a mere blink of an eye in human history—that the Neolithic revolution began and human society switched from hunting and gathering to farming and simple manufacturing. At the same time, human wants grew beyond mere food and shelter to the infinite variety of things that can be *made*. Ever since, all societies have been confronted with three important questions:

1. *Which* goods and services should be produced with society's resources?
2. *How* should they be produced?
3. *Who* should get them?

Together, these three questions constitute the problem of **resource allocation**. The way a society chooses to answer these questions—that is, the method it chooses to allocate its resources—will in part determine the character of its economic system.

Resource allocation A method of determining which goods and services will be produced, how they will be produced, and who will get them.

Let's first consider the *which* question. Should we produce more health care or more movies, more goods for consumers or more capital goods for businesses? Where on its production possibilities frontier should the economy operate? As you will see, there are different methods societies can use to answer these questions.

The *how* question is more complicated. Most goods and services can be produced in a variety of different ways, each method using more of some resources and less of others. For example, there are many ways to dig a ditch. We could use *no capital at all* and have dozens of workers digging with their bare hands. We could use *a small amount of capital* by giving each worker a shovel and thereby use less labor, since each worker would now be more productive. Or we could use *even more capital*—a power trencher—and dig the ditch with just one or two workers. In every economic system, there must always be some mechanism that determines how goods and services will be produced from the infinite variety of ways available.

Finally, the *who* question. Here is where economics interacts most strongly with politics. There are so many ways to divide ourselves into groups: men and women, rich and poor, workers and owners, families and single people, young and old . . . the list is endless. How should the products of our economy be distributed among these different groups and among individuals within each group?

Determining *who* gets the economy's output is always the most controversial aspect of resource allocation. Over the last half-century, our society has become more sensitized to the way goods and services are distributed, and we increasingly ask whether that distribution is fair. For example, men get a disproportionately larger share of our national output than women do, whites get more than African-Americans and Hispanics, and middle-aged workers get more than the very old and the very young. As a society, we want to know *why* we observe these patterns (a positive economic question) and *what* we should do about them (a normative economic question). Our society is also increasingly focusing on the distribution of particular goods and services. Should scarce donor organs be rationed to those who have been waiting the longest so that everyone has the same chance of survival? Or should they be sold to the highest bidder so that those able to pay the most will get them? Should productions of Shakespeare's plays be subsidized by the government to permit more people—especially more poor people—to see them? Or should the people who enjoy these plays pay the full cost of their production?

The Three Methods of Resource Allocation.

Traditional economy An economy in which resources are allocated according to long-lived practices from the past.

The Three Methods of Resource Allocation. Throughout history, every society has relied primarily on one of three mechanisms for allocating resources. In a **traditional economy**, resources are allocated according to the long-lived practices of the past. Tradition was the dominant method of resource allocation for most of human history and remains strong in many tribal societies and small villages in parts of Africa, South America, Asia, and the Pacific. Typically, traditional methods of production are handed down by the village elders, and traditional principles of fairness govern the distribution of goods and services.

Economies in which resources are allocated mostly by tradition tend to be stable and predictable. But these economies have one serious drawback: They don't grow. With everyone locked into the traditional patterns of production, there is little room for innovation and technological change. Traditional economies are therefore likely to be stagnant economies.

Command or centrally planned economy An economic system in which resources are allocated according to explicit instructions from a central authority.

In a **command economy**, resources are allocated mostly by explicit instructions from some higher authority. *Which* goods and services should we produce? The ones we're *ordered* to produce. *How* should we produce them? The way we're *told* to produce them. *Who* will get the goods and services? Whoever the authority *tells* us should get them.

In a command economy, a government body *plans* how resources will be allocated. That is why command economies are also called **centrally planned economies**. But command economies are disappearing fast. Until about 15 years ago, examples would have included the former Soviet Union, Poland, Rumania, Bulgaria, Albania, China, and many others. Beginning in the late 1980s, all of these nations began abandoning central planning. The only examples left today are Cuba and North

Korea, and even these economies—though still dominated by central planning—occasionally take steps away from it.

The third method of allocating resources—and the one with which you are no doubt most familiar—is "the market." In a **market economy,** neither long-held traditions nor commands from above guide most economic behavior. Instead, people are largely free to do what they want with the resources at their disposal. In the end, resources are allocated as a result of individual decision making. *Which* goods and services are produced? Whichever ones producers *choose* to produce. How are they produced? However producers *choose* to produce them. *Who* gets these goods and services? Anyone who *chooses* to buy them.

Market economy An economic system in which resources are allocated through individual decision making.

Of course, in a market system, freedom of choice is constrained by the resources one controls. And in this respect, we do not all start in the same place in the economic race. Some of us—like the Rockefellers and the Kennedys—have inherited great wealth; some—entrepreneur Bill Gates, the novelist Toni Morison, and the model Gisele Bündchen—have inherited great intelligence, talent, or beauty; and some, such as the children of successful professionals, are born into a world of helpful personal contacts. Others, unfortunately, will inherit none of these advantages. In a market system, those who control more resources will have more choices available to them than those who control fewer resources. Moreover, every market economy imposes limits on freeedom of choice. Some restrictions are imposed by government to ensure an orderly, just, and productive society. We cannot kill, steal, or break contracts—even if that is our desire—without suffering serious consequences. And we must pay taxes to fund government services. Still, in spite of the limitations imposed by government and the constraints imposed by limited resources, the market relies heavily on individual freedom of choice to allocate resources.

But wait . . . isn't there a problem here? People acting according to their own desires, without the firm hand of command or tradition to control them? This sounds like a recipe for chaos! How, in such a free-for-all, are resources actually *allocated*?

The answer is contained in two words: *markets* and *prices.*

The Nature of Markets. The market economy gets its name from something that nearly always happens when people are free to do what they want with the resources they possess. Inevitably, people decide to specialize in the production of one or a few things—often organizing themselves into business firms—and then sellers and buyers *come together to trade.* A **market** is a collection of buyers and sellers who have the potential to trade with one another.

Market A group of buyers and sellers with the potential to trade with each other.

In some cases, the market is *global*; that is, the market consists of buyers and sellers who are spread across the globe. The market for oil is an example of a global market, since buyers in any country can buy from sellers in any country. In other cases, the market is local. Markets for restaurant meals, haircuts, and taxi service are examples of local markets.

Markets play a major role in allocating resources by forcing individual decision makers to consider very carefully their decisions about buying and selling. They do so because of an important feature of every market: the *price* at which a good is bought and sold.

The Importance of Prices. A **price** is *the amount of money a buyer must pay to a seller for a good or service.* Price is not always the same as *cost.* In economics, as you've learned in this chapter, cost means *opportunity cost*—the *total* sacrifice

Price The amount of money that must be paid to a seller to obtain a good or service.

needed to buy the good. While the price of a good is a *part* of its opportunity cost, it is not the only cost. For example, the price does not include the value of the time sacrificed to buy something. Buying a new jacket will require you to spend time traveling to and from the store, trying on different styles and sizes, and waiting in line at the cash register.

Still, in most cases, the price of a good is a significant part of its opportunity cost. For large purchases such as a home or automobile, the price will be *most* of the opportunity cost. And this is why prices are so important to the overall working of the economy: They confront individual decision makers with the costs of their choices.

Consider the example of purchasing a car. Because you must pay the price, you know that buying a new car will require you to cut back on purchases of other things. In this way, the opportunity cost to *society* of making another car is converted to an opportunity cost *for you*. If you value a new car more highly than the other things you must sacrifice for it, you will buy it. If not, you won't buy it.

Why is it so important that people face the opportunity costs of their actions? The following thought experiment can answer this question. Imagine that the government passed a new law: When anyone buys a new car, the government will reimburse that person for it immediately. The consequences would be easy to predict. First, on the day the law was passed, everyone would rush out to buy new cars. Why not, if cars are free? The entire stock of existing automobiles would be gone within days—maybe even hours. Many people who didn't value cars much at all, and who hardly ever used them, would find themselves owning several—one for each day of the week or to match the different colors in their wardrobe. Others who weren't able to act in time—including some who desperately needed a new car for their work or to run their households—would be unable to find one at all.

Over time, automobile companies would drastically increase production to meet the surge in demand for cars. So much of our available labor, capital, land, and entrepreneurial talent would be diverted to the automobile industry that we'd have to sacrifice huge quantities of all other goods and services. Thus, we'd end up *paying* for those additional cars in the end, by making do with less education, less medical care, perhaps even less food—all to support the widespread, frivolous use of cars. Almost everyone—even those who love cars—would conclude that society had been made worse-off with the new "free-car" policy. By eliminating a price for automobiles, and severing the connection between the opportunity cost of producing a car and the individual's decision to get one, we would have created quite a mess for ourselves.

 Opportunity Cost

When resources are allocated by the market, and people must pay *for their purchases, they are forced to consider the opportunity cost to society of their individual actions. In this way, markets are able to create a sensible allocation of resources.*

Resource Allocation in the United States. The United States has always been considered the leading example of a market economy. Each day, millions of distinct items are produced and sold in markets. Our grocery stores are always stocked with broccoli and tomato soup, and the drugstore always has Kleenex and aspirin—all due to the choices of individual producers and consumers. The goods that are traded, the way they are traded, and the price at which they trade are determined by the traders themselves. No direction from above is needed to keep markets working.

But even in the United States, there are numerous cases of resource allocation *outside* the market. For example, families are important institutions in the United States, and many economic decisions are made within them. Families tend to operate like traditional villages, not like market economies. After all, few families charge prices for goods and services provided inside the home.

Our economy also allocates some resources by command. Various levels of government collect, in total, about one-third of our incomes as taxes. We are *told* how much tax we must pay, and those who don't comply suffer serious penalties, including imprisonment. Government—rather than individual decision makers—spends the tax revenue. In this way, the government plays a major role in allocating resources—especially in determining which goods are produced and who gets them.

There are also other ways, aside from strict commands, that the government limits our market freedoms. Regulations designed to protect the environment, maintain safe workplaces, and ensure the safety of our food supply are just a few examples of government-imposed constraints on our individual choice.

What are we to make, then, of resource allocation in the United States? Markets are, indeed, constrained. But for each example we can find where resources are allocated by tradition or command, or where government restrictions seriously limit some market freedom, we can find hundreds of examples where individuals make choices according to their own desires. The things we buy, the jobs at which we work, the homes in which we live—in almost all cases, these result from market choices. The market, though not pure, is certainly the dominant method of resource allocation in the United States.

Resource Ownership

So far, we've been concerned with how resources are allocated. Another important feature of an economic system is how resources are *owned*. The owner of a resource—a parcel of land, a factory, or one's own labor time—determines how it can be used and receives income when others use it. And there have been three primary modes of resource ownership in human history.

Under *communal* ownership, resources are owned by everyone—or by no one, depending on your point of view. They are simply there for the taking; no person or organization imposes any restrictions on their use or charges any fees. It is hard to find economies with significant communal ownership of resources. Karl Marx believed that, in time, all economies would evolve toward communal ownership, and he named this predicted system **communism.** In fact, none of the economies that called themselves Marxist (such as the former Soviet Union) ever achieved Marx's vision of communism. This is not surprising: Communal ownership on a broad scale can work only when individuals have no conflicts over how resources are used. Therefore, communism requires the end of *scarcity*—an unlikely prospect in the foreseeable future.

Communism A type of economic system in which most resources are owned in common.

Nevertheless, there are examples of communal ownership on a smaller scale. Traditional villages maintain communal ownership of land and sometimes cattle. In some of the cooperative farms in Israel—called *kibbutzim*—land and capital are owned by all the members. Conflicts may result when individuals differ over how these resources should be used, but these conflicts are resolved by consensus rather than by decree or by charging fees for their use.

Closer to home, most families operate on the principle of communal ownership. The house, television, telephone, and food in the refrigerator are treated as if owned jointly. More broadly, who "owns" our sidewalks, streets, and public beaches? No

Socialism A type of economic system in which most resources are owned by the state.

one does, really. In practice, all citizens are free to use them as much and as often as they would like. This is essentially communal ownership.

Under **socialism,** the *state* owns most of the resources. The prime example is the former Soviet Union, where the state owned all of the land and capital equipment in the country. In many ways, it also owned the labor of individual households, since it was virtually the only employer in the nation and unemployment was considered a crime.

State ownership also occurs in nonsocialist economies. In the United States, national parks, state highway systems, military bases, public colleges and universities, and government buildings are all state-owned resources. Over a third of the land in the country is owned by the federal government. The military, even under our current volunteer system, is an example in which the state owns the labor of soldiers—albeit for a limited period of time.

Capitalism A type of economic system in which most resources are owned privately.

Finally, the third system. When most resources are owned *privately*—as in the United States—we have **capitalism.** Take the book you are reading right now. If you turn to the title page, you will see the imprint of the company that published this book. This is a corporation owned by thousands of individual stockholders. These individuals own the buildings, the land under them, the office furniture and computer equipment, and even the reputation of the company. When these facilities are used to produce and sell a book, the company's profits belong to these stockholders. Similarly, the employees of the company are private individuals. They are selling a resource they own—their labor time—to the company, and they receive income—wages and salaries—in return.

The United States is one of the most capitalistic countries in the world. True, there are examples of state and communal ownership, as we've seen. But the dominant mode of resource ownership in the United States is *private* ownership. Resource owners keep *most* of the income they earn from supplying their resources, and they have broad freedom in deciding how their resources are used.

Types of Economic Systems

We've used the phrase *economic system* a few times already in this book. But now it's time for a formal definition.

Economic system A system of resource allocation and resource ownership.

> An **economic system** *is composed of two features: a mechanism for* allocating *resources and a mode of resource* ownership.

Let's leave aside the rare economies in which communal ownership is dominant and those in which resources are allocated primarily by tradition. That leaves us with four basic types of economic systems, indicated by the four quadrants in Figure 4. In the upper left quadrant, we have *market capitalism.* In this system, resources are *allocated* primarily by the market and *owned* primarily by private individuals. Today, most nations have market capitalist economies, including all of the countries of North America and Western Europe, and most of those in Asia, Latin America, and Africa.

In the lower right quadrant is *centrally planned socialism,* under which resources are mostly allocated by command and mostly owned by the state. This *was* the system in the former Soviet Union and the nations of Eastern Europe until the late 1980s. But since then, these countries' economies have gone through cataclysmic change by moving from the lower right quadrant to the upper left. That is,

HTTP://

The Center for International Comparisons at the University of Pennsylvania (http://pwt.econ. upenn.edu/) is a good source of information on the performance of economies around the world.

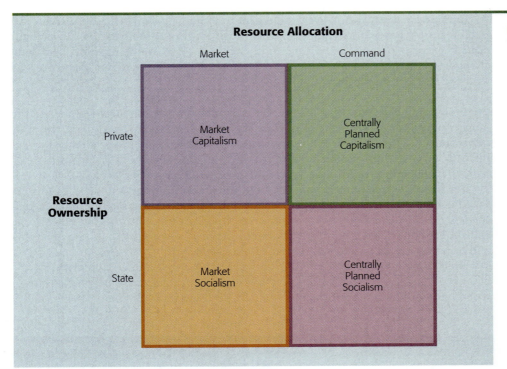

FIGURE 4
Types of Economic Systems

these nations have simultaneously changed both their method of resource allocation and their systems of resource ownership.

Although market capitalism and centrally planned socialism have been the two paramount economic systems in modern history, there have been others. The upper right quadrant represents a system of *centrally planned capitalism,* in which resources are owned by private individuals yet allocated by command. In the recent past, countries such as Sweden and Japan—where the government has been more heavily involved in allocating resources than in the United States—have flirted with this type of system. Nations at war—like the United States during World War II— also move in this direction, as governments find it necessary to direct resources by command in order to ensure sufficient military production.

Finally, in the lower left quadrant is *market socialism,* in which resources are owned by the state yet allocated by the market mechanism. The possibility of market socialism has fascinated many social scientists, who believed it promised the best of both worlds: the freedom and efficiency of the market mechanism and the fairness and equity of socialism. There are, however, serious problems—many would say "unresolvable contradictions"—in trying to mix the two. The chief examples of market socialism in modern history were short-lived experiments—in Hungary and the former Yugoslavia in the 1950s and 1960s—in which the results were mixed at best.

Economic Systems and This Book. In this book, you will learn how market capitalist economies operate. This means that the other three types of economic systems in Figure 4 will be, for the most part, ignored. Until 10 years ago, these statements would have been accompanied by an apology that would have gone something like this: "True, much of the world is characterized by alternative economic systems, but there is only so much time in one course . . ."

In the past decade, however, the world has changed dramatically: About 400 million people have come under the sway of the market as their nations have abandoned centrally planned socialism; another billion or so are being added as China changes course. The study of modern economies is now, more than ever before, the study of market capitalism.

Understanding the Market. The market is simultaneously the most simple and the most complex way to allocate resources. For individual buyers and sellers, the market is simple. There are no traditions or commands to be memorized and obeyed. Instead, we enter the markets we *wish* to trade in and we respond to prices there as we *wish* to, unconcerned about the overall process of resource allocation.

But from the economist's point of view, the market is quite complex. Resources are allocated indirectly, as a *by-product* of individual decision making, rather than through easily identified traditions or commands. As a result, it often takes some skillful economic detective work to determine just how individuals are behaving and how resources are being allocated as a consequence.

How can we make sense of all of this apparent chaos and complexity? That is what economics is all about. And you will begin your detective work in Chapter 3, where you will learn about the most widely used model in the field of economics: the model of supply and demand.

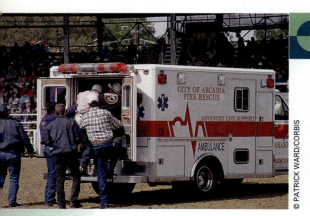

USING THE THEORY
Are We Saving Lives Efficiently?

In this chapter, you learned that if resources are being wasted, we will operate *inside* our PPF rather than on the PPF. For example, suppose "all other goods" are being produced inefficiently. Then, by eliminating the productive inefficiency, we would free up resources. Some of the resources could be used to save more lives and some to produce more of other goods. In Figure 1, this would move us from a point like W to a point like D, where we end up saving more lives *and* having more of other goods.

But there could also be productive inefficiency in the saving of human lives. If that is the case—if it is possible to save more lives without devoting any additional resources to doing so—then we would, once again, be operating inside our PPF. And once again, we could have a free lunch—save more lives *and* have more of other goods—by eliminating the inefficiency.

Some economists have argued that we do, indeed, waste significant amounts of resources in our lifesaving efforts. How have they come to such a conclusion?

The first thing to remember is that saving a life—no matter how it is done—requires the use of resources. Any lifesaving action we might take—putting another hundred police on the streets, building another emergency surgery center, or running an advertising campaign to encourage healthy living—requires certain quantities of resources. In a market economy, resources sell at a price. This allows us to use the dollar cost of a lifesaving method to measure the value of the resources used up by that method.

Moreover, we can compare the "cost per year of life saved" of different methods. For example, in the United States we currently spend about $253 million on heart transplants each year and thereby add about 1,600 years to the lives of heart patients. Thus, the cost per year of life saved from heart transplants is $253,000,000/1,600 = $158,000 (rounded to the nearest thousand).

Method	Cost per Life-Year Saved
Brief physician antismoking intervention:	
Single personal warning from physician to stop smoking	$150
Sickle cell screening and treatment for African-American newborns	$236
Replacing ambulances with helicopters for medical emergencies	$2,454
Intensive physician antismoking intervention:	
Physician identification of smokers among their patients;	
three physician counseling sessions; two further sessions with	
smoking-cessation specialists; and materials—nicotine	
patch or nicotine gum	$2,587
Mammograms: Once every three years, for ages 50–64	$2,700
Chlorination of water supply	$4,000
Next step after suspicious lung X-ray:	
PET Scan	$3,742
Exploratory Surgery	$4,895
Needle Biopsy	$7,116
Vaccination of all infants against strep infections	$80,000
Mammograms: Annually, for ages 50–64	$108,401
Exercise electrocardiograms as screening test:	
For 40-year-old males	$124,374
Heart transplants	$157,821
Mammograms: Annually, for age 40–49	$186,635
Exercise electrocardiograms as screening test:	
For 40-year-old females	$335,217
Seat belts on school buses	$2,760,197
Asbestos ban in automatic transmissions	$66,402,402

TABLE 3
The Cost of Saving Lives

Sources: Electrocardiograms: Charles E. Phelps, *Health Economics,* 2nd ed. (Reading, MA: Addison-Wesley, 1997). Regular exercise: L. Goldman, A. M. Garber, S. A. Grover, & M. A. Hlatky (1996). Task Force 6. Cost-effectiveness of assessment and management of risk factors (Bethesda Conference). *JACC,* 27(5), 1020–1030. Anti-smoking intensive intervention: *Journal of the American Medical Association,* Dec. 3, 1997. Anti-smoking brief intervention: Malcolm Law and Jin Ling Tang, "An Analysis of the Effectiveness of Interventions Intended to Help People Stop Smoking," *Archives of Internal Medicine,* 1995; 155: pp. 1933–1941, and authors' calculations to convert "per life saved" to "per year of life saved." Annual mammograms: Kent Jeffreys, "Progressive Environmentalism: Principles for Regulatory Reform (Policy Report No. 194), National Center for Policy Analysis, June 1995. Benzene emission controls: Tammy O. Tengs et al., "Five Hundred Life-Saving Interventions and Their Cost-Effectiveness," *Risk Analysis,* 1994. All other figures: Tammy O. Tengs, "Dying Too Soon: How Cost-Effectiveness Analysis Can Save Lives," School of Social Ecology, University of California, Irvine, NCPA Policy Report No. 204, May 1997. Replacing ambulances with helicopters: Peter A. Gearhart, Richard Wuerz, A. Russell Localio, "Cost Effectiveness Analysis of Helicopter EMS for Trauma Patients," *Annals of Emergency Medicine,* Oct. 1997, 30:500–506. Chlorination of water supply: Kent Jeffreys, "Guide to Regulatory Reform: The Cost Benefit Rule," National Center for Policy Analysis, *Brief Analysis,* No. 150, January 31, 1995. Strep Vaccination: "A Pound of Prevention," in *News from Harvard Medical, Dental and Public Health Schools,* March 24, 2000 (based on price of $232 for a four-dose vaccination series with Prevnar). Lung cancer screening: M. Ditelin, D. Modka, K. Weber, P. Theiseen, H. Schicha, "Cost Effectiveness of PET in the Management Algorithms of Lung Tumors: Comparison of Health Economic Data," *Nuklearmedizin,* 40(4), August 2001, pp. 122–128, viewed at *http://www.acor.org/cnet/710582.html* (May 2003). Euros have been converted to dollars.

    Table 3 lists several of the methods we currently use to save lives in the United States. Some of these methods reflect legal or regulatory decisions (such as the ban on asbestos) and others reflect standard medical practices (such as annual mammograms for women over 50). Other methods are used only sporadically (such as seat belts in school buses). You can see that the cost per life saved ranges widely—from $150 per year of life saved for a physician warning a patient to quit smoking, to over $66,000,000 per year of life saved from the ban on asbestos in automatic transmissions.

The table indicates that some lifesaving methods are highly cost effective. For example, our society probably exhausts the potential to save lives from brief physician antismoking intervention. Most doctors *do* warn their smoking patients to quit.

But the table also indicates some serious productive *in*efficiency in lifesaving. For example, screening and treating African-American newborns for sickle cell anemia is one of the least costly ways of saving a year of life in the United States—only $236 per year of life saved. Nevertheless, 20 percent of African-American newborns do *not* get this screening at all. Similarly, intensive intervention to discourage smoking is far from universal in the U.S. health care system, even though it has the relatively low cost of $2,587 per year of life saved.

Why is the less than universal use of these lower cost methods *productively inefficient*? To answer, let's do some thought experiments. First, let's imagine that we shift resources from heart transplants to *intensive* antismoking efforts. Then for each year of life we decided *not* to save with heart transplants, we would free up $157,821 in medical resources. If we applied those resources toward intensive antismoking efforts, at a cost of $2,587 per year of life saved, we could then save an additional $157,821/$2,587 = 61 life-years. In other words, we could increase the number of life-years saved without any increase in resources flowing to the health care sector, and therefore, without any sacrifice in other goods and services. If you look back at the definition of productive inefficiency given earlier in this chapter, you'll see why this is an example of it.

But why pick on heart transplants? Our ban on asbestos in automobile transmissions—which requires the purchase of more costly materials with greater quantities of scarce resources—costs us about $66 million for each life-year saved. Suppose these funds were spent instead to buy the resources needed to provide women aged 40 to 49 with annual mammograms (currently *not* part of most physicians' recommendations). Then for each life-year lost to asbestos, we'd save $66 million/186,635 = 354 life-years from earlier detection of breast cancer.

Of course, allocating lifesaving resources is much more complicated than our discussion so far has implied. For one thing, the benefits of lifesaving efforts are not fully captured by "life-years saved" (or even by an alternative measure, which accounts for improvement in *quality* of life). The cost per life-year saved from mandating seat belts on school buses is extremely high—almost $3 million. This is mostly because very few children die in school bus accidents—about 11 per year in the entire United States—and, according to the National Traffic Safety Board, few of these deaths would have been prevented with seat belts. But mandatory seat belts—rightly or wrongly—might decrease the anxiety of millions of parents as they send their children off to school. How should we value such a reduction in anxiety? Hard to say. But it's not unreasonable to include it as a benefit—at least in some way—when deciding about resources.

Another difficulty in allocating our lifesaving resources efficiently—which has become profoundly more serious in the last few years—is uncertainty. Consider, for example, our efforts to prevent a terrorist attack via hijacked airliners. What is the cost per life-year saved? We cannot know. An earlier study of antiterrorist efforts in the mid-1990s had estimated the cost at $8,000,000 per life-year saved, which seems productively inefficient.[4] But this study made two critical assumptions to ar-

---

[4] "The Cost of Anti-terrorist Rhetoric," The Cato Review of Business and Government, Dec. 17, 1996, and authors' calculations to convert "per life saved" to "per year of life saved."

rive at that number. First, that—without the new procedures—37 people would perish each year from airline-related terrorist incidents—equal to the rate we had had in the late 1980s and early 1990s. Second, the study assumed that the safety procedures being evaluated would be 100 percent effective in eliminating attacks.

Both of these assumptions were proven wrong by the events of September 11, 2001. On that day, we discovered that airline hijacking could take many more lives than we had imagined, dramatically reducing the cost per-life-year saved of antiterrorist measures. On the other hand, we also realized that our efforts to prevent such attacks could not be entirely successful—*increasing* the cost per life-year saved.

We confront similar uncertainties in allocating resources to protect against potential bioterrorism. Should our government be stockpiling smallpox vaccine? Should it go further, and press for vaccination of the entire population? The expected cost per life-year saved under each of these policies can range from minuscule to exorbitant, depending on the likelihood of a smallpox attack and how many lives the policy would save—things we can't realistically know. Clearly, trying to gauge and improve our productive efficiency in saving lives—which was never an exact science—has become even *less* exact in the post-9/11 era.

Summary

One of the most fundamental concepts in economics is *opportunity cost*. The opportunity cost of any choice is what we give up when we make that choice. At the individual level, opportunity cost arises from the scarcity of time or money; for society as a whole, it arises from the scarcity of resources—land, labor, capital, and entrepreneurship. To produce and enjoy more of one thing, we must shift resources away from producing something else. The *principle of opportunity cost* tells us that the correct measure of cost is not just the money price we pay, but the opportunity cost: what we must give up when we make a choice. The *law of increasing opportunity cost* tells us that the more of something we produce, the greater the opportunity cost of producing still more.

In a world of scarce resources, each society must have an economic system—its way of organizing economic activity.

All *economic systems* feature *specialization*, where each person and firm concentrates on a limited number of productive activities—and *exchange*, through which we obtain most of what we desire by trading with others. Specialization and exchange enable us to enjoy higher living standards than would be possible under self-sufficiency.

Every economic system determines how resources are owned and how they are allocated. In a market capitalist economy, resources are owned primarily by private individuals and allocated primarily through markets. Prices play an important role in markets by forcing decision makers to take account of society's opportunity cost when they make choices.

Key Terms

Absolute advantage
Capitalism
Centrally planned economy
Command economy
Communism
Comparative advantage
Economic system
Exchange

Explicit cost
Implicit cost
Law of increasing opportunity cost
Market
Market economy
Opportunity cost
Price

Principle of Opportunity Cost
Production possibilities frontier (PPF)
Productive inefficiency
Resource allocation
Socialism
Specialization
Traditional economy

Review Questions

1. "Warren Buffett is one of the world's wealthiest men, worth billions of dollars. For someone like Buffet, the principle of opportunity cost simply doesn't apply." True or false? Explain.

2. What are some reasons why a country might be operating inside its production possibilities frontier (PPF)?

3. Why is a PPF concave—that is, bowed out from the origin? Be sure to give an *economic* explanation.

4. What are three distinct reasons why specialization leads to a higher standard of living?

5. What is the difference between comparative advantage and absolute advantage? Which is more important from an economic viewpoint?

6. List the three questions any resource allocation mechanism must answer. Briefly describe the three primary methods of resource allocation that have evolved to answer these questions.

7. What are the three primary ways in which resources are *owned*? Briefly describe each of them.

8. Why can't the United States economy be described as a *pure market capitalist economy*?

9. True or false?: "Resource allocation and resource ownership are essentially the same thing. Once you know who owns the resources in an economy, you also know by what mechanism those resources will be allocated." Explain your answer.

Problems and Exercises

1. Redraw Figure 1, but this time identify a different set of points along the frontier. Starting at point F (500,000 lives saved, zero production of other goods), have each point you select show equal increments in the quantity of other goods produced. For example, a new point H should correspond to 200,000 units of other goods, point J to 400,000 units, point K to 600,000 units, and so on. Now observe what happens to the opportunity cost of "200,000 more units of other goods" as you move leftward and upward along this PPF. Does the law of increasing opportunity cost apply to the production of "all other goods"? Explain briefly.

2. Suppose that you are considering what to do with an upcoming weekend. Here are your options, from least to most preferred: (1) Study for upcoming midterms; (2) fly to Colorado for a quick ski trip; (3) go into seclusion in your dorm room and try to improve your score on a computer game. What is the opportunity cost of a decision to play the computer game all weekend?

3. How would a technological innovation in lifesaving— say, the discovery of a cure for cancer—affect the PPF in Figure 1?

4. How would a technological innovation in the production of *other* goods—say, the invention of a new kind of robot that speeds up assembly-line manufacturing—affect the PPF in Figure 1?

5. Suppose that one day, Gilligan (the castaway) eats a magical island plant that turns him into an expert at everything. In particular, it now takes him just half an hour to pick a quart of berries, and 15 minutes to catch a fish.
   a. Redo Table 2 in the chapter.
   b. Who—Gilligan or Maryanne—has a comparative advantage in picking berries? In fishing? When the castaways discover each other, which of the two should specialize in which task?

   c. Can *both* castaways benefit from Gilligan's new abilities? How?

6. Suppose that two different castaways, Mr. and Mrs. Howell, end up on a different island. Mr. Howell can pick 1 pineapple per hour, or 1 coconut. Mrs. Howell can pick 2 pineapples per hour, but it takes her two hours to pick a coconut.
   a. Construct a table like Table 2 showing Mr. and Mrs. Howell's labor requirements.
   b. Who—Mr. or Mrs. Howell—has a comparative advantage in picking pineapples? In picking coconuts? Which of the two should specialize in which tasks?
   c. Assume that Mr. and Mrs. Howell had originally washed ashore on different parts of the island, and that they originally each spent 12 hours per day working, spending 6 hours picking pineapples and 6 hours picking coconuts. How will their total production change if they find each other and begin to specialize?

7. You and a friend have decided to work jointly on a course project. Frankly, your friend is a less than ideal partner. His skills as a researcher are such that he can review and outline only two articles a day. Moreover, his hunt-and-peck style limits him to only 10 pages of typing a day. On the other hand, in a day you can produce six outlines or type 20 pages.
   a. Who has an absolute advantage in outlining, you or your friend? What about typing?
   b. Who has a comparative advantage in outlining? In typing?
   c. According to the principle of comparative advantage, who should specialize in which task?

8. Use the information on college costs shown in Table 1 to calculate the average opportunity cost of a year in college for a student at a four-year public institution under the following assumptions:

a. The student receives free room and board at home at no opportunity cost to the parents.

b. The student receives an academic scholarship covering all tuition and fees (in the form of a grant, not a loan or a work study aid).

c. The student works half time while at school at no additional emotional cost.

9. Work the following problems.

a. Use the information on college costs shown in Table 1 to compare the opportunity cost of attending a year of college at a two-year public college, a four-year public college, and a four-year private college.

b. Consider Kylie, who has been awarded academic scholarships covering all tuition and fees at three different colleges. College #1 is a two-year public college. College #2 is a four-year public college, and College #3 is a four-year private college. Explain why, if the decision is based solely on opportunity cost, Kylie will turn down her largest scholarship offers.

c. Given your calculations in part b, what nonmonetary considerations might induce Kylie to go to the college with the highest opportunity cost? How large (in dollar terms) must these nonmonetary benefits be to persuade Kylie to choose the most expensive college?

Challenge Question

1. Suppose that an economy's PPF is a straight line, rather than a bowed out, concave curve. What would this say about the nature of opportunity cost as production is shifted from one good to the other?

 *These exercises require access to Lieberman/Hall Xtra! If Xtra! did not come with your book, visit http://liebermanxtra.swlearning.com to purchase.*

1. Use your Xtra! password at the Hall and Lieberman Web site (http://liebermanxtra.swlearning.com), select Chapter 2, and under Economic Applications, click on EconDebates. Choose *Economic Fundamentals; Scarcity, Choice and Opportunity Cost* and scroll down to find the debate, "Should There Be a Market for Human Organs?" Read the debate, and answer the following questions.

a. How (if at all) would compensation for organ donation offset the opportunity cost of donation?

b. Now click on EconNews. Choose *Economic Fundamentals; Scarcity, Choice and Opportunity Cost* and scroll down to find the article, "What Price for a Life?" Does this form of compensation eliminate the same opportunity cost as organ donation? Why or why not?

2. Use your Xtra! password at the Hall and Lieberman Web site (http://liebermanxtra.swlearning.com), select Chapter 2, and under Economic Applications, click on EconNews. Choose *Economic Fundamentals; Production Possibility Frontier* and scroll down to find the article, "The Federal Budget: What a Difference a Day Makes." Read the summary, and answer the questions below.

a. Does the article imply that the economy is producing efficiently? Why or why not?

b. Draw a PPF between military spending on the horizontal axis, and all other government spending on the vertical axis. Where on the PPF does this article suggest the economy is moving?

c. Is it possible for government to simultaneously increase both military spending and domestic spending?

Supply and Demand

Father Guido Sarducci, a character on the early *Saturday Night Live* shows, once observed that the average person remembers only about five minutes worth of material from college. He therefore proposed the "Five Minute University," where you'd learn only the five minutes of material you'd actually remember and dispense with the rest. The economics course would last only 10 seconds, just enough time for students to learn to recite three words: "supply and demand."

Of course, there is much more to economics than these three words. Still, Sarducci's observation had some truth. Many people *do* regard the phrase "supply and demand" as synonymous with economics. But surprisingly few people actually understand what the phrase means. In a debate about health care, poverty, recent events in the stock market, or the high price of housing, you might hear someone say, "Well, it's just a matter of supply and demand," as a way of dismissing the issue entirely. Others use the phrase with an exaggerated reverence, as if supply and demand were an inviolable physical law, like gravity, about which nothing can be done. So what does this oft-repeated phrase really mean?

First, supply and demand is just an economic model—nothing more and nothing less. It's a model designed to explain *how prices are determined in certain types of markets.*

Why has this model taken on such an exalted role in the field of economics? Because prices themselves play such an exalted role in the economy. In a market system, once the price of something has been determined, only those willing to pay that price will get it. Thus, prices determine which households will get which goods and services and which firms will get which resources. If you want to know why the cell phone industry is expanding while the video rental industry is shrinking, or why homelessness is a more pervasive problem in the United States than hunger, you need to understand how prices are determined. In this chapter, you will learn how the model of supply and demand works and how to use it. You will also learn about the strengths and limitations of the model. It will take more time than Guido Sarducci's 10-second economics course, but in the end you will know much more than just three little words.

MARKETS

Put any compound in front of a chemist, ask him what it is and what it can be used for, and he will immediately think of the basic elements—carbon, hydrogen, oxygen, and so on. Ask an economist almost any question about the economy, and he will immediately think about *markets.*

In ordinary language, a market is a specific location where buying and selling take place: a supermarket, a flea market, etc. In economics, a market is not a place, but rather a collection of *traders.* More specifically,

> *a market is a group of buyers and sellers with the potential to trade with each other.*

Economists think of the economy as a collection of individual markets. In each of these markets, the collection of buyers and sellers will be different, depending on what is being traded. There is a market for oranges, another for automobiles, another for real estate, and still others for corporate stocks, euros, and anything else that is bought and sold.

However, unlike chemistry—in which the set of basic elements is always the same—in economics, we can define a market in *different* ways, depending on our purpose. In fact, in almost any economic analysis, the first step is to define and characterize the market or collection of markets to analyze.

How Broadly Should We Define the Market?

Suppose we want to study the personal computer industry in the United States. Should we define the market very broadly ("the market for computers"), or very narrowly ("the market for ultra-light laptops"), or something in between ("the market for laptops")? The right choice depends on the problem we're trying to analyze.

For example, if we're interested in the price of equipment for connecting to the Internet, there would be no reason to divide computers into desktops and laptops, since the distinction would have nothing to do with e-mail access and would only get in the way. Thus, we'd treat all types of computers as if they were the same

Aggregation The process of combining distinct things into a single whole.

good. Economists call this process **aggregation**—combining a group of distinct things into a single whole.

But suppose we're asking a different question: Why do laptops always cost more than desktops with similar computing power? Then we'd aggregate all laptops together as one good, and all desktops as another, and look at each of these more narrowly defined markets.

The same general principle applies to the *geographic* breadth of the market. If we want to predict how instability in the Persian Gulf will affect gasoline prices around the world, we'd use the "global market for oil," in which the major oil producers in about 20 countries sell to buyers around the globe. But if we want to explain why gasoline is cheaper in the United States than in most of the rest of the world, we'd want to look at the "U.S. market for oil." In this market, global sellers choose how much oil to sell to U.S. buyers.

> In economics, markets can be defined broadly or narrowly, depending on our purpose.

How broadly or narrowly markets are defined is one of the most important differences between *macro*economics and *micro*economics. In macroeconomics, goods and services are aggregated to the highest levels. Macro models even lump all consumer goods—dishwashers, cell phones, blue jeans, and so forth—into the single category "consumption goods" and view them as if they are traded in a single, broadly defined market, "the market for consumption goods." Similarly, instead of recognizing different markets for shovels, bulldozers, computers, and factory buildings, macro models analyze the market for "capital goods." Defining markets this broadly allows macroeconomists to take an overall view of the economy without getting bogged down in the details.

In microeconomics, by contrast, markets are defined more narrowly. Instead of asking how much we'll spend on *consumer goods*, a microeconomist might ask how much we'll spend on *health care* or *video games*. Although microeconomics always involves some aggregation, the process stops before it reaches the highest level of generality.

Buyers and Sellers

A market is composed of the buyers and sellers that trade in it. But who, exactly, *are* these buyers and sellers?

When you think of a seller, your first image might be of a business. In many markets, you'd be right: The sellers *are* business firms. Examples are markets for restaurant meals, airline travel, clothing, and banking services. But businesses aren't the only sellers in the economy. For example, *households* are the primary sellers in labor markets, such as the markets for Web page designers, accountants, and factory workers. Households are also important sellers in markets for used cars, residential homes, and rare artworks. Governments, too, are sometimes important sellers. For example, state governments are major sellers in the market for education through state colleges and universities.

What about buyers? Your first thought may be "people" like yourself, or "households." Indeed, many goods and services are bought primarily by households: college education, movies, housing, clothing, and so on. But businesses and government agencies are the primary buyers in labor markets, and they are also important buyers of personal computers, automobiles, and airline transportation.

As you can see, the buyers in a market can be households, business firms, or government agencies. And the same is true of sellers. Sometimes, it's important to recognize that all three groups are on both sides of a market. But not always. Once again, it depends on our purpose.

Our purpose in this book—and your purpose in taking a college course in economics—is educational. We want to identify the major forces at work in the economy, the ones that cause prices to rise and fall, industries to expand and contract, and so on. Accordingly, we want to keep our models simple, so the important ideas stand out more clearly. This is why we'll usually (but not always) follow this guideline:

> *For the most part, in markets for consumer goods, we'll view business firms as the only sellers, and households as the only buyers.*

Of course, we'll make exceptions whenever decisions by *other* groups of buyers or sellers matter to the problem at hand.

One last simplification should be mentioned. In many of our discussions, we'll be leaving out the "go-between." When analyzing, say, the market for books, we'll view book publishers as selling directly to households, rather than using retailers like Barnes and Noble or Amazon.com to do the selling for them. And in labor markets—such as say, the market for business managers—we'll view business firms as hiring workers directly, rather than using headhunting firms as intermediaries. Except for special issues in which retailers, headhunters or other intermediaries are important, including them would add complexity but not much else.

Competition in Markets

A final issue in defining a market is how individual buyers and sellers view the price of the product. In many cases, individual buyers or sellers have an important influence over the price they charge. For example, in the market for cornflakes, Kellogg's—an individual *seller*—simply sets its price every few months. It can raise the price and sell fewer boxes of cereal or lower the price and sell more. In the market for windshield wiper motors, Ford Motor Company—an individual *buyer*—can influence the price by negotiating special deals or by changing the number of motors it buys. The market for breakfast cereals and the market for windshield wiper motors are examples of *imperfectly competitive* markets.

> *In **imperfectly competitive markets**, individual buyers or sellers can influence the price of the product.*

But now think about the national market for wheat. Can an individual seller have any impact on the market price? Not really. On any given day there is a going price for wheat—say, $5.80 per bushel. If a farmer tries to charge more than that—say, $5.85 per bushel—he won't sell any wheat at all! His customers will instead go to one of his many competitors and buy the identical product from them for less. Each wheat farmer must take the price of wheat as a "given."

The same is true of a single wheat *buyer:* If he tries to negotiate a lower price from a seller, he'd be laughed off the farm. "Why should I sell my wheat to you for $5.75 per bushel, when there are others who will pay me $5.80?" Accordingly, each buyer must take the market price as a given.

HTTP://

The Inomics search engine is devoted solely to economics (http://www.inomics.com/cgi/show). Use it to investigate topics related to supply and demand.

Imperfectly competitive market
A market in which a single buyer or seller has the power to influence the price of the product.

The market for wheat is an example of a *perfectly competitive market.*

Perfectly competitive market
A market in which no buyer or seller has the power to influence the price.

> *In perfectly competitive markets (or just competitive markets), each buyer and seller takes the market price as a given.*

What makes some markets imperfectly competitive and others perfectly competitive? You'll learn the complete answer when you are well into your study of *microeconomics,* along with more formal definitions. But here's a hint: In perfectly competitive markets, there are many small buyers and sellers, each is a small part of the market, and the product is standardized, like wheat. Imperfectly competitive markets, by contrast, have just a few large buyers or sellers, or else the product of each seller is unique in some way.

Using Supply and Demand

Supply and demand is a versatile model. It can be applied to broadly defined goods (the market for food) or narrowly defined goods (the market for Granny Smith apples). Households, business firms, or government agencies can appear in any combination on the buying side or the selling side. The buyers and sellers can reside within a small geographic area or be dispersed around the world.

But there is one important restriction in using supply and demand: We are implicitly assuming that the market is perfectly competitive.

> *The supply and demand model is designed to explain how prices are determined in perfectly competitive markets.*

This suggests that the model isn't very useful. After all, perfectly competitive markets—in which an individual buyer or seller has *no* influence on the market price—are not that common in the real world. However, many markets come reasonably close—close enough, in fact, that we can choose to view them as perfectly competitive.

Think of the market for fast-food hot dogs in a big city. On the one hand, every hot dog stand is somewhat different from every other one in terms of location, quality of service, and so on. This means an individual vendor has *some* influence over the price of his hot dogs. For example, if his competitors are all charging $1.50 for a hot dog, but he sells in a more convenient location, he might be able to charge $1.60 or $1.70 without losing too many customers. In this sense, the market for sidewalk hot dogs does not seem perfectly competitive.

On the other hand, there are rather narrow limits to an individual seller's freedom to change his price. With so many vendors in a big city, who are not *that* different from one another, one who charged $2.00 or $2.25 might soon find that he's lost all of his customers to the other vendors who are charging the market price of $1.50. Since no single seller can deviate *too* much from the market price, we could—if we wanted to—view the market as more or less perfectly competitive.

How, then, do we decide whether to consider a market, such as the market for big-city hot dogs, as perfectly or imperfectly competitive? You won't be surprised to hear that it depends on the question we want to answer. If we want to explain why there are occasional price wars among hot dog vendors, or why some of them routinely charge higher prices than others, viewing the market as perfectly competitive would be counterproductive—it would hide, rather than reveal, the answer. For these questions, the supply and demand model would not work, so we'd choose a *different* model—one designed for a type of *im*perfectly competitive market. (If your current course is *micro*economics, you will soon learn about these models and how to use them.)

But if we want to know why hot dogs are cheaper than most other types of fast foods, the simplest approach is to view the market for hot dogs as perfectly competitive. True, each hot dog vendor does have *some* influence over the price. But that influence is so small, and the prices of different sellers are so similar, that our assumption of perfect competition works pretty well.

Perfect competition then, is a matter of degree, rather than an all-or-nothing characteristic. While there are very few markets in which sellers and buyers take the price as completely given, there are many markets in which a *narrow range* of prices is treated as a given (as in the market for hot dogs). In these markets, supply and demand often provides a good approximation to what is going on. This is why it has proven to be the most versatile and widely used model in the economist's tool kit. Neither laptop computers nor orange juice is traded in a perfectly competitive market. But ask an economist to tell you why the cost of laptops decreases every year, or why the price of orange juice rises after a freeze in Florida, and he or she will invariably reach for supply and demand to find the answer.

Supply and demand are like two blades of a scissors: To analyze a market, we need both of them. In this and the next section, we will be sharpening those blades, learning separately about supply and demand. Then, we'll put them together and put them to use. Let's start with demand.

DEMAND

It's tempting to think of "demand" as just a psychological phenomenon, a pure "want" or "desire." But that notion can lead us astray. For example, you *want* all kinds of things: a bigger apartment, a better car, nicer clothes, more and better vacations. The list is endless. But you don't always *buy* them. Why not?

Because in addition to your wants—which you'd very much like to satisfy—you also face *constraints*. First, you have to *pay*. And in most cases, you don't have any influence over the price of what you buy—you just have to pay up or do without. You also have limited total funds with which to buy things, so every decision to buy one thing is also a decision *not* to buy something else. As a result, every purchase confronts you with an opportunity cost. (Even if you don't spend all of your income during the year, you still face an opportunity cost: Every purchase is money you are not saving for later, so you sacrifice future spending power.) Your "wants," together with the real-world constraints that you face, determine what you will choose to buy in any market. Hence, the following definition:

> A *household's quantity demanded* of a good is the specific amount the household would choose to buy over some time period, given (1) a particular price that must be paid for the good; (2) all other constraints on the household.

Household's quantity demanded The specific amount a household would choose to buy over some time period, given (1) a particular price, (2) all other constraints on the household.

When we add up the buying behavior of all households in a market, we get a similar definition:

Market quantity demanded The specific amount of a good that *all* buyers in the market would choose to buy over some time period, given (1) a particular price, (2) all other constraints they face.

> **Market quantity demanded** (*often just* **quantity demanded**) *is the specific amount of a good that* all *buyers in the market would choose to buy over some time period, given (1) a particular price they must pay for the good; (2) all other constraints on households.*

Since this definition plays a key role in any supply and demand analysis, it's worth discussing briefly exactly what it means and doesn't mean.

Quantity Demanded Implies a *Choice*. Quantity demanded doesn't tell us the amount of a good that households feel they "need" or "desire" in order to be happy. Instead, it tells us how much households would like to buy *when they take into account the opportunity cost* of their decisions. The opportunity cost arises from the constraints households face, such as having to pay a given price for the good, limits on spendable funds, and so on.

Quantity Demanded Is *Hypothetical*. Will households actually be *able* to purchase the amount they want to purchase? Maybe yes, maybe no. There are special situations—analyzed in microeconomics—in which households are frustrated in buying all that they would choose to buy. But quantity demanded makes no assumptions about the availability of the good. Instead, it's the answer to a hypothetical question: How much would households *want* to buy, at a specific price, given real-world limits on their spending power?

Quantity Demanded Depends on *Price*. The price of the good is just one variable among many that influences quantity demanded. But because one of our main purposes in building a supply and demand model is to explain how prices are determined, we try to keep that variable front-and-center in our thinking. This is why for the next few pages we'll assume that all other influences on demand are held constant, so we can explore the relationship between price and quantity demanded.

The Law of Demand

How does a change in price affect quantity demanded? You probably know the answer to this already: When something is more expensive, people tend to buy less of it. This common observation applies to air travel, magazines, education, guitars, and virtually everything else that people buy. For all of these goods and services, price and quantity are *negatively related*: that is, when price rises, quantity demanded falls; when price falls, quantity demanded rises. This negative relationship is observed so regularly in markets that economists call it the *law of demand*.

Law of demand As the price of a good increases, the quantity demanded decreases.

> *The **law of demand** states that when the price of a good rises and everything else remains the same, the quantity of the good demanded will fall.*

Read that definition again, and notice the very important words, "everything else remains the same." The law of demand tells us what would happen *if* all the other influences on buyers' choices remained unchanged, and only one influence—the price of the good—changed.

This is an example of a common practice in economics. In the real world, many variables change *simultaneously*. But to understand changes in the economy, we must first understand the effect of each variable *separately*. So we conduct a series of mental experiments in which we ask: "What would happen if this one variable—and only this variable—were to change?" The law of demand is the result of one such mental experiment, in which we imagine that the price of the good changes, but all other influences on quantity demanded remain constant.

The Demand Schedule and the Demand Curve

To make our discussion more concrete, let's look at a specific market: the market for real maple syrup in the United States. In this market, the buyers are all U.S. residents, whereas the sellers (to be considered later) are maple syrup producers in the United States or Canada.

Table 1 shows a hypothetical **demand schedule** for maple syrup in this market. This is *a list of different quantities demanded at different prices, with all other variables that affect the demand decision assumed constant.* For example, the demand schedule tells us that when the price of maple syrup is $2.00 per bottle, the quantity demanded will be 60,000 bottles per month. Notice that the demand schedule obeys the law of demand: As the price of maple syrup increases, the quantity demanded falls.

Now look at Figure 1. It shows a diagram that will appear again and again in your study of economics. In the figure, each price-and-quantity combination in Table 1 is represented by a point. For example, point *A* represents the price $4.00 and quantity 40,000, while point *B* represents the pair $2.00 and 60,000. When we connect all of these points with a line, we obtain the famous *demand curve*, labeled with a *D* in the figure.

> The **market demand curve** (or just **demand curve**) shows the relationship between the price of a good and the quantity demanded, holding constant all other variables that influence demand. Each point on the curve shows the total quantity that buyers would choose to buy at a specific price.

Notice that the demand curve in Figure 1—like virtually all demand curves—*slopes downward*. This is just a graphical representation of the law of demand.

> The law of demand tells us that demand curves virtually always slope downward.

Shifts vs. Movements Along the Demand Curve

Markets are affected by a variety of events. Some events will cause us to *move along* the demand curve; others will cause the entire demand curve to *shift*. It is crucial to distinguish between these two very different types of effects.

Let's go back to Figure 1. There, you can see that when

Demand schedule A list showing the quantities of a good that consumers would choose to purchase at different prices, with all other variables held constant.

Market demand curve The graphical depiction of a demand schedule; a curve showing the quantity of a good or service demanded at various prices, with all other variables held constant.

Price (per Bottle)	Quantity Demanded (Bottles per Month)
$1.00	75,000
2.00	60,000
3.00	50,000
4.00	40,000
5.00	35,000

TABLE 1
Demand Schedule for Maple Syrup in the United States

FIGURE 1
The Demand Curve

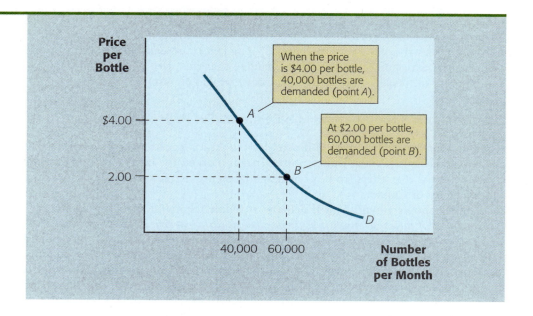

the price of maple syrup rises from $2.00 to $4.00 per bottle, the number of bottles demanded falls from 60,000 to 40,000. This is a movement *along* the demand curve, from point B to point A. In general,

> *a change in the price of a good causes a movement* along *the demand curve.*

In Figure 1, a *fall* in price would cause us to move *rightward* along the demand curve (from point A to point B), and a *rise* in price would cause us to move *leftward* along the demand curve (from B to A).

Remember, though, that when we draw a demand curve, we assume all other variables that might influence demand are *held constant* at some particular value. For example, the demand curve in Figure 1 might have been drawn to give us quantity demanded at each price when average household income in the United States remains constant at, say, $40,000 per year.

But suppose average income increases to $50,000? With more income, we'd expect households to buy more of *most* things, including real maple syrup. This is illustrated in Table 2. At the original income level, households would choose to buy 60,000 bottles of maple syrup at $2.00 per bottle. But after income rises, they would choose to buy more at that price—80,000 bottles, according to Table 2. A similar change would occur at any other price for maple syrup: After income rises, households would choose to buy more than before. In other words, the rise in income *changes the entire relationship between price and quantity demanded.* We now have a *new* demand curve.

Figure 2 plots the new demand curve from the quantities in the third column of Table 2. The new demand curve lies to the *right* of the old curve. For example, at a price of $2.00, quantity demanded increases from 60,000 bottles on the old curve (point B) to 80,000 bottles on the *new* demand curve (point C). As you can see, the rise in household income has *shifted* the demand curve to the right.

Price (per Bottle)	Original Quantity Demanded (Bottles per Month)	New Quantity Demanded After Increase in Income (Bottles per Month)
$1.00	75,000	95,000
2.00	60,000	80,000
3.00	50,000	70,000
4.00	40,000	60,000
5.00	35,000	55,000

TABLE 2
Increase in Demand for Maple Syrup in the United States

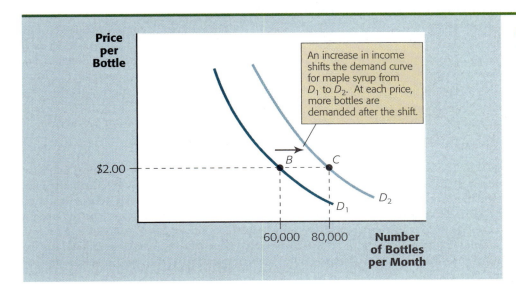

FIGURE 2
A Shift of the Demand Curve

More generally,

a change in any variable that affects demand—except for the good's price—causes the demand curve to shift.

If buyers choose to buy a greater quantity at any price, the demand curve shifts *rightward*. If they decide to buy a smaller quantity at any price, the demand curve shifts *leftward*.

Factors That Shift the Demand Curve

Let's take a closer look at what might cause a change in demand (a shift of the demand curve). Keep in mind that for now, we're exploring *one factor at a time*, always keeping *all other determinants of demand constant*.

Income. In Figure 2, an increase in income shifted the demand for maple syrup to the right. In fact, a rise in income has the same effect on the demand for *most* goods. We call these **normal goods.** Housing, automobiles, health club memberships, and

Income The amount that a person or firm earns over a particular period.

Normal good A good that people demand more of as their income rises.

DANGEROUS CURVES

"Change in Quantity Demanded" vs. "Change in Demand." Language is important when discussing demand. The term *quantity demanded* means a *particular amount* that buyers would choose to buy at a specific price. It's a number represented by a single point on a demand curve. *Demand*, by contrast, means the *entire relationship* between price and quantity demanded, and is represented by the entire demand curve.

For this reason, when a change in the price of a good moves us *along* a demand curve, we call it a **change in quantity demanded**. For example, in Figure 1, the movement from point *A* to point *B* is an *increase* in quantity demanded. This is a change from one number (40,000 bottles) to another (60,000 bottles).

When something *other* than the price changes, causing the entire demand curve to shift, we call it a **change in demand**. In Figure 2, for example, the shift in the curve would be called an *increase in demand*.

Change in quantity demanded A movement along a demand curve in response to a change in price.

Change in demand A shift of a demand curve in response to a change in some variable other than price.

Inferior good A good that people demand less of as their income rises.

Wealth The total value of everything a person or firm owns, at a point in time, minus the total value of everything owed.

real maple syrup are all examples of normal goods.

But not all goods are normal. For some goods—called **inferior goods**—a rise in income would *decrease* demand—shifting the demand curve *leftward*. Regular-grade ground chuck is a good example. It's a cheap source of protein, but not as high in quality as sirloin. With higher income, households could more easily afford better types of meat—ground sirloin or steak, for example. As a result, higher incomes would cause the demand for ground chuck to decrease. For similar reasons, we might expect that Greyhound bus tickets (in contrast to airline tickets) and single-ply paper towels (in contrast to two-ply) are inferior goods.

> *A rise in income will* increase *the demand for a* normal *good, and* decrease *the demand for an* inferior *good.*

Wealth. Your **wealth** at any point in time is the total value of everything you *own* (cash, bank accounts, stocks, bonds, real estate or any other valuable property) minus the total dollar amount you *owe* (home mortgage, credit card debt, auto loan, student loan, and so on). Although income and wealth are different (see the nearby Dangerous Curves box), they have similar effects on demand. Increases in wealth among buyers—because of an increase in the value of their stocks or bonds, for example—gives them more funds with which to purchase goods and services. As you might expect,

> *an increase in wealth will* increase *demand (shift the curve rightward) for a normal good, and* decrease *demand (shift the curve leftward) for an inferior good.*

Substitute A good that can be used in place of some other good and that fulfills more or less the same purpose.

Prices of Related Goods. A **substitute** is a good that can be used in place of another good and that fulfills more or less the same purpose. For example, many people use real maple syrup to sweeten their pancakes, but they could use a number of other things instead: honey, sugar, jam, or *artificial* maple syrup. Each of these can be considered a substitute for real maple syrup.

When the price of a substitute rises, people will choose to buy *more* of the good itself. For example, when the price of jam rises, some jam users will switch to maple syrup, and the demand for maple syrup will increase. In general,

> *a rise in the price of a substitute increases the demand for a good, shifting the demand curve to the right.*

Of course, if the price of a substitute falls, we have the opposite result: Demand for the original good decreases, shifting its demand curve to the left.

There are countless examples in which a change in a substitute's price affects demand for a good. A rise in the price of postage stamps would increase the demand for electronic mail. A drop in the rental price of videos would decrease the demand for movies at theaters. In each of these cases, we assume that the price of the substitute is the only price that is changing.

A **complement** is the opposite of a substitute: It's used *together with* the good we are interested in. Pancake mix is a complement to maple syrup, since these two goods are used frequently in combination. If the price of pancake mix rises, some consumers will switch to other breakfasts—bacon and eggs, for example—that *don't* include maple syrup. The demand for maple syrup will decrease.

Income vs. Wealth It's easy to confuse *income* with *wealth*, because both are measured in dollars and both are sources of funds that can be spent on goods and services. But they are not the same thing. Your income is how much you earn *over a period of time* (such as, $20 *per hour*, $3,500 *per month*, or $40,000 *per year*). Your wealth, by contrast, is the value of what you *own* minus the value of what you *owe* at a moment in time. (Such as, on December 31, 2005, the value of what you own is $12,000, but the value of what you owe is $9,000, so you have $3,000 in wealth.)

To help you see the difference: suppose you get a good job after you graduate, but you have very little in the bank, and you still have large, unpaid student loans. Then you'd have a moderate-to-high *income* (what you earn at your job each period), but your wealth would be negative (since what you would *owe* is greater than what you *own*).

DANGEROUS CURVES

Complement A good that is used *together with* some other good.

> *A rise in the price of a complement decreases the demand for a good, shifting the demand curve to the left.*

For this reason, we'd expect a higher price for automobiles to decrease the demand for gasoline. (To test yourself: How would a lower price for milk affect the demand for breakfast cereal?)

Population. As the population increases in an area, the number of buyers will ordinarily increase as well, and the demand for a good will increase. The growth of the U.S. population over the last 50 years has been an important reason (but not the only reason) for rightward shifts in the demand curves for food, rental apartments, telephones, and many other goods and services.

Expected Price. If buyers expect the price of maple syrup to rise next month, they may choose to purchase more *now* to stock up before the price hike, an increase in demand. If people expect the price to drop, they may postpone buying, hoping to take advantage of the lower price later.

> *In many markets, an expectation that price will rise in the future shifts the* current *demand curve rightward, while an expectation that price will fall shifts the current demand curve leftward.*

Expected price changes are especially important in the markets for financial assets such as stocks and bonds and in the market for real estate. People want to buy more stocks, bonds, and real estate when they think their prices will rise in the near future. This shifts the demand curves for these items to the right.

Tastes. Suppose we know the number of buyers in the United States, their expectations about the future price of maple syrup, the prices of all related goods, and the average levels of income and wealth. Do we have all the information we need to draw the demand curve for maple syrup? Not really. Because we do not yet know how consumers *feel* about maple syrup. How many of them eat breakfast? Of these, how many eat pancakes or waffles? How often? How many of them *like* maple syrup, and how much do they like it? And what about all of the other goods and services competing for consumers' dollars: How do buyers feel about *them*?

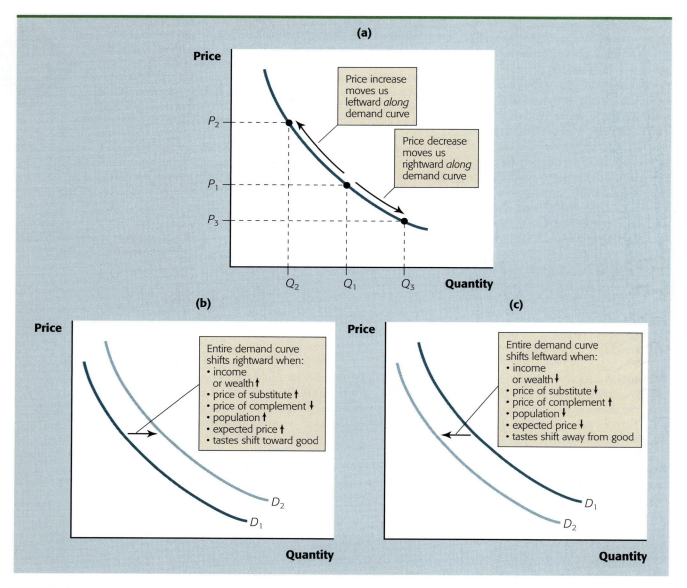

FIGURE 3
Movements Along and
Shifts of the Demand Curve

The questions could go on and on, pinpointing various characteristics about buyers that influence their attitudes toward maple syrup. The approach of economics is to lump all of these characteristics of buyers together and call them, simply, *tastes*. Economists are sometimes interested in where these tastes come from or what makes them change. But for the most part, economics deals with the *consequences* of a change in tastes, whatever the reason for its occurrence.

When tastes change *toward* a good (people favor it more), demand increases, and the demand curve shifts to the right. When tastes change *away* from a good, demand decreases, and the demand curve shifts to the left. An example of this is the change in tastes away from cigarettes over the past several decades. The cause may have been an aging population, a greater concern about health among people of *all* ages, or successful antismoking advertising. But regardless of the cause, the effect has been to decrease the demand for cigarettes, shifting the demand curve to the left.

Figure 3 summarizes the variables we've discussed that affect the demand side of the market, and how their effects are represented with a demand curve. Notice the important distinction between movements *along* the demand curve and *shifts* of the entire curve.

Keep in mind that other variables, besides those listed in Figure 3, can influence demand. For example, weather can affect the demand for many goods: A rise in temperature can increase the demand for ice cream and decrease the demand for sweaters. Expectations other than the future price can matter too. If buyers expect a recession and fear their incomes may fall, demand may decrease for normal goods *now*, even though current income remains unchanged. Some of these other *shift-variables* for the demand curve will be discussed when they become relevant in a specific application. But we'll always use the same logic we used here: If an event makes buyers want to purchase more or less of a good *at any given price*, it causes the demand curve to shift.

Does Supply Affect Demand? A troubling thought may have occurred to you. Among the variables that shift the demand curve in Figure 3, shouldn't we include the amount of syrup available? Or to put the question another way, doesn't supply influence demand?

No—at least not directly. The demand curve answers a series of hypothetical questions about how much buyers *would like* to buy at each different price. A change in the amount available would not affect the answers, and so can't shift the demand curve. As you'll see later, a change in supply *will* change the *price* of the good, but this causes a movement along—not a shift of—the demand curve.

DANGEROUS CURVES

SUPPLY

When most people hear the word *supply*, their first thought is that it's the amount of something "available," as if this amount were fixed in stone. For example, someone might say, "We can only drill so much oil from the ground," or "There are only so many apartments for rent in this town." And yet, the world's known oil reserves—as well as yearly production of oil—have increased dramatically over the last quarter century, as oil companies have found it worth their while to look harder for oil. Similarly, in most towns and cities, short buildings have been replaced with tall ones, and the number of apartments has increased. Supply, like demand, can change, and the amount of a good supplied in a market depends on the *choices* made by those who produce it.

What governs these choices? We assume that business firms' managers have a goal: to earn the highest profit possible. But they also face constraints. First, in a competitive market, the price they can charge for their product is a *given*—the market price. Second, firms have to pay the *costs* of producing and selling their product. These costs will depend on the production process they use, the prices they must pay for their inputs, and more. A firm's desire for profit, together with the real-world constraints that it faces, determines how much it will choose to sell in any market. Hence, the following definition:

> A *firm's quantity supplied* of a good is the specific amount its managers would choose to sell over some time period, given (1) a particular price for the good; (2) all other constraints on the firm.

Firm's quantity supplied The specific amount a firm would choose to sell over some time period, given (1) a particular price for the good; (2) all other constraints on the firm.

When we add up the selling behavior of all firms in a market, we get a similar definition:

Market quantity supplied **The specific amount of a good that *all* sellers in the market would choose to sell over some time period, given (1) a particular price for the good; (2) all other constraints on firms.**

> *Market quantity supplied (often just **quantity supplied**) is the specific amount of a good that all sellers in the market would choose to sell over some time period, given (1) a particular price for the good; (2) all other constraints on firms.*

Let's briefly go over the notion of quantity supplied to clarify what it means and doesn't mean.

Quantity Supplied Implies a *Choice*. We assume that the managers of firms have a simple goal—to earn the highest possible profit. But they also face constraints: the specific price they can charge for the good, the cost of any inputs used, and so on. Quantity supplied doesn't tell us the amount of, say, maple syrup that sellers would like to sell *if* they could charge a thousand dollars for each bottle, and *if* they could produce it at zero cost.

Instead, it's the quantity that gives firms the highest possible profits *when* they take account of the constraints presented to them by the real world. Thus, each firm's quantity supplied reflects a *choice* made by its managers. Adding up those choices for all sellers in the market gives us the market quantity supplied.

Quantity Supplied Is *Hypothetical*. Will firms actually be *able* to sell the amount they want to sell at the going price? At this point, we don't know. But the definition makes no assumptions about firms' *ability* to sell the good. Quantity supplied answers the hypothetical question: How much would firms' managers *want* to sell, given the price of the good and all other constraints they must consider.

Quantity Supplied Depends on *Price*. The price of the good is just one variable among many that influences quantity supplied. But—as with demand—we want to keep that variable foremost in our thinking. This is why for the next few pages we'll assume that all other influences on supply are held constant, so we can explore the relationship between price and quantity supplied.

The Law of Supply

How does a change in price affect quantity supplied? When a seller can get a higher price for a good, producing and selling it become more profitable. Producers will devote more resources toward its production—perhaps even pulling resources out of other types of production—so they can sell more of the good in question. For example, a rise in the price of laptop computers will encourage computer makers to shift resources out of the production of other things (such as desktop computers) and toward the production of laptops.

In general, price and quantity supplied are *positively related:* When the price of a good rises, the quantity supplied will rise as well. This relationship between price and quantity supplied is called the law of supply, the counterpart to the law of demand we discussed earlier.

> The **law of supply** states that when the price of a good rises, and everything else remains the same, the quantity of the good supplied will rise.

Law of supply As the price of a good increases, the quantity supplied increases.

Once again, notice the very important words "everything else remains the same." Although many other variables influence the quantity of a good supplied, the law of supply tells us what would happen if all of them remained unchanged and only one—the price of the good—changed.

The Supply Schedule and the Supply Curve

Let's continue with our example of the market for maple syrup in the United States. Who are the suppliers in this market? Maple syrup producers are located mostly in the forests of Vermont, upstate New York, and Canada. The market quantity supplied is the amount of syrup all of these producers together would offer for sale at each price for maple syrup in the United States.

Table 3 shows the **supply schedule** for maple syrup—a *list of different quantities supplied at different prices, with all other variables held constant.* As you can see, the supply schedule obeys the law of supply: As the price of maple syrup rises, the quantity supplied rises along with it. But how can this be? After all, maple trees must be about 40 years old before they can be tapped for syrup, so any rise in quantity supplied now or in the near future cannot come from an increase in planting. What, then, causes quantity supplied to rise as price rises?

Many things. First, with higher prices, firms will find it profitable to tap existing trees more intensively. Second, evaporating and bottling can be done more carefully, so that less maple syrup is spilled and more is available for shipping. Finally, the product can be diverted from other areas and shipped to the United States instead. For example, if the price of maple syrup rises in the United States but not in Canada, producers would shift deliveries away from Canada so they could sell more in the United States.

Now look at Figure 4, which shows a very important curve—the counterpart to the demand curve we drew earlier. In Figure 4, each point represents a price-quantity pair taken from Table 3. For example, point *F* in the figure corresponds to a price of $2.00 per bottle and a quantity of 40,000 bottles per month, while point *G* represents the price-quantity pair $4.00 and 60,000 bottles. Connecting all of these points with a solid line gives us the *supply curve* for maple syrup, labeled with an *S* in the figure.

> The **market supply curve** (or just **supply curve**) *shows the relationship between the price of a good and the quantity supplied, holding constant the values of all other variables that affect supply. Each point on the curve shows the quantity that sellers would choose to sell at a specific price.*

Price (per Bottle)	Quantity Supplied (Bottles per Month)
$1.00	25,000
2.00	40,000
3.00	50,000
4.00	60,000
5.00	65,000

TABLE 3
Supply Schedule for Maple Syrup in the United States

Supply schedule A list showing the quantities of a good or service that firms would choose to produce and sell at different prices, with all other variables held constant.

Supply curve A graphical depiction of a supply schedule; a curve showing the quantity of a good or service supplied at various prices, with all other variables held constant.

FIGURE 4
The Supply Curve

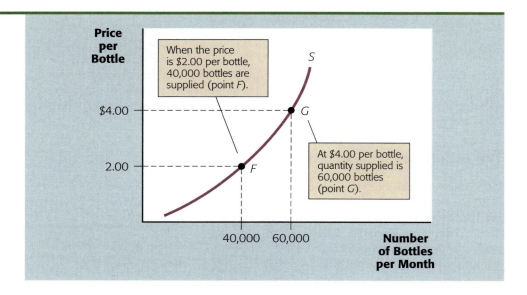

Notice that the supply curve in Figure 4—like all supply curves for goods and services—is *upward sloping*. This is the graphical representation of the law of supply.

> *The law of supply tells us that supply curves slope* upward.

Shifts vs. Movements Along the Supply Curve

As with the demand curve, it's important to distinguish those events that will cause us to *move along* a given supply curve for the good, and those that will cause the entire supply curve to *shift*.

If you look once again at Figure 4, you'll see that if the price of maple syrup rises from $2.00 to $4.00 per bottle, the number of bottles supplied rises from 40,000 to 60,000. This is a movement *along* the supply curve, from point *F* to point *G*. In general,

> *a change in the price of a good causes a movement* along *the supply curve.*

In the figure, a *rise* in price would cause us to move *rightward* along the supply curve (from point *F* to point *G*) and a *fall* in price would move us *leftward* along the curve (from point *G* to point *F*).

But remember that when we draw a supply curve, we assume that all other variables that might influence supply are *held constant* at some particular values. For example, the supply curve in Figure 4 might tell us the quantity supplied at each price when the cost of an important input—transportation from the farm to the point of sale—remains constant.

But suppose the cost of transportation drop. Then, at any given price for maple syrup, firms would find it more profitable to produce and sell it. This is illustrated in Table 4. With the original transportation cost, and a selling price of $4.00 per bottle, firms would choose to sell 60,000 bottles. But after transportation cost falls, they would choose to produce and sell more—80,000 bottles in our example—assuming they could still charge $4.00 per bottle. A similar change would occur for any other

Price (per Bottle)	Original Quantity Supplied (Bottles/Month)	Quantity Supplied After Decrease in Transportation Cost	TABLE 4
$1.00	25,000	45,000	**Increase in Supply of Maple Syrup in the United States**
2.00	40,000	60,000	
3.00	50,000	70,000	
4.00	60,000	80,000	
5.00	65,000	90,000	

price of maple syrup we might imagine: After transportation costs fall, firms would choose to sell more than before. In other words, *the entire relationship between price and quantity supplied has changed*, so we have a *new* supply curve.

Figure 5 plots the new supply curve from the quantities in the third column of Table 4. The new supply curve lies to the *right* of the old one. For example, at a price of $4.00, quantity supplied increases from 60,000 bottles on the old curve (point *G*) to 80,000 bottles on the *new* supply curve (point *J*). The drop in the transportation costs has *shifted* the supply curve to the right.

In general,

"Change in Quantity Supplied" vs. "Change in Supply" As we stressed in our discussion of the demand side of the market, be careful about language when thinking about supply. The term *quantity supplied* means a *particular amount* that sellers would prefer to sell at a particular price. It's a number, represented by a single point on the supply curve. The term *supply*, however, means the *entire relationship* between price and quantity supplied, as represented by the entire supply curve.

For this reason, when the price of the good changes, and we move *along* the supply curve, we have a **change in quantity supplied.** For example, in Figure 4, the movement from point *F* to point *G* is an *increase* in quantity supplied.

When something *other* than the price changes, causing the entire supply curve to shift, we call it a **change in supply.** The shift in Figure 5, for example, would be called an *increase in supply*.

Change in quantity supplied A movement along a supply curve in response to a change in price.

Change in supply A shift of a supply curve in response to some variable other than price.

> *a change in any variable that affects supply—except for the good's price— causes the supply curve to shift.*

If sellers want to sell a greater quantity at any price, the supply curve shifts *rightward.* If sellers would prefer to sell a smaller quantity at any price, the supply curve shifts *leftward.*

Factors That Shift the Supply Curve

Let's take a closer look at some of the *causes* of a change in supply (a shift of the supply curve). As always, we're considering *one* variable at a time, keeping all other determinants of supply constant.

Input Prices. In Figure 5, a drop in transportation costs shifted the supply curve for maple syrup to the right. But producers of maple syrup use a variety of other inputs, too: land, maple trees, evaporators, sap pans, labor, glass bottles, bottling machinery, and more. A lower price for any of these means a lower cost of producing and selling maple syrup, making it more profitable. As a result, we would expect producers to shift resources into maple syrup production, causing an increase in supply.

FIGURE 5
A Shift of the Supply Curve

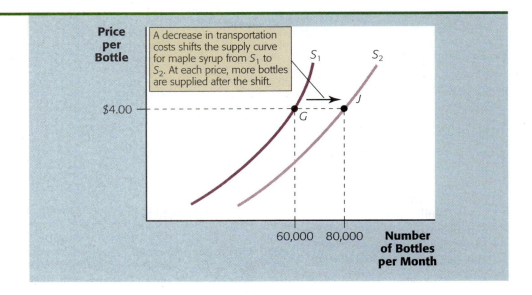

Price per Bottle

A decrease in transportation costs shifts the supply curve for maple syrup from S_1 to S_2. At each price, more bottles are supplied after the shift.

S_1 S_2

$4.00

J

G

60,000   80,000   **Number of Bottles per Month**

In general,

> *a fall in the price of an input causes an increase in supply, shifting the supply curve to the right. A rise in the price of an input causes a decrease in supply, shifting the supply curve to the left.*

If, for example, the wages of maple syrup workers rose, the supply curve in Figure 5 would shift to the left.

Price of Related Goods. Many firms can switch their production rather easily among several different goods or services, all of which require more or less the same inputs. For example, a dermatology practice can rather easily switch its specialty from acne treatments for the young to wrinkle treatments for the elderly. An automobile producer can—without too much adjustment—switch to producing light trucks. And a maple syrup producer could dry its maple syrup and produce maple *sugar* instead. Or it could even cut down its maple trees and sell maple wood as lumber. Other goods that firms *could* produce are called **alternate goods.**

Alternate goods Other goods that a firm could produce, using some of the same types of inputs as the good in question.

For example, if the price of maple *sugar* rose, then at any given price for maple *syrup*, producers would choose to shift some production from syrup to sugar. This would be a decrease in the supply of maple syrup. Alternatively, if firms already are producing maple sugar, and its price *falls,* the supply of syrup would increase. Remember that we are assuming—as always—that every *other* determinant that affects the supply of maple syrup remains unchanged.

> *When the price of an alternate good rises, the supply curve for the good in question shifts leftward. When the price of an alternate falls, the supply curve for the good in question shifts rightward.*

Technology. A *technological advance* in production occurs whenever a firm can produce a given level of output in a new and cheaper way than before. For example, the discovery of a surgical procedure called Lasik—in which a laser is used to reshape the interior of the cornea rather than the outer surface—has enabled eye surgeons to correct their patients' vision with fewer follow-up visits and smaller quantities of medication than were used with previous procedures. This example is a technological advance because it enables firms to produce the same output (eye surgery) more cheaply than before.

Does Demand Affect Supply? In the list of variables that shift the supply curve in Figure 6 we've left out the amount that buyers would like to buy. Is this a mistake? Doesn't demand affect supply?

The answer is no—at least, not directly. The supply curve tells us how much sellers *would* choose to sell at alternative prices. Buyers' decisions don't affect this hypothetical quantity, so they cannot shift the supply curve. But—as you'll soon see—buyers *can* affect the price of the good, which in turn affects quantity supplied. But this is a movement *along* the supply curve—not a shift.

DANGEROUS CURVES

In maple syrup production, a technological advance might be a new, more efficient tap that draws more maple syrup from each tree, or a new bottling method that reduces spillage. Advances like these would reduce the cost of producing maple syrup, making it more profitable, and producers would want to make and sell more of it at any price.

In general,

> *cost-saving technological advances increase the supply of a good, shifting the supply curve to the right.*

Number of Firms. A change in the number of firms in a market will change the quantity that all sellers together would want to sell at any given price. For example, if—over time—more people decided to open up maple syrup farms because it was a profitable business, the supply of maple syrup would increase. And if maple syrup farms began closing down, their number would be reduced and supply would decrease.

> *An increase in the number of sellers—with no other change—shifts the supply curve rightward, while a decrease in the number of sellers shifts it leftward.*

Expected Price. Imagine you're the president of Sticky's Maple Syrup, Inc., and you've determined that the market price of maple syrup—over which you, as an individual seller, have no influence—will rise next month. What would you do? You'd certainly want to postpone selling your maple syrup until the price is higher, and profit greater. Therefore, at any given price *now*, you might slow down production, or just slow down sales by warehousing more of what you produce. If other firms have similar expectations of a price hike, they'll do the same. Thus, an expectation of a *future* price hike will decrease supply *in the present*.

Suppose instead you expect the market price to *drop* next month. Then—at any given price—you'd want to sell more *now*, by stepping up production and even selling out of your inventories. Now, an expected future drop in the price would cause an increase in supply in the present. In terms of our supply curve:

> *In many markets, an expectation of a future price hike shifts the current supply curve leftward. Similarly, an expectation of a future price drop shifts the current supply curve rightward.*

Changes in Weather and Other Natural Events. Weather conditions are an especially important determinant of the supply of agricultural goods.

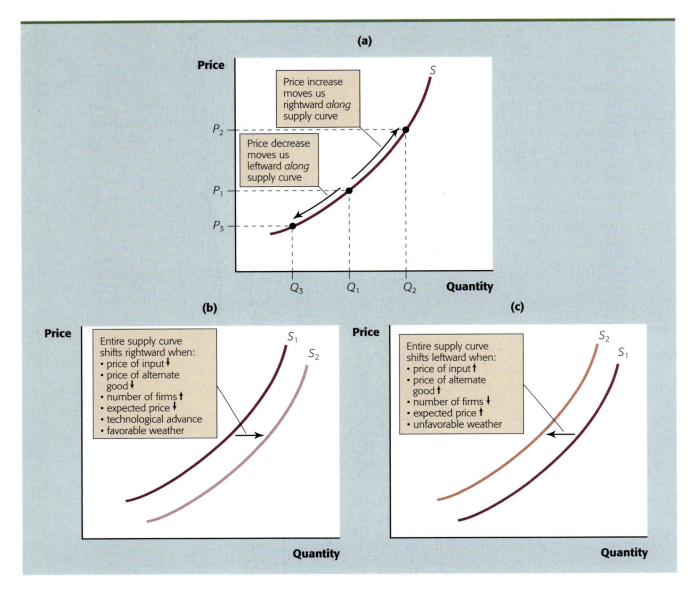

FIGURE 6

Changes in Supply and in Quantity Supplied

Favorable weather *increases crop yields, and causes a* rightward *shift of the supply curve for that crop.* Unfavorable weather *destroys crops and shrinks yields, and shifts the supply curve* leftward.

In addition to bad weather, natural disasters such as fires, hurricanes, and earthquakes can destroy or disrupt the productive capacity of *all* firms in a region. If many sellers of a particular good are located in the affected area, the supply curve for that good will shift leftward. For example, a sudden blight that destroyed many maple trees in Vermont would cause the supply curve to shift leftward in the market we've been analyzing.

Figure 6 summarizes the various factors we've discussed that affect the supply side of the market, and how we illustrate them using a supply curve. But the short list of *shift-variables* for supply is far from exhaustive. For example, a government tax on a good—or a government subsidy paid to producers—will shift the supply curve. So can other government policies, such as environmental and safety regulations. And man-made disasters, such as wars, riots, terrorist attacks, or epidemics, can have the same effects as natural disasters.

Even the *threat* of such events can seriously affect production. In mid-2003, in countries around the world, supply curves for children's toys shifted leftward. The reason? In China—where most of the world's toys are produced—tens of thousands of workers stayed away from their jobs for weeks, fearful of catching SARS (Severe Acute Respiratory Syndrome).

Some of the other shift-variables that shift supply curves will be discussed as they become relevant in future chapters. The basic principle, however, is always the same: Anything that makes sellers want to sell more or less *at any given price* will shift the supply curve.

PUTTING SUPPLY AND DEMAND TOGETHER

What happens when buyers and sellers, each having the desire and the ability to trade, come together in a market? The two sides of the market certainly have different agendas. Buyers would like to pay the lowest possible price, while sellers would like to charge the highest possible price. Is there chaos when they meet, with buyers and sellers endlessly chasing after each other or endlessly bargaining for advantage, so that trade never takes place? A casual look at the real world suggests not. In most markets, most of the time, there is order and stability in the encounters between buyers and sellers. In most cases, prices do not fluctuate wildly from moment to moment, but seem to hover around a stable value. Even when this stability is short-lived—lasting only a day, an hour, or even a minute in some markets—for this short-time the market seems to be at rest. Whenever we study a market, therefore, we look for this state of rest—a price and quantity at which the market will settle, at least for a while.

Economists use the word *equilibrium* when referring to a state of rest. When a market is in equilibrium, both the price of the good and the quantity bought and sold have settled into a state of rest. More formally,

> the **equilibrium price** and **equilibrium quantity** are values for price and quantity in the market that, once achieved, will remain constant—unless and until the supply curve or the demand curve shifts.

What will be the price of maple syrup in the United States? And how much will people actually buy each month? We can rephrase these questions as follows: What is the *equilibrium* price of maple syrup, and what is the *equilibrium* quantity of maple syrup that will be bought and sold? These are precisely the questions that the supply and demand model is designed to answer.

Look at Figure 7, which combines the supply and demand curves for maple syrup. We'll use Figure 7 to find the equilibrium price in this market through the process of elimination.

Let's first ask what would happen if the price was $1.00 per bottle. At this price, buyers would want to buy 75,000 bottles each month, while sellers would offer to sell only 25,000. There would be an **excess demand** of 50,000 bottles. What would happen? Buyers would compete with each other to get more maple syrup than was

HTTP://

Try your hand at a Java-based supply and demand simulation. You can find it at **http://openteach.com/economics/microeconomics.html**.

Equilibrium price The market price that, once achieved, remains constant until either the demand curve or supply curve shifts.

Equilibrium quantity The market quantity bought and sold per period that, once achieved, remains constant until either the demand curve or supply curve shifts.

Excess demand At a given price, the excess of quantity demanded over quantity supplied.

FIGURE 7
Market Equilibrium

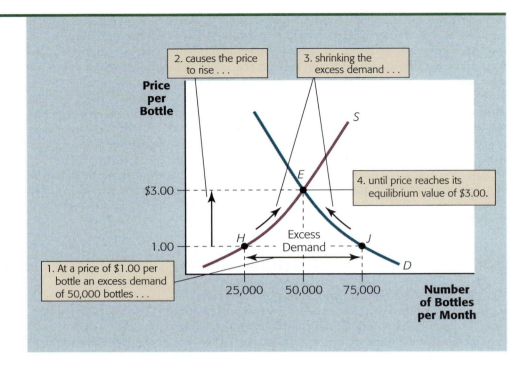

2. causes the price
to rise . . .

3. shrinking the
excess demand . . .

Price
per
Bottle

S

E

$3.00

4. until price reaches its
equilibrium value of $3.00.

H   Excess
1.00   Demand   J

D

1. At a price of $1.00 per
bottle an excess demand
of 50,000 bottles . . .

25,000   50,000   75,000   **Number
of Bottles
per Month**

available, and would offer to pay a higher price rather than do without. The price would then rise.

We conclude that a price of $1.00—or *any* price we might imagine that is less than $3.00—cannot be an equilibrium price. Why not? As we've just seen, if the price starts below $3.00, it would start rising—*not* because the supply curve or the demand curve had shifted, but from natural forces within the market itself. This directly contradicts our definition of equilibrium price.

At this point, we should ask another question: If the price were initially $1.00, would it ever *stop* rising? Yes. Since excess demand is the reason for the price to rise, the process will stop when the excess demand is gone. And as you can see in Figure 8, the rise in price *shrinks* the excess demand in two ways. First, as price rises, buyers demand a smaller quantity—a leftward movement along the demand curve. Second, sellers increase supply to a larger quantity—a rightward movement along the supply curve. Finally, when the price reaches $3.00 per bottle, the excess demand is gone and the price stops rising.

This logic tells us that $3.00 is an *equilibrium* price in this market—a value that won't change as long as the supply and demand curves stay put. But is it the *only* equilibrium price? We've shown that any price *below* $3.00 is not an equilibrium, but what about a price *greater* than $3.00? Let's see.

Suppose the price of maple syrup was, say, $5.00 per bottle. Figure 8 shows us that, at this price, quantity supplied would be 65,000 bottles per month, while quantity demanded would be only 35,000 bottles—an **excess supply** of 30,000 bottles. Sellers would compete with each other to sell more maple syrup than buyers wanted to buy, and the price would fall. Thus, $5.00 cannot be the equilibrium price.

Moreover, the decrease in price would move us along both the supply curve (leftward) and the demand curve (rightward). As these movements continued, the

Excess supply At a given price, the excess of quantity supplied over quantity demanded.

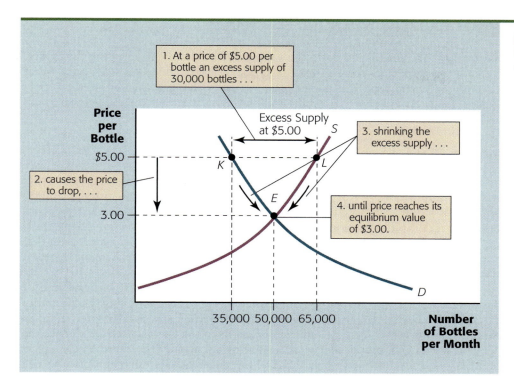

FIGURE 8
Excess Supply and Price Adjustment

1. At a price of $5.00 per bottle an excess supply of 30,000 bottles . . .

2. causes the price to drop, . . .

3. shrinking the excess supply . . .

4. until price reaches its equilibrium value of $3.00.

Excess Supply at $5.00

excess supply of maple syrup would shrink until it disappeared, once again, at a price of $3.00 per bottle. Our conclusion: If the price happens to be above $3.00, it will fall to $3.00 and then stop changing.

You can see that is the equilibrium price—and the *only* equilibrium price—in this market. Moreover, at this price, sellers would want to sell 50,000 bottles—the same quantity that households would want to buy. So, when price comes to rest at $3.00, quantity comes to rest at 50,000 per month—the *equilibrium quantity*.

No doubt, you have noticed that $3.00 happens to be the price at which the supply and demand curves cross. This leads us to an easy, graphical technique for locating our equilibrium:

> *To find the equilibrium price and quantity in a competitive market, draw the supply and demand curves. The equilibrium price and equilibrium quantity can then be found on the vertical and horizontal axes, respectively, at the point where the supply and demand curves cross.*

This graphical insight helps make the logic of equilibrium even more apparent. In equilibrium, the market is operating on *both* the supply curve *and* the demand curve. Therefore, at the going price, quantity demanded and quantity supplied are equal. There are no dissatisfied buyers unable to find goods they want to purchase, nor are there any frustrated sellers unable to sell goods they want to sell. Indeed, this is why $3.00 is the equilibrium price. It's the only price that creates consistency between what buyers choose to buy and sellers choose to sell.

But we don't expect a market to stay at any particular equilibrium forever, as you're about to see.

WHAT HAPPENS WHEN THINGS CHANGE?

Remember that in order to draw the supply and demand curves in the first place, we had to assume particular values for all the other variables—besides price—that affect demand and supply. If one of these variables changes, then either the supply curve or the demand curve will shift, and our equilibrium will change as well. Let's look at some examples.

Income Rises, Causing an Increase in Demand

In Figure 9, point E shows an initial equilibrium in the U.S. market for maple syrup, with an equilibrium price of $3.00 per bottle, and equilibrium quantity of 50,000 bottles per month. Suppose that the incomes of buyers rise because the U.S. economy recovers rapidly from a recession. We know that income is one of the shift-variables in the demand curve (but not the supply curve). We also can reason that maple syrup is a *normal good,* so the rise in income will cause the demand curve to shift rightward. What happens then?

The old price—$3.00—is no longer the equilibrium price. How do we know? Because if the price *did* remain at $3.00, quantity demanded would exceed quantity supplied—an excess demand that would drive the price upward. The new equilibrium—at point E'—is the new intersection point of the curves *after* the shift in the demand curve. Comparing the original equilibrium at point E with the new one at point E', we find that the shift in demand has caused the equilibrium price to rise (from $3.00 to $4.00) and the equilibrium quantity to rise as well (from 50,000 to 60,000 bottles per month).

Notice, too, that in moving from point E to point E', we move *along* the supply curve. That is, a shift of the demand curve has caused a movement along he supply curve. Why is this? The demand shift causes the *price* to rise, and a rise in price always causes a movement *along* the supply curve. But the supply curve itself does not shift, because none of the variables that affect sellers—other than the price of the good—has changed.

In this example, the equilibrium price and quantity changed because income rose. But *any* event that shifted the demand curve rightward would cause both equilibrium price and quantity to rise. For example, if tastes changed in favor of maple syrup, or a substitute good like jam rose in price, or a complementary good like pancake mix became cheaper, the demand curve for

The Endless Loop of Erroneous Logic At some point, you might find yourself caught in an endless loop of erroneous logic about supply and demand. In our example in which income rises and demand increases, you might reason as follows: "The rise in income causes an increase in demand, which causes the price to rise. But a higher price increases supply. Higher supply, in turn, causes the price to fall. But then, when the price falls, demand will increase . . ." and so on. In this logic, the price bobs up and down and never stops moving.

What's the mistake here? The first sentence is indeed correct. But the second sentence—and all that follows from it—is wrong. The second sentence states that "a higher price increases supply," when it *should* say that a higher price increases *quantity supplied.*

This is more than just semantics. An "increase in supply" would be a rightward *shift* of the supply curve, which is what is implied in the incorrect statement. But look again at Figure 9. There is no supply shift, because none of the shift-variables for the supply curve have changed. Only *price* has changed, and that causes a movement *along* the supply curve. So a correct second sentence would be, "And the higher price increases quantity supplied until the new equilibrium is reached, at which point the price stops rising." End of story.

You can avoid this mistake by remembering that *a shift of one curve causes a movement along the other curve to the new equilibrium point.*

maple syrup would shift rightward, just as it did in Figure 9. So, we can summarize our findings as follows:

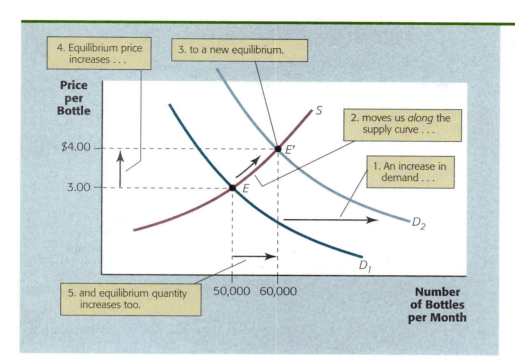

FIGURE 9
A Shift in Demand and a New Equilibrium

4. Equilibrium price increases . . .

3. to a new equilibrium.

2. moves us *along* the supply curve . . .

1. An increase in demand . . .

5. and equilibrium quantity increases too.

Price per Bottle

$4.00

3.00

S

E'

E

D₂

D₁

50,000   60,000

Number of Bottles per Month

A rightward shift in the demand curve causes a rightward movement along the supply curve. Equilibrium price and equilibrium quantity both rise.

An Ice Storm Causes a Decrease in Supply

In January 1998, New England and Quebec were struck by a severe ice storm. Hundreds of thousands of maple trees were downed, and many more were damaged. In Vermont alone, 10 percent of the maple trees were destroyed. How did this affect the market for maple syrup?

As you've learned, weather is a shift-variable for the supply curve.

Figure 10 shows how the ice storm affected this market. Initially, the supply curve for maple syrup was S_1, with the market in equilibrium at Point E. After the ice storm, the supply curve shifted leftward—say, to S_2. The result: a rise in the equilibrium price of maple syrup (from $3.00 to $5.00 in the figure) and a fall in the equilibrium quantity (from 50,000 to 35,000 bottles).

Do Curves Shift Up and Down? Or Right and Left? When describing an increase in demand or supply, it's tempting to substitute "upward" for "rightward," and to substitute "downward" for "leftward" when describing a decrease in demand or supply. But be careful! While this interchangeable language works for the demand curve, it does *not* work for the supply curve. To prove this to yourself, look at Figure 6. There you can see that a rightward shift of the supply curve (an increase in supply) is also a *downward* shift of the curve. In later chapters, it will sometimes make sense to describe shifts as upward or downward. For now, it's best to avoid these terms and stick with *rightward* and *leftward*.

DANGEROUS CURVES

In this case, it was an ice storm that shifted the supply curve leftward. But suppose, instead, that the wages of maple syrup workers had increased or that evaporators became more expensive or that some maple syrup producers went out of business and sold their farms to housing developers. Any of these changes would have

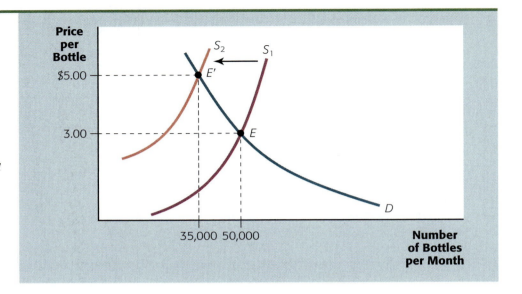

FIGURE 10

A Shift of Supply and a New Equilibrium

An ice storm causes supply to decrease from S_1 to S_2. At the old equilibrium price of $3.00, there is now an excess demand. As a result, the price increases until excess demand is eliminated at point E'. In the new equilibrium, quantity demanded again equals quantity supplied. The price is higher, and fewer bottles are produced and sold.

caused the supply curve for maple syrup to shift leftward, increased the equilibrium price, and decreased the equilibrium quantity.

More generally,

> *any change that shifts the supply curve leftward in a market will increase the equilibrium price and decrease the equilibrium quantity in that market.*

Handheld PCs in 2003: Both Curves Shift

Since shifts in supply and demand work the same way in any market, let's leave maple syrup for now and look at a different market: that for handheld computers like the Palm, HP Ipaq, and Sony Clie. In early 2003, prices for these devices dropped. For example, the price of both Palm's high-end Tungsten T model and Sony's new Clie NX60V dropped from $500 to $400. At the same time, the number of handheld PCs sold dropped—from 3.33 million (in the last quarter of 2002) to 2.45 million (first quarter of 2003). What explains these movements in price and quantity?

In 2003, a decrease in demand caused prices of handheld PCs to fall

To answer this question, we'll use the supply and demand model. In doing so, we're assuming this is a perfectly competitive market, in which each producer sells a standardized product and treats the market price as a given. This is not too far off: Product differences among manufacturers are rather modest, and to stay in business, each producer must charge a price within a rather narrow *range*. Our assumption of perfect competition is, as in most cases, a useful approximation.

Figure 11 shows the market supply and demand curves for handheld PCs in late 2002, labeled S_{2002} and D_{2002}, respectively. Point *A* shows the equilibrium at that time, with an average price of $500 and a quantity of 3.33 million PCs per quarter.

Now, what happened in this market between late 2002 and mid-2003? Let's start with demand, where three factors combined to shift the demand curve leftward.

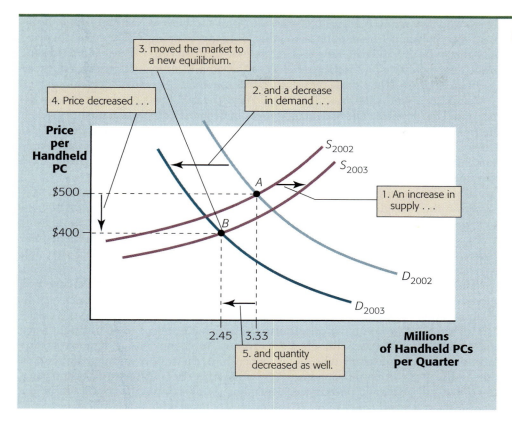

FIGURE 11
Changes in the Market for
Handheld PCs

First, by early 2003, handheld PCs had already been on the market for a few years. Most of those who regarded them as useful had already bought one. Since these first-time buyers had been behind the high demand in earlier periods, their withdrawal from the market amounted to a decrease in demand. (*The shift-variable: a change in market preferences for new handhelds.*)

Second, uncertainties caused by continued slow growth in the U.S. and European economies, and a looming U.S. war with Iraq, caused consumers to worry about their future income. These kinds of worries especially decrease the demand for goods that are relatively expensive and not considered necessities, such as handheld PCs. (*Shift-variable: a change in expectations*, in this case, about future income.)

Finally, in early 2003, cell phones that incorporated some of the key features of handheld PCs were becoming cheaper. Many of those who *would* have bought a handheld PC decided to purchase a cell phone with limited PC-capabilities instead. (*Shift-variable: a decrease in the price of a substitute good.*)

Any one of these three factors, by itself, would have caused a leftward shift in the demand curve for handhelds. When they all occurred together, the result was an even *larger* shift to the left. This is illustrated in Figure 11 by the shift from D_{2002} to D_{2003}.

What about supply? Throughout the early 2000s, new firms—at least, new to handheld PCs—entered the market. And entry continued through 2003, as Dell, Gateway, and Matsushita brought their first handhelds to the market. The entry of new firms increased the number of handhelds that would be offered for sale at any price, shifting the supply curve rightward (from S_{2002} to S_{2003} in the figure). (*Shift-variable: an increase in the number of firms.*)

As you can see in Figure 11, the result of all these events was a change in the market equilibrium—from point *A* to point *B*. In our diagram, the equilibrium price has fallen—from $500 to $400. This should not surprise you: *Either* a leftward shift in the demand curve *or* a rightward shift of the supply curve, by itself, would cause the price to drop. When these two shifts occur together, price drops even more.

But what about equilibrium quantity? Here, the two shifts work in *opposite* directions. The leftward shift in demand works to decrease equilibrium quantity, while the rightward shift in supply tends to increase equilibrium quantity. Figure 11 illustrates what *actually* happened: a decrease in quantity from 3.33 million to 2.45 million units sold. So we know that, over this period, the demand shift was *greater* than the supply shift.

To prove this to yourself, draw a graph that shows a leftward demand shift that is *smaller* than a rightward supply shift. What happens to equilibrium quantity in your diagram? Then draw a graph that shows equilibrium quantity remaining unchanged. If you draw these cases, you'll see that while the price *must* fall when the curves shift in the directions shown in Figure 11, the quantity could either rise, fall, or remain the same; it's *ambiguous*, unless we know the relative *sizes* of the shifts.

This example involves just *one* possible combination of directions that the two curves could shift. But remember that a leftward or rightward shift of one curve can occur together with either a leftward or rightward shift of the other curve. Table 5 lists all the possible combinations. It also shows what happens to equilibrium price and quantity in each case, and when the result is ambiguous (a question mark). For example, the top left entry tells us that when both the supply and demand curves shift rightward, the equilibrium *quantity* will always rise, but the equilibrium price could rise, fall or remain unchanged, depending on the relative *size* of the shifts.

The most general conclusion we can draw from this table is the following:

> *When* just one *curve shifts, and we know the direction of the shift, we can determine the direction that* both *equilibrium price* and *quantity will move.*

> *When* both *curves shift, and we know the* directions *of the shifts, we can determine the direction for* either *price or quantity—but not both. The direction of the other will depend on which curve shifts by more.*

Do *not* try to memorize the entries in Table 5. Instead, remember the advice in Chapter 1: to study economics actively, rather than passively. This would be a good time to put down the book, pick up a pencil and paper, and see whether you can draw a graph to illustrate each of the nine possible results in the table. When you

TABLE 5 **Effect of Supply and Demand Shifts on Equilibrium Price (*P*) and Quantity (*Q*)**	**Increase in Demand (Rightward Shift)**	**No Change in Demand**	**Decrease in Demand (Leftward Shift)**
• **Increase in Supply (Rightward Shift)**	$P?\ Q\uparrow$	$P\downarrow Q\uparrow$	$P\downarrow Q?$
• **No Change in Supply**	$P\uparrow Q\uparrow$	No change in *P* or *Q*	$P\downarrow Q\downarrow$
• **Decrease in Supply (Leftward Shift)**	$P\uparrow Q?$	$P\uparrow Q\downarrow$	$P?\ Q\downarrow$

see a question mark (?) for an ambiguous result, determine which shift would have to be greater for the variable to rise or to fall.

THE PRINCIPLE OF MARKETS AND EQUILIBRIUM

In this chapter, you've seen an example of how economists approach a problem. We began by asking how the prices of the things we buy are actually determined. To answer that question, we abstracted from the complex, real-world economy and viewed it as a number of distinct *markets*. We then chose to analyze one of those markets—the market for maple syrup—by looking for its *equilibrium* price and quantity. The supply-and-demand model is just one example of a more general approach: to identify a market and examine its equilibrium.

> ⚷ *Basic Principle #4: Markets and Equilibrium*
> *To understand how the economy behaves, economists organize the world into separate markets and then examine the equilibrium in each of those markets.*

You have already seen one of the payoffs to this approach: It can explain how the price in a market is determined and what causes that price to change. But the approach takes us even further. It helps us predict important changes in the economy and prepare for them. And it helps us design government policies to accomplish our social goals and avoid policies that are likely to backfire. In the next section, we apply the principle of *markets and equilibrium* to some cases where government intervention is unlikely to accomplish our goals and may even cause unintended harm. In later chapters, you will see some examples of effective government policies that can help market economies work even better.

GOVERNMENT INTERVENTION IN MARKETS

The forces of supply and demand deserve some credit. They force the market price to adjust until something remarkable happens: The quantity that sellers want to sell is also the quantity that buyers want to buy. Thus, no buyer or seller should have trouble turning his intentions into actual market trades.

So, three cheers for supply and demand! Or better make that *two* cheers. Because while everyone agrees that having prices is necessary for the smooth functioning of our economy, not everyone is happy with the prices that supply and demand give us. Apartment dwellers often complain that their rent is too high, and farmers complain that the price of their crops is too low.

Responding to this dissatisfaction, governments will sometimes intervene to *change* the price in a market. In this section, we'll look at two methods governments use to prevent a market price from reaching its equilibrium value.

Price Ceilings

Figure 12 shows our familiar market for maple syrup, with an equilibrium price of $3.00 per bottle. Suppose that maple syrup buyers complain to the government that this price is too high. The government responds by imposing a **price ceiling** in this market—a regulation preventing the price from rising above the ceiling.

Price ceiling A government-imposed maximum price in a market.

FIGURE 12
A Price Ceiling in the Market for Maple Syrup

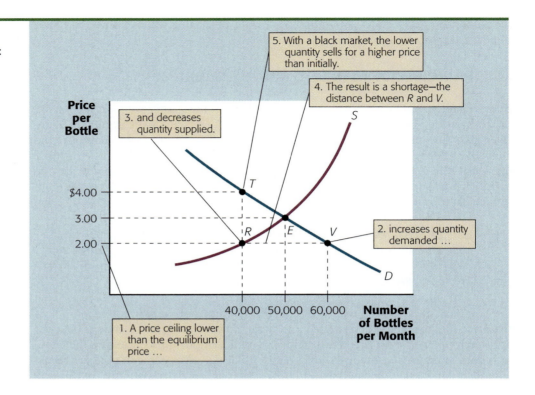

More specifically, suppose the ceiling is $2.00 per bottle, and it is strictly enforced. Then producers will no longer be able to charge $3.00 for maple syrup but will have to content themselves with $2.00 instead. In Figure 12, we will move down along the supply curve, from point *E* to point *R*, decreasing quantity supplied from 50,000 bottles to 40,000. At the same time, the decrease in price will move us along the demand curve, from point *E* to point *V*, increasing quantity demanded from 50,000 to 60,000. These changes in quantities supplied and demanded together create an *excess demand* for maple syrup of 60,000 − 40,000 = 20,000 bottles each month. Ordinarily, the excess demand would force the price back up to $3.00. But now the price ceiling prevents this from occurring. What will happen?

There is a practical observation about markets that helps us arrive at an answer:

> *When quantity supplied and quantity demanded differ, the **short side of the market**—whichever of the two quantities is smaller—will prevail.*

This simple rule follows from the voluntary nature of exchange in a market system: No one can be forced to buy or sell more than they want to. With an excess demand, sellers are the short side of the market. Since we cannot force them to sell any more than they want to (40,000 units) the result is a **shortage** of maple syrup—not enough available to satisfy demand at the going price.

But this is not the end of the story. Because of the shortage, all 40,000 bottles produced each month will quickly disappear from store shelves and many buyers will be disappointed. The next time people hear that maple syrup has become avail-

Short side of the market The smaller of quantity supplied and quantity demanded at a particular price.

Shortage An excess demand not eliminated by a rise in price, so that quantity demanded continues to exceed quantity supplied.

able, everyone will try to get there first, and we can expect long lines at stores. Those who really crave maple syrup may have to go from store to store, searching for that rare bottle. When we include the *opportunity cost* of the time spent waiting in line or shopping around, the ultimate effect of the price ceiling may be a *higher* cost of maple syrup for many consumers.

 Opportunity Cost

> *A price ceiling creates a shortage and increases the time and trouble required to buy the good. While the price decreases, the opportunity cost may rise.*

And there is still more. While the government may be able to prevent maple syrup *producers* from selling above the price ceiling, it may not be able to prevent enterprising individuals from buying maple syrup at the official ceiling price and then reselling it to desperate buyers for a profit. The result is a **black market,** where goods are sold illegally at prices higher than the legal ceiling.

Black market A market in which goods are sold illegally at a price above the legal ceiling.

Ironically, the black market price will typically exceed the original, freely determined equilibrium price—$3.00 per bottle in our example. To see why, look again at Figure 12. With a price ceiling of $2.00, sellers supply 40,000 bottles per month. Suppose all of this is bought by people—maple syrup scalpers, if you will—who then sell it at the highest price they can get. What price can they charge? We can use the demand curve to find out. At $4.00 per bottle (point *T*), the scalpers would just be able to sell all 40,000 bottles. They have no reason, therefore, to charge any less than this.

The unintended consequences of price ceilings—long lines, black markets, and, often, higher prices—explain why they are generally a poor way to bring down prices. Experience with price ceilings has generally confirmed this judgment, so in practice they are rare.

An exception, however, is **rent controls**—city ordinances that specify a maximum monthly rent on many apartments and homes. If you live in a city with rent control, you will be familiar with its consequences. In any case, you may want to reread this section with the market for apartments in mind. How are shortages and long lines manifested? Do rent controls always decrease the cost of apartments to renters? (Think: opportunity cost.) And who are the middlemen—the "apartment scalpers"—who profit in this market?

Rent controls Government-imposed maximum rents on apartments and homes.

Price Floors

Sometimes, governments try to help sellers of a good by establishing a **price floor**— a minimum amount below which the price is not permitted to fall.

Price floor A government-imposed minimum price below which a good or service may not be sold.

For example, suppose that the Maple Syrup Producers Association convinces the government to set a price floor of $5.00 per bottle. To see the effects on the market, look back at Figure 8. At $5.00 per bottle, producers would like to sell 65,000 bottles, while consumers want to purchase only 35,000. The excess supply of 65,000 − 35,000 = 30,000 would ordinarily push the market price down to its equilibrium value, $3.00. But the price floor prevents this. Our short-side rule tells us that buyers would determine the amount actually traded. They would purchase 35,000 of the 65,000 bottles produced, and producers would be unable to sell the remainder.

What would happen then? Producers would have an incentive to violate the price floor by selling some of their maple syrup for less than $5.00. A black market

Floor Above, Ceiling Below! It's tempting to draw a supply and demand diagram with a price floor set *under* the equilibrium price, or a price ceiling *above* the equilibrium price. After all, a floor is usually on the bottom of something, and a ceiling is on the top. Right? In this case, wrong! A price floor set *below* the equilibrium price would have no impact on a market, because the market price would *already* satisfy the requirement that it be higher than the floor. Similarly, a price ceiling set *above* the equilibrium price would have no impact (make sure you understand why). So remember: Always draw an effective price floor *above* the equilibrium price and an effective price ceiling *below* the equilibrium price.

would develop for cheap maple syrup. As you can see, price floors can be just as hard to enforce as price ceilings.

But there is a foolproof strategy the government could use to prevent a black market from developing. It's a strategy that governments around the world typically use when they establish price floors. In our example, the government would establish a special agency—let's call it the Maple Syrup Board—that promises to buy maple syrup from any seller at $5.00 per bottle. With this policy, no supplier would ever sell at any price below $5.00, since it could always sell to the government instead. With the price effectively stuck at $5.00, private buyers will buy 35,000 bottles per month—point *K* on the demand curve in Figure 8. But since quantity supplied is 65,000, the government will find itself buying 65,000 − 35,000 = 30,000 bottles each month. In other words, the government maintains the price floor by buying up the entire excess supply. This prevents the excess supply from doing what it would ordinarily do: drive the price down to its equilibrium value.

And this is not the end of the story. Maintaining a price floor, as described here, would cause the government to endlessly accumulate growing stocks of food. To deal with this, governments will often try to limit supply. Our Maple Syrup Board might gain the power to limit the number of trees each producer could tap. In this way, price floors often get the government deeply involved in production decisions, rather than leaving them to the market.

Governments in many countries have a long history of using price floors in agricultural markets to prop up the incomes of farmers. In the United States, price floors for milk, cheese, eggs, and a variety of fruits and vegetables have been established. This policy has many critics—including most economists. They argue that the government spends too much money buying surplus agricultural products, and that the resulting higher prices distort the public's buying and eating habits—often to their nutritional detriment. Moreover, many of the farmers who benefit from price floors are wealthy individuals or large, powerful corporations, which do not need the assistance.

The Principle of Policy Tradeoffs

In our discussion of government intervention in markets, you may have noticed something interesting: A policy designed to help us achieve one goal causes us to compromise on some other goal. For example, if one of our goals is to maintain high incomes for farmers, we can achieve it by establishing a price floor on farm goods. But we *also* want low tax rates on households and businesses, and the price floor may interfere with this. How? As we've seen, as a result of the price floor, individual farmers will want to sell more farm goods, and individual consumers will want to buy fewer of them. When these reactions from buyers and sellers are taken into account, we discover that there will be a surplus of farm goods on the market that the government will have to deal with. Whether the government decides to establish a costly program to limit production, or to buy the surpluses itself, it will need more tax dollars, and may have to raise tax rates.

This is just one example of a more general principle. In fact, as you will see throughout this text, there are virtually always tradeoffs involved in government policy making. For this reason, we consider government policy tradeoffs to be one of the basic principles of economics.

> ⚶ **Basic Principle #5: Policy Tradeoffs**
> *Government policy is constrained by the reactions of private decision makers. As a result, policy makers face tradeoffs: making progress toward one goal often requires some sacrifice of another goal.*

Economics is famous for making the public aware of policy tradeoffs. Whenever we think we've found an easy solution to one of society's vexing problems, economic analysis makes us aware of some other social goal that must be sacrificed if we pursue that solution. Although this knowledge is sometimes unpleasant, it can help us formulate wiser policies and—at a minimum—prevent even more unpleasant surprises.

Supply and Demand and Normative Economics

Supply and demand offers us important lessons about the economy. The lessons are both positive—telling us *what* will happen when there is a change in a market—and normative—suggesting what sorts of policies we *should or should not* pursue.

Most economists believe that the mechanism of supply and demand is an effective way to allocate resources. "Let the market determine prices," they say, "and let each of us respond to those prices as we wish." When someone proposes to interfere with this mechanism, economists listen—but skeptically. The burden of proof, they believe, should lie with those who favor intervention. Why do economists feel this way?

Answering this question requires a more thorough understanding of the economy than we can provide after just three chapters of this book. Be assured, though, that when you finish your introductory study of economics, you will know why economists treat supply and demand with such respect.

USING THE THEORY
College Administrators Make a Costly Mistake

In the late 1980s, several East Coast colleges purchased expensive equipment that would enable them to switch rapidly from oil to natural gas as a source of heat. The idea was to protect the colleges from a sudden rise in oil prices, like the one they had suffered a decade earlier.

Finally, an event occurred that gave the colleges a chance to put their new equipment to use: In the fall of 1990, Iraq invaded Kuwait. As oil prices skyrocketed, the colleges switched from burning oil to burning natural gas. The college administrators expected big savings on their energy bills. But they were in for a shock. When they received the bills from their local utilities, they found that the price of natural gas—like the price of oil—had risen sharply. As a result, they did not save much in energy costs at all, certainly not enough to justify the costly switching equipment they had purchased. Many of these administrators were angry at the utility companies and accused them of price gouging. Iraq's invasion of Kuwait, they reasoned,

© BOB KRIST/CORBIS

FIGURE 13
The Market for Oil

Before the Iraqi invasion of Kuwait, the oil market was in equilibrium at point E. The invasion and the resulting embargo on Iraqi oil decreased supply to S_2. Price increased to P_2, and the quantity exchanged fell to Q_2.

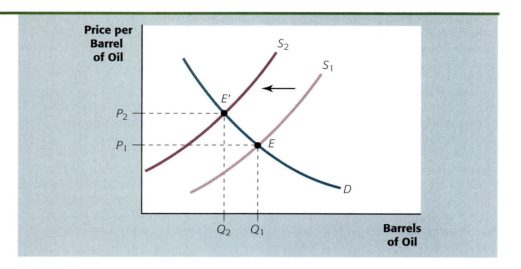

had not affected natural gas supplies at all, so there was no reason for the price of natural gas to rise.

Were the college administrators right? Was this just an example of price gouging by the utility companies who were taking advantage of an international crisis to increase their profits? A simple supply and demand analysis will give us the answer. More specifically, it will enable us to answer two questions: (1) Why did Iraq's invasion of Kuwait cause the price of oil to rise, and (2) Why did the price of natural gas rise as well?

Figure 13 shows supply and demand curves in one of the markets relevant to our analysis: the market for crude oil. In this market, oil producers—including those in Iraq and Kuwait—sell to American buyers. Before the invasion, the market was in equilibrium at E with price P_1 and total output Q_1.

Then came the event that changed the equilibrium: Iraq's invasion and continued occupation of Kuwait—one of the largest oil producers in the world. Immediately after the invasion, the United States led a worldwide embargo on oil from both Iraq and Kuwait. As far as the oil market was concerned, it was as if these nations' oil fields no longer existed—a significant decrease in the oil industry's productive capacity. If you look back at Figure 6 you will see that a decrease in productive capacity shifts the supply curve to the left, and this is just what happened. The new equilibrium at E' occurred at a lower quantity and a higher price. This change in the oil market's equilibrium was well understood by most people—including the college administrators—and no one was surprised when oil prices rose.

But what has all this got to do with natural gas prices? Everything, as the next part of our analysis will show.

Figure 14 shows the next market relevant to our analysis: the market for natural gas. In this market, world producers (which did not include Iraq or Kuwait) sell natural gas to American buyers. In this market, the initial equilibrium—before the invasion and before the rise in oil prices—was at point F. How did the invasion affect the equilibrium?

Oil is a *substitute* for natural gas. A rise in the price of a substitute, we know, will increase the demand for a good. (Look back at Figure 3 if you need a reminder.) In this case, the increase in the price of oil caused the demand curve for natural gas to shift rightward. In Figure 13, the price of natural gas rose from P_3 to P_4.

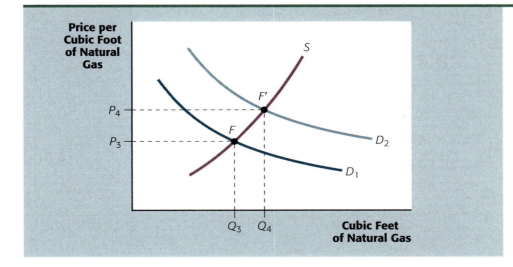

FIGURE 14
The Market for Natural Gas

Oil is a substitute for natural gas. A rise in the price of oil increases the demand for natural gas. Here, demand for natural gas increases from D_1 to D_2 and the price rises from P_3 to P_4.

The administrators were right that the invasion of Kuwait did not affect the supply of natural gas. What they missed, however, was the invasion's effect on the *demand* for natural gas. With a fuller understanding of supply and demand, they could have predicted—*before* investing in their expensive switching equipment—that any rise in oil prices would cause a rise in natural gas prices. Armed with this knowledge, they would have anticipated a much smaller savings in energy costs from switching to natural gas and might have decided that there were better uses for their scarce funds.

Summary

In a market economy, prices are determined through the interaction of buyers and sellers in *markets. Perfectly competitive* markets have many buyers and sellers, and none of them individually can affect the market price. If an individual, buyer, or seller has the power to influence the price of a product, the market is *imperfectly competitive.*

The model of *supply and demand* explains how prices are determined in perfectly competitive markets. The *quantity demanded* of any good is the total amount buyers would choose to purchase at a given price. The *law of demand* states that quantity demanded is negatively related to price; it tells us that the *demand curve* slopes downward. The demand curve is drawn for given levels of income, wealth, tastes, prices of substitute and complementary goods, population, and expected future price. If any of those factors changes, the demand curve will shift.

The *quantity supplied* of a good is the total amount sellers would choose to produce and sell at a given price. According to the *law of supply,* supply curves slope upward. The supply curve will shift if there is a change in the price of an input,

the price of an alternate good, the number of firms, or expectations of future prices.

Equilibrium price and quantity in a market are found where the supply and demand curves intersect. If either of these curves shifts, price and quantity will change as the market moves to a new equilibrium.

The *principle of markets and equilibrium* tells us that to understand how the economy operates, we should think of the economy as a system of markets, and then examine the equilibrium in each of those markets. Equilibrium price and quantity in a market are found where the supply and demand curves intersect. If either of the curves shifts, price and quantity will change as the market moves to a new equilibrium.

Governments often intervene in markets, to change the equilibrium price. *Price ceilings* are imposed in an attempt to hold a price below its equilibrium value. *Price floors* are an attempt to keep the price above the equilibrium value. Economists tend to be skeptical about price ceilings and price floors, since they are often ineffective and have unintended consequences that undermine the government's goals.

Key Terms

Aggregation
Alternate goods
Black market
Change in demand
Change in quantity demanded
Change in quantity supplied
Change in supply
Complement
Demand schedule
Equilibrium price
Equilibrium quantity
Excess demand

Excess supply
Firm's quantity supplied
Household's quantity demanded
Imperfectly competitive market
Income
Inferior good
Law of demand
Law of supply
Market demand curve
Market quantity demanded
Market quantity supplied

Normal good
Perfectly competitive market
Price ceiling
Price floor
Rent controls
Short side of the market
Shortage
Substitute
Supply curve
Supply schedule
Wealth

Review Questions

1. How does the way each of the following terms is used in economics differ from the way it is used in everyday language?
   a. market
   b. demand
   c. normal good
   d. inferior good
   e. supply

2. What is the difference between *demand* and *quantity demanded*?

3. List and briefly explain the factors that can shift a demand curve and the factors that can shift a supply curve.

4. What is the difference between substitutes and complements? Which of the following pairs of goods are substitutes, which are complements, and which are neither?
   a. Coke and Pepsi
   b. Computer hardware and computer software
   c. Beef and chicken
   d. Salt and sugar
   e. Ice cream and frozen yogurt

5. Rank each of the following markets according to how close you think it comes to perfect competition:
   a. Wheat
   b. Personal computer hardware
   c. Gold
   d. Airline tickets from New York to Kalamazoo, Michigan

6. Is each of the following goods more likely to be *normal* or *inferior*?
   a. Lexus automobiles
   b. Secondhand clothes
   c. Imported beer
   d. Baby-sitting services
   e. Recapped tires
   f. Futons
   g. Home haircutting tools
   h. Restaurant meals

7. What does the term *equilibrium* mean in economics?

8. Explain why the price in a free market will not remain above or below equilibrium for long, unless there is outside interference.

9. Determine whether each of the following will cause a change in demand or a change in supply, and in which direction:
   a. Input prices increase.
   b. Income in an area declines.
   c. The price of an alternate good increases.
   d. Tastes shift away from a good.

Problems and Exercises

1. In the late 1990s, beef—which had fallen out of favor in the 1970s and 1980s—became popular again. On a supply and demand diagram, illustrate the effect of such a change on equilibrium price and quantity in the market for beef.

2. In the late 1990s and through 2000, the British public became increasingly concerned about "Mad Cow Disease," which could be deadly to humans if they ate beef from these cattle. Fearing the disease, many consumers switched to other meats, like chicken, pork, or lamb. At the same time, the British government ordered the destruction of thousands of head of cattle. Illustrate the effects of these events on the equilibrium price and quantity in the market for British beef. Can we determine with certainty the direction of change for the quantity? For the price? Explain briefly.

3. Discuss, and illustrate with a graph, how each of the following events will affect the market for coffee:
   a. A blight on coffee plants kills off much of the Brazilian crop.
   b. The price of tea declines.
   c. Coffee workers organize themselves into a union and gain higher wages.
   d. Coffee is shown to cause cancer in laboratory rats.
   e. Coffee prices are expected to rise rapidly in the near future.

4. The following table gives hypothetical data for the quantity of two-bedroom rental apartments demanded and supplied in Peoria, Illinois:

Monthly Rent	Quantity Demanded (Thousands)	Quantity Supplied (Thousands)
$ 800	30	10
$1,000	25	14
$1,200	22	17
$1,400	19	19
$1,600	17	21
$1,800	15	22

   a. Graph the demand and supply curves.
   b. Find the equilibrium price and quantity.
   c. Explain briefly why a rent of $1,000 cannot be the equilibrium in this market.
   d. Suppose a tornado destroys a significant number of apartment buildings in Peoria, but doesn't affect people's desire to live there. Illustrate on your graph the effects on equilibrium price and quantity.

5. The following table gives hypothetical data for the quantity of You-Snooze-You-Lose brand alarm clocks demanded and supplied per month.

Price per Alarm Clock	Quantity Demanded	Quantity Supplied
$ 5	3,500	700
$10	3,000	900
$15	2,500	1,100
$20	2,000	1,300
$25	1,500	1,500
$30	1,000	1,700
$35	500	1,900

   a. Graph the demand and supply curves.
   b. Find the equilibrium price and quantity.
   c. Illustrate on your graph how a decrease in the price of wake-up services would affect the market for You-Snooze-You-Lose alarm clocks.
   d. What would happen if there was a decrease in the price of wake-up services at the same time that the price of the plastic used to manufacture You-Snooze-You-Lose alarm clocks rose?

6. How would each of the following affect the market for blue jeans in the United States? Illustrate each answer with a supply and demand diagram.
   a. The price of denim cloth increases.
   b. An influx of immigrants arrives in the United States. (Explicitly state any assumptions you are making.)
   c. An economic slowdown in the United States causes household incomes to decrease.

7. Indicate which curve shifted—and in which direction—for each of the following. Assume that only one curve shifts.
   a. The price of furniture rises as the quantity bought and sold falls.
   b. Apartment vacancy rates increase while average monthly rent on apartments declines.
   c. The price of personal computers continues to decline as sales skyrocket.

8. Consider the following forecast: "In 2004, we predict that the demand curve for handheld PCs will continue its shift leftward, which will tend to lower price and quantity. However, with a lower price, supply will decrease as well, shifting the supply curve leftward. A leftward shift of the supply curve will tend to raise price and lower quantity. We conclude that as 2004 proceeds, quantity will decrease but the price of handheld PCs may either rise or fall." There is a serious mistake of logic in this forecast. Can you find it? Explain.

9. Draw supply and demand diagrams for market A for each of the following. Then use your diagrams to illustrate the impact of the following events. In each case, determine what happens to price and quantity in each market.
   a. A and B are substitutes, and the price of good B rises.
   b. A and B satisfy the same kinds of desires, and there is a shift in tastes away from A and toward B.
   c. A is a normal good, and incomes in the community increase.
   d. There is a technological advance in the production of good A.
   e. B is an input used to produce good A, and the price of B rises.

10. The market for rice has the following supply and demand schedules:

P (per ton)	Q^D (tons)	Q^S (tons)
$10	100	0
$20	80	30
$30	60	40
$40	50	50
$50	40	60

To support rice producers, the government imposes a price floor of $50 per ton.
   a. What quantity will be traded in the market? Why?

b. What steps might the government have to take to enforce the price floor?

11. The market for one-bedroom apartments in a city has the following supply and demand schedules:

Monthly Rent	Q^D (thousands)	Q^S (thousands)
$1,000	800	300
$1,200	600	350
$1,400	400	400
$1,600	200	450
$1,800	100	500

The government imposes a price ceiling (rent control) of $1,200.

a. With the price ceiling, is there an excess demand, excess supply, or neither? If there is an excess demand or excess supply, state which and give the numerical value.

b. What quantity of one-bedroom apartments will actually be rented?

c. Suppose, instead, that the price ceiling is set at $1,600. What quantity of one-bedroom apartments will be rented now? Is there an excess supply, excess demand, or neither?

Challenge Questions

1. Suppose that demand is given by the equation $Q^D = 500 - 50P$, where Q^D is quantity demanded, and P is the price of the good. Supply is described by the equation $Q^S = 50 + 25P$, where Q^S is quantity supplied. What is the equilibrium price and quantity? (See Appendix)

2. While crime rates have fallen across the country over the past few years, they have fallen especially rapidly in Manhattan. At the same time, there are some neighborhoods in the New York metropolitan area in which the crime rate has remained constant. Using supply and demand diagrams for rental housing, explain how a falling crime rate in Manhattan could make the residents in *other* neighborhoods *worse off*. (Hint: As people from around the country move to Manhattan, what happens to rents there? If someone cannot afford to pay higher rent in Manhattan, what might they do?)

3. A Wall Street analyst observes the following equilibrium price-quantity combinations in the market for restaurant meals in a city over a four-year period:

Year	P	Q (Thousands of Meals per Month)
1	$12	20
2	$15	30
3	$17	40
4	$20	50

She concludes that the market defies the law of demand. Is she correct? Why or why not?

 **ECONOMIC** *Applications*

These exercises require access to Lieberman/Hall Xtra! If Xtra! did not come with your book, visit http://liebermanxtra.swlearning.com to purchase.

1. Use your Xtra! password at the Hall and Lieberman Web site (http://liebermanxtra.swlearning.com), select Chapter 3, and under Economic Applications, click on EconNews. Choose *Economic Fundamentals: Equilibrium,* and scroll down to find the article "Sweet Home Improvement Market." Read the article summary, and answer the questions below.

   a. Show graphically, using supply and demand curves, the impact of the increase in new home sales on the home improvement market.

   b. Now click on EconData. Under Hot Data, scroll down to find *Housing Starts.* Click on it, and read the definition of Housing Starts. Then click on *Diagrams/Data,* and see how the level of housing starts relates to the 30-year mortgage rate. What relationship should this variable have with the mortgage rate? Do you see this in the graph? Why or why not?

   c. Next click on EconNews again. Choose *Economic Fundamental: Supply and Demand* and scroll down to find the article, "PC Price Cuts." Read the article summary, and describe, using supply and demand curves, how the effects of computer price cuts impacts the market for home improvement described in part a.

2. Use your Xtra! password at the Hall and Lieberman Web site (http://hallxtra.swlearning.com), select Chapter 3, and under Economic Applications click on EconDebate.

Choose *Economic Fundamental: Supply and Demand,* and scroll down to find the debate, "Do slave redemption programs reduce the problem of slavery?" Read the debate and answer the questions below.

   a. What incentive problem is mentioned in the debate regarding slave redemption programs? Illustrate this using supply and demand curves.

   b. How could you modify the incentives of slave redemption programs to reduce the problem of increased slave raids?

3. Use your Xtra! password at the Hall and Lieberman Web site (http://liebermanxtra.swlearning.com), select Chapter 3, and under Economic Applications, click on EconNews. Choose *Economic Fundamentals: Equilibrium,* and scroll down to find the article "Students Learn the Hard Way." Read the article summary, and answer the questions below.

   a. As the article points out, many schools are seeing an increase in costs as well as a reduction in state funds available. Illustrate, using a graph of supply and demand in the market for a college education, the effect of increasing costs of producing that education.

   b. Why would student government groups on college campuses with incentives like the ones described in the article be concerned about the quality of the education students were receiving?

APPENDIX

ELASTICITY OF DEMAND

The law of demand tells us that when price increases, quantity demanded will fall, and when price decreases, quantity demanded will rise. But it doesn't tell us *how much* quantity demanded will change. For some goods, quantity demanded is sensitive to price changes, while for other goods, there is almost no sensitivity at all. If we want be more specific about what happens when a price changes, we need a way to measure the sensitivity of quantity demanded to a change in price. Economists have developed just such a measure, called the *price elasticity of demand*.

> *The* price elasticity of demand (E$_D$) *(or just* elasticity of demand, *for short) is the absolute value of the percentage change in quantity demanded divided by the percentage change in price:*
>
> $$E_D = \left| \frac{\%\Delta Q^D}{\%\Delta P} \right|.$$

To understand how the elasticity of demand measures price sensitivity, think about what happens when the price of a good rises by, say, 2 percent. The denominator of our measure will be 2. We know the numerator will be *negative*, because a rise in the price of the good will cause quantity demanded to fall. However, since we take the absolute value of the final fraction, we can ignore the negative sign. Thus, the numerator will tell us the percentage by which quantity demanded falls when the price rises by 2 percent.

Now, the more sensitive quantity demanded is to this 2 percent price change, the greater the fall in quantity demanded, the greater the numerator will be, and the greater E$_D$ will be. Thus, *the more sensitive quantity demanded is to price, the greater will be the price elasticity of demand.* For example, if a 2 percent rise in the price of newspapers causes a 3 percent drop in the quantity of newspapers demanded, then $E_D = |\,\%\Delta Q^D / \%\Delta P\,| = 3\% / 2\% = 1.5$. We would say, "The price elasticity of demand for newspapers is 1.5." If that same 2 percent rise in price instead causes a 6 percent drop in the quantity demanded, then $E_D = |\,\%\Delta Q^D / \%\Delta P\,| = 6\% / 2\% = 3.0$. In the sec-

ond case, quantity demanded is more sensitive to price, and our measure of elasticity is larger: 3.0 rather than 1.5.

The elasticity of demand for a good has a straightforward interpretation: It tells us the percentage change in quantity demanded *per 1 percent increase* in price. An elasticity of 3.0, for example, tells us that when price rises by 1 percent, quantity demanded falls by 3.0 percent. When price rises by 2 percent, quantity demanded falls by 6.0 percent, and so on.

Finally, keep in mind that a demand elasticity number tells us the response of quantity demanded to a price change *when all other influences on demand remain unchanged.* We are interested in the pure effect of a price change on quantity demanded, uncluttered by changes in other prices, income, tastes, or other variables. Elasticity tells us the change in quantity we *would* observe if just the price of the good changed, and nothing else did. In other words,

> *A price elasticity of demand tells us the quantity response to a price change as we move along a demand curve, from one point to another.*

Calculating Price Elasticity of Demand

Suppose that you actually know the demand curve for a product; that is, you know what quantity consumers in a market would like to buy at each possible price. You would still have one more task in order to calculate a demand elasticity: measuring the *percentage change* in both quantity demanded and price.

Percentage Changes for Elasticities. A percentage change is *usually* defined as the change in a variable divided by its starting or base value. (See the mathematical appendix on percentage changes.) But this method of calculating percentage changes can create a problem when determining elasticities. For example, look at Table A1, which shows the quantity of peanuts demanded at two different prices. (For now, ignore the columns referring to macadamia nuts.) Let's first calculate the percentage change in the price of peanuts when the price rises from $1.50 per pound to $2.50 per pound—a change of $1. Since the starting value is

$1.50, the percentage change in price would be $1/$1.50 = 0.66, or 66 percent. But what if—instead of increasing from $1.50 to $2.50—the price had *decreased* from $2.50 to $1.50? In this case, our starting price would be $2.50, and our percentage change in price would now become −$1/$2.50 = −0.40, or −40 percent. This example shows us that, if we calculate percentage changes in the standard way, the number we get will depend on whether the price is rising or falling along any interval. That is, a price change from $1.50 to $2.50 is a percentage rise of 66 percent, while a price change from $2.50 to $1.50 is a percentage fall of 40 percent. The same is true for changes in quantity demanded: The percentage change in quantity demanded—calculated in the standard way—would depend on the *direction* of the change.

But that won't do for calculating an elasticity. Why? Elasticity of demand measures price sensitivity over an *interval* along the demand curve. We want this measure to be the same regardless of which end of the interval we start at. To ensure this, we adopt a special convention for measuring percentage changes for elasticities: *The base value used to calculate a percentage change in a variable is always midway between the initial value and the new value.* Thus, if the price rises from $1.50 to $2.50 or falls from $2.50 to $1.50, we use as our base price the value midway between these two prices, found by calculating their simple average: ($1.50 + $2.50)/2 = $2.00. This way, we are using the same base value, regardless of the direction of the price change. And our percentage change in price will be the same (except for sign) whether price rises from $1.50 to $2.50, or falls from $2.50 to $1.50.

More generally, when price changes from any value P_0 to any other value P_1, we define the percentage change in price as

$$\%\Delta P = \frac{(P_1 - P_0)}{(P_1 + P_0)/2}.$$

The term in the numerator is the change in price; the term in the denominator is the base price—the midpoint between the two prices. If you plug the preceding numbers into this formula, you'll see that when price rises from $1.50 to $2.50, the percentage rise in price is $1.00/$2.00 = 0.50; when price falls from $2.50 to $1.50, the percentage fall is $1.00/$2.00 = 0.50.

The percentage change in quantity demanded is calculated in a similar way. When quantity demanded changes from Q_0 to Q_1, the percentage change is calculated as

$$\%Q^D = \frac{(Q_1 - Q_0)}{(Q_1 + Q_2)/2}.$$

Once again, we are using the number midway between the initial and the new quantity demanded as our base quantity.

Using the Formula. Now let's calculate the elasticity of demand for both peanuts and macadamia nuts, using the hypothetical data in Table A.1. For peanuts, when price rises from $1.50 to $2.50, quantity demanded falls from 500,000 to 490,000, so we have

$$\%\Delta Q^D = \frac{(Q_1 - Q_0)}{[(Q_1 + Q_0)/2]}$$
$$= \frac{(490,000 - 500,000)}{495,000}$$
$$= -0.02, \text{ or } -2.0 \text{ percent}$$
$$\%\Delta P = \frac{(P_1 - P_0)}{[(P_1 + P_0)/2]}$$
$$= \frac{(\$2.50 - \$1.50)}{\$2.00}$$
$$= -0.50, \text{ or } 50.0 \text{ percent}$$
$$E_D = \left|\frac{-2.0 \text{ percent}}{50.0 \text{ percent}}\right| = 0.04.$$

We find that the quantity of peanuts demanded falls by 0.04 percent for each 1 percent increase in price. Not much price sensitivity at all here.

Peanuts		Macadamia Nuts		
Price (per pound)	Quantity (pounds per year)	Price (per pound)	Quantity (pounds per year)	
$1.50	500,000	$8.00	15,000	
$2.50	490,000	$9.00	5,000	

TABLE A.1
Demand Schedules for Peanuts and Macadamia Nuts

For macadamia nuts, the same price change of $1.00—but from $8.00 to $9.00 in this case—causes quantity demanded to fall from 15,000 to 5,000, so we have:

$$\%\Delta Q^D = \frac{(Q_1 - Q_0)}{[(Q_1 + Q_0)/2]}$$

$$= \frac{(5,000 - 15,000)}{10,000}$$

$$= -1.0, \text{ or -100 percent}$$

$$\%\Delta P = \frac{(P_1 - P_0)}{[(P_1 + P_0)/2]}$$

$$= \frac{(\$9.00 - \$8.00)}{\$8.50}$$

$$= 0.118, \text{ or 11.8 percent}$$

$$E_D = \left| \frac{-100 \text{ percent}}{11.8 \text{ percent}} \right| = 8.5$$

Here, each 1 percent increase in price causes quantity demanded to drop by about 8.5 percent. Macadamia nuts, unlike peanuts, exhibit a great deal of price sensitivity.

Categorizing Goods by Elasticity

When the numerical value of the price elasticity of demand is *between 0 and 1.0*, we say that demand is *inelastic*. When demand for a good is inelastic, the elasticity will be smaller than unity, i.e.,

$$\left| \frac{\%\Delta Q^D}{\%\Delta P} \right| < 1$$

Or, rearranging, we obtain

$$\left| \%\Delta Q^D \right| < \left| \%\Delta P \right|$$

In words, inelastic demand means that the percentage change in quantity demanded will be *smaller* than the percentage change in price. For example, if price rises by 4 percent, quantity demanded will fall, but by *less* than 4 percent. When demand is inelastic, quantity demanded is *not* very sensitive to price.

An extreme case of inelastic demand occurs when a change in price causes absolutely no change in quantity demanded at all. In this case, since $\%\Delta Q^D = 0$, the elasticity will equal zero. We call this special case *perfectly inelastic* demand. Panel (a) of Figure A.1 shows what the demand curve for a good would look like if demand were perfectly inelastic at every price. The demand curve is vertical: No matter what the price, quantity demanded is the same.

Although perfectly inelastic demand is interesting from a theoretical point of view, it is difficult to find examples of goods with zero elasticity of demand in the real world. With zero demand elasticity, the good would have to be one that consumers want only in a fixed quantity. One example might be insulin—the drug needed by diabetics to control their blood sugar. Insulin has no use other than in the management of diabetes. For diabetics, quantity requirements for insulin are quite rigid, and there are no substitutes for its use. A drop in price will not encourage diabetics to use more, nor will a modest rise in price cause diabetics to economize on its use.

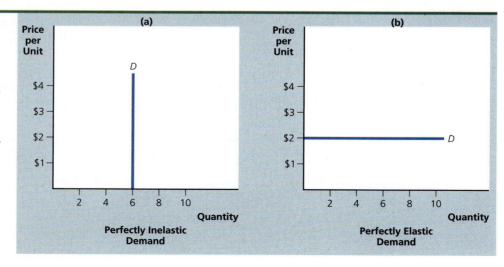

FIGURE A.1
Extreme Cases of Elasticity

The vertical curve of panel (a) represents the case of perfectly inelastic demand. At every price, the same quantity is demanded. The horizontal curve in panel (b) represents perfectly elastic demand. A small change in price would lead to an infinitely large change in quanitity demanded.

When $E_D > 1.0$, we say that demand is *elastic*. In this case, the elasticity will be greater than unity:

$$\left|\frac{\%\Delta Q^D}{\%\Delta P}\right| > 1$$

Or, rearranging, we get

$$\left|\%\Delta Q^D\right| > \left|\%\Delta P\right|$$

When demand is elastic, the percentage change in quantity demanded is *larger* than the percentage change in price. For instance, if price rises by 4 percent, quantity demanded will fall by *more* than 4 percent. Elastic demand means that quantity demanded is *sensitive* to price.

An extreme case of price sensitivity occurs when demand is *perfectly* or *infinitely elastic*. Even the tiniest change in price causes a huge change in quantity demanded, so huge that, for all intents and purposes, we can call the response infinite. When demand is perfectly elastic, then no matter how much people are buying, the demand curve will be a horizontal line—as shown in panel (b) of Figure A.1. The demand for a single brand of salt may fall into this category. If the price of Brand X salt rose a little, while other brands next to it on the supermarket shelf continued to cost the same, virtually everyone would switch to the other brands, causing the quantity of Brand X salt demanded to plummet.

Finally, when elasticity of demand is exactly equal to 1, we have *unitary elasticity*. In this case, we would have $\left|\%\Delta Q^D\right| = \left|\%\Delta P\right|$, and demand for the good is exactly at the boundary between elastic and inelastic. Many consumer products seem to have price elasticities near 1.0. In addition, a price elasticity of 1.0 is important as a benchmark case, as you will see in the next section.

Elasticity and Total Expenditure

When the price of a good increases, the law of demand tells us that people will demand less of it. But this does not necessarily mean that they will *spend* less on it. After the price rises, fewer units will be purchased, but each unit will cost more. It turns out that whether total spending on a good rises or falls depends on the price elasticity of demand for the good.

To see this more formally, note that the total expenditure (*TE*) on a good is defined as

$$TE = P \times Q$$

where P is the price per unit and Q is the quantity purchased. We can use a rule about percentage changes, explained in the Mathematical Appendix: *When two numbers are both changing, the percentage change in their product is the sum of their individual percentage changes.* Applying this to total expenditure, we can write

$$\%\Delta TE = \%\Delta P + \%\Delta Q$$

Now let's assume that P rises by, say, 10 percent. What will happen to total expenditure? If demand is *unitary elastic*, then Q will fall by 10 percent, so we will have

$$\%\Delta TE = 10 \text{ percent} + (-10 \text{ percent}) = 0$$

The percentage change in total expenditure is zero, meaning that total expenditure does not change at all! If demand is *inelastic*, a 10 percent rise in price will cause quantity demanded to fall by *less* than 10 percent, so we have

$$\%\Delta TE = 10 \text{ percent} + (\text{something less negative than } -10 \text{ percent}) > 0$$

The percentage change in total expenditure is greater than zero, so total expenditure rises. Finally, if demand

Where demand is:		A price increase will:	A price decrease will:	TABLE A.2
inelastic	($\%\Delta Q^D < \%\Delta P$)	increase expenditure	decrease expenditure	**Effects of Price Changes on Expenditure**
unitary elastic	($\%\Delta Q^D = \%\Delta P$)	cause no change in expenditure	cause no change in expenditure	
elastic	($\%\Delta Q^D > \%\Delta P$)	decrease expenditure	increase expenditure	

is *elastic*, so that Q falls by more than 10 percent, *TE* will fall:

$$\%\Delta TE = 10 \text{ percent} + (\text{something more negative than} -10 \text{ percent}) < 0$$

Of course, the results we just obtained for a price increase of 10 percent would hold for any price increase. Our conclusions about elasticity and total expenditure are presented in Table A.2. They can be summarized as follows:

> *Where demand is price inelastic, total expenditure moves in the same direction as price. Where demand is elastic, total spending moves in the opposite direction to price. Finally, where demand is unitary elastic, total expenditure remains the same as price changes.*

Let's check the statements in Table A.2, using our hypothetical data for peanuts and macadamia nuts. Repeating the information from our earlier example, and adding a column for total expenditure, we have:

Macadamia Nuts

Price per pound (P)	Quantity Demanded (pounds per year) (Q)	Total Yearly Expenditure (P × Q)
$8.00	15,000	$120,000
$9.00	5,000	$ 45,000

Peanuts

Price per pound (P)	Quantity Demanded (pounds per year) (Q)	Total Yearly Expenditure (P × Q)
$1.50	500,000	$ 750,000
$2.50	490,000	$1,225,000

Notice what happens to total expenditure in each case. Demand for macadamia nuts, you recall, was price elastic ($E_D = 8.5$) when price rose from $8 to $9. According to the rules in Table A.2, we would expect a price rise to reduce total expenditure, and that is exactly what happens: The $1.00 rise in price causes total expenditure to decrease from $120,000 to $45,000. Peanuts, on the other hand, were price inelastic ($E_D = 0.04$) when price rose from $1.50 to $2.50, and our rules tell us that a rise in price should increase total expenditure. Indeed, the $1.00 price hike causes total expenditure on peanuts to rise from $750,000 to $1,225,000.

There is an easy way to see how a change in price changes the total expenditure of buyers, using a graph of the demand curve. At point A in Figure A.2, price is $9 per unit and quantity demanded is 150 units. Total revenue is price × quantity = $9 × 150 = $1,350. But this is exactly equal to the *area* of the blue shaded rectangle, which has a width of 150 and a height of $9. Thus, the area of this rectangle shows total expenditure on the good when price is $9. More generally,

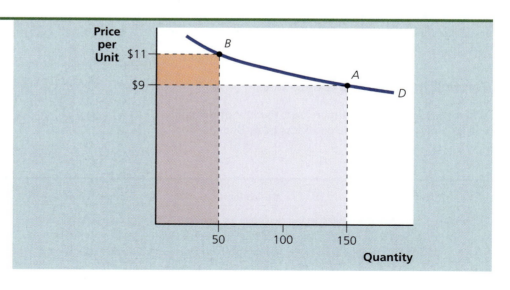

FIGURE A.2
Elasticity and Total Expenditure

Any point along a demand curve defines a rectangle whose area indicates total expenditure on the good at that point. At point A, where price is $9 per unit and 150 units are demanded, expenditure is $1,350. At point B, expenditure is $550. Moving from A to B, expenditure decreases, so demand must be elastic over that range.

At any point on a demand curve, buyers' total expenditure is the area of a rectangle with width equal to quantity demanded and height equal to price.

Now suppose that price rises from $9 to $11, so we move along the demand curve to point *B,* where quantity demanded drops to 50 units. Here, total expenditure is $11 × 50 = $550, given by the area of the red rectangle, with width equal to 50 and height equal to $11. You can see that the area of the wider, blue rectangle is greater than the area of the narrower, red rectangle. This tells us that total expenditure is greater at a price of $9 than it is at $11. In other words, the rise in price from $9 to $11 causes total expenditure to decrease.

As you've learned, a price increase causes total expenditure on a good to decrease only when demand for the good is *elastic*. So our diagram tells us that, for the good depicted in the figure, demand is elastic for a price change from $9 to $11 or from $11 to $9.

Knowing the price elasticity of demand for a good and understanding the link between elasticity and total expenditure is helpful in many different contexts. For example, the total amount that consumers spend on a good is also the *total sales revenue* of firms that sell the good. For this reason, knowing the price elasticity of demand for their product is very important to firms. Producers of goods and services—doctors, bakers, theater owners, manufacturers, and others—use price elasticity of demand to predict the impact of a price change on their total sales revenue. And government policy makers—who need to anticipate how private market participants will respond to government actions—use demand elasticities to price many government services, to make tax policy, and to design programs to help the needy. For example, suppose a city government is considering an increase in mass transit fares, and wants to know the impact on the total revenue of the mass transit system. The answer will depend on the elasticity of demand for mass transit in that city. If the demand is *elastic,* the fare hike will *decrease* revenue; if demand is *inelastic,* revenue will *increase.*

Consumer Choice

You are constantly making economic decisions. Some of them are rather trivial. (Have coffee at Starbucks or more cheaply at home?) Others can have a profound impact on your life. (Live with your parents a while longer or get your own place?) The economic nature of all these decisions is rather obvious, since they all involve *spending*.

But in other cases, the economic nature of your decisions may be less obvious. Did you get up early today in order to get things done, or did you sleep in? Which leisure activities—movies, concerts, sports, hobbies—do you engage in, and how often do you decline an opportunity to have fun for lack of time? At this very moment, what have you decided *not* to do in order to make time to read this chapter? All of these are economic choices, too, because they require you to allocate a scarce resource—your *time*—among different alternatives.

How can we hope to analyze economic decisions when they all seem so different from each other? Our starting point is basic principle #1, maximization subject to constraints, which you first encountered in Chapter 1.

> *The economic approach to understanding a problem is to identify the decision makers and then determine what they are maximizing and the constraints that they face.*

Maximization Subject to Constraints

When we apply this principle to individual decision making, we immediately face two questions: What are individuals trying to maximize? And what are their constraints?

In economics, we assume that most people try to maximize their overall level of *satisfaction*. This may mean just momentary pleasure, but it can also mean self-improvement, a secure future, the right balance between work and play, or anything else that people value. As we attempt to satisfy these desires, we come up against constraints: too little income or wealth to buy everything we might enjoy and too little time to enjoy it all.

In this chapter, you will learn the economic model of individual choice. In most of the chapter, we will focus on choices about *spending*: how people decide what to buy. This is why the theory of individual decision making is often called "consumer theory." Later, in the "Using the Theory" section, we'll see how the theory can be broadened to include decisions about allocating scarce *time* among different activities.

THE BUDGET CONSTRAINT

Virtually all individuals must face two facts of economic life: (1) They have to pay prices for the goods and services they buy, and (2) they have limited funds to spend. These two facts are summarized by the consumer's *budget constraint:*

> *A consumer's **budget constraint** identifies which combinations of goods and services the consumer can afford with a limited budget, at given prices.*

Budget constraint The different combinations of goods a consumer can afford with a limited budget, at given prices.

Consider Max, a devoted fan of both movies and the local music scene, who has a total entertainment budget of $150 each month. Each movie costs Max $10, while the average ticket price for local rock concerts is $30. If Max were to spend all of his $150 budget on concerts at $30 each, he could see at most five each month. If he were to spend it all on movies at $10 each, he could see 15 of them.

But Max could also choose to spend *part* of his budget on concerts and *part* on movies. In this case, for each number of concerts, there is some *maximum* number of movies that he could see. For example, if he goes to one concert per month, it will cost him $30 of his $150 budget, leaving $120 available for movies. Thus, if Max were to choose one concert, the *maximum* number of films he could choose would be $120/$10 = 12.

Figure 1 lists, for each number of concerts, the maximum number of movies that Max could see. Each combination of goods in the table is affordable for Max, since each will cost him exactly $150. Combination *A*, at one extreme, represents no concerts and 15 movies. Combination *F*, the other extreme, represents 5 concerts and no movies. In each of the combinations between *A* and *F*, Max attends both concerts and movies.

The graph in Figure 1 plots the number of movies along the vertical axis and the number of concerts along the horizontal. Each of the points *A* through *F* corresponds to one of the combinations in the table. If we connect all of these points with a straight line, we have a graphical representation of Max's budget constraint, which we call Max's **budget line.**

Budget line The graphical representation of a budget constraint, showing the maximum affordable quantity of one good for given amounts of another good.

FIGURE 1
The Budget Constraint

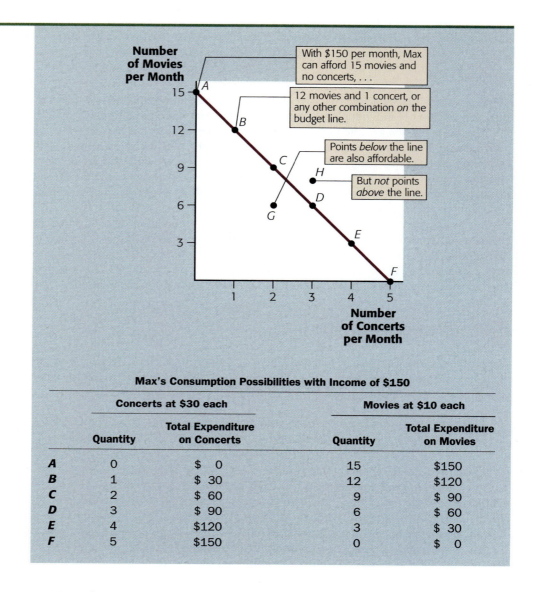

Number of Movies per Month

With $150 per month, Max can afford 15 movies and no concerts, . . .

12 movies and 1 concert, or any other combination *on* the budget line.

Points *below* the line are also affordable.

But *not* points *above* the line.

Number of Concerts per Month

Max's Consumption Possibilities with Income of $150

	Concerts at $30 each		Movies at $10 each	
	Quantity	Total Expenditure on Concerts	Quantity	Total Expenditure on Movies
A	0	$ 0	15	$150
B	1	$ 30	12	$120
C	2	$ 60	9	$ 90
D	3	$ 90	6	$ 60
E	4	$120	3	$ 30
F	5	$150	0	$ 0

Note that any point below or to the left of the budget line is affordable. For example, two concerts and six movies—indicated by point *G*—would cost only $60 + $60 = $120. Max could certainly afford this combination. On the other hand, he *cannot* afford any combination *above* and to the right of this line. Point *H*, representing 3 concerts and 8 movies, would cost $90 + $80 = $170, which is beyond Max's budget. The budget line therefore serves as a *border* between those combinations that are affordable and those that are not.

Let's look at Max's budget line more closely. The *vertical intercept* is 15, the number of movies Max could see if he attended zero concerts. Starting at the vertical intercept (point *A*), notice that each time Max increases one unit along the horizontal axis (attends one more concert), he must decrease 3 units along the vertical (see three fewer movies). Thus, the slope of the budget line is equal to –3. The slope tells us Max's *opportunity cost* of one more concert. That is, the opportunity cost of one more concert is 3 movies foregone.

There is an important relationship between the *prices* of two goods and the opportunity cost of having more of one or the other. The prices Max faces tell us how many dollars he must give up to get another unit of each good. If, however, we divide one money price by another money price, we get what is called a **relative price**, the price of one good *relative* to the other. Since $P_{concert} = \$30$ and $P_{movie} = \$10$, the *relative price of a concert* is the ratio $P_{concert}/P_{movie} = \$30/\$10 = 3$. Notice that 3 is the opportunity cost of another concert in terms of movies; and, except for the minus sign, it is also the slope of the budget line. That is, *the relative price of a concert, the opportunity cost of another concert, and the slope of the budget line* have the same absolute value. This is one example of a general relationship:

The Budget Line's Slope It's tempting to think that the slope of the budget line should be $-P_y/P_x$, where the price of the vertical-axis good, P_y, is in the numerator, rather than in the denominator. But this is wrong. The budget line's slope is the change in *quantity* along the vertical axis divided by the change in *quantity* along the horizontal. As our example shows, when the slope is expressed in terms of *prices* rather than quantities, the formula is $-P_x/P_y$, with the price of the *horizontal*-axis good in the numerator.[1]

DANGEROUS CURVES

Relative price The price of one good relative to the price of another.

Opportunity Cost

> *The slope of the budget line indicates the spending trade-off between one good and another—the amount of one good that must be sacrificed in order to buy more of another good. If P_y is the price of the good on the vertical axis and P_x is the price of the good on the horizontal axis, then the slope of the budget line is $-P_x/P_y$.*

Changes in the Budget Line

To draw the budget line in Figure 1, we have assumed given prices for movies and concerts, and a given income that Max can spend on them. These "givens"—the prices of the goods and the consumer's income—are always *assumed constant* as we move along a budget line; if any one of them changes, the budget line will change as well. Let's see how.

Changes in Income. If Max's available income increases from $150 to $300 per month, then he can afford to see more movies, more concerts, or more of both, as shown by the change in his budget line in Figure 2(a). If Max were to devote *all* of his income to movies, he could now see 30 of them each month, instead of the 15 he was able to see before. Devoting his entire income to concerts would enable him to attend 10, rather than 5. Moreover, for any number of concerts, he will be able to see more movies than before. For example, before, when his budget was only $150, choosing 2 concerts would allow Max to see only 9 movies. Now, with a budget of $300, he can have 2 concerts and *24* movies.

---

[1] For a more general proof, write out the equation for the budget line. Start by recognizing that the price of good y (P_y) times the quantity of good y consumed (Q_y) is the total amount spent on good y ($P_y \times Q_y$). Similarly, the total amount spent on good x is $P_x \times Q_x$. If we are on the budget line, the total amount spent on these two goods must equal the total budget (B), so $P_y \times Q_y + P_x \times Q_x = B$. Solving for Q_y gives us the equation for the budget line: $Q_y = (B - P_x \times Q_x)/P_y$. This can be rewritten as: $Q_y = (B/P_y) + [(-P_x/P_y) \times Q_x]$. The first term in parentheses (B/P_y) is the vertical intercept of budget line. The second term in parentheses ($-P_x/P_y$) is the slope. (See the mathematical appendix to Chapter 1 if you need to review slopes and intercepts.)

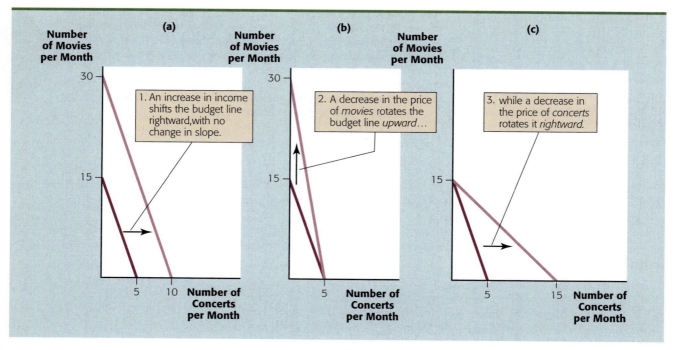

FIGURE 2
Changes in the Budget Line

Notice that the old and new budget lines in Figure 2(a) are parallel; that is, they have the same slope of −3. This is because we changed Max's income but *not* prices. Since the ratio $P_{concert}/P_{movie}$ has not changed, the spending trade-off between movies and concerts remains the same. Thus,

an increase in income will shift the budget line upward (and rightward). A decrease in income will shift the budget line downward (and leftward). These shifts are parallel: Changes in income do not affect the budget line's slope.

Changes in Price. Now let's go back to Max's original budget of $150 and explore what happens to the budget line when a price changes. Suppose the price of a movie falls from $10 to $5. The graph in Figure 2(b) shows Max's old and new budget lines. When the price of a movie falls, the budget line rotates outward; that is, the vertical intercept moves higher. The reason is this: When a movie costs $10, Max could spend his entire $150 on them and see 15; now that they cost $5, he can see a maximum of 30. The horizontal intercept—representing how many concerts Max could see with his entire income—doesn't change at all, since there has been no change in the price of a concert. Notice that the new budget line is also *steeper* than the original one, with slope equal to $-P_{concert}/P_{movie} = -\$30/\$5 = -6$. Now, with movies costing $5, the trade-off between movies and concerts is 6 to 1, instead of 3 to 1.

Panel (c) of Figure 2 illustrates another price change. This time, it's a fall in the price of a *concert* from $30 to $10. Once again, the budget line rotates, but now it is the horizontal intercept (concerts) that changes and the vertical intercept (movies) that remains fixed.

We could draw similar diagrams illustrating a *rise* in the price of a movie or a concert, but you should try to do this on your own. In each case, one of the budget line's intercepts will change, as well as its slope:

> When the price of a good changes, the budget line rotates: Both its slope and one of its intercepts will change.

The budget constraint, as illustrated by the budget line, is one side of the story of consumer choice. It indicates the trade-off consumers *are able to* make between one good and another. But just as important is the trade-off that consumers *want to* make between one good and another, and this depends on consumers' *preferences*, the subject of the next section.

PREFERENCES

How can we possibly speak systematically about people's preferences? After all, people are different. They like different things. American teens delight in having a Coke with dinner, while the very idea makes a French person shudder. What would satisfy a Buddhist monk would hardly satisfy the typical American.

And even among "typical Americans," there is little consensus about tastes. Some read Jane Austen, while others pick John Grisham. Some like to spend their vacations traveling, whereas others would prefer to stay home and sleep in every day. Even those who like Häagen-Dazs ice cream can't agree on which is the best flavor—the company notices consistent, regional differences in consumption. In Los Angeles, chocolate chocolate chip is the clear favorite, while on most of the East Coast, it's butter pecan—except in New York City, where coffee wins hands down. (And economics instructors have different preferences about teaching consumer theory. More on this in a few pages).

In spite of such wide differences in preferences, we can find some important common denominators—things that seem to be true for a wide variety of people. In our theory of consumer choice, we will focus on these common denominators.

Rationality

One common denominator—and a critical assumption behind consumer theory—is that people *have* preferences. More specifically, we assume that you can look at two alternatives and state either that you prefer one to the other or that you are entirely indifferent between the two—you value them equally.

Another common denominator is that preferences are *logically consistent*, or *transitive*. If, for example, you prefer a sports car to a jeep, and a jeep to a motorcycle, then we assume that you will also prefer a sports car to a motorcycle. When a consumer can make choices, and is logically consistent, we say that she has **rational preferences**.

Notice that rationality is a matter of how you make your choices, and not what choices you make. You can be rational and like apples better than oranges, or oranges better than apples. You can be rational even if you like anchovies or brussels sprouts! What matters is that you make logically consistent choices, and most of us usually do.

Rational preferences Preferences that satisfy two conditions: (1) Any two alternatives can be compared, and one is preferred or else the two are valued equally, and (2) the comparisons are logically consistent or transitive.

More Is Better

Another feature of preferences that virtually all of us share is this: We generally feel that *more is better*. Specifically, if we get more of some good or service, and nothing else is taken away from us, we will generally feel better off.

This condition seems to be satisfied for the vast majority of goods we all consume. Of course, there are exceptions. If you hate eggplant, then the more of it you have, the worse off you are. Similarly, a dieter who says, "Don't bring any ice cream into the house. I don't want to be tempted," also violates the assumption. The model of consumer choice in this chapter is designed for preferences that satisfy the "more is better" condition, and it would have to be modified to take account of exceptions like these.

So far, our characterization of consumer preferences has been rather minimal. We've assumed only that consumers are rational and that they prefer more rather than less of every good we're considering. But even this limited information allows us to say the following:

 Maximization Subject to Constraints

> *The consumer will always choose a point on the budget line, rather than a point below it.*

To see why this is so, look again at Figure 1. Max would never choose point *G*, representing 2 concerts and 6 movies, since there are affordable points—on the budget line—that we know make him better off. For example, point *C* has the same number of concerts, but more movies, while point *D* has the same number of movies, but more concerts. "More is better" tells us that Max will prefer *C* or *D* to *G*, so we know *G* won't be chosen. Indeed, if we look at any point below the budget line, we can always find at least one point on the budget line that is preferred, as long as more is better.

Knowing what Max will not do—knowing he *will not* choose a point inside his budget line—is helpful. It tells us that we can narrow our search for the point he *will* choose to just the ones along the budget line *AF*. But how can Max find the one point along the budget line that gives him a higher utility than all the others?

To answer this question, we'll introduce one of the basic principles of economics: *marginal decision making*:

> *Basic Principle #6: Marginal Decision Making*
> *To understand and predict the behavior of individual decision makers, we focus on the incremental or marginal effects of their actions.*

Marginal decision making can be compared to the children's game in which one child is blindfolded and must find a hidden object. As she changes position, the others tell her only "warmer" or "colder" to indicate whether she is moving closer or farther away from the object. Eventually she will find it—without anyone ever telling her where the object is hidden. In consumer theory, we can think of "maximum utility" as the hidden object the consumer is looking for, and we imagine her deciding whether some change in her collection of goods makes her better or worse off—"warmer" or "colder." If she continually makes changes that make her better off, until no such changes are left, then she will discover the combination that makes her as well off as possible.

The Two Approaches to Consumer Choices

Marginal decision making is a central concept in economics in general and consumer theory in particular. But this is where your *instructor's* preferences come in. There are two ways to apply marginal decision making to consumer choices, and they share much in common. First, both assume that preferences are rational. Second, both assume that the consumer would be better off with more of any good we're considering. This means the consumer will always choose a combination of goods *on*, rather than below, his budget line. Finally, both theories come to the same general conclusions about consumer behavior. However, to *arrive* at those conclusions, each theory takes a different road.

The next section presents the "Marginal Utility" approach to consumer decision making. If, however, your instructor prefers the "Indifference Curve" approach, you can skip the next section and go straight to the appendix. Then, come back to the section titled "Income and Substitution Effects," which is where our two roads converge once again.

One warning, though. Both approaches to consumer theory are *models*. They use graphs and calculations to explain how consumers make choices. While the models are logical, they may appear unrealistic to you. And in one sense, they *are* unrealistic: Few consumers in the real world are aware of the techniques we'll discuss, yet they make choices all the time.

Economists don't imagine that, when making choices, households or consumers actually *use* these techniques. Rather, the assumption is that people mostly behave *as if* they use them. Indeed, most of the time, in most markets, household behavior has proven to be consistent with the model of consumer choice. When our goal is to describe and predict how consumers are likely to behave in markets—rather than describe what actually goes on in their minds—our theories of consumer decision making can be very useful.

CONSUMER DECISIONS: THE MARGINAL UTILITY APPROACH

Economists assume that *any* decision maker—a consumer, the manager of a business firm, or officials in a government agency—tries to make the *best* out of any situation. Marginal utility theory treats consumers as striving to maximize their **utility**—an actual *quantitative* measure of well-being or satisfaction. Anything that makes the consumer better off is assumed to raise his utility. Anything that makes the consumer worse off will decrease his utility.

Utility A quantitative measure of pleasure or satisfaction obtained from consuming goods and services.

Utility and Marginal Utility

Figure 3 provides a graphical view of utility—in this case, the utility of a consumer named Lisa who likes ice cream cones. Look first at panel (a). On the horizontal axis, we'll measure the number of ice cream cones Lisa consumes each week. On the vertical axis, we'll measure the utility she derives from consuming each of them. If Lisa values ice cream cones, her utility will increase as she acquires more of them, as it does in the figure. There we see that when she has one cone, she enjoys total utility of 30 "utils," and when she has two cones, her total utility grows to 50 utils, and so on. Throughout the figure, the total utility Lisa derives from consuming ice cream cones keeps rising as she gets to consume more and more of them.

FIGURE 3
Total and Marginal Utility

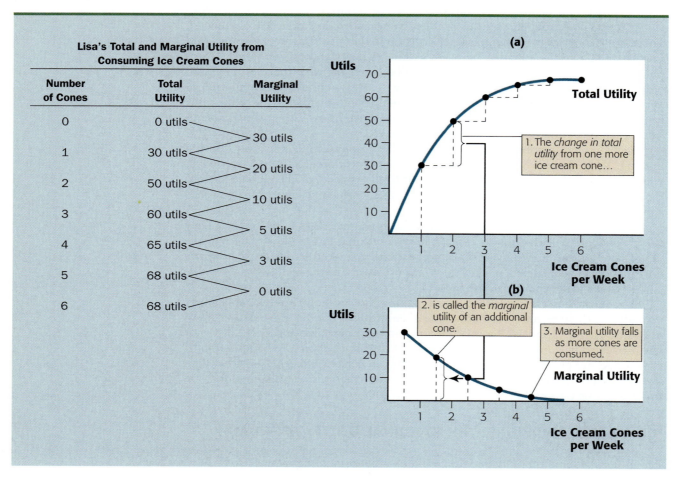

But notice something interesting, and important: Although Lisa's utility increases every time she consumes more ice cream, the *additional* utility she derives from each *successive* cone gets smaller and smaller as she gets more cones. We call the *change in utility* derived from consuming an *additional unit* of a good the *marginal utility* of that additional unit.

Marginal utility The change in total utility an individual obtains from consuming an additional unit of a good or service.

> *Marginal utility is the change in utility an individual enjoys from consuming an additional unit of a good.*

Law of diminishing marginal utility As consumption of a good or service increases, marginal utility decreases.

What we've observed about Lisa's utility can be restated this way: As she eats more and more ice cream cones in a given week, her *marginal utility* from another cone declines. We call this the **law of diminishing marginal utility**, which the great economist Alfred Marshall (1842–1924) defined this way:

> *The marginal utility of a thing to anyone diminishes with every increase in the amount of it he already has.*[2]

According to the law of diminishing marginal utility, when you consume your first unit of some good, like an ice cream cone, you derive some amount of utility. When you get your second cone that week, you enjoy greater satisfaction than when you only had one, but the extra satisfaction you derive from the second is likely to be smaller than the satisfaction you derived from the first. Adding the third cone to your weekly consumption will no doubt increase your utility further, but again the marginal utility you derive from that third cone is likely to be less than the marginal utility you derived from the second.

Figure 3 will again help us see what's going on. The table summarizes the information in the total utility graph. The first two columns show, respectively, the quantity of cones Lisa consumes each week and the total utility she receives each week from consuming them. The third column shows the *marginal* utility she receives from each successive cone she consumes per week. As you can see in the table, Lisa's total utility keeps increasing (marginal utility is always positive) as she consumes more cones (up to five per week), but the rate at which total utility increases gets smaller and smaller (her marginal utility diminishes) as her consumption increases.

Marginal utility is shown in panel (b) of Figure 3. Because marginal utility is the change in utility caused by a change in consumption from one level to another, we plot each marginal utility entry between the old and new consumption levels.

Notice the close relationship between the graph of total utility in panel (a) and the corresponding graph of marginal utility in panel (b). If you look closely at the two graphs, you will see that for every one-unit increment in Lisa's ice cream consumption her marginal utility is equal to the change in her total utility. Diminishing marginal utility is seen in both panels of the figure: in panel (b), by the downward sloping marginal utility curve, and in panel (a), by the positive but decreasing slope (flattening out) of the total utility curve.

One last thing about Figure 3: Because marginal utility diminishes for Lisa, by the time she has consumed a total of five cones per week, the marginal utility she derives from an additional cone has fallen all the way to zero. At this point, she is fully satiated with ice cream and gets no extra satisfaction or utility from eating any more of it in a typical week. Once this satiation point is reached, even if ice cream were free, Lisa would turn it down ("Yechhh! Not more ice cream!!"). But remember from our earlier discussion that one of the assumptions we always make about preferences is that people prefer *more* rather than less of any good we're considering. So when we use marginal utility theory, we assume that marginal utility for every good is positive. For Lisa, it would mean she hasn't yet reached five ice cream cones per week.

Combining the Budget Constraint and Preferences

The marginal utility someone gets from consuming more of a good tells us about his *preferences*. His budget constraint, by contrast, tells us only which combinations of goods he can *afford*. If we combine information about preferences

---

[2] *Principles of Economics*, Book III, Ch. III, Appendix notes 1 & 2. Macmillan & Co., 1930.

(marginal utility values) with information about what is affordable (the budget constraint), we can develop a useful rule to guide us to an individual's utility-maximizing choice.

To develop this rule, let's go back to Max and his choice between movies and concerts. Figure 4 reproduces Max's budget constraint from Figure 1. But now, we've added information about Max's preferences, in the table below the graph.

Each row of the table corresponds to a different point on Max's budget line. For example, the row labeled C corresponds to point C on the budget line. The second entry in each row tells us the number of concerts that Max attends each month, and the third entry tells us the marginal utility he gets from consuming the last concert. For example, at point C, Max attends two concerts, and the second one gives him an additional 1,200 utils beyond the first. Notice that as we move down along the budget line, from point A to B to C and so on, the number of concerts increases and the marginal utility numbers in the table get smaller, consistent with the law of diminishing marginal utility.

The fourth entry in each row shows something new: the marginal utility *per dollar* spent on concerts, obtained by dividing the marginal utility of the last concert by the price of a concert ($MU_{concerts}/P_{concerts}$). This tells us the gain in utility Max gets *for each dollar he spends* on the last concert. For example, at point C, Max gains 1,200 utils from his second concert during the month, so his marginal utility *per dollar* spent on that concert is 1,200 utils/$30 = 40 utils per dollar. Marginal utility per dollar, like marginal utility itself, declines as Max attends more concerts. After all, marginal utility itself decreases, and the price of a concert isn't changing, so the ratio of marginal utility to price must decrease as he sees more concerts.

The last three entries in each row give us similar information for movies: the number of movies attended, the marginal utility derived from the last movie, and the marginal utility per dollar spent on the last movie (MU_{movies}/P_{movies}). As we travel *up* this column, Max attends more movies, and both marginal utility and marginal utility per dollar decline—once again, consistent with the law of diminishing marginal utility.

Now, Max's goal is to find the affordable combination of movies and concerts—the point on his budget line—that gives him the highest possible utility. As you are about to see, this will be the point at which *the marginal utility per dollar is the same for both goods.*

To see why, imagine that Max is searching along his budget line for the utility-maximizing point, and he's currently considering point B, which represents 1 concert and 12 movies. Is he maximizing his utility? Let's see. Comparing the fourth and seventh entries in row B of the table, we see that Max's marginal utility per dollar spent on concerts is 50 utils, while his marginal utility per dollar spent on movies is only 10 utils. Since he gains more additional utility from each dollar spent on concerts than from each dollar spent on movies, he will have a net gain in utility if he shifts some of his dollars from movies to concerts. To do this, he must travel farther down his budget line.

Next suppose that, after shifting his spending from movies to concerts, Max arrives at point C on his budget line. What should he do then? At point C, Max's *MU* per dollar spent on concerts is 40 utils, while his *MU* per dollar spent on movies is 15 utils. Once again, he would gain utility by shifting from movies to concerts, traveling down his budget line once again.

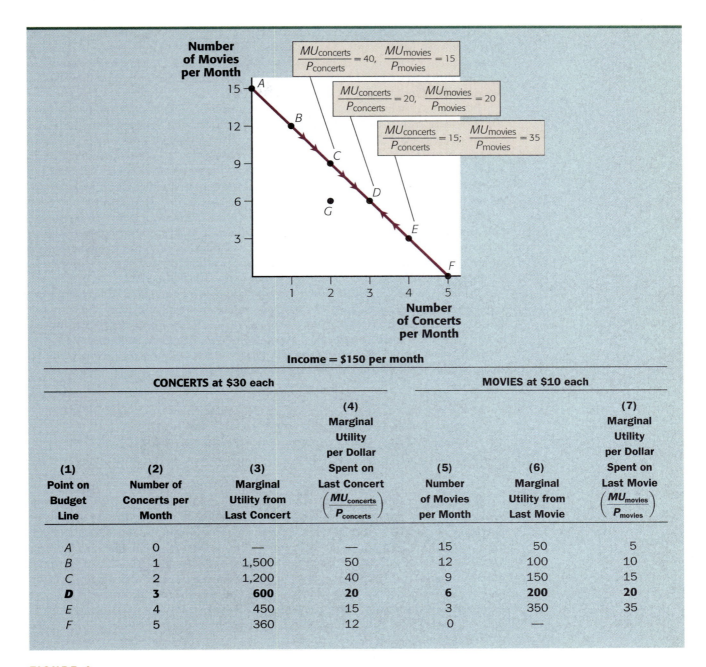

Income = $150 per month

	CONCERTS at $30 each			MOVIES at $10 each		
(1) Point on Budget Line	**(2)** Number of Concerts per Month	**(3)** Marginal Utility from Last Concert	**(4)** Marginal Utility per Dollar Spent on Last Concert $\left(\dfrac{MU_{concerts}}{P_{concerts}}\right)$	**(5)** Number of Movies per Month	**(6)** Marginal Utility from Last Movie	**(7)** Marginal Utility per Dollar Spent on Last Movie $\left(\dfrac{MU_{movies}}{P_{movies}}\right)$
A	0	—	—	15	50	5
B	1	1,500	50	12	100	10
C	2	1,200	40	9	150	15
D	**3**	**600**	**20**	**6**	**200**	**20**
E	4	450	15	3	350	35
F	5	360	12	0	—	

FIGURE 4
Consumer Decision Making

The budget line shows the maximum number of movies Max could attend for each number of concerts he attends. He would never choose an interior point like G because there are affordable points—on the line—that make him better off. Max will choose the point on the budget line at which the marginal utilities per dollar spent on movies and concerts are equal. From the table, this occurs at point D.

Now suppose that Max arrives at point *D*. At this point, the *MU* per dollar spent on both movies and concerts is the same: 20 utils. There is no further gain from shifting spending from movies to concerts. At point *D*, Max has exploited all opportunities to make himself better off by moving down the budget line. He has maximized his utility.

But wait . . . what if Max had started at a point on his budget line *below* point *D?* Would he still end up at the same place? Yes, he would. Suppose Max finds himself at point *E*, with 4 concerts and 3 movies. Here, marginal utilities per dollar are 15 utils for concerts and 35 utils for movies. Now, Max could make himself better off by shifting spending away from concerts and toward movies. He will travel *up* the budget line, once again arriving at point *D*, where no further move will improve his well-being.

As you can see, it doesn't matter whether Max begins at a point on his budget line that's above point *D* or below it. Either way, if he keeps shifting spending toward the good with greater marginal utility per dollar, he will always end up at point *D*. And because marginal utility per dollar is the same for both goods at point *D*, there is nothing to gain by shifting spending in either direction.

What is true for Max and his choice between movies and concerts is true for *any* consumer and *any* two goods. We can generalize our result this way: For any two goods *x* and *y*, with prices P_x and P_y, whenever $MU_x/P_x > MU_y/P_y$, a consumer is made better off shifting spending away from *y* and toward *x*. When $MU_y/P_y > MU_x/P_x$, a consumer is made better off by shifting spending away from *x* and toward *y*. This leads us to an important conclusion:

Marginal Decision Making

> *A utility-maximizing consumer will choose the point on the budget line where marginal utility per dollar is the same for both goods ($MU_x/P_x = MU_y/P_y$). At that point, there is no further gain from reallocating expenditures in either direction.*

We can generalize even further. Suppose there are more than two goods an individual can buy. For example, we could imagine that Max wants to divide his entertainment budget among movies, concerts, football games, and what have you. Or we can think of a consumer who must allocate her entire income among thousands of different goods and services each month: different types of food, clothing, entertainment, transportation, and so on. Does our description of the optimal choice for the consumer still hold? Indeed, it does. No matter how many goods there are to choose from, when the consumer is doing as well as possible, it must be true that $MU_x/P_x = MU_y/P_y$ for any pair of goods *x* and *y*. If this condition is *not* satisfied, the consumer will be better off consuming more of one and less of the other good in the pair.[3]

---

[3] There is one exception to this statement: Sometimes the optimal choice is to buy *none* of some good. For example, suppose that $MU_y/P_y > MU_x/P_x$ no matter how small a quantity of good *x* a person consumes. Then the consumer should always reduce consumption of good *x* further, until its quantity is zero. Economists call this a "corner solution," because when there are only two goods being considered, the individual will locate at one of the end points of the budget line in a corner of the diagram.

What Happens When Things Change?

If every one of our decisions had to be made only once, life would be much easier. But that's not how life is. Just when you think you've figured out what to do, things change. In a market economy, as you've learned, prices can change for any number of reasons. (See Chapter 3.) A consumer's income can change as well. He may lose a job or find a new one; she may get a raise or a cut in pay. Changes in our incomes or the prices we face cause us to rethink our spending decisions: What maximized utility before the change is unlikely to maximize it afterward. The result is a change in our behavior.

Why Use Marginal Utility *per Dollar?* In finding the utility-maximizing combination of goods for a consumer, why do we use marginal utility *per dollar* instead of just marginal utility? Shouldn't the consumer always shift spending wherever *marginal utility* is greater? The answer is no. The following thought experiment will help you see why. Imagine that you like to ski and you like going out for dinner. Further, given your current combination of skiing and dining out, your marginal utility for one more skiing trip is 2,000 utils, and your marginal utility for an additional dinner is 1,000 utils. Should you shift your spending from dining out to skiing? It might seem so, since skiing has the higher marginal utility.

But what if skiing costs $200 per trip, while a dinner out costs only $20? Then, while it's true that another ski trip will give you twice as much utility as another dinner out, it's also true that *skiing costs 10 times as much.* You would have to sacrifice 10 restaurant meals for 1 ski trip, and that would make you *worse* off. Instead, you should shift your spending in the other direction: from skiing to dining out. Money spent on additional ski trips will give you 2,000 utils/$200 = 10 utils per dollar, while money spent on additional dinners will give you 1,000 utils/$20 = 50 utils per dollar. Dining out clearly gives you "more bang for the buck" than skiing. The lesson: When trying to find the utility-maximizing combination of goods, compare marginal utilities *per dollar,* not marginal utilities of the two goods.

DANGEROUS CURVES

Changes in Income. Figure 5 illustrates how an increase in income might affect Max's choice between movies and concerts. As before, we assume that movies cost $10 each, that concerts cost $30 each, and that these prices are not changing. Initially, Max has $150 in income to spend on the two goods, so his budget line is the line from point A to point F. As we've already seen, under these conditions, Max would choose point D (three concerts and six movies) to maximize utility.

Now suppose Max's income increases to $300. Then his budget line will shift upward and outward in the figure. How will he respond? As always, he will search along his budget line until he finds the point where the marginal utility per dollar spent on both goods is the same. But where will this point be? Without more information—such as that provided in the table in Figure 4—we can't be certain which of the points on Max's new budget line will satisfy this condition. But we can discuss some of the possibilities.

Figure 5 illustrates three alternative possibilities. If Max's best combination ends up being point *H*, he would attend 12 movies and 6 concerts. If we compare his initial choice (point *D*) with this new choice (point *H*), we see that the rise in income has caused him to consume more of *both* goods. As you learned in Chapter 3, when an increase in income causes a consumer to buy *more* of something, we call that thing a *normal good*. If, for Max, point *H* happens to be where the marginal utilities per dollar for the two goods are equal, then, for him, both movies and concerts are normal goods.

Alternatively, Max's marginal utilities per dollar might be equal at a point like *H'*, with 9 concerts and 3 movies. In this case, the increase in income would cause Max's consumption of concerts to increase (from 3 to 9), but his consumption of movies to *fall* (from 6 to 3). Movies would be an *inferior good* for Max—one for which demand decreases when income increases—while concerts would be a *normal* good.

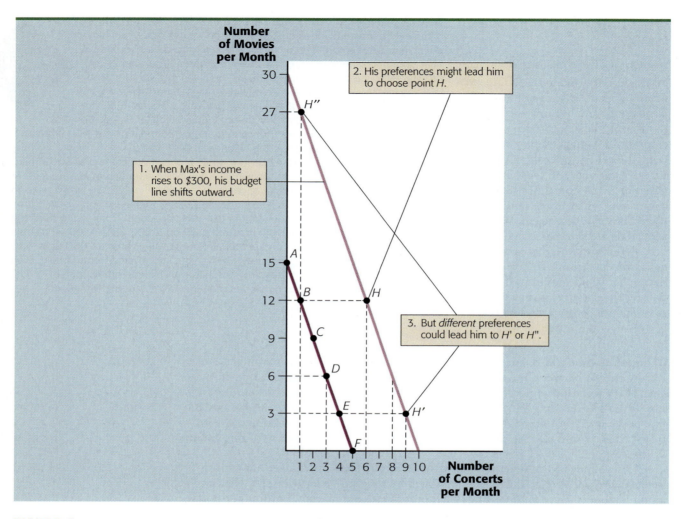

FIGURE 5
Effects of an Increase in Income

Finally, let's consider another possible outcome for Max: point *H″*. At this point, he attends more movies and fewer concerts compared to point *D*. If point *H″* is where Max's marginal utilities per dollar are equal after the increase in income, then *concerts* would be the inferior good, while movies would be normal.

> *A rise in income—with no change in prices—leads to a new quantity demanded for each good. Whether a particular good is normal (quantity demanded increases) or inferior (quantity demanded decreases) depends on the individual's preferences, as represented by the marginal utilities for each good, at each point along his budget line.*

Changes in Price. Let's explore what happens to Max when the price of a concert decreases from $30 to $10 while his income remains at $150 and the price of a movie remains $10. The drop in the price of concerts will rotate Max's budget line rightward, pivoting around its vertical intercept, as illustrated in the

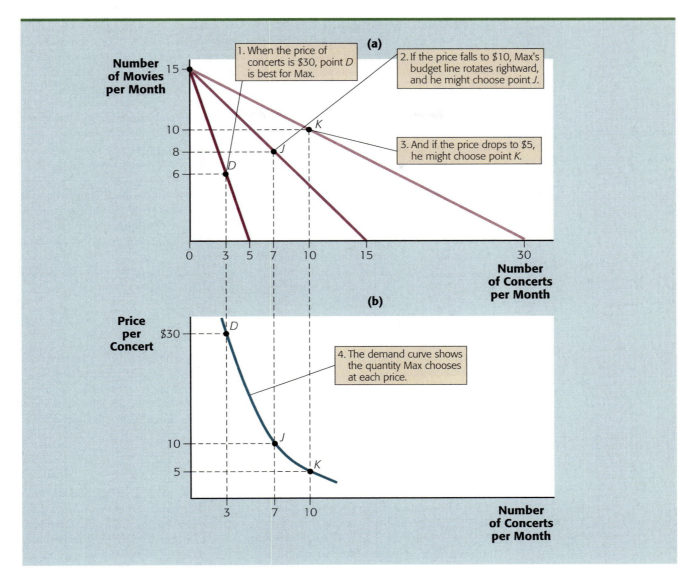

FIGURE 6
Deriving the Demand Curve

upper panel of Figure 6. What will Max do after his budget line rotates in this way? Again, he will select the combination of movies and concerts on his budget line that makes him as well off as possible. This will be the combination at which the marginal utility per dollar spent on both goods is the same. In the figure, we assume that this occurs at point *J* on the new budget line, where Max consumes 7 concerts and 8 movies.

   If the price of concerts drops once again, to $5, the budget line rotates rightward again. In the figure, Max chooses point *K*, attending 10 concerts and 10 movies.

The Individual's Demand Curve

You've just seen that each time the price of concerts changes, so does the quantity of concerts Max will want to see. The lower panel of Figure 6 highlights this relationship by plotting the quantity of concerts demanded on the horizontal axis and the price of concerts on the vertical axis. For example, in both the upper and lower panels, point *D* tells us that when the price of concerts is $30, Max will see three of them. When we connect points like *D*, *J*, and *K* in the lower panel, we get Max's **individual demand curve**, which shows *the quantity of a good he demands at each different price*. Notice that Max's demand curve for concerts slopes downward—a fall in the price of concerts increases the quantity demanded—showing that Max's responses to price changes obey the law of demand.

But if Max's preferences—and his marginal utility values—had been different, could his response to a price change have *violated* the law of demand? The answer is yes . . . and no. Yes, it is theoretically possible. (As a challenge, try identifying points on the three budget lines that would give Max an *upward-sloping* demand curve.) But no, it does not seem to happen in practice.

To understand why and to gain other insights, the next section takes a deeper look into the effects of a price change on quantity demanded.

Individual demand curve A curve showing the quantity of a good or service demanded by a particular individual at each different price.

INCOME AND SUBSTITUTION EFFECTS

Whether you've studied the marginal utility approach (the previous section) or the indifference curve approach (appendix), you've learned a logical process that leads directly to an individual's demand curve. But the demand curve actually summarizes the impact of *two* separate effects of a price change on quantity demanded. As you are about to see, these two effects sometimes work together, and sometimes oppose each other.

The Substitution Effect

Suppose the price of a good falls. Then it becomes less expensive *relative to* other goods whose prices have not fallen. Some of these other goods are *substitutes* for the now cheaper good—they are different goods, but they are used to satisfy the same general desire. When *one* of the ways of satisfying a desire becomes relatively cheaper, consumers tend to purchase more of it (and tend to purchase less of the substitute goods).

In Max's case, concerts and movies, while different, both satisfy his desire to be entertained. When the price of concerts falls, so does its relative price (relative to movies). Max can now get more entertainment from his budget by substituting concerts in place of movies, so he will demand more concerts.

This impact of a price decrease is called a **substitution effect**: the consumer substitutes *toward* the good whose price has decreased, and away from other goods whose prices have remained unchanged.

Substitution effect As the price of a good falls, the consumer substitutes that good in place of other goods whose prices have not changed.

> *The **substitution effect** of a price change arises from a change in the relative price of a good, and it always moves quantity demanded in the opposite direction to the price change. When price decreases, the substitution effect works to increase quantity demanded; when price increases, the substitution effect works to decrease quantity demanded.*

The substitution effect is a powerful force in the marketplace. For example, while the price of cellular phone calls has fallen in recent years, the price of pay phone calls has remained more or less the same. This fall in the relative price of cell phone calls has caused consumers to substitute toward them and away from using regular pay phones. As a result, many private providers of pay phones are having financial difficulty.

The substitution effect is also important from a theoretical perspective: It is the main factor responsible for the law of demand. Indeed, if the substitution effect were the *only* effect of a price change, the law of demand would be more than a law; it would be a logical necessity. But as we are about to see, a price change has another effect as well.

The Income Effect

In Figure 6, when the price of concerts decreases from $30 to $10, Max's budget line rotates rightward.[4] Max now has a wider range of options than before: He can consume more concerts, more movies, or *more of both*. The price decline of *one* good has increased Max's total purchasing power over *both* goods.

A price cut gives the consumer a gift, which is rather like an increase in *income*. Indeed, in an important sense, it *is* an increase in *available* income: Point D (3 concerts and 6 movies) originally cost Max $150, but after the decrease in the price of concerts, the same combination would cost him just $(6 \times \$10) + (3 \times \$10) = \$90$, leaving him with $60 in *available income* to spend on more movies or concerts or both. This leads to the second effect of a change in price:

> The **income effect** of a price change arises from a change in purchasing power over both goods. A drop in price increases purchasing power, while a rise in price decreases purchasing power.

How will a change in purchasing power influence the quantity of a good demanded? That depends. Recall that an increase in income will increase the demand for normal goods and decrease the demand for inferior goods. The same is true for the *income effect* of a price cut: It can work to either *increase* or *decrease* the quantity of a good demanded, depending on whether the good is normal or inferior. For example, if concerts are a normal good for Max, then the income effect of a price cut will lead him to consume more of them; if concerts are inferior, the income effect will lead him to consume fewer.

Combining Substitution and Income Effects

Now let's look again at the impact of a price change, considering the substitution and income effects together. A change in the price of a good changes both the relative price of the good (the substitution effect) and the overall purchasing power of the consumer (the income effect). The ultimate impact of the price change on quantity demanded will depend on *both* of these effects. For normal goods, these two

Cheaper cell phone calls, and the substitution effect, may soon drive pay phones out of the market.

Income effect As the price of a good decreases, the consumer's purchasing power increases, causing a change in quantity demanded for the good.

---

[4] If you've studied the indifference curve approach, refer to Figure A.5 in the appendix to this chapter.

effects work together to push quantity demanded in the same direction. But for inferior goods, the two effects oppose each other. Let's see why.

Normal Goods. When the price of a normal good falls, the substitution effect *increases* quantity demanded. The price drop will also increase the consumer's purchasing power—and for a normal good—*increase* quantity demanded even further. The opposite occurs when price increases: The substitution effect decreases quantity demanded, and the decline in purchasing power further decreases it. Figure 7 summarizes how the substitution and income effects combine to make the price and quantity of a normal good move in opposite directions:

> *For normal goods, the substitution and income effects work together, causing quantity demanded to move in the opposite direction of the price. Normal goods, therefore, must always obey the law of demand.*

Inferior Goods. Now let's see how a price change affects the demand for *inferior* goods. As an example, consider inter-city bus service. For many consumers, this is an inferior good: with a higher income, these consumers would choose quicker and more comfortable alternatives (such as air or train travel), and therefore demand *less* bus service. Now, if the price of bus service falls, the substitution effect would work, as always, to *increase* quantity demanded. The price cut will also, as always, increase the consumer's purchasing power. But if bus service is inferior, the rise in purchasing power will *decrease* quantity demanded. Thus, we have two opposing effects: the substitution effect, increasing quantity demanded, and the income effect, decreasing quantity demanded. In theory, either of these effects could dominate the other, so the quantity demanded could move in either direction.

In practice, however, the substitution effect almost always dominates for inferior goods.

Why? Because we consume such a wide variety of goods and services that a price cut in any one of them changes our purchasing power by only a small amount. For example, suppose you have an income of \$20,000 per year, and you spend \$500

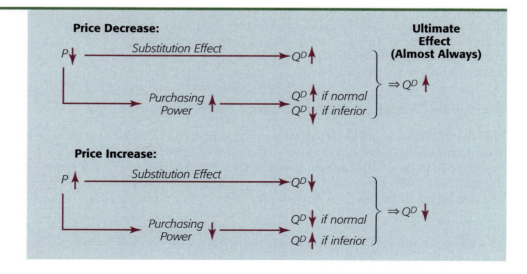

FIGURE 7
Income and Substitution Effects

per year on bus tickets. If the price of bus travel falls by, say, 20 percent, this would save you $100—like a gift of $100 in income. But $100 is only ½ percent of your income. Thus, a 20 percent fall in the price of bus travel would cause only a ½ percent rise in your purchasing power. Even if bus travel is, for you, an inferior good, we would expect only a tiny decrease in your quantity demanded when your purchasing power changes by such a small amount. Thus, the income effect should be very small. On the other hand, the *substitution* effect should be rather large: With bus travel now 20 percent cheaper, you will likely substitute away from other purchases and buy more bus travel.

> *For inferior goods, the substitution and income effects of a price change work against each other. The substitution effect moves quantity demanded in the opposite direction of the price, while the income effect moves it in the same direction as the price. But since the substitution effect virtually always dominates, consumption of inferior goods—like normal goods—will virtually always obey the law of demand.*

CONSUMERS IN MARKETS

Since the market demand curve tells us the quantity of a good demanded by *all* consumers in a market, it makes sense that we can derive it by adding up the individual demand curves of every consumer in that market.

Figure 8 illustrates how this can be done in a small local market for bottled water, where, for simplicity, we assume that there are only three consumers—Jerry, George, and Elaine. The first three diagrams show their individual demand curves. If the market price were, say, $2 per bottle, Jerry would buy 4 bottles each week (point *c*), George would buy 6 (point *c'*), and Elaine would buy zero (point *c"*). Thus, the market quantity demanded at a price of $2 would be 4 + 6 + 0 = 10, which is point *C* on the market demand curve. To obtain the entire market demand curve, we repeat this procedure at each different price, adding up the quantities demanded by each individual to obtain the total quantity demanded in the market. (Verify on your own that points *A, B, D,* and *E* have been obtained in the same way.) In effect, we obtain the market demand curve by summing horizontally across each of the individual demand curves:

> *The market demand curve is found by horizontally summing the individual demand curves of every consumer in the market.*

Notice that as long as each individual's demand curve is downward sloping (and this will virtually always be the case), then the market demand curve will also be downward sloping. More directly, if a rise in price makes each consumer buy fewer units, then it will reduce the quantity bought by *all* consumers as well. Indeed, the market demand curve can still obey the law of demand even when *some* individuals violate it. Thus, although we are already quite confident about the law of demand at the individual level, we can be even *more* confident at the market level. This is why we always draw market demand curves with a downward slope.

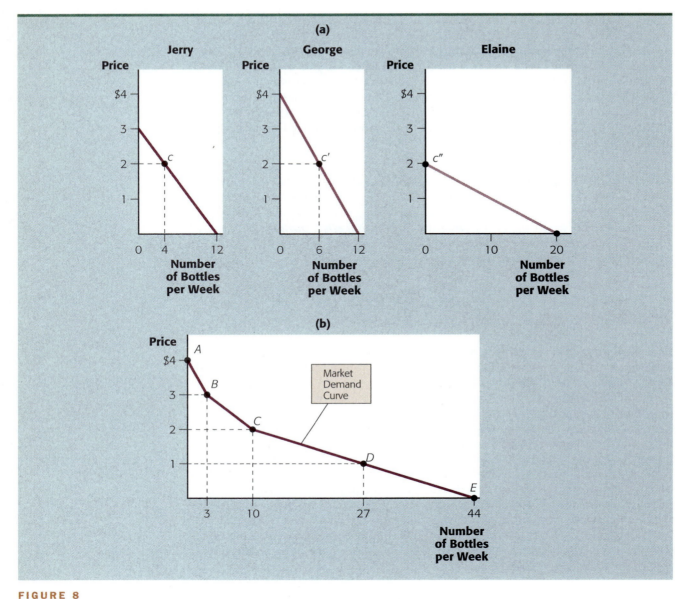

FIGURE 8
From Individual to Market Demand

The individual demand curves show how much bottled water will be demanded by Jerry, George, and Elaine at different prices. As the price falls, each demands more. The market demand curve in panel (b) is obtained by adding up the total quantity demanded by all market participants at different prices.

CONSUMER THEORY IN PERSPECTIVE

Our model of consumer theory—whether using marginal utility or indifference curves—may strike you as rather simple. Indeed, it was *purposely* kept simple, to bring out the "big ideas" more clearly. But can it explain and predict behavior in more complicated, real-world situations? In many cases, yes—with appropriate modification. In other cases, . . . no.

Extensions of the Model

One problem our simple model ignores is *uncertainty*. In our model, the consumer knows with certainty the outcome of any choice—so many movies and concerts—and knows with certainty how much income is available for spending. But in many real-world situations, you make your choice and you take your chances. When you buy a car, it might be a lemon; when you pay for some types of surgery, there is a substantial risk that it will be unsuccessful; and when you buy a house, you cannot be sure of its condition or how much you will like the neighborhood. Income, too, is often uncertain. Employees risk being laid off, and self-employed lawyers, doctors, and small-business owners might have a good year or a bad year. When uncertainty is an important aspect of consumer choice, economists use other, more complex models. But even these models are based on the one you have learned in this chapter.

Another problem is *imperfect information*. In our model, consumers are assumed to *know* exactly what goods they are buying and the prices at which they can buy them. But in the real world, we must sometimes spend time and money to get this information. Prices can be different in different stores and on different days, depending on whether there is a sale, so we might have to make phone calls or shop around. To be sure of the quality of our purchases, we may have to subscribe to *Consumer Reports* magazine or spend time inspecting goods or getting advice from others. Over the past few decades, economists have been intensely interested in imperfect information and its consequences for decision-making behavior. And our simple model—modified to take account of the *cost* of acquiring information—has proven very useful.

A third problem is that people can spend more than their incomes in any given year, by borrowing funds or spending out of savings. Or they may spend less than their incomes because they choose to save or pay back debts. This, too, is easily handled by our model of consumer choice, for example, by defining one of the goods as "future consumption."

Finally, you might think that consumer theory always regards people as relentlessly selfish, concerned only about their own consumption. In fact, when people trade in impersonal markets this is mostly true: People *do* try to allocate their spending among different goods to achieve the greatest possible satisfaction. But in many areas of economic life, people act unselfishly. This, too, has been incorporated into the traditional model of consumer theory.

For example, Max's *own* utility might depend on the utility enjoyed by someone else—either a member of his own family, or others in his neighborhood or community, or even the average level of utility in the world. In fact, the "utility of others" can be treated as "another good" in the model. Useful analyses of charitable giving, bequests, and voting behavior have been based on this modification of the model.

Challenges to the Model

From our discussion, you can see that the model of consumer choice is quite versatile, capable of adapting to more aspects of economic behavior than one might think. But economists have long observed that certain types of behavior do not fit the model at all. For example, people will sometimes *judge quality by price*. Diamonds, designer dresses, men's suits, doctors' services, and even automobiles are sometimes perceived as being better if their prices are higher. This means that the consumer cannot choose among different combinations of goods by themselves; she must first know their prices. And when prices change, so will her preferences—violating our description of rational preferences.

Behavioral economics A subfield of economics focusing on behavior that deviates from the standard assumptions of economic models.

Behavioral Economics. In recent years, a broader challenge has emerged from a new subfield of economics known as **behavioral economics.** Behavioral economists try to incorporate facts about actual human behavior—often pointed out by psychologists—that deviate from the standard assumptions of economic models. While economists—dating back to Adam Smith—have often reached outside the field for broader insights, behavioral economists do so in a more systematic and formal way. And while their models incorporate some of the traditional tools of economic analysis, others are conspicuously left out. Behavioral economists are represented on the faculties of the most prestigious universities, win major professional awards, and are the subject of much attention in the media.[5]

To understand what's different about behavioral economics, let's take a broad look at the more standard approach of economics. As a rule, economists view decision makers as striving to achieve a well-defined goal: typically, the goal of *maximizing some quantity.* In this chapter, for example, consumers are viewed as trying to maximize their utility or well-being. In later chapters, business firms are striving to *maximize profit.* Even when households or firms are recognized as *groups* of individuals with different agendas, economists typically assume that maximization is involved. For example, while a firm's owners might want the firm to maximize profits, the managers might want to consider their own incomes, power, prestige, or job security. When the goals conflict, the behavior of the firm will depend on how the conflict is resolved. Still, each individual or group within the firm is depicted as trying to maximize something. Economists have often disagreed over *what* is being maximized, but have usually accepted the idea that *something* is.

Behavioral economists, however, point out that some human behavior is not consistent with *any* type of maximization. For example, stock market investors will often hold on to shares when the price has fallen, refusing to sell until the price rises enough to prevent any loss. They do so even when selling the stock and using the money for other purposes—such as buying a new car—would make them better off. Their desire to avoid regret over a past loss seems to get in the way of maximizing their current utility.

Another example: Dieters will often refuse to have ice cream in the house, to help them avoid temptation. This might seem innocuous, but it's inconsistent with our notion of the rational, utility-maximizing consumer. After all, if a consumer can select the utility-maximizing choice among all available options, he should never try to limit the options available. Or—more simply—a rational consumer should be able to say no, and not be harmed by the option of saying yes.

Indeed, there are many examples where emotion seems to trump narrowly defined rationality: procrastination, drug addiction, and even honesty—especially when telling the truth is costly and a lie would not be discovered. And how can it be rational to spend $3 on gas and wear and tear on your car when driving to a slightly less-expensive supermarket, where you'll save only $2 at checkout? Moreover, why would someone make this drive for groceries, but not to save $3 on a $1,000 personal computer?

Behavioral economists have offered explanations for these and other examples of economic behavior that wholly or partially abandon the idea of maximization. Instead, they incorporate notions about people's *actual thinking process* in making decisions. And they point out that such behavior by large groups of people can alter a market's equilibrium.

---

[5] A brief summary of behavioral economics, and some of the controversy surrounding it, is in Roger Lowenstein's "Exuberance Is Rational," *New York Times Magazine,* February 11, 2001. For further insights, consult the list of behavioral economics and finance resources, compiled by the librarians at the University of California at Berkeley: *http://www.lib.berkeley.edu/BUSI/pdfs/behave.pdf.*

However, before you start wondering why you've bothered to learn about the utility-maximizing consumer, or why you should go on to read about the profit-maximizing firm, a little perspective is in order. While we do, indeed, observe many cases where behavior is *not* rational, we observe far many more cases where it *is*. While the questions raised by behaviorists are fascinating, and their insights valuable, even its strongest proponents would *not* use behavioral models to explain why gasoline prices rise and fall, or how bad weather might affect Florida orange growers. In fact, they wouldn't use behavioral models to explain most of what happens in the vast majority of markets around the world, because the standard economic models work so much better for this purpose.

So while behavioral economics is often portrayed in the media as an "alternative" or even a "replacement" for traditional economic theory, few if any economists see it that way. Instead, behavioral economics is more commonly viewed as an addition to the existing body of economic theory—an extra limb that extends the theory's reach to some anomalous behavior.

USING THE THEORY
Improving Education

© SUSAN VAN ETTEN

So far in this chapter, we've considered the problem of a consumer trying to maximize utility by selecting the best combination of goods and services. But consumer theory can be extended to consider almost *any* decision between two alternatives, including activities that cost us time rather than dollars. In this section, we apply the model of consumer choice to an important issue: the quality of education.[6]

Billions of dollars have been spent over the past few decades trying to improve the quality of education in our schools, colleges, and universities. In 2003 alone, the U.S. Department of Education spent about $3 billion on research to assess and implement new educational techniques. For example, suppose it is thought that computer-assisted instruction might help students learn better or more quickly. A typical research project to test this hypothesis would be a *controlled experiment* in which one group of students would be taught with the computer-assisted instruction and the other group would be taught without it. Then students in both groups would be tested. If the first group scores significantly higher, computer-assisted instruction will be deemed successful; if not, it will be deemed unsuccessful. To the disappointment of education researchers, most promising new techniques are found to be unsuccessful: Students seem to score about the same, no matter which techniques are tried.

Economists find these studies highly suspect, since the experiments treat students as passive responders to stimuli. Presented with a stimulus (the new technique), students are assumed to give a simple response (scoring higher on the exam). Where in this model, economists ask, are students treated as *decision makers,* who must make *choices* about allocating their scarce time?

[6] This section is based on ideas originally published in Richard B. McKenzie and Gordon Tullock, *The New World of Economics,* 3d ed. (Burr Ridge, IL: Irwin, 1981).

FIGURE 9
Time Allocation

Panel (a) shows combinations of French and economics test scores that can be obtained for a given amount of study time. The slope of −2 indicates that each additional point in French requires a sacrifice of 2 points in economics. The student chooses point C. Panel (b) shows that computer-assisted French instruction causes the budget line to rotate outward; French points are now less expensive. The student might move to point D, attaining a higher French score. Or she might choose F, using all of the time freed up in French to study economics. Or she might choose an intermediate point such as E.

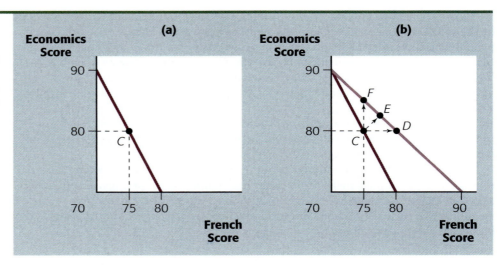

Let's apply our model of consumer choice to a student's time allocation problem. To keep things simple, we'll assume a bleak world in which there are only two activities: studying economics and studying French. Instead of costing money, each of these activities costs *time,* and there is only so much time available. And instead of buying quantities of two goods, students "buy" points on their exams with hours spent studying.

Panel (a) of Figure 9 shows how we can represent the time allocation problem graphically. The economics test score is measured on the vertical axis and the French score on the horizontal axis. The straight line in the figure is the student's budget line, showing the trade-off between economics and French scores. Our student can achieve any combination of scores on this budget line with her scarce time.

A few things are worth noting about the budget line in the figure. First, the more study time you devote to a subject, the better you will do on the test. But that means *less* study time for the other subject and a lower test score there. Thus, the opportunity cost of scoring better in French is scoring lower in economics, and vice versa. This is why the budget line has a negative slope: the higher the score in French, the lower the score in economics. As our student moves downward along the budget line, she is shifting hours away from studying economics and toward studying French.

Second, notice that the vertical and horizontal axes both start at 70 rather than 0. This is to keep our example from becoming too depressing. If our student devotes *all* her study time to economics and none to French, she would score 90 in economics but still be able to score 70 (rather than zero) in French, just by attending class and paying attention. If she devotes all her time to French, she would score 80 in French and 70 in economics. (*Warning:* Do not try to use this example to convince your economics instructor you deserve at least a 70 on your next exam.)

Finally, the budget line in our example is drawn as a straight line with a slope of −2. So each additional point in French requires our student to sacrifice two points in economics. This assumption helps make the analysis more concrete. But none of our conclusions would be different if the budget line had a different slope, or even if it were curved so that the trade-off would change as we moved along it. But let's take a moment to understand what our example implies.

As you've learned, the slope of any budget line is $-P_x/P_y$, where x is the good measured on the horizontal axis and y is the good measured on the vertical axis. In our example, $-P_x/P_y$ translates into $-P_{\text{French point}}/P_{\text{econ point}}$. But what is the "price" of a test point in French or economics? Unlike the case of Max, who had to allocate his scarce *funds* between concerts and movies, our student must allocate her scarce *time* between the two "goods" she desires: test points in French and test points in economics. The *price* of a test point is therefore not a money price, but rather a *time price*: the number of study hours needed to achieve an additional point. For example, if it takes an additional two hours of studying to achieve another point in French, then the price per point in French is two hours. Moreover, in the figure, we assume that the price per point in economics is one-half the price per point in French, so if $P_{\text{French point}} = 2$, then $P_{\text{econ point}} = 1$. The slope of the budget line is therefore $-P_{\text{French point}}/P_{\text{econ point}} = -2$.

Now let's turn our attention to student decision making. Our student derives satisfaction of utility from both her economics score and her French score—the greater either score, the better off she is. But among all those combinations of scores on her budget line, which is the best choice? That depends on the student's preferences, whether characterized by the marginal utility approach or the indifference curve approach. Suppose that initially, this student's best choice is at point C, where she scores 80 in economics and 75 in French.

Now, let's introduce a new computer-assisted technique in the French class, one that is, in fact, remarkably effective: It enables students to learn more French with the same study time or to study less and learn the same amount. This is a *decrease* in the price of French points—it now takes fewer hours to earn a point in French—so the budget line will rotate outward, as shown in panel (b) of Figure 9. On the new budget line, if our student devotes all of her time to French, she can score higher than before—90 instead of 80—so the horizontal intercept moves rightward. But since nothing has changed in her economics course, the vertical intercept remains unaffected. Notice, too, that the budget line's slope has changed to –1. Now, the opportunity cost of an additional point in French is one point in economics rather than two.

After the new technique is introduced in the French course, our *decision-making* student will locate at a point on her new budget line based once again on her preferences. Panel (b) illustrates some alternative possibilities. At point D, her performance in French would improve, but her economics performance would remain the same. This seems to be the kind of result education researchers have in mind when they design their experiments: If a successful technique is introduced in the French course, we should be able to measure the impact with a French test.

Point F illustrates a different choice: *Only* the economics performance improves, while the French score remains unchanged. Here, even though the technique in French is successful (it does, indeed, shift the budget line), none of its success shows up in higher French scores.

But wait: How can a new technique in the French course improve performance in economics but not at all in French? The answer is found by breaking down the impact of the new technique into our familiar income and substitution effects. The new technique lowers the student's time cost of getting additional points in French. The substitution effect (French points are relatively cheaper) will tend to improve her score in French, as she substitutes her time away from studying economics and toward studying French. But there is also an *"income"* effect: The "purchasing power" of her time has increased, since now she could use her fixed allotment of study time to "buy" higher scores in *both* courses. If performance in French is a "normal good," this increase in "purchasing power" will work to increase her French score, but if it is an "inferior good," it could work to *decrease* her French score. Point *F* could come about because French performance is *such* an inferior good that the negative income effect exactly cancels out the positive substitution effect. In this case, the education researchers will incorrectly judge the new technique a complete failure—it does not affect French scores at all.

Could this actually happen? Perhaps. It is easy to imagine a student deciding that 75 in French is good enough and using any study time freed up from better French instruction to improve her performance in some other course. More commonly, we expect a student to choose a point such as *E,* somewhere between points *D* and *F,* with performance improving in *both* courses. But even in this case, the higher French score measures just a *part* of the impact of the technique; the remaining effect is seen in a higher economics score.

This leads us to a general conclusion: When we recognize that students make *choices,* we expect only *some* of the impact of a better technique to show up in the course in which it is used. In the real world, college students typically take several courses at once and have other competing interests for their time as well (cultural events, parties, movies, telephone calls, exercising, and so on). Any time saved due to better teaching in a single course might well be "spent" on *all* of these alternatives, with only a little devoted to that single course. Thus, we cannot fully measure the impact of a new technique by looking at the score in one course alone. This suggests why educational research is conducted as it is: A more accurate assessment would require a thorough accounting for all of a student's time, which is both expensive and difficult to achieve. Nevertheless, we remain justified in treating this research with some skepticism.

Summary

Graphically, the budget constraint is represented by the *budget line*. Only combinations on or below the budget line are affordable. An increase in income shifts the budget line outward. A change in the price of a good causes the budget line to rotate. Whenever the budget line shifts or rotates, the consumer moves to a point on the *new* budget line. The consumer will always choose the point that provides the greatest level of satisfaction or *utility,* and this will depend on the consumer's unique preferences.

There are two alternative ways to represent consumer preferences, which lead to two different approaches to consumer decision making. The *marginal utility approach* is presented in the body of the chapter. In this approach, a utility-maximizing consumer chooses the combination of goods along her budget line at which the marginal utility per dollar spent is the same for all goods. When income or price changes, the consumer once again equates the marginal utility per dollar of both goods, resulting in a choice along the *new* budget line.

In the *indifference curve approach,* presented in the appendix, a consumer's preferences are represented by a collection of her *indifference curves,* called her *indifference map.* The highest level of utility or satisfaction is achieved at the point on the budget line that is also on the highest possible indifference curve. When income or price changes, the consumer moves to the point on the *new* budget line that is on the highest possible indifference curve.

Using either of the two approaches, we can trace the quantity of a good chosen at different prices for that good, and generate a downward sloping *demand* curve for that good. The downward slope reflects the interaction of the *substitution effect* and the *income effect.* For a normal good, both effects contribute to the downward slope of the demand curve. For an inferior good, we can have confidence that the substitution effect dominates the income effect, so—once again—the demand curve will slope downward.

Key Terms

Behavioral economics	Individual demand curve	Relative price
Budget constraint	Law of diminishing marginal utility	Substitution effect
Budget line	Marginal utility	Utility
Income effect	Rational preferences	

Review Questions

1. What variables are assumed constant along a budget line?

2. What kinds of changes will shift or rotate the budget line?

3. [Uses the Marginal Utility Approach] Explain the relationship between a total quantity and a marginal quantity.

4. [Uses the Marginal Utility Approach] State and explain the law of diminishing marginal utility. Can you think of a good or service you consume that is not subject to this law? Could marginal utility be negative? Give an example.

5. Economists usually assume that consumer preferences are logically consistent. What does that mean? What are some other assumptions economists make about preferences?

6. Discuss the following statement: "Economists' assumption of consumer rationality is too strong. For example, anyone who smokes cigarettes is clearly being irrational."

7. What condition will be satisfied when a consumer has chosen the combination of goods that maximizes utility subject to a budget constraint? Use either the Marginal Utility Approach or Indifference Curve Approach.

8. What are income and substitution effects? How are they related to the law of demand?

9. "The demand curve for an inferior good is upward sloping." True or false? Explain.

10. How is a market demand curve derived?

Problems and Exercises

1. Parvez, a pharmacology student, has allocated $120 per month to spend on paperback novels and used CDs. Novels cost $8 each; CDs cost $6 each. Draw his budget line.
   a. Draw and label a second budget line that shows what happens when the price of a CD rises to $10.
   b. Draw and label a third budget line that shows what happens when the price of a CD rises to $10 *and* Parvez's income rises to $240.

2. [Uses the Marginal Utility Approach] Now go back to the original assumptions of problem 1 (novels cost $8, CDs cost $6, and income is $120). Suppose that Parvez is spending $120 monthly on paperback novels and used CDs. For novels, $MU/P = 5$; for CDs, $MU/P = 4$. Is he maximizing his utility? If not, should he consume (1) more novels and fewer CDs or (2) more CDs and fewer novels? Explain briefly.

3. [Uses the Marginal Utility Approach] Anita consumes both pizza and Pepsi. The following tables show the amount of utility she obtains from different amounts of these two goods:

Pizza		Pepsi	
Quantity	Utility	Quantity	Utility
4 slices	115	5 cans	63
5 slices	135	6 cans	75
6 slices	154	7 cans	86
7 slices	171	8 cans	96

Suppose Pepsi costs $0.50 per can, pizza costs $1 per slice, and Anita has $9 to spend on food and drink. What combination of pizza and Pepsi will maximize her utility?

4. Three people have the following individual demand schedules for Count Chocula cereal that show how many boxes each would purchase monthly at different prices:

Price	Person 1	Person 2	Person 3
$5.00	0	1	2
$4.50	0	2	3
$4.00	0	3	4
$3.50	1	3	5

a. What is the market demand schedule for this cereal? (Assume that these three people are the only buyers.) Draw the market demand curve.

b. Why might the three people have different demand schedules?

5. Suppose that 1,000 people in a market *each* have the same monthly demand curve for bottled water, given by the equation $Q^D = 100 - 25P$, where P is the price for a 12-ounce bottle in dollars.

a. How many bottles would be demanded in the entire market if the price is $1?

b. How many bottles would be demanded in the entire market if the price is $2?

c. Provide an equation for the *market* demand curve, showing how the market quantity demanded by all 1,000 consumers depends on the price.

6. What would happen to the market demand curve for polyester suits, an inferior good, if consumers' incomes rose?

7. Larsen E. Pulp, head of Pulp Fiction Publishing Co., just got some bad news: The price of paper, the company's most important input, has increased.

a. On a supply/demand diagram, show what will happen to the price of Pulp's output (novels).

b. Explain the resulting substitution and income effects for a typical Pulp customer. For each effect, will the customer's quantity demanded increase or decrease? Be sure to state any assumptions you are making.

8. "If a good is inferior, a rise in its price will cause people to buy more of it, thus violating the law of demand." True or false? Explain.

9. Which of the following descriptions of consumer behavior violates the assumption of *rational preferences*? In each case, explain briefly.

a. Joseph is confused: He doesn't know whether he'd prefer to take a job now or go to college full-time.

b. Brenda likes mustard on her pasta, in spite of the fact that pasta is not meant to be eaten with mustard.

c. Brewster says, "I'd rather see an action movie than a romantic comedy, and I'd rather see a romantic comedy than a foreign film. But given the choice, I think I'd rather see a foreign film than an action movie."

10. [Uses the Indifference Curve Approach] Howard spends all of his income on magazines and novels. Illustrate each of the following situations on a graph, with the quantity of magazines on the vertical axis and the quantity of novels on the horizontal axis. Use two budget lines and two indifference curves on each graph.

a. When the price of magazines rises, Howard buys fewer magazines and more novels.

b. When Howard's income rises, he buys more magazines *and* more novels.

c. When Howard's income rises, he buys more magazines but *fewer* novels.

11. [Uses the Indifference Curve Approach]

a. Draw a budget line for Cameron, who has a monthly income of $100. Assume that he buys steak and potatoes, and that steak costs $10 per pound and that potatoes cost $2 per pound. Add an indifference curve for Cameron that is tangent to his budget line at the combination of 5 pounds of steak and 25 pounds of potatoes.

b. Draw a new budget line for Cameron, if his monthly income falls to $80. Assume that potatoes are an inferior good to Cameron. Draw a new indifference curve tangent to his new budget constraint that reflects this inferiority. What will happen to Cameron's potato consumption? What will happen to his steak consumption?

12. [Uses the Indifference Curve Approach]

a. Draw a budget line for Rafaella, who has a weekly income of $30. Assume that she buys chicken and eggs, and that chicken costs $5 per pound while eggs cost $1 each. Add an indifference curve for Rafaella that is tangent to her budget line at the combination of 4 pounds of chicken and 10 eggs.

b. Draw a new budget line for Rafaella, if the price of chicken falls to $3 per pound. Assume that Rafaella views chicken and eggs as substitutes. What will happen to her chicken consumption? What will happen to her egg consumption?

Challenge Questions

1. When an economy is experiencing inflation, the prices of most goods and services are rising but at different rates. Imagine a simpler inflationary situation in which *all* prices, and all wages and incomes, are rising at the same rate, say 5 percent per year. What would happen to consumer choices in such a situation? (*Hint:* Think about what would happen to the budget line.)

2. [Uses the Indifference Curve Approach] With the quantity of popcorn on the vertical axis and the quantity of ice cream on the horizontal axis, draw indifference maps to illustrate each of the following situations. (*Hint:* Each will look different from the indifference maps in the appendix, because each violates one of the assumptions we made there.)

   a. Larry's marginal rate of substitution between ice cream and popcorn remains constant, no matter how much of each good he consumes.

   b. Heather loves ice cream but hates popcorn.

   c. When Andy eats ice cream, he tends to get addicted: The more he has, the more he wants still more, and he's willing to give up more and more popcorn to get the same amount of additional ice cream.

3. [Uses the Indifference Curve Approach] The appendix to this chapter states that when a consumer is buying the optimal combination of two goods x and y, then $MRS_{y,x} = P_x / P_y$. Draw a graph, with an indifference curve and a budget line, and with the quantity of y on the vertical axis, to illustrate the case where the consumer is buying a non-optimal combination on his budget line for which $MRS_{y,x} > P_x / P_y$.

 *These exercises require access to Lieberman/Hall Xtra! If Xtra! did not come with your book, visit http://liebermanxtra.swlearning.com to purchase.*

1. Use your Xtra! password at the Hall and Lieberman Web site (http://liebermanxtra.swlearning.com), select this chapter, and under Economic Applications, click on EconNews. Choose *Microeconomics: Elasticity,* and scroll down to find the articles, "Health Maintenance Organizations Fail to Maintain Health Benefits" and "Higher Health-Care Costs: Who Pays?" Read the article summaries and answer the following questions:

   a. Construct a budget line for two goods: health care and all other goods, assuming the following information: you have an income level of $30,000, one unit of health care (office visits, for example) costs $100, one unit of all other goods costs $50. You currently have no health insurance. Be sure to label your axes and your intercept points.

   b. Now assume that you receive health care from your employer at a cost to you of $2,000 per year, but as a result of your purchase of health care, all costs are covered (you are 100% insured). How does your budget line change from that in a? (*Hint:* now that you are fully insured, what is the price of health care?) Draw a new budget line in the graph you made in part a.

   c. After reading the articles, it is clear that employers are taking steps to reduce the burden they assume in

   covering employees' medical expenses. If the cost of coverage remained the same, but only 80% of medical costs were covered by insurance (in effect, you now have a 20% copayment), what would happen to your budget line in b? Draw this in the same graph as before.

   d. Did this have the effect desired by employers and health maintenance organizations? Why or why not?

2. Use your Xtra! password at the Hall and Lieberman Web site (http://liebermanxtra.swlearning.com), select this chapter, and under Economic Applications, click on EconNews. Choose *Microeconomics: Utility and Consumer Choice* and scroll down to find the article, "Does the Anti-sweatshop Movement Help or Harm Workers In Low-Wage Economies?" Read the debate and consider the following question: Much of the discussion, in economic terms, revolves around the relative differences in marginal utility of production and wage rates paid between developing and developed countries. According to the article, how does a firm use the *principle of marginal decision making* and maximize its own utility when deciding to move operations, for example, from the United States to a developing country?

APPENDIX

THE INDIFFERENCE CURVE APPROACH

This appendix presents an alternative approach to consumer decision making, and can be read in place of the approach in the body of the chapter ("Consumer Decisions: The Marginal Utility Approach"). We're naming it the "Indifference Curve Approach" after a graph that you will soon encounter.

Let's start by reviewing what we've already discussed about preferences. We assume that an individual (1) can compare any two options and decide which is best, or that both are equally attractive, (2) makes choices that are logically consistent, and (3) prefers more of every good to less. The first two assumptions are summarized as rational preferences; the third tells us that a consumer will always choose to be *on* her budget line, rather than below it.

But now, we'll go a bit further.

AN INDIFFERENCE CURVE

In Figure A.1, look at point *G,* which represents 20 movies and 1 concert per month. Suppose we get Max to look at this figure with us, and ask him to imagine how satisfied he would be to have the combination at point *G.* Max thinks about it for a minute, then says, "Okay, I know how satisfied I would be." Next, we say to Max, "Suppose you are at point *G* and we give you *another* concert each month, for a total of 2. That would make you even *more* satisfied, right?" Since Max likes concerts, he nods his head. But then we ask, "After giving you this additional concert, how many movies could we *take away* from you and leave you no better or worse off than you were originally, at point *G?*" Obliging fellow that he is, Max thinks about it and answers, "Well, if I'm starting at point *G,* and you give me another concert, I suppose you could take away 9 movies and I'd be just as happy as I was at *G.*"

Max has essentially told us that he is *indifferent between* point *G* on the one hand and point *H* on the

other. We know this because starting at point *G,* adding 1 more concert and taking away 9 movies puts us at point *H.*

But let's keep going. Now we get Max to imagine that he's at point *H,* and we ask him the same question, and this time he answers, "I could trade 5 movies for 1 more concert and be equally well off." Now Max is telling us that he is indifferent between point *H* and *J,* since *J* gives him 1 more concert and 5 fewer movies than point *H.*

So far, we know Max is indifferent between point *G* and point *H,* and between point *H* and point *J.* So long as he is rational, he must be entirely indifferent among all three points—*G, H,* and *J*—since all three give him the same level of satisfaction. By continuing in this way, we can trace out a set of points that—as far as Max is concerned—are equally satisfying. When we connect these points with a curved line, we get one of Max's *indifference curves.*

> An **indifference curve**[7] *represents all combinations of two goods that make the consumer equally well off.*

Notice two things about the indifference curve in Figure A.1. First, it slopes downward. This follows from our assumption about preferences that "more is better." Every time we give Max another concert, we make him better off. In order to find another point on his indifference curve, we must make him worse off by the same amount, *taking away* some movies.

Second, notice the *curvature* of the indifference curve. As we move downward and rightward along it, the curve becomes flatter (the absolute value of its slope decreases). Why is this?

---

[7] Key Terms found in this appendix are defined at the end of the appendix and in the glossary.

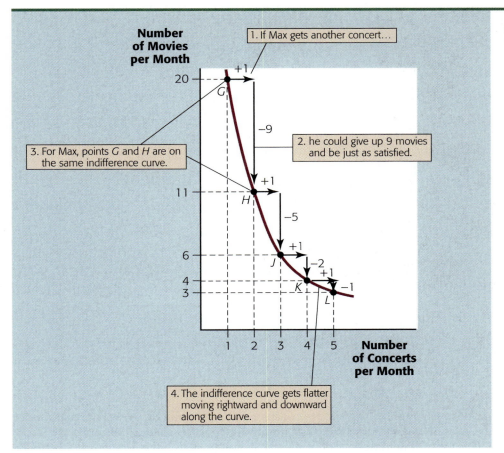

FIGURE A.1
An Indifference Curve

Boxes in figure:

1. If Max gets another concert…

2. he could give up 9 movies and be just as satisfied.

3. For Max, points G and H are on the same indifference curve.

4. The indifference curve gets flatter moving rightward and downward along the curve.

Axis labels: Number of Movies per Month; Number of Concerts per Month

The Marginal Rate of Substitution

We can better understand the shape of the indifference if we first think a bit more about what its slope means. Think of the slope (without the minus sign) as the maximum number of movies that Max would *willingly trade* for one more concert. For example, going from point G to point H, Max gives up 9 movies for 1 concert and remains indifferent. Therefore, from point G, if he gave up *10* movies for 1 concert, he'd be *worse off*, and he would not willingly make that trade. Thus, at point G, the *greatest* number of movies he'd sacrifice for another concert would be 9.

This notion of "willingness to trade," as you'll soon see, has an important role to play in our model of consumer decision making. And there's a technical term for it: the *marginal rate of substitution of movies for concerts.* More generally, when the quantity of good *y* is

measured on the vertical axis, and the quantity of good *x* is measured on the horizontal axis,

> the **marginal rate of substitution of good y for good x** (MRS$_{y,x}$) along any segment of an indifference curve is the absolute value of the slope along that segment. The MRS tells us the maximum amount of y a consumer would willingly trade for one more unit of x.

This gives us another way of describing the shape of the indifference curve: As we move downward along the curve, the *MRS* (the number of movies Max would willing trade for another concert) gets smaller and smaller. To see why the *MRS* behaves this way, consider point G, high on Max's indifference curve. At this point, Max is seeing a lot of movies and relatively few concerts compared to points lower down, such as *J, K,* or *L*. With so

FIGURE A.2
An Indifference Map

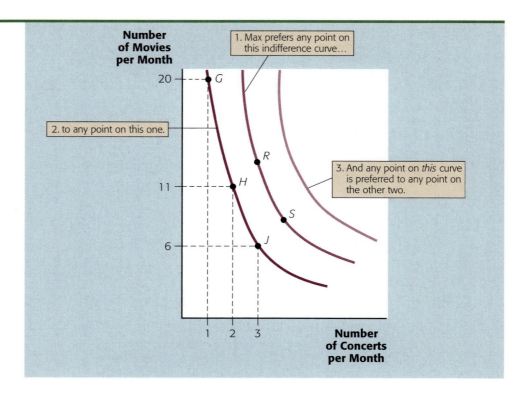

few concerts, he'd value another one very highly. And with so many movies, each one he gives up doesn't harm him much. So, at a point like *G,* he'd be willing to trade a large number of movies for even one more concert. His $MRS_{movies, concerts}$ is relatively large, and since the *MRS* is the absolute value of the indifference curve's slope, the curve is relatively steep at point *G.*

But as we continue traveling down his indifference curve, from *G* to *H* to *J* and so on, movies become scarcer for Max, so each one given up hurts him a bit more. At the same time, he's attending more and more concerts, so adding another one doesn't benefit him as much as before. At a point like *K,* then, Max is more reluctant to trade movies for concerts. To get another concert, he'd willingly trade fewer movies at point *K* than at point *G.* So at point *K,* the *MRS* is relatively small and the curve is relatively flat.

THE INDIFFERENCE MAP

To trace out the indifference curve in Figure A.1, we began at a specific point—point *G.* Figure A.2 reproduces that same indifference curve through *G, H,* and *J.* But

now consider the new point *R,* which involves more movies *and* more concerts than at point *H.* We know that point *R* is preferred to point *H* ("more is better"), so it is not on the indifference curve that goes through *H.* However, we can use the same procedure we used earlier to find a *new* indifference curve, connecting all points indifferent to point *R.* Indeed, we can repeat this procedure for any initial starting point we might choose, tracing out dozens or even hundreds of Max's indifference curves, as many as we'd like.

The result would be an **indifference map,** a set of indifference curves that describe Max's preferences, like the three curves in Figure A.2. We know that Max would always prefer any point on a higher indifference curve to any point on a lower one. Equivalently, if we imagine that Max's level of satisfaction can be measured quantitatively as his level of **utility,** we can say the following: all the points on any one indifference curve give Max the same level of utility, but a higher indifference cuve provides more utility than a lower indifference curve.

For example, consider the points *H* and *S. S* represents more concerts but fewer movies than *H.* How can we know if Max prefers *S* to *H,* or *H* to *S?* Max's indifference map tells us that he *must* prefer *S* to *H*. Why? We know that he prefers *R* to *H*, since *R* has more of both goods. We also know that Max is indifferent between *R* and *S*, since they are on the same indifference curve. Since he is indifferent between *S* and *R*, but prefers *R* to *H*, then he must also prefer *S* to *H*.

The same technique could be used to show that

> *any point on a higher indifference curve is preferred to any point on a lower one.*

Thus, Max's indifference map tells us how he ranks all alternatives imaginable. This is why we say that an indifference map gives us a complete characterization of someone's preferences: It allows us to look at any two points and—just by seeing which indifference curves they are on—immediately know which, if either, is preferred.

Two Mistakes with Indifference Curves First, don't allow the ends of an indifference curve to "curl up," like the curve through point *B* in the following figure, so that the curve slopes upward at the ends. This violates our assumption of "more is better." To see why, notice that point *A* has more of both goods than point *B*. So as long as "more is better," *A* must be preferred to *B*. But then *A* and *B* are not indifferent, so they cannot lie on the same indifference curve. For the same reason, points *M* and *N* cannot lie on the same indifference curve. Remember that indifference curves cannot slope upward.

Second, don't allow two indifference curves to cross. For example, look at the two indifference curves passing through point *V*. *T* and *V* are on the same indifference curve, so the consumer must be indifferent between them. But *V* and *S* are also on the same indifference curve, so the consumer is indifferent between them, too. Since rationality requires the consumer's preferences to be consistent, the consumer must then also be indifferent between *T* and *S*, but this is impossible because *S* has more of both goods than *T*, a violation of "more is better." Remember that indifference curves cannot cross.

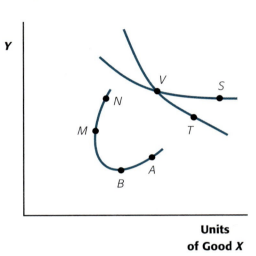

CONSUMER DECISION MAKING

Now we can combine everything you've learned about budget lines in the chapter, and what you've learned about indifference curves in this appendix, to determine the combination of movies and concerts that Max should choose. Figure A.3 adds Max's budget line to his indifference map. In drawing the budget line, we assume that Max has a monthly entertainment budget of $150, and that a concert costs $30 and a movie costs $10.

We assume that Max—like any consumer—wants to make himself as well off as possible (to "maximize his utility"). Max's optimal combination of movies and concerts will satisfy two criteria: (1) it will be a point on his budget line; and (2) it will lie on the highest indifference curve possible. Max can find this point by traveling down his budget line from *A*. As he does so, he will pass through a variety of indifference curves. (To see this clearly, you can pencil in additional indifference curves *between* the ones drawn in the figure.) At first, each in-

difference curve is higher than the one before, until he reachest the highest curve possible. This occurs at point *D*, where Max sees six movies and three concerts each month. Any further moves down the budget line will put him on lower indifference curves, so these moves would make him worse off. Point *D* is Max's optimal choice.

Notice something interesting about point *D*. First, it occurs where the indifference curve and the budget line are tangent—where they touch but don't cross. As you can see in the diagram, when an indifference curve actually crosses the budget line, we can always find some other point on the budget line that lies on a higher indifference curve.

Second, at point *D*, the slope of the indifference curve is the same as the slope of the budget line. Does this make sense? Yes, when you think about it this way: The absolute value of the indifference curve's slope—the *MRS*—tells us the rate at which Max would *willingly* trade movies for concerts. The slope of the budget line, by contrast, tells us the rate at which Max is *actually able* to trade movies for concerts. If there's

FIGURE A.3
Consumer Decision Making with Indifference Curves

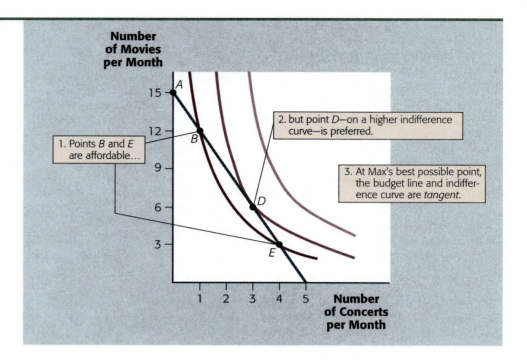

any difference between the rate at which Max is *willing* to trade one good for another and the rate at which he is *able* to trade, he can always make himself better off by moving to another point on the budget line.

For example, suppose Max were at point *B* in Figure A.3. The indifference there is steeper than his budget line. In fact, the indifference curve appears to have a slope of about −6, so Max's *MRS* there is about 6; he'd willingly give up 6 movies for 1 more concert. But his budget line—as you learned earlier in the chapter—has a slope of −3. Thus, at point *B*, Max would be *willing* to trade about 6 movies for one concert. But according to his budget line, he is *able* to trade just 3 movies for each concert. If trading 6 movies for a concert would leave him indifferent, then trading just 3 movies for a concert must make him better off. We conclude that when Max's indifference curve is steeper than his budget line, he should spend more on concerts and less on movies.

Using similar reasoning, convince yourself that Max should make the opposite move—spending less on concerts and more on movies—if his indifference curve is *flatter* than his budget line, as it is at point *E*. Only when the indifference curve and the budget line have the same slope—when they touch but do not cross—is Max as well off as possible. This is the point where the

indifference curve is *tangent* to the budget line. When Max, or any other consumer, strives to be as well off as possible, he will follow this rule:

> *The optimal combination of goods for a consumer is the point on the budget line where an indifference curve is tangent to the budget line.*

We can also express this decision-making rule in terms of the *MRS* and the prices of two goods. Recall that the slope of the budget line is $= -P_x / P_y$, so the absolute value of the budget line's slope is P_x / P_y. As you've just learned, the absolute value of the slope of an indifference curve is $MRS_{y,x}$. This allows us to state the decision-making rule as follows:

> *The optimal combination of two goods x and y is that combination on the budget line for which* $MRS_{y,x} = P_x / P_y$

If this condition is not met, there will be a difference between the rate at which a consumer is *willing* to trade good *y* for good *x*, and the rate at which he is *able* to trade them. This will always give the consumer an opportunity to make himself better off.

WHAT HAPPENS WHEN THINGS CHANGE?

So far, as we've examined Max's search for the best combination of movies and concerts, we've assumed that Max's income, and the prices of each good, have remained unchanged. But in the real world, an individual's income, and the prices of the things they buy, *can* change. How would these changes affect a consumer's choice?

Changes in Income

Figure A.4 illustrates how an increase in income might affect Max's choice between movies and concerts. We assume that movies cost $10 each, concerts cost $30 each, and that these prices are not changing. Initially,

Max has $150 to spend on the two goods, so his budget line is the lower line through point *D*. As we've already seen, under these conditions, the optimal combination for Max is point *D* (3 concerts and 6 movies).

Now suppose Max's income increases to $300. Then his budget line will shift upward and rightward in the figure. How will he respond? As always, he will search along his budget line until he arrives at the highest possible indifference curve, which will be tangent to the budget line at that point.

But where will this point be? There are several possibilities, and they depend on Max's preferences, as reflected in his indifference map. In the figure, we've used an indifference map for Max that leads him to point *H*, enjoying 6 concerts and 12 movies per month. As you

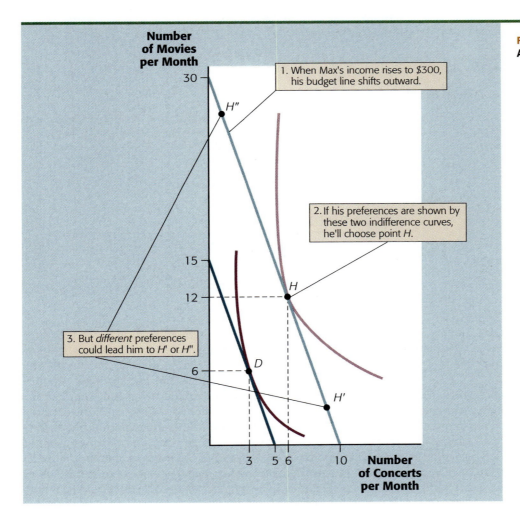

FIGURE A.4
An Increase in Income

Number of Movies per Month

1. When Max's income rises to $300, his budget line shifts outward.

2. If his preferences are shown by these two indifference curves, he'll choose point *H*.

3. But *different* preferences could lead him to *H'* or *H"*.

Number of Concerts per Month

FIGURE A.5
Deriving the Demand Curve

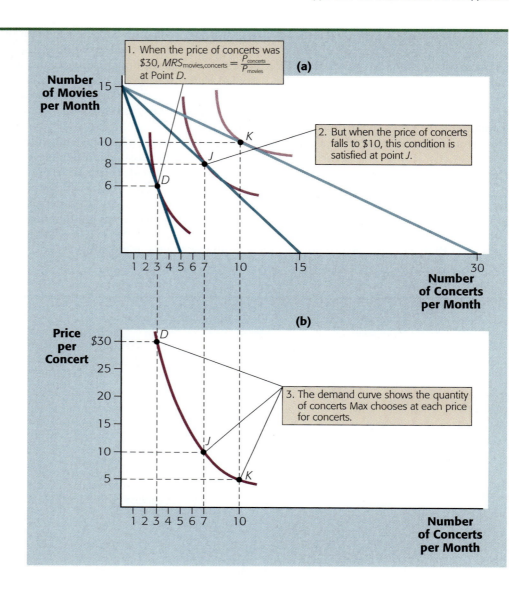

1. When the price of concerts was $30, $MRS_{movies,concerts} = \frac{P_{concerts}}{P_{movies}}$ at Point D.

(a)

2. But when the price of concerts falls to $10, this condition is satisfied at point J.

(b)

3. The demand curve shows the quantity of concerts Max chooses at each price for concerts.

can see in the figure, at this point, he has reached the highest possible indifference curve that his budget allows. It's also the point at which $MRS_{movies, concerts} = P_{concerts}/P_{movies} = 3$.

Notice that, in moving from D to H, Max chooses to buy more concerts (6 rather than 3) and more movies (12 rather than 6). As discussed in Chapter 3, if an increase in income (with prices held constant) increases the quantity of a good demanded, the good is *normal*. For Max, with the indifference map we've assumed in Figure A.4, both concerts and movies would be normal goods.

But what if Max's preferences, and his indifference map, had been different from the one in the figure? For example, suppose that after income increased, the tangency between his budget line and the highest indifference curve he could reach occurred at a point like H′, with 9 concerts and 3 movies. In this case, the increase in income would cause Max's consumption of concerts to increase (from 3 to 9), but his consumption of movies to *fall* (from 6 to 3). If so, movies would be an *inferior good* for Max, one for which demand decreases when income increases, while concerts would be a normal good.

It's also possible for Max to have preferences that lead him to point H''—with more movies and fewer concerts compared to point D. In this case, *concerts* would be the inferior good and movies would be normal.

A rise in income, with no change in prices, leads to a new quantity demanded for each good. Whether a particular good is normal (quantity demanded increases) or inferior (quantity demanded decreases) depends on the individual's preferences, as represented by his indifference map.

Changes in Price

Let's explore what happens to Max when the price of a concert decreases from $30 to $10, while his income and the price of a movie remain unchanged. The drop in the price of concerts rotates Max's budget line rightward, pivoting around its vertical intercept, as illustrated in the upper panel of Figure A.5. What will Max do after his budget line rotates in this way? Based on his indifference curves—as they appear in the figure—he'd choose point J. This is the new combination of movies and concerts on his budget line that makes him as well off as possible (puts him on the highest possible indifference curve that he can afford). It's also the point at which $MRS_{\text{movies, concerts}} = P_{\text{concerts}}/P_{\text{movies}} = 1$, since movies and concerts now have the same price.

What if we dropped the price of concerts again, this time, to $5? Then Max's budget line rotates further rightward, and he will once again find the best possible point. In the figure, Max is shown choosing point K, attending 10 concerts and 10 movies.

THE INDIVIDUAL'S DEMAND CURVE

You've just seen that each time the price of concerts changes, so does the quantity of concerts Max will want to attend. The lower panel of Figure A.5 illustrates this relationship by plotting the quantity of concerts demanded on the horizontal axis and the *price* of concerts on the vertical axis. For example, in both the upper and lower panels, point D tells us that when the price of concerts is $30, Max will see three of them. When we connect points like D, J, and K in the lower panel, we get Max's **individual demand curve**, which shows the quantity of a good he demands at each different price. Notice that Max's demand curve for concerts slopes downward—a fall in the price of concerts increases the quantity demanded—showing that for Max, concerts obey the law of demand.

But if Max's preferences—and his indifference map—had been different, could his response to a price change have *violated* the law of demand? The answer is yes . . . and no. Yes, it is theoretically possible. (As a challenge, try penciling in a new set of indifference curves that would give Max an *upward-sloping* demand curve in the figure.) But no, it does not seem to happen in practice. To find out why, it's time to go back to the body of the chapter, to the section titled, "Income and Substitution Effects."

Key Terms

Indifference curve A curve representing all combinations of two goods that make the consumer equally well off.

Indifference map A set of indifference curves that represent an individual's preferences.

Individual demand curve A curve showing the quantity of a good or service demanded by a particular individual at each different price.

Marginal rate of substitution ($MRS_{y,x}$) The maximum amount of good y a consumer would willingly trade for one more unit of good x. Also, the slope of a segment of an indifference curve.

Utility A quantitative measure of pleasure or satisfaction obtained from consuming goods and services.

Production and Cost

On September 5, 2001, Hewlett Packard announced that it planned to buy one of its major competitors, Compaq Computer, for $25 billion—the largest merger in the history of the computer industry. The announcement ignited a firestorm of controversy. Although management at both companies and most of *Compaq*'s shareholders were enthusiastic about the plan, a group of influential Hewlett Packard shareholders was vehemently opposed. Each side had its eye on March 19, 2002—the official date of a yes-or-no vote among Hewlett Packard shareholders.

For the next six months, the two sides campaigned with full-page ads in major newspapers, daily appearances on CNBC, MSNBC, and CNN, and behind-the-scenes lobbying. As the vote neared, the conflict occasionally strayed into questions about motives, accusations of unethical conduct, and even personal attacks. But the debate always returned to one of the central issues: the effect of the proposed merger on *costs*. Specifically, Hewlett Packard's managers claimed that within a couple of years the merger would create annual cost savings of $2.5 billion for the two companies. The opposition did not believe them. In the end, the shareholders approved, and the two companies merged into one on May 3, 2002.

Although this particular transaction was unusually lively, mergers are anything but unusual. In a typical year, more than a thousand U.S. corporations—with a total value of close to $1 trillion—are acquired by other companies. Thousands more companies are acquired each year in Europe and Asia. In most cases, the stockholders of both firms end up favoring these deals. And in most cases, a major reason for the move—and the stockholders' approval—is the impact on costs.

This chapter is mostly about costs: how to think about them, how to measure them, and how business decisions cause them to change. By the time you've finished the chapter, you'll understand why costs play such an important role in mergers and acquisitions. But since this chapter also begins our study of business firms, some general but important questions will be addressed first. What *are* business firms? Why are they so prevalent in our economy—and in every market economy? Why do so many of us work for them, instead of striking out on our own? In the next section, we begin to answer these questions.

THE NATURE OF THE FIRM

What is a business firm? In the most general sense,

> *a business firm is an organization, owned and operated by private individuals, that specializes in* production.

Business firm An organization, owned and operated by private individuals, that specializes in production.

When you hear the word *production*, your first thought is probably about *goods*. You might imagine a busy, noisy factory where *things* are assembled, piece-by-piece, and then carted off to a warehouse for eventual sale. Large manufacturers might come to mind: General Motors, Boeing, or U.S. Steel. But in economics, production is a more general concept.

> *Production is the process of combining inputs to make goods or services, often called* outputs.

Notice that production also encompasses *services*. Indeed, many of the largest business firms in the U.S. produce services: Think of Citicorp (banking services), American Airlines (transportation services), Verizon (telecommunications services), and Wal-Mart (retailing services).

Figure 1 illustrates the relationships between the firm and those it deals with. Notice that we have put the firm's management in the center of the diagram. It is the managers who must decide what the firm will do, both day-to-day and over a longer time horizon. When we refer to the firm as a *decision maker,* we mean the manager or managers who actually make the decisions.

As you can see in the figure, the firm must deal with a variety of individuals and organizations. It sells its output to *customers*—which can be households, government agencies, or other firms—and receives *revenue* from them in return. For example, Ford Motor Company sells its automobiles to households, to other firms (such as rental car companies), and to government agencies (such as local police departments). Ford earns revenue from all of these customers.

FIGURE 1
The Firm and Its Environment

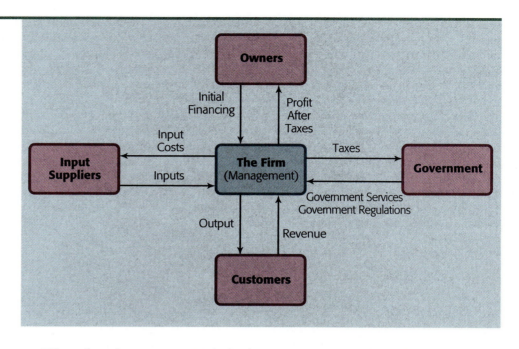

Where does the revenue go? Much of it goes to *input suppliers*. Ford must pay for labor, machinery, steel, rubber, electricity, factory buildings and the land underneath them, and much, much more. The total of all of these payments makes up the firm's *costs* of production.

Profit Total revenue minus total cost.

When costs are deducted from revenue, what remains is the firm's **profit**:

$$\text{Profit} = \text{Revenue} - \text{Costs}.$$

Figure 1 shows that the firm's profit (after taxes) accrues to the *owners* who provided the firm's initial financing.

Finally, every firm must deal with the government. On the one hand, it pays taxes to the government, and must obey government laws and regulations. On the other hand, firms receive valuable services from the government. These include the use of public capital, like roads and bridges, as well as the presence of a legal and financial system that help the economy run smoothly.

Types of Business Firms

Sole proprietorship A firm owned by a single individual, who receives all of the firm's profit as household income.

Business firms can be divided into three major categories, based on the rules and conditions of ownership. The greatest number of firms are **sole proprietorships**, in which a single individual owns the firm, takes responsibility for it, and receives all of the profits as part of his or her household income. Common examples of sole proprietorships include shops and restaurants that are owned by just one person, and the businesses of free-lance consultants, writers, and artists.

Partnership A firm owned by two or more people, who receive all of the firm's profit as household income.

Other firms are **partnerships**, in which ownership and responsibility are shared among two or more co-owners. Small professional practices—such as medical, dental or law practices—are often partnerships. In partnerships, like sole proprietorships, the owners receive all of the firms' profits as part of their household income.

Corporation A firm owned and ultimately controlled by all those who buy shares of stock in the firm, who may receive part of the firm's profit as dividend payments.

The largest firms—such as General Motors, Time Warner, Starbucks, and Sony—almost always fall into the third category: **corporations**. In a corporation, ownership is divided among those who buy shares of *stock*. Each share of stock gives its holder (1) a vote for the board of directors, which, in turn, hires the corporation's top management; and (2) a fraction of the corporation's total profit. While some of the profit may be paid out to the shareholders as *dividends*, it's not uncommon for most or all of it to remain with the corporation, where it can be used to fund new projects.

THINKING ABOUT PRODUCTION

When you think of production, it is quite natural to think of *outputs*—the things firms *make*—and *inputs*—the things firms *use* to make outputs. Inputs include resources (labor, capital, land, and entrepreneurship), as well as other inputs. For example, to produce this book, South-Western used a variety of resources: *labor* (including that provided by the authors, editors, artists, printers, and company managers); *human capital* (the knowledge and skills possessed by each of the preceding workers); *physical capital* (including computers, delivery trucks, and a company headquarters building in Cincinnati); and *land* (under the headquarters). The company also used other inputs, including raw materials such as paper and ink, as well as the services of trucking companies, telephone companies, and Internet access providers.

A firm's **technology** refers to the variety of methods the firm can use to turn its inputs into goods and services. We leave it to engineers and scientists to spell out a firm's technology and to discover ways to improve it. When thinking about the firm, economists treat technology as a given, a constraint on the firm's production. This constraint is spelled out by the firm's *production function*:

> *For each different combination of inputs, the **production function** tells us the maximum quantity of output a firm can produce over some period of time.*

Technology A method by which inputs are combined to produce a good or service.

Production function A function that indicates the maximum amount of output a firm can produce over some period of time from each combination of inputs.

The idea behind a production function is illustrated in Figure 2. Quantities of each input are plugged into the box representing the production function, and the maximum quantity of goods or services produced pops out. The production function itself—the box—is a mathematical function relating inputs and outputs.

When a firm uses many different inputs, production functions can be quite complicated. This is true even of small firms. For example, the production function for a video and DVD rental store would tell us how many movies it could rent per day with different combinations of floor space, shelving, salesclerks, cash registers, movies in stock, lighting, air conditioning, and so on.

In this chapter, to keep things simple, we'll spell out the production function for a mythical firm that uses only two inputs: capital and labor. Our firm is Spotless Car Wash, whose output is a service: the number of cars washed. The firm's capital is the number of automated car-washing lines, and its labor is the number of full-time workers who drive the cars onto the line, drive them out, towel them down at the end, and deal with customers.[1]

---

[1] Of course, a car wash would use other inputs besides just capital and labor: water, washrags, soap, electricity, and so on. But the costs of these inputs would be minor when compared to the costs of labor and capital. To keep our example simple, we ignore these other inputs.

FIGURE 2
The Firm's Production Function

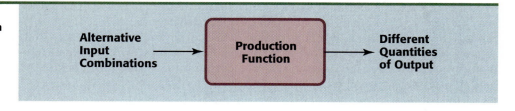

The Short Run and the Long Run

When a firm alters its level of production, its input requirements will change. Some inputs, such as labor, can be adjusted relatively quickly. Other inputs—for example, capital equipment—may be more difficult to change. Why? Leases or rental agreements may commit the firm to keep paying for equipment over some period of time, whether the equipment is used or not. Or there may be practical difficulties in adjusting capital, like a long lead time needed to acquire new equipment or sell off existing equipment. These considerations make it useful to categorize firms' decisions into one of two sorts: *long-run decisions* and *short-run decisions*.

Long run A time horizon long enough for a firm to vary all of its inputs.

> *The **long run** is a time horizon long enough for a firm to vary* all *of its inputs.*

The long run will be different for different firms. For a surgeon who would need several months to obtain a new surgical laser, to find a buyer for the one he has, or to find a larger or a smaller office, the long run is several months or more. At Spotless Car Wash, it might take a year to acquire and install an additional automated line or to sell the ones it already has. For Spotless, then, the long run would be any period longer than a year.

When a firm makes long-run decisions, it makes choices about *all* of its inputs. But firms must also make decisions over shorter time horizons, during which some of its inputs *cannot* be adjusted. We call these **fixed inputs**. Any input which is *not* fixed is called a **variable input**. Using this terminology, we can define the short-run planning horizon as follows:

Fixed input An input whose quantity must remain constant, regardless of how much output is produced.

Variable input An input whose usage can change as the level of output changes.

> *The **short run** refers to any time horizon over which at least one of the firm's inputs cannot be varied.*

Short run A time horizon during which at least one of the firm's inputs cannot be varied.

For Spotless Car Wash, the short run would be any period *less* than a year, the period during which it is stuck with a certain number of automated lines.

You can think of the short run and long run as two different lenses that a firm's managers must look through to make decisions. The short-run lens makes at least one of the inputs appear to be fixed, but the long-run lens makes all inputs appear variable. To guide the firm over the next several years, the manager must use the long-run lens; to determine what the firm should do next week, the short-run lens is best.

PRODUCTION IN THE SHORT RUN

When firms make short-run decisions, there is nothing they can do about their fixed inputs: They are stuck with whatever quantity they have. They can, however, make choices about their variable inputs. Indeed, we see examples of such short-run decisions all the time. Boeing might decide *this month* to cut its production of aircraft by 5 percent and lay off thousands of workers, even though it cannot change its factory buildings or capital equipment for another year or more. For Boeing (using a time horizon of less than a year) labor is variable, while its factory and equipment are fixed. Levi Strauss might decide to increase production of blue jeans over the next quarter by obtaining additional workers,

TABLE 1
Short-Run Production at Spotless Car Wash

Quantity of Capital	Quantity of Labor	Total Product (Cars Washed per Day)
1	0	0
1	1	30
1	2	90
1	3	130
1	4	161
1	5	184
1	6	196

cotton cloth, and sewing machines, yet continue to make do with the same factories because there isn't time to expand them or acquire new ones. Here, workers, cloth, and sewing machines are all variable, while only the factory buildings are fixed.

Spotless Car Wash uses only two inputs to produce its output, labor and capital. In the short run, we'll assume that labor is the variable input, and capital is the fixed input. The three columns in Table 1 describe Spotless's production function in the short run. Column 1 shows the quantity of the fixed input, capital (K); column 2 the quantity of the variable input, labor (L). Note that in the short run, Spotless is stuck with one unit of capital—one automated line—but it can take on as many or as few workers as it wishes. Column 3 shows the firm's *total product* (Q).

> *Total product is the maximum quantity of output that can be produced from a given combination of inputs.*

Total product The maximum quantity of output that can be produced from a given combination of inputs.

For example, the table shows us that with one automated line but no labor, total product is zero. With one line and six workers, output is 196 cars washed per day.

Figure 3 shows Spotless's *total product curve*. The horizontal axis represents the number of workers, while the vertical axis measures total product. (The amount of capital—which is held fixed at one automated line—is not shown on the graph.) Notice that each time the firm hires another worker, output increases, so the total product curve slopes upward. The vertical arrows in the figure show precisely *how much* output increases with each one-unit rise in employment. We call this rise in output the *marginal product of labor*.

Using the Greek letter Δ ("delta") to stand for "change in," we can define marginal product this way:

> *The **marginal product of labor** (**MPL**) is the change in total product (ΔQ) divided by the change in the number of workers employed (ΔL):*
>
> $$MPL = \frac{\Delta Q}{\Delta L}$$
>
> *The MPL tells us the rise in output produced when one more worker is hired.*

Marginal product of labor The additional output produced when one more worker is hired.

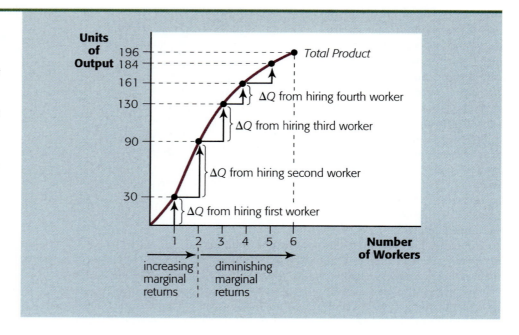

For example, if employment rises from 2 to 3 workers, total product rises from 90 to 130, so the marginal product of labor for *that* change in employment is calculated as $(130 − 90) / 1 = 40$ units of output.

Marginal Returns to Labor

Look at the vertical arrows in Figure 3, which measure the marginal product of labor, and you may notice something interesting. As more and more workers are hired, the *MPL* first increases (the vertical arrows get longer) and then decreases (the arrows get shorter). This pattern is believed to be typical at many types of firms, so it's worth exploring.

Increasing marginal returns to labor The marginal product of labor increases as more labor is hired.

Increasing Marginal Returns to Labor. When the marginal product of labor rises as employment rises, there are **increasing marginal returns to labor.** Each time a worker is hired, total output rises by more than it did when the previous worker was hired. Why does this happen? One reason is that additional workers may allow production to become more specialized. Another reason is that at very low levels of employment, there may not be enough workers to properly operate the available capital. In either case, the additional worker not only produces some additional output as an individual, but also makes all other workers more productive.

Figure 3 tells us that Spotless Car Wash experiences increasing returns to labor up to the hiring of the second worker. While one worker *could* operate the car wash alone, he or she would have to do everything: drive the cars on and off the line, towel them down, and deal with customers. Much of this worker's time would be spent switching from one task to another. The result, as we see in Table 1, is that one worker can wash only 30 cars each day. Add a second worker, though, and now specialization is possible. One worker can collect money and drive the cars onto the line, and the other can drive them off and towel them down. Thus, with two workers, output rises all the way to 90 car washes per day; the second worker adds more to production (60 car washes) than the first (30 car washes) by making *both* workers more productive.

Diminishing Returns to Labor. When the marginal product of labor is decreasing, we say there are **diminishing marginal returns to labor.** Output rises when another worker is added, so marginal product is positive. But the rise in output is smaller and smaller with each successive worker. Why does this happen? For one thing, as we keep adding workers, additional gains from specialization will be harder and harder to achieve. Moreover, each worker will have less and less of the fixed inputs with which to work.

Diminishing marginal returns to labor The marginal product of labor decreases as more labor is hired.

This last point is worth stressing. It applies not just to labor but to any variable input. In all kinds of production, if we keep increasing the quantity of any one input, while holding the others fixed, diminishing marginal returns will eventually set in. If a farmer keeps adding additional pounds of fertilizer to a fixed amount of land, the yield may continue to increase, but eventually the *size* of the increase—the marginal product of fertilizer—will begin to come down. If a small bakery continues to acquire additional ovens without hiring any workers or enlarging its floor space, eventually the additional output of bread—the marginal product of ovens—will decline. This tendency is so pervasive and widespread that it has been deemed a law, and economists have given that law a name:

> The **law of diminishing (marginal) returns** states that as we continue to add more of any one input (holding the other inputs constant), its marginal product will eventually decline.

Law of diminishing marginal returns As more and more of any input is added to a fixed amount of other inputs, its marginal product will eventually decline.

The law of diminishing returns is a physical law, not an economic one. It is based on the nature of production—on the physical relationship between inputs and outputs with a given technology.

At Spotless, diminishing returns set in after two workers have been hired. Beyond this point, the firm is crowding more and more workers into a car wash with just one automated line. Output continues to increase, since there is usually *something* an additional worker can do to move the cars through the line more quickly, but the increase is less dramatic each time.

This section has been concerned with *production*—the *physical* relationship between inputs and outputs. But a more critical concern for a firm is: What will it *cost* to produce any level of output? Cost is measured in dollars and cents, not in physical units of inputs or outputs. But as you are about to see, what you've learned about production will help you understand the behavior of costs.

THINKING ABOUT COSTS

Talk to people who own or manage businesses, and it won't be long before the word *cost* comes up. People in business worry about measuring costs, controlling costs, and—most of all—reducing costs. This is not surprising: Owners want their firms to earn the highest possible profit, and costs must be subtracted from a firm's revenue to determine its profit. We will postpone a thorough discussion of profit until the next chapter. Here, we focus on just the *costs* of production: how economists think about costs, how costs are measured, and how they change as the firm adjusts its level of output.

Let's begin by revisiting a familiar notion. In Chapter 2 you learned that economists always think of cost as *opportunity cost*—what we must give up in order to do something. This concept applies to the firm as well:

Opportunity Cost

> *A firm's total cost of producing a given level of output is the opportunity cost of the owners—everything they must give up in order to produce that amount of output.*

This notion—that the cost of production is its opportunity cost—is at the core of economists' thinking about costs. It can help us understand which costs matter—and which don't—when making business decisions.

The Irrelevance of Sunk Costs

HTTP://

Dwight Lee's "Opportunity cost and hidden invention" is an interesting debunking of the myth that corporations try to suppress inventions that make their products obsolete. (The location of Lee's essay changes frequently. To find the current page, go to http://www.google.com and enter both author and title.)

Suppose that last year, Acme Pharmaceutical Company spent $10 million developing a new drug to treat acne that, if successful, promised to generate annual sales revenue many times that amount. At first, it seemed that the drug worked as intended. But then, just before launching production, management discovered that some early test results had been misinterpreted. The new drug, it turns out, doesn't cure acne at all—but it's remarkably effective in treating a rare underarm fungus. In this smaller, less lucrative market, annual sales revenue would be just $30,000. Now management must decide: Should they sell the drug as an antifungus remedy?

When confronted with a problem like this, some people will answer something like this: "Acme should *not* sell the drug. You don't sell something for $30,000 a year when it cost you $10 million to make it." Others will respond this way: "Of course Acme should sell the drug. If they don't, they'd be wasting that huge investment of $10 million." But neither approach to answering this question is correct, because both use the $10 million development cost to reach a conclusion. The $10 million is completely *irrelevant* to the decision.

The $10 million already spent on developing the drug is an example of a *sunk cost*. More generally,

Sunk cost A cost that has been paid or must be paid, regardless of any future action being considered.

> *a sunk cost is one that already has been paid, or must be paid, regardless of any future action being considered.*

In the case of Acme, the development cost has been paid already, and the firm will not get this money back, whether it chooses to sell the drug in this new smaller market, or *not* to sell the drug there. Since it's not part of the opportunity cost of either choice—something that would have to be sacrificed *for* that choice—it should have no bearing on the decision. For Acme, as for any business,

> *Sunk costs should not be considered when making decisions.*

What *should* be considered are the costs that *do* depend on the decision about producing the drug, namely, the cost of actually manufacturing it and marketing it for the smaller market. If the $30,000 Acme could earn in annual revenue exceeds these costs, Acme should produce it.

Look again at the definition of sunk cost and you'll see that even a *future* payment can be sunk, if an *unavoidable commitment to pay it has already been made.* Suppose, for example, Acme Pharmaceuticals has signed an employment contract with a research scientist, legally binding the firm to pay her annual salary for three years even if she is laid off. Although some or all of the payments haven't yet been made, all three years of salary are sunk costs for Acme because they *must* be made no matter what Acme does. As sunk costs, they are irrelevant to Acme's decisions.

Explicit Versus Implicit Costs

In Chapter 2, in discussing the opportunity cost of education, you learned that there are two types of costs: **explicit** (involving actual payments) and **implicit** (no money changes hands). The same distinction applies to costs for a business firm.

Suppose you're thinking about opening up a restaurant in a building that you already own. You wouldn't have to pay any rent, so there's no explicit rental payment. Does this mean that using the building is free?

To an accountant—who focuses on actual money payments—the answer is yes. But to an economist—who thinks of opportunity cost—the answer is *absolutely not.* By choosing to use your own building for your restaurant, you would be sacrificing the opportunity to rent it to someone else. This *foregone rent* is an implicit cost, and it is as much a cost of production as the rent you would pay if you rented the building from someone else. In both cases, something is given up to produce your output.

Now suppose that instead of *borrowing* money to buy ovens, dishes, tables, chairs, and an initial inventory of food for your restaurant, you used your *own* money. You would then have no loans or interest to pay back. However, that money of yours *could* have been put in a bank account, lent to someone else, or invested elsewhere. With these options, you could earn investment income on your money. Economists measure the opportunity cost of funds you invest in a business as the income you *could* earn by investing the funds elsewhere. This *foregone investment income* is an implicit cost of doing business.

Finally, suppose you decided to manage your restaurant yourself. Have you escaped the costs of hiring a manager? Not really, because you are still bearing an opportunity cost: You *could* do something else with your time. We measure the value of your time as the income you *could* earn by devoting your labor to your next-best

Any sunk costs of pharmaceutical development are irrelevant to the decision to market a new drug.

Explicit costs Money actually paid out for the use of inputs.

Implicit costs The cost of inputs for which there is no direct money payment.

Explicit Costs	Implicit Costs	
Rent paid out	Opportunity cost of:	
Interest on loans	Owner's land and buildings (rent foregone)	
Managers' salaries	Owner's money (investment income	
Hourly workers' wages	foregone)	
Cost of raw materials	Owner's time (labor income foregone)	

TABLE 2
A Firm's Costs

income-earning activity. This *foregone labor income*—the wage or salary you could be earning elsewhere—is an implicit cost of your business, and therefore part of its opportunity cost.

Table 2 summarizes our discussion by listing some common categories of costs that business firms face, both explicit (on the left) and implicit (on the right).

COSTS IN THE SHORT RUN

Managers must answer questions about costs over different time horizons. One question might be, "How much will it cost us to produce a given level of output *this year*?" Another might be, "How much will it cost us to produce a given level of output *three years from now and beyond*?" In this section, we'll explore managers' view of costs for a time horizon—perhaps a month, a few months, or a year—during which *at least one* of the firm's inputs is fixed. That is, we'll be looking at costs with a *short-run* planning horizon.

Remember that no matter how much output is produced, the quantity of a fixed input *must* remain the same. Other inputs, by contrast, can be varied as output changes. Because the firm has these two different types of inputs in the short run, it will also face two different types of costs.

Fixed costs Costs of fixed inputs.

The costs of a firm's fixed inputs are called, not surprisingly, **fixed costs**. Like the fixed inputs themselves, fixed costs must remain the same no matter what the level of output. Typically, we treat rent and interest—whether explicit or implicit— as fixed costs, since producing more or less output in the short run will not cause any of these costs to change. Managers typically refer to fixed costs as their *overhead costs*, or simply, overhead.

Variable costs Costs of variable inputs.

The costs of obtaining the firm's variable inputs are its **variable costs**. These costs, like the usage of variable inputs themselves, will rise as output increases. Most businesses treat the wages of hourly employees and the costs of raw materials as variable costs, since quantities of both labor and raw materials can usually be adjusted rather rapidly.

Measuring Short-Run Costs

In Table 3, we return to our mythical firm—Spotless Car Wash—and ask: What happens to *costs* as output changes in the short run? The first three columns of the table give the relationship between inputs and outputs—the production function— just as in Table 1 a few pages earlier. But there is one slight difference: In Table 3, we've reversed the order of the columns, putting total output first. We are changing our perspective slightly: Now we want to observe how a change in the quantity of *output* causes the firm's *inputs*—and therefore its *costs*—to change.

In addition to Spotless's production function, we need to know one more thing before we can analyze its costs: what it must *pay* for its inputs. In Table 3, the price of labor is set at $60 per worker per day, and the price of each automated car-washing line at $75 per day.

How do Spotless's short-run costs change as its output changes? Get ready, because there are a surprising number of different ways to answer that question, as illustrated in the remaining columns of Table 3.

(1) Output (per Day)	(2) Capital	(3) Labor	(4) TFC	(5) TVC	(6) TC	(7) MC	(8) AFC	(9) AVC	(10) ATC
	Labor cost = $60 per day					Capital cost = $75 per day			
0	1	0	$75	$ 0	$ 75		—	—	—
						$2.00			
30	1	1	$75	$ 60	$135		$2.50	$2.00	$4.50
						$1.00			
90	1	2	$75	$120	$195		$0.83	$1.33	$2.17
						$1.50			
130	1	3	$75	$180	$255		$0.58	$1.38	$1.96
						$1.94			
161	1	4	$75	$240	$315		$0.48	$1.49	$1.96
						$2.61			
184	1	5	$75	$300	$375		$0.44	$1.63	$2.04
						$5.00			
196	1	6	$75	$360	$435		$0.41	$1.84	$2.22

TABLE 3
Short-Run Costs for Spotless Car Wash

Total Costs. Columns 4, 5, and 6 in the table show three different types of total costs. In column 4, we have Spotless's **total fixed cost** (TFC), the cost of all inputs that are fixed in the short run. Like the quantity of fixed inputs themselves, fixed costs remain the same no matter what the level of output.

Total fixed cost The cost of all inputs that are fixed in the short run.

For Spotless Car Wash, the daily cost of renting or owning one automated line is $75, so total fixed cost is $75. Running down the column, you can see that this cost—because it is fixed—remains the same no matter how many cars are washed each day.

Column 5 shows **total variable cost** (TVC), the cost of all variable inputs. For Spotless, labor is the only variable input. As output increases, more labor will be needed, so TVC will rise. For example, to wash 90 cars each day requires 2 workers, and each worker must be paid $60 per day, so TVC will be 2 × $60 = $120. But to wash 130 cars requires 3 workers, so TVC will rise to 3 × $60 = $180.

Finally, column 6 shows us that

Total variable cost The cost of all variable inputs used in producing a particular level of output.

total cost (TC) *is the sum of all fixed and variable costs:*

TC = TFC + TVC.

Total cost The costs of all inputs—fixed and variable.

For example, at 90 units of output, TFC = $75 and TVC = $120, so TC = $75 + $120 = $195. Because total variable cost rises with output, total cost rises as well.

Now look at Figure 4, where we've graphed all three total cost curves for Spotless Car Wash. Both the TC and TVC curves slope upward, since these costs increase along with output. Notice that there are *two* ways in which TFC is represented in the graph. One is the TFC curve, which is a horizontal line, since TFC has the same value at any level of output. The other is the *vertical distance* between the rising TVC and TC curves, since TFC is always the *difference* between TVC and TC. In the graph, this vertical distance must remain the same, at $75, no matter what the level of output.

FIGURE 4
The Firm's Total Cost Curves

At any level of output, total cost (TC) is the sum of total fixed cost (TFC) and total variable cost (TVC).

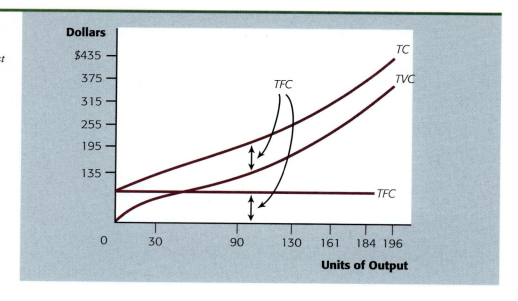

Average Costs. While total costs are important, sometimes it is more useful to track a firm's costs *per unit* of output, which we call its *average cost*. There are three different types of average cost, each obtained from one of the total cost concepts just discussed.

Average fixed cost Total fixed cost divided by the quantity of output produced.

> *The firm's **average fixed cost** (AFC) is its total fixed cost divided by the quantity (Q) of output:*
>
> $$\text{AFC} = \frac{\text{TFC}}{\text{Q}}.$$

No matter what kind of production or what kind of firm, *AFC* will always fall as output rises. Why? Because *TFC* remains constant, so a rise in *Q must* cause the ratio *TFC/Q* to fall. Business managers often refer to this decline in *AFC* as "spreading their overhead" over more output. For example, a restaurant has overhead costs for its buildings, furniture, and cooking equipment. The more meals it serves, the lower will be its overhead cost per meal. Does *AFC* fall with output at Spotless Car Wash? Look at Table 3, column 8. When output is 30 units, *AFC* is $75/30 = $2.50. But at 90 units of output, *AFC* drops to $75/90 = $0.83. And *AFC* keeps declining as we continue down the column. The more output produced, the lower is fixed cost per unit of output.

Average variable cost Total variable cost divided by the quantity of output produced.

> *Average variable cost (AVC) is the cost of the variable inputs per unit of output:*
>
> $$\text{AVC} = \frac{\text{TVC}}{\text{Q}}.$$

AVC is shown in column 9 of the table. For example, at 30 units of output, *TVC* = $60, so *AVC* = *TVC/Q* = $60/30 = $2.00.

What happens to *AVC* as output rises? Based on mathematics alone, we can't be sure. On the one hand, a rise in *Q* raises the denominator of the fraction *TVC/Q*. On the other hand, *TVC* increases, so the numerator rises as well. Thus, it's possible for *AVC* to either rise or fall, depending on whether *TVC* or *Q* rises by a greater percentage. But if you run your finger down the *AVC* column in Table 3, you'll see a pattern: The *AVC* numbers first decrease and then increase. Economists believe that this pattern of decreasing and then increasing average variable cost is typical at many firms. When plotted in Figure 5, this pattern causes the *AVC* curve to have a U shape. We'll discuss the reason for this characteristic U shape a bit later.

> *Average total cost* (ATC) *is the total cost per unit of output:*
>
> $$ATC = \frac{TC}{Q}.$$

Average total cost Total cost divided by the quantity of output produced.

Values for *ATC* are listed in column 10 of Table 3. For example, at 90 units of output, *TC* = $195, so *ATC* = *TC/Q* = $195/90 = $2.17. As output rises, *ATC*, like *AVC*, can either rise or fall, since both the numerator and denominator of the fraction *TC/Q* rises. (See Table 3, column 10.) But we usually expect *ATC*, like *AVC*, to first decrease and then increase, so the *ATC* curve will also be U-shaped. However—as you can see in Figure 5—it is not identical to the *AVC* curve. At each level of output, the vertical distance between the two curves is equal to average *fixed* cost (*AFC*). Since *AFC* declines as output increases, the *ATC* curve and the *AVC* curve must get closer and closer together as we move rightward.

Marginal Cost. The total and average costs we've considered so far tell us about the firm's cost at a particular *level* of output. For many purposes, however, we are more interested in how cost *changes* when output *changes*. This information is provided by another cost concept:

> *Marginal cost* (MC) *is the change in total cost* (ΔTC) *divided by the change in output* (ΔQ):
>
> $$MC = \frac{\Delta TC}{\Delta Q}.$$
>
> *It tells us how much cost rises* per unit *increase in output.*

Marginal cost The increase in total cost from producing one more unit of output.

For Spotless Car Wash, marginal cost is entered in column 7 of Table 3 and graphed in Figure 5. Since marginal cost tells us what happens to total cost when output *changes*, the entries in the table are placed *between* one output level and another. For example, when output rises from 0 to 30, total cost rises from $75 to $135. For this change in output, we have Δ*TC* = $135 − $75 = $60, while Δ*Q* = 30, so *MC* = $60/30 = $2.00. This entry is listed *between* the output levels 0 and 30 in the table.

Explaining the Shape of the Marginal Cost Curve

Marginal cost is graphed in Figure 5. As in the table, each value of marginal cost is plotted *between* output levels. For example, the marginal cost of increasing output

FIGURE 5
Average and Marginal Costs

Average variable cost (AVC) *and average total cost* (ATC) *are U-shaped, first decreasing and then increasing. Average fixed cost* (AFC), *the vertical distance between* ATC *and* AVC, *becomes smaller as output increases.*

The marginal cost (MC) *curve is also U-shaped, reflecting first increasing and then diminishing marginal returns to labor.* MC *passes through the minimum points of both the* AVC *and* ATC *curves.*

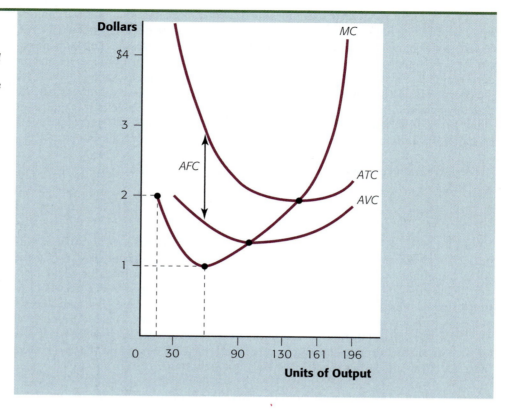

from 0 to 30 is $2, and this is plotted at output level 15—midway between 0 and 30. Similarly, when going from 30 to 90 units of output, the MC is plotted midway between 30 and 90. (For now, ignore the other bulleted points.)

The marginal cost curve has an important relationship to the total cost curve. As you can see in Figure 4, the total cost (TC) is plotted on the vertical axis, and quantity (Q) on the horizontal axis, so the slope along any interval is just $\Delta TC / \Delta Q$. But this is exactly the definition of marginal cost.

> *The marginal cost for any change in output is equal to the* slope *of the total cost curve along that interval of output.*

If you look carefully at the TC curve in Figure 4, you'll see that while its slope is always positive, it first decreases (the TC curve gets flatter), then increases (gets steeper). Correspondingly, in Figure 5, MC first declines and then rises. Why is this? Here, we can use what we learned earlier about marginal returns to labor. At low levels of employment and output, there are increasing marginal returns to labor: $MPL = \Delta Q/\Delta L$ is rising. That is, each worker hired adds more to production than the worker before. But that means that *fewer additional workers are needed to produce an additional unit of output*. Now, since additional labor is this firm's only cost of increasing production, the cost of an additional unit of output (MC) must be falling. Thus, as long as MPL is rising, MC must be falling.

For Spotless, since MPL rises when employment increases from zero to one and then one to two workers, MC must fall as the firm's output rises from zero to 30 units (produced by one worker) and then from 30 to 90 units (produced by two workers).

At higher levels of output, we have the opposite situation: Diminishing marginal returns set in and the marginal product of labor ($\Delta Q/\Delta L$) falls. Therefore, additional units of output require *more* and *more* additional labor. As a result, each additional unit of output costs more and more to produce. Thus, as long as *MPL* is falling, *MC* must be rising.

For Spotless, diminishing marginal returns to labor occur for all workers beyond the second, so *MC* rises for all increases in output beyond the change from 30 to 90.

To sum up:

> *When the marginal product of labor (MPL) rises, marginal cost (MC) falls. When MPL falls, MC rises. Since MPL ordinarily rises and then falls, MC will do the opposite: It will fall and then rise. Thus, the MC curve is U-shaped.*

The Relationship Between Average and Marginal Costs

Although marginal cost and average cost are not the same, there is an important relationship between them. Look again at Figure 5 and notice that all three curves—*MC*, *AVC*, and *ATC*—first fall and then rise, but not all at the same time. The *MC* curve bottoms out before either the *AVC* or *ATC* curve. Further, the *MC* curve intersects each of the average curves *at their lowest points*. These graphical features of Figure 5 are no accident; indeed, they follow from the laws of mathematics. To understand this, let's consider a related example with which you are probably more familiar.

An Example: Average and Marginal Test Scores. Suppose you take five tests in your economics course during the term, with the results listed in Table 4. To your immense pleasure, you score 100 on your first test. Your total score—the total number of points you have received thus far during the term—is 100. Your marginal score—the *change* in your total caused by the most recent test—will also be 100, since your total rose from 0 to 100. Your average score so far is 100 as well.

Number of Tests Taken	Total Score	Marginal Score	Average Score
0	0		—
		100	
1	100		100
		50	
2	150		75
		60	
3	210		70
		70	
4	280		70
		80	
5	360		72

TABLE 4
Average and Marginal Test Scores

Now suppose that, for the second test, you forget to study actively. Instead, you just read the text while simultaneously watching music videos and eavesdropping on your roommate's phone conversations. As a result, you get a 50. Your marginal score is 50. Since this score is lower than your previous average of 100, the second test will pull your average down. Indeed, whenever you score lower than your previous average, you will always decrease the average. In the table, we see that your average after the second test falls to 75.

Now you start to worry, so you turn off the TV while studying, and your performance improves a bit: You get a 60. Does the improvement in your score—from 50 to 60—increase your *average* score? Absolutely not. Your average will decrease once again, because your *marginal* score of 60 is *still* lower than your previous average of 75. As we know, when you score lower than your average, it pulls the average down, even if you're improving. In the table, we see that your average now falls to 70.

For your fourth exam, you study a bit harder and score a 70. This time, since your score is precisely *equal* to your previous average, the average remains unchanged at 70.

Finally, on your fifth and last test, your score improves once again, this time to 80. This time, you've scored *higher* than your previous average, pulling your average up from 70 to 72.

This example may be easy to understand because you are used to figuring out your average score in a course as you take additional exams. But the relationship between marginal and average spelled out here is universal: It is the same for grade point averages, batting averages—*and* costs.

Average and Marginal Cost. Now let's apply our previous discussion to a firm's cost curves. Whenever marginal cost is below average cost, we know that the cost of producing *one more* unit of output is *less* than the average cost of all units produced so far. Therefore, producing one more unit will bring the average down. That is, when marginal cost is below average cost, average cost will come down. This applies to both average *variable* cost and average *total* cost.

For example, when Spotless is producing 30 units of output, its *ATC* is $4.50 and its *AVC* is $2.00 (see Table 3). But if it increases output from 30 to 90 units, the marginal cost of these *additional* units is just $1.00. Since *MC* is less than both *ATC* and *AVC* for this change, it pulls both averages down. Graphically, when the *MC* curve lies below one of the average curves (*ATC* or *AVC*), that average curve will slope downward.

Now consider a change in output from 90 units to 130 units. Marginal cost for this change is $1.50. But the *AVC* at 90 units is $1.33. Since *MC* is greater than *AVC*, this change in output will pull *AVC* up. Accordingly, the *AVC* curve begins to slope upward. However, *ATC* at 90 units is $2.17. Since *MC* is still *less* than *ATC*, the *ATC* curve will continue to slope downward.

Finally, consider what happens at higher levels of output, such as a change from 161 to 184 units. For this change in output, *MC* is $2.61, which is greater than the previous values of both *AVC* ($1.49) and *ATC* ($1.96). If the firm makes this move, both *AVC* and *ATC* will rise.

Now, let's put together what we know about marginal cost and what we know about the relationship between marginal and average cost. Remember that marginal cost drops rapidly when the firm begins increasing output from low levels of production, due to increasing marginal returns to labor. Thus, *MC* will initially drop *below* AVC and ATC, pulling these averages down. But if the firm keeps increasing its output, diminishing returns to labor will set in. *MC* will keep on rising, until it *exceeds* AVC and ATC. Once this happens, further increases in output will *raise* both AVC and ATC.

> *At low levels of output, the* MC *curve lies below the* AVC *and* ATC *curves, so these curves will slope downward. At higher levels of output, the* MC *curve will rise above the* AVC *and* ATC *curves, so these curves will slope upward. Thus, as output increases, the average curves will first slope downward and then slope upward. That is, they will have a U shape.*

This explains why, in Figure 5, both the *AVC* and *ATC* curves are U-shaped.

There is one more important observation to make before we leave the short run. We've just seen that whenever the *MC* curve lies *below* the *ATC* curve, *ATC* is falling. But when the *MC* curve crosses the *ATC* curve and rises *above* it, *ATC* will be rising. As a result, the *MC* curve must intersect the *ATC* curve at its *minimum* point, as it does in Figure 5. And the same is true of the *AVC* curve.

> *The* MC *curve will intersect the minimum points of the* AVC *and* ATC *curves.*

Time to Take a Break. By now, your mind may be swimming with concepts and terms: total, average, and marginal cost curves; fixed and variable costs; explicit and implicit costs. . . . We are covering a lot of ground here and still have a bit more to cover: production and cost in the *long run*.

As difficult as it may seem to keep these concepts straight, they will become increasingly easy to handle as you use them in the chapters to come. But it's best not to overload your brain with too much new material at one time. So if this is your first trip through this chapter, now is a good time for a break. Then, when you're fresh, come back and review the material you've read so far. When the terms and concepts start to feel familiar, you are ready to move on to the long run.

PRODUCTION AND COST IN THE LONG RUN

Most of the business firms you have contact with—such as your supermarket, the stores where you buy new clothes, your telephone company, and your Internet service provider—plan to be around for quite some time. They have a long-term planning horizon, as well as a short-term one. But so far, we've considered the behavior of costs only in the short run.

In the long run, costs behave differently, because the firm can adjust *all* of its inputs in any way it wants:

> *In the long run, there are no fixed inputs or fixed costs; all inputs and all costs are variable. The firm must decide what combination of inputs to use in producing any level of output.*

How will the firm choose? Its goal is to earn the highest possible profit, and to do this, it must follow the *least cost rule:*

HTTP://

Examples of economies of scale can be found at **http://bized.ac.uk/stafsup/options/notes/econ204.htm.**

> *To produce any given level of output, the firm will choose the input mix with the lowest cost.*

The Least Cost Rule When you read the *least cost rule* of production, you might think that the firm's long-run goal is to have the *least possible cost*. But this is not true. To convince yourself, just realize that the least possible cost would be zero, and in the long run this could be achieved by not using any inputs and producing nothing!

DANGEROUS CURVES

The least cost rule says that any *given* level of output should be produced at the lowest possible cost. The firm's goal is to maximize *profit*, and the least cost rule helps it do that. For example, if the firm is considering producing 10 units of output, and there are two ways to produce that number of units—one costing $6,000 and the other costing $5,000—the firm should always choose the latter way because it is cheaper. But notice that $5,000 is not the "lowest possible cost" for the firm; *it is the lowest possible cost for producing 10 units.*

Let's apply the least cost rule to Spotless Car Wash. Suppose we want to know the cost of washing 196 cars per day. In the short run, of course, Spotless does not have to worry about how it would produce this level of output: It is stuck with one automated line, and the only way to wash 196 cars is to hire six workers (see Table 3). Total cost in the short run will be $6 \times \$60 + \$75 = \$435$.

In the long run, however, Spotless can vary the number of automated lines as well as the number of workers. Its *long-run* production function will tell us all the different combinations of *both* inputs that can be used to produce any output level. Suppose four different input combinations can be used to wash 196 cars per day. These are listed in Table 5. Combination *A* uses the least capital and the most labor—no automated lines at all and nine workers washing the cars by hand. Combination *D* uses the most capital and the least labor—three automated lines with only three workers. Since each automated line costs $75 per day and each worker costs $60 per day, it is easy to calculate the cost of each production method. Spotless will choose the one with the lowest cost: combination *C*, with two automated lines and four workers, for a total cost of $390 per day.

Retracing our steps, we have found that if Spotless wants to wash 196 cars per day, it will examine the different methods of doing so and select the one with the least cost. Once it has determined the cheapest production method, the other, more expensive methods can be ignored.

Table 6 shows the results of going through this procedure for several different levels of output. The second column, **long-run total cost** *(LRTC)*, tells us the cost of producing each quantity of output *when the least-cost input mix is chosen.* For each output level, different production methods are examined, the cheapest one is chosen, and the others are ignored. Notice that the *LRTC* of zero units of output is $0. This will always be true for any firm. In the long run, all inputs can be adjusted as the firm wishes, and the cheapest way to produce zero output is to use *no* inputs at all. (For comparison, what is the *short*-run total cost of producing zero units? Why can it never be $0?)

Long-run total cost The cost of producing each quantity of output when all inputs are variable and the least-cost input mix is chosen.

	Method	Quantity of Capital	Quantity of Labor	Cost
TABLE 5 **Four Ways to Wash 196 Cars per Day**	A	0	9	$540
	B	1	6	$435
	C	2	4	$390
	D	3	3	$405

Output	LRTC	LRATC
0	$ 0	—
30	$ 100	$3.33
90	$ 195	$2.17
130	$ 255	$1.96
161	$ 315	$1.96
184	$ 360	$1.96
196	$ 390	$1.99
250	$ 650	$2.60
300	$1,200	$4.00

TABLE 6
Long-Run Costs for Spotless Car Wash

The third column in Table 6 gives the **long-run average total cost** *(LRATC)*, the cost per unit of output in the long run:

$$LRATC = \frac{LRTC}{Q}.$$

Long-run average total cost The cost per unit of producing each quantity of output in the long run, when all inputs are variable.

Long-run average total cost is similar to average total cost, which was defined earlier. Both are obtained by dividing total cost by the level of output. There is one important difference, however: To calculate *ATC*, we used total cost *(TC)*, which pertains to the short run, in the numerator. In calculating *LRATC,* we use *long-run* total cost *(LRTC)* in the numerator. Thus, *LRATC* tells us the cost per unit when the firm can vary *all* of its inputs and always chooses the cheapest input mix possible. *ATC,* however, tells us the cost per unit when the firm is stuck with some collection of fixed inputs.

The Relationship Between Long-Run and Short-Run Costs

If you compare Table 6 (long run) with Table 3 (short run), you will see something important: For some output levels, *LRTC* is smaller than *TC.* For example, Spotless can wash 196 cars for an *LRTC* of $390. But earlier, we saw that in the short run, the *TC* of washing these same 196 cars was $435. To understand the reason for this difference, look back at Table 5, which lists the four different ways of washing 196 cars per day. In the short run, the firm is stuck with just one automated line, so its only option is method *B.* In the long run, however, the firm can adjust *all* of its inputs, so it can choose any of the four methods of production, including method *C,* which is cheapest. In many cases, the freedom to choose among different production methods enables the firm to select a cheaper input mix in the long run than it can in the short run. Thus, in the long run, the firm may be able to save money.

But not always. At some output levels, the freedom to adjust all inputs doesn't save the firm a dime. To wash 130 cars, for example, the long-run cost—the cost when using the cheapest input mix—is the same as the short-run total cost (*LRTC* = *TC* ($255). For this output level, it must be that the *short-run* input mix is also the least-cost input mix. Thus, if Spotless wants to wash 130 cars per day, it would choose in the long run the same production method it is already using in the short run. At this output level, the firm could not save money by adjusting its capital in the long run. (There are other output levels listed in the tables for which $LRTC = TC$. Can you find them?)

What we have found for Spotless Car Wash is true for all firms:

> *The long-run total cost of producing a given level of output can be less than or equal to, but not greater than, the short-run total cost* (LRTC ≤ TC).

We can also state this relationship in terms of *average* costs. That is, we can divide both sides of the inequality by Q and obtain $LRTC/Q \le TC/Q$. Using our definitions, this translates to $LRATC \le ATC$.

> *The long-run average cost of producing a given level of output can be less than or equal to, but not greater than, the short-run average total cost* (LRATC ≤ ATC).

Average Cost and Plant Size. Often, economists refer to the collection of fixed inputs at the firm's disposal as its *plant*. For example, the plant of a computer manufacturer such as Dell would include its factory buildings and the assembly lines inside them. The plant of the Hertz car-rental company would include all of its automobiles and rental offices. For Spotless Car Wash, we've assumed that the plant is simply the company's capital equipment—the automated lines for washing cars. If Spotless were to add to its capital, then each time it acquired another automated line, it would have a different, and larger, plant. Viewed in this way, we can distinguish between the long run and the short run as follows: *In the long run, the firm can change the size of its plant; in the short run, it is stuck with its current plant.*

Now think about the *ATC* curve, which tells us the firm's average total cost in the short run. This curve is always drawn for a specific plant. That is, the *ATC* curve tells us how average cost behaves in the short run, *when the firm uses a plant of a given size.* If the firm had a different-size plant, it would be moving along a different *ATC* curve. In fact, there is a different *ATC* curve for each different plant the firm could have. In the long run, then, the firm can choose on which *ATC* curve it wants to operate. And, as we know, to produce any level of output, it will always choose that *ATC* curve—among all of the *ATC* curves available—that enables it to produce at lowest possible average total cost. This insight tells us how we can graph the firm's *LRATC* curve.

Graphing the *LRATC* Curve. Look at Figure 6, which shows several different *ATC* curves for Spotless Car Wash. There is a lot going on in this figure, so let's take it one step at a time. First, find the curve labeled ATC_1. This is our familiar *ATC* curve—the same one shown in Figure 5—which we used to find Spotless's average total cost in the short run, when it was stuck with one automated line.

The other *ATC* curves refer to *different* plants that Spotless *might* have had instead. For example, the curve labeled ATC_0 shows how average total cost would behave if Spotless had a plant with *zero* automated lines; ATC_2 shows average total cost with *two* automated lines, and so on. Since, in the long run, the firm can choose which size plant to operate, it can also choose on which of these *ATC* curves it wants to operate. And, as we know, in the long run, it will always choose the plant with the lowest possible average total cost.

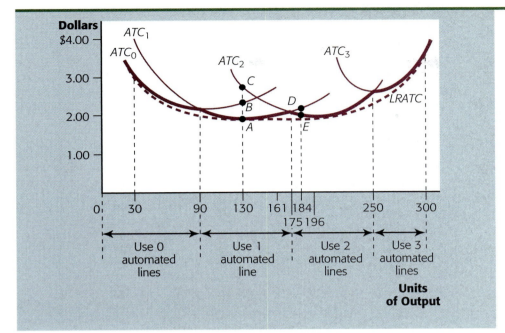

FIGURE 6
Long-Run Average Total Cost

Average-total cost curves ATC_0, ATC_1, ATC_2, *and* ATC_3 *show average costs when the firm has zero, one, two, and three production lines, respectively. The LRATC curve combines portions of all the firm's ATC curves. The firm will choose the lowest-cost ATC curve for each level of output.*

Let's take a specific example. Suppose that Spotless thinks that it might wash 130 cars per day. In the long run, what size plant should it choose? Scanning the different *ATC* curves in Figure 6, we see that the lowest possible per-unit cost—$1.96 per car—is at point *A* along ATC_1. The best plant for washing 130 cars per day, therefore, will have just one automated line. For this output level, Spotless would never choose a plant with zero lines, since it would then have to operate on ATC_0 at point *B*. Since point *B* is higher than point *A*, we know that point *B* represents a larger per-unit cost. Nor would the firm choose a plant with two lines—operating on ATC_2 at point *C*—for this would mean a still larger per-unit cost. Of all the possibilities, only point *A* along ATC_1 enables Spotless to achieve the lowest per-unit cost for washing 130 cars. Thus, to produce 130 units of output in the long run, Spotless would choose to operate at point *A* on ATC_1. Point *A* is the *LRATC* of 130 units.

Now, suppose instead that Spotless wanted to produce 184 units of output in the long run. A plant with one automated line is no longer the best choice. Instead, the firm would choose a plant with *two* automated lines. How do we know? For an output of 184, the firm could choose point *D* on ATC_1, or point *E* on ATC_2. Since point *E* is lower, it is the better choice. At this point, average total cost would be $1.96, so this would be the *LRATC* of 184 units.

Continuing in this way, we could find the *LRATC* for *every* output level Spotless might produce. To produce any given level of output, the firm will always operate on the *lowest ATC* curve available. As output increases, it will move along an *ATC* curve until another, lower *ATC* curve becomes available—one with lower costs. At that point, the firm will increase its plant size, so it can move to the lower *ATC* curve. In the graph, as Spotless increases its output level from 90 to 175 units of output, it will continue to use a plant with one automated line and move along ATC_1. But if it wants to produce *more* than 175 units in the long run, it will increase its plant to *two* automated lines and begin moving along ATC_2.

Thus, we can trace out Spotless's *LRATC* curve by combining just the lowest portions of all the *ATC* curves from which the firm can choose. In Figure 6, this is the thick, scallop-shaped curve.

A firm's *LRATC* curve combines portions of each *ATC* curve available to the firm in the long run. For each output level, the firm will always choose to operate on the *ATC* curve with the lowest possible cost.

Figure 6 also gives us a view of the different options facing the firm in the short run and the long run. Once Spotless builds a plant with one automated line, its options in the short run are limited: It can only move along ATC_1. If it wants to increase its output from 130 to 184 units, it must move from point *A* to point *D*. But in the long run, it can move along its *LRATC* curve—from point *A* to point *E*—by changing the size of its plant.

More generally,

> *in the short run, a firm can only move along its current* ATC *curve. In the long run, however, it can move from one* ATC *curve to another by varying the size of its plant. As it does so, it will also be moving along its* LRATC *curve.*

Explaining the Shape of the *LRATC* Curve

In Figure 6, the *LRATC* curve has a scalloped look because the firm can only choose among four different plants. But many firms—especially large ones—can choose among hundreds or even thousands of different plant sizes. Each plant would be represented by a different *ATC* curve, so there would be hundreds of *ATC* curves crowded into the figure. As a result, the scallops would disappear, and the *LRATC* curve would appear as a smooth curve, like the dashed line in Figure 6.

In Figure 7, which reproduces this smoothed-out *LRATC* curve, you can see that the curve is U-shaped—much like the *AVC* and *ATC* curves you learned about earlier. That is, as output increases, long-run average costs first decline, then remain constant, and finally rise. Although there is no law or rule of logic that requires an *LRATC* curve to have all three of these phases, in many industries this seems to be the case. Let's see why, by considering each of the three phases in turn.

Economies of Scale. When an increase in output causes *LRATC* to decrease, we say that the firm is enjoying **economies of scale**: the more output produced, the lower the cost per unit.

Economies of scale Long-run average total cost decreases as output increases.

On a purely mathematical level, economies of scale mean that long-run total cost is rising by a smaller proportion than output. For example, if a doubling of output (Q) can be accomplished with less than a doubling of costs, then the ratio $LRTC/Q = LRATC$ will decline, and—voilà!—economies of scale.

> *When long-run total cost rises proportionately less than output, production is characterized by economies of scale, and the* LRATC *curve slopes downward.*

So much for the mathematics. But in the real world, *why* should total costs ever increase by a smaller proportion than output? Why should a firm experience economies of scale?

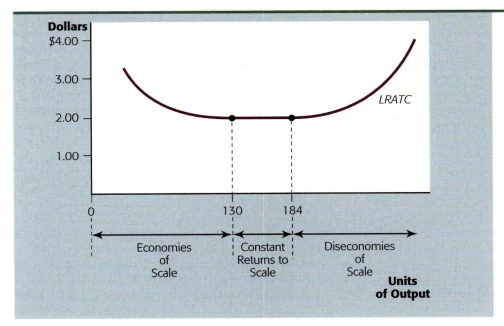

FIGURE 7
The Shape of *LRATC*

If long-run total cost rises proportionately less than output, production reflects economies of scale, and LRATC slopes downward. If cost rises proportionately more than output, there are diseconomies of scale, and LRATC slopes upward. Between those regions, cost and output rise proportionately, yielding constant returns to scale.

Gains from Specialization. One reason for economies of scale is gains from specialization. At very low levels of output, workers may have to perform a greater variety of tasks, slowing them down and making them less productive. But as output increases and workers are added, more possibilities for specialization are created. At Spotless, an increase in output and employment might permit one worker to specialize in taking cash from customers, a second to drive the cars onto the line, a third to towel them down, a fourth to work on advertising, and so on. Since each worker is more productive, output will increase by a greater proportion than costs.

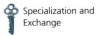
Specialization and Exchange

The greatest opportunities for increased specialization occur when a firm is producing at a relatively low level of output, with a relatively small plant and small workforce. Thus, economies of scale are more likely to occur at lower levels of output.

More Efficient Use of Lumpy Inputs. Another explanation for economies of scale involves the "lumpy" nature of many types of plant and equipment. **Lumpy inputs** are inputs that cannot be increased in tiny increments, but rather must be increased in large jumps.

Lumpy input An input whose quantity cannot be increased gradually as output increases, but must instead be adjusted in large jumps.

A doctor, for example, needs the use of an X-ray machine in order to serve her patients. Unless she can share with other doctors (which may not be possible), she must buy one or more *whole* machines; she cannot buy a half or a fifth of an X-ray machine. Suppose a single machine can service up to 500 patients per month and costs $2,000 per month (in interest payments or foregone investment income). Then the more patients the doctor sees (up to 500), the lower will be the cost of the machine per patient. For example, if she sees 100 patients each month, the cost per patient will be $2,000/100 = $20. If she sees 500 patients, the cost per patient drops to $2,000/500 = $4. If much of the doctor's plant and equipment are lumpy in this way, her *LRATC* curve might continue to decline over some range of output.

We see this phenomenon in many types of businesses: Plant and equipment must be purchased in large lumps, and a low cost per unit is achieved only at high levels of output. If you decide to start a pizza delivery business on campus, you will have to purchase or rent at least one pizza oven. If you can make 200 pizzas per day with a single oven, then your total oven costs will be the same whether you bake 1, 10, 50, 100, or 200 pizzas. The more pizzas you make, the lower will be your oven costs *per pizza*.

Other inputs besides equipment can also be lumpy in this way. Restaurants must pay a yearly license fee and are not permitted to buy part of a license if their output is small. An answering service must have a receptionist on duty at all times, even if only a few calls come in each day. A theater must have at least one ticket seller and one projectionist, regardless of how many people come to see the show. In all of these cases, an increase in output allows the firm to spread the cost of lumpy inputs over greater amounts of output, lowering the cost *per unit of output*.

Making more efficient use of lumpy inputs will have more impact on *LRATC* at low levels of output when these inputs make up a greater proportion of the firm's total costs. At higher levels of output, the impact is smaller. For example, suppose a restaurant must pay a yearly license fee of $1,000. If output doubles from 1,000 to 2,000 meals per year, license costs per meal served will fall from $1 to $0.50. But if output doubles from 10,000 to 20,000 meals, license costs per meal drop from $0.10 to $0.05—a hardly noticeable difference. Thus, spreading lumpy inputs across more output—like the gains from specialization—is more likely to create economies of scale at relatively low levels of output. This is another reason why the typical *LRATC* curve—as illustrated in Figure 7—slopes downward at relatively low levels of output.

A look back at Table 6 shows that there are, indeed, economies of scale for Spotless at low levels of output. It costs $100 to wash 30 cars and $195 to wash 90 cars. As output triples from 30 to 90, costs increase by only *$95/$100*, or 95 percent, so *LRATC* falls. Spotless is clearly enjoying economies of scale. Indeed, Figure 7 shows that it will experience economies of scale for all output levels up to 130 units.

Diseconomies of Scale. As output continues to increase, most firms will reach a point where bigness begins to cause problems. This is true even in the long run, when the firm is free to increase its plant size as well as its workforce. Large firms may require more layers of management, so communication and decision making become more time consuming and costly. Huge corporations like IBM, General Motors, and Verizon each have several hundred high-level managers, and thousands more at lower levels. Indeed, for much of the 1980s, IBM was criticized by its stockholders for the failure of its large, sluggish, managerial bureaucracy to keep up with rapid changes in the market for small computers. Large firms may also have a harder time screening out misfits among new hires and monitoring those already working at the firm, so there is an increase in mistakes, shirking of responsibilities, and even theft from the firm. These problems contribute to rises in *LRTC* as output increases, and work in the opposite direction to the forces helping to create economies of scale. When the firm reaches a certain size—and has exploited all major cost savings from "bigness"—these problems will start to dominate. And as the firm continues to grow larger, *LRATC* will rise.

More generally,

Diseconomies of scale Long-run average total cost increases as output increases.

when long-run total cost rises more than in proportion to output, there are diseconomies of scale, and the LRATC curve slopes upward.

While economies of scale are more likely at low levels of output, *dis*economies of scale are more likely at higher output levels. In Figure 7, you can see that Spotless does not experience diseconomies of scale until it is washing more than 184 cars per day.

Constant Returns to Scale. In Figure 7, you can see that for output levels between 130 and 184, the smoothed-out *LRATC* curve is roughly flat. Over this range of output, *LRATC* remains approximately constant as output increases. Here, output and *LRTC* rise by roughly the same proportion:

> *When both output and long-run total cost rise by the same proportion, production is characterized by **constant returns to scale**, and the* LRATC *curve is flat.*

Constant returns to scale Long-run average total cost is unchanged as output increases.

Why would a firm experience constant returns to scale? We have seen that as output increases, cost savings from specialization and more efficient use of lumpy inputs will eventually be exhausted. But production may still have room to expand before the costly problems of "bigness" kick in. The firm will then have a range of output over which average cost neither rises nor falls as production increases—constant returns to scale. Notice that constant returns to scale, if present at all, are most likely to occur at some *intermediate* range of output.

In sum, when we look at the behavior of *LRATC*, we often expect a pattern like the following: economies of scale (decreasing *LRATC*) at relatively low levels of output, constant returns to scale (constant *LRATC*) at some intermediate levels of output, and diseconomies of scale (increasing *LRATC*) at relatively high levels of output. This is why *LRATC* curves are typically U-shaped.

Of course, even U-shaped *LRATC* curves will have different appearances for firms in different industries. And as you're about to see, these differences in *LRATC* curves have much to tell us about the economy.

USING THE THEORY
Long-Run Costs, Market Structure, and Mergers

If you want to buy a television, you can choose from among dozens of brands—Sony, Panasonic, Philips, JVC, Hitachi, and more—from among dozens of stores—Circuit City, Fry's, Best Buy, and other large chains, as well as a selection of small local stores. But if you want to hook up to cable, there will be only one company you can call: the one cable service provider in your area.

The same applies in many other markets in which you buy goods and services. For some purchases, you can choose from among many suppliers, such as manufacturers (of furniture, shoes, or computers) and retailers (of books, cars, and clothes). For other purchases, you've got only a few choices (such as cell phone service), and occasionally, just one (such as cross-country trains, regular mail delivery, and—in most areas—electricity).

The number of firms in a market is an important aspect of *market structure,* a general term for the environment in which trading takes place. What accounts for these differences in the number of sellers in the market? The shape of the *LRATC* curve plays an important role in the answer.

© JEFF ZARUBA/CORBIS

LRATC and the Size of Firms

Figure 8 shows how the *LRATC* curve might look for four different firms, each producing different types of goods in different markets. (For now, to make our analysis as general as possible, we won't name the specific goods.) Look first at panel (a) (ignore the demand curve for now). Notice that the *LRATC* curve for this firm displays economies of scale (slopes downward) up to an output level of 1,000 units per month, and then hits bottom before rising sharply. The output level at which the *LRATC* first hits bottom is known as the **minimum efficient scale (MES)** for the firm, the lowest level of output at which it can achieve minimum cost per unit. In the figure, if this firm were producing at its MES of 1,000 units, its long-run cost per unit would be $80. Moreover, if this *LRATC* curve is typical of *all* firms in the market, then $80 is the *lowest possible long-run price* in this market. We know this because if the price were any *less* than $80, the typical firm would eventually go out of business (it would be charging less for the good than the lowest possible cost of producing it).

Once we know the lowest possible price for this good, we can also determine the *maximum possible total quantity demanded* by using the market demand curve. In panel (a), for example, the market demand curve tells us that when price is $80, quantity demanded is 100,000 units. If the price can't be any lower than $80 in the long run, then market quantity demanded can't be any *greater* than 100,000 units.

Now let's apply these two curves—the *LRATC* for the *typical firm,* and the demand curve for the *entire market*—to market structure. When the MES is small relative to the maximum potential market as in panel (a), firms that are *relatively small* will have a cost advantage over relatively large firms. In the figure, a firm supplying just 1 percent of the maximum market (1,000 units out of 100,000) will put the firm at point *E* on its *LRATC* curve, with cost per unit of $80. The cost per unit of a larger firm—say, one producing 3,000 units at point *F*—would be $160. A firm this large would be unable to compete with its smaller rivals.

Accordingly, we'd expect a market in which firms have this type of *LRATC* curve to be populated by many small firms, each producing for only a tiny share of the market. In most cities, markets for personal services fit this pattern—haircuts, shoe repair, home remodeling, plumbing, lawn care, massages, and so on. For such businesses, economies of scale—from specialization and spreading lumpy inputs over more production—are exhausted rather rapidly, and then significant diseconomies of scale set in—perhaps from the difficulties of monitoring employees who are "in the field" performing services.

Panel (b) shows the opposite extreme: significant economies of scale that continue as output increases, even to the point where a typical firm is supplying the maximum possible quantity demanded. In such a market, a single, large firm enjoys a cost advantage over a smaller one. Once a single firm enters and expands production to reach most of the potential quantity demanded, it has already achieved a lower cost per unit than any new competitor could hope to achieve. Since this market will gravitate naturally toward *monopoly,* a market with just one seller, we call the market—as well as the single firm operating there—a **natural monopoly.** Regular mail delivery, cable television service, and city subway systems are all examples of natural monopolies, where the required lumpy inputs are so costly that even producing for the entire market does not exhaust economies of scale.

Minimum efficient scale The lowest output level at which the firm's *LRATC* curve hits bottom.

Natural monopoly A market in which a single firm's production is characterized by economies of scale, even when its output expands to serve the entire market.

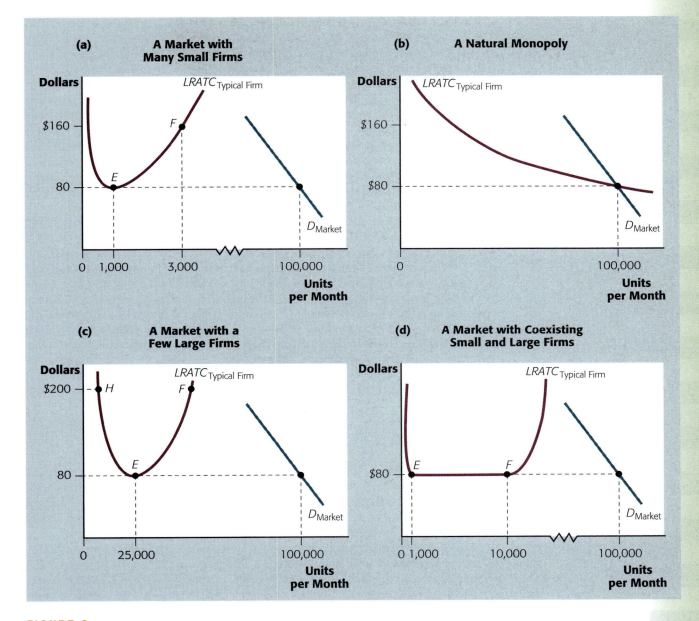

FIGURE 8

How *LRATC* Helps Explain Market Structure

In panel (a), the typical firm's MES occurs at an output level of 1,000—very small compared to the maximum potential market of 100,000. A small firm producing at point E has a cost advantage over a large firm producing at point F.

In panel (b), the typical firm's MES occurs beyond the maximum potential market. A single large firm producing at or near point E has a cost advantage over a smaller firm producing for just part of the market.

In panel (c), the typical firm's MES occurs at a relatively large fraction of the maximum potential market. A large firm producing at or near point E has a cost advantage over a smaller firm producing at point H, or an even larger firm producing at point F.

In panel (d), the MES occurs at a small fraction of the maximum potential market. But neither a small firm producing at point E nor a large firm producing at point F has a cost advantage over the other.

Panel (c) shows a third possibility. Here, the MES occurs at 25,000 units, which is 25 percent of the maximum potential market. In this type of market, we'd expect to see a few large competitors. Each of them would have a cost advantage over any single firm that tried to supply for the entire market on its own, but also have a cost advantage over a very small firm. This market has room for a few large competitors, but just a few. (Use the graph to prove to yourself that a smaller firm producing, say, just 5,000 units, or a larger firm producing, say, 50,000 units would have higher cost per unit than the 25,000-unit firm.) Examples of markets like this—where we'd expect to see (and do see) just a few firms—are manufacturers of passenger aircraft, airlines, pharmaceuticals, college textbook publishers, and online booksellers. In each of these cases, there are significant lumpy inputs that create economies of scale until each firm has expanded to produce for a relatively large share of the market.

Finally, look at panel (d). The MES of the typical firm in this market is 1,000 units, the lowest output level at which it reaches minimum cost per unit. But for firms in this market, diseconomies of scale don't set in until output exceeds 10,000 units. In between, firms experience constant returns to scale. Since both small and large firms can have equally low average costs, with neither having any advantage over the other, firms of varying sizes can coexist. Examples are orange producers (where large conglomerates coexist with small farmers), clothing stores (Macy's and the Gap coexist with the local men's and women's clothing shops), electronics retailers, law firms, and colleges. (More than half of all colleges and universities in the United States have fewer than 2,000 students. But they coexist with dozens of mega-universities, such as the University of Texas at Austin [the largest public] with 49,000 students, or New York University [the largest private] with 37,000 students.)

The Urge to Merge

Look again at panel (c), but now imagine that—for some reason—this market has 10 firms each with the *LRATC* shown there, and each is operating at point *H*, with cost per unit of $200. We'll assume that price is *at least* $200, so these firms can survive for the moment (which means that market quantity demanded must be *less* than its maximum potential of 100,000).

Each of these firms would want to expand in order to achieve the cost efficiencies that economies of scale makes possible. But they can't *all* expand to their MES of 25,000, because then market output would be 10 × 25,000 = 250,000, larger than the maximum potential quantity demanded. We'd expect to see cutthroat competition, with each firm trying to steal market share from the others. Eventually, some firms might expand, while others, seeing their market shrink further and their costs rise, might be forced out of business.

But something else might happen as well: Two of these small firms might realize that, by merging to form a larger, single firm with double the output, they could slide down the *LRATC* curve in the figure and enjoy a significant cost advantage over the other, still-smaller firms. This is a market that is ripe for a merger wave. In fact, any firm that *didn't* merge with another, or find some other way to expand, would likely be forced out of business, unable to compete with its larger and lower-cost rivals.

When market conditions are stable for long periods of time, we'd expect that firms would have already expanded to exploit economies of scale, through mergers or other means. So a sudden merger wave is usually set off by some *change* in the market. And recent history gives us some examples.

Consider the banking industry. For decades, commercial banks were prohibited from operating in more than one state. While estimates of the MES for banking have been controversial, it was likely that banks, especially in small states with smaller markets, were operating at output levels below their MES. Then, in the 1990s, a series of government policy changes, culminating in the Interstate Banking and Branching Efficiency Act of 1994, effectively ended the restrictions on interstate banking. The result was a wave of bank mergers that decreased the number of commercial banks by 30 percent—from 12,370 in 1990 to 8,698 in 1999. At the same time, the size of the average U.S. commercial bank almost doubled.

Another example is Hewlett Packard and Compaq, discussed at the beginning of this chapter. While these two firms make many products, and there were several benefits to be gained by a merger, we'll focus on just the personal computer market here.

Two major events shook the market for personal computers in 2001. One was a leftward shift in the market demand curve, largely caused by a souring economy. By itself, a shrinking market would affect all suppliers there, causing them to move leftward along their *LRATC* curves and raising cost per unit. But a second event was the determination of a nimble competitor, Dell Computer, to *gain* market share. Through cost-cutting innovations in taking orders and building machines, Dell succeeded: Its share of the world PC market rose from 9.7 percent in 1999 to 13.1 percent in early 2001. Much of this growth came at the expense of Hewlett Packard and Compaq, who each suffered a declining share of a shrinking total market. As these two firms moved leftward along their *LRATC* curves, they saw their cost per unit rising. Managers at both firms believed that a merger could reverse this move by creating one large firm with lower cost per unit.

Market structure in general, and mergers and acquisitions in particular, raise many important issues for public policy. Low-cost production can benefit consumers . . . *if* it results in lower prices. But when lower costs arise from mergers—which can reduce competition among the remaining firms—prices can rise even as costs fall. And in special markets, mergers often create special controversies. For example, in mid-2003, a Federal Communications Commission ruling made it easier for corporations to expand into local media markets, where significant, unexploited economies of scale may exist. The prospect of small, local television and radio stations being acquired by national media companies stirred a heated debate over access to diverse sources of news. We'll return to some of the public policy issues raised by different market structures in later chapters.

Summary

Business firms combine inputs to produce outputs—goods and services. A firm's *production function* describes the maximum output it can produce using different quantities of inputs. In the *short run,* at least one of the firm's inputs is fixed. In the *long run,* all inputs can be varied.

A firm's *cost of production* is the opportunity cost of its owners—everything they must give up in order to produce output. In the short run, some costs are *fixed* and independent of the level of production. Other costs—*variable costs*—change as production increases. *Marginal cost* is the change in total cost from producing one more unit of output. The *marginal cost curve* has a U shape, reflecting the underlying marginal product of labor. A variety of average cost curves can be defined. The *average variable cost curve* and the *average total*

cost curve are each U-shaped, reflecting the relationship between average and marginal cost.

In the long run, all costs are variable. The firm's *long-run total cost curve* indicates the cost of producing each quantity of output with the least-cost input mix. The related *long-run average total cost (LRATC) curve* is formed by combining portions of different *ATC* curves, each portion representing a different plant size. The shape of the *LRATC* curve reflects the nature of returns to scale. It slopes downward when there are economies of scale, slopes upward when there are diseconomies of scale, and is flat when there are constant returns to scale. Variations in the shape of the typical firm's *LRATC* curve can help explain the number of firms and the average size of firms in different industries.

Key Terms

Average fixed cost	Implicit costs	Production function
Average total cost	Increasing marginal returns to labor	Profit
Average variable cost	Law of diminishing marginal returns	Short run
Business firm	Long run	Sole proprietorship
Constant returns to scale	Long-run average total cost	Sunk costs
Corporation	Long-run total cost	Technology
Diminishing marginal returns to labor	Lumpy inputs	Total cost
Diseconomies of scale	Marginal cost	Total fixed cost
Economies of scale	Marginal product of labor	Total product
Explicit costs	Minimum efficient scale	Total variable cost
Fixed costs	Natural monopoly	Variable costs
Fixed input	Partnership	Variable input

Review Questions

1. Discuss the distinction between the short run and the long run as those terms relate to production.

2. Which of the following inputs would likely be classified as fixed and which as variable over a time horizon of one month? Why?
   a. Ovens to the Nabisco bakery
   b. Wood to the La-Z-Boy Chair Co.
   c. Oranges to Minute Maid Juice Co.
   d. Labor to a McDonald's hamburger franchise
   e. Cars to Hertz Rent-a-Car Co.

3. Explain the difference between the total output of a firm and the marginal product of labor (*MPL*) at that firm. How are they related?

4. Classify the following as fixed or variable costs for a time horizon of six months. Justify your categorization.
   a. General Motors' outlay for steel
   b. Pillsbury's rent on its corporate headquarters
   c. The cost of newsprint for the *New York Times*

5. What is the difference between marginal cost and total variable cost?

6. "Average fixed cost is the same at all levels of output." Is this statement true or false? Explain briefly.

7. ""Whenever a firm experiences diminishing returns to labor, it will experience diseconomies of scale." Is this statement true or false? Explain briefly.

Problems and Exercises

1. The following table shows total output (in tax returns completed per day) of the accounting firm of Hoodwink and Finagle:

Number of Accountants	Number of Returns per Day
0	0
1	5
2	12
3	17
4	20
5	22

Assuming the quantity of capital (computers, adding machines, desks, etc.) remains constant at all output levels:
   a. Calculate the marginal product of each accountant.
   b. Over what range of employment do you see increasing returns to labor? Diminishing returns?
   c. Explain why *MPL* might behave this way in the context of an accounting firm.

2. The following table gives the short-run and long-run total costs for various levels of output of Consolidated National Acme, Inc.:

Q	TC_1	TC_2
0	0	350
1	300	400
2	400	435
3	465	465
4	495	505
5	560	560
6	600	635
7	700	735

   a. Which column, TC_1 or TC_2, gives long-run total cost, and which gives short-run total cost? How do you know?

   b. For each level of output, find short-run *TFC, TVC, AFC, AVC,* and *MC.*
   c. At what output level would the firm's short-run and long-run input mixes be the same?
   d. Starting from producing two units, Consolidated's managers decide to double production to four units. So they simply double all of their inputs in the long run. Comment on their managerial skill.
   e. Over what range of output do you see economies of scale? Diseconomies of scale? Constant returns to scale?

3. In a recent year, a long, hard winter gave rise to stronger-than-normal demand for heating oil. The following summer was characterized by strong demand for gasoline by vacationers. Show what these two events might have done to the short-run *MC, AVC,* and *ATC* curves of Continental Airlines. (*Hint:* How would these events affect the price of oil?)

4. Ludmilla's House of Schnitzel is currently producing 10 schnitzels a day at point *A* on the following diagram. Ludmilla's business partner, Hans (an impatient sort), wants her to double production immediately.

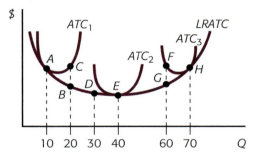

   a. What point will likely illustrate Ludmilla's cost situation for the near future? Why?
   b. If Ludmilla wants to keep producing 20 schnitzels, at what point does she want to be eventually? How can she get there?

c. Eventually, Ludmilla and company do very well, expanding until they find themselves making 70 schnitzels a day. But after a few years, Ludmilla discovers that profit was greater when she produced 20 schnitzels per day. She wants to scale back production to 20 schnitzels per day, laying off workers, selling off equipment, renting less space, and producing fewer schnitzels. Hans wants to reduce output by just cutting back on flour and milk and laying off workers. Who's right? Discuss the situation with reference to the relevant points on the diagram.

d. Does the figure tell us what output Ludmilla should aim for? Why or why not?

5. Clean 'n' Shine is a competitor to Spotless Car Wash. Like Spotless, it must pay $75 per day for each automated line it uses. But Clean 'n' Shine has been able to tap into a lower-cost pool of labor, paying its workers only $50 per day. Clean 'n' Shine's production technology is given in the table below. To determine its short-run cost structure, fill in the blanks in the table.

a. Over what range of output does Clean 'n' Shine experience increasing marginal returns to labor? Over what range does it experience decreasing marginal returns to labor?

b. As output increases, do average fixed costs behave as described in the text? Explain.

c. As output increases, do marginal cost, average variable cost, and average total cost behave as described in the text? Explain.

d. Looking at the numbers in the table, but without drawing any curves, is the relationship between MC and AVC as described in the text? What about the relationship between MC and ATC?

Short-Run Costs for Clean 'n' Shine Car Wash

(1) Output (per Day)	(2) Capital	(3) Labor	(4) TFC	(5) TVC	(6) TC	(7) MC	(8) AFC	(9) AVC	(10) ATC
0	1	0	$___	$___	$___		—	—	—
						$___			
30	1	1	$___	$___	$___		$___	$___	$___
						$___			
70	1	2	$___	$___	$___		$___	$___	$___
						$___			
120	1	3	$___	$___	$___		$___	$___	$___
						$___			
160	1	4	$___	$___	$___		$___	$___	$___
						$___			
190	1	5	$___	$___	$___		$___	$___	$___
						$___			
210	1	6	$___	$___	$___		$___	$___	$___

6. In Table 3, when output rises from 130 to 161 units, marginal cost is $1.94. For this change in output, marginal cost is greater than the previous AVC ($1.38) but less than the previous ATC ($1.96). According to the relationship between marginals and averages you learned in this chapter:

a. What should happen to AVC due to this change in output? Does it happen?

b. What should happen to ATC due to this change in output? Does it happen? (*Hint:* Calculate ATC to the third decimal place.)

7. A soft drink manufacturer that uses just labor (variable) and capital (fixed) paid a consulting firm thousands of dollars to calculate short-run costs at various output levels. But after the cost table (on the next page) was handed over to the president of the soft drink company, he spilled Dr Pepper on it, making some of the entries illegible. The consulting firm, playing tough, is demanding another payment to provide a duplicate table.

a. Should the soft drink president pay up? Or can he fill in the rest of the entries on his own? Fill in as many entries as you can to determine your answer. (*Hint:* First, determine the price of labor.)

b. Do MC, AVC, and ATC have the relationship to each other that you learned in this chapter? Explain.

Output per day	Units of Capital	Number of Workers	TFC	TVC	TC	MC	AFC	AVC	ATC
0	10	0	$1,000	?	?		?	?	?
						?			
20,000	10	100	?	$9,000	?		?	?	?
						?			
40,000	10	?	?	?	?		?	?	$0.325
						?			
60,000	10	225	?	?	?		?	?	?
						?			
80,000	10	?	?	?	$27,000		?	?	?

8. "If a firm has diminishing returns to labor over some range of output, it cannot have economies of scale over that range." True or false? Explain briefly.

9. Down On Our Luck Studios has spent $100 million producing an awful film, *A Depressing Story About a Miserable Person.* If the studio releases the film, the most cost-effective marketing plan would cost an additional $5 million, bringing the total amount spent to $105 million. Box office sales under this plan are predicted to be $12 million, which would be split evenly between the theaters and the studio. Additional studio revenue from video and DVD sales would be about $2 million. Should the studio release the film? If no, briefly explain why not. If yes, explain how it could make sense to release a film that cost $105 million but earns only $12 million.

10. The term "orphan drug" refers to a product that treats a rare disease affecting fewer than 200,000 Americans. Given the high cost of developing drugs, and given the limited demand for orphan drugs, use *LRATC* and demand diagrams to show a situation in which an orphan drug will not be produced at all.

Challenge Questions

1. Draw the long-run total cost and long-run average cost curves for a firm that experiences:
   a. Constant returns to scale over all output levels.
   b. Diseconomies of scale over low levels of output, constant returns to scale over intermediate levels of output, and economies of scale over high output levels. Does this pattern of costs make sense? Why or why not?

2. A firm has the strange *ATC* curve drawn to the right. Sketch in the marginal cost curve this firm must have. (*Hint:* Use what you know about the marginal-average relationship. Note that this *MC* curve does *not* have a standard shape.)

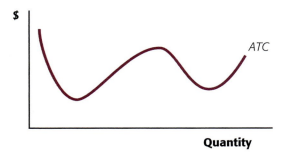

1. Use your Xtra! Password at the Hall and Lieberman Web site (http://liebermanxtra.swlearning.com), select this chapter, and under Economic Applications, click on EconNews Online. Select *Microeconomics: Production and Costs,* and scroll down to find the articles, "Precision Plowing" and "Optimizing Operations." Read the summaries there.

   a. Is the utilization of GPS-guided tractors and wireless technologies examples of long-run production adjustments, or short-run production adjustment? Why?
   b. Are there any sunks, or unavoidable, costs incurred with these new technologies? If so, what are they?
   c. In what ways are GPS-guided tractors and wireless technologies similar forms of production advances?

How Firms Make Decisions: Profit Maximization

In 2001, the managers of Nintendo America, Inc., knew that they had another winner on their hands: the Game Boy Advance handheld game machine. The new product ran 17 times faster than its predecessor (Game Boy Color), and displayed 32,768 colors on its 2.9 inch screen. It was sure to dazzle consumers, displaying images more spectacular and faster-moving than any competing product.

Then came the hard questions. Where should the new product be produced: Japan, the United States, or perhaps Hong Kong? How should the company raise the funds to pay the costs of production? When should it bring the product to market? How much should it spend on advertising, and in which types of media? And finally, what price should the company charge, and how many units should it plan to produce?

These last decisions—how much to produce and what price to charge—are the focus of this chapter. In the end, Nintendo planned to produce 23 million units for the first year, and decided to charge $99.95. But why didn't it charge a lower price that would allow it to sell more units? Or a higher price that would give it more profit on each unit sold?

Although this chapter concentrates on firms' decisions about price and output level, the tools you will learn apply to many other firm decisions. How much should MasterCard spend on advertising? How late should Starbucks keep its coffee shops open? How many copies should *Newsweek* give away free to potential subscribers? Should movie theaters offer Wednesday afternoon showings that only a few people attend? This chapter will help you understand how firms answer these sorts of questions.

THE GOAL OF PROFIT MAXIMIZATION

To analyze decision making at the firm, let's start with a very basic question: What is the firm trying to maximize?

Economists have given this question a lot of thought. Some firms—especially large ones—are complex institutions in which many different groups of people work together. A firm's owners will usually want the firm to earn as much profit as possible. But the workers and managers who actually run the firm may have other agendas. They may try to divert the firm away from profit maximization in order to benefit themselves. For now, let's assume that workers and managers are faithful servants of the firm's owners. That is,

> *we will view the firm as a single economic decision maker whose goal is to maximize its owners' profit.*

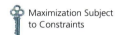 Maximization Subject to Constraints

Why do we make this assumption? Because it has proven so *useful* in understanding how firms behave. True, this assumption leaves out the details of these other agendas that often are present in real-world firms. But remember that every economic model *abstracts* from reality. To stay simple and comprehensible, it leaves out many real-world details and includes only what is relevant for the purpose at hand. If the purpose is to explain conflict within the firm or deviations from profit-maximizing behavior, or even fraudulent accounting practices by management (such as the 2002 corporate scandals at Enron, WorldCom, and other firms), then the differing goals of managers and owners should be a central element of the model.

But when the purpose is to explain how firms decide what price to charge and how much to produce, or whether to enter a new market or permanently leave a current one, the assumption of profit maximization has proven to be sufficient. It explains what firms actually do with reasonable—and sometimes remarkable—accuracy.

Why? Part of the reason is that managers who deviate *too* much from profit maximizing for *too* long are typically replaced. The managers may be sacked by the current dissatisfied owners or by other firms that acquire the underperforming firm.

Another reason is that so many managers are well trained in the tools of profit maximization. This is in contrast to our model of consumer behavior, in which we asserted that consumers act *as if* they are using the model's graphs and calculations—although we recognize that most consumers never actually do. The basic economic model of the firm's behavior, however, is well understood *and used* by most managers, who have typically taken several economics courses as part of their management education. In fact, economists' thinking about firm behavior has so permeated the language and culture of modern business that it's sometimes hard to distinguish where theory ends and practice begins.

UNDERSTANDING PROFIT

Profit is defined as the firm's *sales revenue* minus its *costs of production*. There is widespread agreement over how to measure the firm's revenue—the flow of money into the firm. But there are two different conceptions of the firm's costs, and each of them leads to a different definition of profit.

Two Definitions of Profit

One conception of costs is the one used by accountants. With a few exceptions, accountants consider only *explicit* costs, where money is actually paid out.[1] If we deduct only the costs recognized by accountants, we get one definition of profit:

Accounting profit Total revenue minus accounting costs.

Accounting profit = Total revenue − Accounting costs.

But economics, as you have learned, has a much broader view of cost—*opportunity cost*. For the firm's owners, opportunity cost is the total value of *everything* sacrificed to produce output. This includes not only the explicit costs recognized by accountants—such as wages and salaries and outlays on raw materials—but also *implicit costs,* when something is given up but no money changes hands. For example, if an owner contributes his own time or money to the firm, there will be foregone wages or foregone investment income—both implicit costs for the firm.

This broader conception of costs leads to a second definition of profit:

Economic profit Total revenue minus all costs of production, explicit and implicit.

Economic profit = Total revenue − All costs of production
= Total revenue − (Explicit costs + Implicit costs)

The difference between economic profit and accounting profit is an important one; when they are confused, some serious (and costly) mistakes can result. An example might help make the difference clear.

Suppose you own a firm that produces T-shirts and you want to calculate your profit over the year. Your bookkeeper provides you with the following information:

Total Revenue from Selling T-shirts	**$300,000**
Cost of raw materials	$ 80,000
Wages and salaries	150,000
Electricity and phone	20,000
Advertising cost	40,000
Total Explicit Cost	**290,000**
Accounting Profit	**$ 10,000**

[1] One exception is *depreciation,* a charge for the gradual wearing out of the firm's plant and equipment. Accountants include this as a cost even though no money is actually paid out.

From the looks of things, your firm is earning a profit, so you might feel pretty good. Indeed, if you look only at *money* coming in and *money* going out, you have indeed earned a profit: $10,000 for the year . . . an *accounting* profit.

But suppose that in order to start your business you invested $100,000 of your own money—money that could have been earning $6,000 in interest if you'd put it in the bank instead. Also, you are using two extra rooms in your own house as a factory—rooms that could have been rented out for $4,000 per year. Finally, you are managing the business full-time, without receiving a separate salary, and you could instead be working at a job earning $40,000 per year. All of these costs—the interest, rent, and salary you *could* have earned—are implicit costs that have not been taken into account by your bookkeeper. They are part of the opportunity cost of your firm, because they are sacrifices you made to operate your business.

Now let's look at this business from the economist's perspective and calculate your *economic* profit.

Total Revenue from Selling T-shirts		$300,000
Cost of raw materials	$ 80,000	
Wages and salaries	150,000	
Electricity and phone	20,000	
Advertising cost	40,000	
Total Explicit Costs	**$290,000**	
Investment income foregone	$ 6,000	
Rent foregone	4,000	
Salary foregone	40,000	
Total Implicit Costs	**$ 50,000**	
Total Costs		**$340,000**
Economic Profit		**−$ 40,000**

From an economic point of view, your business is not profitable at all, but is actually losing $40,000 per year! But wait—how can we say that your firm is suffering a loss when it takes in more money than it pays out? Because, as we've seen, your *opportunity cost*—the value of what you are giving up to produce your output—includes more than just money costs. When *all* costs are considered—implicit as well as explicit—your total revenue is not sufficient to cover what you have sacrificed to run your business. You would do better by shifting your time, your money, and your spare room to some alternative use.

Which of the two definitions of profit is the correct one? Either one of them, depending on the reason for measuring it. For tax purposes, the government is interested in profits as measured by accountants. The government cares only about the money you've earned, not what you *could* have earned had you done something else with your money or your time.

However, for our purposes—understanding the behavior of firms—economic profit is clearly better. Should your T-shirt factory stay in business? Should it expand or contract in the long run? Will other firms be attracted to the T-shirt industry? It is economic profit that will help us answer these questions, because it is economic profit that you and other owners care about.

Opportunity Cost

> *The proper measure of profit for understanding and predicting the behavior of firms is* economic profit. *Unlike accounting profit, economic profit recognizes all the opportunity costs of production—both explicit costs and implicit costs.*

Why Are There Profits?

When you look at the income received by households in the economy, you see a variety of payments. Those who provide firms with land receive *rent*—the payment for land. Those who provide labor receive a wage or salary. And those who lend firms money so they can purchase capital equipment receive interest. The firm's profit goes to its owners. But what do the owners of the firm provide that earns them this payment?

Economists view profit as a payment for two contributions of entrepreneurs, who are just as necessary for production as are land, labor, or machinery. These two contributions are *risk taking* and *innovation*.

Consider a restaurant that happens to be earning profit for its owner. The land, labor, and capital the restaurant uses to produce its meals did not simply come together magically. Someone—the owner—had to be willing to take the initiative to set up the business, and this individual assumed the risk that the business might fail and the initial investment be lost. Because the consequences of loss are so severe, the reward for success must be large in order to induce an entrepreneur to establish a business.

On a larger scale, Ted Turner risked hundreds of millions of dollars in the late 1970s when he created Cable News Network (CNN). Now that CNN has turned out to be so successful, it is easy to forget how risky the venture was at the outset. At the time, many respected financial analysts forecast that the project would fail and Turner would be driven into bankruptcy.

Profits are also a reward for *innovation*. Ted Turner was the first to create a 24-hour global news network, just as Pierre Omidyar—when he founded eBay in 1995—was the first to establish a commercially viable online auction market. These are obvious innovations.

But innovations can also be more subtle, and they are more common than you might think. When you pass by a successful laundromat, you may not give it a second thought. But someone, at some time, had to be the first one to realize, "I bet a laundromat in this neighborhood would do well"—an innovation. There can also be innovations in the production process, such as the improvement in mass production that made the disposable contact lens possible.

In almost any business, if you look closely, you will find that some sort of innovation was needed to get things started. Innovation, like taking on the risk of losing substantial wealth, makes an essential contribution to production. Profit is, in part, a reward to those who innovate.

THE FIRM'S CONSTRAINTS

If the firm were free to earn whatever level of profit it wanted, it would earn virtually infinite profit. This would make the owners very happy. Unfortunately for owners, though, the firm is not free to do this; it faces *constraints* on both its revenue and its costs.

The Demand Constraint

The constraint on the firm's revenue arises from a familiar concept: the demand curve. This curve always tells us the quantity of a good buyers wish to buy at different prices. But which buyers? And from which firms are they buying? Depending on how we answer these questions, we might be talking about different types of demand curves.

Market demand curves—like the ones you studied in Chapter 3—tell us the quantity demanded by *all* consumers from *all* firms in a market. In this chapter, we look at yet another kind of demand curve:

> The **demand curve facing the firm** *tells us, for different prices, the quantity of output that customers will choose to purchase from that firm.*

Maximization Subject to Constraints

Demand curve facing the firm
A curve that indicates, for different prices, the quantity of output that customers will purchase from a particular firm.

Notice that this new demand curve—the demand curve facing the firm—refers to only *one* firm, and to *all buyers* who are potential customers of that firm.

Let's consider the demand curve faced by Ned, the owner and manager of Ned's Beds, a manufacturer of bed frames. Figure 1 lists the different prices that Ned could charge for each bed frame and the number of them (per day) he can sell at each price. The figure also shows a graph of the demand curve facing Ned's firm. For each price (on the vertical axis), it shows us the quantity of output the firm can sell (on the horizontal axis). Notice that, like the other types of demand curves we have studied, the demand curve facing the firm slopes downward. In order to sell more bed frames, Ned must lower his price.[2]

The definition of the demand curve facing the firm suggests that once it selects a price, the firm has also determined how much output it will sell. But we can also flip the demand relationship around: Once the firm has selected an output level, it has also determined the maximum price it can charge. This leads to an alternative definition:

> The demand curve facing the firm *shows us the maximum price the firm can charge to sell any given amount of output.*

Looking at Figure 1 from this perspective, we see that the horizontal axis shows alternative levels of output and the vertical axis shows the price Ned should charge if he wishes to sell each quantity of output.

These two different ways of defining the firm's demand curve show us that it is, indeed, a constraint for the firm. The firm can freely determine *either* its price *or* its level of output. But once it makes the choice, the other variable is automatically determined by the firm's demand curve. Thus, the firm has only *one* choice to make. Selecting a particular price *implies* a level of output, and selecting an output level *implies* a particular price. Economists typically focus on the choice of output level, with the price implied as a consequence. We will follow that convention in this textbook.

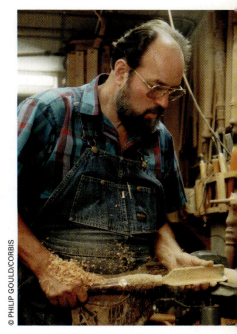

Like other firms, a furniture manufacturer must determine either its price for its products, or its level of output; once it chooses price, its level of output is determined, and vice versa.

---

[2] The downward-sloping demand curve tells us that Ned's Beds sells its output in an *imperfectly competitive market*, a market where the firm can *set* its price. Most firms operate in this type of market. If a manager thinks, "I'd like to sell more output, but then I'd have to lower my price, so let's see if it's worth it," we know he operates in an imperfectly competitive market. In a *perfectly competitive market*, by contrast, the firm would have to accept the market price as given. We assumed that markets were perfectly competitive in Chapter 3, and in the next chapter we'll examine them in more detail.

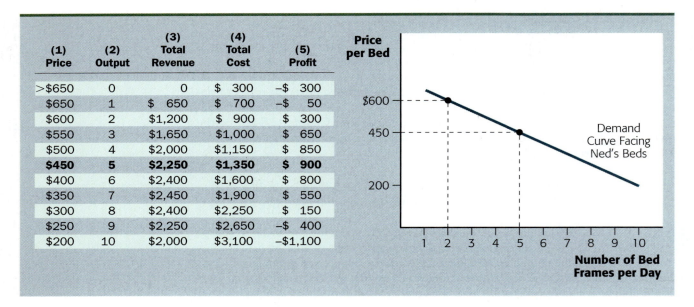

(1) Price	(2) Output	(3) Total Revenue	(4) Total Cost	(5) Profit
>$650	0	0	$ 300	–$ 300
$650	1	$ 650	$ 700	–$ 50
$600	2	$1,200	$ 900	$ 300
$550	3	$1,650	$1,000	$ 650
$500	4	$2,000	$1,150	$ 850
$450	**5**	**$2,250**	**$1,350**	**$ 900**
$400	6	$2,400	$1,600	$ 800
$350	7	$2,450	$1,900	$ 550
$300	8	$2,400	$2,250	$ 150
$250	9	$2,250	$2,650	–$ 400
$200	10	$2,000	$3,100	–$1,100

FIGURE 1
The Demand Curve Facing the Firm

The table presents information about Ned's Beds. Data from the first two columns are plotted in the figure to show the demand curve facing the firm. At any point along that demand curve, the product of price and quantity equals total revenue, which is given in the third column of the table.

Total revenue The total inflow of receipts from selling a given amount of output.

Total Revenue. A firm's **total revenue** is the total inflow of receipts from selling output. Each time the firm chooses a level of output, it also determines its total revenue. Why? Because once we know the level of output, we also know the highest price the firm can charge. Total revenue, which is the number of units of output times the price per unit, follows automatically.

The third column in Figure 1 lists the total revenue of Ned's Beds. Each entry is calculated by multiplying the quantity of output (column 2) by the price per unit (column 1). For example, if Ned's firm produces 2 bed frames per day, he can charge $600 for each of them, so total revenue will be 2 × $600 = $1,200. If Ned increases output to 3 units, he must lower the price to $550, earning a total revenue of 3 × $550 = $1,650. Because the firm's demand curve slopes downward, Ned must lower his price each time his output increases, or else he will not be able to sell all he produces. With more units of output, but each one selling at a lower price, total revenue could rise or fall. Scanning the total revenue column, we see that for this firm, total revenue first rises and then begins to fall. This will be discussed in greater detail later on.

The Cost Constraint

Every firm struggles to reduce costs, but there is a limit to how low costs can go. These limits impose a second constraint on the firm. Where do the limits come from? They come from concepts that you learned about in Chapter 5. Let's review them briefly.

First, the firm has a given production function, which is determined by its production technology. The production function tells us all the different ways in which the firm can produce any given level of output. In the long run, when all inputs are variable, the firm can use *any* method in its production function. In the short run, it is even more constrained: It can use only *some* of the methods in that production function, because one or more of its inputs are *fixed*.

Second, the firm must pay *prices* for each of the inputs that it uses, and we assume there is nothing the firm can do about those prices. Together, the production function and the prices of the inputs determine what it will cost to produce any given level of output. And once the firm chooses the *least cost* method available, it has driven the cost of producing that output level as low as it can go.

> *The firm uses its production function, and the prices it must pay for its inputs, to determine the least cost method of producing any given output level. Therefore, for any level of output the firm might want to produce, it must pay the cost of the "least cost method" of production.*

Maximization Subject to Constraints

The fourth column of Figure 1 lists Ned's total cost—the lowest possible cost of producing each quantity of output. More output always means greater costs, so the numbers in this column are always increasing. For example, at an output of zero, total cost is $300. This tells us we are looking at costs in the short run, over which some of the firm's costs are *fixed*. (What would be the cost of producing 0 units if this were the long run?) If output increases from 0 to 1 bed frame, total cost rises from $300 to $700. This increase in total costs—$400—is caused by an increase in *variable* costs, such as labor and raw materials.

THE PROFIT-MAXIMIZING OUTPUT LEVEL

In this section, we ask a very simple question: How does a firm find the level of output that will earn it the greatest possible profit? We'll look at this question from several angles, each one giving us further insight into the behavior of the firm.

The Total Revenue and Total Cost Approach

At any given output level, we know (1) how much revenue the firm will earn and (2) its cost of production. We can then easily calculate profit, which is just the difference between total revenue (*TR*) and total cost (*TC*).

> *In the total revenue and total cost approach, the firm calculates* Profit = TR − TC *at each output level and selects the output level where profit is greatest.*

Let's see how this works for Ned's Beds. Column 5 of Figure 1 lists total profit at each output level. If the firm were to produce no bed frames at all, total revenue (*TR*) would be 0, while total cost (*TC*) would be $300. Total profit would be *TR* − *TC* = 0 − $300 = −$300. We would say that the firm earns a profit of negative $300 or a **loss** of $300 per day. Producing one bed frame would raise total revenue to $650 and total cost to $700, for a loss of $50. Not until the firm produces 2 bed frames does total revenue rise above total cost and the firm begin to make a profit. At 2 bed frames per day, *TR* is $1,200 and *TC* is $900, so the firm earns a profit of $300. Remember that as long as we have been careful to include *all* costs in *TC*—implicit as well as explicit—the profits and losses we are calculating are *economic* profits and losses.

In the total revenue and total cost approach, finding the profit-maximizing output level is straightforward: We just scan the numbers in the profit column until we

Loss The difference between total cost (*TC*) and total revenue (*TR*), when *TC* > *TR*.

find the largest value, $900, and the output level at which it is achieved, 5 units per day. We conclude that the profit-maximizing output for Ned's Beds is 5 units per day.

The Marginal Revenue and Marginal Cost Approach

There is another way to find the profit-maximizing level of output. This approach, which uses *marginal* concepts, gives us some powerful insights into the firm's decision-making process. Recall that *marginal* cost is the *change* in total cost per unit increase in output. Now, let's consider a similar concept for revenue.

Marginal revenue The change in total revenue from producing one more unit of output.

> *Marginal revenue* (**MR**) *is the change in the firm's total revenue* (ΔTR) *divided by the change in its output* (ΔQ):
>
> $$MR = \Delta TR/\Delta Q$$
>
> MR *tells us how much revenue rises* per unit *increase in output.*

Table 1 reproduces the *TR* and *TC* columns from Figure 1, but adds columns for marginal revenue and marginal cost. (In the table, output is always changing by one unit, so we can use Δ*TR* alone as our measure of marginal revenue.) For example, when output changes from 2 to 3 units, total revenue rises from $1,200 to $1,650.

Maximize Profit, Not Revenue You may be tempted to forget about profit and think that the firm should produce where its total revenue is maximized. As you can see in Figure 1 (column 3), total revenue is greatest when the firm produces 7 units per day, but at this output level, profit is not as high as it could be. The firm does better by producing only 5 units. True, revenue is lower at 5 units, but so are costs. It is the difference between revenue and cost that matters, not revenue alone.

DANGEROUS CURVES

For this output change, *MR* = $450. As usual, marginals are placed *between* different output levels because they tell us what happens as output *changes* from one level to another.

There are two important things to notice about marginal revenue. First, when *MR* is *positive*, an increase in output causes total revenue to *rise*. In the table, *MR* is positive for all increases in output from 0 to 7 units. When *MR* is *negative*, an increase in output causes total revenue to *fall*, as occurs for all increases beyond 7 units.

The second thing to notice about *MR* is a bit more complicated: Each time output increases, *MR* is *smaller* than the price the firm charges at the new output level. For example, when output increases from 2 to 3 units, the firm's total revenue rises by $450—even though it sells the third unit for a price of $550. This may seem strange to you. After all, if the firm increases output from 2 to 3 units, and it gets $550 for the third unit of output, why doesn't its total revenue rise by $550?

The answer is found in the firm's downward-sloping demand curve, which tells us that to sell more output, the firm must cut its price. Look back at Figure 1 of this chapter. When output increases from 2 to 3 units, the firm must lower its price from $600 to $550. Moreover, the new price of $550 will apply to *all three* units the firm sells.[3] This means it *gains* some revenue—$550—by selling that third unit.

---

[3] Some firms can charge two or more different prices for the same product. We'll explore some examples in the appendix to Chapter 8.

Output	Total Revenue	Marginal Revenue	Total Cost	Marginal Cost	Profit
0	0		$ 300		−$300
		$650		$400	
1	$ 650		$ 700		−$50
		$550		$200	
2	$1,200		$ 900		$300
		$450		$100	
3	$1,650		$1,000		$650
		$350		$150	
4	$2,000		$1,150		$850
		$250		$200	
5	$2,250		$1,350		$900
		$150		$250	
6	$2,400		$1,600		$800
		$ 50		$300	
7	$2,450		$1,900		$550
		−$ 50		$350	
8	$2,400		$2,250		$150
		−$150		$400	
9	$2,250		$2,650		−$400
		−$250		$450	
10	$2,000		$3,100		−$1,100

TABLE 1
More Data for Ned's Beds

But it also *loses* some revenue—$100—by having to lower the price by $50 on each of the two units of output it could have otherwise sold at $600. Marginal revenue will always equal the *difference* between this gain and loss in revenue—in this case, $550 − $100 = $450.

> *When a firm faces a downward-sloping demand curve, each increase in output causes a revenue gain, from selling additional output at the new price, and a revenue loss, from having to lower the price on all previous units of output. Marginal revenue is therefore less than the price of the last unit of output.*

Using *MR* and *MC* to Maximize Profits. Now we'll see how marginal revenue, together with marginal cost, can be used to find the profit-maximizing output level. The logic behind the *MC* and *MR* approach is this:

> *An increase in output will always raise profit as long as marginal revenue is greater than marginal cost (MR > MC).*

Notice the word *always*. Let's see why this rather sweeping statement must be true. Table 1 tells us that when output rises from 2 to 3 units, *MR* is $450, while *MC* is $100. This change in output causes both total revenue and total cost to rise, but it causes revenue to rise by *more* than cost ($450 > $100). As a result, profit must increase. Indeed, looking at the profit column, we see that increasing output from 2 to 3 units *does* cause profit to increase, from $300 to $650.[4]

The converse of this statement is also true:

> *An increase in output will always lower profit whenever marginal revenue is less than marginal cost* (MR < MC).

For example, when output rises from 5 to 6 units, *MR* is $150, while *MC* is $250. For this change in output, both total revenue and total cost rise, but cost rises *more*, so profit must go down. In Table 1, you can see that this change in output does indeed cause profit to decline, from $900 to $800.

These insights about *MR* and *MC* lead us to the following simple guideline the firm should use to find its profit-maximizing level of output:

Marginal Decision Making

> To *find the profit-maximizing output level, the firm should increase output whenever* MR > MC, *and decrease output when* MR < MC.

Let's apply this rule to Ned's Beds. In Table 1 we see that when moving from 0 to 1 unit of output, *MR* is $650, while *MC* is only $400. Since *MR* is larger than *MC*, making this move will increase profit. Thus, if the firm is producing 0 beds, it should always increase to 1 bed. Should it stop there? Let's see. If it moves from 1 to 2 beds, *MR* is $550, while *MC* is only $200. Once again, *MR* > *MC*, so the firm should increase to 2 beds. You can verify from the table that if the firm finds itself producing 0, 1, 2, 3, or 4 beds, *MR* > *MC* for an increase of 1 unit, so it will always make greater profit by increasing production.

Until, that is, output reaches 5 beds. At this point, the picture changes: From 5 to 6 beds, *MR* is $150, while *MC* is $250. For this move, *MR* < *MC*, so profits would decrease. Thus, if the firm is producing 5 beds, it should *not* increase to 6. The same is true at every other output level beyond 5 units: The firm should *not* raise its output, since *MR* < *MC* for each increase. We conclude that Ned maximizes his profit by producing 5 beds per day—the same answer we got using the *TR* and *TC* approach earlier.[5]

Profit Maximization Using Graphs

Both approaches to maximizing profit (using totals or using marginals) can be seen even more clearly when we use graphs. In Figure 2(a) and (b), the data from Table 1 have been plotted—the *TC* and *TR* curves in the upper panel, and the *MC* and *MR* curves in the lower one.

The marginal revenue curve has an important relationship to the total revenue curve. As you can see in Figure 2(a), total revenue (*TR*) is plotted on the vertical

[4] You may have noticed that the rise in profit ($350) is equal to the difference between *MR* and *MC* in this example. This is no accident. *MR* tells us the *rise* in revenue; *MC* tells us the *rise* in cost. The difference between them will always be the *rise* in profit.

[5] It sometimes happens that *MR* is precisely equal to *MC* for some change in output, although this does not occur in Table 1. In this case, increasing output would cause *both* cost and revenue to rise by equal amounts, so there would be *no* change in profit. The firm should not care whether it makes this change in output or not.

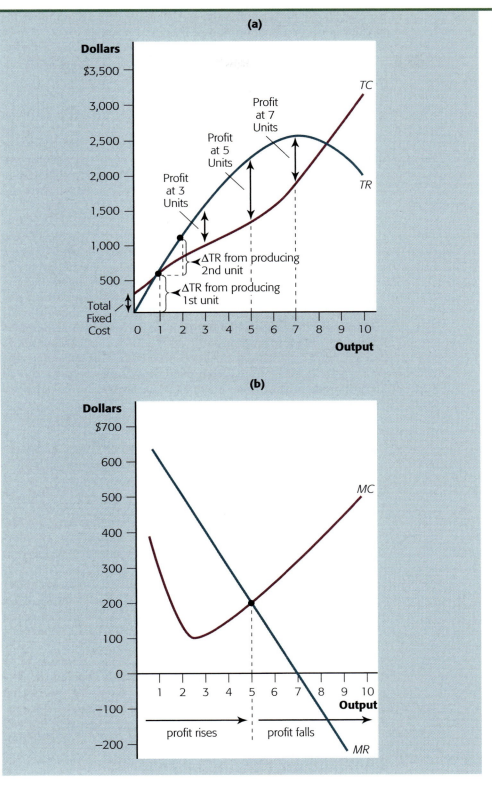

(a)

FIGURE 2
Profit Maximization
Panel (a) shows the firm's total revenue (TR) and total cost (TC) curves. Profit is the vertical distance between the two curves at any level of output. Profit is maximized when that vertical distance is greatest—at 5 units of output. Panel (b) shows the firm's marginal revenue (MR) and marginal cost (MC) curves. (As long as MR lies above the horizontal axis, the TR curve slopes upward.) Profit is maximized at the level of output closest to where the two curves cross—at 5 units of output.

axis, and quantity (Q) on the horizontal axis, so the slope along any interval is just $\Delta TR/\Delta Q$. But this is exactly the definition of marginal revenue.

> *The marginal revenue for any change in output is equal to the* slope *of the total revenue curve along that interval.*

Thus, as long as the *MR* curve lies above the horizontal axis *(MR > 0)*, *TR* must be increasing and the *TR* curve must slope upward. In the figure, *MR* > 0, and the *TR* curve slopes upward from zero to 7 units. When the *MR* curve dips below the horizontal axis (*MR* < 0), *TR* is decreasing, so the *TR* curve begins to slope downward. In the figure, this occurs beyond 7 units of output. As output increases in Figure 2, *MR* is first positive and then turns negative, so the *TR* curve will first *rise* and then *fall*.

The *TR* and *TC* Approach Using Graphs.

Now let's see how we can use the *TC* and *TR* curves to guide the firm to its profit-maximizing output level. We know that the firm earns a profit at any output level where *TR* > *TC* —where the *TR* curve lies *above* the *TC* curve. In Figure 2(a), you can see that all output levels between 2 and 8 units are profitable for the firm. The *amount* of profit is simply the *vertical distance* between the *TR* and *TC* curves, whenever the *TR* curve lies above the *TC* curve. Since the firm cannot sell part of a bed frame, it must choose whole numbers for its output, so the profit-maximizing output level is simply the whole-number quantity at which this vertical distance is greatest—5 units of output. Of course, the *TR* and *TC* curves in Figure 2 were plotted from the data in Table 1, so we should not be surprised to find the same profit-maximizing output level—5 units—that we found before when using the table.

We can sum up our graphical rule for using the *TR* and *TC* curves this way:

> *To maximize profit, the firm should produce the quantity of output where the vertical distance between the* TR *and* TC *curves is greatest and the* TR *curve lies above the* TC *curve.*

The *MR* and *MC* Approach Using Graphs.

Figure 2 also illustrates the *MR* and *MC* approach to maximizing profits. As usual, the marginal data in panel (b) are plotted *between* output levels, since they tell us what happens as output changes from one level to another.

In the diagram, as long as output is less than 5 units, the *MR* curve lies above the *MC* curve (*MR* > *MC*), so the firm should produce more. For example, if we consider the move from 4 to 5 units, we compare the *MR* and *MC* curves at the midpoint between 4 and 5. Here, the *MR* curve lies above the *MC* curve, so increasing output from 4 to 5 will increase profit.

But now suppose the firm is producing 5 units and considering a move to 6. At the midpoint between 5 and 6 units, the *MR* curve has already crossed the *MC* curve, and now it lies *below* the *MC* curve. For this move, *MR* < *MC*, so raising output would *decrease* the firm's profit. The same is true for every increase in output beyond 5 units: The *MR* curve always lies below the *MC* curve, so the firm will decrease its profits by increasing output. Once again, we find that the profit-maximizing output level for the firm is 5 units.

Notice that the profit-maximizing output level—5 units—is the level closest to where the *MC* and *MR* curves cross. This is no accident. For each change in output that *increases* profit, the *MR* curve will lie above the *MC* curve. The first time that an output change *decreases* profit, the *MR* curve will cross the *MC* curve and dip below it. Thus, the *MC* and *MR* curves will always cross closest to the profit-maximizing output level.

With this graphical insight, we can summarize the *MC* and *MR* approach this way:

> *To maximize profit, the firm should produce the quantity of output closest to the point where* MC = MR—*that is, the quantity of output at which the* MC *and* MR *curves intersect.*

 Marginal Decision Making

This rule is very useful, since it allows us to look at a diagram of *MC* and *MR* curves and *immediately* identify the profit-maximizing output level. In this text, you will often see this rule. When you read, "The profit-maximizing output level is where *MC* equals *MR*," translate to "The profit-maximizing output level is closest to the point where the *MC* curve crosses the *MR* curve."

A Proviso. There is, however, one important exception to this rule. Sometimes the *MC* and *MR* curves cross at two different points. In this case, the profit-maximizing output level is the one at which the *MC* curve crosses the *MR* curve *from below.*

Figure 3 shows why. At point *A*, the *MC* curve crosses the *MR* curve from *above.* Our rule tells us that the output level at this point, Q_1, is *not* profit maximizing. Why not? Because at output levels lower than Q_1, MC > MR, so profit *falls* as output increases toward Q_1. Also, profit *rises* as output increases *beyond* Q_1, since MR > MC for these moves. Since it never pays to increase *to* Q_1, and profit rises when increasing *from* Q_1, we know that Q_1 cannot possibly maximize the firm's profit.

Misusing the Gap Between *MR* and *MC* A common error is assuming that the firm should produce the level of output at which the difference between *MR* and *MC* is as large as possible, like 2 or 3 units of output in Figure 2. Let's see why this is wrong. If the firm produces 2 or 3 units, it would leave many profitable increases in output unexploited—increases where *MR* > *MC*. As long as *MR* is even a tiny bit larger than *MC*, it pays to increase output, since doing so will add more to revenue than to cost. The firm should be satisfied only when the difference between *MR* and *MC* is as *small* as possible, not as *large* as possible.

DANGEROUS CURVES

But now look at point *B*, where the *MC* curve crosses the *MR* curve from below. You can see that when we are at an output level lower than Q^*, it always pays to increase output, since MR > MC for these moves. You can also see that, once we have arrived at Q^*, further increases will reduce profit, since MC > MR. Q^* is thus the profit-maximizing output level for this firm—the output level at which the *MC* curve crosses the *MR* curve *from below.*

What About Average Costs?

You may have noticed that this chapter has discussed *most* of the cost concepts introduced in Chapter 5. But it has not yet referred to *average* cost. There is a good reason for this. We have been concerned about how much the firm should produce

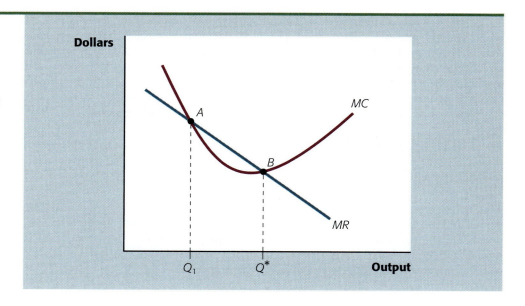

if it wishes to earn the greatest possible level of profit. To achieve this goal, the firm should produce more output whenever doing so *increases* profit, and it needs to know only *marginal* cost and *marginal* revenue for this purpose. The different types of average cost (*ATC, AVC,* and *AFC*) are simply irrelevant. Indeed, a common error—sometimes made even by business managers—is to use *average* cost in place of *marginal* cost in making decisions.

For example, suppose a yacht maker wants to know how much his total cost will rise in the short run if he produces another unit of output. It is tempting—*but wrong*—for the yacht maker to reason this way: "My cost per unit (*ATC*) is currently $50,000 per yacht. Therefore, if I increase production by 1 unit, my total cost will rise by $50,000; if I increase production by 2 units, my total cost will rise by $100,000, and so on."

There are two problems with this approach. First, *ATC* includes many costs that are *fixed* in the short run—including the cost of all fixed inputs such as the factory and equipment and the design staff. These costs will *not* increase when additional yachts are produced, and they are therefore irrelevant to the firm's decision making in the short run. Second, *ATC changes* as output increases. The cost per yacht may rise above $50,000 or fall below $50,000, depending on whether the *ATC* curve is upward or downward sloping at the current production level. Note that the first problem—fixed costs—could be solved by using *AVC* instead of *ATC*. The second problem—*changes* in average cost—remains even when *AVC* is used.

The correct approach, as we've seen in this chapter, is to use the *marginal cost* of a yacht and to consider increases in output one unit at a time. The firm should produce the output level where its *MC* curve crosses its *MR* curve from below. Average cost doesn't help at all; it only confuses the issue.

Does this mean that all of your efforts to master *ATC* and *AVC*—their definitions, their relationship to each other, and their relationship to *MC*—were a waste of time? Far from it. As you'll see, average cost will prove *very* useful in the chapters to come. You'll learn that whereas marginal values tell the firm *what* to do, averages can tell the firm *how well* it has done. But average cost should *not* be used in place of marginal cost as a basis for decisions.

The Marginal Approach to Profit

The *MC* and *MR* approach for finding the profit-maximizing output level is actually a very specific application of a more general principle:

> *The **marginal approach to profit** states that a firm should take any action that adds more to its revenue than to its costs.*

 Marginal Decision Making

Marginal approach to profit
A firm maximizes its profit by taking any action that adds more to its revenue than to its cost.

In this chapter, the action being considered is whether to increase output by 1 unit. We've learned that the firm should take this action whenever *MR* > *MC*.

But the same logic can be applied to *any other decision* facing the firm. Should a restaurant owner take out an ad in the local newspaper? Should a convenience store that currently closes at midnight stay open 24 hours instead? Should a private kindergarten hire another teacher? Should an inventor pay to produce an infomercial for her new gizmo? Should a bank install another ATM? The answer to all of these questions is yes—*if* the action would add more to revenue than to costs. In future chapters, we'll be using the marginal approach to profit to analyze some other types of firm decisions.

DEALING WITH LOSSES

So far, we have dealt only with the pleasant case of profitable firms and how they select their profit-maximizing output level. But what about a firm that cannot earn a positive profit at *any* output level? What should it do? The answer depends on what time horizon we are looking at.

The Short Run and the Shutdown Rule

In the short run, the firm must pay for its fixed inputs, because there is not enough time to sell them or get out of lease and rental agreements. But the firm can *still* make decisions about production. And one of its options is to *shut down*—to stop producing output, at least temporarily.

At first glance, you might think that a loss-making firm should always shut down its operation in the short run. After all, why keep producing if you are not making any profit? In fact, it makes sense for some unprofitable firms to continue operating.

Imagine a firm with the *TC* and *TR* curves shown in the upper panel of Figure 4 (ignore the *TVC* curve for now). No matter what output level the firm produces, the *TC* curve lies above the *TR* curve, so it will suffer a loss—a negative profit. For this firm, the goal is still profit maximization. But now, the highest profit will be the one with the *least negative value*. In other words, profit maximization becomes *loss minimization*.

If the firm keeps producing, then the smallest possible loss is at an output level of *Q**, where the distance between the *TC* and *TR* curves is smallest. *Q** is

The firm shown here cannot earn a positive profit at any level of output. If it produces anything, it will minimize its loss by producing where the vertical distance between TR and TC is smallest. Because TR exceeds TVC at Q*, the firm will produce there in the short run.

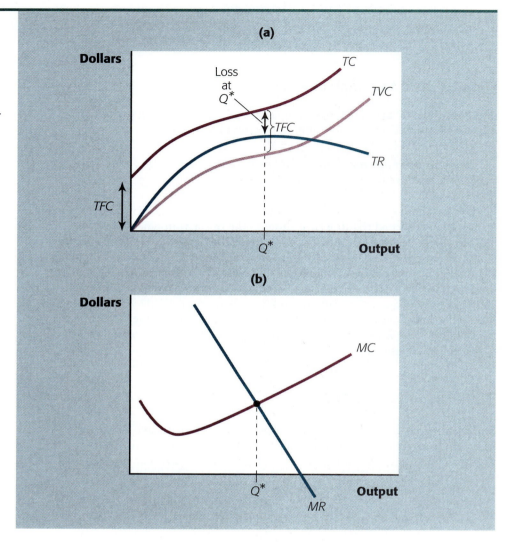

also the output level we would find by using our marginal approach to profit (increasing output whenever that adds more to revenue than to costs). This is why, in the lower panel of Figure 4, the MC and MR curves must intersect at (or very close to) Q*.

The question is: Should this firm produce at Q* and suffer a loss? The answer is yes—*if* the firm would lose even *more* if it stopped producing and shut down its operation. Remember that, in the short run, a firm must continue to pay its total fixed cost (TFC) no matter what level of output it produces—even if it produces nothing at all. If the firm shuts down, it will therefore have a loss equal to its TFC, since it will not earn any revenue. But if, by producing some output, the firm can cut its loss to something *less* than TFC, then it should stay open and keep producing.

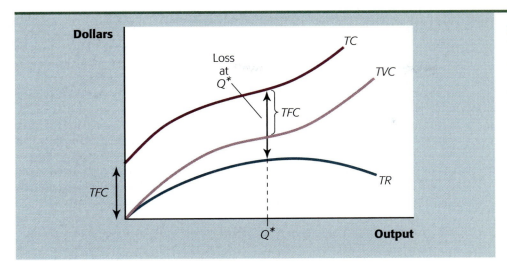

FIGURE 5
Shut Down

At Q*, this firm's total variable cost exceeds its total revenue. The best policy is to shut down, produce nothing, and suffer a loss equal to TFC in the short run.

To understand the shutdown decision more clearly, let's think about the firm's total variable costs. Business managers often call *TVC* the firm's *operating cost*, since the firm only pays these variable costs when it continues to operate. If a firm, by staying open, can earn *more* than enough revenue to cover its operating costs, then it is making an *operating profit* (*TR > TVC*). It should not shut down because its operating profit can be used to help pay its fixed costs. But if the firm cannot even cover its operating cost when it stays open—that is, if it would suffer an *operating loss* (*TR < TVC*)—it should definitely shut down. Continuing to operate only *adds* to the firm's loss, increasing the total loss beyond fixed costs.

This suggests the following guideline—called the **shutdown rule**—for a loss-making firm:

> *Let Q* be the output level at which* MR = MC. *Then, in the short run:*
> *If* TR > TVC *at Q*, the firm should keep producing.*
> *If* TR < TVC *at Q*, the firm should shut down.*
> *If* TR = TVC *at Q*, the firm should be indifferent between shutting down and producing.*

Shutdown rule In the short run, the firm should continue to produce if total revenue exceeds total variable costs; otherwise, it should shut down.

Look back at Figure 4. At *Q**, the firm is making an operating profit, since its *TR* curve is above its *TVC* curve. This firm, as we've seen, should continue to operate.

Figure 5 is drawn for a different firm, one with the same *TC* and *TVC* curves as the firm in Figure 4, but with a lower *TR* curve. This firm *cannot* earn an operating profit, since its *TR* curve lies below its *TVC* curve everywhere—even at *Q**. This firm should shut down.

The shutdown rule is a powerful predictor of firms' decisions to stay open or cease production in the short run. It tells us, for example, why some seasonal businesses—such as ice cream shops in summer resort areas—shut down in the winter, when *TR* drops so low that it becomes smaller than *TVC*. And it tells us why producers of steel, automobiles, agricultural goods, and television sets will often keep producing output for some time even when they are losing money.

The Long Run: The Exit Decision

The shutdown rule applies only in the short run, a time horizon too short for the firm to escape its commitments to pay for fixed inputs such as plant and equipment. In fact, we only use the term *shut down* when referring to the short run.

But a firm can also decide to stop producing in the long run. In that case, we say the firm has decided to **exit** the industry.

Exit A permanent cessation of production when a firm leaves an industry.

The long-run decision to exit is different than the short-run decision to shut down. That's because in the long run, there *are* no fixed costs, since all inputs can be varied. Therefore, a firm that exits, by reducing all of its inputs to zero, will have *zero* costs (an option not available in the short run). And since exit also means zero revenue, a firm that exits will earn zero profit. When would a firm decide to exit and earn zero profit? When its only other alternative is to earn *negative* profit.

> A firm should exit the industry in the long run when—at its best possible output level—it has any loss at all.

We will look more closely at the exit decision and other long-run considerations in the next chapter.

© GEORGE HALL/CORBIS

USING THE THEORY
Getting It Wrong and Getting It Right

Today, almost all managers have a good grasp of the concepts you've learned in this chapter, largely because microeconomics has become an important part of every business school curriculum. But if we go back a few decades—to when fewer managers had business degrees—we can find two examples of how management's failure to understand the basic theory of the firm led to serious errors. In one case, ignorance of the theory caused a large bank to go bankrupt; in the other, an airline was able to outperform its competitors because *they* remained ignorant of the theory.

Getting It Wrong: The Failure of Franklin National Bank

In the mid-1970s, Franklin National Bank—one of the largest banks in the United States—went bankrupt. The bank's management had made several errors, but we will focus on the most serious one.

First, a little background. A bank is very much like any other business firm: It produces output (in this case a service, making loans) using a variety of inputs (including the funds it lends out). The price of the bank's output is the interest rate it charges to borrowers. For example, with a 5 percent interest rate, the price of each dollar in loans is 5 cents per year.

Unfortunately for banks, they must also *pay* for the money they lend out. The largest source of funds is customer deposits, for which the bank must pay interest. If a bank wants to lend out *more* than its customers have deposited, it can obtain funds from a second source, the *federal funds market*, where banks lend money to one another. To borrow money in this market, the bank will usually have to pay a higher interest rate than it pays on customer deposits.

In mid-1974, John Sadlik, Franklin's chief financial officer, asked his staff to compute the average cost to the bank of a dollar in loanable funds. At the time, Franklin's funds came from three sources, each with its own associated interest cost:

Source	Interest Cost
Checking Accounts	2.25 percent
Savings Accounts	4 percent
Borrowed Funds	9–11 percent

What do these numbers tell us? First, each dollar deposited in a Franklin *checking* account cost the bank 2.25 cents per year,[6] while each dollar in a *savings* account cost Franklin 4 cents. Also, Franklin, like other banks at the time, had to pay between 9 and 11 cents on each dollar borrowed in the federal funds market. When Franklin's accountants were asked to figure out the average cost of a dollar in loans, they divided the total cost of funds by the number of dollars they had lent out. The number they came up with was 7 cents.

This average cost of 7 cents per dollar is an interesting number, but, as we know, it should have *no relevance to a profit-maximizing firm's decisions*. And this is where Franklin went wrong. At the time, all banks, including Franklin, were charging interest rates of 9 to 9.5 percent to their best customers. But Sadlik decided that since money was costing an *average* of 7 cents per dollar, the bank could make a tidy profit by lending money at 8 percent—earning 8 cents per dollar. Accordingly, he ordered his loan officers to approve any loan that could be made to a reputable borrower at 8 percent interest. Needless to say, with other banks continuing to charge 9 percent or more, Franklin National Bank became a very popular place from which to borrow money.

But where did Franklin get the additional funds it was lending out? That was a problem for the managers in *another* department at Franklin, who were responsible for *obtaining* funds. It was not easy to attract additional checking and savings account deposits, since, in the 1970s, the interest rate banks could pay was regulated by the government. That left only one alternative: the federal funds market. And this is exactly where Franklin went to obtain the funds pouring out of its lending department. Of course, these funds were borrowed not at 7 percent, the average cost of funds, but at 9 to 11 percent, the cost of borrowing in the federal funds market.

To understand Franklin's error, let's look again at the average cost figure it was using. This figure included an irrelevant cost: the cost of funds obtained from customer deposits. This cost was irrelevant to the bank's lending decisions, since *additional* loans would not come from these deposits, but rather from the more expensive federal funds market. Further, this average figure was doomed to rise as Franklin expanded its loans. How do we know this? The *marginal* cost of an additional dollar of loans—9 to 11 cents per dollar—was greater than the *average* cost—7 cents. As you know, whenever the marginal is greater than the average, it pulls the average up. Thus, Franklin was basing its decisions on an average cost figure that not only included irrelevant sunk costs but was bound to increase as its lending expanded.

More directly, we can see Franklin's error through the lens of the marginal approach. The *marginal revenue* of each additional dollar lent out at 8 percent was 8 cents, while the *marginal cost* of each additional dollar—since it came from the federal funds market—was 9 to 11 cents. *MC* was greater than *MR*, so Franklin was actually losing money each time its loan officers approved another loan! Not

---

[6] This cost was not actually a direct interest payment to depositors, since in the 1970s banks generally did not pay interest on checking accounts. But banks *did* provide free services such as check clearing, monthly statements, free coffee, and even gifts to their checking account depositors, and the cost of these freebies was computed to be 2.25 cents per dollar of deposits.

surprisingly, these loans—which never should have been made—caused Franklin's profits to *decrease,* and within a year the bank had lost hundreds of millions of dollars. This, together with other management errors, caused the bank to fail.

Getting It Right: The Success of Continental Airlines

In the early 1960s, Continental Airlines was doing something that seemed like a horrible mistake. All other airlines at the time were following a simple rule: They would offer a flight only if, on average, 65 percent of the seats could be filled with paying passengers, since only then could the flight break even. Continental, however, was flying jets filled to just 50 percent of capacity and was actually expanding flights on many routes. When word of Continental's policy leaked out, its stockholders were angry, and managers at competing airlines smiled knowingly, waiting for Continental to fail. Yet Continental's profits—already higher than the industry average—continued to grow. What was going on?

There *was,* indeed, a serious mistake being made, but by the *other* airlines, not Continental. This mistake should by now be familiar to you: using average cost instead of marginal cost to make decisions. The "65 percent of capacity" rule used throughout the industry was derived more or less as follows: The total cost of the airline for the year (TC) was divided by the number of flights during the year (Q) to obtain the average cost of a flight ($TC/Q = ATC$). For the typical flight, this came to about $4,000. Since a jet had to be 65 percent full in order to earn ticket sales of $4,000, the industry regarded any flight that repeatedly took off with less than 65 percent as a money loser and canceled it.

As usual, there are two problems with using ATC in this way. First, an airline's average cost per flight includes many costs that are irrelevant to the decision to add or subtract a flight. These *sunk costs* include the cost of running the reservations system, paying interest on the firm's debt, and fixed fees for landing rights at airports—none of which would change if the firm added or subtracted a flight. Also, average cost ordinarily *changes* as output changes, so it is wrong to assume it is constant in decisions about *changing* output.

Continental's management, led by its vice-president of operations, had decided to try the marginal approach to profit. Whenever a new flight was being considered, every department within the company was asked to determine the *additional* cost they would have to bear. Of course, the only additional costs were for additional *variable* inputs, such as additional flight attendants, ground crew personnel, inflight meals, and jet fuel. These additional costs came to only about $2,000 per flight. Thus, the *marginal* cost of an additional flight—$2,000—was significantly less than the marginal revenue of a flight filled to 65 percent of capacity—$4,000. The marginal approach to profits tells us that when $MR > MC$, output should be increased, which is just what Continental was doing. Indeed, Continental correctly drew the conclusion that the marginal revenue of a flight filled at even 50 percent of capacity—$3,000—was *still* greater than its marginal cost, and so offering the flight would increase profit. This is why Continental was expanding routes even when it could fill only 50 percent of its seats.

In the early 1960s, Continental was able to outperform its competitors by using a secret—the marginal approach to profits. Today, of course, the secret is out, and all airlines use the marginal approach when deciding which flights to offer.[7]

---

[7] For more information about Continental's strategy, see "Airline Takes the Marginal Bone," *Business Week,* April 20, 1963, pp. 111–114.

Summary

In economics, we view the firm as a single economic decision maker with the goal of maximizing the owners' profit. Economic profit is total revenue minus *all* costs of production, explicit and implicit. In their pursuit of maximum profit, firms face two constraints. One is embodied in the demand curve the firm faces; it indicates the maximum price the firm can charge to sell any amount of output. This constraint determines the firm's revenue at each level of production. The other constraint is imposed by costs: More output always means greater costs. In choosing the profit-maximizing output, the firm must consider both revenues and costs.

One approach to choosing the optimal level of output is to measure profit as the difference between total revenue and total cost at each level of output, and then select the output level at which profit is greatest. An alternate approach uses *marginal revenue* (MR), the change in total revenue from producing one more unit of output, and *marginal cost* (MC), the change in total cost from producing one more unit. The firm should increase output whenever $MR > MC$, and lower output when $MR < MC$. The profit-maximizing output level is the one closest to the point where $MR = MC$.

If profit is negative, but total revenue exceeds total variable cost, the firm should continue producing in the short run. Otherwise, it should shut down and suffer a loss equal to its fixed cost. A firm with negative profit in the long run should exit the market.

Key Terms

Accounting profit

Demand curve facing the firm

Economic profit

Exit

Loss

Marginal approach to profit

Marginal revenue

Shutdown rule

Total revenue

Review Questions

1. What is the difference between accounting profit and economic profit?

2. Can a firm earn an accounting profit at the same time it is suffering an economic loss? If so, give a numerical example. Can a firm earn an economic profit at the same time it is suffering an accounting loss? Again, if this is possible, give a numerical example.

3. Name two contributions to the production process for which profit is a payment. Pick a local business, and briefly explain how the entrepreneur behind it has made each of these contributions.

4. What are the two kinds of demand curves we have discussed in this chapter? What does each tell us?

5. What are the constraints on the firm's ability to earn profit? How does each constraint arise?

6. How does the firm select the level of output where profit is greatest in:
   a. The total revenue and total cost approach?
   b. The marginal revenue and marginal cost approach? How is each approach illustrated graphically?

Problems and Exercises

1. You have a part-time work/study job at the library that pays $10 per hour, 3 hours per day on Saturdays and Sundays. Some friends want you to join them on a weekend ski trip leaving Friday night and returning Monday morning. They estimate your share of the gas, motel, lift tickets, and other expenses to be around $30. What is your total cost (considering both explicit and implicit costs) for the trip?

2. Until recently, you worked for a software development firm at a yearly salary of $35,000. Now, you decide to open your own business. Planning to be the next Bill Gates, you quit your job, cash in a $10,000 savings account (which pays 5 percent interest), and use the money to buy the latest computer hardware to use in your business. You also convert a basement apartment in your house, which you have been renting for $250 a month, into a workspace for your new software firm.

You lease some office equipment for $3,600 a year and hire two part-time programmers, whose combined salary is $25,000 a year. You also figure it costs around $50 a month to provide heat and light for your new office.

a. What are the total annual explicit costs of your new business?
b. What are the total annual implicit costs?
c. At the end of your first year, your accountant cheerily informs you that your total sales for the year amounted to $55,000. She congratulates you on a profitable year. Are her congratulations warranted? Why or why not?

3. The following data are price/quantity/cost combinations for Titan Industry's mainframe computer division:

Quantity	Price per Unit	Total Cost of Production
0	above $225,000	$200,000
1	$225,000	$250,000
2	$175,000	$275,000
3	$150,000	$325,000
4	$125,000	$400,000
5	$90,000	$500,000

a. What is the marginal revenue if output rises from 2 to 3 units? (*Hint:* Calculate total revenue at each output level first.) What is the marginal cost if output rises from 4 to 5 units?
b. What quantity should Titan produce to maximize total revenue? Total profit?
c. What is Titan's fixed cost? How do Titan's marginal costs behave as output increases? Provide a plausible explanation as to why a computer manufacturer's marginal costs might behave in this way.

4. Each entry in this table shows marginal revenue and marginal cost when a firm increases output to the given quantity:

Quantity	MR	MC
10		
	30	25
11		
	29	23
12		
	27	22
13		
	25	25
14		
	23	27
15		
	21	29
16		
	19	31
17		

What is the profit-maximizing level of output?

5. The following tables give information about demand and total cost for two firms. In the short run, how much should each produce?

Firm A

Quantity	Price	Total Cost
0	above $125	$250
1	$125	$400
2	$100	$500
3	$ 75	$550
4	$ 50	$600
5	$ 25	$700

Firm B

Quantity	Price	Total Cost
0	above $500	$ 500
1	$500	$ 700
2	$400	$ 900
3	$300	$1,100
4	$200	$1,300
5	$100	$1,500

6. At its best possible output level, a firm has total revenue of $3,500 per day and total cost of $7,000 per day. What should this firm do in the short run if:
a. the firm has total *fixed* costs of $3,000 per day?
b. the firm has total *variable* costs of $3,000 per day?

7. Suppose you own a restaurant that serves only dinner. You are trying to decide whether or not to rent out your dining room and kitchen during mornings to another firm, The Breakfast Club, Inc., that will serve only breakfast. Your restaurant currently has the following monthly costs:

Rent on building:	$2,000
Electricity:	$1,000
Wages and salaries:	$15,000
Advertising:	$2,000
Purchases of food and supplies:	$8,000
Your foregone labor income:	$4,000
Your foregone interest:	$1,000

a. Which of your current costs are implicit, and which are explicit?
b. Suppose The Breakfast Club, Inc. offers to pay $800 per month to use the building. They promise to use only their own food, and also to leave the place spotless when they leave each day. If you believe them, should you rent out your restaurant to them? Or does it depend? Explain.

8. Suppose that, due to a dramatic rise in real estate taxes, Ned's Beds' total fixed cost rises from $300 to $1,300 per day. Use the data of Table 1 to answer the following:
   a. What does the tax hike do to Ned's *MC* and *MR* curves?
   b. In the short run, how many beds should Ned produce after the rise in taxes?
   c. In the long run, how many beds should Ned produce after the rise in taxes?

9. Suppose Ned's Beds does *not* have to lower the price in order to sell more beds. Specifically, suppose Ned can sell all the beds he wants at a price of $275 per bed.

   a. What will Ned's *MR* curve look like? (*Hint:* How much will his revenue rise for each additional bed he sells?)
   b. In Table 1, how would you change the numbers in the marginal revenue column to reflect the constant price for beds?
   c. Using the marginal cost and *new* marginal revenue numbers in Table 1, find the number of beds Ned should sell.

Challenge Questions

1. A firm's *marginal profit* can be defined as the change in its profit when output increases by one unit.
   a. Compute the marginal profit for each change in Ned's Beds' output in Table 1.
   b. State a complete rule for finding the profit-maximizing output level in terms of marginal profit.

2. Howell Industries specializes in precision plastics. Their latest invention promises to revolutionize the electronics industry, and they have already made and sold 75 of the miracle devices. They have estimated average costs as given in the following table:

Unit	ATC
74	$10,000
75	$12,000
76	$14,000

Backus Electronics has just offered Howell $150,000 if it will produce the 76th unit. Should Howell accept the offer and manufacture the additional device?

These exercises require access to Lieberman/Hall Xtra! If Xtra! did not come with your book, visit http://liebermanxtra.swlearning.com to purchase.

1. Use your Xtra! Password at the Hall and Lieberman Web site (http://liebermanxtra.swlearning.com), select this chapter, and under Economic Applications, click on EconNews. Click on *Microeconomics: Profit Maximization*, and scroll down to find the article, "To Charge or Not to Charge." Is Pitegoff classifying tourism as a variable input, or a fixed input? Why? How does this influence his decision on whether to keep prices constant?

2. Use your Xtra! Password at the Hall and Lieberman Web site (http://liebermanxtra.swlearning.com), select this chapter, and under Economic Applications, click on EconNews, then on *Microeconomics: Profit Maximization*. Find the article "Money for Nothing." Explain why Sony's decision to buy out Mariah Carey's contract had no impact on its profit (focus solely on the buy-out of the contract, not the secondary effects, such as reduced marketing costs, etc.

Perfect Competition

No one knows exactly how many different goods and services are offered for sale in the United States, but the number must be somewhere in the tens of millions. Each of these goods is traded in a market, where buyers and sellers come together, and these markets have several things in common. Sellers want to sell at the *highest* possible price; buyers seek the *lowest* possible price; and all trade is *voluntary*. But here, the similarity ends.

When we observe buyers and sellers in action, we see that different goods and services are sold in vastly different ways. Take advertising, for example. Every day, we are inundated with sales pitches on television, radio, and newspapers for a long list of products: toothpaste, perfume, automobiles, Internet Web sites, cat food, banking services, and more. But have you ever seen a farmer on television, trying to convince you to buy *his* wheat, rather than the wheat of other farmers? Do shareholders of major corporations like General Motors sell their stock by advertising in the newspaper? Why, in a world in which virtually *everything* seems to be advertised, do we not see ads for wheat, shares of stock, corn, crude oil, gold, copper, or foreign currency?

Or consider profits. Anyone starting a business hopes to make as much profit as possible. Yet some companies—Microsoft, Quaker Oats, and PepsiCo, for example—

earn sizable profit for their owners year after year, while at other companies, such as Delta Air Lines and most small businesses, economic profit is generally low.

We could say, "That's just how the cookie crumbles," and attribute all of these observations to pure randomness. But economics is all about *explaining* such things, finding patterns amidst the chaos of everyday economic life. When economists turn their attention to differences in trading, such as these, they think immediately about *market structure,* the subject of this and the next chapter. We've used this term informally elsewhere in the text, but now it's time for a formal definition:

> By **market structure**, *we mean all the characteristics of a market that influence the behavior of buyers and sellers when they come together to trade.*

Market structure The characteristics of a market that influence how trading takes place.

To determine the structure of any particular market, we begin by asking three simple questions:

1. *How many* buyers and sellers are there in the market?
2. Is each seller offering a *standardized product,* more or less indistinguishable from that offered by other sellers, or are there significant differences between the products of different firms?
3. Are there any *barriers to entry or exit,* or can *outsiders* easily enter and leave this market?

The answers to these questions help us to classify a market into one of four basic types: *perfect competition, monopoly, monopolistic competition,* or *oligopoly.* The subject of this chapter is perfect competition. In the next chapter, we'll look carefully at the other market structures.

WHAT IS PERFECT COMPETITION?

Does the phrase "perfect competition" sound familiar? It should, because you encountered it earlier, in Chapter 3. There you learned (briefly) that the famous supply and demand model explains how prices are determined in *perfectly competitive markets.* Now we're going to take a much deeper and more comprehensive look at perfectly competitive markets. By the end of this chapter, you will understand very clearly how perfect competition and the supply and demand model are related.

Let's start with the word *competition* itself. When you hear that word, you may think of an intense, personal rivalry, like that between two boxers competing in a ring or two students competing for the best grade in a small class. But there are other, less personal forms of competition. If you took the SAT exam to get into college, you were competing with thousands of other test takers in rooms just like yours, all across the country. But the competition was *impersonal:* You were trying to do the best that you could do, trying to outperform others in general, but not competing with any one individual in the room. In economics, the term "competition" is used in the latter sense. It describes a situation of diffuse, impersonal competition in a highly populated environment. The market structure you will learn about in this chapter—perfect competition—is an example of this notion.

The Three Requirements of Perfect Competition

Perfect competition
A market structure in which there are many buyers and sellers, the product is standardized, and sellers can easily enter or exit the market.

> *Perfect competition* is a market structure with three important characteristics:
>
> 1. *There are large numbers of buyers and sellers, and each buys or sells only a tiny fraction of the total quantity in the market.*
> 2. *Sellers offer a standardized product.*
> 3. *Sellers can easily enter into or exit from the market.*

These three conditions probably raise more questions than they answer, so let's see what each one really means.

A Large Number of Buyers and Sellers. In perfect competition, there must be many buyers and sellers. How many? It would be nice if we could specify a number—like 32,456—for this requirement. Unfortunately, we cannot, since what constitutes a large number of buyers and sellers can be different under different conditions. What is important is this:

> *In a perfectly competitive market, the number of buyers and sellers is so large that no individual decision maker can significantly affect the price of the product by changing the quantity it buys or sells.*

Think of the world market for wheat. On the selling side, there are hundreds of thousands of individual wheat farmers—more than 250,000 in the United States alone. Each of these farmers produces only a tiny fraction of the total market quantity. If any one of them were to double, triple, or even quadruple its production, the impact on total market quantity and market price would be negligible. The same is true on the buying side: There are so many small buyers that no one of them can affect the market price by increasing or decreasing its quantity demanded.

Most agricultural markets conform to the large-number-of-small-firms requirement, as do markets for precious metals such as gold and silver and markets for the stocks and bonds of large corporations. For example, more than 2 million shares of General Motors stock are bought and sold *every day,* at a price (as this is written) of about $40 per share. A decision by a single stockholder to sell, say, $1 million dollars worth of this stock—about 25,000 shares—would cause only a barely noticeable change in quantity supplied on any given day.

But now think about the U.S. market for athletic shoes. In 2002, four large producers—Nike, Reebok, Adidas, and New Balance—accounted for 72 percent of total sales. If any one of these producers decided to change its output by even 10 percent, the impact on total quantity supplied—and market price—would be *very* noticeable. The market for athletic shoes thus fails the large-number-of-small-firms requirement, so it is not an example of perfect competition.

A Standardized Product Offered by Sellers. In a perfectly competitive market, buyers do not perceive significant differences between the products of one seller and another. For example, buyers of wheat will ordinarily have no preference for one farmer's wheat over another's, so wheat would surely pass the standardized product test. The same is true of many other agricultural products—for example, corn syrup and soybeans. It is also true of commodities like crude oil or pork bellies, precious metals like gold or silver, and financial instruments such as the stocks and bonds of a particular firm. (One share of AT&T stock is indistinguishable from another.)

When buyers *do* notice significant differences in the outputs of different sellers, the market is not perfectly competitive. For example, most consumers perceive differences among the various brands of coffee on the supermarket shelf and may have strong preferences for one particular brand. Coffee, therefore, fails the standardized product test of perfect competition. Other goods and services that would fail this test include personal computers, automobiles, houses, colleges, and medical care.

Easy Entry into and Exit from the Market. Entry into a market is rarely free; a new seller must always incur *some* costs to set up shop, begin production, and establish contacts with customers. But a perfectly competitive market has no *significant* barriers to discourage new entrants: Any firm wishing to enter can do business on the same terms as firms that are already there. For example, anyone who wants to start a wheat farm can do so, facing the same costs for land, farm equipment, seeds, fertilizer, and hired labor as existing farms. The same is true of anyone wishing to open up a dry cleaning shop, restaurant, or dog-walking service. Each of these examples would pass the easy-entry test of perfect competition.

In many markets, however, there are significant barriers to entry. These are often *legal barriers*. An example: For the last 70 years, the number of taxicabs licensed to operate in New York City has been fixed, with only occasional small changes, at around 12,000. Unless the city issues more licenses in the future, true entry into this market will be impossible—the licenses may change hands, but the total number of legally operated taxis cannot increase. Another example of legal barriers to entry is *zoning laws*. These place strict limits on how many businesses such as movie theaters, supermarkets, or hotels can operate in a local area.

Aside from laws, significant barriers to entry can arise simply because existing sellers have an important advantage that new entrants cannot duplicate. The brand loyalty enjoyed by existing producers of breakfast cereals, instant coffee, and soft drinks would require a new entrant to wrest customers away from existing firms—a very costly undertaking. Or as you saw in Chapter 5, significant economies of scale may give existing firms a cost advantage over new entrants. We will discuss these and other barriers to entry in more detail in later chapters.

In addition to easy entry, perfect competition is characterized by easy *exit:* A firm suffering a long-run loss must be able to sell off its plant and equipment and leave the industry for good, without obstacles. Some markets satisfy this requirement, and some do not. Plant-closing laws or union agreements can require lengthy advance notice and high severance pay when workers are laid off. Or capital equipment may be so highly specialized—like an assembly line designed to produce just one type of automobile—that it cannot be sold off if the firm decides to exit the market. These and other barriers to exit do not conform to the assumptions of perfect competition.

Toward the end of this chapter, you'll see that easy entry and exit have important implications for competitive markets in the long run.

Is Perfect Competition Realistic?

The three assumptions a market must satisfy to be perfectly competitive (or just "competitive," for short) are rather restrictive. Do any markets satisfy all these requirements? How broadly can we apply the model of perfect competition when we think about the real world?

First, remember that perfect competition is a *model*—an abstract representation of reality. No model can capture *all* of the details of a real-world market, nor should it. Still, in some cases, the model fits remarkably well. We have seen that the market for wheat, for example, passes all three tests for a competitive market: many buyers and sellers, standardized output, and easy entry and exit. Indeed, most agricultural markets satisfy the strict requirements of perfect competition quite closely, as do many financial markets and some markets for consumer goods and services.

But in the vast majority of markets, one or more of the assumptions of perfect competition will, in a strict sense, be violated. This might suggest that the model can be applied only in a few limited cases. Yet when economists look at real-world markets, they use the perfect competition model more than any other market model. Why is this?

First, the model of perfect competition is powerful. Using simple techniques, it leads to important predictions about a market's response to changes in consumer tastes, technology, and government policies. While other types of market structure models also yield valuable predictions, they are often more cumbersome and their predictions less definitive. Second, many markets, while not strictly perfectly competitive, come *reasonably* close. The more closely a real-world market fits the model, the more accurate our predictions will be when we use it.

We can even, with some caution, use the model to analyze markets that violate all three assumptions. Take the worldwide market for television sets. There are about a dozen major sellers in this market. Each of them knows that its output decisions will have *some* effect on the market price, but no one of them can have a *major* impact on price. Consumers do recognize the difference between one brand and another, but their preferences are not very strong, and most recognize that quality has become so standardized that all brands are actually close substitutes for each other. And there are indeed barriers to entry—existing firms have supply and distribution networks that would be difficult for new entrants to replicate—but these barriers are not *so* great that they would keep out new entrants if they saw the potential for high profit. Thus, although the market for televisions does not strictly satisfy any of the requirements of perfect competition, it is not *too* far off on any one of them. The model will not perform as accurately for televisions as it does for wheat, but, depending on how much accuracy we need, it may do just fine.

In sum, perfect competition can approximate conditions and yield accurate-enough predictions in a wide variety of markets. This is why you will often find economists using the model to analyze the markets for crude oil, consumer electronic goods, fast-food meals, medical care, and higher education, even though in each of these cases one or more of the requirements may not be strictly satisfied.

THE PERFECTLY COMPETITIVE FIRM

When we stand at a distance and look at conditions in a competitive market, we get one view of what is occurring; when we stand close and look at the individual competitive *firm*, we get an entirely different picture. But these two pictures are very closely related. After all, a market is a collection of individual decision makers, much as a human body is a collection of individual cells. In a perfectly competitive market, the individual cells (firms and consumers) and the overall body (the market) affect each other through a variety of feedback mechanisms. This is why, in learning about the competitive firm, we must also discuss the competitive market in which it operates.

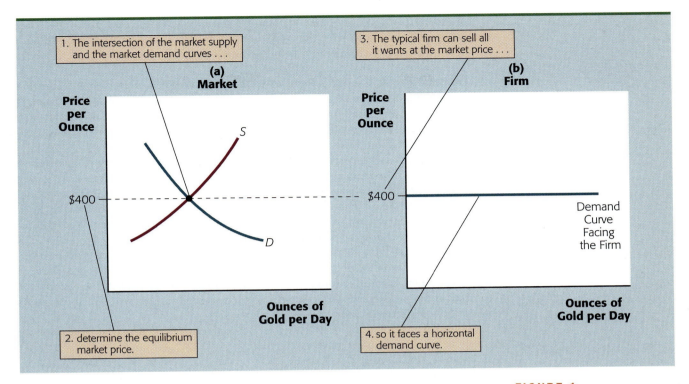

1. The intersection of the market supply and the market demand curves . . .

3. The typical firm can sell all it wants at the market price . . .

(a)
Market

(b)
Firm

Price per Ounce

Price per Ounce

S

$400

$400

D

Demand Curve Facing the Firm

Ounces of Gold per Day

Ounces of Gold per Day

2. determine the equilibrium market price.

4. so it faces a horizontal demand curve.

FIGURE 1
The Competitive Industry and Firm

Figure 1(a) applies the tools you have already learned—supply and demand—to the competitive market for gold. The market demand curve slopes downward: As price falls, buyers will want to purchase more. The supply curve slopes upward: As price rises, the total quantity supplied by firms in the market will rise. The intersection of the supply and demand curves determines the equilibrium price of gold, which, in the figure, is $400 per troy ounce.[1] This is all familiar territory. But now let's switch lenses and see how Small Time Gold Mines, an individual mining company, views this market.

Goals and Constraints of the Competitive Firm

Small Time's goal—like that of any business firm—is to *maximize profit*. And, like any firm, it faces constraints. For example, it must use some given production technology to produce its output, and must pay some given prices for its inputs. As a result, Small Time faces a familiar cost constraint; just like Spotless Car Wash in Chapter 5 and Ned's Beds in Chapter 6, Small Time Gold Mines faces a total cost of production for any level of output it might want to produce. In addition to *total* cost, Small Time has *ATC*, *AVC*, and *MC* curves, and these have the familiar shapes you learned about in the previous two chapters.

A perfectly competitive firm faces a cost constraint like any other firm. The cost of producing any given level of output depends on the firm's production technology and the prices it must pay for its inputs.

Maximization Subject to Constraints

---

[1] Gold is sold by the troy ounce, which is about 10 percent heavier than a regular ounce.

In addition to a cost constraint, Small Time Gold Mines faces a demand constraint, as does any firm. But there is something different about the demand constraint for a perfectly competitive firm like Small Time.

The Demand Curve Facing a Perfectly Competitive Firm.

Panel (b) of Figure 1 shows the demand curve facing Small Time Gold Mines. Notice the special shape of this curve: It is horizontal, or infinitely price elastic. This tells us that no matter how much gold Small Time produces, it will always sell it at the same price—$400 per troy ounce. Why should this be?

First, in perfect competition, output is standardized—buyers do not distinguish the gold of one mine from that of another. If Small Time were to charge a price even a tiny bit higher than other producers, it would lose all of its customers; they would simply buy from Small Time's competitors, whose prices would be lower. The horizontal demand curve captures this effect. It tells us that if Small Time raises its price above $400, it will not just sell *less* output, it will sell *no* output.

Second, Small Time is only a tiny producer relative to the entire gold market. No matter how much it decides to produce, it cannot make a noticeable difference in market quantity supplied and so cannot affect the market price. Once again, the horizontal demand curve describes this effect perfectly: The firm can increase its production without having to lower its price.

All of this means that Small Time has no control over the price of its output—it simply accepts the market price as given:

Price taker Any firm that treats the price of its product as given and beyond its control.

> *In perfect competition, the firm is a **price taker**: It treats the price of its output as given.*

The horizontal demand curve facing the firm and the resulting price-taking behavior of firms are hallmarks of perfect competition. If a manager thinks, "If we produce more output, we will have to lower our price," then the firm faces a *downward-sloping* demand curve and is not a competitive firm. The manager of a competitive firm will always think, "We can sell all the output we want at the going price, so how much should we produce?"

Notice that, since a competitive firm takes the market price as given, its only decision is *how much output to produce and sell*. Once it makes that decision, we can determine the firm's cost of production, as well as the total revenue it will earn (the market price times the quantity of output produced). Let's see how this works in practice with Small Time Gold Mines.

Cost and Revenue Data for a Competitive Firm

Table 1 shows cost and revenue data for Small Time. In the first two columns are different quantities of gold that Small Time could produce each day and the maximum price that it could charge. Because Small Time is a competitive firm, a price taker, the price remains constant at $400 per ounce, no matter *how* much gold it produces.

Run your finger down the total revenue and marginal revenue columns. Since price is always $400, each time the firm produces another ounce of gold, total revenue rises by $400. This is why marginal revenue—the additional revenue from selling one more ounce of gold—remains constant at $400.

Figure 2 plots Small Time's total revenue and marginal revenue. Notice that the total revenue (*TR*) curve in panel (a) is a *straight line* that slopes upward; each time

(1) Output (Troy Ounces of Gold per Day)	(2) Price (per Troy Ounce)	(3) Total Revenue	(4) Marginal Revenue	(5) Total Cost	(6) Marginal Cost	(7) Profit
0	$400	$ 0		$ 550		−$550
			$400		$450	
1	$400	$ 400		$1,000		−$600
			$400		$200	
2	$400	$ 800		$1,200		−$400
			$400		$ 50	
3	$400	$1,200		$1,250		−$ 50
			$400		$100	
4	$400	$1,600		$1,350		$250
			$400		$150	
5	$400	$2,000		$1,500		$500
			$400		$250	
6	$400	$2,400		$1,750		$650
			$400		$350	
7	$400	$2,800		$2,100		$700
			$400		$450	
8	$400	$3,200		$2,550		$650
			$400		$550	
9	$400	$3,600		$3,100		$500
			$400		$650	
10	$400	$4,000		$3,750		$250

TABLE 1
Cost and Revenue Data for Small Time Gold Mines

output increases by one unit, *TR* rises by the same $400. That is, the slope of the *TR* curve is equal to the price of output.

The marginal revenue (*MR*) curve is a *horizontal* line at the market price. In fact, the *MR* curve is the same horizontal line as the demand curve. Why? Remember that marginal revenue is the additional revenue the firm earns from selling an additional unit of output. For a price-taking competitive firm, that additional revenue will always be the price per unit, no matter how many units it is already sells.

> *For a competitive firm, marginal revenue at each quantity is the same as the market price. For this reason, the marginal revenue curve and the demand curve facing the firm are the same: a horizontal line at the market price.*

In panel (b), we have labeled the horizontal line "*d = MR*," since this line is both the firm's demand curve (*d*) *and* its marginal revenue curve (*MR*).[2]

Columns 5 and 6 of Table 1 show total cost and marginal cost for Small Time. There is nothing special about cost data for a competitive firm. In Figure 2, you

---

[2] In this and later chapters, lowercase letters for quantities and demand curves refer to the individual firm, and uppercase letters to the entire market. For example, the demand curve facing the firm is labeled *d*, while the market demand curve is labeled *D*.

FIGURE 2
Profit Maximization in Perfect Competition

Panel (a) shows a competitive firm's total revenue (TR) and total cost (TC) curves. TR is a straight line with slope equal to the market price. Profit is maximized at 7 ounces per day, where the vertical distance between TR and TC is greatest. Panel (b) shows that profit is maximized where the marginal cost (MC) curve intersects the horizontal demand (d) and marginal revenue (MR) curves.

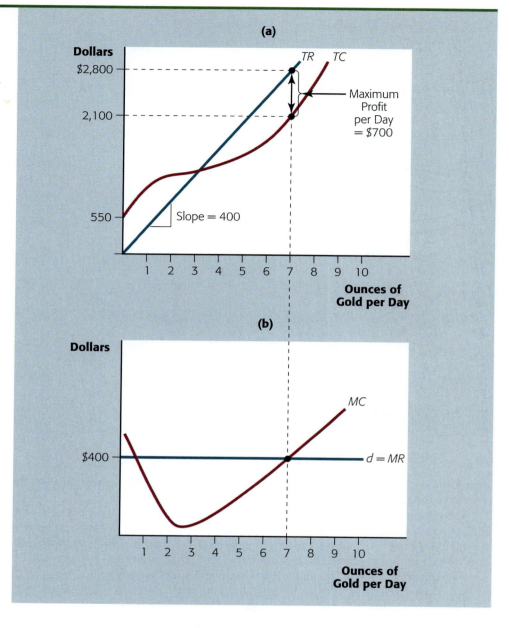

can see that marginal cost (*MC*)—as usual—first falls and then rises. Total cost, therefore, rises first at a decreasing rate and then at an increasing rate. (You may want to look at Chapter 5 to review why this cost behavior is so common.)

Finding the Profit-Maximizing Output Level

A competitive firm—like any other firm—wants to earn the highest possible profit, and to do so, it should use the principles you learned in Chapter 6. Although the diagrams look a bit different for competitive firms, the ideas behind them are the same. We can use either Table 1 or Figure 2 to find the profit-maximizing output level. And we can use the techniques you have already learned: the total revenue and total cost approach, or the marginal revenue and marginal cost approach.

The Total Revenue and Total Cost Approach. The *TR* and *TC* approach is the most direct way of viewing the firm's search for the profit-maximizing output level. Quite simply, at each output level, subtract total cost from total revenue to get total profit:

$$\text{Total Profit} = TR - TC$$

Then we just scan the different output levels to see which one gives the highest number for profit.

In Table 1, total profit is shown in the last column. A simple scan of that column tells us that $700 is the highest daily profit that Small Time Gold Mines can earn. Tracing along the row to the first column, we see that to earn this profit, Small Time must produce 7 ounces per day, its profit-maximizing output level.

The same approach to maximizing profit can be seen graphically, in the upper panel of Figure 2. There, total profit at any output level is the distance between the *TR* and *TC* curves. As you can see, this distance is greatest when the firm produces 7 units, verifying what we found in the table.

This approach is simple and straightforward, but it hides the interesting part of the story: the way that *changes* in output cause total revenue and total cost to change. The other approach to finding the profit-maximizing output level focuses on these changes.

The Marginal Revenue and Marginal Cost Approach. In the *MR* and *MC* approach, the firm should continue to increase output as long as marginal revenue is greater than marginal cost. You can verify, using Table 1, that if the firm is initially producing 1, 2, 3, 4, 5, or 6 units, *MR* > *MC*, so producing more will raise profit. Once the firm is producing 7 units, however, *MR* < *MC*, so further increases in output will reduce profit. Alternatively, using the graph in panel (b) of Figure 2, we look for the output level at which *MR* = *MC*. As the graph shows, there are two output levels at which the *MR* and *MC* curves intersect. However, we can rule out the first crossing point because there, the *MC* curve crosses the *MR* curve from above. Remember that the profit-maximizing output is found where the *MC* curve crosses the *MR* curve from *below*. Once again, this occurs at 7 units of output.

You can see that finding the profit-maximizing output level for a competitive firm requires no new concepts or techniques; you have already learned everything you need to know in Chapter 6. In fact, the only difference is one of appearance. Ned's Beds—our firm in Chapter 6—did *not* operate under perfect competition. As a result, both its demand curve and its marginal revenue curve sloped *downward*. Small Time, however, operates under perfect competition, so its demand and *MR* curves are the same horizontal line.

Measuring Total Profit

You have already seen one way to measure a firm's total profit on a graph: the vertical distance between the *TR* and *TC* curves. In this section, you will learn another graphical way to measure profit.

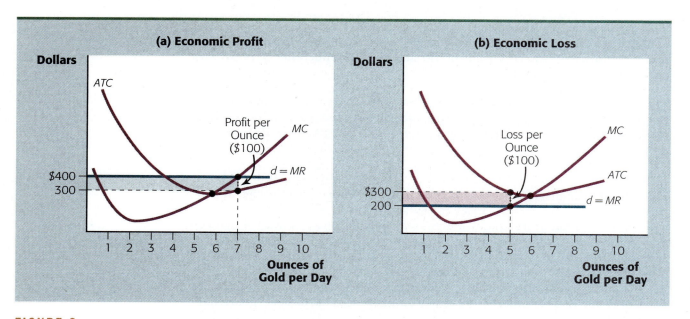

FIGURE 3
Measuring Profit or Loss

The competitive firm in panel (a) produces where marginal cost equals marginal revenue, or 7 units of output per day. Profit per unit at that output level is equal to revenue per unit ($400) minus cost per unit ($300), or $100 per unit. Total profit (indicated by the blue-shaded rectangle) is equal to profit per unit times the number of units sold, $100 × 7 = $700. In panel (b), the firm faces a lower market price of $200 per ounce. The best it can do is to produce 5 ounces per day and suffer a loss shown by the red area. It loses $100 per ounce on each of those 5 ounces produced, so the total loss is $500—the area of the red-shaded rectangle.

To do this, we start with the firm's *profit per unit*, which is the revenue it gets on each unit minus the cost per unit. Revenue per unit is just the price (*P*) of the firm's output, and cost per unit is our familiar *ATC*, so we can write:

$$\text{Profit per unit} = P - ATC.$$

In Figure 3(a), Small Time's *ATC* curve has been plotted (based on the data in Table 1). When the firm is producing at the profit-maximizing output level, 7 units, its *ATC* is $300. Since the price of output is $400, profit *per unit* = *P* − *ATC* = $400 − $300 = $100. This is just the vertical distance between the firm's demand curve and its *ATC* curve at the profit-maximizing output level.

Once we know Small Time's profit per unit, it is easy to calculate its *total* profit: Just multiply profit per unit by the number of units sold. Small Time is earning $100 profit on each ounce of gold, and it sells 7 ounces in all, so total profit is $100 × 7 = $700.

Now look at the blue-shaded rectangle in Figure 3(a). The height of this rectangle is profit per unit, and the width is the number of units produced. The *area* of the rectangle—height × width—equals Small Time's profit:

> *A firm earns a profit whenever* P > ATC. *Its total profit at the best output level equals the area of a rectangle with height equal to the distance between* P *and* ATC, *and width equal to the level of output.*

In the figure, Small Time is fortunate: At a price of $400, there are several output levels at which it can earn a profit. Its problem is to select the one that makes its profit as large as possible. (We should all have such problems.)

But what if the price had been lower than $400—so low, in fact, that Small Time could not make a profit at *any* output level? Then the best it can do is to choose the smallest possible loss. Just as we did in the case of profit, we can measure the firm's total loss using the *ATC* curve.

Panel (b) of Figure 3 reproduces Small Time's *ATC* and *MC* curves from panel (a). This time, however, we have assumed a lower price for gold—$200—so the firm's $d = MR$ curve is the horizontal line at $200. Since this line lies everywhere below the *ATC* curve, profit per unit ($P - ATC$) is always negative: Small Time cannot make a positive profit at *any* output level.

With a price of $200, the *MC* curve crosses the *MR* curve from below at 5 units of output. Unless Small Time decides to shut down (we'll discuss shutting down for competitive firms later), it should produce 5 units. At that level of output, *ATC* is $300, and profit per unit is $P - ATC = \$200 - \$300 = -\$100$, a *loss* of $100 per unit. The total loss is loss per unit (negative profit per unit) times the number of units produced, or $-\$100 \times 5 = -\$500$. This is the area of the red-shaded rectangle in Figure 3(b), with height of $100 and width of 5 units:

> A firm suffers a loss whenever $P < ATC$ at the best level of output. Its total loss equals the area of a rectangle with height equal to the distance between P and ATC, and width equal to the level of output.

The Firm's Short-Run Supply Curve

A competitive firm is a price taker: It takes the market price as given and then decides how much output it will produce at that price. If the market price changes for any reason, the price taken as given will change as well. The firm will then have to find a new profit-maximizing output level. Let's see how the firm's choice of output changes as the market price rises or falls.

Misusing Profit per Unit It is tempting—but *wrong*—to think that the firm should produce where profit *per unit* ($P - ATC$) is greatest. The firm's goal is to maximize *total* profit, not profit per unit. Using Table 1 or Figure 3(a), you can verify that while Small Time's profit *per unit* is greatest at 6 units of output, its *total* profit is greatest at 7 units.

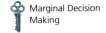

Figure 4(a) shows *ATC*, *AVC*, and *MC* curves for a competitive producer of wheat. The figure also shows five hypothetical demand curves the firm might face, each corresponding to a different market price for wheat. If the market price were $3.50 per bushel, the firm would face demand curve d_1, and its profit-maximizing output level—where $MC = MR$—would be 7,000 bushels per year. If the price dropped to $2.50 per bushel, the firm would face demand curve d_2, and its profit-maximizing output level would drop to 5,000 bushels. You can see that the profit-maximizing output level is always found by traveling from the price, across to the firm's *MC* curve, and then down to the horizontal axis. In other words,

> as the price of output changes, the firm will slide along its *MC* curve in deciding how much to produce.

Marginal Decision Making

But there is one problem with this: If the firm is suffering a loss—a loss large enough to justify shutting down—then it will *not* produce along its *MC* curve; it will produce zero units instead. Thus, in order to know for certain how much output the firm will produce, we must bring in the shutdown rule you learned in Chapter 6.

The Shutdown Price. Suppose the price in Figure 4(a) drops down to $2 per bushel. At this price, the best output level is 4,000 bushels, and the firm suffers a loss, since $P < ATC$. Should the firm shut down? Let's see. At 4,000 bushels, it is

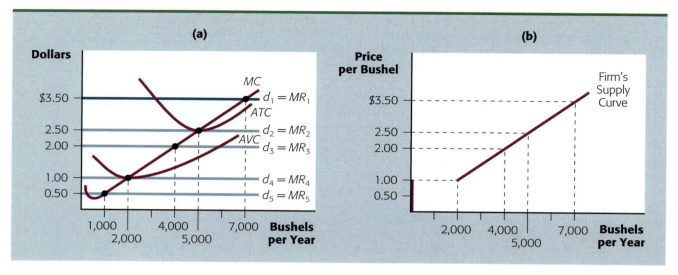

FIGURE 4
Short-Run Supply Under Perfect Competition

Panel (a) shows a typical competitive firm facing various market prices. For prices between $1 and $3.50 per bushel, the profit-maximizing quantity is found by sliding along the MC curve. Below $1 per bushel, the firm is better off shutting down, because P < AVC, and so TR < TVC. Panel (b) shows that the firm's supply curve consists of two segments. Above the shutdown price of $1 per bushel it follows the MC curve; below that price, it is coincident with the vertical axis.

Shutdown price The price at which a firm is indifferent between producing and shutting down.

also true that $P > AVC$, since the demand curve lies above the AVC curve at this output level. Multiplying both sides of the last inequality by Q gives us

$$P \times Q > AVC \times Q.$$

Since $AVC \times Q$ is just TVC, this inequality is the same as

$$TR > TVC.$$

As we know from Chapter 6, a firm should *never* shut down when $TR > TVC$. Thus, at a price of $2, the firm will stay open and produce 4,000 units of output.

Now, suppose the price drops all the way down to $0.50 per bushel. At this price, $MR = MC$ at 1,000 bushels, but notice that here $P < AVC$. Once again, we multiply both sides by Q to obtain

$$P \times Q < AVC \times Q$$

or

$$TR < TVC.$$

A firm should *always* shut down when $TR < TVC$, so at a price of $0.50, this firm will produce *zero* units of output.

Finally, let's consider a price of $1. At this price, $MR = MC$ at 2,000 bushels, and here we have $P = AVC$ or $TR = TVC$. At $1, therefore, the firm will be indifferent between staying open and shutting down. We call this price the firm's **shutdown price**, since it will shut down at any price lower and stay open at any price higher. The output level at which the firm will shut down must occur at the *minimum* of the AVC curve. Why? Note that as the price of output decreases, the best output level is found by sliding along the MC curve, until MC and AVC cross. At that point, the firm will shut down. But—as you learned in Chapter 5—MC will always cross AVC at its minimum point.

Now let's recapitulate what we've found about the firm's output decision. For all prices above the minimum point on the AVC curve, the firm will stay open and will produce the level of output at which $MR = MC$. For these prices, the firm slides along its *MC* curve in deciding how much output to produce. But for any price below the minimum *AVC*, the firm will shut down and produce zero units. We can summarize all of this information in a single curve—the **firm's supply curve**—which tells us how much output the firm will produce at any price:

> *The competitive firm's supply curve has two parts. For all prices above the minimum point on its AVC curve, the supply curve coincides with the MC curve. For all prices below the minimum point on the AVC curve, the firm will shut down, so its supply curve is a vertical line segment at zero units of output.*

Firm's supply curve A curve that shows the quantity of output a competitive firm will produce at different prices.

In panel (b) of Figure 4, we have drawn the supply curve for our hypothetical wheat farmer. As price declines from $3.50 to $1, output is determined by the firm's *MC* curve. For all prices *below* $1—the shutdown price—output is zero and the supply curve coincides with the vertical axis.

COMPETITIVE MARKETS IN THE SHORT RUN

Recall that the short run is a time period too short for the firm to vary *all* of its inputs: The quantity of at least one input remains fixed. For example, in the short run, a wheat farmer will be stuck with a certain plot of land and a certain number of tractors. Now let's extend the concept of the short run from the firm to the market as a whole. It makes sense that if the short run is insufficient time for a firm to vary its fixed inputs, then it is also insufficient time for a *new* firm to acquire those fixed inputs and *enter* the market. Similarly, it is too short a period for firms to reduce their fixed inputs to zero and *exit* the market. We conclude that

> *in the short run, the number of firms in the industry is fixed.*

The (Short-Run) Market Supply Curve

Once we know how to find the supply curve of each *individual* firm in a market, we can easily determine the short-run **market supply curve**, showing the amount of output that all sellers in the market will offer at each price.

Market supply curve A curve indicating the quantity of output that all sellers in a market will produce at different prices.

> *To obtain the market supply curve, we add up the quantities of output supplied by all firms in the market at each price.*

To keep things simple, suppose there are 100 identical wheat farms and that each one has the supply curve shown in Figure 5(a)—the same supply curve we derived in Figure 4. Then at a price of $3.50, each firm would produce 7,000 bushels. With 100 such firms, the market quantity supplied will be $7,000 \times 100 = 700,000$ bushels. At a price of $2.50, each firm would supply 5,000 bushels, so market supply would be 500,000. Continuing in this way, we can trace out the market supply curve shown in panel (b) of Figure 5. Notice that once the price drops below $1— the shutdown price for each firm—the market supply curve jumps to zero.

The market supply curve in the figure is a *short-run* market supply curve, since it gives us the combined output level of just those firms *already* in the industry. As

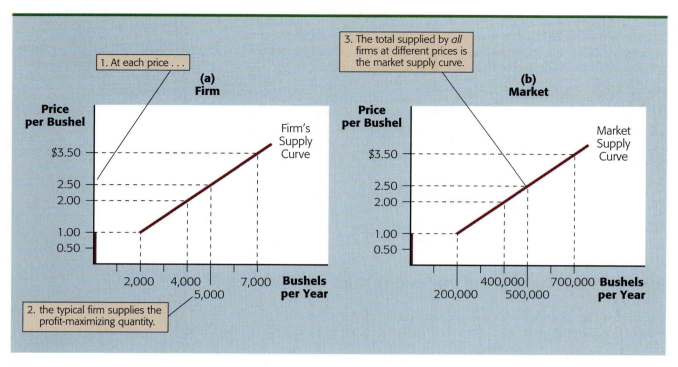

FIGURE 5
Deriving the Market
Supply Curve

we move along this curve, we are assuming that two things are constant: (1) the fixed inputs of each firm and (2) the number of firms in the market.

Short-Run Equilibrium

How does a perfectly competitive market achieve equilibrium? We've already addressed this question in Chapter 3, in our study of supply and demand. But now we'll take a much closer look, paying attention to the individual firm and individual consumer as well as the market.

Figure 6 puts together the pieces we've discussed so far, including those from Chapter 4 on consumer choice, to paint a complete picture of how a competitive market arrives at a short-run equilibrium. On the right side, we add up the quantities supplied by all firms to obtain the market supply curve. On the left side, we add up the quantities demanded by all consumers to obtain the market demand curve. The market supply and demand curves show if/then relationships: *If* the price were such and such, *then* firms would supply this much and consumers would buy that much. Up to this point, the prices and quantities are purely hypothetical. But once we bring the two curves together and find their intersection point, we know the *equilibrium* price: the price at which trading will actually take place. Finally, we confront each firm and each consumer with the equilibrium price to find the actual quantity each consumer will buy and the actual quantity each firm will produce.

Figure 7 gets more specific, illustrating two possible short-run equilibriums in the wheat market. In panel (a), if the market demand curve were D_1, the short-run equilibrium price would be $3.50. Each firm would face the horizontal demand

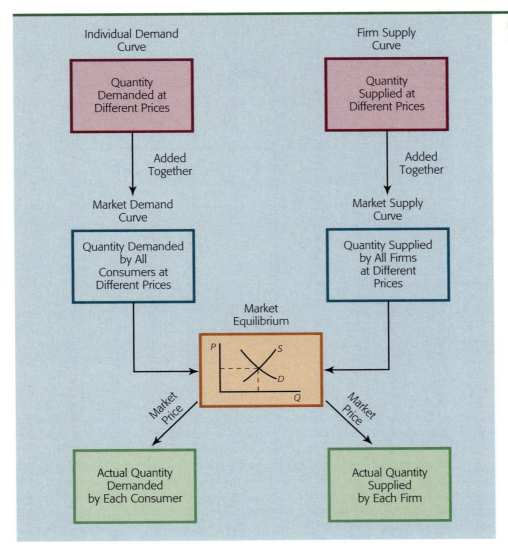

FIGURE 6
Perfect Competition

curve d_1 (panel (b)) and decide to produce 7,000 bushels. With 100 such firms, the equilibrium market quantity would be 700,000 bushels. Notice that, at a price of $3.50, each firm is enjoying an economic profit, since $P > ATC$.

If the market demand curve were D_2 instead, the equilibrium price would be $2. Each firm would face demand curve d_2, and produce 4,000 bushels. With 100 firms, the equilibrium market quantity would be 400,000. Here, each firm is suffering an economic loss, since $P < ATC$. These two examples show us that *in short-run equilibrium, competitive firms can earn an economic profit or suffer an economic loss.*

We are about to leave the short run and turn our attention to what happens in a competitive market over the long run. But before we do, let's look once more at how a short-run equilibrium is established. One part of this process—combining supply and demand curves to find the market equilibrium—has been familiar to you

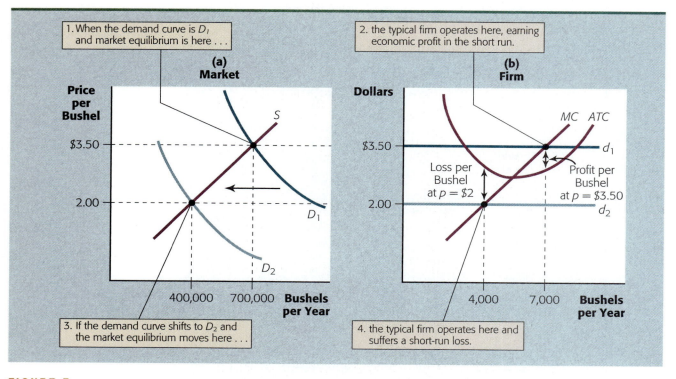

1. When the demand curve is D_1 and market equilibrium is here . . .

2. the typical firm operates here, earning economic profit in the short run.

(a) Market

(b) Firm

3. If the demand curve shifts to D_2 and the market equilibrium moves here . . .

4. the typical firm operates here and suffers a short-run loss.

FIGURE 7
Short-Run Equilibrium in Perfect Competition

all along. But now you can better appreciate how much information is contained within each of these curves and what an impressive job the market does coordinating millions of decisions made by people who may never even meet each other.

Think about it: So many individual consumers and firms, each with its own agenda, trading in the market. Not one of them has any power to decide or even influence the market price. Rather, the price is determined by *all* of them, adjusting until *total* quantity supplied is equal to *total* quantity demanded. Then, facing this equilibrium price, each consumer buys the quantity he or she wants, each firm produces the output level that it wants, and we can be confident that all of them will be able to realize their plans. Each buyer can find willing sellers, and each seller can find willing buyers.

Markets and Equilibrium

> *In perfect competition, the market sums up the buying and selling preferences of individual consumers and producers, and determines the market price. Each buyer and seller then takes the market price as given, and each is able to buy or sell the desired quantity.*

This process is, from a certain perspective, a thing of beauty, and it happens each day in markets all across the world—markets for wheat, corn, barley, soybeans, apples, oranges, gold, silver, copper, and more. And something quite similar happens in other markets that do not strictly satisfy our requirements for perfect competition—markets for television sets, books, air conditioners, fast-food meals, oil, natural gas, bottled water, blue jeans. The list is virtually endless.

COMPETITIVE MARKETS IN THE LONG RUN

So far, we've explored the short run only, and assumed that the number of firms in the market is fixed. But perfect competition becomes even *more* interesting in the long run, when entry and exit can occur. After all, the long run is a time horizon long enough for firms to vary *all* of their inputs. It should therefore be long enough for *new* firms to acquire fixed inputs and enter the market, and for firms already in the industry to sell off their fixed inputs and *exit* from the market.

But what makes firms want to enter or exit a market? The driving force behind entry is economic profit, and the force behind exit is economic loss.

Profit and Loss and the Long Run

Recall that economic profit is the amount by which total revenue exceeds *all* costs of doing business. The costs to be deducted include implicit costs like foregone investment income and foregone wages for an owner who devotes money and time to the business. Thus, when a firm earns positive economic profit, we know the owners are earning *more* than they could by devoting their money and time to some other activity.

A temporary episode of positive economic profit will not have much impact on a competitive industry, other than the temporary pleasure it gives the owners of competitive firms. But when positive profit reflects basic conditions in the industry and is expected to continue, major changes are in the works. Outsiders, hungry for profit themselves, will want to enter the market and—since *there are no barriers to entry*—they can do so.

Similarly, if firms in the market are suffering economic losses, they are not earning enough revenue to cover all their costs, so there must be other opportunities that would more adequately compensate owners for their money or time. If this situation is expected to continue over the firm's long-run planning horizon—a period long enough to vary *all* inputs—there is only one thing for the firm to do: exit the market by selling off its plant and equipment, thereby reducing its loss to zero.

> *In a competitive market, economic profit and loss are the forces driving long-run change. The expectation of continued economic profit causes outsiders to enter the market; the expectation of continued economic losses causes firms in the market to exit.*

In the real world of business, entry and exit occur literally every day. In some cases, we see entry occur through the formation of an entirely new firm. For example, in the late 1990s, the high profits of the earliest Internet service providers (ISPs)—such as America Online, CompuServe, and Prodigy—led to the establishment of more than 7,000 new ISPs by the end of the decade. Entry can also occur when an existing firm adds a new product to its line. For example, among the firms that entered the ISP market were many firms that had been established years before there *was* such as thing as an ISP, such as Sprint (which entered with Earthlink), Microsoft (the Microsoft Network), and AT&T. Although these were not *new firms*, they were *new participants* in the market for Internet service.

Exit, too, can occur in different ways. A firm may go out of business entirely, selling off its assets and freeing itself once and for all from all costs. In 2000 and

Kozmo.com—*an Internet-based service that delivered videos and snacks—was one of thousands of online retailers that exited their markets in 2000 and 2001.*

2001, for example, thousands of Internet firms exited their markets in this way, or were purchased by other firms that subsequently exited themselves. These failing firms included the toy seller Toysmart; home delivery services Kozmo.com, Urban-fetch, and Webvan; and pet suppliers pets.com and petstore.com.

But exit can also occur when a firm switches out of a particular product line, even as it continues to produce other things. For example, publishing companies often decide to abandon unsuccessful magazines, yet they continue to thrive by publishing other magazines and books.

Long-Run Equilibrium

Entry and exit—however they occur—are powerful forces in real-world competitive markets. They determine how these markets change over the long run, how much output will ultimately be available to consumers, and the prices they must pay. To explore these issues, let's see how entry and exit move a market to its long-run equilibrium from different starting points.

From Short-Run Profit to Long-Run Equilibrium. Suppose that the market for wheat is initially in a short-run equilibrium like point A in panel (a) of Figure 8, with market supply curve S_1. The initial equilibrium price is $4.50 per bushel. In panel (b), we see that a typical competitive firm—producing 9,000 bushels—is earning economic profit, since $P > ATC$ at that output level. As long as we remain in the short run, with no new firms entering the market, this situation will not change.

But as we enter the long run, much will change. First, economic profit will attract new entrants, increasing the number of firms in the market. Now remember (from Chapter 3) when we draw a market supply curve like S_1, we draw it for some *given* number of firms, and we hold that number constant. But in the long run, as the number of firms increases, the market supply curve will *shift rightward;* a greater quantity will be supplied at any given price. As the market supply curve shifts rightward, several things happen:

1. The market price begins to fall—from $4.50 to $4.00 to $3.50 and so on.
2. As market price falls, the demand curve facing each firm shifts downward.
3. Each firm—striving as always to maximize profit—will slide down its marginal cost curve, decreasing output.[3]

This process of adjustment, in the market and the firm, continues until . . . well, until when? To answer this question, remember why these adjustments are occurring in the first place: Economic profit is attracting new entrants and shifting the market supply curve rightward. Thus, all of these changes will stop when the *reason* for entry—positive profit—no longer exists. And this, in turn, requires the market supply curve to shift rightward enough, and the price to fall enough, so that *each existing firm is earning zero economic profit.* Panels (c) and (d) in Figure 8 show the final, long-run equilibrium. First, look at panel (c), which shows long-run market equilibrium at point E. The market supply curve has shifted to S_2, and the price has fallen to $2.50 per bushel. Next, look at panel (d), which tells us why the

---

[3] There is one other possible consequence that we ignore here: Entry into the industry, which changes the demand for the industry's inputs, may also change input prices. If this occurs, firms' ATC curves will shift. For now, we will assume that entry (and exit) do not affect input prices, so that the ATC curve does not shift.

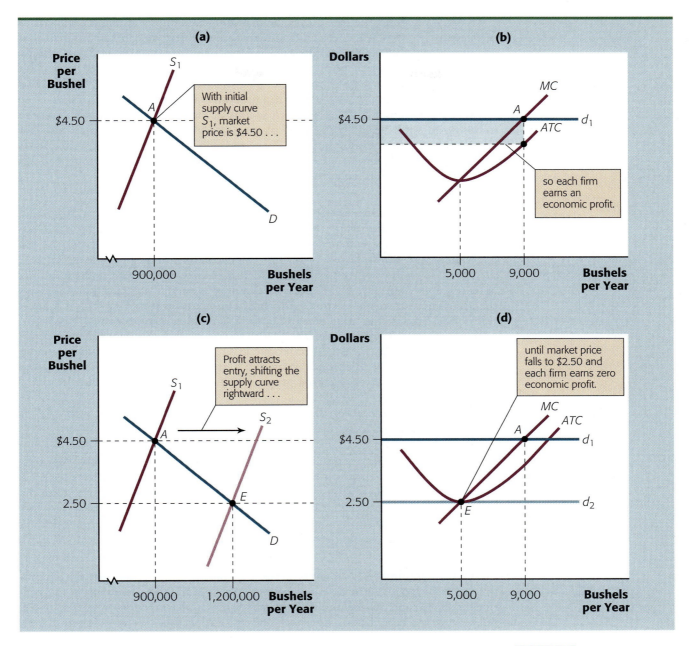

(a)

With initial supply curve S_1, market price is $4.50 . . .

(b)

so each firm earns an economic profit.

(c)

Profit attracts entry, shifting the supply curve rightward . . .

(d)

until market price falls to $2.50 and each firm earns zero economic profit.

FIGURE 8
From Short-Run Profit to Long-Run Equilibrium

market supply curve stops shifting when it reaches S_2. With that supply curve, each firm is producing at the lowest point of its *ATC* curve, with $P = ATC = \$2.50$, and each is earning zero economic profit. With no economic profit, there is no further reason for entry, and no further shift in the market supply curve.

In a competitive market, positive economic profit continues to attract new entrants until economic profit is reduced to zero.

Now you can see the role played by one of our assumptions about competitive markets: *easy entry*. With no significant barriers to entry, we can be confident that economic profit at the typical firm will attract new firms to the industry, driving down the market price until the economic profit disappears. If a permanent barrier—legal or otherwise—prevented new firms from coming into the market, this mechanism would not work, so long-run economic profit would be possible.

Before proceeding further, take a close look at Figure 8. As the market moves to its long-run equilibrium (point *E* in panels (c) and (d)), output at each firm *decreases* from 9,000 to 5,000 bushels. But in the market as a whole, output *increases* from 900,000 to 1,200,000 bushels. How can this be? (See if you can answer this question yourself. *Hint:* entry!)

From Short-Run Loss to Long-Run Equilibrium.

We have just seen how, beginning from a position of short-run profit at the typical firm, a competitive market will adjust until the profit is eliminated. But what if we begin from a position of loss? As you might guess, the same type of adjustments will occur, only in the opposite direction.

This is a good opportunity for you to test your own skill and understanding. Study Figure 8 carefully. Then see if you can draw a similar diagram that illustrates the adjustment from short-run *loss* to long-run equilibrium. Start with a market price of $1.50. Use the same demand curve as in Figure 8, but draw in a new, appropriate market supply curve. Then let the market work. Show what happens in the market, and at each firm, as economic loss causes some firms to exit. If you do this correctly, you'll end up once again at a market price of $2.50, with each firm earning zero economic profit. Your graph will illustrate the following conclusion:

In a competitive market, economic losses continue to cause exit until the losses are reduced to zero.

Notice the role played by our assumption of *easy exit* in competitive markets. When there are no significant barriers to exit, we can be confident that economic loss will eventually drive firms from the industry, raising the market price until the typical firm breaks even again. Significant barriers to exit (such as a local law forbidding a plant from closing down) would prevent this mechanism from working, and economic losses would persist even in the long run.

Distinguishing Short-Run from Long-Run Outcomes.

You've seen that the equilibrium in a competitive market can be very different in the short run than in the long run. In short-run equilibrium, competitive firms can earn profits or suffer losses. But in long-run equilibrium, after entry or exit has occurred, economic profit is always zero. The distinction between short-run and long-run equilibrium is important, and not just in competitive markets. In *any* market, our analysis will depend on the time period we are considering, and the appropriate period to use depends on the question we are asking. If we want to predict what happens several years after a change in demand, we should ask what the new *long-run* equilibrium will be. If we want to know what happens a few *months* after a change in demand, we'll look for the new *short-run* equilibrium.

When economists look at a market, they automatically think of the short run versus the long run and then choose the period more appropriate for the question at hand. As you'll see, this way of thinking is applied again and again in economics. It is one of the basic principles you will learn in this book:

Basic Principle #7: Short-Run versus Long-Run Outcomes
Markets behave differently in the short run and the long run. In solving a problem, we must always know which of these time horizons we are analyzing.

The Notion of Zero Profit in Perfect Competition

From the preceding discussion, you may wonder why anyone in his or her right mind would ever want to set up shop in a competitive industry or stay there for any length of time, since—in the long run—they can expect zero economic profit. Indeed, if you want to become a millionaire, you would be well advised not to buy a wheat farm. But most wheat farmers—like most other sellers in competitive markets—do not curse their fate. On the contrary, they are likely to be quite content with the performance of their businesses. How can this be?

Remember that zero *economic* profit is not the same as zero *accounting* profit. When a firm is making zero *economic* profit, it is still making some accounting profit. In fact, the accounting profit is just enough to cover all of the owner's implicit costs, including compensation for any foregone investment income or foregone salary. Suppose, for example, that a wheat farmer paid $100,000 for land and works 40 hours per week. Suppose, too, that the money *could* have been invested in some other way and earned $6,000 per year, and the farmer *could* have worked equally pleasantly elsewhere and earned $40,000 per year. Then the farm's implicit costs will be $46,000, and zero economic profit means that the farm is earning $46,000 in *accounting profit* each year. This won't make a wheat farmer ecstatic, but it will make it worthwhile to keep working the farm. After all, if the farmer quits and takes up the next best alternative, he or she will do no better. To emphasize that zero economic profit is not an unpleasant outcome, economists often replace it with the term **normal profit**, which is a synonym for "zero economic profit," or "just enough accounting profit to cover implicit costs." Using this language, we can summarize long-run conditions at the typical firm this way:

Normal profit Another name for zero economic profit.

> *In the long run, every competitive firm will earn* normal profit—*that is, zero economic profit.*

Perfect Competition and Plant Size

There is one more characteristic of competitive markets in the long run that we have not yet discussed: the plant size of the competitive firm. It turns out that the same forces—entry and exit—that cause all firms to earn zero economic profit *also* ensure that:

> *In long-run equilibrium, every competitive firm will select its plant size and output level so that it operates at the minimum point of its* LRATC *curve.*

 Short-Run versus Long-Run Outcomes

To see why, let's consider what would happen if this condition were violated. Figure 9(a) illustrates a firm in a perfectly competitive market. The firm faces a market price of P_1 and produces quantity q_1, where $MC_1 = MR_1$. With its current plant, the firm has average costs given by ATC_1. Note that the firm is earning zero profit, since average cost is equal to P_1 at the best output level.

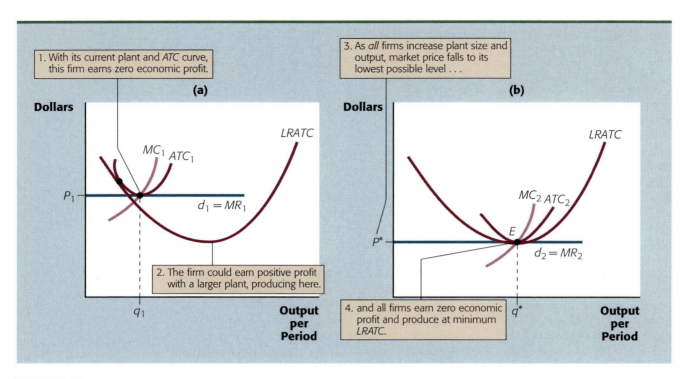

FIGURE 9
**Perfect Competition and
Plant Size**

But panel (a) does *not* show a true long-run equilibrium. How do we know this? First, in the long run, the typical firm will want to expand. Why? Because by increasing its plant size, it could slide down its *LRATC* curve and produce more output at a lower cost per unit. Since it is a perfectly competitive firm—a small participant in the market—it can expand in this way *without* affecting market price. As a result, the firm, after expanding, could operate on a new, lower *ATC* curve, so that *ATC* is less than *P*. That is, by expanding, the firm could potentially earn an economic profit.

Second, this same opportunity to earn positive economic profit will attract new entrants that will establish larger plants from the outset. Expansion by existing firms and entry by new ones increase market output and bring down the market price. The process will stop—and a long-run equilibrium will be established—only when there is no potential to earn positive economic profit with *any* plant size. As you can see in panel (b), this condition is satisfied only when each firm is operating at the minimum point on its *LRATC* curve, using the plant represented by ATC_2, and producing output of q^*. Entry and expansion must continue in this market until the price falls to P^*, because only then will each firm—doing the best that it can do—earn zero economic profit. (*Question:* In the long run, what would happen to the firm in panel (a) if it refused to increase its plant size?)

A Summary of the Competitive Firm in the Long Run

Panel (b) of Figure 9 summarizes everything you have learned about the competitive firm in long-run equilibrium. The typical firm, taking the market price P^* as given, produces the profit-maximizing output level q^*, where $MR = MC$. Since this is the long run, each firm will be earning zero economic profit, so we also know that $P^* = ATC$. But since $P^* = MC$ and $P^* = ATC$, it must also be true that $MC =$

ATC. As you learned in Chapter 5, *MC* and *ATC* are equal only at the minimum point of the *ATC* curve. Thus, we know that each firm must be operating at the lowest possible point on the *ATC* curve for the plant it is operating. Finally, each firm selects the plant that makes its *LRATC* as low as possible, so each operates at the minimum point on its *LRATC* curve.

As you can see, there is a lot going on in Figure 9 (b). But we can put it all together with a very simple statement:

> *At each competitive firm in long-run equilibrium,* P = MC = *minimum* ATC = *minimum* LRATC.

In Figure 9(b), this equality is satisfied when the typical firm produces at point *E,* where its demand, marginal cost, *ATC,* and *LRATC* curves all intersect. This is a figure well worth remembering, since it summarizes so much information about competitive markets in a single picture. (Here is a useful self-test: Close the book, put away your notes, and draw a set of diagrams in which one curve at a time does *not* pass through the common intersection point of the other three. Then explain which principle of firm or market behavior is violated by your diagram. Do this separately for all four curves.)

Figure 9(b) also explains one of the important ways in which perfect competition benefits consumers: In the long run, each firm is driven to the plant size and output level at which its cost per unit is as low as possible. This lowest possible cost per unit is also the price per unit that consumers will pay. If price were any lower than P^*, it would not be worthwhile for firms to continue producing the good in the long run. Thus, given the *LRATC* curve faced by each firm in this industry—a curve that is determined by each firm's production technology and the costs of its inputs—P^* is the lowest possible price that will ensure the continued availability of the good. In perfect competition, consumers are getting the best deal they could possibly get.

WHAT HAPPENS WHEN THINGS CHANGE?

So far, you've learned how competitive firms make decisions, how these decisions lead to a short-run equilibrium in the market, and how the market moves from short- to long-run equilibrium through entry and exit. Now, it's time to ask: *What happens when things change?* In this section, we'll deal with a change in demand for the product and, in the process, learn some important additional features of perfect competition. In the section titled "Using the Theory," we'll look at changes in technology.

A Change in Demand

In Figure 10, panel (a) shows a competitive market that is initially in long-run equilibrium at point *A*, where the market demand curve D_1 and supply curve S_1 intersect. Panel (b) shows conditions at the firm, which faces demand curve d_1 and produces the profit-maximizing quantity q_1.

But now suppose that the market demand curve shifts rightward to D_2 and remains there. (This shift could be caused by any one of several factors. If you can't list some of them, turn back to Chapter 3 and look again at Figure 3.) Panels (c) and (d) show what happens. In the *short run*, the shift in demand moves the market equilibrium to point *B*, with market output Q_{SR} and price P_{SR}. At the same time,

HTTP://
Economists have tried to simulate the behavior of competitive markets through experiments. The University of Arizona's Market. Econ is an Internet-based example
http://market.econ.arizona.edu/default.asp.

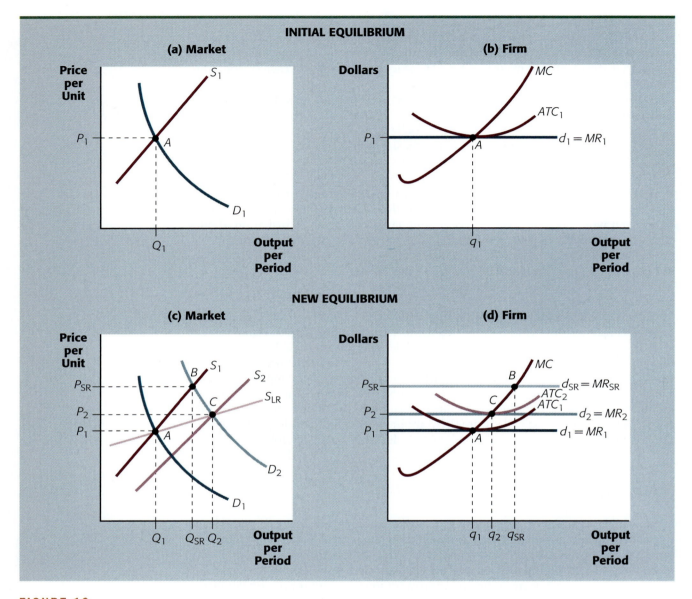

FIGURE 10
An Increasing-Cost Industry

At point A in panel (a), the market is in long-run equilibrium. The typical firm in panel (b) earns zero economic profit. If demand increases, market price rises. Individual firms increase output and earn an economic profit at point B. Profit attracts entry, increasing market supply but also driving up ATC. When long-run equilibrium is reestablished at point C in panel (c), price is higher, but the typical firm again earns zero economic profit. The long-run market supply curve is an upward-sloping line found by connecting points like A and C in panel (c).

the demand curve facing each firm shifts upward, and each firm raises output to the new profit-maximizing level q_{SR}. At this output level, $P > ATC$, so each firm is earning economic profit. Thus, the short-run impact of an increase in demand is (1) a rise in market price, (2) a rise in market quantity, and (3) economic profits.

When we turn to the long run, we know that economic profit will attract the entry of new firms. And, as you learned a few pages ago, an increase in the number of firms shifts the market supply curve rightward, which drives down the price until the economic profit is eliminated. But how far must the price fall in order to bring this about? That is, how far can we expect the market supply curve to shift? In answering this question, we'll add one more detail to our model that we've ignored until now.

Think about what happens as entry occurs in an industry. With more firms, output increases, so the industry will demand more *inputs*—more raw materials, more labor, more capital, and more land. We can usually expect the prices of these inputs to rise.

Now, a rise in input prices will affect a firm's *ATC* curve. Why? Whenever we draw the *ATC* curve, we assume that the firm's production technology and the prices it must pay for its inputs remain constant. But when inputs become more expensive, cost per unit will be greater at *any* level of output. As a result, the *ATC* curve will shift upward. For example, expansion of the artichoke industry would increase the demand for land suitable for growing this crop, cause the price of this land to rise, and force up the *ATC* curve facing each artichoke producer.[4]

Let's sum up what we know so far. After the demand curve shifts, we arrive at point B in panel (c) in the short run. At this point, the price is higher and the typical firm is earning economic profit. Profit attracts entry, so the market supply curve begins to shift rightward, bringing the price back down. At the same time, the expansion of output in the industry raises input prices and shifts the typical firm's *ATC* curve upward. In panel (d), the *ATC* curve shifts upward to the curve ATC_2.

Now comes our important conclusion: Since the *ATC* curve has shifted upward, zero profit will occur at a price *higher* than the initial price P_1. In panel (d), the typical firm will earn zero profit when the price is P_2. Thus, entry will cease, and the market supply curve will *stop* shifting rightward, when the market price reaches P_2. In the figure, this occurs when the market supply curve reaches S_2. The final, long-run equilibrium occurs at point C, with price P_2, industry output at Q_2, and the typical firm producing q_2.

There is a lot going on in Figure 10. But we can make the story simpler if we *skip over* the short-run equilibrium at point B, and just ask: What happens in the *long run* after the demand curve shifts rightward? The answer is: The market equilibrium will move from point A to point C. A line drawn through these two points tells us, in the long run, the market price we can expect for any quantity the market provides. In Figure 10, this is the thin line, which is called the *long-run supply curve* (S_{LR}).

Misinterpreting the Supply Shift in Figure 10 In Chapter 3, you learned that a rightward shift in demand does *not* cause a rightward shift in supply. Instead, it raises the price and causes *a movement along* the supply curve. But in Figure 10, the demand curve shifts rightward from D_1 to D_2, the price rises, and then . . . the supply curve shifts rightward! So, now you may be wondering whether demand shifts *do* cause supply shifts.

The answer is: They *don't*—not by themselves. In the figure you can see that the shift in demand first raises the price, moving us *along* the supply curve S_1 from point A to point B. This is just as you learned in Chapter 3. But now, we're extending our analysis further, into the long run. The rise in price, if it creates profit for firms already in the market, will cause new firms to enter. It's this *increase in the number of firms* that causes the supply curve to shift.

DANGEROUS CURVES

> The **long-run supply curve** shows the relationship between market price and market quantity produced after all long-run adjustments have taken place.

Long-run supply curve A curve indicating the quantity of output that all sellers in a market will produce at different prices, after all long-run adjustments have taken place.

[4] Notice that, in Figure 10, we've kept the diagram simple by shifting up the *ATC* curve, but not the *MC* curve. This would be entirely accurate if the inputs whose prices are rising are *lumpy inputs*. Over some range of output, the quantity of these inputs would not vary with output, leaving marginal cost unchanged. But even when both the *MC* and the *ATC* curves shift upward, our conclusions remain the same.

If input prices rise when an industry expands (as in our example), then an increase in market quantity will require an increase in the price. This is why the long-run supply curve S_{LR} has an *upward slope* in Figure 10.

Increasing, Decreasing and Constant Cost Industries.

In Figure 10, an increase in demand led to a higher price, after all long-run adjustments in the market were completed. But, things don't *have* to end up as in Figure 10. It depends on what happens to input prices as new firms enter the industry and begin demanding inputs along with the firms already there. In Figure 10, the increase in demand for inputs causes the price of those inputs to *rise*. That's why the *ATC* curve shifts upward, and that's why the long-run supply curve slopes upward. This type of industry—which is the most common—is called an *increasing cost industry*.

Increasing cost industry An industry in which the long-run supply curve slopes upward because each firm's *ATC* curve shifts upward as industry output increases.

> In an **increasing cost industry**, *entry causes input prices to rise, which shifts up the typical firm's ATC curve, and raises the market price at which firms earn zero economic profit. As a result, the long-run supply curve slopes upward.*

But there are two other possibilities. First, an industry might use such a small percentage of total inputs that, even as new firms enter, there is no noticeable effect on input prices. For example, suppose we want to analyze the effect of an increase in demand for bicycles in the United States. The bicycle industry uses only a tiny fraction of the nation's labor, capital, aluminum, rubber, and almost any other basic input we can think of. This industry could expand considerably without any noticeable rise in input prices. As a result, the *ATC* curve would stay put as new firms entered the industry and—as you are asked to verify in an end-of-chapter challenge question—the long-run supply curve would be horizontal. This type of industry is a *constant cost industry*.

Constant cost industry An industry in which the long-run supply curve is horizontal because each firm's *ATC* curve is unaffected by changes in industry output.

> In a **constant cost industry**, *entry has no effect on input prices, so the typical firm's ATC curve stays put and the market price at which firms earn zero economic profit does not change. As a result, the long-run supply curve is horizontal.*

Another possibility is that of a *decreasing cost industry*, in which entry into an industry by new firms actually *decreases* input prices. For example, suppose that a modest size city has just a few sushi restaurants. Periodically, a partially loaded truck makes a special trip from a distant larger city to deliver raw fish, nori seaweed, wasabi, and other special ingredients to these few restaurants. Transportation costs—part of the price of the ingredients—will be rather high.

Now suppose that demand for sushi meals increases. Profits at the existing restaurants attracts entry. With more restaurants ordering ingredients, the same delivery truck makes the same trip, but now it is fully loaded and the transportation costs are shared among more restaurants. As a result, transportation costs at *each* restaurant decrease—and each restaurant's *ATC* curve shifts down. Competition among the restaurants then ensures that prices will drop to match the lower *ATC*. As a result, the long-run effect of an increase in demand is a *lower* price for eating sushi at a restaurant—a downward sloping long-run supply curve. (Another end-of-chapter challenge question will ask you to draw the relevant graphs.)

> *In a **decreasing cost industry**, entry causes input prices to* fall, *which causes the typical firm's ATC curve to shift* downward, *and* lowers *the market price at which firms earn zero economic profit. As a result, the long-run supply curve slopes* downward.

Decreasing cost industry An industry in which the long-run supply curve slopes downward because each firm's *ATC* curve shifts downward as industry output increases.

Market Signals and the Economy

The previous discussion of changes in demand included a lot of details, so let's take a moment to go over it in broad outline. You've seen that an *increase* in demand always leads to an *increase* in market output in the short run, as existing firms raise their output levels, and an even *greater* increase in output in the long run, as new firms enter the market.

We could also have analyzed what happens when demand *decreases,* but you are encouraged to do this on your own instead, drawing the diagram and tracing through the logic. If you do it correctly, you'll find that the leftward shift of the demand curve will cause a drop in output in the short run and an even greater drop in the long run. The effect on price will depend on the nature of the industry, i.e., whether input prices rise or fall as exit takes place. (Once again, you'll be drawing some of these graphs in an end-of chapter challenge question.)

But now let's step back from these details and see what they really tell us about the economy. We can start with a simple fact: In the real world, the demand curves for different goods and services are constantly shifting. For example, over the last decade, Americans have developed an increased taste for bottled water. The average American gulped down 8 gallons of the stuff in 1990, and more than twice that much—18 gallons—in 2001. As a consequence, the *production* of bottled water has increased dramatically. This seems like magic: Consumers want more bottled water and, presto!, the economy provides it. What our model of perfect competition shows us are the workings behind the magic, the logical sequence of events leading from our desire to consume more bottled water and its appearance on store shelves.

The secret—the trick up the magician's sleeve—is this: As demand increases or decreases in a market, *prices change.* And price changes act as *signals* for firms to enter or exit an industry. How do these signals work? As you've seen, when demand increases, the price tends to initially *overshoot* its long-run equilibrium value during the adjustment process, creating sizable temporary profits for existing firms. Similarly, when demand decreases, the price falls *below* its long-run equilibrium value, creating sizable losses for existing firms. These exaggerated, temporary movements in price, and the profits and losses they cause, are almost irresistible forces, pulling new firms into the market or driving existing firms out. In this way, the economy is driven to produce whatever collection of goods consumers prefer.

For example, as Americans shifted their tastes toward bottled water, the market demand curve for this good shifted rightward and the price rose. Initially, the price rose *above* its new long-run equilibrium value, leading to high profits at existing bottled water firms such as Poland Spring and Arrowhead. High profits, in turn, attracted entry—especially the entry of new brands from established firms not previously selling bottled water, such as Pepsi's Aquafina and Coke's Dasani. As a result, production expanded to match the increase in demand by consumers. More of our land, labor, capital, and entrepreneurial skills are now used to produce bottled water. Where did these resources come from?

In large part, they were freed up from those industries that experienced a *decline* in demand. In these industries, lower prices have caused exit, freeing up land, labor, capital, and entrepreneurship to be used in other, expanding industries, such as the bottled water industry.

Market signals Price changes that cause changes in production to match changes in consumer demand.

> *In a market economy, price changes act as **market signals**, ensuring that the pattern of production matches the pattern of consumer demands. When demand increases, a rise in price signals firms to enter the market, increasing industry output. When demand decreases, a fall in price signals firms to exit the market, decreasing industry output.*

Importantly, in a market economy, no single person or government agency directs this process. There is no central command post where information about consumer demand is assembled, and no one tells firms how to respond. Instead, existing firms and new entrants, in their *own* search for higher profits, respond to market signals and help move the overall market in the direction it needs to go. This is what Adam Smith meant when he suggested that individual decision makers act—as if guided by an *invisible hand*—for the overall benefit of society, even though, as individuals, they are merely trying to satisfy their own desires.

© LYNDA RICHARDSON/CORBIS

USING THE THEORY

Changes in Technology

In this chapter, you've learned that perfectly competitive markets deliver the goods consumers want to buy at the lowest possible price. Moreover, you've seen that production in perfectly competitive markets follows consumer demand. Demand for a good increases, and production rises. Demand decreases, production falls.

But the service of competitive markets extends to other types of changes as well. In this section, we'll explore how competitive markets ensure that the benefits of technological advances are enjoyed by consumers.

One industry that has experienced especially rapid technological changes in the 1990s is farming. By using genetically altered seeds, farmers are able to grow crops that are more resistant to insects and more tolerant of herbicides. This lowers the total—and average—cost of producing any given amount of the crop.

Figure 11 illustrates the market for corn, but it could just as well be the market for soybeans, cotton, or many other crops. In panel (a), the market begins at point A, where the price of corn is \$3 per bushel. In panel (b), the typical farm produces 1,000 bushels per year and—with average cost curve ATC_1—earns zero economic profit.

Now let's see what happens when new, higher-yield corn seeds are made available. Suppose first that only one farm uses the new technology. This farm will enjoy

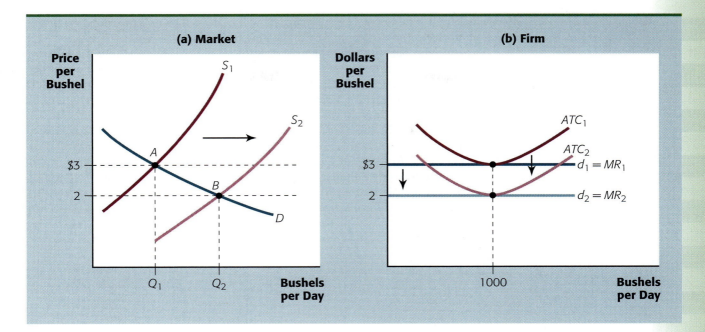

(a) Market

(b) Firm

FIGURE 11

Technological Change in Perfect Competition

Technological change may reduce ATC. *In panel (b), any farm that adopts new technology will earn an economic profit if it can produce at the old market price of $3 per bushel. That profit will lead its competitors to adopt the same technology and will also attract new entrants. As market supply increases, price falls until each farm is once again earning zero economic profit.*

a downward shift in its *ATC* curve from ATC_1 to ATC_2. Since it is so small relative to the market, it can produce all it wants and continue to sell at $3. Although we have not drawn in the farm's *MC* curve, you can see that the farm has several output levels from which to choose where $P > ATC$ and it can earn economic profit.

But not for long. In the long run, economic profit at this farm will cause two things to happen. First, all other farmers in the market will have a powerful incentive to adopt the new technology—to plant the new, genetically engineered seed themselves. Under perfect competition, they can do so; there are no barriers that prevent any farmer from using the same technology as any other. As these farms adopt the new seed technology, their *ATC* curves, too, will drop down to ATC_2.

Second, outsiders will have an incentive to enter this industry with plants utilizing the new technology, shifting the market supply curve rightward (from S_1 to S_2) and driving down the market price. The process will stop only when the market price has reached the level at which *farms using the new technology* earn zero economic profit. In Figure 11, this occurs at a price of $2 per bushel.[5]

From this example, we can draw two conclusions about technological change under perfect competition. First, what will happen to a farmer who is reluctant to change his technology? As *other* farms make the change, and the market price falls from $3 to $2, the reluctant farmer will find himself suffering an economic loss, since his average cost will remain at $3. His competitors will leave him to twist in

---

[5] In this example, we assume that the price of the new technology remains the same as it is adopted throughout the industry. If the price of the new technology were to rise, then—in the long run—the typical firm's *ATC* curve could still shift downward, but not as far as ATC_2; the market supply curve would then shift rightward, but not as far as S_2; and the price would drop, but not all the way to $2.

the wind, and if he refuses to shape up, he will be forced to exit the industry. In the end, *all* farms in the market must use the new technology.

Second, who benefits from the new technology in the long run? Not the farmers who adopt it. *Some* farmers—the earliest adopters—may enjoy *short-run* profit before the price adjusts completely. But in the long run, all farmers will be right back where they started, earning zero economic profit. The gainers are *consumers* of corn, since they benefit from the lower price.

Although some of the data in this example are hypothetical, the story is not. The average American farmer today feeds 129 people, double the amount fed only a few years ago. And as our example suggests, powerful forces push farmers to adopt new productivity-enhancing technology. From 1995 to 2003, the fraction of U.S. corn acreage planted with genetically modified seeds increased from zero to 38 percent, and is still growing rapidly. For soybeans, the comparable figures are zero to 80 percent.

More generally, we can summarize the impact of technological change as follows:

Short-Run versus
Long-Run Outcomes

> *Under perfect competition, a technological advance leads to a rightward shift of the market supply curve, decreasing market price. In the short run, early adopters may enjoy economic profit, but in the long run, all adopters will earn zero economic profit. Firms that refuse to use the new technology will not survive.*

Technological advances in many competitive industries—mining, lumber, communication, entertainment, and others—have indeed spread quickly, shifting market supply curves rapidly and steadily rightward over the past 100 years. While this has often been hard on individual competitive firms, which must continually adapt to new technologies in order to survive, it has led to huge rewards for consumers.

Summary

Perfect competition is a market structure in which (1) there are large numbers of buyers and sellers and each buys or sells only a tiny fraction of the total market quantity; (2) sellers offer a standardized product; and (3) sellers can easily enter or exit from the market. While few real markets satisfy these conditions precisely, the model is still useful in a wide variety of cases.

Each perfectly competitive firm faces a horizontal demand curve; it can sell as much as it wishes at the market price. The firm chooses its profit-maximizing output level by setting marginal cost equal to the market price. Its *short-run supply curve* is that part of its MC curve that lies above the average variable cost curve. Total profit is profit per unit $(P - ATC)$ times the profit-maximizing quantity.

In the short run, market price is determined where the market supply curve—the horizontal sum of all firms' supply curves—crosses the market demand curve. In short-run equilibrium, existing firms can earn a profit (in which case new firms will enter) or suffer a loss (in which case existing firms will exit). Entry or exit will continue until, in the long run, each firm is earning zero economic profit. At each competitive

firm in long-run equilibrium, price = marginal cost = minimum average total cost = minimum long-run average total cost.

When demand curves shift, prices change more in the short run than in the long run. The temporary, exaggerated price movements act as market signals, ensuring that output expands and contracts in each industry to match the pattern of consumer preferences.

In the long run, an increase in demand can result in a higher, lower, or unchanged market price, depending on whether the good is produced, respectively, in an *increasing cost industry*, *decreasing cost industry*, or *constant cost industry*. The long-run supply curve slopes upward in an increasing cost industry and slopes downward for a decreasing cost industry. In a constant cost industry, the long-run supply curve will be horizontal.

A technological advance in a perfectly competitive market causes the equilibrium price to fall and equilibrium quantity to rise. Each competitive firm must use the new technology in order to survive, but consumers reap all the benefits by paying a lower price.

Key Terms

Constant cost industry
Decreasing cost industry
Firm's supply curve
Increasing cost industry

Long-run supply curve
Market signals
Market structure
Market supply curve

Normal profit
Perfect competition
Price taker
Shutdown price

Review Questions

1. What are the three characteristics that typify a perfectly competitive market? Explain the importance of each characteristic.

2. How do economists justify using the perfectly competitive model to analyze markets that clearly do not satisfy one or more of the assumptions of that model?

3. On a scale of 1 to 5, with 5 being full satisfaction and 1 being no satisfaction at all, rank the following markets in terms of their satisfaction of the three characteristics of the perfectly competitive model. Assign a score for each characteristic and justify your assignment.
   a. Clothing stores
   b. Restaurants
   c. Book publishing
   d. Home video game production
   e. Jet aircraft production

4. Why is the demand curve facing a perfectly competitive firm infinitely elastic?

5. "To maximize profit, a perfectly competitive firm should produce the level of output at which marginal cost is equal to price." True, false, or uncertain? Explain.

6. To calculate profit (or loss) for a perfectly competitive firm, we look at the difference between P and ATC, but to determine the profit-maximizing (or loss-minimizing) level of output, we focus on price and marginal cost. Why?

7. Discuss the following statement: "Economists need to pay more attention to the real business world. Their model of perfect competition predicts that firms in a market will end up earning no profit, nothing above costs. As any accountant can tell you, if you look at the balance sheets of most businesses in any industry, their revenue exceeds their costs; they do, in fact, make a profit."

8. True, false, or uncertain? Explain your answer.
   a. A perfectly competitive firm is profitable when price exceeds minimum AVC.
   b. A competitive firm's supply curve is just its MC curve.

9. What is the fundamental characteristic that distinguishes the short run from the long run in the analysis of a competitive market?

10. True or false? In a perfectly competitive market, an increase in output requires a high price in the short run, but not in the long run. Justify your answer.

Problems and Exercises

1. In 1999, (1) sales of sport utility vehicles (SUVs) skyrocketed, and (2) the price of gasoline rose. Because SUVs get lower gasoline mileage than the automobiles they replaced, their owners ended up buying more gasoline even as the price per gallon rose. Is this a violation of the law of demand?

2. Suppose that a perfectly competitive firm has the following total variable costs (TVC):

Quantity:	0	1	2	3	4	5	6
TVC:	$0	$6	$11	$15	$18	$22	$28

It also has fixed costs of $6. If the market price is $5 per unit:
   a. Find the firm's profit-maximizing quantity using the marginal revenue and marginal cost approach.
   b. Check your results by re-solving the problem using the total revenue and total cost approach. Is the firm earning a positive profit, suffering a loss, or breaking even?

3. Assume that the market for cardboard is perfectly competitive (if not very exciting). In each of the following scenarios, should a typical firm continue to produce or

should it shut down in the short run? Draw a diagram that illustrates the firm's situation in each case.
a. Minimum *ATC* = $2.00
   Minimum *AVC* = $1.50
   Market price = $1.75
b. *MR* = $1.00
   Minimum *AVC* = $1.50
   Minimum *ATC* = $2.00

4. The following table gives quantity supplied and quantity demanded at various prices in the perfectly competitive meat-packing market:

Price (per lb.)	Q_S	Q_D
	(in millions of lbs.)	
$1.00	10	100
$1.25	15	90
$1.50	25	75
$1.75	40	63
$2.00	55	55
$2.25	65	40

Assume that each firm in the meat-packing industry faces the following cost structure:

Pounds	*TC*
60,000	$110,000
61,000	$111,000
62,000	$112,000
63,000	$115,000

a. What is the profit-maximizing output level for the typical firm? (*Hint:* Calculate *MC* for each change in output, then find the equilibrium price, and calculate *MR* for each change in output.)
b. Is this market in long-run equilibrium? Why or why not? (*Hint:* Calculate *ATC*.)
c. What do you expect to happen to the number of meat-packing firms over the long run? Why?

5. Assume that the kitty litter industry is perfectly competitive and is presently in long-run equilibrium:
a. Draw diagrams for both the market and a typical firm, showing equilibrium price and quantity for the market, and *MC*, *ATC*, *AVC*, *MR*, and the demand curve for the firm.
b. Your friend has always had a passion to get into the kitty litter business. If the market is in long-run equilibrium, will it be profitable for him to jump in head-first (so to speak)? Why or why not?
c. Suppose people begin to prefer dogs as pets, and cat ownership declines. Show on your diagrams from part (a) what happens in the industry and the firm in the long run, assuming that this is a constant cost industry.

6. In a perfect competitive, increasing cost industry, is the long-run supply curve always flatter than the short-run market supply curve? Explain.

7. "A *profit-maximizing* competitive firm will produce the quantity of output at which price *exceeds* cost per unit by the greatest possible amount." True or false? Explain briefly. [*Hint:* see Figure 3(a)]

8. In the "Using the Theory" section of this chapter, you learned that technological advances lead to falling prices, increasing output, and only a temporary burst of profit for early adopters, with long-run profit returning to zero. Would any of these results change if the market demand for the good were completely inelastic? (Draw a diagram similar to Figure 11 to make your case.)

9. "My economics professor must be confused. First he tells us that in perfect competition, the demand curve is completely flat—horizontal. But then he draws a supply and demand diagram that has a downward-sloping demand curve. What gives?" Resolve this confusion in a single sentence.

10. Assume that the firm shown in this table produces output using one fixed input and one variable input.

Output	Price	Total Revenue	Marginal Revenue	Total Cost	Marginal Cost	Profit
0	$50	$0		$5		
					$35	
1	$50					
					$15	
2	$50					
					$35	
3	$50					
					$55	
4	$50					
					$65	

a. Complete this table and use it to find this firm's short-run profit-maximizing quantity of output. How much profit will this firm earn?
b. Redo the table and find the profit-maximizing quantity of output, if the price of the firm's fixed input rose from $5 to $10. How much profit will this firm earn now?
c. Now redo the original table and find the profit-maximizing quantity of output, if the price of the firm's variable input rose so that *MC* increased by $20 at each level of output. How much profit will this firm earn in this case?

11. Assume that the firm shown in this table produces output using one fixed input and one variable input.
    a. Complete this table and use it to find this firm's short-run profit-maximizing quantity of output. How much profit will this firm earn?
    b. Redo the table and find the profit-maximizing quantity of output, if the price of the firm's fixed input fell from $1,000 to $500. How much profit will this firm earn now?
    c. Now redo the original table and find the profit-maximizing quantity of output, if the price of the firm's variable input fell so that *MC* fell by half at each level of output. How much profit will the firm earn in this case?

Output	Price	Total Revenue	Marginal Revenue	Total Cost	Marginal Cost	Profit
0	$3500	$0		$1000		
					$4000	
1	$3500					
					$3000	
2	$3500					
					$2000	
3	$3500					
					$1000	
4	$3500					
					$3000	
5	$3500					
					$4000	
6	$3500					
					$9000	
7	$3500					
					$36,000	
8	$3500					

Challenge Questions

1. Figure 10 in the chapter shows the long-run adjustment process after an increase in demand. The figure assumes that input prices *rise* as industry output expands. However, in a *decreasing cost industry*, input prices *fall* as output expands.
    a. Redraw Figure 10 under the assumption that input prices *fall* as industry output expands. Illustrate what happens in the short run and in the long run after the market demand curve shifts rightward.
    b. Trace out the long-run supply curve for this industry. How does it differ from the long-run supply curve in Figure 10?

2. Figure 10 in the chapter shows the long-run adjustment process after an increase in demand. The figure assumes that input prices rise as industry output expands. However, in a *constant cost industry*, input prices *remain constant* as output expands.
    a. Redraw Figure 10 under the assumption that input prices *do not change* as industry output expands. Illustrate what happens in the short run and in the long run after the market demand curve shifts rightward.
    b. Trace out the new long-run supply curve for this industry. How does it differ from the long-run supply curve in Figure 10? How can it be that more output is offered by the market after the increase in

demand, when each firm in the industry is producing the same quantity of output as they were at price P_1?

3. Figure 10 in the chapter shows the long-run adjustment process after an increase in demand. In this problem, you will be analyzing the effect of a *decrease* in demand in different types of industries.
    a. Redraw Figure 10 under the assumption that the industry in question is an *increasing cost industry*, and illustrate what happens in the short run and in the long run after the market demand curve shifts *leftward* instead of rightward.
    b. Redraw Figure 10 under the assumption that the industry in question is a *constant cost industry*, and illustrate what happens in the short run and in the long run after the market demand curve shifts *leftward* instead of rightward.
    c. Redraw Figure 10 under the assumption that the industry in question is a *decreasing cost industry*, and illustrate what happens in the short run and in the long run after the market demand curve shifts *leftward* instead of rightward.

4. In rare cases, existing technologies are found to be polluting or physically dangerous, and are banned. Review the "Using the Theory" section of this chapter. Then, show graphically the effects of banning a technology that is in

common use in a competitive industry. (*Hint:* After the technology is banned, what will happen to the average cost curve?)

5. If a firm's demand curve is horizontal, *must* its *MR* curve be horizontal as well? If a firm's *MR* curve is horizontal, *must* its demand curve be horizontal as well? Explain in each case.

ECONOMIC *Applications*   *These exercises require access to Lieberman/Hall Xtra! If Xtra! did not come with your book, visit http://liebermanxtra.swlearning.com to purchase.*

1. Use your Xtra! password at the Hall and Lieberman Web site (http://liebermanxtra.swlearning.com) and under Economic Applications click on EconNews. Click on *Microeconomics: Production and Costs*, and read the article, "Precision Plowing." Why would a perfectly competitive firm like a farm purchase such expensive equipment if it is producing the same good as its competitors? Carefully explain, making sure to distinguish between the long run and short run in your answer.

2. Use your Xtra! password at the Hall and Lieberman Web site (http://liebermanxtra.swlearning.com) and under Economic Applications click on EconNews. Select *Microeconomics: Perfect Competition*, and read the article, "One Farmer's Loss Is Another's Grain." Carefully explain, using a diagram with cost and revenue curves, the long-run adjustment that is taking place in this article.

Monopoly and Imperfect Competition

As you learned in the last chapter, we can use the perfectly competitive model to answer some important questions about markets—even markets that do not strictly satisfy its requirements. But the perfectly competitive model will not always be the best choice. In some cases, the questions we want to answer center on a market's *departures* from perfect competition, rather than its approximate fit.

Consider the question of profit. Many small businesses, and some large ones, earn high profits for their owners year after year. The perfectly competitive model is not much use if we want to explain these long-run profits, since the model predicts *zero* economic profit in the long run.

Or think about the problem of pricing. When Braun develops a new electric toothbrush, or Toshiba develops a new laptop computer, they might spend months analyzing what price to charge before bringing their products to market. Moreover, they might consider charging *different* prices to *different* consumers. Toshiba, for example, might give a special discount to computer stores at colleges and universities. If we want to understand pricing decisions like these, the perfectly competitive model would be useless. A perfectly competitive firm is a *price taker*—it takes the market price as given. For such a firm, there is *no* price decision at all.

231

Or consider the way businesses interact with their rivals. Before the managers of Kellogg breakfast cereals make any important business decision, they will think very carefully about how its rivals—Post, Quaker, and General Mills—will react. If Kellogg introduces a new cereal, or lowers its prices, what will these rivals do? Once again, the perfectly competitive model cannot help us answer this question. A competitive firm *never* needs to worry about its rivals, since it can sell all the output it wants at the market price, and nothing it does will affect that price.

Finally, there are markets for which the perfectly competitive model would be *entirely* inappropriate. For example, think about local markets for cable television. Consumers must buy from the one firm that serves their area, and that firm has no direct competitors. We would never analyze such a market with the tools of Chapter 7.

As you can see, while the perfectly competitive model can be applied very widely, it cannot be applied to *all* markets. This is why economists have identified other market structures besides perfect competition and have developed models to help us analyze them. In this chapter, you will learn about three new market structures: *monopoly, oligopoly,* and *monopolistic competition.*

MONOPOLY

Monopoly is as close as economics comes to a dirty word. It is typically associated with extraordinary power, unfairly high prices and exploitation. For example, in the board game *Monopoly*, when you take over a neighborhood by buying up adjacent properties, you exploit other players by charging them exorbitantly higher rent.

The negative reputation of monopoly is in many ways deserved. Adam Smith's "invisible hand"—which channels the behavior of perfectly competitive firms into a socially beneficial outcome—doesn't poke, prod or even lay a finger on a monopoly firm. Monopolies, therefore, present a problem that nations around the world address with the very *visible* hand of government.

At the same time, a mythology has developed around monopolies. The media often portrays their power as absolute and unlimited, and their behavior as capricious and unpredictable. One sometimes hears that monopoly should be treated like an infectious disease: prevent it from arising, and destroy it when it does.

As you are about to see, this negative characterization goes too far. A monopoly's power may be formidable, but it's far from umlimited. Monopoly behavior—far from capricious—is remarkably predictable. And while monopolies should be avoided in most cases, it is sometimes the best way to organize production. In such cases, we would do better to *manage* the monopoly, rather than destroy it.

What Is a Monopoly?

In most of your purchases—a haircut, a car, a college education—more than one seller is competing for your dollars. But in some markets, you have no choice at all. If you want to mail a letter for normal delivery, you must use the U.S. Postal Service. If you want cable television service, you must use the one cable television company in your area. And if you live in a very small town, you may have just one doctor, one gas station, or one movie theater to select from. These are all examples of *monopolies:*

Monopoly firm The only seller of a good or service that has no close substitutes.

Monopoly market The market in which a monopoly firm operates.

> A *monopoly firm* is the only seller of a good or service with no close substitutes. *The market in which the monopoly firm operates is called a monopoly market.*

A key concept in the definition of monopoly is the notion of *substitutability*. There is usually more than one way to satisfy a desire, and a single seller of a good or service is *not* considered a monopoly if other firms sell products—close substitutes—that satisfy that same desire. For example, only one firm in the country—Kellogg—sells Kellogg's Corn Flakes. But other cereal companies sell their own brands of cornflakes, and other similar flaky cereals, all of which are very close substitutes for Kellogg's. This is why we do not consider Kellogg to be a monopoly firm.

But now imagine that you live in a small, rural town, and there is only one dental practice in the region. While there may be alternatives—traveling to a dentist in another distant town, or yanking out your own infected tooth with a pliers—these are not close substitutes for the services of the local practice. Accordingly, we would regard the sole dental practice in the area as a monopoly.

Why Monopolies Exist

The mere existence of a monopoly means that *something* is causing other firms to stay out of the market rather than enter and compete with the firm already there. Broadly speaking, there must be some *barrier to entry*. Three common types of barriers are: economies of scale, legal barriers, and network externalities.

Economies of Scale Recall from Chapter 5 that economies of scale in production cause a firm's long-run average cost curve to slope downward. That is, the more output the firm produces, the lower will be its cost per unit. If economies of scale persist to the point where a single firm is producing for the entire market, we call the market a *natural monopoly*:

> A natural monopoly exists when, due to economies of scale, one firm can produce at a lower cost per unit than can two or more firms.

The monopoly firm, or the market in which is operates, is called a *natural* monopoly for good reason: Unless the government intervenes, only one seller would survive. The market would *naturally* become a monopoly. Why?

Although we've already discussed the answer (in Chapter 5), let's step through it in a bit more detail here. Figure 1 is a larger and more specific version of panel (b) from Figure 8 in Chapter 5. It shows the *LRATC* curve for a typical dry cleaner operating in a small town. Dry cleaners use several "lumpy inputs"—inputs that must be purchased in some minimum quantities for a wide range of output. For example, whether it cleans 1 article of clothing each week or 300, the dry cleaner will need the same small parcel of land for its shop, a single employee to handle customers, the same amount of electricity for the lights. For all output levels from 0 to 300, it will need either the same amount of machinery (if it cleans the clothes on site) or the same amount of transportation services (if the clothes are cleaned elsewhere). Clearly, the more clothes cleaned, the lower the firm's cost per piece of clothing, creating economies of scale (a downward-sloping *LRATC* curve). As you can see, for any market quantity in our diagram, a single dry cleaning shop could sell it at lower cost per unit than could two or more dry cleaners.

The figure also shows the market demand curve (D_{market}) for dry cleaning in this small town. Notice that it crosses the *LRATC* curve at 300 units, and then drops below it. This tells us that the *maximum* potential market for dry cleaning in this town is 300 pieces per week. Why? In order for quantity demanded in this market to exceed 300 pieces—say, 350—price would have to drop down to $5 per piece (point C). But this amount of cleaning wouldn't be offered in the town without driving the cost per unit *above* $5 per piece. For example, a single cleaner servicing all 350 pieces would have a cost per unit of $12 per piece (point B) and would go out of business charging the most the market would pay for that quantity, which is $5 per piece. Two firms splitting the market would be in even worse shape: Their cost per unit would be even larger. But in order to get enough customers to clean 350 pieces between them, they could charge only $5.00—less than their cost per unit. Therefore, the maximum amount of dry cleaning that can be done in this market, while permitting the dry cleaning industry to survive in the long run, is 300 pieces per week.

Let's suppose that this town already has such a business—Incumbent Cleaning—and its owner is making a nice profit. (We'll examine how the existing cleaner selects his price to maximize profit in a couple of pages.) Another resident is considering opening a competing firm in the town. Should she do it? Not if she's smart. In order to attract customers, she'd have to at least match, or maybe undercut, the price charged by Incumbent Cleaners. But in any competition over price, Incumbent has an advantage: It's already cleaning more clothes than the newcomer could, even if the newcomer were able to capture half the market. Thus, Incumbent's cost per unit is already lower than the newcomer could hope to achieve. Threatened by the newcomer, Incumbent could always lower its price to just a shade above its low cost per unit and still earn a small profit. But if the newcomer (with fewer initial customers and a much higher cost per unit) tried to match Incumbent's low price, it would suffer a loss.

Since there is time and expense involved in setting up a new dry cleaning shop—and closing it down if it fails—a potential entrant would not want to bear these costs for nothing. She would most likely look for another business, one with *LRATC* and market demand curves that do *not* look like Figure 1.

Small local monopolies are often *natural* monopolies. Think of the sole gas station in a small town. Since it needs a minimum set of certain inputs no matter how

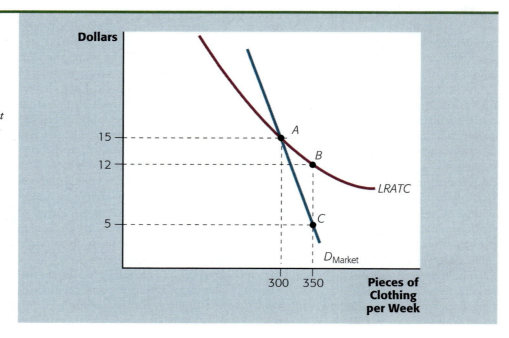

FIGURE 1
A Natural Monopoly

The market quantity of dry cleaning could never be 350 pieces per week because the lowest possible cost per unit of cleaning 350 pieces is $12 (point B), which exceeds the price people would willingly pay. The maximum potential market is 300 pieces. For any quantity up to the maximum potential market, a single firm has a cost advantage over two or more firms that split the market among themselves.

little gas it sells (a pump for each type of gas, space for cars to pull up), each additional gallon sold lowers the station's cost per unit. By producing for the entire (small town) market, it achieves the smallest possible cost per unit. Under these circumstances, a potential new entrant would have to think very hard about coming into this market, since it would not be able to survive a price war with the firm already there. The same logic can explain the monopoly position held by the sole food market, attorney, or dentist in a small town. These are all natural monopolies, because they continue to enjoy economies of scale up to the point at which they are serving the entire market.

Legal Barriers Many monopolies arise because of legal barriers. Of course, since laws are created by human beings, this immediately raises the question: Why would anyone purposely create barriers that lead to monopoly? As you'll see, the answer varies depending on the type of barrier being erected. Here, we'll consider two of the most important legal barriers that give rise to monopolies: protection of intellectual property and government franchise.

Protection of Intellectual Property. The words you are reading right now are an example of *intellectual property,* which includes literary, artistic, and musical works, as well as scientific inventions. Most markets for a specific intellectual property are monopolies: One firm or individual owns the property and is the sole seller of the rights to use it. There is both good and bad in this. As you will learn in this chapter, prices tend to be higher under monopoly than under perfect competition, and monopolies often earn economic profit as a consequence. This is good for the monopoly and bad for everyone else. On the other hand, it is just this promise of monopoly profit that encourages the creation of original products and ideas, which certainly benefits the rest of us. The Palm Pilot personal organizer, the Visex laser for reshaping the eye's cornea, and Internet search engines such as Google, Vivisimo, and Teoma were all launched by innovators who bore considerable costs and risks with an expectation of future profits. The same is true of every compact disc you listen to, every novel you read, and every movie you see.

 Policy Tradeoffs

In dealing with intellectual property, government strikes a compromise: It allows the creators of intellectual property to enjoy a monopoly and earn economic profit, but only for a limited period of time. Once the time is up, other sellers are allowed to enter the market, and it is hoped that competition among them will bring down prices.

The two most important kinds of legal protection for intellectual property are *patents* and *copyrights*. New scientific discoveries and the products that result from them are protected by a **patent** obtained from the federal government. The patent prevents anyone else from selling the same discovery or product for about 20 years. For example, in 1981, the Eli Lilly Company took out a patent on the chemical fluoxetine, the active ingredient in Prozac. As the first antidepressant without serious side effects, Prozac proved enormously profitable for Lilly. The drug earned Lilly as much as $13.5 million in profit *per day* before its patent expired in August 2001. Other pharmaceutical companies, forced to work around Lilly's patent, took much longer to develop their own, similar drugs. In the meantime, Lilly was the sole seller of a product with no close substitutes.

Patent A temporary grant of monopoly rights over a new product or scientific discovery.

Copyright A grant of exclusive rights to sell a literary, musical, or artistic work.

Literary, musical, and artistic works are protected by a **copyright,** which grants exclusive rights over the material for at least 50 years. For example, the copyright on this book is owned by South-Western/Thomson Learning. No other company or individual can print copies and sell them to the public, and no one can quote from the book at length without obtaining South-Western's permission.

Copyrights and patents are often sold to another person or firm, but this does not change the monopoly status of the market, since there is still just one seller. For example, the song "Happy Birthday" was originally written in 1893 but first received copyright protection in 1935. Since then, the copyright has changed hands numerous times and is currently owned by Time Warner. While you are free to sing this song at a private birthday party, anyone who wants to sing it on radio or television—that is, anyone who wants to profit from the song—must obtain a license from Time Warner and pay a small royalty.

Government Franchise. The large firms we usually think of as monopolies—utility, telephone, and cable television companies—have their monopoly status guaranteed through **government franchise,** a grant of exclusive rights over a product. Here, the barrier to entry is quite simple: Any other firm that enters the market will be prosecuted!

Government franchise A government-granted right to be the sole seller of a product or service.

Governments usually grant franchises when they think the market is a *natural monopoly.* In this case, a single large firm enjoying economies of scale would have a lower cost per unit than multiple smaller firms, so government tries to serve the public interest by *ensuring* that there are no competitors. In exchange for its monopoly status, the seller must submit to either government ownership and control or else government regulation over its prices and profits.

This is the logic behind the monopoly status of the U.S. Postal Service. No matter how many letters it delivers, a postal firm must have enough letter carriers to reach every house every day. Two postal companies would need many more carriers to deliver the same total number of letters, raising costs and, ultimately, the price of mailing a letter. Thus, mail delivery is a natural monopoly, one that the federal government has chosen to own and control rather than merely regulate. Federal law prohibits any other firm from offering normal letter delivery service.

Local governments, too, create monopolies by granting exclusive franchises in a variety of industries believed to be natural monopolies. These include utility companies that provide electricity, gas, and water, as well as garbage collection services.

Since ordinary letter delivery is a natural monopoly, the U.S. Postal Service has been granted an exclusive government franchise to deliver the mail.

Network Externalities Imagine that one day, in a flash of brilliance, you hit upon a simple idea that enables you to create a new, superior operating system for personal computers. You spend the next six months writing the computer code, and you succeed. Compared to Microsoft Windows, your operating system is less vulnerable to viruses, works 10 percent faster, and uses 10 percent less memory. It even allows the user to turn off the caps-lock key, which most people use only by mistake.

Now all you need is a few million dollars to launch your new product. You manage to get appointments with several venture capital firms, specialists in funding new projects. But every time you make your pitch, and the venture capital people realize what you're proposing, you get the same reaction: hysterical laughter. "But really," you say. "It works better than Windows. I can prove it." "We believe you," they always respond. And they do. And then . . . they start laughing again.

Why? Because you're trying to enter a market with significant *network externalities*.[1]

> *Network externalities* *exist when an increase in the network's membership (more users of the product) increase its value to current and potential members.*

Network externalities A situation in which the value of a good or service to each user increases as more people use it.

When network externalities are present, joining a large network is more beneficial than joining a small network, even if the product in the larger network is somewhat inferior to the product in the smaller one. Once a network reaches a certain size, additional consumers will want to join just because so many others already have. And if joining the network requires you to buy a product produced by only one firm, that firm can rapidly become the leading supplier in the market.

All of this applies to the market for computer operating systems. First, when you buy a Windows computer, you benefit by having a huge number of other computers—owned by friends and coworkers—that you can easily operate, and a large number of people with whom you can easily share documents. And, by buying the Windows machine, you enlarge the network, benefitting your friends and coworkers.

Second, you gain access to many software programs, such as PowerPoint, that are designed for Windows and not for the alternatives (Apple or Linux). Of course, by buying a Windows machine and enlarging the network, you and millions of people like you provide even more incentive to software developers to direct their efforts toward Windows users.

Third, if you've ever had a problem with your computer and tried getting help from a software seller's support line, you've learned the time you can save by just calling a knowledgeable friend or coworker. By joining the huge Windows network, you increase the number of friends who would be able to help you in a pinch. (And you become another person who can help them.)

Windows, the first operating system to be used by tens of millions of people, has clearly benefited from network externalities. And today, with the system installed on more than 80 percent of all personal computers sold in the United States, Windows's leading position in personal computer operating systems would be difficult to overcome. For a new operating system to gain a foothold, the seller would have to incur substantial costs beyond just writing new code. It would have to create a new word processor and spreadsheet, or subsidize sellers of existing software to create versions for the new operating system. It would have to promote its product heavily. And it would have to endure a lengthy period of low prices in order to induce customers to switch.

The reason that venture capitalists would not be willing to bankroll your new operating system is that the costs of all these efforts—beyond your original creation of the operating system—would probably be greater than the revenue that your products would bring in.

Network externalities can also explain the leading positions of eBay in the market for online auctions and Amazon in online retailing. (See if you can identify the network externalities for eBay and Amazon.)

---

[1] The term *externality* will be defined formally in Chapter 10. But if you're curious, an externality is a by-product of a transaction that affects someone other than the buyer or seller (someone external to the transaction). In the case of network externalities, by paying to join the network (e.g., buying a Windows computer), you make the network larger, benefiting others (current and potential members) who weren't involved in your transaction.

Monopoly Goals and Constraints

The goal of a monopoly, like that of any firm, is to earn the highest profit possible. And, like other firms, a monopolist faces constraints.

Reread that last sentence because it is important. It is tempting to think that a monopolist—because it faces no direct competitors in its market—is free of constraints. Or that its constraints are special ones, unlike those of any other firm. For example, many people think that the only force preventing a monopolist from charging outrageously high prices is public outrage. In this view, your cable company would charge $200, $500, or even $10,000 per month if only it could "get away with it."

But with a little reflection, it is easy to see that a monopolist faces purely *economic* constraints that limit its behavior—constraints that are similar to those faced by other, nonmonopoly firms. What are these constraints?

First, there is a constraint on the monopoly's *costs*: For any level of output the monopolist might produce, it must pay some total cost to produce it. This cost constraint is determined by the monopolist's production technology—which tells it how much output it can produce with different combinations of inputs—and also by the prices it must pay for those inputs. In other words, the constraints on the monopolist's costs are the same as on any other type of firm, such as the perfectly competitive firm we studied in the previous chapter.

There is also a *demand constraint*. The monopolist's demand curve—which is also the market demand curve—tells us the maximum price the monopolist can charge to sell any given quantity of output.[2]

To sum up:

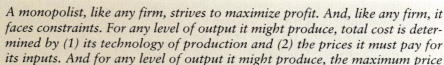

Maximization Subject to Constraints

A monopolist, like any firm, strives to maximize profit. And, like any firm, it faces constraints. For any level of output it might produce, total cost is determined by (1) its technology of production and (2) the prices it must pay for its inputs. And for any level of output it might produce, the maximum price it can charge is determined by the market demand curve for its product.

Monopoly Price or Output Decision

Notice that the title of this section reads "price *or* output decision," not "price *and* output decision." The reason is that noncompetitive firms—such as monopolies—do *not* make two separate decisions about price and quantity, but rather *one* decision. More specifically, once the firm determines its output level, it has also determined its price (the maximum price it can charge and still sell that output level). Similarly, once the firm determines its price, it has also determined its output level (the maximum output the firm can sell at that price).

Of course, any *change* in output also implies a *change* in price, and vice versa. And these changes will affect both the firm's revenue and its costs. Let's first examine the effect on total revenue.

---

[2] We're currently analyzing the behavior of a *single-price monopoly*—one that charges the same price for every unit it sells. When you see the term *monopoly* by itself, it means *single-price monopoly*. The Appendix to this chapter will analyze the case of *price-discriminating firms*, which can charge several different prices simultaneously (for example, by charging different prices to different customers).

Output and Revenue. Suppose a monopolist is considering selling more output. Then, since it faces a downward-sloping demand curve, it will have to lower its price. However, the new, lower price must be charged *not* just on the new, additional units it wants to sell, but on *all* units of output, including those it was previously selling at a higher price. For example, if your local cable television company wants more subscribers, it will have to lower its rates for everyone, including those who already subscribe at the current rate. Thus, lowering price and increasing output have two offsetting effects on total revenue: On the one hand, more output is sold, tending to *increase* total revenue; on the other hand, *all* units now go for a lower price, tending to *decrease* total revenue. The net effect may be a rise or fall in total revenue, or—another way to say the same thing—the firm's *marginal revenue* may be positive or negative.

This should sound familiar to you. In Chapter 6, Ned's Beds faced a downward-sloping demand curve and had to lower its price on all of its bed frames in order to sell more of them. Although Ned was not necessarily the only seller in his market, his total and marginal revenue behaved in much the same way as we are describing here.

Figure 2 illustrates the demand and marginal revenue curves for Zillion-Channel Cable, a monopoly that sells cable television services to the residents of a town. We will assume that Zillion-Channel is free from government regulation. In the figure, the demand curve shows the number of subscribers at each monthly price for cable. The demand curve is both a *market* demand curve and the demand curve *facing the firm*, since Zillion-Channel is the only firm in its market.

Let's see what happens to Zillion-Channel's revenue as we move from point *A* to point *B* along its demand curve. At point *A*, the firm charges a monthly price of $50 and attracts 5,000 paid subscribers, for a total revenue of 5,000 × $50 = $250,000. If it lowers its price to $48, moving to point *B*, 1,000 more people will

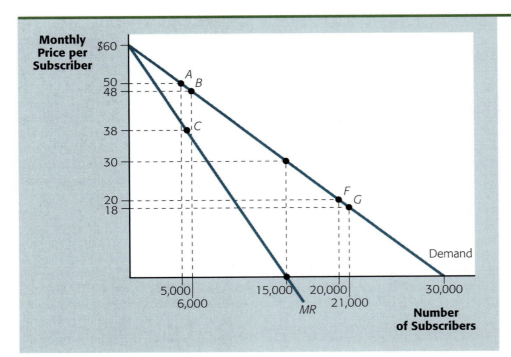

FIGURE 2
Demand and Marginal Revenue

A monopoly faces a downward-sloping market demand curve. To sell additional output, the firm must lower its price. Marginal revenue (MR) shows the change in total revenue that results from a one-unit increase in output. MR is less than price; to sell an additional unit, the monopoly must lower the price on that unit and on previous units.

subscribe, for a total revenue of 6,000 × $48 = $288,000. Thus, in moving from point *A* to point *B*, total revenue rises by $38,000. The marginal revenue for this move, which tells us the increase in revenue per additional unit of output, can be calculated as follows:

$$MR = \frac{\Delta TR}{\Delta Q} = \frac{(\$288,000 - \$250,000)}{(6,000 - 5,000)} = \frac{\$38,000}{1,000} = \$38$$

This value for marginal revenue—$38—is plotted at point *C*, which is midway between points *A* and *B*. Notice that *MR* is *less* than the new price of output, $48. This follows from the two competing effects just discussed: On the one hand, the monopoly is selling more output and getting $48 on each additional unit; on the other hand, it has to charge a lower price on the previous 5,000 units of output it was selling. In the move from *A* to *B*, it turns out that total revenue rises, and marginal revenue is positive, but less than $48.

> *When any firm, including a monopoly, faces a downward-sloping demand curve, marginal revenue is less than the price of output. Therefore, the marginal revenue curve will lie below the demand curve.*

For other moves along the demand curve, total revenue may decline, so marginal revenue will be negative. (Verify this for the move from point *F* to point *G*.) For such changes, the marginal revenue curve lies below the horizontal axis.

The marginal revenue curve alone tells us something about the monopoly's output decision:

> *A monopoly will produce at an output level where marginal revenue is positive.*

How can we be sure? Look again at Figure 2. When Zillion-Channel reaches 15,000 subscribers, its marginal revenue is zero. Raising output any further (say, from 15,000 to 16,000 subscribers) pushes *MR* into the negative zone. But negative marginal revenue means that *total* revenue decreases. Thus, by raising output beyond 15,000, total revenue goes down.

What about costs? We know that pushing output higher than 15,000 will increase total costs, just as does *any* rise in output. So, putting this together: Raising output beyond 15,000 causes revenue to decrease and costs to increase. Profit must therefore fall—not a good move. Thus, the firm will not want to push output into the region where marginal revenue is negative. And if it's in that region, it should go into reverse and *decrease* output, since that would *raise* profit. So in the end, it will produce somewhere in the region where *MR* is positive.

The Profit-Maximizing Output Level.
Knowing that a monopoly will produce only where marginal revenue is positive narrows down the possibilities somewhat . . . but not enough. Which of the many output levels smaller than 15,000 units will Zillion-Channel choose? To answer, we return to our (now familiar) rule from Chapter 6, which tells us how *any* firm can find its profit-maximizing output level:

Marginal Decision
Making

> *To maximize profit, a monoply—like any firm—should produce the quantity where* MC = MR *and the* MC *curve crosses the* MR *curve from below.*

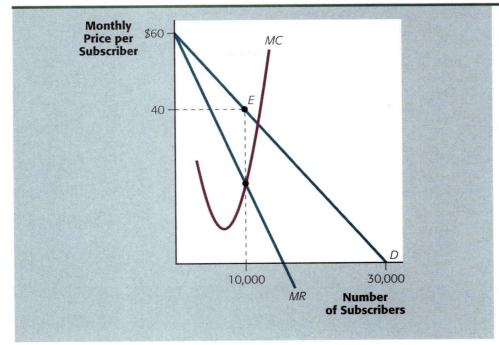

FIGURE 3
**Monopoly Price and Output
Determination**

*Like any firm, the monopolist
maximizes profit by producing
where MC equals MR. Here, that
quantity is 10,000 units. The
price charged ($40) is read off the
demand curve. It is the highest
price at which the monopolist
can sell that level of output.*

Figure 3 adds Zillion-Channel's marginal cost curve to the demand and marginal revenue curves of Figure 2. The greatest profit possible occurs at an output level of 10,000, where the *MC* curve crosses the *MR* curve from below. In order to sell this level of output, the firm will charge a price of $40, locating at point *E* on its demand curve. You can see that for a monopoly, *price and output are not independent decisions, but different ways of expressing the same decision.* Once Zillion-Channel determines its profit-maximizing output level (10,000 units), it has also determined its profit-maximizing price ($40), and vice versa.

Profit and Loss

In Figure 3, we can determine Zillion-Channel's price and output level, but we cannot see whether the firm is making an economic profit or loss. This will require one more addition to the diagram—the average cost curve. Remember that

Profit per Unit = $P - ATC$.

Now, the price, *P*, at any output level is read off the demand curve. Profit per unit, then, is just the distance between the firm's demand curve and its *ATC* curve.

Figure 4(a) is just like Figure 3 but adds Zillion-Channel's *ATC* curve. As you can see, at the profit-maximizing output level of 10,000, price is $40 and average total cost is $32, so profit per unit is $8.

Now look at the blue rectangle in the figure. The height of this rectangle is profit

A Monopoly Supply Curve? A question may have occurred to you: Where is the monopoly's *supply curve*? The answer is that *there is no supply curve for a monopoly.* A firm's supply curve tells us how much output a firm will want to produce and sell when it is *presented* with different prices. This makes sense for a perfectly competitive firm that takes the market price as given and responds by deciding how much output to produce. A monopoly, by contrast, is *not* a price taker; it *chooses* its price. Since the monopolist is free to choose any price it wants—and it will always choose the *profit-maximizing* price and no other—the notion of a supply curve does not apply to a monopoly.

DANGEROUS CURVES

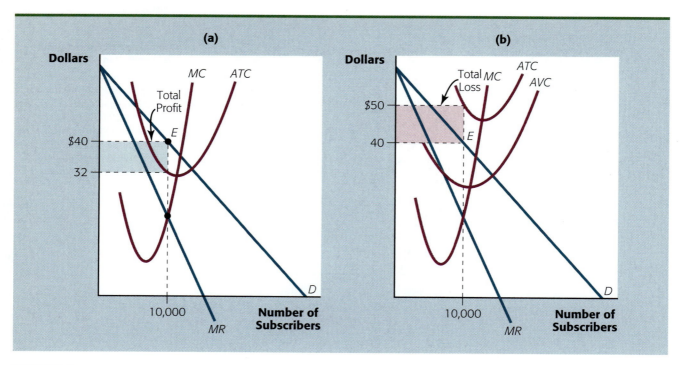

FIGURE 4
Monopoly Profit and Loss

In panel (a), the monopolist's profit is the difference between price and average total cost (ATC) multiplied by the number of units sold. The blue area indicates a profit of $80,000. Panel (b) shows a monopolist suffering a loss. At the best level of output, ATC exceeds price. The red rectangle shows a loss of $100,000.

per unit ($8), and the width is the number of units produced (10,000). The *area* of the rectangle—height × width—equals Zillion-Channel's total profit, or $8 × 10,000 = $80,000.

> *A monopoly earns a profit whenever P > ATC. Its total profit at the best output level equals the area of a rectangle with height equal to the distance between P and ATC and width equal to the level of output.*

This should sound familiar: It is exactly how we represented the profit of a perfectly competitive firm (compare with Figure 3(a) in Chapter 7). The diagram looked different under perfect competition because the firm's demand curve was horizontal, whereas for a monopoly it is downward sloping.

However, a monopoly will not *necessarily* earn economic profit. Figure 4(b) illustrates the case of a monopoly suffering a loss. Here, costs are higher than in panel (a), and the *ATC* curve lies everywhere above the demand curve, so the firm will suffer a loss at any level of output. At the best output level—10,000—*ATC* is $50, so the loss per unit is $10. The total loss ($100,000) is the area of the red rectangle, whose height is the loss per unit ($10) and width is the best output level (10,000). Being a monopolist is no guarantee of profit. If costs are too high, or demand is insufficient, a monopolist may break even or suffer a loss.

> *A monopoly suffers a loss whenever P < ATC. Its total loss at the best output level equals the area of a rectangle with height equal to the distance between ATC and P and width equal to the level of output.*

The Shut-Down Decision

What if a monopoly suffers a loss in the short run? Then it will have to make the same decision as any other firm: to shut down or not to shut down. The rule you learned in Chapter 6—that a firm should shut down if $TR < TVC$ at the output level where marginal revenue and marginal cost are equal—applies to any firm, including a monopoly. And (as you learned in Chapter 7), the statement "$TR < TVC$" is equivalent to the statement "$P < AVC$." Therefore,

> *any firm—including a monopoly—should shut down if* $P < AVC$ *at the output level where* $MR = MC$.

That is, if the firm's price per unit cannot cover its variable or operating costs per unit at its best output level (where $MR = MC$), then the firm should shut down.

In Figure 4(b), Zillion-Channel is suffering a loss. But since $P = \$40$ and AVC is less than \$40 at an output of 10,000, we have $P > AVC$: The firm should keep operating. On your own, draw in an alternative AVC curve in panel (b) that would cause Zillion-Channel to shut down. (*Hint:* It will be higher than the existing AVC curve.)

In some cases, the shutdown rule will accurately and realistically predict when a monopoly will shut down in the short run. In other cases, it will not. Many monopolies produce a vital service, such as transportation or communications, and these monopolies typically operate under government regulation. Suppose the monopoly experiences a temporary upward shift in its AVC curve, say, because the price of a variable input rises. Or suppose it experiences a temporary leftward shift of its demand curve, say, because household income decreases. In either case, if the monopoly suddenly finds that $P < AVC$, government may not allow it to shut down, but instead use tax revenue to make up for the firm's losses.

HTTP://

Macrosoft is a monopoly simulation written by Peter Wilcoxen of the University of Texas. Try it at **http://maxwell.insightworks. com/games/macrosoft/**.

Monopoly in the Long Run

In the short run, a monopoly may earn an economic profit or suffer an economic loss. (It may, of course, break even as well; see if you can draw this case on your own.) But what about the long run? The most important insight of the previous chapter was that perfectly competitive firms *cannot* earn a profit in long-run equilibrium. Profit attracts new firms into the market, and market production increases. This, in turn, causes the market price to fall, eliminating any temporary profit earned by a competitive firm.

But there is no such process at work in a monopoly market, where barriers *prevent* the entry of other firms into the market. Outsiders will *want* to enter an industry when a monopoly is earning above economic profit, but they will be *unable to do so*. Thus, the market provides no mechanism to eliminate monopoly profit.

> *Unlike perfectly competitive firms, monopolies may earn economic profit in the long run.*

What about economic loss? If a monopoly is a government franchise, and it faces the prospect of long-run loss, the government may decide to subsidize it in order to keep it running—especially if it provides a vital service like mail delivery or mass transit. But if the monopoly is privately owned and controlled, it will not tolerate long-run losses. A monopoly suffering an economic loss that it expects to continue indefinitely should always exit the industry, just like any other firm.

> *A privately owned monopoly suffering an economic loss in the long run will exit the industry, just as would any other business firm. In the long run, therefore, we should not find privately owned monopolies suffering economic losses.*

Comparing Monopoly to Perfect Competition

We have already seen one important difference between monopoly and perfectly competitive markets: In perfect competition, economic profit is relentlessly reduced to zero by the entry of other firms; in monopoly, economic profit can continue indefinitely.

But monopoly also differs from perfect competition in another way:

Markets and Equilibrium

> *We can expect a monopoly market to have a higher price and lower output than an otherwise similar perfectly competitive market.*

To see why this is so, let's explore what would happen if a single firm took over a perfectly competitive market, changing the market to a monopoly. Figure 5 illustrates a competitive market consisting of 100 identical firms. The market is in long-run equilibrium at point *E*, with a market price of $10 and market output of 100,000 units. In panel (b), the typical firm faces a horizontal demand curve at $10, produces output of 1,000 units, and earns zero economic profit.

Now, imagine that a single company buys all 100 firms, to form a monopoly. The new monopoly market is illustrated in panel (c). Under monopoly, the horizontal demand curve facing each firm becomes irrelevant. Instead, the demand curve facing the monopoly is the downward-sloping *market* demand curve *D*—the same as the market demand curve in panel (a). Since the demand curve slopes downward, marginal revenue will be less than price, and the *MR* curve will lie everywhere below the demand curve. To maximize profit, the monopoly will want to find the output level at which *MC = MR*. But what is the new monopoly's *MC* curve?

We'll assume that the monopoly doesn't change the way output is produced: Each previously competitive firm will continue to produce its output with the same technology as before, only now it operates as one of 100 different plants that the monopoly controls. With this assumption, *the monopoly's marginal cost curve will be the same as the market supply curve in panel (a).* Why? First, remember that the market supply curve is obtained by adding up each individual firm's supply curve, that is, each individual firm's marginal cost curve. Therefore, the market supply curve tells us the marginal cost—at *some* firm—of producing another unit of output for the market. When the monopoly takes over each of these individual firms, the market supply curve tells us how much it will cost the monopoly to produce another unit of output at one of its plants. For example, point *E* on the market supply curve tells us that, when total supply is 100,000, with each plant producing 1,000, increasing output by one more unit will cost the monopoly $10, because that is the marginal cost at each of its plants. The same is true at every other point along the old competitive market supply curve: It will always tell us the monopoly's cost of producing one more unit at one of the plants it now owns. In other words, the

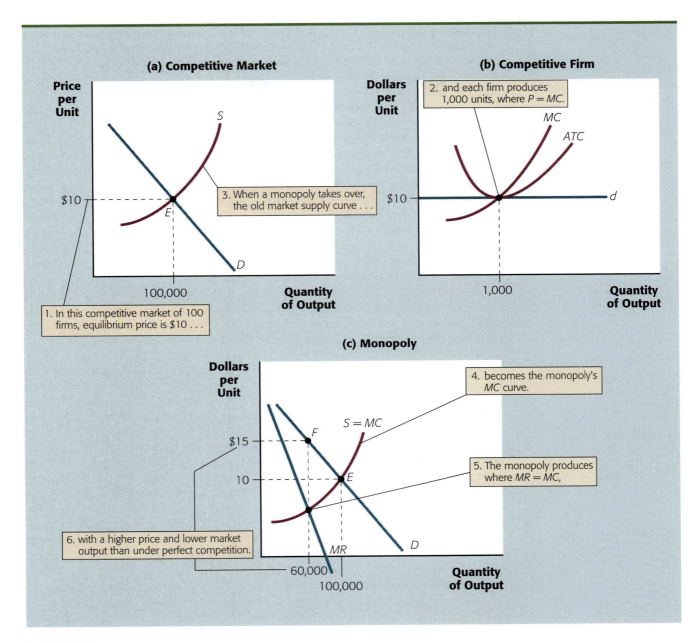

(a) Competitive Market

Price per Unit

S

10 ---- E

3. When a monopoly takes over, the old market supply curve . . .

D

100,000

Quantity of Output

1. In this competitive market of 100 firms, equilibrium price is $10 . . .

(b) Competitive Firm

Dollars per Unit

2. and each firm produces 1,000 units, where $P = MC$.

MC

ATC

10 ---- d

1,000

Quantity of Output

(c) Monopoly

Dollars per Unit

4. becomes the monopoly's MC curve.

F

$S = MC$

15 ---- F

10 ---- E

5. The monopoly produces where $MR = MC$,

6. with a higher price and lower market output than under perfect competition.

MR

D

60,000

100,000

Quantity of Output

FIGURE 5
Comparing Monopoly and Perfect Competition

Panel (a) shows a competitive market with 100 identical firms. The market price is $10 per unit; at that price, each firm (panel b) sells 1,000 units and earns zero economic profit. A monopolist that buys up all these firms will face the market demand curve D in panel (c). It will produce 60,000 units, where MR = MC. *The monopolist produces less than the competitive firms did and charges a higher price ($15 rather than $10).*

upward-sloping curve in panel (c), which is the market supply curve when the market is competitive, becomes the marginal cost curve for a single firm when the market is monopolized. This is why the curve is labeled both S (the old market supply) and MC (the new marginal cost of the monopolist).

Now we have all the information we need to find the monopoly's choice of price and quantity. In panel (c), the monopoly's *MC* curve crosses the *MR* curve from below at 60,000 units of output. This will be the monopoly's profit-maximizing output level. To sell this much output, the monopoly will charge $15 per unit—point *F* on its demand curve.

Notice what has happened in our example: After the monopoly takes over, the price rises from $10 to $15, and market quantity drops from 100,000 to 60,000. The monopoly, compared to a competitive market, would *charge more and produce less*.

Now let's see who gains and who loses from the takeover. By raising price and restricting output, the new monopoly earns economic profit. We know this because if the firm were to charge $10—the competitive price—each of its plants would break even, giving it zero economic profit. But we've just seen that $10 is *not* the profit maximizing price—$15 is. So, the firm must make higher profit at $15 than at $10, or higher than zero economic profit. Consumers, however, lose in two ways: They pay more for the output they buy, and, due to higher prices, they buy less output. The changeover from perfect competition to monopoly thus benefits the owners of the monopoly and harms consumers of the product.

Keep in mind, though, an important proviso concerning this result: Comparing monopoly and perfect competition, we see that price is higher and output is lower under monopoly *if all else is equal*. In particular, we have assumed that after the market is monopolized, the technology of production remains unchanged at each previously competitive firm.

But a monopoly may be able to *change* the technology of production, so that all else would *not* remain equal. For example, a monopoly may have each of its new plants *specialize* in some part of the production process, or it may be able to achieve efficiencies in product planning, employee supervision, bookkeeping, or customer relations. If these cost savings enable the monopoly to use a less costly input mix for any given output level, then the monopoly's marginal cost curve in panel (c) would be *lower* than the competitive market supply curve in panel (a). If you add another, lower *MC* curve to panel (c), you'll see that this tends to *decrease* the monopoly's price and *increase* its output level—exactly the reverse of the effects discussed earlier. If the cost savings are great enough, and the *MC* curve drops low enough, a profit-maximizing monopoly could even charge a lower price and produce more output than would a competitive market. (See if you can draw a diagram to demonstrate this case.) The general conclusion is this:

The monopolization of a competitive industry leads to two opposing effects. First, for any given technology of production, monopolization leads to higher prices and lower output. Second, changes in the technology of production made possible under monopoly may lead to lower prices and higher output. The ultimate effect on price and quantity depends on the relative strengths of these two effects.

The Future of Monopoly

The past century was not kind to monopolies. In the first half of the century, vigorous antitrust legislation and enforcement broke up many long-standing monopolies, such as Standard Oil in 1911 and Alcoa in 1945. For the rest of the century, many monopolies and would-be monopolies came under the scrutiny of government regulators, and were unable to fully maximize profit. Today, monopolies face a different threat: the relentless advance of technology.

Consider, for example, the natural monopoly of local phone service. The service, which currently takes place over local telephone wires, is characterized by economies of scale: A single company can produce at a lower cost per unit than could several competitors. But soon, cable television companies will have the technology to offer local telephone service over *cable* wires. When this technology is put in place, every household will have two suppliers from which to choose: the existing local phone company *and* the local cable company. At this point, the monopoly status of local telephone companies will come to an end.

Even the old standard of monopolies, the post office, is being threatened by technology. Computerized inventory tracking and fuel-efficient jets have enabled companies such as Federal Express and DHL to offer low-cost overnight letter delivery services, while e-mail and bill paying by phone are cutting into the volume of old-fashioned letters. It is not hard to imagine a time in the future when you will receive all your mail on the Internet, and the notion of *hand-delivered* letters will become a thing of the past, a quaint practice you can tell your children about.

Technology is even threatening the monopolies enjoyed by patent and copyright holders. Almost every college student knows about Napster or its descendants—"sharing services" that enable Internet users to download copyrighted songs from other users, without paying for them. Each time the recording industry defends its intellectual property rights with legal challenges that put one sharing service out of business, another springs up. New printing and scanning techniques enable counterfeiters to reproduce exact replicas not only of patented goods, but also their labels and packaging. According to the FBI, U.S. businesses lose more than $200 billion per year from the production and sale of counterfeit products, including clothing, toys, pharmaceuticals, computer hardware, watches, and more.[3]

This is not to say that monopolies are taking their last breaths. Just as technological progress weakens some monopolies, it can also help to preserve existing monopolies or create new ones. For example, technology is being called into service to help preserve monopolies created by patents and copyrights, as governments and companies experiment with new techniques for detecting counterfeit products, analogous to those used to detect counterfeit currency.

The latest scientific discoveries may be laying the groundwork for future monopolies in products and services we can't yet imagine. Finally, some small-town monopolies—especially those that provide personal services such as medical care or legal representation—may remain immune to the technological threats. It's safe to say that monopolies in many forms will be with us for some time.

MONOPOLISTIC COMPETITION

In perfect competition, there are so many firms selling the same product, that none of them can affect the market price. In monopoly, there is just *one* seller in the market, so it sets the price as it wishes. Most markets for goods and services, however, are neither perfectly competitive nor purely monopolistic. Instead, they lie somewhere *between* these two extremes, with more than one firm, but not enough firms to qualify for perfect competition. We call such markets *imperfectly competitive*:

---

[3] *Source:* "A World of Fakes," *U.S. News and World Report,* July 14, 2003.

Imperfect Competition A market structure with more than one firm, but in which one or more of the requirements of perfect competition are violated.

> *Imperfect competition* refers to market structures between perfect competition and monopoly. In imperfectly competitive markets, there is more than one seller, but still too few to create a perfectly competitive market. In addition, imperfectly competitive markets often violate other conditions of perfect competition, such as the requirement of a standardized product or free entry and exit.

There are two different types of imperfect competition. *Monopolistic competition*—the subject of this section—and *oligopoly,* which we take up in the next section.

Monopolistic Competition A market structure in which there are many firms selling products that are differentiated, yet are still close substitutes, and in which there is free entry and exit.

> *Monopolistic competition* is a market structure with three fundamental characteristics:
>
> 1. *many buyers and sellers;*
> 2. *sellers offer a differentiated product*
> 3. *sellers can easily enter into or exit from the market.*

Note that monopolistic competition combines features of both perfect competition and monopoly—hence its name. Like perfect competition, there are many buyers and sellers and easy entry and exit. Restaurants, photocopy shops, dry cleaners, and small retail stores are typically monopolistic competitors. In each case, there are many sellers in the market, and it is easy to set up a business or to exit if things don't go well. But unlike perfect competitors, each seller produces a somewhat different product from the others. No two coffeehouses, photocopy shops, or food markets are exactly the same. For this reason, a monopolistic competitor can raise its price (up to a point) and lose only *some* of its customers. The others will stay with the firm because they like its product, even when it charges somewhat more than its competitors. Thus, a monopolistic competitor faces a *downward-sloping demand curve* and, in this sense, is more like a monopolist than a perfect competitor:

> Because it produces a differentiated product, a monopolistic competitor faces a downward-sloping demand curve: When it raises its price a modest amount, quantity demanded will decline (but not all the way to zero).

What makes a product differentiated? Sometimes, it is the *quality* of the product. By many objective standards—room size, service, and other amenities—the Hilton has better hotel rooms than Motel 6. In other cases, the difference is a matter of taste, rather than quality. In terms of measurable characteristics, Colgate toothpaste is probably neither better nor worse than Crest, but each has its own flavor and texture, and each appeals to different people.

Another type of differentiation arises from differences in *location*. Even if two bookstores are identical in every other respect—range of selection, atmosphere, service—you will still prefer the one closer to your home or office.

Ultimately, product differentiation is a subjective matter: A product is different whenever people *think* that it is, whether their perception is accurate or not. You may know, for example, that all bottles of bleach have identical ingredients—5.25 percent sodium hypochlorite and 94.75 percent water. But if some buyers think that Clorox bleach is different and would pay a bit more for it, then Clorox bleach is a differentiated product. Thus, whenever a firm faces a downward-sloping demand curve, we can assume that it produces a differentiated product. The reason for the downward slope may be a difference in product quality, consumer tastes, or location, or it may be entirely illusory, but the economic implications are always the same: The firm can raise its price without losing all of its business. A monopolistic competitor, therefore, is *not* a price taker, but rather a "price setter"—it *chooses* its price.

Monopolistic Competition in the Short Run

The individual monopolistic competitor behaves very much like a monopoly. Its constraints are its given production technology, the prices it must pay for its inputs, and the downward-sloping demand curve that it faces. And, like any other firm, its goal is to maximize profit, which it does by producing where $MR = MC$. The result may be economic profit or loss in the short run.

The key difference is this: While a monopoly is the *only* seller in its market, a monopolistic competitor is one of many sellers. When a *monopoly* raises its price, its customers must pay up or buy less in the market. When a *monopolistic competitor* raises its price, its customers have one additional option: They can buy a similar good from some other firm. Thus, all else equal, the demand curve facing a firm should be flatter under monopolistic competition than under monopoly. That is, since closer substitutes are available under monopolistic competition than under monopoly, a given rise in price should cause a greater fall in quantity demanded.

Figure 6 illustrates the situation of a monopolistic competitor, Kafka Exterminators. The figure shows the demand curve, d_1, that the firm faces, as well as the marginal revenue, marginal cost, and average total cost curves. As a monopolistic competitor, Kafka Exterminators competes with many other extermination services in its local area. Thus, if it raises its price, it will lose some of its customers to the competition. If Kafka had a *monopoly* on the local extermination business, we would expect the same rise in price to cause a smaller drop in quantity demanded, since customers would have to buy from Kafka or else get rid of their bugs on their own.

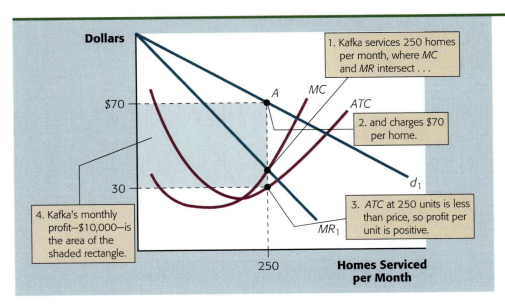

1. Kafka services 250 homes per month, where *MC* and *MR* intersect . . .

2. and charges $70 per home.

3. *ATC* at 250 units is less than price, so profit per unit is positive.

4. Kafka's monthly profit—$10,000—is the area of the shaded rectangle.

FIGURE 6
A Monopolistically Competitive Firm in the Short Run

Like any other firm, Kafka Exterminators will produce where $MR = MC$. As you can see in Figure 6, when Kafka faces demand curve d_1 and the associated marginal revenue curve MR_1, its profit-maximizing output level is 250 homes served per month, and its profit-maximizing price is $70 per home. In the short run, the firm may earn an economic profit or an economic loss, or it may break even. In the figure, Kafka is earning an economic profit: Profit per unit is $P - ATC = \$70 - \$30 = \$40$, and total monthly profit—the area of the blue rectangle—is $\$40 \times 250 = \$10,000$.

Monopolistic Competition in the Long Run

If Kafka Exterminators were a monopoly, Figure 6 might be the end of our story. The firm would continue to earn economic profit forever, since barriers to entry would keep out any potential competitors. But under monopolistic competition—in which there are no barriers to entry and exit—the firm will not enjoy its profit for long. As new sellers enter the market, attracted by the profits that can be earned there, some of Kafka's customers will sign up with the new entrants. At any given price, Kafka will find itself servicing fewer homes than before, and the demand curve it faces will shift leftward. Entry will continue to occur, and the demand curve will continue to shift leftward, until Kafka and other firms are earning zero economic profit. This process of adjustment is shown in Figure 7. As the demand curve shifts leftward (from d_1 to d_2), the marginal revenue curve shifts left as well (from MR_1 to MR_2). Why is this? First, a leftward shift in demand is also a *downward* shift in demand: Now that is has more competitors, Kafka must charge a lower price than before in order to sell any given quantity. But if price is lower, then—starting at any quantity—selling an *additional* unit will *add less* to total revenue than it did before. Thus, at any output level, marginal revenue is lower than before—a downward shift in the MR curve. And, as you can see in the figure, a downward shift in the MR curve is also a leftward shift of that curve.

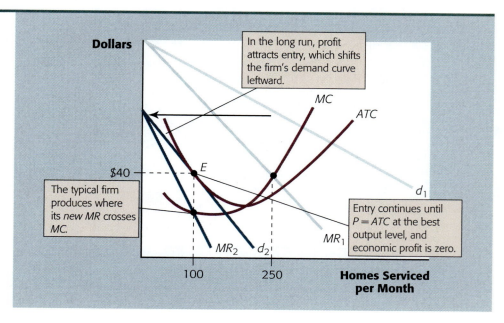

FIGURE 7
A Monopolistically Competitive Firm in the Long Run

Kafka's new profit-maximizing output level, 100, is found at the intersection point between its marginal cost curve and its *new* marginal revenue curve. Kafka's new price—found on its demand curve d_2 at 100 units—is $40. Finally, since *ATC* is also $40 at that output level, Kafka is earning zero economic profit—the best it can do in the long run.[4] In long-run equilibrium, the profit-maximizing price, $40, will always equal the average total cost of production.

We can also reverse these steps. If the typical firm is suffering an economic loss (draw this diagram on your own), *exit* will occur. With fewer competitors, those firms that remain in the market will gain customers, so their demand curves will shift *rightward*. Exit will cease only when the typical firm is earning zero economic profit, at point *E* in Figure 7. Thus, point *E* represents the long-run equilibrium of the typical firm whether we start from a position of economic profit or economic loss:

> *Under monopolistic competition, firms can earn positive or negative economic profit in the short run. But in the long run, free entry and exit will ensure that each firm earns zero economic profit, just as under perfect competition.*

Short-Run versus
Long-Run Outcomes

Is this prediction of our model realistic? Indeed it is: In the real world, monopolistic competitors often earn economic profit or loss in the short run, but, given enough time, profits attract new entrants and losses result in an industry shakeout, until firms are earning zero economic profit. In the long run, restaurants, retail stores, hair salons, and other monopolistically competitive firms earn zero economic profit for their owners. That is, there is just enough accounting profit to cover the implicit costs of doing business, which is just enough to keep the owners from shifting their time and money to some alternative enterprise.

Think of your own city or town. Has a certain kind of business been springing up everywhere? Is another type of business gradually disappearing? If you look around, you will see entry and exit occurring, as monopolistically competitive markets adjust from short-run to long-run equilibrium.

Nonprice Competition

If a monopolistic competitor wants to increase its output, one way is to cut its price. That is, it can move *along* its demand curve. But a price cut is not the only way to increase output. Since the firm produces a differentiated product, it can sell more by convincing people that its own output is better than that of competing firms. Such efforts, if successful, will *shift* the firm's demand curve rightward.

> *Any action a firm takes to increase the demand for its output—other than cutting its price—is called nonprice competition.*

Nonprice competition Any action a firm takes to increase the demand for its product, other than cutting its price.

Better service, product guarantees, free home delivery, more attractive packaging, as well as advertising to inform customers about these things, are all examples of nonprice competition. Fast-food restaurants are notorious for nonprice competition.

---

[4] Other things may also happen as the industry expands. For example, the increased demand for inputs may raise or lower the typical firm's *ATC* and *MC* curves, depending on whether we are dealing with an increasing- or decreasing-cost industry. (See Chapter 7.) This does not change our result, however: Entry into the market will continue until the typical firm earns zero economic profit, even if its *MC* and *ATC* curves have shifted.

When Burger King says, "Have it your way," the company is saying, "Our hamburgers are better than those at McDonald's because *we* make them to order." When McDonald's responds with an attractive, fresh-faced young woman behind the counter, smiling broadly when you order a Happy Meal, it is saying, in effect, "So what if we don't make your burgers to order; our staff is better looking and more upbeat than Burger King's."

Nonprice competition is another reason why monopolistic competitors earn zero economic profit in the long run. If an innovative firm discovers a way to shift its demand curve rightward—say, by offering better service or more clever advertising—then in the *short run*, it may be able to earn a profit. This means that other, less innovative firms will experience a leftward shift in *their* demand curves, as they lose sales to their more innovative rival.

But not for long. In monopolistic competition, the "easy entry" assumption includes the ability of new entrants, as well as existing firms, to copy the successful business practices of others. If product guarantees are enabling some firms to earn economic profit, then *all* firms will offer product guarantees. If advertising is doing the trick, then *all* firms will start ad campaigns. In the long run, we can expect *all* monopolistic competitors to run advertisements, to be concerned about service, and to take whatever actions have proven profitable for other firms in the industry. All this nonprice competition is costly—one must *pay* for advertising, for product guarantees, for better staff training—and these costs must be included in each firm's *ATC* curve, shifting it upward. But none of this changes our conclusion that monopolistic competitors will earn zero economic profit in the long run.

Indeed, nonprice competition strengthens our conclusions. In the short run, a firm may earn profit because it has relatively few competitors or because it has discovered a new way to attract customers. But in the long run, the profitable firm will find its demand curve shifting leftward due to the entry of new firms, or the imitation of its successful nonprice competition, or both. In the end, each firm will find itself back in the situation depicted in Figure 7. Because of the costs of nonprice competition, each firm's *ATC* curve will be higher than it would otherwise be. However, it will still touch, but not cross, the demand curve, and the firm will still earn zero economic profit. We will take a closer look at one form of nonprice competition, advertising, in the "Using the Theory" section at the end of the chapter.

OLIGOPOLY

A monopolistic competitor enjoys a certain amount of independence. There are so many *other* firms selling in the market—each one such a small fish in such a large pond—that each of them can make decisions about price and quantity without worrying about how the others will react. For example, if a single pharmacy in a large city cuts its prices, it can safely assume that any other pharmacy that could benefit from price cutting has already done so, or will shortly do so, *regardless of its own actions*. Thus, there is no reason for the price-cutting pharmacy to take the reactions of other pharmacies into account when making its own pricing decisions.

But in some markets, most of the output is sold by just a few firms. These markets are not monopolies (there is more than one seller), but they are not monopolistically competitive either. There are so few firms that the actions taken by any one will *very much* affect the others and will likely generate a response. For example, more than 60 percent of the automobiles sold in the United States are made by one of the "Big Three": General Motors, Ford, and DaimlerChrysler. If GM were to lower its price in order to increase its output, then Ford and Chrysler would suffer a significant drop in their own sales. They would not be happy about this and would probably respond with price cuts of their own. GM's output, in turn, would be affected by the price cuts at Ford and Chrysler.

When just a few large firms dominate a market, so that the actions of each one have an important impact on the others, it would be foolish for any one firm to ignore its competitors' reactions. On the contrary, in such a market, each firm recognizes its *strategic interdependence* with the others. Before the management team makes a decision, it must reason as follows: "If we take action *A*, our competitors will do *B*, and then we would do *C*, and they would respond with *D* . . . ," and so on. This kind of thinking is the hallmark of the market structure we call *oligopoly:*

> An **oligopoly** is a market dominated by a small number of strategically interdependent firms.

Oligopoly A market structure in which a small number of firms are strategically interdependent.

There are many different types of oligopolies. The output may be more or less identical among firms, such as copper wire, or differentiated, such as laptop computers. An oligopoly market may be international, as in the market for automobile tires; mostly national, as in the market for breakfast cereals; or local, as in the market for some daily newspapers. There may be one dominant firm whose share of the market far exceeds all the others, such as Nike, which manufactured 39 percent of all athletic shoes in 2002—more than three times the output of the next largest firm (Reebok). Or there may be two or more large firms of roughly similar size, like Boeing and Airbus in the global market for large passenger aircraft. You can see that oligopoly markets can have different characteristics, but in all cases, *a small number of strategically interdependent firms produce the dominant share of output in the market.*

Why Oligopolies Exist

Oligopoly firms do not always earn economic profit in the long run, but even when they do, entry into the market does not occur—a few large firms continue to dominate the industry. Thus, our search for the origin of oligopolies is really a search for the specific *barriers to entry* that keep out competitors and maintain the dominance of just a few firms. What are these barriers?

Economies of Scale: Natural Oligopolies. In Chapter 5, you learned that economies of scale can limit the number of firms that can survive in a market. (If you need to refresh your memory, look back at panel (c) of Figure 8 in that chapter.) When the minimum efficient scale (MES) for a typical firm is a relatively large percentage of the market, a large firm, supplying a large share of the market, will have lower cost per unit than a small firm. Since small firms can't compete, only a few large firms survive, and the market becomes an oligopoly. And because this tends to happen on its own unless there is government intervention, such a market is often called a **natural oligopoly,** analogous to natural monopoly. Airlines, college

Natural oligopoly A market that tends naturally toward oligopoly because the minimum efficient scale of the typical firm is a large fraction of the market.

textbook publishers, and passenger jet manufacturers are all examples of oligopolies in which economies of scale play a large role.

Reputation as a Barrier. A new entrant may suffer just from being new. Established oligopolists are likely to have favorable reputations. In many oligopolies—like the markets for soft drinks and breakfast cereals—heavy advertising expenditure has also helped to build and maintain brand loyalty. A new entrant might be able to catch up to those already in the industry, but this may require a substantial period of high advertising costs and low revenues. In some cases, where the potential profits are great, investors may decide it is worth the risk and accept the initial losses in order to enter the industry. Ted Turner took such a risk and sustained several years of losses before his cable ventures (Cable News Network, Turner Network Television, and Turner Broadcasting System) earned a profit. But in other industries, the initial losses may be too great and the probability of success too low for investors to risk their money starting a new firm.

Strategic Barriers. Oligopoly firms often pursue strategies designed to keep out potential competitors. They can maintain excess production capacity as a signal to a potential entrant that, with little advance notice, they could easily saturate the market and leave the new entrant with little or no revenue. They can make special deals with distributors to receive the best shelf space in retail stores or make long-term arrangements with customers to ensure that their products are not displaced quickly by those of a new entrant. And they can spend large amounts on advertising to make it difficult for a new entrant to differentiate its product.

Legal Barriers. Patents and copyrights, which can be responsible for monopoly, can also create oligopolies. For example, all three government-approved drugs commonly prescribed to treat symptoms of Alzheimer's disease are still protected by patents. Until these patents expire, or several new drugs are developed, the market for Alzheimer's drugs will continue to be an oligopoly consisting of just three large pharmaceutical companies.

Like monopolies, oligopolies are not shy about lobbying the government to preserve their market domination. One of the easiest targets is foreign competition. U.S. steel companies are relentless in their efforts to limit the amount of foreign—especially Japanese—steel sold in the U.S. market. In the past, they have succeeded in getting special taxes on imported steel and financial penalties imposed upon successful foreign steel companies. Other U.S. industries, including automobiles, textiles, and lumber, have had similar successes.

Legal barriers can operate against *domestic* entrants, too. Zoning regulations may prohibit the building of a new supermarket, movie theater, or auto repair shop in a local market, preserving the oligopoly status of the few firms already established there. Lobbying by established firms is often the source of these restrictive practices.

Oligopoly Behavior

Of the market structures you have studied in this book, oligopoly presents the greatest challenge to economists. In the other types of markets—perfect competition, monopoly, and monopolistic competition—each firm acts independently, without worrying about the reactions of other firms. The firm's task is a simple one: to select an output level along its demand curve that gives it maximum profit.

But this approach doesn't describe an oligopolist. The essence of oligopoly, remember, is *strategic interdependence*, wherein each firm anticipates the actions of its rivals when making decisions. Thus, we cannot analyze one firm's decisions in isolation from other firms. In order to understand and predict behavior in oligopoly markets, economists have had to modify the tools used to analyze the other market structures and to develop entirely new tools as well.

Let's look at an example of strategic interdependence more closely and see why the tools we've used to analyze the other market structures will not work for oligopoly. Remember Kafka Exterminators? Because it was a monopolistic competitor, it could raise or lower its price, and move along its demand curve in Figure 6, without having to worry that it would cause a change in a *substitute's price*. But what if Kafka had been an oligopolist—say, one of two exterminators in a small town? Then, if Kafka lowered its price, the location of its demand curve would *depend on the actions of its rival*. If the rival chose *not* to change its price, Kafka's demand curve would stay put. But if the rival lowered its price to match Kafka's, Kafka's demand curve would shift leftward—because a substitute good (the services of Kafka's rival) had decreased. Thus, Kafka could not predict whether it would end up on its old demand curve or some new one without taking into account how its competitor would *react* to its decision. Kafka could not use the simple $MR=MC$ rule, because the position of Kafka's MR curve—like the position of its demand curve—would depend on the reaction of its rival. You can see why oligopoly presents such a challenge, not only to the firms themselves, but also to economists studying them. However, one approach, called **game theory**, has yielded rich insights into oligopoly behavior.

The Game Theory Approach. The word *game* applied to oligopoly decision making might seem out of place. Games—like poker, basketball, or chess—are usually played for fun, and even when money is at stake, the sums are usually small. What do games have in common with important business decisions, where hundreds of millions of dollars and thousands of jobs may be at stake?

In fact, quite a bit. In all games—except those of pure chance, such as roulette—a player's strategy must take account of the strategies followed by other players. This is precisely the situation of the oligopolist. Game theory analyzes oligopoly decisions as if they were games by looking at the rules players must follow, the payoffs they are trying to achieve, and the strategies they can use to achieve them.

Game theory An approach to modeling the strategic interaction of oligopolists in terms of moves and countermoves.

Simple Oligopoly Games. Imagine a town with just two gas stations: Gus's Gas and Filip's Fillup. This is an example of an oligopoly with just two firms, called a **duopoly**. We will regard Gus and Filip as *players* in a *game* in which they must make their decisions independently, without knowing in advance what the other will do.

Figure 8 shows the **payoff matrix** for this game—a listing of the payoffs that each player will receive for each possible combination of strategies that might be selected. The payoff matrix presents a lot of information at once, so let's take it step-by-step.

First, notice that each *column* represents a strategy that Gus might choose: to charge a low price for his gas, or a high price.[5] Second, each *row* represents a strategy that Filip might select: a low price, or a high price. Thus, each of the four boxes

Duopoly An oligopoly market with only two sellers.

Payoff Matrix A table showing the payoffs to each of two firms for each pair of strategies they choose.

---

[5] In a real-world market for gasoline—even one with just two gas stations—there would be many prices from which to choose. Our assumption of just two prices is a "simplifying assumption" that makes it easier to see what is going on.

FIGURE 8
A Duopoly Game

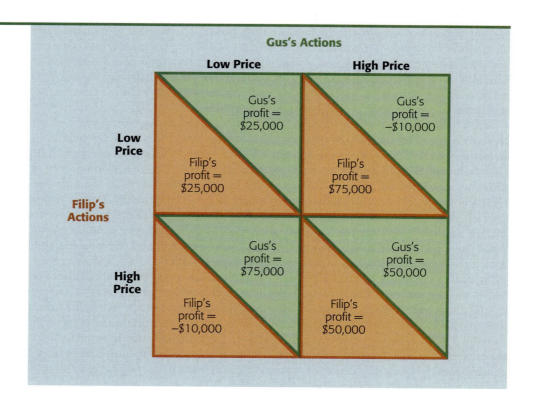

in the payoff matrix represents one of four possible strategy combinations that might be selected by the two players in this game:

1. Upper left box: Both Gus and Filip charge a low price.
2. Lower left box: Gus charges a low price and Filip charges a high price.
3. Upper right box: Gus charges a high price and Filip charges a low price.
4. Lower right box: Both Gus and Filip charge a high price.

Let's make two additional (temporary) assumptions: First, each player must decide on his strategy without knowing what the other will do. Second, once the strategy is selected, the player is stuck with it for some time. (These assumptions are actually realistic in some oligopoly markets, especially those in which prices are negotiated with customers privately and in which it is costly to change prices after they are set.)

Let's now look at the game from Gus's point of view. The entries shown in *green* in each box are Gus's possible *payoffs*—the yearly profit he will earn in each case. (Ignore the orange entries for now.) For example, the lower left square shows that when Gus charges a low price and Filip charges a high price, Gus's yearly profit will be $75,000.

Gus wants the best possible profit for himself, but he is not sure what Filip will do. So Gus asks himself which strategy would be best *if* Filip were to charge a low price. The *top row* of the matrix guides us through his reasoning. "If Filip decides to charge a low price, my best choice would be to charge a low price too, because then I'd earn $25,000 in profit, rather than a loss of $10,000." Next, Gus determines the best strategy if Filip were to charge a *high* price. As the *bottom row* shows, he'll reason as follows: "If Filip charges a high price, my best choice would be to charge a low price, because then I'd earn $75,000 in profit, rather than $50,000."

Let's recap: If Filip charges a low price, Gus's best choice is a low price. If Filip charges a high price, Gus's best choice is—once again—to charge a low price. Thus, regardless of Filip's strategy, Gus's best choice is to charge a low price. In this game, the strategy "low price" is an example of a *dominant strategy* for Gus.

> A **dominant strategy** is a strategy that is best for a player regardless of the strategy of the other player.

Maximization Subject to Constraints

Dominant Strategy A strategy that is best for a firm no matter what strategy its competitor chooses.

If a player has a dominant strategy in a game, we can safely assume that he will follow it.

What about Filip? He is presented with the same set of options and payoffs as his partner—as shown by the orange entries in the payoff matrix. When Filip looks down each *column,* he can see his possible payoffs for each strategy that Gus might follow. As you can see (and make sure that you can, by going through all the possibilities), Filip also has a dominant strategy—charge the low price. We can now predict that *both* players will follow the strategy of charging a low price, and that the outcome of the game—the upper left-hand corner—is a low price for each player, with each earning $25,000 in profit.

When each decision maker is charging the lower price, he is doing the best that he can do, given the actions of the other. Therefore, once they reach the upper left-hand corner, neither Gus nor Filip will have any incentive to change his price. The *market equilibrium* price, in this case, is the low price.

Markets and Equilibrium

Oligopoly Games in the Real World. While our simple example helps us understand the basic ideas of game theory, real-world oligopoly situations are seldom so simple. First, there will typically be more than two strategies from which to choose (for example, a variety of different prices or several different amounts to spend on *non-*price competition such as advertising). Also, there will usually be more than two players, so a two-dimensional payoff matrix like the one in Figure 8 would not suffice. Still, as long as each firm has a dominant strategy, we can predict the outcome of the game—the market equilibrium—although we might need the help of a computer in the more complex cases.

Second, in some games, one or more players may *not* have a dominant strategy. For example, if we alter just one entry in the figure—changing Gus's payoff of $75,000 (lower left-hand box) to $40,000—Gus would no longer have a dominant strategy. As you can verify on your own, if Filip charges a low price, Gus should charge a low price; but if Filip charges a high price, Gus should charge a high price too. Thus, Gus's choice depends on Filip's choice. However, since we have not changed any of Filip's payoffs, he still has a dominant strategy—to charge a low price. Since Gus knows that Filip will select a low price, Gus will always select a low price, too. Thus, we can still predict the market equilibrium: a low price for both firms. This example shows us that, *when one player has a dominant strategy, we can still predict the game's outcome, whether the other player has a dominant strategy or not.*

But what if we *also* change Filip's payoff of $75,000 (upper right-hand corner) to $40,000? Then, as you can verify, *neither* player will have a dominant strategy, so predicting a competitor's strategy can be more of a challenge. Moreover, we, as outside observers, would need a more sophisticated analysis to predict an outcome to the game.

Finally, in our example, we've limited the players to *one* play of the game. While this might make sense in cases where the players get only one chance to

Repeated play A situation in which strategically interdependent sellers compete over many time periods.

make a decision, it is not realistic for most oligopoly markets. In reality, for gas stations and almost all other oligopolies, there is **repeated play,** where both players select a strategy, observe the outcome of that trial, and play the game again and again, as long as they remain rivals. Repeated play can fundamentally change the way players view a game and lead to new strategies based on long-run considerations. One possible result of repeated trials is *cooperative behavior,* to which we now turn.

Cooperative Behavior in Oligopoly

In the real world, oligopolists will usually get more than one chance to choose their prices. Pepsi and Coca-Cola have been rivals in the soft drink market for most of this century, as have Ford, DaimlerChrysler, and GM in the automobile market and Kellogg, Post (Kraft Foods), Quaker, and General Mills in the breakfast cereal market. These firms can change their strategies based on the responses of their rivals.

The equilibrium in a game with repeated plays may be very different from the equilibrium in a game played only once. Often, firms will evolve some form of *cooperation* in the long run.

For example, look again at Figure 8. If this game were played only once, we would expect each player to pursue its dominant strategy, select a low price, and end up with $25,000 in yearly profit. But there is a better outcome for both players. If each were to charge a high price, each would make a profit of $50,000 per year. If Gus and Filip remain competitors year after year, we would expect them to realize that by cooperating, they would both be better off. And there are many ways for the two to cooperate.

Explicit collusion Cooperation involving direct communication between competing firms about setting prices.

Explicit Collusion. The simplest form of cooperation is **explicit collusion,** in which managers meet face to face to decide how to set prices. In our example, Gus and Filip might strike an agreement that each will charge a high price, moving the outcome of the game to the lower right-hand corner in Figure 8, where each earns $50,000 in yearly profit instead of $25,000.

Cartel A group of firms that selects a common price that maximizes total industry profits.

The most extreme form of explicit collusion is the creation of a **cartel**—a group of firms that tries to maximize the total profits of the group as a whole. To do this, the group of firms behaves as if it were a monopoly, treating the market demand curve as the "monopoly's" demand curve. Then, it finds the point on the demand curve—the price and quantity of output—that maximizes total profit. Each member is instructed to charge the agreed-upon price (cartels are often called *price-fixing* agreements), and each is allotted a share of the cartel's total output. This last step is crucial: If any member produces and sells more than its allotted portion, then the group's total *output* rises and the price will fall below the agreed-upon profit maximizing price.

The most famous cartel in recent years has been OPEC—the Organization of Petroleum Exporting Countries—which meets periodically to influence the price of oil by setting the amount that each of its members can produce. In the mid-1970s, OPEC quadrupled its price per barrel in just two years, leading to a huge increase in profits for the cartel's members. In the late 1990s, OPEC exerted its muscle once again, doubling the price of oil over a period of 18 months.

If explicit collusion to raise prices is such a good thing for oligopolists, why don't they all do it? A major reason is that it's usually *illegal.* OPEC was not considered illegal by any of the oil-producing nations, but cartels are against the law in the United States, the European Union, and most of the developed nations. Explicit collusion must therefore be conducted with the utmost secrecy. And the penalties, if the oligopolists are caught, can be severe.

For example, in 2001, a former chairman of Sotheby's auction house was sentenced to jail for his involvement in a price-fixing agreement with competitor Christie's. (The two auction houses together controlled more than 90 percent of the world's live auction market in rare art, jewelry, and other collectibles, and had agreed to cooperate in setting auction commissions.) The same year, a cartel of eight vitamin manufacturers were collectively fined a total of nearly $1 billion by the European Union.

The chances of getting caught, and the severe penalties at stake, are important reasons why *explicit* collusion seems to be rare in the United States and Europe. But as you might guess from the italics on "explicit," oligopolists can collude in other, *implicit* ways.

Tacit Collusion. Any time firms cooperate *without* an explicit agreement, they are engaging in **tacit collusion**. Typically, players adopt strategies along the following lines: "In general, I will set a high price. If my rival also sets a high price, I will go on setting a high price. If my rival sets a low price this time, I will punish him by setting a low price next time." You can see that if both players stick to this strategy, they will both likely set the high price. Each is waiting for the other to go first in setting a low price, so it may never happen.

This type of strategy is often called **tit-for-tat,** defined as doing to the other player what he has just done to you. In our gas station duopoly, for example, Gus will pick the high price whenever Filip has set the high price in the previous play, and Gus will pick the low price if that is what Filip did in the previous play. With enough plays of the game, Filip may eventually catch on that he can get Gus to set the desired high price by setting the high price himself and that he should not exploit the situation by setting the low price, because that will cause Gus to set the low price next time. The result of every play will then be a *cooperative outcome:* The players move to the lower right-hand corner of Figure 8, with each firm earning the higher $50,000 in profit.

Tit-for-tat strategies are prominent in the airline industry. When one major airline announces special discounted fares, its rivals almost always announce identical fares the next day. The response from the rivals not only helps them remain competitive, but also provides a signal to the price-cutting airline that it will not be able to offer discounts that are unmatched by its rivals.

However, the gentle reminder of tit for tat is not always effective in maintaining tacit collusion, and an oligopolist will sometimes go further, attempting to *punish* a firm that threatens to destroy tacit cooperation. The airline industry is famous for such efforts, which often—to the delight of travelers—lead to price wars.

A typical example occurred during August 2002, when American Airlines, in an effort to gain revenue with a small price cut, quietly began offering 10 percent discounts on tickets sold by certain travel agents. The discounts were not published on American's computer reservation system, where they would have been seen by competitors. But Northwest Airlines found out anyway, and immediately responded with its own 10 percent price cuts on routes it shared with American. This, by itself, would have been a tit-for-tat strategy. But Northwest went one step further by announcing its discounts on its public computer system, thereby applying them to *all* fares on those routes. The next day, American countered by extending *its*

Tacit collusion Any form of oligopolistic cooperation that does not involve an explicit agreement.

Tit-for-tat A game-theoretic strategy of doing to another player this period what he has done to you in the previous period.

Price leadership A form of tacit collusion in which one firm sets a price that other firms copy.

discounts to all flights and one day later, Northwest increased its discounts to 20 percent. . . . By the time the price war ended, both airlines had cut their ticket prices by 40 percent, and several other airlines had joined the price war as well.[6]

Another form of tacit collusion is **price leadership,** in which one firm, the *price leader,* sets its price, and other sellers copy that price. The leader may be the dominant firm in the industry (the one with the greatest market share, for example), or the position of leader may rotate from firm to firm. During the first half of this century, U.S. Steel typically acted as the price leader in the steel industry: When it changed its prices, other firms would automatically follow. In recent decades, Goodyear has been the acknowledged leader in the tire industry, its price increases virtually always matched within days by Michelin, Bridgestone, and most other tire makers.

With price leadership, there is no formal agreement. Rather, the choice of the leader, the criteria it uses to set its price, and the willingness of other firms to follow come about because the firms realize—without formal discussion—that the system benefits all of them. To keep the price-following firms from cheating—taking large amounts of business by setting a lower price than the price leader—the leader and the firms that choose to follow must be able to punish a cheater. They can do this by setting a low price as quickly as possible after anyone cheats. The expectation of that response may be enough to prevent the cheating in the first place.

The Limits to Collusion. It is tempting to think that collusion—whether explicit or tacit—gives oligopolies absolute power over their markets, leaving them free to jack up prices and exploit the public without limit. But oligopoly power, even with collusion, has its limits.

First, even colluding firms are constrained by the market demand curve: A rise in price will always reduce the quantity demanded from *all* firms together. There is one price—the cartel monopoly price—that maximizes the total profits of all firms in the market, and it will never serve the group's interest to charge any price higher than this.

Second, collusion, even when it is tacit, may be illegal. Although it may be difficult to prove, companies that even *appear* to be colluding may find themselves facing close government scrutiny. Indeed, hardly a month goes by without the announcement of one or more new investigations of collusion by the Justice Department.

Third, collusion is limited by powerful incentives to cheat on any agreement. Cheating is an endemic problem among colluding oligopolists and often leads to the collapse of even the most formal agreements.

The Future of Oligopoly

Some people think that the U.S. and other Western economies are moving relentlessly toward oligopoly as the dominant market structure. Technological change is often cited as the reason. For example, in the early part of the century, several dozen U.S. firms manufactured passenger cars. With the development of mass-production

---

[6] Sources: "U.S. Airlines in Summer Price War," *Airwise News,* August 8, 2002; "Business Fliers Rejoice— Price War!" *Business Week Online,* August 26, 2002; "American Cuts Business Fares," *Aviation News,* August 2002.

technology, the number has steadily fallen to three. Stories like this suggest an economy in which markets are increasingly controlled and manipulated by a few players who, by colluding, exploit the public for their own gain. In 1932, two economists—Adolf Berle and Gardiner Means—noted the trend toward big business and predicted that, unless something were done to stop it, the 200 largest U.S. firms would control the nation's entire economy by 1970.

Berle and Means's prediction has not come true. Today, there are hundreds of thousands of ongoing businesses in the United States. In Chapter 5, we identified one reason: In many markets, the minimum efficient scale of production is so small relative to the size of the market that large firms have no cost advantage over small ones. But the prevalence of oligopoly in the national and world economies is anything but stable. Some forces in our society are helping to keep market dominance in check, while others encourage it. Let's consider some of the major forces affecting the future of oligopoly.

Antitrust Legislation and Enforcement. Antitrust policies in the United States and many other countries are designed to protect the interests of consumers by ensuring adequate competition in the marketplace. In practice, antitrust enforcement has focused on three types of actions: (1) preventing collusive agreements among firms, such as price-fixing agreements; (2) breaking up or limiting the activities of large firms—oligopolists and monopolists—whose market dominance harms consumers; and (3) preventing mergers that would lead to harmful market domination.

The impact of antitrust actions goes far beyond the specific companies called into the courtroom. Managers of firms even *considering* anticompetitive moves have to think long and hard about the consequences of acts that might violate the antitrust laws. For example, many economists believe that in the late 1940s and early 1950s, General Motors would have driven Ford and Chrysler out of business or bought them out were it not for fear of antitrust action. On the other hand, antitrust and other government policies toward business are a part of our *political* system. While the thrust of these policies is always to preserve competition, the type of competition preserved—and the zeal with which the policies are applied—can shift. In Chapter 5, we saw that legislative changes in the 1990s, enabling banks to operate across state lines, led to a merger wave in the banking sector. In mid-2003, a decision by the Federal Communications Commission made it easier for large media companies to acquire local radio and television stations. If this decision holds, then economies of scale may be a driving *economic* force toward market dominance by a few firms, but a change in government policy will have made it possible.

The Globalization of Markets. Recall that when the minimum efficient scale (MES) of the typical firm is large relative to the size of the market, a large firm has a cost advantage over a small one, and the result is a natural oligopoly. But what if the *size of the market* increases? Then an unchanged MES becomes *relatively* smaller, when compared to the market. A larger number of firms can survive there. By enlarging markets from national ones to global ones, international trade can increase the number of firms in a market, thus decreasing market dominance by a few, and increasing competition.

Although oligopolists often try to prevent it, they face increasingly stiff competition from foreign producers. Some economists have argued, for example, that the

U.S. market for automobiles now has so many foreign sellers that it resembles monopolistic competition more than oligopoly. Similar changes have occurred in the U.S. markets for color televisions, stereo equipment, computers, beer, and wine. At the same time, the entry of U.S. producers has helped to increase competition in foreign markets for movies, television shows, clothing, household cleaning products, and prepared foods.

On the other hand, globalization also enables firms that have *not* reached their MES (say, because of domestic government restrictions) to become bigger players in the new, global market. And large global firms can force many smaller, national companies out of business. Thus, although globalization may give consumers in each nation access to a greater number of firms, these may be larger and more powerful firms—creating greater likelihood of strategic interaction and the danger of collusion.

Technological Change. One way that technological change works to *increase* competition is by creating new substitute goods. For example, e-mail has provided a substitute for many types of hard copy: personal letters, bills, and some types of documents. The result is tough competition for one of our oldest monopolies—the U.S. Postal Service—as well as competition for a long-standing oligopoly—overnight package delivery services.

Technology can also reduce barriers to entry in much the same way that globalization does: by increasing the size of the market. A small town, for example, might be able to support only a few stores selling, say, luggage, file cabinets, or CDs, because the MES of a brick-and-mortar store is large relative to the small market there. But technology—the Internet—has enabled residents in many smaller towns to choose among a dozen or more online sellers of the same merchandise. By connecting the town's residents to the national market for retail services, the Internet has increased the size of the market in which they are buyers. In that larger, national market, because the MES is smaller relative to the market, several firms can compete.

However, this trend can also be seen as *encouraging* oligopoly. By extending the reach of large national retailers, the Internet enables them to become still larger. And if the small brick-and-mortar stores can't compete in this larger market and go out of business, then the texture of retail service in the country changes. There are more firms competing for the business of residents in any town, but there are fewer of these firms nationwide, and they are larger. The result could be strategic interaction—and possibly collusion—among large national players.

Finally, some technologies actually *increase* the MES of the typical firm, thereby encouraging the formation of oligopolies. For example, producers of digital products—like entertainment, software, and information—have very high up-front costs (lumpy inputs) in creating their goods and services, but almost nonexistent costs of duplicating them to produce and sell another unit. The cost to a software firm of having another buyer download the program, for example, is almost nonexistent. For this reason, a firm in a digital market can continue to experience economies of scale until it serves a relatively large fraction of a national or even global market. Microsoft, Disney, and Time Warner, are examples of companies for which new technology has led to a larger market share.

USING THE THEORY
Advertising in Monopolistic Competition and Oligopoly

On any given day, you are probably exposed to hundreds of advertisements. The morning newspaper announces sales on clothes, computers, and paper towels. You will likely spend more time watching advertisements for breakfast cereals on television than you will spend eating them. And as you search for information on the Internet, ads for video cameras, credit cards, and diet pills flash before your eyes. No doubt about it: Advertising is everywhere in the economy.

Or is it? Actually, in two of the market structures you've learned about—perfect competition and monopoly—firms do little, if any, advertising. Indeed, perfectly competitive firms *never* advertise, since there is no point to it. Each firm in a competitive market produces the same product as any other, so what would they advertise? And in any case, because each firm can sell all it wants at the market price, advertising would only raise costs without any benefit to the firm. Monopolists *sometimes* advertise, but—as the only seller of a product with no close substitutes—they are under no pressure to do so.

Where, then, is all this advertising coming from?

The answer, for the most part, is: from monopolistic competitors and oligopolists. Why? Because monopolistic competitors always produce a differentiated product, and oligopolists often do. In these types of markets, the firm gains customers by convincing them that its product is different and better in some way than that of its competitors. Advertising, whether it merely informs customers about the product ("The new Toyota Corolla gets 45 miles per gallon on the highway") or attempts to influence them more subtly and psychologically ("Our exotic perfume will fill your life with mystery and intrigue"), is one way to sharply differentiate a product in the minds of consumers. Since other firms will take advantage of the opportunity to advertise, any firm that *doesn't* advertise will be lost in the shuffle. In this section, we use the tools we've learned in this chapter to look at some aspects of the economics of advertising.

Advertising and Market Equilibrium
Under Monopolistic Competition

A monopolistic competitor advertises for two reasons: to shift its demand curve rightward (greater quantity demanded at each price) and to make demand for its output *less* elastic (so it can raise price and suffer a smaller decrease in quantity demanded). Advertising costs money, so in addition to its impact on the demand curve, it will also affect the firm's *ATC* curve. What is the ultimate impact of advertising on the typical firm?

Figure 9(a) shows demand and *ATC* curves for a company, Narcissus Fragrance, that manufactures and sells perfume. Initially, when there is no advertising at all in the industry, Narcissus is in long-run equilibrium at point *A*, in panel (a), where its demand curve ($d_{\text{no ads}}$) and *ATC* curve ($ATC_{\text{no ads}}$) touch. The firm charges $60 per bottle, sells 1,000 bottles each month, and earns zero economic profit.

Now suppose that Narcissus decides to run a costly television ad campaign and, for now, that no other firm advertises. Then the cost of advertising will shift the

FIGURE 9
Advertising in Monopolistic Competition

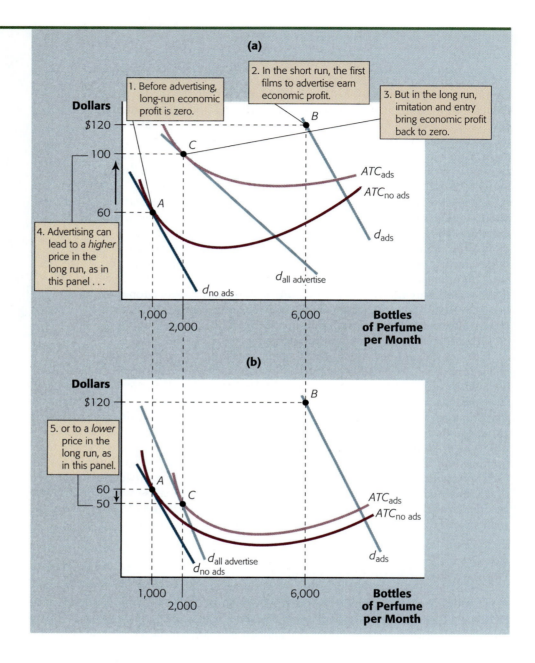

(a)

1. Before advertising, long-run economic profit is zero.

2. In the short run, the first films to advertise earn economic profit.

3. But in the long run, imitation and entry bring economic profit back to zero.

Dollars

$120

100

60

C

B

A

ATC_{ads}

$ATC_{no\ ads}$

d_{ads}

$d_{all\ advertise}$

$d_{no\ ads}$

4. Advertising can lead to a *higher* price in the long run, as in this panel . . .

1,000   2,000   6,000   **Bottles of Perfume per Month**

(b)

Dollars

$120

B

5. or to a *lower* price in the long run, as in this panel.

60
50

A

C

ATC_{ads}

$ATC_{no\ ads}$

$d_{all\ advertise}$

$d_{no\ ads}$

d_{ads}

1,000   2,000   6,000   **Bottles of Perfume per Month**

company's *ATC* curve upward, to ATC_{ads}. Cost per unit will be greater at every output level. Notice, however, that the rise is smaller at higher output levels, where the cost of the ad is spread over a larger number of units. In addition to the shift in *ATC*, the ad campaign would shift the demand curve rightward and make it steeper. Since Narcissus is the *only* firm advertising, the effect on the demand curve would be substantial, shifting it all the way to d_{ads}. Notice that there are many points along this new demand curve where Narcissus could earn a profit; the greatest profit will be the output level at which its new *MC* and *MR* curves (not shown) intersect. In panel (a), we assume that this occurs at 6,000 bottles per month. The firm will thus operate at point *B* along its new demand curve, charge a price of $120 per bottle, and earn an economic profit, since *P* > *ATC*.

Narcissus will not be able to remain at point *B* for long. In the long run, its profit will tempt other firms to initiate ad campaigns of their own. (Remember that under monopolistic competition, we assume that firms can imitate the successful business policies of their competitors.) As other firms advertise, they will take back some of Narcissus's new business, shifting its demand curve leftward. Narcissus's demand curve, however, doesn't shift *all* the way back to its original position; we assume that advertising will increase the overall demand for perfume, so demand for each firm—including Narcissus—will be higher than when no firm advertises. In the end, Narcissus will end up at a point like *C* on demand curve $d_{all\ advertise}$, where *P* = *ATC* = $100, and the firm earns zero economic profit.

Notice that, once other firms are advertising, Narcissus *must* advertise as well. Why? If it chooses not to advertise, its *ATC* curve will return to $ATC_{no\ ads}$, but its demand curve will lie somewhere to the *left* of $d_{no\ ads}$. (The demand curve was $d_{no\ ads}$ when *no* firm was advertising. But now, with its competitors running ad campaigns, if Narcissus chooses *not* to advertise, it will sell less output at any price than it did originally.) With average costs given by $ATC_{no\ ads}$, and the demand curve somewhere to the left of $d_{no\ ads}$, Narcissus would suffer a loss at *any* output level. Thus, if it wants to stay in business in the long run, it *must* advertise.

We can summarize the impact of advertising as illustrated in panel (a) this way: The output of the typical firm has increased (from 1,000 to 2,000 units), and thus, advertising has increased the total size of the market: more perfume is being bought than before. But the individual firm does not benefit from this. Since each firm must pay the costs of advertising (and more competitors may have entered the market), Narcissus and its competitors are each earning normal economic profit—just as they were originally.

But what about consumers? We would think that costly advertising will raise the price to consumers, and in panel (a), that is what has happened: Advertising has raised the price from $60 to $100 in the long run.

But this is not the *only* possible result. Panel (b) illustrates the somewhat surprising case where advertising leads to *lower* costs per unit and a *lower* price for consumers. As before, we begin with Narcissus at point *A* with no advertising in the market, then move to point *B* when Narcissus is the only firm running ads, and end up at point *C* after imitation by other firms and entry have eliminated Narcissus's economic profit.

Notice that, in panel (b), the ultimate impact of advertising is to decrease both cost per unit and price from $60 to $50. How can this be? By advertising, each firm is able to produce and sell more output. This remains true even when *all* firms advertise because total market demand has increased. Since the firm was originally on the downward-sloping portion of its *ATC* curve, we know that its *non*advertising costs per unit will decline as output expands. If this decline is great enough—as in panel (b)—then costs per unit will drop, even when the cost of advertising is included. In other words, because you and I and everyone else is buying more perfume, each producer can operate closer to capacity output, with lower costs per unit. In the long run, entry will force each firm to pass the cost savings on to us.

Our analysis suggests the following conclusion:

> *Under monopolistic competition, advertising may increase the size of the market, so that more units are sold. But in the long run, each firm earns zero economic profit, just as it would if no firm were advertising. The price to the consumer may either rise or fall.*

Advertising and Collusion In Oligopoly

In this chapter, you've learned that oligopolists have a strong incentive to engage in tacit collusion. But such collusion is difficult to detect. When one firm raises its prices and others follow, that may be evidence of price leadership, or it may be that costs in the industry have risen, and *all* firms—affected in the same way—have decided independently to raise their prices. But in some cases, such as strategic decisions about oligopoly, we can use a simple game theory model to show that collusion is almost certainly taking place.

Let's take the airline industry as an example. Polls have shown that passengers have been very concerned about airline safety. This was true before the infamous hijacking of four airliners on September 11, 2001, when thousands died. Since that incident, safety has weighed even more heavily on the minds of those considering flying. Any airline that could convince the public of its superior safety record would profit considerably.

In theory, *any* airline should be able to claim superior safety. After all, there are many different ways to interpret safety data. By searching hard enough, almost any airline could come up with a measure by which it would appear the "safest." And any airline that actually imposed special passenger and baggage screening procedures could tout the changes in its ads, taking business from other airlines. Yet no airline has ever run an advertisement with information about its security policies or attacked those of a competitor. Let's see why.

Figure 10 shows some hypothetical payoffs from this sort of advertising as seen by two firms, United Airlines and American Airlines, competing on a particular route. Focus first on the top, green-shaded entries, which show the payoffs for American. If neither firm ran safety ads, American would earn a level of profit we will call *medium,* as a benchmark. If American ran ads touting its own safety, but United did not, American's profit would certainly increase—to "high" in the payoff matrix. If both firms ran safety ads—especially negative ads that attacked their rival— the public's demand for airline tickets would certainly decline. Reminded of the dangers of flying, more consumers would choose to travel by train, bus, or car. American's profit in this case would be lower than if *neither* firm ran ads, so we have labeled it "low" in the payoff matrix. Finally, the worst possible result for American—"very low" in the figure—occurs when United touts its own safety record, but American does not.

Now consider American's possible strategies. If United decides to run the ads (the top row), American's best action is to run them as well. If United does not run the ads (bottom row), American's best action is still to run the ads. Thus, American has a dominant strategy: Regardless of what United does, it should run the safety ads.

As you can verify, United, whose payoffs are the lower, orange-shaded entries, faces an entirely symmetrical situation, and it, too, has the same dominant strategy:

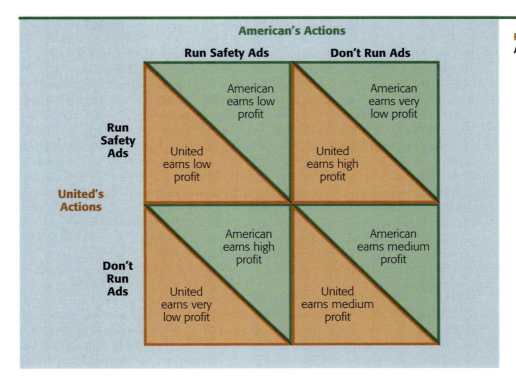

FIGURE 10
An Advertising Game

Run the ads. Thus, when each airline acts independently, the outcome of this game is shown in the upper left-hand corner, where each airline runs ads and earns a low profit. So why don't we observe that outcome?

The answer is that the airlines are playing against each other repeatedly and reach the kind of cooperative equilibrium we discussed earlier. Each airline can punish its rival next time if it fails to cooperate this time. In the cooperative outcome, each airline plays the strategy that it will *not* run the ads as long as its rival does not. The game's outcome moves to the lower right-hand corner. Here, neither firm runs ads, and each earns medium rather than low profit. This is the result we see in the airline industry.

Should we be surprised at the cooperative outcome in this case? Not really. Recall that the ability to get away with cheating is one of the chief obstacles to cooperation. But when the agreement involves *advertising*, cheating would be instantly detected and would therefore be unlikely to occur. This makes advertising a particularly good opportunity for cooperation.

Until the 1980s, a similar collusive understanding seemed to characterize the automobile industry. As long as the "Big Three" dominated auto sales in the United States, the word *safety* was never heard in their advertising. There seemed to be an understanding that all three would earn greater profits if consumers were *not* reminded of the dangers of driving. Things changed in the 1980s, however, as foreign firms' share of the U.S. market rose dramatically. One of the new players, Volvo, decided that its safety features were so far superior to its competitors that it no longer paid to play by the rules. Volvo began running television advertisements that not only stressed its own safety features, but implied that competing products were dangerous. (On a rainy night, a worried father stops his son at the door, hands him some keys, and says, "Here, son, take the Volvo.") Once Volvo began running ads like these, the other automakers had no choice but to reciprocate. Now, automobile ads routinely mention safety features like antilock brakes and air bags.

Something similar *almost* happened in the airline travel industry. But the "Volvo" in this case was not an airline but an aircraft manufacturer. In November 1999, Airbus ran ads designed to convince the public that its four-engine A340 jets were safer for transatlantic travel than Boeing's twin-engine 777s. A print ad—taken out in more than a dozen newspapers and magazines, including the *Economist, Fortune,* and the *Wall Street Journal*—shows a lone Airbus A340 flying under ominous, dark skies, with a choppy sea below. The caption read, "If you're over the middle of the Pacific, you want to be in the middle of four engines." Not surprisingly, Boeing condemned the ad, declaring that "this not so subtle scare-tactic . . . is a dramatic departure from the high standards our industry has traditionally met. Airbus's actions have, rightfully so, raised a considerable amount of displeasure in our industry." The major airlines reacted even more strongly. The CEO of Continental Airlines, Gordon Bethune, informed Airbus that the ad "makes it more unlikely we would put our confidence in you or your products."[7] Airbus soon stopped running the ads.

Until July 2002, that is, when Airbus did it again at the Air Show in Farnborough, England. This time, Airbus installed a huge billboard at the edge of the runway with a new slogan: "A340—4 ENGINES 4 LONG HAUL." Once again, full-page ads appeared in daily newspapers and air show magazines. And once again, Airbus was attacked by the industry. But this time, a spokesman for Boeing's marketing department launched an odd counterattack against rival Airbus: "Think of it this way. If you have two engines, there are two chances of engine failure. If you have four engines, there are four chances of engine failure. The chance of engine failure doesn't go down with four engines; it goes up."[8] Although the logic behind this response is confounding, the fact that Boeing responded at all is significant. Perhaps the gloves are coming off now.

THE FOUR MARKET STRUCTURES: A POSTSCRIPT

You have now been introduced to the four different market structures: perfect competition, monopoly, monopolistic competition, and oligopoly. Each has different characteristics, and each leads to different predictions about pricing, profit, nonprice competition, and firms' responses to changes in their environments.

Table 1 summarizes some of the assumptions and predictions associated with each of the four market structures. While the table is a useful review of the *models* we have studied, it is not a how-to guide for analyzing real-world markets: We cannot simply look at the array of markets we see around us and say, "This one is perfectly competitive," "That one is an oligopoly," and so on. Why not? Because markets in the real world will typically have characteristics of more than one kind of market structure. A barbecue restaurant, for example, may be viewed as a mo-

[7] "Competitor's 'scare tactic' vexes Boeing," *Herald Net,* November 6, 1999 (*www.heraldnet.com*); "Airlines Blast New Ads from Airbus . . ." *Wall Street Journal,* November 22, 1999.
[8] Quoted in Kathleen Hanser, "An Airbus Advertising Campaign at the Farnborough Air Show Stoked the Fires in the Debate Between . . . Two Engines & Four Engines," *Boeing Frontiers* (Vol. 1, Issue 5), September 2002 (*http://www.boeing.com/news/frontiers/archive/2002/september/i_ca1.html*)

	Perfect Competition	Monopolistic Competition	Oligopoly	Monopoly
ASSUMPTIONS ABOUT:				
Number of Firms	Very many	Many	Few	One
Output of Different Firms	Identical	Differentiated	Identical or differentiated	—
View of Pricing	Price taker	Price setter	Price setter	Price setter
Barriers to Entry or Exit?	No	No	Yes	Yes
Strategic Interdependence?	No	No	Yes	—
PREDICTIONS:				
Price and Output Decisions	$MC = MR$	$MC = MR$	Through strategic Interdependence	$MC = MR$
Short-Run Profit	Positive, zero, or negative	Positive, zero, or negative	Positive, zero, or negative	Positive, zero, or negative
Long-Run Profit	Zero	Zero	Positive or zero	Positive or zero
Advertising?	Never	Almost always	Yes, if differentiated product	Sometimes

TABLE 1
A Summary of Market Structures

nopolistic competitor in the market for *restaurants* in Memphis, or an oligopolist in the market for *barbecue* restaurants in Memphis, or a monopolist in the market for barbecue restaurants *within walking distance of Graceland*.

You've seen how market structure models help us organize and understand the apparent chaos of real-world markets. But now, it seems, we've ended up with a different type of chaos: We can usually choose among two, three, or even four different models when studying a particular market.

But, as we've seen several times in this text, our choice of model is not really arbitrary; rather, it depends on the *questions we are trying to answer.* Suppose we're interested in barbecue restaurants. To explain why a *particular* barbecue restaurant with no nearby competitors earns economic profit year after year, or why it spends so much of its profit on rent-seeking activity (lobbying the local zoning board), we would most likely use the monopoly model. If we want to explain why *most* barbecue restaurants do *not* earn much economic profit, or why they pay for advertisements in the yellow pages and the local newspapers, we would use the model of monopolistic competition. To explain a price war among the few restaurants in a neighborhood, or to explore the possibility of explicit or tacit collusion in pricing or advertising, we would use the oligopoly model. And if we're interested in barbecue restaurants as an example of *restaurants in general*, and we want general explanations about restaurant prices, or the expansion or contraction of the restaurant industry in a city or country, we would use the perfectly competitive model, which ignores the distinctions between different restaurants and any barriers to entry that might exist.

We will come back to markets for goods and services again (in Chapter 10) when we consider the operation of the microeconomy as a whole, the notion of economic efficiency, and the proper role of government in the economy. But first we must explore another type of market, one that, until now, we've ignored.

Summary

A *monopoly firm* is the only seller of a good or service with no close substitutes. Monopoly arises because of some barrier to entry such as: economies of scale, legal barriers or network externalities. As the only seller, the monopoly faces the demand curve for the entire market, and must decide what price to charge in order to maximize profit.

Like other firms, a monopolist will produce where $MR = MC$ and set that maximum price consumers are willing to pay for that quantity. Monopoly profit ($P - ATC$ multiplied by the quantity produced) can persist in the long run because of barriers to entry.

Imperfect competition refers to market structures with more than one firm, but in which one or more of the requirements of pure competition are violated. Monopolistic competition is one type of imperfect competition. In this type of market, there are many small buyers and sellers, no significant barriers to entry or exit, and firms sell differentiated profits. As in monopoly, each firm faces a downward-sloping demand curve, chooses the profit-maximizing quantity where $MR = MC$, and charges the maximum price it can for that quantity. As in perfect competition, economic profit eventually attracts new entrants, causing all firms to earn zero economic profit in the long run.

Oligopoly is another type of imperfect competition. The market is dominated by a small number of strategically interdependent firms. New entry is deterred by economies of scale, reputational barriers, strategic barriers, and legal barriers.

In the game theory approach to oligopoly, a *payoff matrix* indicates the payoff to each firm for each combination of strategies adopted by that firm and by its rivals. A *dominant strategy* is a strategy that is best for a particular firm regardless of what its rival does. If a firm has a dominant strategy, it will always play it, and that helps predict the outcome of the game.

With repeated play, oligopolists may learn to cooperate in an effort to increase profits. *Explicit collusion,* where managers meet to set prices, is illegal in the United States and many other countries. As a result, other forms of *tacit collusion* have evolved. Still, collusion is limited by a number of factors: cheating by firms, government antitrust enforcement, market globalization, and technological change.

Key Terms

Cartel	Imperfect competition	Oligopoly
Copyright	Monopolistic competition	Patent
Dominant strategy	Monopoly firm	Payoff matrix
Duopoly	Monopoly market	Price leadership
Explicit collusion	Natural oligopoly	Repeated play
Game theory	Network externalities	Tacit collusion
Government franchise	Nonprice competition	Tit-for-tat

Review Questions

1. Why do monopolies arise? Discuss the most common factors that explain the existence of a monopoly.

2. How can the government create a monopoly? Why might the government want to do this?

3. Drunk with power, the CEO of Monolith, Inc., a single-price monopoly, assumes that he can set any price he wants and sell as many units as he wants at that price. Is he correct? Why or why not?

4. True or false? "A firm's marginal cost curve is always its supply curve." Explain.

5. Why might a monopoly earn an economic profit in the long run? How does this differ from the situation faced by a perfectly competitive firm?

6. Explain why, if a monopoly takes over all the firms in a perfectly competitive industry, its marginal cost curve will be the same as the perfectly competitive industry's supply curve.

7. Firm A maximizes profit at an output of 1,000 units, where Price = 50 and $MC = 50$. Firm B maximizes profit at an output of 2,000 units, where Price = 5 and $MC = 3$. Which firm is likely to be a monopoly and which perfectly competitive? Explain your reasoning.

8. How do output and price for a monopoly compare with output and price if the same market were perfectly competitive?

9. What features does a monopolistically competitive market share with a perfectly competitive market? With a monopoly market?

10. True or false? "The only way for a monopolistic competitor to increase its sales is to lower its price." Explain.

11. Classify each of the following business firms as perfectly competitive, monopolistically competitive, oligopolistic, or monopolistic. Justify your answer. That is, discuss what characteristic(s) of the market designation you assign are likely to be present.
   a. General Motors
   b. An Iowa corn farmer
   c. Kinko's copy shop (large city)
   d. Kinko's copy shop (the only copy center within a two-mile radius of your campus)
   e. Ben & Jerry's ice cream (national)
   f. Daily newspaper (one of two in a medium-size city)
   g. Spanish-language newspaper (the only one in the Hispanic community of a medium-size southwestern city)

12. What is the difference between a natural oligopoly and a natural monopoly?

13. Discuss some factors that might keep new entrants out of an oligopolistic market.

14. The minimum efficient scale in a certain industry is 2,300 units. Exactly what additional information do you need in order to predict whether this industry will be perfectly (or monopolistically) competitive, an oligopoly, or a monopoly?

Problems and Exercises

1. In a certain large city, hot dog vendors are *perfectly competitive*, and face a market price of $1.00 per hot dog. Each hot dog vendor has the following total cost schedule:

Number of Hot Dogs per Day	Total Cost
0	$63
25	73
50	78
75	88
100	103
125	125
150	153
175	188
200	233

a. Add a *marginal cost* column to the right of the total cost column. (*Hint:* Don't forget to divide by the *change* in quantity when calculating *MC*.)

b. What is the profit-maximizing quantity of hot dogs for the typical vendor, and what profit (loss) will he earn (suffer)? Give your answer to the nearest 25 hot dogs.

One day, Zeke, a typical vendor, figures out that if he were the only seller in town, he would no longer have to sell his hot dogs at the market price of $1.00. Instead, he'd face the following demand schedule:

Price per Hot Dog	Number of Hot Dogs per Day
> $6.00	0
6.00	25
5.50	50
4.00	75
3.25	100
2.75	125
2.25	150
1.75	175
1.25	200

c. Add *total revenue* and *marginal revenue* columns to the table above. (*Hint:* Once again, don't forget to divide by the *change* in quantity when calculating *MR*.)

d. As a monopolist with the cost schedule given in the first table, how many hot dogs would Zeke choose to sell each day? What price would he charge?

e. A lobbyist has approached Zeke, proposing to form a new organization called "Citizens to Eliminate Chaos in Hot Dog Sales." The organization will lobby the city council to grant Zeke the only hot dog license in town, and it is guaranteed to succeed. The only problem is, the lobbyist is asking for a payment that amounts to $200 per business day as long as Zeke stays in business. On purely economic grounds, should Zeke go for it?

2. a. Draw demand, *MR,* and *ATC* curves that show a monopoly that is just breaking even.
   b. Redraw your graph from part (a). Show what will happen in the short run if the prices of the firm's variable inputs rise.
   c. Redraw your graph from part (a). Show what will happen in the short run if the prices of the firm's variable inputs fall.

3. Below is demand and cost information for Warmfuzzy Press, which holds the copyright on the new best-seller, *Burping Your Inner Child.*

Q (No. of Copies)	P (per Book)	ATC (per Book)
100,000	$100	$20
200,000	$ 80	$15
300,000	$ 60	$16⅔
400,000	$ 40	$22½
500,000	$ 20	$31

   a. Determine what quantity of the book Warmfuzzy should print, and what price it should charge in order to maximize profit.
   b. What is Warmfuzzy's maximum profit?
   c. Prior to publication, the book's author renegotiates his contract with Warmfuzzy. He will receive a great big hug from the CEO, along with a one-time bonus of $1,000,000, payable when the book is published. This payment was not part of Warmfuzzy's original cost calculations.
   How many copies should Warmfuzzy publish now? Explain your reasoning.

4. Draw demand, *MR, AVC,* and *ATC* curves that show a monopolist that is operating while incurring an economic loss. Show how a technological change could keep this monopolist from shutting down, first if the change affected only the monopolist's fixed costs, and then if the change affected only its variable costs.

5. Answer the following:
   a. Complete the following table and use it to find this monopolist's short-run profit-maximizing level of output. How much profit will this firm earn?
   b. Redo the table to show what will happen to the short-run profit-maximizing level of output if the monopolist's marginal costs rise by $1 at each level of output. How much profit will the firm earn now?
   c. Redo the original table to show what will happen to the short-run profit-maximizing level of output if the monopolist's marginal costs fall by $0.40 at each level of output. How much profit would the firm earn in this case?

   d. A change in the price of what kind of input would result in a change in marginal cost?

Output	Price	Total Revenue	Marginal Revenue	Total Cost	Marginal Cost	Profit
0	$5.60			$ 0.50		
1	$5.50			$ 3.50		
2	$5.40			$ 5.45		
3	$5.30			$ 6.45		
4	$5.20			$ 6.90		
5	$5.10			$ 8.90		
6	$5.05			$13.40		
7	$4.90			$20.40		

6. Draw the relevant curves to show a monopolistic competitor suffering a loss in the short run. What will this firm do in the long run if the situation does not improve? How would this action affect *other* firms in this market?

7. The owner of an optometry practice, in a city with more than a hundred other such practices, has the following demand and cost schedules for eye exams:

Price per Eye Exam	Eye Exams per Week	Total Cost per Week	Total Revenue per Week	Marginal Revenue	Marginal Cost
$100	100	$10,500			
80	140	$10,800			
60	200	$11,300			
40	310	$12,290			
20	550	$14,762			

   a. Fill in the columns for total revenue, marginal revenue, and marginal cost. (Remember to put *MR* and *MC between* output levels.)
   b. Briefly explain why an optometry practice (like this one) might face a downward-sloping demand curve, even if it is one out of more than a hundred. (*Hint:* What might make this market monopolistically competitive rather than perfectly competitive?)
   c. Use the data you filled in for the marginal revenue and marginal cost columns to find the profit-maximizing price and the profit-maximizing number of eye exams per week for this practice.

8. Tino owns a taco stand in Houston, Texas, where there are dozens of other taco stands. He faces the following demand and cost schedules for his taco plates (two tacos and a side of refried beans):

Price per Taco Plate	Taco Plates per Week	Total Cost per Week	Total Revenue per Week	Marginal Revenue	Marginal Cost
$5	50	$30			
4	80	$50			
3	150	$176			
2	800	$1476			
1	1100	$2136			

a. Fill in the columns for total revenue, marginal revenue, and marginal cost and use the table to find the profit-maximizing price and the profit-maximizing number of taco plates per week for Tino's Taco Stand. (Remember to put *MR* and *MC* *between* output levels.)

b. What will likely happen to Tino's profits if his biggest competitor starts a successful "buy one-get one free" campaign?

c. Redo the table to show what will happen if Tino spends $100 on an advertising campaign that increases the quantity demanded at each output level by 20%. What will happen to his profit-maximizing price and profit-maximizing number of taco plates per week? Do you expect this outcome to persist? Explain.

9. Suppose that the cost data in Problem 7 are for the short run, and that the owner of the practice suddenly realizes that she forgot to include her only fixed cost: her license fee of $2,600 per year (which is $50 per week). Should the practice shut down in the short run? Why or why not?

10. Assume that the plastics business is monopolistically competitive.

a. Draw a graph showing the long-run equilibrium situation for a typical firm in the industry. Clearly label the demand, *MR*, *MC*, and *ATC* curves.

b. One of the major inputs into plastics is oil. Draw a new graph illustrating the short-run position of a plastics company after an increase in oil prices. Again, show all relevant curves.

c. If oil prices remain at the new, higher level, what will happen to get firms in the plastics industry back to a long-run equilibrium?

11. Draw a diagram, including demand, marginal revenue, marginal cost, and any other curves necessary, to illustrate each of the following two situations for a monopolistic competitor:

a. The firm is suffering a loss, and should shut down in the short run.

b. The firm is suffering a loss, but should stay open in the short run.

12. In a small Nevada town, Ptomaine Flats, there are only two restaurants, the Road Kill Cafe and, for Italian fare, Sal Monella's. Each restaurant has to decide whether to clean up its act or to continue to ignore health code violations.

Each restaurant currently makes $7,000 a year in profit. If they both tidy up a bit, they will attract more patrons but must bear the (substantial) cost of the cleanup; so they will both be left with a profit of $5,000. However, if one cleans up and the other doesn't, the influx of diners to the cleaner joint will more than cover the costs of the scrubbing; the more hygienic place ends up with $12,000, and the grubbier establishment incurs a loss of $3,000.

a. Write out the payoff matrix for this game, clearly labeling strategies and payoffs to each player.

b. What is each player's dominant strategy?

c. What will be the outcome of the game? Explain your answer.

d. Suppose the two restaurants believe they will face the same decision repeatedly. How might the outcome differ? Why?

e. Assume that if one cleans up and one stays dirty, the cleaner restaurant makes only $6,000 in profit. All other payoffs are the same as before. What will the outcome of the game be now without cooperation? With cooperation?

13. Assume that Nike and Adidas are the only sellers of athletic footwear in the United States. They are deciding how much to charge for similar shoes. The two choices are "High" (H) and "Outrageously High" (OH). Nike's payoffs are in the lower left of each cell in the payoff matrix:

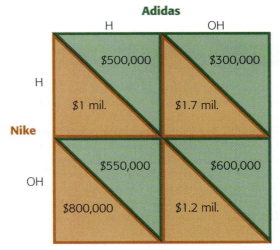

a. Do both companies have dominant strategies? If so, what are they?

b. What will be the outcome of the game?

c. If Nike becomes the acknowledged price leader in the industry, what will be its dominant strategy? What will be the outcome of the game? Why?

Challenge Questions

1. Let a single-price monopoly's demand curve be given by $P = 20 - 4Q$, where P is price and Q is quantity demanded. Marginal revenue is $MR = 20 - 8Q$. Marginal cost is $MC = Q^2$. How much should this firm produce in order to maximize profit?

2. Suppose that the government has decided to tax all the firms in a monopolistically competitive industry. Specifically, suppose it levies a fixed tax on each firm; that is, the amount of the tax is the same regardless of how much output the firm produces. In the short run, how would that tax affect the price, output level, and profit of the typical firm in that industry? What would be the effect in the long run?

3. In the next column you will find the payoff matrix for a two-player game, where each player has three possible strategies: *A, B,* and *C.* The payoff for player 1 is listed in the lower left portion of each cell. Assume there is no cooperation among players.
   a. Does either player have a dominant strategy? If so, which player or players, and what is the dominant strategy?
   b. Can we predict the outcome of this game using the concept of dominant strategies? Why or why not?

c. Suppose that strategy *C* is no longer available to either player. Does either player have a dominant strategy now? Can we now predict the outcome of the game using dominant strategies? Explain. (*Hint:* Assume that players know the payoffs—both for themselves and for the other players—for every strategy.)

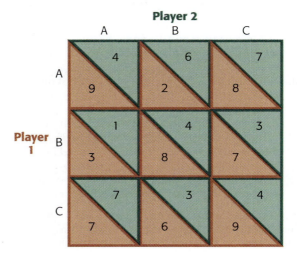

 These exercises require access to Lieberman/Hall Xtra! If Xtra! did not come with your book, visit *http://liebermanxtraxtra. swlearning.com* to purchase.

1. Use your Xtra! password at the Hall and Lieberman Web site (http://liebermanxtra.swlearning.com) and under Economic Applications click on EconNews. Select *Microeconomics: Monopoly,* and read the article, "Dentsply Monopoly: A Test of Antitrust Law's Teeth." Then go to EconDebate and again select *Microeconomics: Monopoly.* Find the debate, "Is Microsoft a Monopoly?" Why did the Department of Justice accuse each firm of being a monopoly if they have other competitors in their market? Does this satisfy the definition of monopoly as given in this chapter? Why or why not?

2. Use your Xtra! password at the Hall and Lieberman Web site (http://liebermanxtra.swlearning.com) and under Economic Applications click on EconNews. Select *Microeconomics: Monopolistic Competition,* and read the article "Just-in-Time State-of-the-Art Fashion." Explain what form of nonprice competition the firm uses to gain an edge on its rivals.

3. Use your Xtra! password at the Hall and Lieberman Web site (http://liebermanxtra.swlearning.com) and under Eco-

nomic Applications click on EconNews. Click on *Microeconomics: Oligopoly* and read the article "Fair Oil Prices," then answer the questions below.
   a. Using a game theory model of cartels, is Venezuela's strategy credible? Why or why not? Would your answer change if the Venezuelan president were visiting only OPEC nations?
   b. Now go to EconDebate. Again select *Microeconomics: Oligopoly* and find the debate, "Should the Strategic Petroleum Reserve Be Used to Reduce Fluctuations in Oil Prices?" Read the debate. In terms of game theory, would using the Strategic Petroleum Reserve be effective against a cartel like OPEC? Why or why not?
   c. In light of Venezuela's request to increase the price of oil, should we use the SPR to provide additional oil? Why or why not?

APPENDIX
PRICE DISCRIMINATION

In this chapter, we've analyzed the decisions of *single-price firms*—those that charge the same price on every unit that they sell. But not all firms operate this way. For example, telephone companies charge different rates for calls made by people on different calling plans; movie theaters charge lower prices to senior citizens; airlines charge lower prices to those who book their flights in advance; and supermarkets and food companies charge lower prices to customers who clip coupons from their local newspaper.

In some cases, the different prices are due to differences in the firm's costs of production. For example, it may be more expensive to deliver a product a great distance from the factory, so a firm may charge a higher price to customers in outlying areas. But in other cases, the different prices arise not from cost differences, but from the firm's recognition that *some customers are willing to pay more than others:*

> *Price discrimination occurs when a firm charges different prices to different customers for reasons other than differences in costs.*

The term *discrimination* in this context requires some getting used to. In everyday language, *discrimination* carries a negative connotation: We think immediately of discrimination against someone because of his or her race, sex, or age. But a price-discriminating firm does not discriminate based on prejudice, stereotypes, or ill will toward any person or group; rather, it divides its customers into different categories based on their *willingness to pay* for the good—nothing more and nothing less. By doing so, the firm can squeeze even more profit out of the market. Why, then, doesn't *every* firm practice price discrimination?

Requirements for Price Discrimination

Although every firm would *like* to practice price discrimination, not all of them can. To successfully price discriminate, three conditions must be satisfied:

1. *There must be a downward-sloping demand curve for the firm's output.* In order to price discriminate,

a firm must be able to raise its price to at least *some* customers without losing their business. A competitive firm cannot price discriminate: If it were to raise its price even slightly to some customers, they would simply buy the identical output from some other firm that is selling at the market price. This is one reason why there is no price discrimination in perfectly competitive markets like those for wheat, soybeans, and silver.

When a firm faces a downward-sloping demand curve, however, we know that some customers will continue to buy even when the price increases. Monopolies and imperfectly competitive firms satisfy the downward-sloping demand requirement.

2. *The firm must be able to identify consumers willing to pay more.* In order to determine which prices to charge to which customers, a firm must identify how much different customers are willing to pay. But this is often difficult. Suppose your barber or hairstylist wanted to price discriminate. How would he determine how much you are willing to pay for a haircut? He could *ask* you, but . . . let's be real: You wouldn't tell him the truth, since you know he would only use the information to charge you more than you've been paying. Price-discriminating firms—in most cases—must be a bit sneaky, relying on more indirect methods to gauge their customers' willingness to pay.

For example, airlines know that business travelers, who must get to their destination quickly, are willing to pay a higher price for air travel than are tourists or vacationers, who can more easily travel by train, bus, or car. Of course, if airlines merely *announced* a higher price for business travel, then no one would admit to being a business traveler when buying a ticket. So the airlines must find some way to identify business travelers without actually asking. Their method is crude but reasonably effective: Business travelers typically plan their trips at the last minute and don't stay over Saturday night, while tourists and vacationers generally plan long in advance and do stay over Saturday. Thus, the airlines give a discount to any customer who books a flight several weeks in advance and stays over, and they charge a higher price to those who book at the last minute and don't stay over. Of course, some business travelers may be able to do advance planning and pay the lower price, and some personal travelers who cannot plan in advance might be priced out of the market. But on the whole, the airlines are able to charge a higher price to a group of people—business travelers—who are willing to pay more.[9]

Catalog retailers—such as Victoria's Secret—have an easily available clue for determining who is willing to pay more: the customer's address. People who live in high-income zip codes are mailed catalogs with higher prices than people who live in lower-income areas. Some Internet retailers have even used software to track customers' past purchases to gauge whether each is a free spender or a careful shopper. Only the careful shoppers get the low prices.[10]

3. *The firm must be able to prevent low-price customers from reselling to high-price customers.* Preventing a product from being resold by low-price customers can be a vexing problem for a would-be discriminator. For example, when airlines began price discriminating, a resale market developed: Business travelers could buy tickets at the last minute from intermediaries, who had booked in advance at the lower price and then advertised their tickets for sale. To counter this, the airlines imposed the additional requirement of a Saturday stayover in order to buy at the lower price. By adding this restriction, the airlines were able to substantially reduce the reselling of low-price tickets to business travelers.

It is often easy to prevent resale of a *service* because of its personal nature. A hairstylist can charge different prices to different customers without fearing that one customer will sell her haircut to another. The same is true of the services provided by physicians, attorneys, and music teachers.

Resale of *goods*, however, is much harder to prevent, since goods can be easily transferred from person to person without losing their usefulness. A classic example of how far a company might have to go to prevent resale of a good is the case of Rohm and Haas, a chemical firm. In the 1940s, Rohm and Haas sold methyl methacrylate powder, used to make durable plastic, at two prices. Industrial users, who had many other options, paid 85 cents per pound; dental laboratories, which had no other choice of material for making dentures and were willing to pay more, were charged $22 per pound. In spite of Rohm and Haas's diligent efforts to prevent it, this price differential led to a flourishing resale market, in which industrial users were buying methyl methacrylate at 85 cents per pound and selling it for substantially more to dental laboratories. Internal memos at Rohm and Haas revealed that the company, desperate for a solution, considered (but did not finally adopt) a plan to put lead or even arsenic (!) in all powder sold at the lower price so that dental laboratories would be unable to use it.[11]

Effects of Price Discrimination

Price discrimination always benefits the owners of a firm: When the firm can charge different prices to different consumers, it can use this ability to increase its

---

[9] It is sometimes argued that airlines' pricing behavior is based entirely on a cost difference to the airline. For example, it is probably more costly for an airline to keep seats available until the last minute, because there is a risk that they will go unsold. The higher price for last-minute bookings would then compensate the airline for the unsold seats. (See, for example, the article by John R. Lott, Jr., and Russell D. Roberts in *Economic Inquiry,* January 1991.) But we know that cost differences are not the only reason for the price differential, or else the airlines would not have added the Saturday stayover requirement, which has nothing to do with their costs.

[10] Woolley, Scott, "I Got It Cheaper than You," *Forbes,* November 2, 1998. For a general discussion of Internet pricing, see Robert E. Hall, *Digital Dealing* (W. W. Norton, 2002).

[11] From George W. Stocking and Myron W. Watkins, *Cartels in Action: Case Studies in International Business Diplomacy* (New York: The Twentieth Century Fund, 1946), p. 403

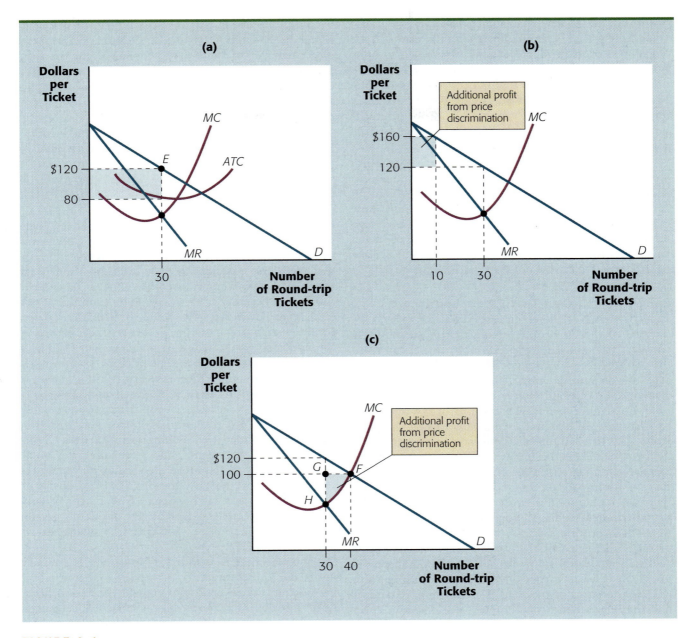

FIGURE A.1

Price Discrimination

Panel (a) shows a single-price monopoly airline selling 30 round-trip tickets per day at $120 each and earning a profit of $1,200 per day. Panel (b) shows the same airline if it can charge a higher price to its business travelers. The shaded rectangle shows the additional profit the airline earns by price discriminating; total profit is now $1,600. Panel (c) shows an alternative strategy. In addition to selling 30 regular tickets at $120 each, the airline attracts an additional 10 passengers at a lower student fare of $100. So profit rises by the area of the shaded region.

profit. But the effects on consumers can vary. To understand how price discrimination affects the firm and the consumers of its product, let's take a simple example. Imagine that only one company—No-Choice Airlines—offers direct, small-plane flights between Omaha, Nebraska and Salina, Kansas. (What barrier to entry might explain No-Choice's monopoly on this route? If you're stumped, look again at the section on the sources of monopoly in this chapter.)

Panel (a) of Figure A.1 illustrates what No-Choice would do if it could *not* price discriminate and had to operate as a single-price firm. Since $MR = MC$ at 30 round-trip tickets per day, No-Choice's profit-maximizing price would be $120 per ticket. The firm's average total cost for 30 round-trips is $80, so its profit per ticket would be $120 − $80 = $40. Total profit is $40 × 30 = $1,200, equal to the area of the shaded rectangle.

Price Discrimination That Harms Consumers.

Now suppose that No-Choice discovers that on an average day, 10 of the 30 people buying tickets are business travelers who are willing to pay more, and it can identify them by their *un*willingness to book in advance and stay over on Saturday night. No-Choice could price discriminate by offering two prices: $120 for those who book in advance and stay over on Saturday, and $160 to all others. In effect, No-Choice is raising the price from $120 to $160 for its 10 business customers.

Let's calculate the impact on No-Choice's profit. Since it continues to sell the same 30 round-trip tickets, there is no impact on its costs. Its revenue, however, will rise: It charges $40 more than before on 10 of its round-trip tickets. Thus, No-Choice will earn an additional daily profit of $40 × 10 = $400. This *increase* in profit is identified as the shaded rectangle in Figure A.1(b). Total profit is now the sum of two numbers: the profit No-Choice earned *before* price discrimination ($1,200, the area of the shaded rectangle in panel (a)) and the *increase* in profit due to price discrimination ($400, the area of the shaded rectangle in panel (b)). By price discriminating, No-Choice has raised its total profit from $1,200 to $1,600 per day.

What about consumers? Since 10 customers each pay $40 more than before, they lose 10 × $40 = $400 from paying the higher price. Other travelers, who continue to pay $120 for their tickets, are unaffected by the higher price.

Summing up, in this case the impact of price discrimination—compared to a single-price policy—is a direct transfer of funds from consumers to the firm. The increase in the firm's profit is equal to the additional payments by consumers. This conclusion applies more generally as well:

> *When price discrimination raises the price for some consumers above the price they would pay under a single-price policy, it harms consumers. The additional profit for the firm is equal to the monetary loss of consumers.*

Price Discrimination That Benefits Consumers.

Let's go back to the initial situation facing No-Choice and suppose that, instead of charging a higher price to business travelers, it decides to price discriminate in a different way. No-Choice discovers that students who travel to college in Salina are going by train, because it is cheaper. However, at a price of $100, the airline could sell an average of 10 round-trip tickets per day to the students. No-Choice's new policy is this: $120 for a round-trip ticket, but a special price of $100 for students who show their ID cards. The result is shown in panel (c). Although the decision to sell an additional 10 tickets pushes No-Choice beyond the output level at which $MC = MR$, this is no problem. The MR curve was drawn under the assumption that No-Choice charges a single price and must lower the price on all tickets in order to sell more. But this is no longer the case. With price discrimination, the MR curve no longer tells us what will happen to No-Choice's revenue when output increases. As you are about to see, the firm will be able to increase its profit by selling the additional tickets.

The reasoning is as follows: No-Choice is now selling 10 *additional* round-trip tickets, so in this case both its cost and its revenue will change. Each additional ticket adds $100 to the firm's revenue; this is the new marginal revenue. Each additional ticket also adds an amount to costs given by the firm's MC curve. Thus, the distance between $100 and the MC curve gives the *additional profit* earned on each additional ticket, and the total additional profit is the shaded area HGF in panel (c) of Figure A.1.

What about consumers? The original 30 consumers are unaffected, since their ticket price has not changed.

But the new customers—the 10 students—come out ahead: Each is able to take the flight rather than the longer train trip. In this case, price discrimination benefits the monopoly at the same time as it benefits a group of consumers—the students who were not buying the service before, but who *will* buy it at a lower price and gain some benefits by doing so. Since no one's price is raised, no one is harmed by this policy:

> *When price discrimination lowers the price for some consumers below what they would pay under a single-price policy, it benefits consumers as well as the firm.*

Of course, it is possible for a firm to combine *both* types of price discrimination. That is, it could raise the price above what it would charge as a single-price monopoly for some consumers and lower it for others. This kind of price discrimination would increase the firm's profit, while benefiting some consumers and harming others. (For practice, draw a diagram showing the change in total profit if No-Choice were to charge three prices: a basic price of $120, a price of $160 for business travelers, and a price of $100 for students. Who would gain and who would lose?)

Key Terms

Price discrimination Charging different prices to different customers for reasons other than differences in cost.

The Labor Market and Wage Rates

When we went to do the deals for Shrek 2, *they were made in one day. It was that fast and that easy. It was also probably the biggest payday in movie history. They were each paid $10 million for what is in effect 18 hours of work.*
Jeffrey Katzenberg, cofounder of DreamWorks SKG, referring to payments made to Eddie Murphy, Mike Myers, and Cameron Diaz for voiceovers.[1]

Imagine, for a pleasant moment, that you are Eddie Murphy, Mike Myers, or Cameron Diaz. Your typical workday begins in a limousine, escorting you to the site of the day's recording. There you are doted on by assistants whose sole job is to keep you happy, who look at you respectfully, even worshipfully. Finally, you perform the day's work: a few hours worth of reading from a script. If you make a mistake, everyone laughs good-naturedly, and you get another chance to get it right—as many chances as you need. And after doing this each day for a few weeks, you pick up a check for $10 million.

Now, switch gears and imagine that you have a less-rewarding job, say, as a short-order cook at a coffeehouse. You spend the day sweating over a hot grill, spinning a little metal wheel with an endless supply of orders, each one determining

---

[1] "Question and Answer: Movie Mogul Jeffrey Katzenberg," *Reel West* (Vol. 17, No. 4) July–August 2002.

what you must do for the next three minutes. You cook several hundred meals that day, all the while suffering the short tempers of waiters and waitresses who want you to do it faster, who glare at you if you forget that a customer wanted french fries instead of home fries, and who call you everything but your proper name. At the end of the day, your face is covered with grease, your eyes are red from smoke, and your feet are sore from standing. And for toiling in this way day after day, for an entire year, you earn $20,000.

Why does Eddie Murphy earn so much more for his work than a short order cook? Indeed, why do most lawyers, doctors, and corporate managers earn more than most teachers, truck drivers, and assembly-line workers? And why do these workers, in turn, earn more than farmworkers, store clerks, and waiters? As you'll learn in this chapter, we can explain much about wage differences once we understand how labor markets work.

LABOR MARKETS IN PERSPECTIVE

Labor markets differ in an important way from the other markets we've considered so far in this book. When we analyzed the markets for soybeans, bed frames, TV cable service, gasoline and more, we were studying *product markets*, in which firms sell goods and services to households or other firms. Of course, goods and services aren't produced out of thin air. Firms need *resources*—labor, capital, land, and entrepremeurship—to make goods and services. Firms obtain these resources by purchasing them from their owners in **resource markets**.

Figure 1 illustrates the essential difference between product markets and resource markets. Notice that, in product markets, households demand goods and services, and firms supply them. In resource markets, these roles are typically reversed: Firms demand resources, and households—which own the resources—are the suppliers.

We can identify three general categories of resource markets. Firms purchase factory buildings, office buildings, computers, cash registers, and other plant and equipment in *markets for capital*. They buy or rent real estate for their operations in various *markets for land*. And finally, when firms hire workers, they act as buyers in *markets for labor*.

The basic approach we will take in studying labor markets may initially strike you as a bit heartless: We will treat labor as a commodity—something that is bought and sold in the marketplace. We'll regard the *wage rate*—what a firm pays for an hour of labor—as the price of that commodity. In other words, we explain how a wage rate is determined in much the same way we'd explain how the price of a bushel of soybeans is determined. We do this for one simple reason: It works.

Of course, labor *is* different from other things that are traded. Sellers of soybeans do not care who buys their product, as long as they get the market price. Sellers of labor, on the other hand, care about other things besides the price they receive for their time, such as working conditions, friendly coworkers, commuting distance, possibilities for advancement, prestige, a sense of fulfillment, and more.

A second distinct feature of labor is the special meaning of the price in this market: the wage rate. Most of the income people earn over their lifetimes will come from their jobs—from selling their labor—so their wage rate will determine how well they can feed, clothe, house, and otherwise provide for themselves and their

Resource markets Markets in which households sell resources—land, labor, and natural resources—to firms.

families. Differences in wages thus bring up vital issues of *equity* and *fairness* in the economy. Economics has much to say about how and why wages differ, as you will see in this chapter.

Defining a Labor Market

If you are like most college students, you will be looking for a full-time job shortly after you graduate. From the economic point of view, you will become a seller in a labor market. But which labor market? Most broadly, you will be selling in the market for college graduates. But we could also define your labor market more narrowly—perhaps the market for economics B.A.s, or even the market for economics B.A.s in Scranton.

> *How broadly or narrowly we define a labor market depends on the specific questions we wish to answer.*

For example, suppose we are interested in explaining why college graduates, on average, earn more than those with just high school diplomas. Then we would want to analyze two very broadly defined labor markets: the national market for college-educated labor and the national market for high-school educated labor. In either of these markets, you would be one of millions of sellers, and each employer would be one of hundreds of thousands of employers.

On the other hand, we might be interested in finding out how salaries in some specific profession are determined. For this purpose, we would use a narrower definition: the market for, say, entry-level investment research analysts in the United States. In this market, the sellers would be all qualified individuals (those with bachelors' degrees in economics or business) who want to do this type of work, and the buyers would be all the securities firms, banks, and other financial institutions that hire them. Or, we could go even narrower, and ask why the wages of entry-level investment analysts are higher in New York City than elsewhere in the country. Here, the buyers and sellers would be limited to those who are qualified and who live in the New York area, or those who could move there within the period we are considering. In this chapter, since we'll be asking different types of questions about labor markets, we'll need to look at both broadly and narrowly defined markets.

Competitive Labor Markets

Perfectly competitive labor market Market with many indistinguishable sellers of labor and many buyers, and with easy entry and exit of workers.

In most of this chapter, we'll be viewing both product and labor markets are *perfectly competitive.* So let's begin by defining perfect competition in a labor market.

> *A perfectly competitive labor market has the following three characteristics:*
> 1. *There are large numbers of buyers (firms) and sellers (households), and each individual firm or household is only a tiny part of the labor market.*
> 2. *All workers in the labor market appear the same to firms.*
> 3. *Workers can easily enter into or exit from the labor market.*

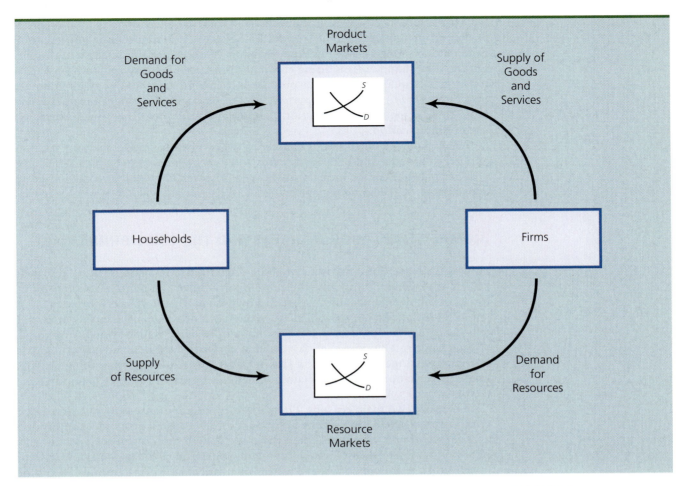

FIGURE 1
Product Markets and Resource Markets

In product markets, households demand goods and services, and firms supply them. In resource markets, the roles are reversed: Firms demand resources—such as labor, capital, land, or entrepreneurship. Households supply them.

Do these conditions sound familiar? They should, since they are almost identical to the features of perfect competition in a product market (Chapter 7). The only difference is that here it is labor, rather than a good or service, that is being traded.

Very few labor markets *strictly* satisfy all three of these requirements. But many markets come close enough to make the perfectly competitive model a useful approximation. The more closely a particular labor market satisfies the conditions, the more accurate our analysis will be.

For example, consider the requirement that all workers are the same. We know that no two workers are ever precisely the same, just as no two pocket PCs made by different companies are identical. But in Chapter 3, when we wanted to explain price changes for pocket PCs in general, we ignored the difference between one brand and another and assumed that consumers viewed pocket PCs as a standardized product. Similarly, when we want to explain changes in the wage rate for large groups of workers, it will often make sense to ignore the differences among workers, and assume that employers view all workers in a labor market as essentially the same.

This assumption will be more realistic in some labor markets than in others. A farmer hiring apple pickers may indeed make few distinctions among different job candidates, as long as they meet the minimum requirements for strength and agility. On the other hand, a firm hiring computer programmers may be acutely aware of differences in quality. Still, if our purpose is to analyze changes in pay for computer programmers *in general* (rather than why some computer programmers are paid more than others), our assumption that all workers appear the same to firms is a useful simplification.

We will devote much of this chapter to the competitive model, because it can be applied so broadly and because it serves as a benchmark against which other types of labor markets can be measured. We will, however, also look at some important departures from perfect competition.

COMPETITIVE LABOR MARKETS AND THE EQUILIBRIUM WAGE

How is the wage rate—the price of labor—determined in a competitive labor market? It is determined just like the price in any other competitive market: by the forces of supply and demand. Figure 2 shows the market for factory workers in Orlando, Florida. The curve labeled L^D is the labor demand curve in this market. It tells us the number of factory workers that all firms in Orlando would want to hire at each wage rate. Notice that this demand curve, like the demand curve in any labor market, slopes downward: a rise in the wage rate—with everything else that might affect labor demand remaining unchanged—causes firms to employ fewer factory workers. Why is this?

There are two main reasons. First, a rise in the wage raises any one firm's *marginal costs* of production. (Why marginal cost? Because it costs more to produce an *additional* unit of output when the wage is high than when the wage is low.) But—as you'll be asked to show in an end-of-chapter problem—an upward shift in the firm's marginal cost curve causes its profit-maximizing output level to decrease. As output decreases, so does the number of workers the firm needs for production. For example, if the going wage for factory workers were to rise, then a shirt factory in Orlando would decide to produce fewer shirts and need fewer workers. The same would happen at other factories in Orlando: Higher wages would lead to higher marginal costs, lower output, and a decrease in the quantity of labor demanded.

Second, a rise in the wage of factory workers would cause the price of this input to rise *relative to other inputs*. Firms may then wish to substitute the other inputs (whose prices have *not* risen) for factory workers (whose price *has* risen). For example, a shirt factory might purchase computer-controlled sewing machines. In this way, they would be substituting capital (the new sewing machines) and other types of labor (computer programmers and operators) for factory workers.

> *The labor demand curve in any labor market slopes downward because a rise in the wage rate (1) increases firms' costs, causing them to decrease production and employ fewer workers; and (2) increases the relative cost of labor from that market, causing firms to substitute other inputs, such as capital or other types of labor.*

Now let's switch gears, and look at the curve labeled L^S—the labor supply curve. It slopes *upward*, telling us that as the wage rate rises, more people will offer to sell their labor in this market. Why does a rise in the wage rate increase labor supply? After all, won't people who need jobs want to work at virtually *any wage rate*? So at higher wage rates, won't the same number of people offer to sell their labor as at lower wage rates?

The answer to this last question is no. First, it is *not* true that everyone who might offer to sell their labor would do so at any wage. Many people choose not to work at low wages, but might be induced to work if the wage were high enough. Students, the retired and those currently supporting themselves with past savings are just three examples. Think about yourself. If you are not currently working, isn't there *some* hypothetical wage that would make you quit college and seek work immediately? And if you *are* currently working, can you imagine a wage that is so low that you would decide to quit? Now, realize that millions of others have similar criteria for working: there is some critical wage rate beyond which they would choose to work, and below which they would *not* want to work. As the wage rate rises, it reaches more and more individuals' critical wage rate, and so more and more people decide to offer their labor services for sale.

There is a second reason that an increase in the wage rate causes an increase in the quantity of labor supplied to a market. As the wage rate rises, some people will *switch into* the now, more lucrative labor market from other labor markets. For example, a rise in factory wage rates in Orlando would attract factory workers from other areas, such as Miami. It might also induce other workers in Orlando—cab drivers, store clerks, and waiters—to switch to factory work.

The labor supply curve in any labor market slopes upward because a rise in the wage rate (1) induces some of those not currently working to seek work; and (2) attracts some of those who are currently working in other labor markets.

Now let's return to the question that brought us to Figure 2 in the first place: How is the wage rate determined in a competitive labor market? As you have no

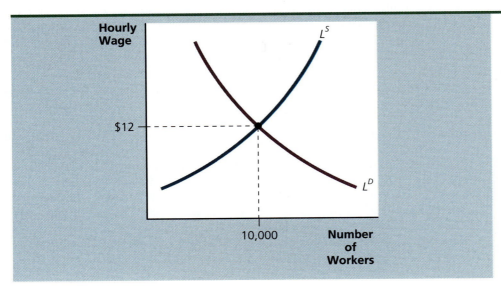

FIGURE 2
A Competitive Labor Market

The diagram shows the labor market for factory workers in Orlando, Florida. The demand for labor curve (L^D) slopes downward, and the supply of labor curve (L^S) slopes upward. The intersection of the two curves determines the equilibrium wage ($12), and the equilibrium number of factory workers is 10,000.

doubt guessed by now: the equilibrium wage will be determined by the intersection of the labor supply curve (L^S) and the labor demand curve (L^D). At any other wage rate, there would be either an excess demand for labor or an excess supply of labor, forcing the wage rate to move to its equilibrium value. In Figure 2, the equilibrium wage is $12 per hour. At this wage, firms will want to hire 10,000 factory workers—the same number of people who want jobs as factory workers. Thus, the equilibrium level of employment is 10,000.

Markets and Equilibrium

> *The forces of supply and demand will drive a competitive labor market to its equilibrium point—the point where the labor supply and labor demand curves intersect.*

WHY DO WAGES DIFFER?

Consider Table 1, which shows hourly earnings in 2001 for full-time workers in selected occupations. Each row of the table lists not only the median wage rate (in bold) for an occupation, but also the wage rate at each percentile. For example, the first row shows that 10 percent of full-time physicians earned $18.56 per hour or less, while 90 percent earned $129.48 or less (so the top 10 percent earned $129.48 or more). And the bolded middle column tells us that in 2001, half of physicians earned less than $62.50 per hour while the other half earned more.

Note the significant inequality in wage rates among *different* occupations. These sharp differences occur even for jobs in the same industry, in which the work is often similar. Compare, for example, the median hourly wage rate of a business professor ($40.85) and a political science professor ($26.04), or that of a physician ($62.50) and a registered nurse ($21.06).

But you can also see sharp differences in earnings *within* many occupations. For physicians, the wage rate at the 90th percentile is six or seven times higher than at the 10th. Even in the lowest-paying occupations, wage rates at the 90th percentile can be two or three times greater than those at the 10th.

The table tells us that there is substantial wage inequality among and within occupations in the U.S. labor market. Moreover, wage inequality is *persistent*. Both the highest-paid and lowest-paid occupations have been so for decades, and the highest-paid workers within each occupation have consistently earned substantially more than the lowest.

Moreover, Table 1—and the Bureau of Labor Statistics data on which it is based—underestimates the full extent of wage inequality in the U.S. labor market. It does not include bonuses, fringe benefits, or other additional labor earnings that are substantially greater for the highest-paying occupations and the highest-paid workers within each job. It also leaves out those at the very top—such as chief executive officers of top corporations, sports celebrities, and movie stars. For example, Eddie Murphy's wage rate on most films is between $10,000 and $20,000 per hour, and—if the quote at the beginning of this chapter is accurate—he earned an astounding $550,000 per hour on *Shrek 2*. Baseball star Alex Rodriguez earns $50,000 each time he steps to the plate.

How can an hour of human labor have such different values in the market?

Occupation	10th Percentile	25th Percentile	Median (50th Percentile)	75th Percentile	90th Percentile
Physicians	$18.56	$36.06	**$62.50**	$102.55	$129.48
Business and Marketing Teachers (College and University)	$21.36	$25.29	**$40.85**	$ 59.81	$ 74.53
Marketing, Advertising, and Public Relations Managers	$19.23	$24.40	**$36.29**	$ 46.18	$ 57.69
Computer Systems Analysts	$20.16	$24.69	**$30.04**	$ 35.91	$ 42.66
Political Science Teachers (College and University)	$20.56	$23.22	**$26.04**	—	$ 38.38
Elevator Installers and Repairers	$21.48	$22.10	**$24.86**	$ 31.76	—
Registered Nurses	$16.82	$18.51	**$21.06**	$ 25.06	$ 29.61
Elementary School Teachers	$12.75	$15.16	**$18.83**	$ 22.02	$ 28.61
Lathe and Turning Machine Operators	$10.50	$12.25	**$14.38**	$ 17.68	$ 22.00
Cabinetmakers	$ 7.50	$ 9.31	**$13.51**	$ 15.00	$ 20.00
Bank Tellers	$ 7.65	$ 8.78	**$ 9.65**	$ 11.14	$ 12.20
Apparel Sales Workers	$ 6.85	$ 7.62	**$ 8.77**	$ 10.40	$ 21.63
Kitchen Workers, Food Preparation	$ 5.86	$ 6.65	**$ 7.97**	$ 9.33	$ 10.65
Cashiers	$ 5.98	$ 6.29	**$ 7.27**	$ 8.50	$ 11.00

Source: Selected data from *National Compensation Survey: Occupational Wages in the United States, January 2001,* (Supplemental Tables), Bureau of Labor Statistics, released January 2003. The BLS data is based on surveys of about 18,000 business establishments employing about 86 million workers.

TABLE 1
Hourly Earnings of Full-time Workers in Selected Occupations, 2001

An Imaginary World

To understand why wages differ in the real world, let's start by imagining an *unreal* world, with three features:

1. Except for differences in wages, all jobs are equally attractive to all workers.
2. All workers are equally able to do any job.
3. All labor markets are perfectly competitive.

In such a world, we would expect every worker to earn an identical wage in the long run. Let's see why.

Figure 3 shows two different labor markets that initially have different wage rates. Panel (a) shows a local market for elementary school teachers, with an initial equilibrium at point *A* and a wage of $20 per hour. Panel (b) shows the market for computer systems analysts, who, at point *B*, earn $30 per hour. In our imaginary world, could this diagram describe the *long-run* equilibrium in these markets? Absolutely not.

Imagine that you are an elementary school teacher. By our first assumption, you would find being a systems analyst just as attractive as teaching school. But since systems analysts earn more, you would prefer to be one. By our second assumption, you are *qualified* to be a systems analyst, and by our third assumption, there are no barriers to prevent you from becoming one. Thus, you—and many of your fellow

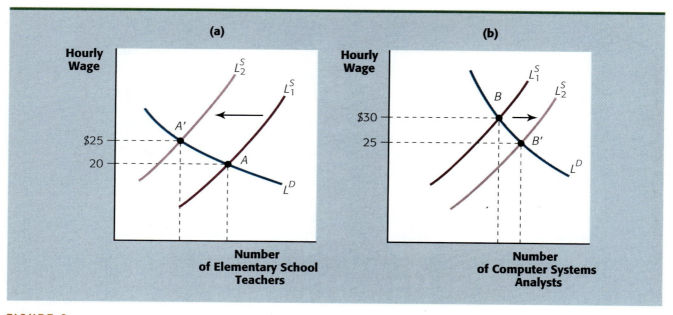

FIGURE 3
Disappearing Wage Differentials

Initially, the supply and demand for elementary school teachers in panel (a) determine an equilibrium wage of $20 per hour— at point A. In panel (b), the equilibrium wage for systems analysts is initially $30 per hour. If these markets are competitive, if the two jobs are equally attractive, and if all workers are equally able to do both jobs, this wage differential cannot persist. Some elementary school teachers give up that occupation, reducing supply in panel (a), and become systems analysts, increasing supply in panel (b). This migration will continue until the wage in both markets is $25.

teachers—will begin looking for jobs as systems analysts. In panel (a) the labor supply curve will shift leftward (exit from the market for elementary school teachers), and in panel (b) the labor supply curve will shift rightward (entry into the market for systems analysts). As these shifts occur, the market wage rate of elementary school teachers will rise and that of systems analysts will fall.

When will the entry and exit stop? When there is no longer any reason for an elementary school teacher to want to be a systems analyst—that is, when both labor markets are paying the same wage rate ($25 in our example). In the long run, the market for elementary school teachers reaches equilibrium at point A' and the market for systems analysts at point B'.

Note that these long-run adjustments will occur even if no one actually *switches* jobs. If systems analysts are paid more, then *new* entrants into the labor force— choosing their occupation for the first time—will pick that job over elementary school teaching. As more schoolteachers retire than enter the profession, their number will shrink. Meanwhile, more systems analysts enter the profession than retire, so their number will grow. These changes will continue until, at points A' and B', the long-run wage rate is equal in both markets.

Our conclusion about elementary school teachers and computer systems analysts would apply to *any* pair of labor markets we might choose. In our imaginary world, bank tellers and physicians, kitchen workers and nurses—all would earn the same wage. In this world, different labor markets are like water in the same pool: If the level rises at one end, water will flow into the other end until the level is the same everywhere. In the same way, workers will flow into labor markets with higher wages, evening out the wages in different jobs . . . *if* our three critical assumptions are satisfied.

But take any one of these assumptions away, and the equal-wage result disappears. This tells us where to look for the sources of wage inequality in the real world: a *violation* of one or more of our three assumptions.

Compensating Differentials

In our imaginary world, all jobs were equally attractive to all workers. But in the real world, jobs differ in hundreds of ways that matter to workers. When one job is intrinsically more or less attractive than another, we can expect their wages to differ by a *compensating wage differential:*

> *A* ***compensating wage differential*** *is the difference in wage rates that makes two jobs equally attractive to workers.*

To see how compensating wage differentials come about, let's consider some of the important ways in which jobs can differ.

Nonmonetary Job Characteristics. Suppose you clean offices inside a skyscraper, and you find you could earn $1 more per hour washing the building's windows . . . from the *outside*. Would you "flow" to the window washer's labor market, like water in a pool? Probably not. The higher risk of death just wouldn't be worth it.

Danger is an example of a **nonmonetary job characteristic.** It is an aspect of a job—good or bad—that is not easily measured in dollars. When you think about a career, whether you are aware of it or not, you are evaluating hundreds of nonmonetary job characteristics: the risk of death or injury, the cleanliness of the work environment, the prestige you can expect in your community, the amount of physical exertion required, the degree of intellectual stimulation, the potential for advancement . . . the list goes on and on. You will also think about the geographic location of the job and the characteristics of the community in which you would live and work: weather, crime rates, pollution levels, the transportation system, cultural amenities, and so on.

What does all this suggest about differing wages in the long run? Remember that in long-run equilibrium, all adjustments that might affect wage rates have already occurred. This, in turn, requires that people have no incentive to leave one labor market and enter another, for such changes would shift labor supply curves and change the wage in each market. But workers will be satisfied to stay in a job they consider less desirable only if it pays a compensating wage differential. The compensating differential will be just enough to keep workers from migrating from one labor market to another.

Let's see how compensating differentials figure into our example of elementary school teachers and computer systems analysts. Look back at Figure 3. Earlier, we saw that if both jobs were equally attractive, both would pay the same wage rate in the long run. But now let's make an extreme assumption: that everyone in the population has the same tastes for different occupations, and they all prefer the human interaction of school teaching to the abstraction of working with computer systems. Further, suppose it takes a wage differential of $10 in favor of computers to make the two jobs equally attractive. Then the long-run equilibrium would remain at the initial points *A* and *B*, with systems analysts earning a compensating wage differential of $10 per hour to make up for the less desirable features of their job. Even with the higher wage rate for systems analysts, there would be no shift of elementary school teachers to the systems analyst market.

> *The nonmonetary characteristics of different jobs give rise to compensating wage differentials. Jobs considered intrinsically less attractive will tend to pay higher wages, other things being equal.*

Compensating wage differential
A difference in wages that makes two jobs equally attractive to a worker.

Nonmonetary job characteristic
Any aspect of a job—other than the wage—that matters to a potential or current employee.

 Markets and Equilibrium

What about unusually *attractive* jobs? These jobs will generally pay *negative* compensating differentials. For example, many new college graduates are attracted to careers in the arts or the media. Since entry-level jobs in these industries are so desirable for nonmonetary reasons, they tend, on average, to pay lower wages than similar jobs in other industries. For the same reason, people will accept lower wages when a job offers a high probability of advancement and a higher salary in the future. It comes as no surprise, then, that management trainees at large corporations are often paid relatively low salaries.

Of course, different people have different tastes for working and living conditions. While some prefer a quiet, laid-back work environment like a library or laboratory, others like the commotion of a loading dock or a trading floor. While most people are extremely averse to risking their lives, some actually prefer to live dangerously, as in police work or rescue operations. Therefore, we cannot use our own preferences to declare a job as less attractive or more attractive, or to decide which jobs should pay a positive or negative compensating differential. Rather, when labor markets are perfectly competitive, the entry and exit of workers automatically determines the compensating wage differential in each labor market.

Compensating wage differentials are one reason most economists are skeptical about the idea of *comparable worth*, which holds that a government agency should determine the skills required to perform different jobs and mandate the wage differences needed between them. Although this policy could correct some inequities when labor markets are imperfectly competitive, it could also introduce serious inequities of its own, since no one can know how different workers would value the hundreds of characteristics of each job. Economists generally prefer policies to increase competition and eliminate discrimination, so that the market itself can determine comparable worth.

A Digression: It Pays to Be Unusual. One implication of compensating wage differentials is that workers with unusual tastes often have a monetary advantage in the labor market. For example, only a small fraction of workers *like* dangerous jobs, such as police work. As long as the labor market is competitive, and there is relatively high demand for workers in dangerous jobs, police officers will earn more than those in other, similar jobs that have a lower risk of death or injury. But if you are one of those unusual people who *like* danger, you will earn the same compensating wage differential as all other police officers, even though you would have chosen to be a police officer anyway.

Similarly, if you like the frigid winter weather in Alaska, if you like washing windows on the 90th floor, or if you think it would be fun to defend the cigarette industry in the media, you can earn a higher wage by putting your somewhat unusual tastes to work.

Cost-of-Living Differences. Many people would find living in Cleveland and living in Philadelphia about equally attractive. Yet wages in Philadelphia are about 10 percent higher than in Cleveland. Why? One major reason is that prices in Philadelphia are about 10 percent higher than in Cleveland. If wages were equal in the two cities, many people deciding where to live would prefer Cleveland, where their earnings would have greater purchasing power. The supply of labor in Philadelphia's labor markets would shrink, increasing the wage there, while the supply in Cleveland's labor markets would rise, driving down the wage in Cleveland. In the end, the wage difference would be sufficient to compensate Philadelphians for the higher cost of living in their city.

Differences in living costs can cause compensating wage differentials. Areas where living costs are higher than average will tend to have higher-than-average wages.

Difference in Human Capital Requirements. All else equal, jobs that require more education and training will be less attractive. In order to attract workers, these jobs must offer higher pay than other jobs that are similar in other ways, but require less training.

Let's go back to Figure 3, but this time imagine that we're comparing the market for elementary school teachers in the left panel with the market for *physicians* in the right panel, with an initial equilibrium wage of $62.50. Would we expect labor supply curves in these two markets to shift until wage rates were equal for both? No, because physicians must complete an additional three years of medical school after college, plus a residency and sometimes further training. If these jobs were equally attractive in all other ways, then the point at which the labor supply curves would stop shifting would leave physicians earning substantially more to compensate for the higher costs (such as tuition and foregone income) of becoming a doctor.

Differences in human capital requirements can give rise to compensating wage differentials. Jobs that require more costly training will tend to pay higher wages, other things equal.

Compensating differentials explain much of the wage differential between jobs requiring college degrees and those that require only a high school diploma. In early 2003, the median hourly wage rate of college graduates was $22.57 per hour, but for high school graduates, only $13.72.[2] The especially high earnings of doctors, attorneys, research scientists and college professors reflect—at least in part—compensating differentials for the high human capital requirements—and human capital costs—of entering their professions.

The idea of compensating wage differentials dates back to Adam Smith, who first observed that unpleasant jobs seem to pay more than other jobs that require similar skills and qualifications. It is a powerful concept, and it can explain many of the differences we observe in wages . . . but not all of them.

Differences in Ability

In December 2000, at the age of 26, Alex Rodriguez signed a 10-year contract to play baseball for the Texas Rangers at an average salary of $25 million per year. Was this salary so high because of a compensating differential for the unpleasantness of playing professional baseball? Or was there an unusually high risk of death on this job? Was the cost of living in Dallas hundreds of times greater than in other cities? Had Rodriguez, at the age of 26, spent more years honing his skills than the average attorney, doctor, architect, or engineer—or even more than the average baseball player?

[2] "Usual Weekly Earnings of Wage and Salary Workers: First Quarter 2003," *Bureau of Labor Statistics News,* April 17, 2003.

The answer to all of these questions is no. We have overlooked the obvious explanation: Rodriguez is an *outstanding* baseball player, better than 99.999 percent of the population could ever hope to be with *any* amount of practice. This is partly because of his *endowments*—the valuable characteristics he possesses due to birth or childhood experiences but that did not require any opportunity cost on his part. In Rodriguez's case, these would include his natural speed, agility, and coordination. Of course, Rodriguez also had the skill and perseverance to exploit his talent. Together, his endowments of talent and his work at exploiting them have made Rodriguez an outstanding athlete.

While Alex Rodriguez may be an extreme case, the principle applies across the board. Not everyone has the intelligence needed to be a research scientist, the steady hand to be a neurosurgeon, the quick-thinking ability to be a commodities trader, the well-organized mind to be a business manager, or the talent to be an artist or a ballet dancer. This violates our imaginary-world principle that all workers have equal ability to do any job—or at least equal ability to acquire the skills needed. And that explains much of the wage inequality we observe in the real world.

We can understand this in terms of Figure 3 of this chapter. A wage differential between two otherwise equal jobs could persist if those working for lower wages (point *A* in panel (a)) cannot enter the high-wage market (point *B* in panel (b)) because—regardless of how much human capital they acquire—they can never perform well enough.

Wage rate inequality, and income inequality more generally, increased during the 1990s and early 2000s. Part of the reason may be that differences in abilities have become more important in the labor market. Scientific discoveries and technological advances have increased the skill requirements of many jobs, and the abilities needed to *acquire* those skills. For example, it takes more ability to learn to repair an automatic elevator than to learn how to operate a manual elevator. If significant numbers of workers are unable to master the skills needed for higher-paying jobs, then movement from one labor market to another may be stopped short. This would result in a persistent—and increasing—wage differential between high-skilled and low-skilled workers.

Our discussion so far, centering on Figure 3, explains wage differences *between* occupations. But that is only part of the story. Substantial pay differences also exist *within* each occupation, as you can see by the wage rates at different percentiles in Table 1. Here, too, ability plays an important role. In any job, workers' talents, intelligence, and physical abilities—and their value to firms—vary considerably. For example, suppose two advertising account managers have equal education and training, but manager A, being more talented, can design better ad campaigns and attract twice as many high-paying clients than can manager B. Then, in an otherwise competitive labor market, a firm will be willing to pay manager A twice as much as manager B.

> *In general, those with greater ability to do a job well—based on their talent, intelligence, motivation, or perseverance—will be more valuable to firms. As a result, firms will be willing to pay them a higher wage rate, beyond any compensating differential for their human capital investment.*

Differences in ability also help explain why workers' pay tends to rise with age and experience on the job. Experience not only adds to a worker's human capital, but also provides a signal of ability to employers. Hiring a new, untested worker—

even one who seems to have great talent—is always a bit risky, since the worker's ability hasn't yet been proven. By contrast, hiring or continuing to employ someone with a history of advancement and accomplishments reduces this risk. All else equal, firms will typically pay more for a worker with a proven track record. Not surprisingly, when wage rates within an occupation are broken down by age (not shown in the table), those who are older—and have been in their occupation longer—dominate the higher percentiles, while younger and newer entrants are more prevalent in the lower percentiles.

The Economics of Superstars. Why was the owner of the Texas Rangers willing to pay $25 million per year to have Alex Rodriguez play for his team? The immediate answer is: because he is so *good*. Alex Rodriguez is an example of a *superstar*—an individual widely viewed as among the top few in their professions. In recent years, superstars have included actors such as Mel Gibson, Eddie Murphy, and Julia Roberts; talk show hosts Jay Leno and David Letterman; news announcers Dan Rather and Peter Jennings; novelists Stephen King and J. K. Rowling; and film director Stephen Spielberg.

But when we try to explain the extremely high wage rates of these superstars based on their exceptional abilities alone, we confront a puzzle. Clearly Alex Rodriguez has more athletic ability, and more skill in honing it, than almost anyone in the population, including other major-league baseball players. But can this explain a salary that is *25 times* that of the median major-league player? By any measure, is Rodriguez *25 times better*?

Or consider other superstars. ABC news anchor Peter Jennings may deliver the evening news better than most local news anchors. But is he "better enough" to justify a salary estimated to be 100 times higher?[3] And most would agree that Eddie Murphy's voice work for *Shrek 2* was better than, say, the voiceovers on the Saturday morning cartoon shows. But Murphy's hourly pay was about 3,000 times greater than that of the typical cartoon voice actor.[4] Is he *that much better*? Huge wage rate differentials like this are seen in many professions, especially those involving the media. The very top writers, rock stars, comedians, talk show hosts, and movie directors all earn wage premiums that seem vastly out of proportion to their additional abilities. Why?

The explanation in all these cases *is* based on ability—and also the exaggerated rewards the market bestows on those deemed the best or one of the best in a field.[5] Say you like to read one mystery novel a month for entertainment. If you can choose between the best novel published that month or one that is almost—but not quite— as good, you will naturally choose the one you think is best. Only people who read *two* novels each month would choose the best *and* the second best, and only those

© MITCHELL GERBER/CORBIS

Although Eddie Murphy's acting talent may not be a thousand times better than the average, he earns more than a thousand times the average actor's salary because he is at the top of his profession.

---

[3] According to the BLS, the average news anchor earns $83,400 (Bureau of Labor Statistics, U.S. Department of Labor, *Occupational Outlook Handbook, 2002–03 Edition, News Analysts, Reporters, and Correspondents*, on the Internet at *http://www.bls.gov/oco/ocos088.htm*). Peter Jennings's salary is typically reported at $10 million. (See, for example, "Jennings Signs ABC Contract," *Online News Hour*, Public Broadcasting Service, November 18, 2002 (*http://www.pbs.org/newshour/media/media_watch/july-dec02/jennings_11-18-02.html*). Both sites visited July 03, 2003.

[4] Voice actors on Saturday morning cartoons are paid $636 for a four-hour session (not counting time spent rehearsing and auditioning). Patrick Goldstein, "The Big Picture: A Voice Actor Speaks for Herself," *Los Angeles Times*, December 18, 2001.

[5] See, for example, Robert H. Frank and Philip J. Cook, *The Winner Take All Society* (New York: The Free Press, 1995).

who read three will choose the top three. If most people rank recent mystery novels in the same order, then the best will sell millions of copies, the second best might sell hundreds of thousands, and the third best might sell only thousands. Even though all three novels might be very close in quality, a publisher will earn *10 times* more revenue selling the best novel (compared to the second best), and 10 times more revenue selling the second best (compared to the third best), and so on. Accordingly, a publisher will be willing to pay the same multiples in advances and royalties when bidding for contracts with mystery novelists of different rankings. Even if the top author is viewed as only *slightly* better than the next one down, as long as the vast majority of readers agree on the ranking, she can end up earning 10 times as much.

The same thing happens in markets for athletes, rock concerts, action movies, and news broadcasts. In all these cases, where the service is sold to millions of people and where there is wide agreement about who are the top few superstars, the differences in rewards can be vastly disproportionate to differences in ability. The owner of the Texas Rangers was willing to pay Alex Rodriguez $25 million each year because he believed that Rodriguez, as a superstar, would bring in *at least* that much additional revenue each year—from ticket sales, skybox rentals, TV and radio broadcasting fees, concession sales, parking fees, and more.

But the phenomenon is not limited to media markets or media stars. Suppose you are wealthy and you need a heart transplant. How much more would you be willing to pay to have one of the top 10 surgeons perform your operation, compared to one ranked in the *next* 10?

Barriers to Entry

In our imaginary world, there were no barriers to entering any trade or profession. The absence of barriers is an important element of our assumption that the labor market is competitive. But in some labor markets, barriers keep out would-be entrants, resulting in higher wages in those markets.

In Figure 3 we saw that if systems analysts were paid higher wages than elementary school teachers, entry into the market for systems analysts would help equalize wages in the two jobs. But what if systems analysts were *protected* from competition by a barrier to entry, one that kept newcomers from becoming systems analysts? Then the labor supply curve in panel (b) would *not* shift rightward, and the higher wage for systems analysts could persist. Going back to the analogy of water flowing to equalize the water level at both ends of a pool, a barrier to entry is like a wall in the middle of the pool. It blocks the flow, allowing one end to have a higher water level than the other.

Since barriers to entry help maintain high wages for those protected by the barriers (those who already have jobs in the protected market), we should not be surprised to find that in almost all cases, it is those already employed who are responsible for erecting the barriers. But it is not enough to simply put up a sign, "Newcomers, stay out!" The pull of higher wages is a powerful force, and preventing entry requires a force at least as powerful. What keeps newcomers out of a market, thus maintaining a higher-than-competitive wage for those already working there?

Occupational Licensing. In many labor markets, occupational licensing laws keep out potential entrants. Highly paid professionals such as doctors, lawyers, and dentists, as well as those who practice a trade, like barbers, beauticians, and plumbers, cannot legally sell their services without first obtaining a license. In many states you cannot even sell the service of braiding hair without a license. In order to get the license, you must complete a long course in cosmetology and pass an exam.

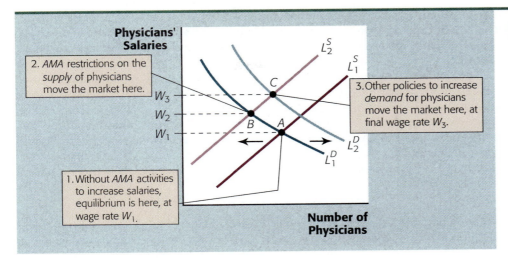

FIGURE 4
The Market for Physicians

Physicians' Salaries

2. *AMA* restrictions on the *supply* of physicians move the market here.

3. Other policies to increase *demand* for physicians move the market here, at final wage rate W_3.

1. Without *AMA* activities to increase salaries, equilibrium is here, at wage rate W_1.

Number of Physicians

The American Medical Association (AMA)—a professional organization to which almost half of American physicians belong—is perhaps the strongest example of occupational licensing as a barrier to entry. The AMA portrays itself as a vigilant defender of high standards in health care, through its regulation of medical schools, its certification of specialists, and its government lobbying. Economists tend to have a much different view of the AMA. While not denying that the AMA's efforts do raise the quality of physicians, they see it primarily as an instrument to maintain high incomes for doctors.

Figure 4 shows the market for physicians in the United States. In the absence of any income-raising activity, labor supply curve L_1^S would intersect labor demand curve L_1^D at point *A*, resulting in equilibrium wage W_1. Whether this wage would be relatively high or low is not known; since 1847, when the AMA was founded, this competitive equilibrium has never been attained.

Much of the AMA's activity has been designed to decrease the *supply* of doctors. Immediately after its founding, it imposed strict licensing procedures that increased entry costs for *new* doctors; existing practitioners were exempted from the new requirements. In spite of these restrictions, there was a rapid increase in the number of physicians toward the end of the century. In response, between 1900 and 1920, the AMA closed down almost half of the nation's medical schools.[6] These and other efforts to restrict the supply of doctors have resulted in a supply curve for physicians like L_2^S, lying to the left of L_1^S, moving the equilibrium to point *B*, and raising salaries to W_2.

But this is not the end of the story. The AMA has also increased the *demand* for physicians' services by preventing nonphysicians from competing. Throughout its history, the association has moved aggressively to limit competition from midwives, chiropractors, homeopathists, and other health professionals. By limiting access to these alternative health professionals, the AMA increases the demand for the services of its own members. The impact of these policies has been a rightward shift in the demand curve for doctors, to L_2^D, moving the equilibrium to a point like *C* and raising salaries further, to W_3.

(If you think maintaining high standards is the main motivation for these policies, consider this: AMA policy allows a physician to practice in *any* area of medicine, even

---

[6] "Doctors Operate to Cut Out Competition," *Business and Society Review*, Summer, 1986, pp. 4–9.

one in which he has no specialized training. For example, a dermatologist with no training or experience in obstetrics can legally deliver a baby; a midwife with extensive experience might be arrested if she delivers a baby without the supervision of an M.D.)

In the late 1980s, rising health care costs led to increased public scrutiny of the AMA, and its anticompetitive practices came under heavy attack. Some restrictions were eased, and the number of doctors per 100,000 people increased from 169 in 1975 to 233 in 1990. At the same time, the Federal Trade Commission and the courts pressured the AMA to remove its ban on physician advertising. For the first time, new entrants could compete with established practices by advertising their prices and services. Not surprisingly, many physicians began to complain about falling incomes.

Union Wage Setting. A labor union represents the collective interests of its members. Unions have many functions, including pressing for better and safer working conditions, operating apprenticeship programs, and administering pension programs. But a major objective of a union is to raise its members' pay. Federal law prohibits a union from creating an overt barrier to entry; it is illegal for a firm to agree to hire only union members. Instead, the union negotiates a higher-than-competitive wage with the firm. But at a higher wage, the firm will employ fewer workers. Thus, many potential workers are kept out of union jobs because the firm will not hire them at the union wage.

The higher union wage is contrary to the interests of the employer, so why does the employer agree? Because the union has the power to strike. During a strike—when the firm's workers refuse to come to work—the firm suffers a loss. Rather than take the risk of a strike, employers will often agree to the higher wage demanded by the union.

Figure 5 illustrates how unions can create wage differences. We assume that jobs in two industries—long-haul trucking and short-haul trucking—are equally attractive in all respects other than the wage rate. With no labor union, these two markets would reach equilibrium at points A and B, respectively, where both pay the same wage, W_1.

Now suppose instead that long-haul truckers are organized into a union, which has negotiated a higher wage, W_2, with employers. At this wage, employment of long-haul truckers drops from 300,000 to 250,000, while the number who would like to work in this market rises to 350,000. Now there is an excess supply of long-haul truckers equal to $350,000 - 250,000 = 100,000$. Ordinarily, we would expect an excess supply of labor to force the wage down, but the union wage agreement prevents this. With fewer jobs available in the unionized sector, some former long-haul truckers will look for work as *nonunion*, short-haul truckers. Thus, in panel (b), the labor supply curve shifts rightward. In equilibrium, the number of short-haul truckers rises from 200,000 to 225,000, and the wage of short-haul truckers drops to W_3. The end result is a union–nonunion wage differential of $W_2 - W_3$. Notice that only *part* of the differential ($W_2 - W_1$) represents an increase in union wages; the other part ($W_1 - W_3$) comes from a decrease in *nonunion* wages.

Markets and Equilibrium

> *In a competitive labor market, a union—by raising the wage firms must pay—decreases total employment in the union sector. This, in turn, causes wages in the nonunion sector to drop. The combined result is a wage differential between union and nonunion wages.*

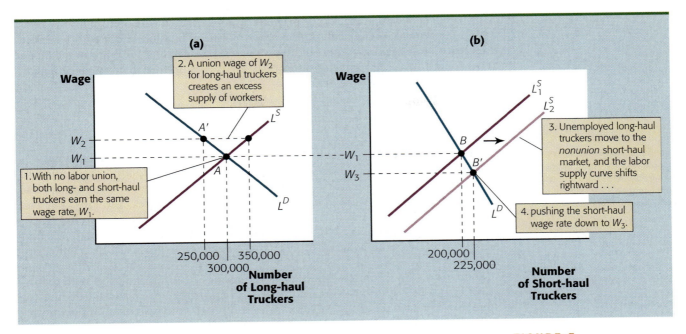

(a)

Wage

2. A union wage of W_2 for long-haul truckers creates an excess supply of workers.

L^S

A'

W_2

W_1

A

1. With no labor union, both long- and short-haul truckers earn the same wage rate, W_1.

L^D

250,000 | 350,000
300,000

Number of Long-haul Truckers

(b)

Wage

L_1^S

L_2^S

B

W_1

B'

W_3

3. Unemployed long-haul truckers move to the *nonunion* short-haul market, and the labor supply curve shifts rightward . . .

L^D

4. pushing the short-haul wage rate down to W_3.

200,000
225,000

Number of Short-haul Truckers

FIGURE 5
Union Wage Differentials

In the end, how big is the union–nonunion wage differential? H. Gregg Lewis[7] reviewed more than 200 studies that asked precisely this question and determined that between 1967 and 1979, union members earned, on average, about 15 percent more than otherwise similar nonunion workers.

Given the conflict that has surrounded many union–management wage negotiations, and the media attention devoted to them, this difference may seem rather small. But keep in mind that a 15 percent differential—about $2.30 per hour at today's average wage rate for hourly production workers—would amount to $4,700 per year, continuing year after year. After 40 years on the job, the average union member would earn about $188,000 more than the average nonunion member, enough to put a down payment on a house *and* put a child through college with no student loans. And if each year's differential were put in the bank at 5 percent interest, it would amount to about $600,000 after 40 years. So a 15 percent wage differential is nothing to sneeze at.

The differential has most likely declined since 1979, however, as unions' bargaining power has weakened. This is partly reflected in a decline in union membership: In the mid-1950s, 25 percent of the U.S. labor force was unionized; today, only about 13 percent of the labor force are union members. Nevertheless, unions still maintain a significant (though declining) presence in many industries, such as automobiles, steel, coal, construction, mining, and trucking, and they are certainly responsible for at least *some* of the higher wages earned in those industries.

Of course, we're viewing unions here from one perspective only: to explain how wage differences can arise. The full effect of unions on labor markets is much more complex. For example, many of the features of modern work that we take for granted today—such as paid vacations and overtime pay—originated in union struggles with management.

[7] H. G. Lewis, *Union Relative Wage Effects: A Survey* (Chicago: University of Chicago Press, 1986).

Moreover, through grievance procedures and other forms of communications with management, unions can raise worker morale and reduce labor turnover. And if higher morale makes workers more productive, the demand for labor in the union sector could increase, reducing (and possibly reversing) the drop in employment caused by the higher wage.

DISCRIMINATION AND WAGES

Discrimination When a group of people have different opportunities because of personal characteristics that have nothing to do with their abilities.

Discrimination occurs when *the members of a group of people have different opportunities because of characteristics that have nothing to do with their abilities.* Throughout American history, discrimination against women and minorities has been widespread in housing, business loans, consumer services, and jobs. The last arena—jobs—is our focus here. While tough laws and government incentive programs have lessened overt job discrimination—such as the help wanted ads that asked for white males as late as the 1950s—less obvious forms of discrimination remain.

Our first step in understanding the economics of discrimination is to distinguish two words that are often confused. *Prejudice* is an emotional dislike for members of a certain group; *discrimination* refers to the restricted opportunities offered to such a group. As you will see, prejudice does not always lead to discrimination, nor is prejudice necessary for discrimination to occur.

Employer Prejudice

When you think of job discrimination, your first image might be a manager who refuses to hire members of some group, such as African-Americans or women, because of pure prejudice. As a result, the victims of prejudice, prevented from working at high-paying jobs, must accept lower wages elsewhere. No doubt, many employers hire according to their personal prejudices. But it may surprise you to learn that economists generally consider employer prejudice one of the *least* important sources of labor market discrimination.

To see why, look at Figure 6, which shows the labor market divided into two broad sectors, A and B. To keep things simple, we'll assume that all workers have the same qualifications and that they find jobs in either sector equally attractive. Under these conditions, if there were *no* discrimination, both sectors would pay the same wage, W_1. (Can you explain why?)

Now suppose the firms in sector A decide they no longer wish to employ members of some group—say, women. What would happen? Women would begin looking for jobs in the *nondiscriminating* sector B, and the labor supply curve there would shift rightward. The equilibrium would move from F to F', decreasing the wage to W_2. At the same time, with women no longer welcome in sector A, the labor supply curve there would shift leftward, moving the market from E to E' and driving the wage up to W_3. It appears that employer discrimination would create a gender wage differential equal to $W_3 - W_2$.

But the differential would be only temporary. Why? With the wage rate in sector B now lower, *men* would exit that market and seek jobs in the higher-paying sector A. These movements would reverse the changes in labor supply, and, in the end, both sectors would pay the same wage again. Employer prejudice against women might lead to a permanent change in the *composition* of labor in each

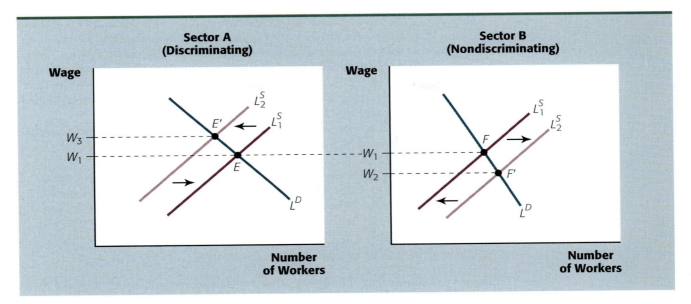

FIGURE 6
Employer Discrimination and Wage Rates

sector—with only men working in sector A and both sexes working in sector B—but *no change in wage rates.*

But employer prejudice might not even change the composition of labor in either sector, because there is another force working to eliminate this form of discrimination altogether: the product market. Since biased employers must initially pay higher wages to employ men, they will have higher average costs than unbiased employers. If biased firms sell their product in a competitive market, they will suffer losses and ultimately be forced to exit their industries. Over the long run, prejudiced employers should be replaced with unprejudiced ones. Even if the product market is imperfectly competitive, the firm will still have its stockholders or owners to contend with. Unless *their* prejudice is so strong that they are willing to forego profit, management will be under pressure to hire qualified women rather than pay a premium to hire men. In either case,

when prejudice originates with employers, competitive labor markets work to discourage discrimination and reduce or eliminate any wage gap between the favored and the unfavored group.

Employee and Customer Prejudice

What if *workers*, rather than employers, are prejudiced? Then our conclusions are very different. If, for example, a significant number of male assembly-line workers dislike supervision by women, then hiring female supervisors might reduce productivity, raise costs for any level of output, and therefore decrease profit. In a competitive product market, a *nondiscriminating* firm would be forced out of business. And even in imperfectly competitive product markets, stockholders will *want* the firm to discriminate against female supervisors, even if they themselves are not prejudiced. In this case, we cannot count on the market to solve the problem at all.

In the absence of discrimination, the wage rate would be W_1 in both sector A and sector B. If firms in sector A discriminate against some group—such as women—the group would seek work in the nondiscriminating sector, B. The increased labor supply in sector B causes the wage there to fall to W_2, while the decreased supply in sector A causes the wage there to rise to W_3. But this wage differential is only temporary if the discrimination results from employer prejudice. As men migrate from sector B to the now-higher wage sector A, the labor supply changes in both sectors are reversed. The wage returns to W_1 in both sectors.

The same argument applies if the prejudice originates with the firm's *customers*. For example, if many automobile owners distrust female mechanics, then an auto repair shop that hires them would lose some customers and sacrifice profit. True, excluding qualified female mechanics is costly; it means paying higher wages to men and charging higher prices. But customers will be willing to *pay* a higher price, since they prefer male mechanics. Even in the long run, then, women might be excluded from the auto mechanics trade.

More generally, if worker or customer prejudice is common in high-wage industries, then women would be forced into low-wage jobs.

Markets and Equilibrium

> When prejudice originates with the firm's employees or its customers, market forces may encourage, rather than discourage, discrimination and can lead to a permanent wage gap between the favored and unfavored groups.

Statistical Discrimination

Suppose you are in charge of hiring 10 new employees at your firm. Suppose, too, that young, married women in your industry are twice as likely to quit their jobs within two years than men (say, because they decide to have children) and that quits are very costly to your firm: New workers must be recruited and trained, and production is disrupted when there is a temporary gap in staffing. Let's say that 20 people apply for the 10 positions—half men and half women. All are equally qualified, and you have no way of knowing which *individuals* among them are more likely to quit within two years. Whom will you hire?

If your sole goal is to maximize the firm's profit, there is no question: You will hire the men. (If you have goals other than profit maximization, you might not last very long at that firm.) Notice that in this example, there was no mention of prejudice. Indeed, even if there isn't a trace of prejudice in you, in the firm's employees, or in its customers, profit maximization may still dictate hiring the men.

Statistical discrimination When individuals are excluded from an activity based on the statistical probability of behavior in their group, rather than their personal characteristics.

Statistical discrimination—so called because individuals are excluded based on the statistical probability of behavior in their group, rather than their own personal traits—is a case of discrimination without prejudice. It can lead an unbiased profit-maximizing employer to discriminate against an individual member of a group, even though that particular individual might never engage in the feared behavior.

But, as some observers have pointed out, statistical discrimination can also be a cover for prejudice. For example, consider statistical discrimination against women. True, women are more likely to leave work to care for their children. But men are more likely to develop alcohol and drug problems, which can lead to poor judgment and costly accidents on the job. If there were no prejudice, then the risks associated with hiring men would be thrown into the equation. According to critics of the statistical discrimination theory, the negative behavior of a favored group (such as men) is rarely considered by employers.

Dealing with Discrimination

As you've seen, discrimination due to pure employer prejudice is unlikely to have much of an impact on labor markets. As long as some employers are *not* prejudiced, those who *are* prejudiced will be at a competitive disadvantage. In the long run, the market helps to *eliminate* this type of discrimination.

But for other types of discrimination—such as statistical discrimination or discrimination due to worker or consumer prejudice—market incentives work in the opposite way, leading to a permanent and stubborn problem. In these cases, many economists and other policy makers believe that government action is needed. This is especially so when the groups discriminated against are already poor or disadvantaged in some way.

Some favor affirmative action programs, which actively encourage firms to expand opportunities for women and minorities; others favor stricter enforcement of existing antidiscrimination laws and stiffer penalties when discriminatory hiring occurs. Both approaches to policy force *all* firms to bear the costs of nondiscriminatory hiring, so that no single firm is at a disadvantage. For example, by forcing *all* firms to hire women—and to bear the costs of possibly greater quit rates or of alienating workers or customers who might be prejudiced—no single firm is put at a disadvantage by hiring women.

Discrimination and Wage Differentials

How much have the wages of victimized groups been reduced because of discrimination? As you are about to see, this is a very difficult question to answer.

A starting point—but *only* a starting point—is Table 2, which shows median earnings for different groups of full-time workers in the population. Notice the substantial earnings gap between men and women of either race and between whites and blacks of either sex. Doesn't this prove that the impact of discrimination on wages is substantial? Not necessarily.

Consider the black–white differential for men. In 2003, black men earned 24 percent less than white men, on average. But *some* of this difference is due to differences in education, job experience, job choice, and geographic location between whites and blacks. For example, the proportion of black adults with college degrees is a little more than half that of white adults. Even if all firms were completely color-blind in their hiring and wage payments, disproportionately fewer blacks would have higher-paying jobs requiring college degrees, and this would produce an earnings differential in favor of whites. The same would apply if blacks were more likely to live in low-wage areas or, on average, had fewer years of prior experience when applying for jobs.

Several studies suggest that if we limit comparisons to whites and blacks with the same educational background, geographic location, and, in some cases, the

	Median Income	Percent of White Male Income
White Males	$761	100%
Black Males	$582	76%
Hispanic Males	$503	66%
White Females	$590	78%
Black Females	$512	67%
Hispanic Females	$403	53%

Source: Bureau of Labor Statistics News Release, *"Usual Weekly Earnings,"* April 17, 2003. Data are for first quarter of 2003. (*Note:* Persons of Hispanic origin may be of any race.)

TABLE 2
Median Weekly Earnings, 2001 (of Full-time Wage and Salary Workers Over Age 25)

same ability (measured by a variety of different tests), 50 percent or more of the earnings difference disappears.[8]

Does this mean that discrimination accounts for half or less of the earnings differential? Not at all: Many of the observed differences in education, geographic location, and ability are the *result* of job market discrimination. Figure 7 illustrates a vicious cycle of discrimination in the labor market. First, job discrimination causes a wage differential between equally qualified whites and blacks. With a lower wage, blacks have less incentive to remain in the labor force or to invest in human capital, since they reap smaller rewards for these activities. The result is that blacks, on average, have less education and less job experience than whites, and even color-blind employers will hire disproportionately fewer blacks in high-paying jobs, perpetuating their lower wages.

In addition to job market discrimination, there is *premarket* discrimination—unequal treatment in education and housing—that occurs *before* an individual enters the labor market. For example, regardless of black families' incomes, housing

FIGURE 7
The Vicious Cycle of Discrimination

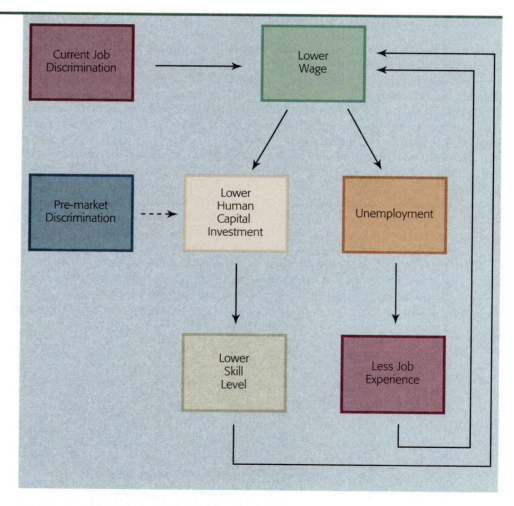

[8] See, for example, June O'Neill, "The Role of Human Capital in Earnings Differences between Black and White Men," *Journal of Economic Perspectives* (Fall 1990), pp. 25–45.

discrimination may exclude them from neighborhoods with better public schools, resulting in fewer blacks being admitted to college. Discriminatory treatment by teachers within a school may contribute to lowered aspirations and diminished job-market expectations. All of these contribute to the low-wage syndrome.

Similar reasoning applies to the earnings gap between women and men. On the one hand, we have a large earnings gap. In 2003, for example, the earnings of white female workers were only 78 percent of those of white men. On the other hand, studies suggest that a third or more of the male–female wage gap is due to differences in skills and job experience. But for women, as well as blacks and other minorities, differences in skills and experience can be the *result* of lower wages: Since women know they will earn less than men and will have more trouble advancing on the job, they have less incentive to invest in human capital and to stay in the labor force. Premarket discrimination plays a role, too. Several studies have suggested that different treatment of girls in secondary school may lower their job market aspirations. And even before school, girls may be socialized to prefer different (and lower-paying) career paths than boys, such as nursing rather than medicine.

In the end, we do not know nearly as much about the impact of discrimination on wages as we would like to know, but research is proceeding at a rapid pace. As we've seen, the data must always be interpreted with care:

> *In measuring the impact of job market discrimination on earnings, the wage gap between two groups gives an overestimate, since it fails to account for differences in skills and experience. However, comparing only workers with similar skills and experience leads to an underestimate, since skill and experience are themselves influenced by discrimination—both in the job market and outside of it.*

USING THE THEORY
The Minimum Wage

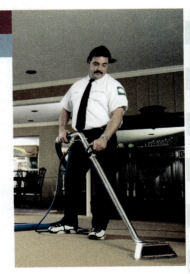

A minimum wage law is motivated by a desire to raise the wages of the lowest paid workers. The law makes it illegal to hire a worker for less than a specified wage, in any labor market covered by the law. When the federal minimum wage rate was first established in the United States in 1938, the minimum was set at 25 cents per hour, and applied to industries employing only 43 percent of the workforce. In 2003, the minimum wage was $5.15 per hour and covered almost 90 percent of the workforce.

Of course, prices rose between 1938 and 2003 as well. Even though the minimum wage has increased in *dollars* during those years, its purchasing power has fallen by about 34 percent. As a result, several states now have their own, higher minimum wage rates. In 2003, the highest were in Alaska ($7.15) and Washington state ($7.01). In both of these states, the minimum wage automatically rises with the overall level of prices.

When most people think about the minimum wage, they see it as a means to increase living standards for the lowest paid workers, and their analysis stops there. After all, a full-time worker earning the federal minimum wage of $5.15 per hour would earn only $10,712 per year—less than enough to support a single parent and child above the government's official poverty line. Indeed, the minimum wage *does* raise living standards for some workers above what they would otherwise be. But the minimum wage also serves as a *barrier to entry* in labor markets covered by the law. And this can have paradoxical side effects that hurt some of the people the minimum wage is supposed to help.

To understand the effect of the minimum wage, we'll divide the U.S. labor market into three parts: (1) the market for skilled labor; (2) the market for unskilled labor in industries *covered* by the minimum wage law; and (3) the market for unskilled labor in industries effectively *not covered* by the law, either because it does not apply (waiters, house cleaners, and nannies) or because firms routinely violate it (typically, very small firms that are difficult to monitor).

Figure 8 shows the long-run equilibrium in these markets if *no* minimum were in effect. The wage rate in both unskilled labor markets (panels (a) and (b)) is initially $4.00 per hour, at points A and B. It's the same in both markets because in the absence of a minimum wage law, workers would migrate to whichever market had the higher wage until the wage rates were equal. In the skilled labor market in panel (c), the wage rate is considerably higher at $20, for all the reasons we've discussed in this chapter.

Now let's impose a minimum wage of $5.15 on the *covered unskilled* sector in panel (a), and trace through the effects. First, employment in that sector falls, from N_1 to N_2. Since quantity demanded is less than quantity supplied, and since no firm can be forced to hire more workers than it wants to, there will be an excess supply of labor equal to $N_3 - N_2$. Part of this excess is due to an increase in quantity supplied from N_1 to N_3 (with a higher wage rate, more people want to work in the covered, unskilled sector). But part of it is also due to a *decrease* in quantity *demanded*, from N_1 to N_2. You can already see that while some unskilled workers benefit (those who keep their jobs and are paid more), others are hurt: They lose their jobs.

The job losses in panel (a) can be especially harmful to young workers who are not college bound and who need to establish a job record. A good performance at a first job, even a minimum wage job, can enable an unskilled worker to seek other employment later, at more than the minimum wage. (This is somewhat analogous to the way college students use unpaid internships—which are not covered by minimum wage law—to beef up their résumés and improve their employment prospects.) But the effects in panel (a) are just the beginning.

Some of those who lose their jobs in the covered sector will move to the only sector where jobs are still available—the uncovered sector in panel (b). There the labor supply curve will shift rightward, from L_1^S to L_2^S, and the market wage will fall below its initial value—to $3.00 in our example. Thus the impact of the minimum wage spills over into the sector not covered by it. Increased competition for jobs drives down the wages of *all* workers there, even those who were already employed before the minimum wage was imposed. More specifically, we would expect a decline in the wages of waiters, house cleaners, and unskilled workers who work in law-breaking firms.

> *A minimum wage—by raising wage rates in covered industries, and lowering them in uncovered industries—creates a wage differential among the least-skilled workers, depending on the industry in which they work.*

What about skilled workers? Are they affected by minimum wage legislation? You might think not, since they are already earning more than the minimum. But when the wage of unskilled labor rises in the covered sector, employers there will,

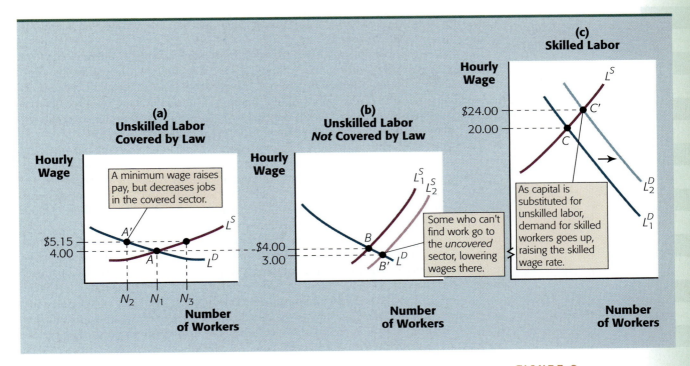

(a)
Unskilled Labor
Covered by Law

Hourly Wage

A minimum wage raises pay, but decreases jobs in the covered sector.

L^S

$5.15
4.00

A'
A

L^D

N_2 N_1 N_3

Number of Workers

(b)
Unskilled Labor
Not Covered by Law

Hourly Wage

L_1^S L_2^S

B

Some who can't find work go to the *uncovered* sector, lowering wages there.

$4.00
3.00

B' L^D

Number of Workers

(c)
Skilled Labor

Hourly Wage

L^S

$24.00
20.00

C'
C

As capital is substituted for unskilled labor, demand for skilled workers goes up, raising the skilled wage rate.

L_2^D

L_1^D

Number of Workers

FIGURE 8
The Minimum Wage

to some degree, substitute skilled workers and capital equipment for unskilled labor. For example, a dishwasher might be replaced by a sophisticated dishwashing machine that requires maintenance and repair by skilled workers. An unskilled product packager might be replaced by a high-tech machine designed and maintained by skilled workers. Substitution toward capital that is produced, operated and maintained by skilled labor will shift the labor demand curve in panel (c) rightward, from L_1^D to L_2^D. As a result, the wage rate in the skilled sector will increase, from $20 to $24 in our example.

> *A minimum wage—by causing firms to substitute away from unskilled labor toward capital and skilled labor—can increase the wage differential between skilled and unskilled workers.*

You can see that the minimum wage sets off a chain of events. In the end, some unskilled workers benefit in the form of higher pay. Other unskilled workers are harmed by lower pay or unemployment. There is only one group in which everyone benefits: skilled workers. It should come as no surprise, then, that for many decades the most vocal advocates of raising the minimum wage have been labor unions, whose membership is disproportionately made up of skilled workers.

What do economists think about the minimum wage? There is both agreement and disagreement. Surveys consistently show that a large majority of economists agree with the analysis presented here, as well as its most important conclusion: that the minimum wage law causes unemployment among unskilled workers. For example, in a 1995 survey of economists who specialize in the study of labor markets, 87 percent agreed that "a minimum wage increases unemployment among young and unskilled workers."[9]

Further, most economists regard the minimum wage as an *inefficient* policy for helping poor working families. More than half of those directly affected by the minimum wage are young adults who are not supporting families. Some of these may be teenagers living at home with well-off families, and not in need of help. Others who *do* need help may be harmed, if they are unable to find a job in the covered sector, or if they are unlucky enough to be working in the uncovered sector.

As a rule, economists prefer policies that target assistance directly to those in need and exclude those who are well off. In the United States, the earned income tax credit (EITC)—which supplements the incomes of low-income workers—is an example of such a policy. In 2002, the EITC for a low-income worker supporting two children could reach $4,100 from the federal government, and another $1,000 or so from a state EITC. Unlike the minimum wage, the EITC helps *only* the poor, and it deprives no one of a job. And the funds come out of general tax revenues, most of which is collected from moderate- and high-income taxpayers and profitable corporations. The cost of the minimum wage, by contrast, is paid by business owners and their customers, who may not be well off.

You might think, then, that economists would overwhelmingly *oppose* any increase in the minimum wage. But that is not the case. In the 1995 survey, a majority of labor economists (57 percent) believed that the minimum wage should be increased, in spite of the rise in unemployment it would cause. Similar support was found in another, more recent survey of economists.[10] What explains this support?

First, there is a *positive economic* disagreement—a disagreement about the facts of how the economy works. Those who *favor* an increase in the minimum wage tend to believe the effect on unemployment is much *smaller* than those who oppose an increase.

But there may be other reasons for these survey results. For example, some economists—even if they view an EITC-like program as superior—may feel that the current EITC level is too low. They may favor a hike in the minimum wage because—even with all of its problems—it is more politically achievable than higher EITC benefits. Others may believe that higher unemployment, as a more visible problem than low wages, is more likely to influence public policy in a direction they favor, such as an increase in funding for programs to improve job skills.

You can see that the minimum wage, like most issues of public policy, is not as simple as it appears at first glance, or even at second glance. But as you've seen, it serves as one among many barriers to entry into labor markets. And like occupational licensing and union wage setting, it provides another reason for wage differentials.

[9] Robert Whaples, "Is There Consensus among American Labor Economists? Survey Results on Forty Propositions," *Journal of Labor Research*, Vol. XVII, No. 4 (Fall 1996) pp. 730–731.

[10] Fuchs, Victor R., Alan B. Krueger, and James M. Poterba, "Economists' Views About Parameters, Values, and Policies: Survey Results in Labor and Public Economics." *The Journal of Economic Literature*, Vol. 36, No. 3 (September, 1998), pp. 1387–1425.

Summary

Firms need *resources*—land, labor, capital, and entrepreneurship—in order to produce output. These resources are traded in *resource markets* in which firms are demanders and households are suppliers. *Labor markets* are key resource markets. A *perfectly competitive labor market*—the type of labor market explored in this chapter—is one in which there are many buyers and sellers, all workers appear the same to firms, and there are no barriers to entry or exit.

The labor demand curve in any labor market slopes downward for two reasons. First, a higher wage rate raises firms' marginal costs, causing a decrease in output and employment. Second, a higher wage rate raises the *relative* cost of labor from a particular market, causing firms to substitute other inputs, such as capital or other types of labor.

The labor supply curve in any labor market slopes upward for two reasons. First, a higher wage rate induces some of those not currently working to seek work. Second, a higher wage rate attracts those who are currently working in *other* labor markets.

Labor supply and demand curves can help us understand why wages vary so widely among the population. For a given category of labor, the intersection of the supply and demand curves determines the market wage and employment. In an imaginary world that satisfied three conditions—(1) all jobs are equally attractive to all workers (except for wage differences); (2) all workers are equally able to do any job; and (3) all labor markets are perfectly competitive—the wages of all workers would be identical. Thus, differences in wages must arise from a violation of one or more of these conditions.

When the attractiveness of two jobs differs, *compensating wage differentials* will emerge to offset those differences. When the productivity of workers differs, the more productive workers will earn higher wages. And in some cases, barriers to entry—violating the conditions of perfect competition—contribute to higher wages for protected workers.

Another reason for wage differentials is prejudice, which creates barriers to entry for unfavored groups of workers. When employer prejudice exists, market forces work to discourage discrimination and reduce wage gaps between groups. However, employee and customer prejudice encourage discrimination and can lead to permanent wage gaps.

The federal minimum wage law is designed to address some of the disparity in wages among the population. In particular, it is designed to help those who earn the lowest wages by increasing their wage rate above the equilibrium value. While many low-wage workers are helped by the minimum wage, it also has side effects that undermine its purpose. These include higher unemployment in labor markets covered by the minimum wage and lower wages for unskilled workers in the uncovered sector. Another unintentional side effect is to raise the wages of skilled workers who end up replacing the now-more-expensive unskilled workers.

Key Terms

Compensating wage differential

Discrimination

Nonmonetary job characteristic

Perfectly competitive labor market

Resource markets

Statistical discrimination

Review Questions

1. For each of the following jobs, would you expect the compensating wage differential to be positive or negative? (In each case, compare to a job as a computer programmer.) Describe what nonmonetary job characteristics and human capital requirements might be at work in each case.
   a. Worker in a slaughterhouse
   b. College professor
   c. Attorney
   d. Bartender at a tropical resort
   e. New York City police officer

2. In this chapter, you learned about several explanations for wage inequality. Which explanation (or explanations) best explains each of the following?

   a. A paralegal in New York earns more than a paralegal doing the same work in Keokuk, Iowa.
   b. Although they work on the same cases and do many of the same things, an attorney's salary is many times that of a paralegal.
   c. Larry King earns more as a talk show host than the morning host of a New York radio show.
   d. A professor of philosophy with a Ph.D. earns less than an accountant with only a B.A.
   e. Construction workers in Germany, which has strong unions and extensive apprenticeship programs, are paid higher wage rates than American workers in the same trades.

3. Why are earnings not always proportional to ability?

4. True or false? Discrimination does not always arise from prejudice. Explain.

5. Explain how market forces tend to:
    a. Encourage discrimination when the prejudice comes from a firm's employees or customers.
    b. Discourage discrimination when the prejudice comes from employers.

6. What is "statistical discrimination"? What are some possible remedies for it?

7. Explain how the union–nonunion wage differential can arise. Illustrate with relevant graphs.

8. Discuss the advantages that the earned income tax credit (EITC) has over the minimum wage as a tool for helping poor working families.

Problems and Exercises

1. The labor markets for factory workers and construction workers are in equilibrium: The wage in both is W_0, and the number employed is N_0. Assume that both labor markets are perfectly competitive, there are no barriers to entry or exit of workers, and workers are equally qualified to do both jobs and find them equally attractive.
    a. Unexpectedly, demand for factory output soars. Using graphs, show the short-run effect on the equilibrium wage and number employed in factories.
    b. Draw graphs that illustrate the long-run equilibrium position in the two industries.

2. Suppose the demand for unskilled labor were completely insensitive with respect to the wage rate (i.e., a vertical labor demand curve). Using graphs similar to those in Figure 4, but modified to reflect this new assumption, explain how a minimum wage above the equilibrium wage for covered unskilled workers would affect employment and the wage rate among:

    a. covered, unskilled workers;
    b. uncovered, unskilled workers; and
    c. skilled workers.

3. State how each of the following would affect the average wage of college professors relative to other professionals in the long run. In each case, illustrate with a supply and demand diagram.
    a. Requirements to become a college professor are increased from one to two Ph.D. degrees.
    b. Urban colleges around the country relocate to rural areas.
    c. The college-age population decreases.
    d. The number of courses college professors have to teach each year is reduced by 25%. (*Note:* Be sure to state any assumptions you use to arrive at your answer.)

Challenge Questions

1. [Requires Appendix to Chapter 3] Some advocates of the minimum wage argue that any decrease in the employment of the unskilled will be slight. They assert that an increase in the minimum wage will actually increase the total amount paid to unskilled workers (i.e., wage × number of unskilled workers employed). Discuss what assumptions they are making about the "wage elasticity of labor demand."

1. Use your Xtra! password at the Hall and Lieberman Web site (http://lieberman.swlearning.com), select this chapter, and under Economic Applications, click on EconDebate. Choose *Microeconomics: Income Distribution and Poverty*, and scroll down to find the debate, "Does a Gender Wage Gap Still Exist?" Read the debate carefully, and answer the questions below.
    a. What forms of market-based discrimination can explain part of the wage differential between men and women?

    b. Scroll further down the page, and under Primary Sources and Data, find the report by the Council of Economic Advisors, "Explaining Trends in the Gender Wage Gap." Click on this link, and read the Executive Summary of this report. What arguments does this report give to support the absence of nonmarket gender wage discrimination?

Economic Efficiency and the Role of Government

In nations around the world, virtually every disagreement about the economy ultimately leads to the government. And some disagreements start there as well.

In the United States, for example, hardly a day goes by without a speech in Congress attacking or applauding the government's spending on defense, education, environmental programs, and more. There are also sharp disagreements about the *role* the government should play in our economic life. Should it help people send their children to private schools by giving them vouchers? Should it discourage the merger of two large airlines? Should local governments be collecting the trash and running the prisons, rather than contracting these services out to private firms? Even events that originate almost entirely in the private economy—such as an accounting scandal at a major corporation, the closing of a large factory, or a drop in stock prices—invariably lead to a sharp disagreement over what government should do. Similar controversies exist in other developed market economies, such as the nations of the European Union or Japan.

But all of these disagreements tend to obscure a remarkable degree of *agreement* about the economy, and the government's role in it. For example, the vast majority of goods and services that you buy in stores, over the Internet, or obtain in other ways are provided by *private firms,* and almost everyone agrees that's how it should be. Hardly anyone proposes that the government should be providing the economy's books, jeans, computers, restaurant meals, entertainment, or soft drinks. At the same time, there is widespread agreement that certain goods and services *should* be provided by government, and government alone, such as general police protection, the court system, and national defense.

Much of this agreement is based on ideas about *economic efficiency*—the organizing theme of this chapter. As you'll see, there is more to the concept of efficiency than appears at first glance. It enables us to understand why markets often perform so well, and why they sometimes don't. And efficiency helps us define a role for government involvement in the economy about which there is broad agreement.

THE MEANING OF EFFICIENCY

What, exactly, do we mean by the word *efficiency*? We all use this word, or its opposite, in our everyday conversation: "I wish I could organize my time more efficiently," "He's such an inefficient worker," "Our office is organized very efficiently," and so on. In each of these cases, we use the word *inefficient* to mean "wasteful" and *efficient* to mean "the absence of waste."

In economics, too, efficiency means the absence of waste, although a very specific kind of waste: *the waste of an opportunity to make someone better off without harming anyone else.* More specifically,

> economic efficiency *is achieved when we cannot rearrange the production or allocation of goods to make one person better off without making anybody else worse off.*

Notice that economic efficiency is a limited concept. While it is an important goal for a society, it is not the only goal. Most of us would list fairness as another important social goal. But an economy can be efficient even if most people are extremely poor and a few are extraordinarily rich, a situation that many of us would regard as unfair.

> *An efficient economy is not necessarily a fair economy.*

Why, then, do economists put so much stress on efficiency, rather than on issues of fairness? Largely because it is so much easier for people to agree about efficiency. We all define fairness differently, depending on our different ethical and moral views. Issues of fairness must therefore be resolved politically.

But virtually all of us would agree that if we fail to take actions that would make some people in our society better off *without harming anyone*—that is, if we fail to achieve economic efficiency—we have wasted a valuable opportunity. Economics—by helping us understand the preconditions for economic efficiency and teaching us how we can bring about those preconditions—can make a major contribution to our material well-being.

PARETO IMPROVEMENTS

Imagine the following scenario: A boy and a girl are having lunch in elementary school. The boy frowns at a peanut butter and jelly sandwich, which, on this particular day, makes the girl's mouth water. She says, "Wanna trade?" The boy looks at her chicken sandwich, considers a moment, and says, "Okay."

This little scene, which is played out thousands of times every day in schools around the country, is an example of a trade in which both parties are made better off and no one is harmed. And as simple as it seems, such trading is at the core of the concept of economic efficiency. It is an example of a *Pareto* (pronounced puh-RAY-toe) *improvement,* named after the Italian economist, Vilfredo Pareto (1848–1923), who first systematically explored the issue of economic efficiency.

> A ***Pareto improvement*** *is any action that makes at least one person better off, and harms no one.*

Pareto improvement An action that makes at least one person better off, and harms no one.

In a market economy such as that in the United States, where trading is voluntary, literally hundreds of millions of Pareto improvements take place every day. Almost every purchase is an example of a Pareto improvement. If you pay $30 for a pair of jeans, then the jeans must be worth more to you than the $30 that you parted with or you wouldn't have bought them. Thus, you are better off after making the purchase. On the other side, the owner of the store must have valued your $30 more highly than he valued the jeans or he wouldn't have sold them to you. So she is better off, too. Your purchase of the jeans, like virtually every purchase made by every consumer every day, is an example of a Pareto improvement.

The notion of a Pareto improvement helps us arrive at a formal definition of economic efficiency:

> *Economic efficiency is achieved when every possible Pareto improvement is exploited.*

This definition can be applied to an individual market or to the economy as a whole. For example, suppose we look at the market for laser printers and cannot identify a single Pareto improvement in that market that has not already been exploited. No matter how hard we look, we cannot find a change in price or output level, or any other change for that matter, that would make some producer or some consumer better off without harming anyone. Then we would say that the market for laser printers is economically efficient.

Alternatively, we can look at the economy as a whole. If we discover remaining Pareto improvements that are not occurring—say, a change in the price of some good or a change in the quantity of a good produced—then we would deem the economy economically inefficient.

Of course, no economy can exploit *every* Pareto improvement, so no society can ever be completely economically efficient according to our definition. But achieving something close to economic efficiency is an important goal. When we look at real-world markets and real-world economies, it is best to view economic efficiency as a continuum. At one end of the continuum are economies in which, in most markets, most opportunities for Pareto improvements are exploited. At the other end of the continuum are economies in which many markets are economically inefficient—where many opportunities for mutual gain remain unexploited. As you will see in this chapter, perfectly competitive markets tend to be economically efficient, and well-functioning market economies tend to lie close to the economically efficient end of the spectrum.

Side Payments and Pareto Improvements

The examples of Pareto improvements we've considered so far involve easily arranged transactions, in which one person trades with another and both come out ahead. Since both parties benefit, they have every incentive to find each other and trade.

But there are more complicated situations in which a Pareto improvement will come about only if one side makes a special kind of payment to the other, which we call a *side payment*. These are situations in which an action, without the side payment, would benefit one group and harm another.

Here's a simple example. Suppose the owner of an empty lot wants to build a movie theater on her property. Many people might gain from the theater: the owner of the empty lot, moviegoers, the theater's employees, and more. But the residents in the immediate vicinity might be harmed, because the theater will bring noise and traffic congestion.

Imagine that we can measure the dollar value of the gains and losses for each person in the town, and when we sum them up, we find that the total benefits to the gainers are valued at $100,000 while the total harm to the losers is valued at $70,000.

Building the theater—by itself—would *not* be a Pareto improvement, because while some would benefit, others would be hurt. But suppose we could easily arrange for the gainers to pay, say, an $80,000 *side payment* to those harmed. Then, as long as the side payment is made, and distributed properly, *everyone* would come out ahead: Building the theater would be a Pareto improvement.

How do we know that everyone would come out ahead? Because the gainers' benefits of $100,000 are large enough to pay the $80,000 side payment and still have some gains left over. The harm to the losers of $70,000 is small enough so that, when they receive the $80,000 side payment, they actually are better off. These results can be easily seen in the scorecard below:

Action: Build the movie theater (with $80,000 side payment).

Gainers	Effect before side payment:	+$100,000
(theater owner,	Side payment (given):	−$ 80,000
moviegoers, etc.)	Net effect:	+$ 20,000
Losers	Effect before side payment:	−$ 70,000
(nearby residents)	Side payment (received):	+$ 80,000
	Net effect:	+$ 10,000

If you experiment around a bit, you'll see that *any* side payment greater than $70,000 and less than $100,000 would turn this action into a Pareto improvement.

More generally,

if an action creates greater total benefits for gainers than total harm to losers, then a side payment exists which, if transferred from gainers to losers, would make the action a Pareto improvement.

Any side payment with a value between the total benefits to the gainers and the total losses to the losers will do the trick.

This has an important implication for economic efficiency. If there is an action that benefits some more than it harms others, and *if an appropriate side payment can be easily arranged*, then *not* taking the action is a waste of an opportunity to make everyone better off. Economic efficiency requires that we find, and exploit, opportunities that—with side payments—would be Pareto improvements.

But reread the italicized words in the paragraph above. The appropriate side payment—as you'll see later in the chapter—is *not* always easy to arrange. In many instances, arranging a side payment to ensure that everyone benefits has high costs. It may be that, after deducting these costs, too little would be left to adequately compensate the losers while still leaving the gainers better off. When a side payment *cannot* be made—or for any reason is *not* made—then even though the action might create greater gain than harm, it might not be considered fair. Achieving the efficient outcome then becomes *one* consideration, but not the only one. We'll come back to this important issue of side payments later in the chapter and see how it justifies, on efficiency grounds, many instances of government involvement.

MARKETS AND ECONOMIC EFFICIENCY

Now let's turn our attention from the isolated example of a single action—building the movie theater—to consider Pareto improvements and economic efficiency in *markets*. Remember that in a market system, firms and consumers are largely free to produce and consume as they wish, without anyone orchestrating the process from above. Can we expect such unsupervised trading to be economically efficient? That is, will the quantity bought and sold in each market exploit all possible Pareto improvements?

In this section, you'll see that the answer is a conditional yes . . . as long as trading takes place in *perfectly competitive markets*. To demonstrate this, we'll return to the tools we've used to analyze competitive markets: demand and supply curves. But we'll look at them in a slightly different way.

Reinterpreting the Demand Curve

Figure 1 shows a market demand curve for guitar lessons: the quantity demanded per week at each price. It also indicates who would be taking each lesson. For example, at a price of $25, only Flo—who values guitar lessons the most—takes a lesson, so quantity demanded in the market is one. If the price drops to $23, Joe will take one weekly lesson, so quantity demanded is two. At $21, Flo will decide to take a second lesson each week, so quantity demanded rises to three. This is the standard way of thinking about a market demand curve.

But we can also view the curve in a different way: It tells us the maximum price someone would be willing to pay for each unit of the good. Therefore, it tells us how much that unit is *worth* to the person who buys it. In Figure 1, for example, the maximum value of the first lesson to some consumer in the market is just a tiny bit greater than $25. How do we know this? Because Flo, who values this lesson more highly than anyone else, will not buy it at any price greater than $25. But if the price falls to $25, she will buy it. When she decides to buy it, she must be getting at least a tiny bit more in value than the $25 she is giving up. So the value of that first lesson must be

FIGURE 1
The Value of Another
Guitar Lesson

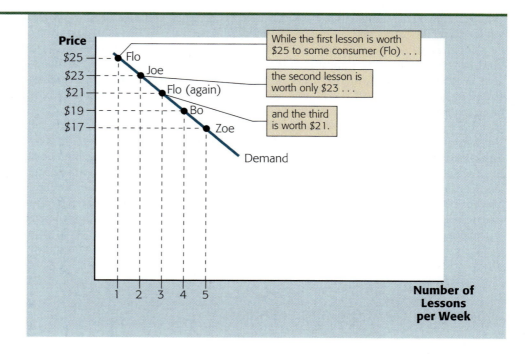

FIGURE 1
The Value of Another Guitar Lesson

just a tiny bit more than $25. Ignoring for the moment the phrase "tiny bit more," we can say that the first lesson in the market is worth $25 to some consumer (Flo), the second is worth $23 to some consumer (Joe), and the third is worth $21 (Flo again).

Notice that each guitar lesson in the market has a different value. In part, this is because consumers differ in their incomes and tastes. (For example, based on differences in their incomes or tastes, Flo values one lesson per week more than does Joe.) But also, for each individual, the value of additional lessons declines as more lessons are taken. Flo, for example, values her first weekly lesson at $25, but her second at only $21.

Of course, in Figure 1, we've simplified by assuming there are very few consumers in the market for guitar lessons. This makes the graph easier to read. But the point is the same whether there are 5 consumers in the market, or 500, or 50,000. In general,

> *the height of the market demand curve at any quantity shows us the value— to someone—of the last unit of the good consumed.*

Reinterpreting the Supply Curve

Now let's look at the other side of the market: those who *supply* guitar lessons. Figure 2 shows us a supply curve for guitar lessons: the quantity offered each week at various prices. The figure also indicates who would be supplying each lesson. For example, at a price of $13, Martin would offer one lesson each week. If the price rose to $15, Martin would offer two lessons per week, and at $17, another teacher—Gibson—would enter the market and offer a third.

But this supply curve also tells us the minimum price a seller must get in order to supply that lesson. For example, for the first lesson, the price would have to be at least $13. At any price less than that, no one will offer it. Similarly, $15 is the

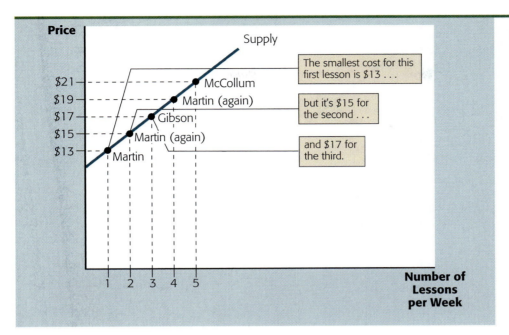

FIGURE 2
The Additional Cost
of Guitar Lessons

minimum price it would take to get some producer in this market (Martin again) to supply the second lesson, and $17 is what it would take for the third lesson to be supplied (Gibson this time).

Why does it take higher prices to get more lessons? Because offering lessons is *costly* to guitar teachers. Not only do they have to rent studio space, but they must also use their time, which comes at an opportunity cost. In order to convince a teacher to supply a guitar lesson, the price must *at least* cover the additional costs of giving that lesson. And even if studio rental costs remain the same for all teachers and all lessons, guitar teachers will still value the opportunity cost of their time differently.

The minimum price that would convince Martin, Gibson, or any other teacher to supply a lesson will be the amount that just barely compensates for the additional cost of that lesson—and a tiny bit more. Ignoring the phrase "a tiny bit more," we can say that

> the height of the market supply curve at any quantity shows us the additional cost—to some producer—of each unit of the good supplied.[1]

The Efficient Quantity of a Good

Figure 3 combines the supply and demand curves for guitar lessons. Remember that the demand curve shows us the *value* of each lesson to some *consumer* and the supply curve shows us the additional *cost* of each lesson to some producer. We can then find the efficient quantity of weekly guitar lessons by using the following logical principle:

---

[1] If you've been reading the chapters in order, you'll recognize *additional cost* as *marginal cost,* first introduced in Chapter 5 and discussed in later chapters. That is, the height of the supply curve tells us the lowest marginal cost at which each unit could be supplied in the market.

FIGURE 3
Efficiency in the Market for Guitar Lessons

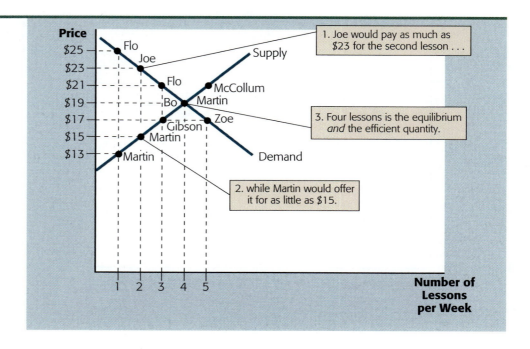

> *Whenever—at some quantity—the demand curve is higher than the supply curve, the value of one more unit to some consumer is greater than its additional cost to some producer.*

This means that when the demand curve lies above the supply curve, we can always find a price for one more unit that makes both the consumer and the producer better off: a Pareto improvement.

Here's an example: Look at the *second* lesson in the figure. Tracing up vertically, we see that the demand curve (with a height of $23) lies above the supply curve (with a height of $15). That tells us that some consumer—Joe—values this lesson more than it would cost some teacher—Martin—to provide it. If Joe can *buy* the lesson at any price *less than $23,* he comes out ahead; if Martin can *sell* it for any price *greater than $15,* he comes out ahead. So, at any price *between $15 and $23,* both will come out ahead and no one is harmed: a Pareto improvement.

The scorecard below illustrates what would happen at one such price: $17. (In case you're wondering, we're purposely avoiding the equilibrium price in this market, in order to show that these calculations can be made for more than one price.)

Action: Provide the second weekly guitar lesson at a price of $17.

Martin	Effect before payment:	−$15
(sells lesson)	Payment (received):	+$17
	Net effect:	+$ 2
Joe	Effect before payment:	+$23
(buys lesson)	Payment (given):	−$17
	Net effect:	+$ 6

When the price is $17, Joe comes out ahead by $6 and Martin by $2. But if you change the price to any value between $15 and $23, and construct a similar scorecard, you'll see that while the *distribution* of the net gains between Joe and Martin will change, they will both still come out ahead. Moreover, their *total* gain will always be $8—the difference between the value of the lesson to Joe and the cost of producing it to Martin.

Continuing in this way, we find that the third lesson, and even the fourth, could be offered as Pareto improvements. (The fourth would be only a *slight* Pareto improvement, because its value is just a tiny bit greater than $19 and its cost a tiny bit less than $19.)

What about lessons for which the demand curve is *lower* than the supply curve—such as the fifth? Then there is *no* price at which both could come out ahead. To Zoe, the consumer who values the fifth weekly lesson the most, it's worth only $17. And for McCollum, the one who could provide it at the lowest additional cost, that cost would be $21. Producing this lesson could not be a Pareto improvement—no matter what the price—since the lowest cost of providing it is greater than its highest value to anyone in the market. Someone must be harmed: either the buyer or seller, or possibly both. (An end-of-chapter problem asks you to show that, if the fifth lesson *were* being produced, then *not* producing it—along with a possible side payment—would be a Pareto improvement.)

Let's recap: Whenever the demand curve lies *above* the supply curve, producing the lesson is a Pareto improvement. Whenever the demand curve lies *below* the supply curve, producing the lesson can*not* be a Pareto improvement. This tells us that the efficient quantity of guitar lessons—the quantity at which all Pareto improvements are exploited—is where the demand curve and supply curve intersect. At this quantity, the value of the last unit produced will be equal to (or possibly a tiny bit greater than) the cost of providing it.

If the market for guitar lessons is perfectly competitive, the equilibrium quantity will be the efficient quantity.

© MICHAEL NEWMAN/PHOTOEDIT, INC.

> *The efficient quantity of a good is the quantity at which the market demand curve and market supply curves intersect.*

Perfect Competition and Efficiency

As you learned in Chapter 3 (and again in Chapter 7), when markets behave as the model of perfect competition predicts, the price adjusts until the market quantity reaches its *equilibrium:* where the market demand curve and market supply curve intersect. But we've just seen that this quantity is also the *economically efficient* quantity—the one that exploits all possible Pareto improvements. This gives us a very important and powerful result:

> *In a well-functioning, perfectly competitive market, the* equilibrium *quantity is also the* efficient *quantity.*

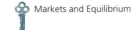

Markets and Equilibrium

Let's consider this statement carefully. It tells us that, if we leave producers and consumers alone to trade with each other as they wish, then—as long as the market is working well and it's perfectly competitive—the market will exploit every opportunity to make someone better off that doesn't harm anyone else. No special side payments need to be arranged, because the price paid for the good *is itself* the side payment.

Furthermore, we know that the *types* of goods produced in competitive markets will reflect consumer preferences. Goods that are valued by some people greater than the additional cost it would take to provide them *will* be provided in the market. The mutual gain possible for buyers and sellers creates the incentive for trading. But if a good has such low value, relative to its cost, that the demand curve lies below the supply curve at *all* quantities, it will *not* be provided. Mutual gain from providing the good is not possible. (You may want to draw the supply and demand graph for such a good to see what it looks like.) This is why you don't find chocolate-covered Brussels sprouts in any store, even though there may be a few people who would pay some small amount for them.

The notion that perfect competition—where many buyers and sellers each try to do the best for themselves—actually delivers efficient markets is one of the most important ideas in economics. The great British economist of the 18th century, Adam Smith, coined the term *invisible hand* to describe the force that leads a competitive economy relentlessly and automatically toward economic efficiency:

> *[The individual] neither intends to promote the public interest, nor knows how much he is promoting it . . . he intends only his own gain, and he is in this, as in many other cases, led by an* invisible hand *to promote an end which was not part of his intention.*[2]

We can recognize the *end* promoted by the invisible hand as the economically efficient outcome.

The Efficiency Role of Government

When a well-functioning, perfectly competitive market is permitted to reach its equilibrium, the outcome is efficient: No opportunities for mutual gain remain unexploited. But government can, and does, *contribute* to the economic efficiency of markets, in two crucial ways.

First, the government provides the infrastructure that permits markets to function. Part of the infrastructure is physical—roads, bridges, airports, waterways, and buildings. Equally important is the market system's institutional infrastructure—laws, courts, and regulatory agencies. Although maintaining the institutional infrastructure uses only a small fraction of the nation's resources, the market economy would collapse without it.

The second way government supports market activity is by stepping in when markets are not working properly, that is, when they leave Pareto improvements unexploited.

The rest of this chapter explores these two government contributions to economic efficiency.

THE INSTITUTIONAL INFRASTRUCTURE OF A MARKET ECONOMY

Americans take their institutional infrastructure almost completely for granted. The best way to appreciate the infrastructure of the United States is to visit another country that has a poor one. In many countries, the police are more likely to steal from citizens than to protect them from thievery. In some nations, the people have no effective rights to their own property: Somebody can start building a shack on

---

[2] Adam Smith, *The Wealth of Nations* (Modern Library Classics edition, 2000), p. 423.

their land, and the government won't stop him. If a person is injured by a drunk driver, there may be no system for compensating her or punishing the driver. Many nations suffer from powerful mafias that extort protection money by threatening to shut down businesses or physically harm their owners.

For example, a study commissioned by the World Bank estimated that Russian households pay $3 billion in bribes each year, about half the amount they pay in income taxes. Most of the bribes paid by households went to education workers (including teachers!) and traffic police. Russian businesses pay even more in bribes: about $33 billion.[3]

Indonesia has a similar problem. More than half of households and businesses surveyed have been asked for bribes by government officials and others. And almost half of the government officials surveyed acknowledged receiving "unofficial payments."[4] (Teachers—once again—were frequent bribe takers.)

Although these are extreme examples, all too many nations suffer from problems of this type. But in nations with highly developed and stable legal infrastructures, such incidents are the exception rather than the rule. For example, very few students in the United States would even *think* of offering cash to an instructor for a better grade.

Figure 4 shows that when countries are divided into three groups, according to the quality of their institutional infrastructure, there is a strong relation between infrastructure and output per worker. The countries on the left—the ones with the lowest-quality infrastructures—were able to produce only about $3,000 in output per-worker per-year in 1988. These are the nations where property rights are weak, contracts are not enforced, and the government is more often predator than protector of economic activity. In the middle of the figure are countries with medium-quality infrastructures, averaging about $5,500 in output per worker per year. On the right are the best-organized countries, averaging $17,000 in output per worker. In this group, nations with the very best infrastructures—such as the United States—achieved output levels more than double that average.

The Legal System

The backbone of a market economy's institutional infrastructure is the legal system. Of course, the legal system is also important for noneconomic reasons. The law protects us from physical and emotional harm, and guarantees us freedom of speech and other vital civil liberties. Here, we will focus on the purely economic role of the legal system—the ways that it supports markets and helps us achieve economic efficiency. We'll look at five very broad categories: criminal law, property law, contract law, tort law, and antitrust law.

Criminal Law. While criminal law has important moral and ethical dimensions, its central economic function is to limit exchanges to voluntary ones. Since both parties agree to a voluntary exchange, they must each benefit from it. Therefore, as long as no third party is harmed, such an exchange will always be a Pareto improvement. But an *in*voluntary exchange—robbery, for example—always harms one side.

---

[3] "A Russian Tilts at Graft," *New York Times,* February 10, 2003; and "Report: Russian Society Saturated by Corruption," *Helsingin Sanomat,* International Edition, August 13, 2002 (*http://www.helsinki-hs.net/archive.asp*).

[4] "A Diagnostic Study of Corruption in Indonesia," Partnership for Governance Reform, *Final Report,* February 2002.

FIGURE 4
**Government Infrastructure and
Output per Worker**

Countries with low-quality infrastructures produced an average of only $3,000 per worker per year in 1988. These countries tend to have corrupt governments, poor enforcement of contracts, and weak property rights. Countries with higher-quality infrastructures, including the United States, produced an average of $17,000 per worker per year.

Source: Robert E. Hall and Charles I. Jones, "The Productivity of Nations," Working Paper 5812, National Bureau of Economic Research, November 1997; Robert E. Hall and Charles I. Jones, "Why Do Some Countries Produce So Much More Output per Worker than Others?" *Quarterly Journal of Economics,* 114:83–116, February 1999.

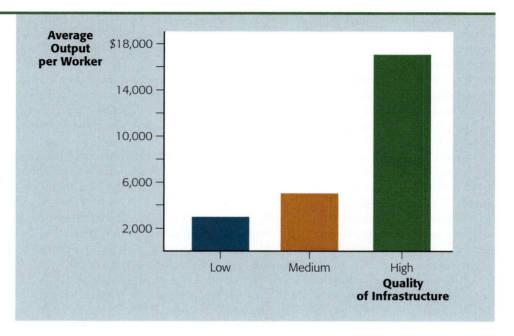

> *By making most involuntary exchanges illegal, criminal law helps to channel our energies into exchanges and productive activities that benefit all parties involved: Pareto improvements. In this way, criminal law contributes to economic efficiency.*

Of course, to be effective, it's not enough to merely define which activities are harmful; the criminal code must also be enforced, with penalties serious enough and certain enough to dissuade people from committing harmful crimes. In some cases, it has proven much easier to draft a criminal code than to provide for enforcement.

Russia, for example, enacted a sophisticated new criminal code in the mid-1990s, but has been unable to effectively enforce it, due to massive corruption in local governments and police forces. As a result, a disproportionate number of Russian citizens pursue activities that harm others, such as running protection rackets that victimize small businesses, or eliminating business competitors through threats and even assassinations.

Another example of the inefficiency caused by deficient law enforcement occurred after the U.S. occupation of Iraq in 2003. In the months following the invasion, the country's former government had ceased to operate, but the U.S. military had not exercised control in most of the country. It was not clear what laws were in effect, and no one was enforcing them in any case. As U.S. Army and Iraqi crews desperately tried to restore electric power to the country, they encountered a frequent problem: Looters would remove a length of copper wire from the unguarded power grid to sell on the black market for about $5. Each theft caused thousands of dollars of damage to the power grid and deprived millions of people of electricity for additional days, causing far greater harm to the country than benefits for the thief.[5]

[5] "Iraq Trip Report," Representative Frank Wolf, May 2003 (*http://www.house.gov/wolf/iraq-report-low.pdf*); Daniel Yergin, "Oil Shortage," CERA Newsroom, May 25, 2003 (*http://www.cera.com/news/details/1,1308,5577,00.html*), and various television news broadcasts.

Property Law. Property law gives people precisely defined, enforceable rights over the things they own. Without property law, people would spend a good part of their time dealing with others who claimed to own their house, their farm, or their factory. In the United States and other advanced countries, highly secure systems keep track of who owns land, cars, shares of stock, airplanes, patents, and other important pieces of property.

When property rights are poorly defined, much time and energy are wasted in disputes about ownership, and people spend time trying to capture resources from others—time that could have been spent producing valuable goods and services. As a result, countries with poorly defined property rights do not produce as much output from their resources as they could with better-defined property rights. This is inefficient: Benefits that buyers and sellers *could* gain from the additional output do not occur.

> *Property law—by reducing disputes about property, and channeling resources into production rather than the capture of property belonging to others—contributes to economic efficiency by increasing total production, thus raising the total benefits that markets can provide.*

Contract Law. In 1995, two 25-year-old Stanford graduate students, Larry Page and Sergey Brin, had an idea for a new Internet search engine, one that would find and organize Web sites according to their likely importance to the searcher. Initially, they funded the enterprise by borrowing money on credit cards and from parents and friends. But by 1998, in order to compete with existing search engines like Yahoo and Alta Vista, they needed more money than these resources could provide. Where could they get it?

Like many entrepreneurs before them, Page and Brin turned to strangers—people with money who were looking for a new company in which to invest. The young entrepreneurs signed contracts promising their investors a portion of the company's future profits.

It turned out that the new search engine—called Google—was indeed a success. Over the next several years, its traffic grew by 20 percent per month, and by the end of 2002, Google had about 300 employees and fielded 2,000 searches *per second*. The company had become highly profitable, earning half of its income by selling its search technique to other firms, and the other half from carrying advertising.

But what guaranteed that Page and Brin would honor all their contracts with investors and hand over the appropriate shares of the company's profits? In countries in which contract law is less well defined or less strictly enforced, investors would worry that they would not be able to collect their share. In the United States and other countries with a strong legal system, that worry rarely arises because contracts can be enforced.

A contract is a mutual promise. Often, as in the example of Google, one party does something first (investors provided millions of dollars) and the other party promises to do something later (Page and Brin promised to run the business and pay their investors a share of the profit). As long as no third parties are harmed, the exchange that occurs under a contract is always a Pareto improvement: It's a voluntary deal that won't happen unless both sides are made better off.

Contracts play a special role in a market economy. Without them, only Pareto improvements involving simultaneous exchange could take place: You get a bag of apples from a farmer and simultaneously hand over some money. Contracts enable us to make exchanges in which one person goes first. That person has to be able to rely on the other person to make good on the promise later. Without this assurance, whoever goes first would not be willing to make the deal in the first place. Thus, contracts make it possible to form new companies and to hire the services of experts who specialize in such things as auto repair, plumbing, roof repair, dentistry, and legal services—all cases in which someone goes first.

Specialization and Exchange

> *Contracts enable us to make exchanges that take place over time and in which one person must act first. In this way, contracts help society enjoy the full benefits of specialization and exchange.*

Legal enforcement of contracts is not the only force that makes people keep promises. Parents, religious organizations, and schools teach people that keeping a promise is a moral obligation. And a reputation for failing to keep promises would be harmful to a business or a person. Still, contracts and the infrastructure for enforcing them play a vital role in making the economy more efficient. There are enough would-be cheaters to create problems, and contract law provides an effective way to deal with them.

Tort Law. Contract law deals with people or businesses that are economically involved with each other, such as suppliers and their customers, or partners in a business deal. Tort law, on the other hand, deals with interactions among strangers or people not linked by contracts.

Tort A wrongful act that harms someone.

More specifically, a **tort** is a wrongful act—such as manufacturing an unsafe product—that causes harm to someone. Tort law defines the types of harm for which someone can seek legal remedy, and what sorts of compensation the injured person can expect.

When people and businesses are held responsible for injuries they cause, they act more carefully. Tort law in the United States provides incentives for drivers to drive carefully, for doctors to examine their patients more completely, and for manufacturers of products such as power mowers to control hazards through proper design. Tort law also protects against *fraud,* in which a seller of something—a product, a business, shares of stock—lies to the buyer in order to make the sale.

Antitrust Law. Antitrust law is designed to prevent businesses from making agreements or engaging in other behavior that limits competition and harms consumers. More specifically, antitrust law operates in three areas:

1. *Agreements among competitors.* U.S. antitrust law—expressed in Section 1 of the Sherman Act—prohibits "contracts, combinations, or conspiracies" among competing firms that would harm consumers by raising prices. The most flagrant agreements prohibited by this law are those that directly fix prices. But the law also prohibits agreements that raise prices indirectly, by limiting competition among sellers. An agreement by firms to allocate markets among them—so that one seller serves one group of customers exclusively, while other sellers are assigned their own groups of exclusive customers—may violate the law. For example, in the mid-1990s, the only two important sellers of review courses for the bar exam taken by prospective lawyers divided up their territory to avoid competition. The courts outlawed their agreement because it reduced competition.
2. *Monopolization.* Section 2 of the Sherman Act makes it illegal to monopolize or attempt to monopolize a market. As the law is now interpreted, it is illegal

for one seller to harm a rival by interfering with its operations or hobbling the rival in certain ways. For example, it is illegal for a company to spread false information about a rival's product as part of an attempt to drive that rival out of the market. But the law does not prohibit monopoly or harm to competitors. Rather, it prohibits *certain steps* to acquire or maintain a monopoly or to harm competitors. A firm that harms its rivals by selling a better product, thus taking business away from them, is not in violation of the law.

3. *Mergers.* In a merger, two firms combine to form one new firm. Mergers can sometimes result in higher prices from oligopoly or monopoly. For example, if the largest firm in a market has a 40 percent share of total sales and the second-largest has a 30 percent share, we can expect that the rivalry between them will benefit consumers. But if they merge to form a single firm with a 70 percent share, the rivalry would disappear and prices would rise. Mergers of this type are often blocked by the U.S. government based on Section 7 of the Clayton Act.

Regulation

Regulation is another important part of the institutional infrastructure that supports a market economy. Under regulation, a government agency—such as the Food and Drug Administration (FDA), the Environmental Protection Agency (EPA), or a state public utilities commission—has the power to direct businesses to take specific actions. The EPA has detailed control over what substances a business can release into the atmosphere or into the water. Public utilities commissions set the prices for electricity, gas, and telephone service. Often, regulators must approve business actions before they are undertaken, as in the case of the FDA's approval of new drugs.

Regulation differs from the use of legal procedures in a fundamental way: Regulators reach deep into the operations of businesses to tell them what to do, while legal procedures typically result in fines or other penalties if businesses do something wrong. To help see the distinction, consider the different ways in which regional and long-distance telephone companies are treated. Because they are regulated, regional telephone companies (such as Bell South or Cincinnati Bell) are *told* what price to charge. Long-distance phone companies, by contrast, are largely unregulated, so they can charge whatever price they wish. But if long-distance companies are caught breaking the law in setting prices (such as, by entering into illegal agreements to restrict competition), they will have to pay fines, and their managers may even have to go to jail.

Law and Regulation in Perspective

The invisible hand of the market system cannot operate on its own. The legal system, along with our regulatory agencies, creates an environment in which the invisible hand can do its job. Almost every Pareto improvement that we can think of relies on the legal and regulatory infrastructure. Recall the last time you bought a meal in a restaurant. If you paid cash, the criminal law against counterfeiting enabled the restaurant to more readily accept your paper currency. If you paid by credit card, contract law assured the restaurant that it would eventually be paid by the credit card company. The restaurant itself couldn't function without contracts with its suppliers, landlord, and employees. You could be reasonably confident that the food was not contaminated, in part because of inspections by local regulatory agencies and also because tort law provides legal disincentives for harmful products.

But what about cases where law and regulation don't seem to be working perfectly? After all, we still have crimes against people and property. Unsafe products like poorly designed automobiles or tainted frozen dinners *are* produced and only sometimes recalled before someone is harmed. Businesses *do* fix prices and are only sometimes caught. Accounting frauds—such as those that occurred at Enron, WorldCom, and some other major corporations in the early 2000s—*do* occur and cause serious harm to employees and stockholders. Do these and countless other examples mean that our institutional infrastructure is failing us?

Yes . . . and no. While instances like these are never welcome, our society has chosen not to eliminate them entirely. We could, if we wanted to, eliminate all crime, all unsafe products, and all other detriments to economic life by enacting more stringent laws and regulations and enforcing them to the hilt. But doing so would require even larger expenditures on legal and regulatory enforcement than we currently make. In deciding whether to make these expenditures, we must balance the benefits—safer products, reduced crime, and the like—against the costs.

For example, in part because of our strong tort law, the United States is one of the safest countries of the world, and is growing safer. Adult on-the-job death rates have fallen dramatically. But even the United States has chosen not to *completely eliminate* safety hazards: Each year, about 30 people out of every 100,000 die from accidents of some kind. Why do we accept this? Because the complete (or almost complete) elimination of fatal accidents would require too many of our resources to be diverted from other uses. Most of us would think it is simply not worth it. For example, to eliminate all preventable fatal accidents, we would have to require that every automobile be inspected dozens of times each month; that drivers enroll in a refresher course each year, perhaps each month, updating and reinforcing their driving skills and safety consciousness; and that all restaurants have laboratories to inspect every meal for *E. coli* contamination before serving it. Moreover, all of these requirements would have to be strictly enforced, requiring more police and inspectors to catch violators and more courts and jails to prosecute and penalize them. In such a world, our standard of living would plummet, and we'd all agree that we'd be better off taking on *some* additional risk of accidents in order to free up resources for increased production.

Policy Tradeoffs

> *A legal and regulatory system that ensured the complete elimination of crime, unsafe products, and other unwelcome activities would be less efficient than a system that tolerated some amount of these activities. An efficient infrastructure must consider the costs, as well as the benefits, of achieving our legal and regulatory goals.*

MARKET FAILURES

The social infrastructure we've been discussing largely helps to create fertile ground for markets to operate and generate Pareto improvements. But there is another vitally important role for government: to intervene in situations of *market failure.*

Market failure A market that fails to take advantage of every Pareto improvement.

> *A **market failure** occurs when a market equilibrium—even with the proper institutional support—is economically inefficient.*

Here, we'll focus on three general types of market failures to which economists have devoted a lot of attention: (1) monopoly power; (2) externalities; and (3) public goods. As you'll see, government involvement can often help deal with, and even cure, a market failure. But government involvement has costs as well as benefits, and sometimes government policies create problems of their own. While economists and policy makers agree in theory on what causes a market failure, dealing with real-world market failures remains one of the most controversial aspects of government policy.

MONOPOLY AND MONOPOLY POWER

A firm has *monopoly power* when it can influence the price that it charges for its product. Monopolists, oligopolists, and monopolistic competitors all have some monopoly power, because they *set* their price in order to maximize profit rather than take the price as given. However, competition among monopolistic competitors limits their monopoly power and helps keeps prices low. But a market with just one seller, or a few oligopolists who cooperate and behave as a monopoly, is a more serious market failure.

Why does monopoly power amount to a market failure? Let's consider an example. Imagine a perfectly competitive market for guitar lessons in a large city, with hundreds of teachers and thousands of students. Now imagine that this market is taken over by a single firm. We'll assume this new monopoly treats each of the old sellers as an independent operation . . . with one exception: The monopoly owner will now set the price of all lessons in the market, so as to maximize its total profit.

Figure 5 shows the market from the perspective of the new monopoly. Each additional lesson is provided by the part of the monopoly's operation that can produce it at the lowest additional cost—that is, by the supplier who provided that lesson before, when the market was perfectly competitive. Thus, the monopoly's *marginal cost* curve—showing the additional cost of another lesson—is the same as the original market supply curve. The demand curve, too, is the same as the original demand curve: At each price, people in the market will still choose to buy the same quantity of lessons they would buy before.

The monopoly maximizes profit by choosing the number of lessons per week at which marginal revenue and marginal cost are equal. However, the monopoly—unlike competitive suppliers—must drop the price on *all* lessons in order to sell one more. That's why the monopoly's marginal revenue curve lies below the demand curve: Marginal revenue is less than the price of the last lesson.

In the figure, you can see that the monopoly's profit-maximizing output level is 2,500 lessons per week, and it charges the highest price—$22—at which it can sell that number of lessons.

To understand the inefficiency caused by monopolization of this market, remember that each unit up to 4,000 *could* be provided at an additional cost (given by the height of the *MC* curve) that is lower than its value to some consumer (given by the height of the demand curve). So 4,000 is the *efficient* quantity, and also the *equilibrium* quantity under perfect competition. But the monopoly does not provide any of the lessons 2,501 through 4,000. Providing these lessons would be Pareto improvements . . . but they aren't provided. Why not? Buyers will only buy lessons whose value is greater than the price. But *the monopoly charges a price that is greater than marginal cost*. Therefore, buyers will choose *not* to buy some lessons

FIGURE 5
The Inefficiency of Monopoly

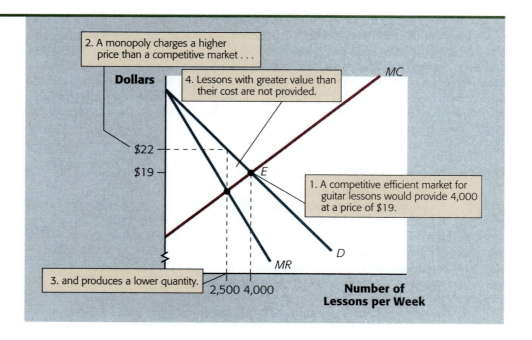

even though their value exceeds the additional cost of providing them. For example, in the figure, buyers do not buy the 2,501st lesson because its value is slightly less than $22. But the *marginal cost* of the 2,501st lesson is *substantially* below $22, so an efficient market would provide it.[6]

Our example generalizes to other firms that face a downward-sloping demand curve—that is, other firms with monopoly power:

> *Monopoly and imperfectly competitive markets—in which firms charge a price greater than marginal cost—are generally inefficient. Price is too high, and output is too low, to create the efficient outcome.*

What can the government do to make this monopoly market more efficient?

Antitrust Law as a Remedy

In the case of the guitar-lesson monopoly, there may be a solution: Since this market would function very well under competitive conditions, the government could use *antitrust law* to break the monopoly into several competing firms. But breaking up a monopoly would *not* make sense in other cases where the market would perform even worse with more competition.

For example, monopolies that arise from patents and copyrights, as discussed in Chapter 8, provide an incentive for artistic creations and scientific discovery. Break-

---

[6] Note that if the monopoly could *price discriminate*—continuing to charge $22 on lessons 1 through 2,500, and then charge $19 *just* for lessons 2,501 through 4,000—it *would* choose to supply the efficient quantity. (You may want to review price discrimination in the appendix to Chapter 8; in this case, the *MR* curve would be a horizontal line at $19 for all quantities between 2,501 to 4,000.) But not all firms can price discriminate. A *single-price* monopoly, like the one in Figure 5, will be inefficient.

ing up a monopoly in, say, a particular drug—by removing its patent before it expired—would lead to a greater and closer-to-efficient quantity of *that* drug. But it would also reduce incentives to develop *future* drugs. Over a long period of time, the benefits from the drug industry as a whole could be reduced. Drug prices are controversial: There are hot debates about the duration of drug patents and what should qualify as a patentable drug. But no one seriously proposes destroying temporary drug monopolies by eliminating patents and turning the market into anything resembling perfect competition.

Similarly, monopoly power that arises from *network externalities*—discussed in Chapter 8—offers benefits that would be hard to achieve under more competitive conditions. Microsoft, for example, takes advantage of its market power in several ways. But the Windows network, which provides substantial benefits, could not exist unless a single firm produced the operating system used by most personal computers.

Finally, when a monopoly arises as a *natural monopoly,* using antitrust law to break it up or even to prevent its formation in the first place is a poor remedy. Because this type of monopoly presents special challenges, it's worth its own discussion.

The Special Case of Natural Monopoly

In Chapter 5 and again in Chapter 8, you learned that a *natural monopoly* exists when, due to economies of scale, one firm can produce for the entire market at a lower cost per unit than can two or more firms. If the government steps aside, such a market will naturally evolve toward monopoly.

Figure 6 presents an example of a natural monopoly: a local cable company in a small city.

A cable company has important *lumpy inputs*—inputs needed in fixed amounts over a wide range of output. For example, whether the number of subscribers in the city is 1,000 or 100,000, a cable company must still lay the same, costly, underground cable to every neighborhood, and use up the same resources repairing and maintaining it. Similarly, the company's legal department must negotiate (and periodically renegotiate) contracts with each of its entertainment providers—the same number of contracts whether the company has just a few subscribers or 100,000. Spreading these costs over more subscribers reduces cost per unit. In the figure, these economies of scale continue until the entire market is served: The *LRATC* curve slopes downward through its intersection point with the market demand curve, *D*.

To serve an *additional* household, however, is *not* very costly to a cable company: just the installation appointment, some additional, above-ground cable, periodic replacement of the cable box, and handling the occasional complaint. Therefore, *marginal* cost for a cable company is relatively low. In Figure 6, we assume that marginal cost is a constant $15 per additional household—no matter how many households are served. Accordingly, the marginal cost curve is a horizontal line at $15.

If the market for cable service in the city is left to itself, one firm would become the sole supplier. In the absence of any government intervention, it would then sign up the profit-maximizing number of households, where marginal revenue (*MR*) and marginal cost (*MC*) are equal. In the figure, the *MR* and *MC* curves intersect at point *F*, and the cable monopoly will sign up 50,000 households. The price, at point *A* on the demand curve, is $60 per month and profit is equal to the shaded rectangle.

But point *A*—with an output of 50,000—is *inefficient*. In fact, the efficient level of output in the figure is found at point *B*, *where the* MC *curve crosses the demand curve* and the firm serves 100,000 households. The 50,001st through the 100,000th

FIGURE 6
Regulating a Natural Monopoly

Left unregulated, the cable mo-
nopoly would serve 50,000
households, where MC = MR.
This is inefficient, because units
50,001 to 100,000 have value to
some consumer greater than
their marginal cost.

By mandating a price of $15,
government regulators could
achieve the efficient outcome—
100,000 households—at point B.
But with price less than LRATC,
the monopoly would suffer a
loss, so it would have to be sub-
sidized or go out of business.

The alternative, which is typ-
ically chosen, is to set price at
$29—the lowest achievable av-
erage cost in this market, which
includes a "fair rate of return."
At this price, the monopoly
serves 85,000 households. This
is not the efficient quantity of
100,000, but is closer to the effi-
cient outcome than would be
achieved without regulation.

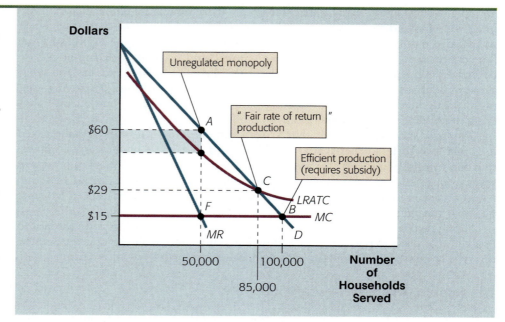

households still value cable service more than the additional cost of providing it to
them, so it would be efficient to provide them with the service. Once output has
risen to 100,000, further increases are worth less than $15 to consumers but would
cost the firm $15 to provide. Thus, serving 100,000 households, and no more, is
the efficient outcome. Because no household beyond the 50,000th will actually *buy*
cable service as long as the monopoly charges $60, the cable monopoly is a market
failure. What can the government do?

Using antitrust law to break the natural monopoly into several competing firms
would not make sense. With several firms—each supplying to only a part of the market—each firm's cost per unit would be even higher than the monopoly's cost per unit.
Therefore, the price in a more competitive market could never be $15 (the price needed
to get us to the efficient point *B*). In fact, competition, by raising cost per unit, might
result in an even *higher* price than under monopoly, creating even more inefficiency.

But if breaking up a natural monopoly is not advisable, what *can* government
do to bring us closer to economic efficiency? One option is public *ownership* and
operation of cable service, as is done with the post office, another natural monopoly. Public takeover of private business is rare, except when certain conditions are
present (to be discussed later in this chapter). That leaves one other option, and the
one local governments actually choose for the cable industry: *regulation*.

Regulation of Natural Monopoly

At the beginning of this chapter, you learned that under regulation, a government
agency digs deep into the operations of a business and takes some of the firm's decisions under its own control. In the case of a natural monopoly, regulators tell the
firm what price it can charge.

At first glance, you might think that natural monopoly regulators have an easy job. For example, in Figure 6, we know that the efficient quantity is 100,000 households—just the number of households that will purchase the service if the price is $15. Therefore, all the regulators have to do is set the official price at $15 and—voila!—an efficient market.

Unfortunately, it's not that easy. First, there is the matter of information: The regulators must be able to trace out the firm's *MC* curve as well as the market demand curve. This job is especially difficult when the monopoly's managers, hoping for a higher price, have an incentive to overstate costs. Even with a cooperative monopoly, the job is extremely complex, and the best regulators can hope for is a crude approximation to the actual curves.

More important, even with perfect information about the monopolist's cost and demand curves, regulators have a serious problem. If you look again at Figure 6, you'll notice that the *MC* curve lies everywhere *below* the *LRATC* curve. This must be the case for a natural monopoly, since economies of scale—the reason for the natural monopoly—means that the *LRATC* curve slopes downward, and this can occur only when marginal cost is less than average cost. (See Chapter 6 on the marginal–average relationship if you've forgotten why. Here, both marginal cost and average cost refer to the long run.)

Now you can see the problem for regulators: If they set the efficient price of $15 so that buyers demand the efficient quantity of 100,000, the firm's cost per unit is *greater* than $15. The firm will suffer a loss. In the long run, it will go out of business.

This problem leaves the regulator with two alternatives. First, it can set price equal to *MC* ($15 in our example) and *subsidize* the monopoly from the general budget, to make up for the loss. But this would require taxpayers in general, rather than just the monopoly's customers, to help pay for the product.

In practice, however, regulators in market economies around the world have usually chosen a different solution. The regulators determine a price that gives owners a "fair rate of return" for funds they've put into the monopoly. This fair rate of return is designed to be the same rate of return they could have earned in a similar, alternative investment. In other words, the fair rate of return should give the monopoly what economists call *normal profit*—a profit just high enough to cover all of the owners' opportunity costs, including the foregone interest on their own funds.

What price will accomplish this? Remember that we've included all costs into our cost curves, including the opportunity cost of owners' funds. Thus, a fair rate of return is already built into the *LRATC* curve in Figure 6. If the firm charges a price equal to average cost, it will cover all the costs of the operation, including the fair rate of return for owners. You can see that at point *C*—with a price of $29—the firm is charging the lowest possible price that prevents it from suffering a loss. This strategy—called *average cost pricing*—is the most common solution chosen by regulators of natural monopolies. More generally,

> *with average cost pricing, regulators strive to set the price equal to cost per unit where the* LRATC *curve crosses the demand curve. At this price, the natural monopoly makes zero economic profit, which provides its owners with a fair rate of return and keeps the monopoly in business.*

Average cost pricing is not a perfect solution. For one thing, it does not quite make the market efficient. For example, notice that in Figure 6, only 85,000 units are produced, instead of the efficient quantity of 100,000. Nevertheless, compared to no regulation at all, average cost pricing lowers the price to consumers and increases the quantity they buy, bringing us closer to the efficient level.

EXTERNALITIES

If you live in a dormitory, you have no doubt had the unpleasant experience of trying to study while the stereo in the next room is blasting through your walls—and usually not your choice of music. This may not sound like an economic problem, but it is one. The problem is that your neighbor, in deciding to listen to loud music, is considering only the private costs (the sacrifice of his own time) and private benefits (the enjoyment of music) of his action. He is not considering the harm it causes to you. Indeed, the harm you suffer might be greater than the benefit he gets from blasting his music. In this case, his turning down the volume could be a Pareto improvement, with an appropriate side payment. And unless he does turn down the volume, the situation remains inefficient.

When a private action has side effects that affect other people in important ways, we have the problem of externalities:

Externality A by-product of a good or activity that affects someone not immediately involved in the transaction.

> *An **externality** is a by-product of a good or activity that affects someone not immediately involved in the transaction.*

For example, the by-product of your neighbor blasting his stereo is the noise coming into your room. We call this a negative externality, because the by-product is harmful. When the by-product is *beneficial* to a third party, it is a positive externality. We'll consider examples of positive externalities a bit later.

The Private Solution to a Negative Externality

Under certain conditions, the inefficiency that would be caused by a negative externality will automatically be resolved by the parties themselves. Remember our example, early in the chapter, of the movie theater that would create benefits for some residents worth $100,000, but $70,000 worth of harm for others?

Imagine that instead of many residents, the harm would be inflicted on only *one* resident: Fernando, the owner of a private Zen mediation center next to the empty lot on which the theater is to be built. Because of the traffic congestion the theater would bring—and the associated engine noise, blaring horns, and pollution— Fernando would have to move his meditation center to another location. Moreover, he has determined that the time, trouble, and expense of moving would bring his total harm to $70,000.

Let's also imagine that the $100,000 in *benefits* would be received by just one person: Grace, the owner of the empty lot, who wants to build the theater on it.

In this situation, there is a negative externality of $70,000 affecting Fernando. Will the theater be built? The answer is: almost certainly *yes*. And—surprisingly— the result remains the same, regardless of who has the *legal rights* in this case.

Suppose Grace, the owner of the empty lot, has the legal right to build whatever she wants there. Then she will do so—and Fernando will move his center and suffer the $70,000 in harm, without compensation. This may or may not be fair, but *the theater will be built*.

Now suppose, instead, that Fernando has the legal right to *block* the sale. (Say, the city zoning law is written to prevent any theaters from being built without approval of those immediately next door.) Would Fernando want the theater to be built? You might think no, since the theater causes him harm. But, in fact, Fernando will almost certainly, in the end, favor the theater and be happy to move. Why?

If Fernando has the power to block the sale, Grace will realize that the only way to come out ahead is to *compensate* Fernando. Any side payment Grace makes under $100,000 still leaves her with a gain. Suppose she offers $80,000. Then by moving, Fernando would come out $10,000 ahead ($80,000 in cash minus the $70,000 in harm). In fact, while we can't predict the exact size of the side payment, we do know that it will end up somewhere between $70,000 and $100,000. We also know that (1) both sides have a powerful incentive to come to an agreement, because they can both gain from it; and (2) with only two parties involved, the costs of arranging the side payment will likely be low. Once again, even though building the theater forces Fernando to move, and he has the legal power to stop it, *the theater will be built.*

Note that building the theater is the *efficient* outcome given our assumptions. After all, the gains to the gainers are greater than the losses to the losers.

What if building the theater is *not* efficient, because it causes greater harm than benefits? Then side payments will ensure that it will not be built. (An end-of-chapter problem asks you to show this with a specific example.)

The Coase Theorem. As you've seen in our example, whether the theater will or will not be built depends entirely on whether it is the *efficient* or *in*efficient outcome, regardless of who holds the legal rights. Therefore, in our example, the negative externality is *solved* by the market. No government intervention is required, other than the initial assignment of legal rights.

This rather surprising result is known as the *Coase theorem*, named after the economist Ronald Coase

> The **Coase theorem** states that—when side payments can be negotiated and arranged without cost—the private market will solve the externality problem on its own, always arriving at the efficient outcome. While the initial distribution of legal rights will determine the allocation of gains and losses among the parties, it will not affect the action taken.

Coase theorem When a side payment can be arranged without cost, the market will solve an externality problem—and create the efficient outcome—on its own.

Note that the Coase theorem requires that side payments can be arranged *without cost*—or, in practice, that the cost is so low relative to the gains or losses at stake that it doesn't matter. This requirement is most likely to be satisfied when all three of the following conditions are present: (1) legal rights are clearly established; (2) legal rights can be easily transferred; and (3) the number of people involved is very small.

Unfortunately, many-real world situations do not satisfy these conditions. Legal rights are often in dispute. Suppose, for example, that the zoning law makes vague references to prohibiting "businesses known to create serious disturbance." Then, Grace and Fernando are very likely to end up in court, each having a different view about whether a movie theater is that kind of business. Since courts are often more concerned about fairness or legal interpretation than efficiency, the outcome may not be the efficient one. (This is not necessarily bad; fairness, as we've stressed, is a concern as well as efficiency.)

Furthermore, once a court decides the issue, legal rights may not be transferable. For example, if Fernando wins the court case and blocks the sale, the court may not allow Fernando to transfer his court victory to Grace even if she offers him a substantial side payment.

But the biggest problem in applying the Coase theorem to many real-world externalities is the third condition: Often, a large number of people are involved. Earlier in this chapter, we assumed—more realistically—that building the movie theater would affect *many* people in the town, positively and negatively. It would be very costly to determine the gains and losses for each one, get them all together, and then come up with a solution that would please everyone. Moreover, when many people are involved, achieving efficiency with side payments is plagued by an often insoluble problem, to which we turn now.

The Free Rider Problem. Once again, suppose that the efficient outcome is to build the theater. Suppose, too, that those who would be harmed have the legal power to block the sale, and a side payment has, indeed, been negotiated by representatives of the gainers and the losers—one that makes everyone come out ahead. The total side payment is $80,000, with each gainer told to contribute, say, $500. Now, we face another problem: A gainer may try to get a *free ride,* refusing to pay, reasoning that his own part of the payment is so small—just a "drop in the bucket"—that the theater will be built regardless. He may claim that he doesn't receive benefits, or just laugh off anyone who comes to collect. (Remember: the government is not involved at this point.) If *many* of those who should be part of the side payment reason this way and attempt to get a free ride, we have the *free rider problem.*

Free rider problem When the efficient outcome requires a side payment but individual gainers will not contribute.

> The **free rider problem** *occurs when the efficient outcome requires a side payment but individual gainers—each obligated to pay a small share of the side payment—will not contribute.*

The free rider problem, if extensive enough, can shrink the side payment until it isn't large enough to compensate losers and still leave the gainers better off. In that case, the private arrangement—based on voluntary participation rather than government coercion—will break down and the efficient outcome will not be achieved. Indeed, the free rider problem stands in the way of many Pareto improvements. And it is one of the main reasons why we typically turn to government to deal with important externalities that affect many people.

Market Externalities and Government Solutions

A competitive market has, by definition, many buyers and sellers. So when a negative externality affects a *market,* the private (Coase theorem) solution may not work.

Many negative externalities in markets are caused by some form of *pollution.* Cities pollute rivers and lakes with sewage, and industries pollute them with chemicals. Cars and power plants pollute the atmosphere. As you are about to see, the market for a good that creates pollution—like markets with other negative externalities—is inefficient.

Panel (a) of Figure 7 illustrates an inefficiency in the market for gasoline, which pollutes the air with carbon monoxide and soot, dust, and other visible and microscopic solids. In the figure, we assume that the market is perfectly competitive. (Ignore the curve labeled *MSC* for now.) The supply curve *S*—like every market

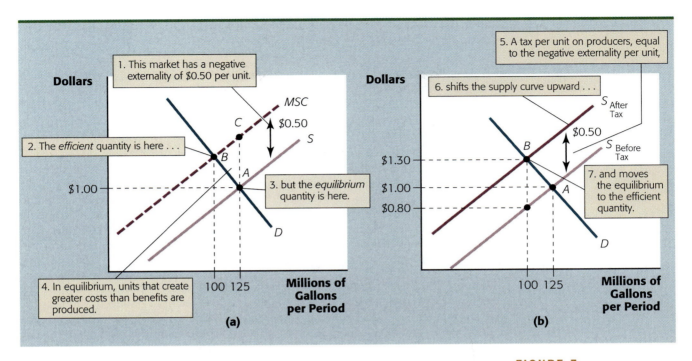

FIGURE 7
A Tax on Producers to Correct a Negative Externality

supply curve we've considered so far—reflects the costs of inputs used by *gasoline producers*. The height of the supply curve at any output level tells us the marginal cost (MC) of producing the last unit of output.

But the supply curve does *not* reflect any costs to the general public—such as the health and environmental damage caused by pollution—because (before government involvement) the firm does not have to pay them. The market reaches equilibrium at point *A*, where the supply curve *S* and the demand curve *D* intersect. The equilibrium quantity of gasoline is 125 million gallons per period, and the price is $1.00 per gallon.

But if gasoline causes a negative externality, 125 million is *not* the efficient output level. We can see this by incorporating the negative externality into our diagram. Let's suppose that each gallon of gas imposes a cost to the general public of $0.50. When we add this cost to the marginal cost already paid by gasoline producers, we get the **marginal social cost** (*MSC*) of another unit of gasoline. *MSC* includes *all* costs of producing another unit of gas: the resources used up and paid for by the industry, *and* the costs imposed on third parties. Because *MSC* is the fuller concept of costs, whenever there is a negative externality, *MSC* > *MC* at any level of output. This is why the *MSC* curve in Figure 7 lies *above* the market supply curve.

Once we draw the *MSC* curve in Figure 7, panel (a), we discover that the *efficient* level of output is 100 million gallons, where the *MSC* curve intersects the demand curve at point *B*. Why? Efficiency requires that the market provide only those units that are valued more highly by consumers than they cost to produce. The *MSC* curve tells us what it *really* costs to produce gas, when *all* costs are considered. For all units up to 100 million, the demand curve lies above the *MSC* curve, so those units are more highly valued than their costs. An efficient market would provide these 100 million units. But for all units *beyond* 100 million, the *MSC* curve lies

Marginal social cost (*MSC*) The full cost of producing another unit of a good, including the marginal cost to the producer *and* any harm caused to third parties.

above the demand curve. These units should *not* be produced, because they cost more—in the fullest sense—than their value to consumers.

> *A market with a negative externality associated with producing or consuming a good will produce* more *than the efficient quantity.*

How can we achieve the efficient result of 100 million gallons? One way is to change the *equilibrium* quantity to 100 million. Perhaps we could somehow raise the supply curve to the position of the *MSC* curve in Figure 7, panel (a). Indeed, if the Coase theorem applied—and everyone affected could negotiate and enforce an agreement without cost—the private market could accomplish this on its own.

Unfortunately, with so many people involved, it would take too much time and trouble for individual gasoline producers and consumers to arrange the appropriate side payments and production cutbacks, and in any case, the free rider problem would effectively destroy the arrangement. The efficient outcome, therefore, requires *government intervention* in the market.

Taxing a Negative Externality. One method the government could use to move the gasoline market to point *B* would be a tax on producers. In panel (b) of Figure 7, we show the effect of a tax of $0.50 per gallon, which is the harm caused by each additional gallon of gas. In addition to its other inputs, each firm would have to pay $0.50 per gallon to the government. As each firm's marginal cost rose by $0.50, the market supply curve would shift upward by $0.50, raising it to the position of the *MSC* curve. Once the tax is in place, the market would reach a new equilibrium at point *B*—producing the efficient quantity of 100 million gallons.

Notice that, in the new equilibrium, the price of gasoline to consumers rises from $1.00 to $1.30. Producers, meanwhile, keep only $0.80 of that $1.30, because they have to pay $0.50 to the government on each gallon they sell at $1.30. Thus, the payment of the externality tax is shared between consumers and producers.

> *A tax on each unit of a good, equal to the external harm it causes, can correct a negative externality and bring the market to an efficient output level.*

Let's take a step back and consider the logic of this result. The tax cures the inefficiency because it forces the market to *internalize the externality*—to take account of the harm caused by gasoline. After the tax, the harm caused by gasoline affects the decisions of *both* producers and consumers. The firm receives 20 cents less for each gallon it sells, so it decides to produce less. Consumers pay 30 cents more, so they decide to buy less.

This logic suggests that a tax on *consumers* of gasoline would work just as well as a tax on producers. If a tax of $.50 per gallon were imposed on consumers, the market demand curve would shift *downward* by that amount, and the end result would be the same as in our example: Consumers would pay $1.30 (including the tax), producers would get $0.80, and the market would once again arrive at the same efficient quantity of 100 million. (An end-of-chapter problem asks you to illustrate this.)

Taxes to correct negative externalities have been used in countries around the world: Sweden has imposed a tax on each kilogram of nitrogen oxide emitted by power plants. Denmark imposes taxes on businesses that produce, and households that consume, products that cause carbon dioxide emissions. Malaysia taxes harmful by-products of palm oil mills. And Vietnam has imposed a tax on coal production—

HTTP://

Jeffrey Frankel's "Greenhouse Gas Emissions" is an interesting analysis of an important negative externality. You can find it at http://www.brook.edu/comm/ PolicyBriefs/pb052/pb52.htm.

largely because of the harm to tourism caused by unsightly coal mines.[7] In the United States, however, negative externalities are more often corrected with other methods.

Regulation and Tradable Permits.

A tax is not the only way to correct a negative externality. Government can also use *regulation* to move a market closer to the efficient point. For example, in the gasoline market, regulators could tell car owners how much they could drive, or tell car producers how much pollution their vehicles are allowed to create. Indeed, this last regulation—state pollution restrictions on new automobiles—has been the method of choice for reducing pollution from automobiles in the United States.

But in the last two decades, the U.S. government has also relied increasingly on an innovative technique—called *tradable permits*—to reduce several types of pollution. This method is based on an understanding of Pareto improvements.

A **tradable permit** is a license that allows a company to release a unit of pollution into the environment over some period of time. By issuing a fixed number of permits, the government determines the total level of pollution that can be legally emitted each period. However, firms can sell their government-issued permits to other firms in an organized market.

A firm whose technology would make it very costly to reduce pollution generally *buys* permits in the market. By buying a permit at a price lower than its cost of reducing pollution by another unit, the high-cost firm comes out ahead. At the same time, a firm whose technology enables it to reduce pollution rather cheaply will *sell* permits. By giving up permits, the low-cost firm takes on the obligation to reduce its pollution further. But by selling the permit at a price greater than its pollution-control cost, the low-cost firm gains as well.

The trading of permits shifts the costs of any given level of environmental improvement toward those firms who can do so more cheaply. The general public, however, is not affected by the trade, since total pollution remains unchanged. Therefore, for any given level of pollution, allowing firms to buy and sell licenses generates Pareto improvements. Viewed another way, tradable permits—by making it cheaper to lower pollution—has enabled the U.S. government to impose stricter environmental standards with the same total burden on producers.

Tradable permits have been used since the early 1980s to reduce several types of pollution. Permits for adding lead to gasoline virtually eliminated leaded gasoline from the market within five years. And a system of tradable permits begun in 1990 for sulfur dioxide (the pollutant that causes acid rain) cut emissions in half within five years—well ahead of schedule and at much lower cost than anticipated. Tradable permits are catching on in other countries as well, and are being considered, along with other policies, in international efforts to address the problem of global warming.

> **Tradable permit** A license that allows a company to release a unit of pollution into the environment over some period of time.

Left to itself, a market with a negative externality will produce too much output. Taxes, regulation, and tradable permits are examples of government intervention to decrease output toward the efficient level.

Dealing with a Positive Externality.

What about the case of a positive externality, in which the by-product of a good or service *benefits* other parties rather than harms them? Once again, the market will not arrive at the economically efficient output level; in this case, output will be *too low.*

[7] International Institute for Sustainable Development Web page (*http://iisd.ca/susprod/displaydetails.asp?id=74*).

Marginal social benefit (MSB)
The full benefit of producing another unit of a good, including the benefit to the consumer *and* any benefits enjoyed by third parties.

To see why, consider the market for a college education. In deciding whether to go to college, each of us takes account of the costs to us (tuition, room and board, what we could have earned instead of going to college) and the benefits to us (a higher-paying and more interesting job in the future, the enjoyment of learning). But by becoming educated, you also benefit other members of society in many ways. For example, you will be a more informed voter and thereby help to steer the government in directions that benefit many people besides you. If you major in chemistry, biology, or mechanical engineering, you may invent something that benefits society at large more than it benefits you. Or you may learn concepts and skills that make you a more responsible member of your community. Thus, the market for college education involves a positive externality.

Let's see why a competitive market in college education, with no government interference, would not produce the economically efficient amount of education.

Figure 8, panel (a), shows the market for bachelor's degrees. The height of the supply curve *S* reflects the costs of providing each degree at colleges and universities, and the height of the demand curve measures the value of each degree—*to the person who gets it.* But the demand curve does *not* reflect any of the benefits that college provides to the general public. Without government intervention, the market reaches equilibrium at point *A,* where the supply curve *S* and the demand curve *D* intersect. The equilibrium number of degrees is 800,000 per year, and the four-year price of a degree is $100,000.

But since college confers benefits on society at large, 800,000 is *not* the efficient output level. We can see this by incorporating the positive externality into our diagram. Let's suppose that each bachelor's degree gives the general public $30,000 in benefits. When we add this benefit to the benefit for the degree holders themselves, we get the **marginal social benefit** (*MSB*) of another degree. *MSB* includes *all* the benefits of producing another bachelor's degree—the benefits to the holder *and* the benefits to society at large. This is why the *MSB* curve in Figure 8, panel (a), lies *above* the market demand curve. The distance between the curves is $30,000—the value of the positive externality.

Once we draw the *MSB* curve in Figure 8, panel (a), we discover that the *efficient* level of output is 1 million college degrees, where the *MSB* curve intersects the supply curve at point *B.* Why? Efficiency requires that the market provide any unit that has more value than it would cost to produce. The *MSB* curve tells us what the value of each degree *really* is, when *all* benefits are considered. For all units up to 1 million, the *MSB* curve lies above the supply curve, so those units provide greater value than their costs. An efficient market would provide these 1 million units, but a competitive market—left to itself—provides only 800,000.

A market with a positive externality associated with producing or consuming a good will produce less than the efficient quantity.

How can we achieve the efficient result of 1 million college degrees each year? One way is to *change* the demand curve so it is the same as the *MSB* curve in panel (a) of Figure 8. If everyone affected could negotiate and enforce an agreement without cost (the Coase theorem, which applies to positive externalities as well as negative), then the private market could solve the problem. People who benefit from *others'* degrees could be asked to give a side payment to those in college. This side payment would be included as part of the value of the degree for those considering

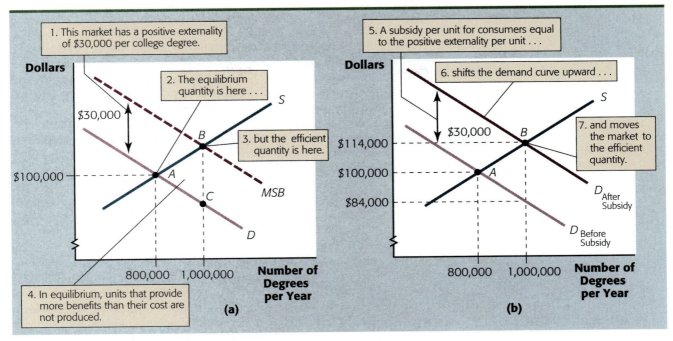

(a)

1. This market has a positive externality of $30,000 per college degree.

2. The equilibrium quantity is here . . .

3. but the efficient quantity is here.

4. In equilibrium, units that provide more benefits than their cost are not produced.

Dollars

$30,000

$100,000

S

B

A

C

D

MSB

800,000   1,000,000

Number of Degrees per Year

(b)

5. A subsidy per unit for consumers equal to the positive externality per unit . . .

6. shifts the demand curve upward . . .

7. and moves the market to the efficient quantity.

Dollars

$30,000

$114,000

$100,000

$84,000

S

B

A

$D_{After Subsidy}$

$D_{Before Subsidy}$

800,000   1,000,000

Number of Degrees per Year

FIGURE 8
A Subsidy for Consumers to Correct a Positive Externality

college, shifting the demand curve upward. With a side payment of $30,000 per student, the market demand curve would rise to the position of the *MSB* curve and the market would provide 1 million degrees, the efficient level.

Of course, the time, trouble, and expense of arranging such a system privately would be prohibitive. And the free rider problem would be unmanageable. (Imagine someone passing the hat for voluntary contributions to support strangers in college!) Efficiency, once again, requires *government intervention.*

In most countries, the method of choice for government in the education market is *subsidies*—a payment to a producer or consumer for each unit provided. In the figure, we imagine that the subsidy is paid to students. (An end-of-chapter question asks you to explore the case where the subsidy is paid to colleges.) In Figure 8, panel (b), a subsidy of $30,000 per degree causes each student to add $30,000 to the value he or she places on a college education, thereby shifting up the demand curve by that amount. Each student would now be willing to pay $30,000 more than before, because they will receive that sum from the government.

The subsidy causes the market to *internalize* the positive externality of benefits from college degrees. That is, it forces consumers and producers to consider these benefits when making decisions. In the new equilibrium, the price of a degree rises, from $100,000 to $114,000 in the figure. This encourages colleges to increase enrollments. But students, after accounting for the subsidy, pay only $114,000 − $30,000 = $84,000. This is why more of them choose to attend college.

A subsidy on each unit of a good, equal to the external benefits it creates, can correct a positive externality and bring the market to an efficient output level.

PUBLIC GOODS

One of the major roles of government in the economy is to provide *public goods*. These are goods that the market—if left to itself—will not provide at all, or will not provide efficiently even if there is no other market failure. It is left to the government to provide public goods in the efficient quantities, usually free of charge. (A more formal definition of public goods will come a bit later.)

To understand what makes a good public rather than private, let's begin by discussing two important features of *private goods*. First, a private good is characterized by **rivalry** in consumption—if one person consumes it, someone else cannot. If you rent an apartment, then someone else will *not* be able to rent that apartment. The same applies to virtually all goods that you buy in markets—food, computers, air travel, and so on. Rivalry also applies to privately provided services: the time you spend with your doctor, lawyer, or career counselor is time that someone else will *not* spend with that professional.

> **Rivalry** A situation in which one person's consumption of a unit of a good or service means that no one else can consume that unit.

Most of the goods and services we've considered so far in this text are rival goods. By allowing the market to provide rival goods at a *price*, we ensure that people take account of the opportunity costs to society of their decisions to use these goods. If they were provided free of charge, people would tend to use them even if their value were less than the value of the resources used to produce them. Moreover, offering a rival good free of charge enables some people who don't value the good very highly to grab up all available supplies, depriving others who might value the goods even more. Thus, leaving such goods to the market—where a price reflecting marginal cost is charged—tends to promote economic efficiency.

If a good is rivalrous, efficiency requires that people pay a price for its use. In the absence of any market failure, private provision will lead to the efficient level of production.

> **Excludability** The ability to exclude those who do not pay for a good from consuming it.

A second feature of a private good is **excludability,** the ability to exclude those who do not pay for a good from consuming it. When you go to the supermarket, you are not permitted to eat frozen yogurt unless you pay for it. The same is true when you go to the movies or purchase a car. But if firms can*not* prevent nonpayers from consuming a good, the market will be *unable* to provide it, since few consumers would pay if they can consume it without paying. Excludability is what makes it *possible* for private firms to provide a good.

If a good is excludable, it can *be provided by the private market.*

Let's sum up so far: Rivalry means that a price *must* be charged to achieve efficiency. Excludability means that private firms—who *do* charge a price—*can* produce it. If a good has both of these characteristics, it is called a *pure private good*.

> **Pure private good** A good that is both rivalrous and excludable.

A good that is both rivalrous and excludable is a **pure private good.** *In the absence of any significant market failure, private firms will provide these goods at close to efficient levels.*

But not all goods have these two characteristics. Consider, for example, an urban park located in an area where many people pass by during the day. People will enjoy walking by the park, just because it is pretty to look at. But to provide and maintain it requires many resources and raw materials: the labor of landscape architects and gardeners, gardening tools, fertilizer, flower bulbs, and so on. However, a walk-by park is, essentially, *nonexcludable*. If a private firm provided the park, the firm could not limit the benefits of walking by to those who paid for it. (Yes, it could construct a giant fence, but that would prevent *everyone* who walked by from seeing and enjoying the park.) For this reason, a private firm would have difficulty surviving by creating and maintaining an urban, walk-by park.

"But wait," you may think. "Couldn't the firm *ask* people to contribute according to the importance they place on the park?" Yes, but then each individual would have an incentive to downplay its importance and pay nothing. This is the *free rider problem* mentioned earlier in this chapter: When a good is nonexcludable, people have an incentive to become free riders—to let others pay for the good, so they can enjoy it without paying.

Thus, a private firm is generally unable to provide a nonexcludable good at all; it would not be able to stay in business.

> *When a good is nonexcludable, the private sector will generally be unable to provide it. In most cases, if we want such a good, government must provide it.*

In addition to being nonexcludable, urban parks are *nonrival*: One person can consume or enjoy passing by the park without anyone else consuming or enjoying less of it. Moreover, it uses up *no more of society's resources* when the benefits of the park are extended to an additional person. For this reason, even if the private sector *could* somehow charge us according to our consumption of the view as we walk by the park, it *should not* charge us. Why not? Because by charging a price each time we walk by, it would force each of us to consider a personal cost that does *not* correspond to any opportunity cost for society. Each time an additional person sees the park, a Pareto improvement takes place: That person gains and no one loses. Thus, to be economically efficient, *everyone* who places *any value at all* on seeing the park should be able to see it. But this will only happen if the price of seeing the park is *zero*.

This leads us to an important conclusion: Since the economically efficient price for the park is zero, private firms—which would have to charge a positive price—should not be the ones to provide it. That is, even if a firm *could* exclude those who do not pay, it *should not* do so. By charging a positive price, the number of people deciding to pay and enjoy the park would be below the economically efficient level.

> *When a good or service is nonrival, the market cannot provide it efficiently. Rather, to achieve economic efficiency, the good or service would have to be provided free of charge.*

Now let's combine these features. If a good is nonrival, the private market cannot provide it *efficiently*, since efficiency requires a zero price. If it's nonexcludable, the private market will usually not provide the good *at all*. If a good has both of these characteristics, it is called a *pure public good*.

> *A good that is both nonrivalrous and nonexcludable is a **pure public good**.*

Pure public good A good that is both nonrivalrous and nonexcludable.

A pure public good, if it could provide benefits to some people that are greater than the cost of providing it to them, is a market failure. Producing the good would be efficient. But because the good is nonexcludable, the private market generally ignores it. This means that if we rely on the private market, we not only don't get the efficient quantity, we generally get *no* quantity. Furthermore, even if the private market *could* provide such a good, it could usually not do so efficiently, because charging *any* positive price for a nonrivalrous good would be inefficient.

Although we've been discussing rivalry and excludability—and their opposites—as absolutes, these characteristics are often murky. Some of the benefits of consuming a good can be rival, and some nonrival. Some of the benefits can be excludable, and some not. Consider a newspaper. Consumption of the paper is mostly rival: The paper I buy at the newsstand and take home can't be bought and taken home by you. It's also partly excludable: You can't buy it from the newsstand unless you pay. But an important aspect of this good is the *information* inside it, which is largely *nonrival* (if I tell you what I've read, you gain knowledge of the news without diminishing my knowledge) and somewhat *nonexcludable* (if I tell you the news, you get the information without having to pay the newspaper company).

Accordingly, it makes sense to view rivalry and excludability as a matter of *degree,* rather than absolute categories. This is why, in Figure 9, different goods are positioned at different points along a spectrum for rivalry and excludability. Goods that appear farthest toward the upper left corner are the *purest private goods*—those with a very *high degree* of excludability and rivalry. These include most of the goods we've discussed in earlier chapters, such as bed frames, car washes, wheat, extermination services, and so on. The market almost always provides these goods and—with the government's help when necessary to correct for externalities and limit monopoly power—can provide them in close-to-efficient quantities.

Goods that appear farthest toward the lower right corner are the *purest public goods:* almost entirely nonrival and nonexcludable. National defense, for example, has both characteristics: My being defended to any degree doesn't mean you are defended any less. And it is virtually impossible to exclude those who don't pay from the benefits of national defense, as long as they remain in the country.

Many considerations go into the *relative* positions of the goods in Figure 9, and you may disagree with our choices. For example, we've made cable television more nonexludable than highways (it's easier to hook up cable illegally than to bypass a highway tollbooth once it's installed). Similarly, we've positioned cable television as more *rivalrous* than software, because *certain* aspects of cable service—the installation appointment, the cable box, repairs—use up resources that others can't use simultaneously.

Mixed Goods

Goods that appear in the upper right and lower left corners can be called *mixed goods,* because they share features of both public and private goods. These goods are becoming increasingly important in our society, and they are responsible for some growing social tension and controversy.

Excludable but Nonrivalrous Goods. Consider first goods near the upper right-hand corner, which are excludable but nonrivalrous. This category includes most information products. The problem with this type of mixed good is that although the private sector can (and often does) supply it, it does not do so in the efficient quantity. As you've learned, efficiency in the market for a nonrivalrous good is achieved only when additional units are available without charge.

For example, Microsoft and other software companies have considerable power to *exclude* you from using their software unless you pay, by encoding discs with copy protection and limiting the number of installations permitted. And although some

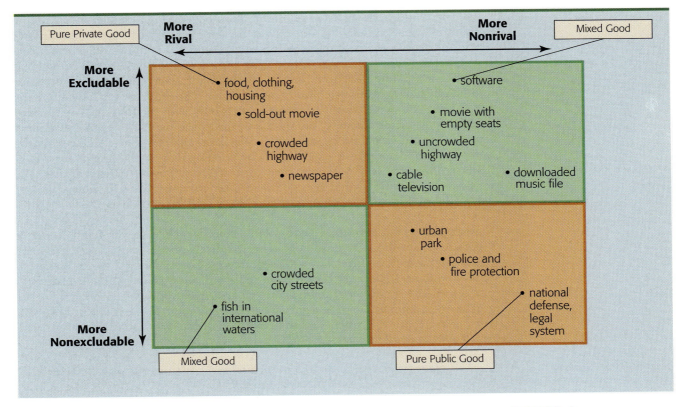

FIGURE 9
Pure Private, Pure Public, and Mixed Goods

people can break these codes, most cannot. Yet providing someone with an *additional* copy of its software hardly costs Microsoft anything at all. And if not for the embedded copy protection, people could copy the software from their friends, using up no resource other than the space on their own hard drive. Software, then, is an essentially nonrivalrous good, but an excludable one. It is neither pure public nor pure private.

Digital music files are another example of this type of mixed good. Over the past few years, millions of people have downloaded copyrighted songs from file-sharing servers such as Morpheus, Gnutella, Kazaa, WinMX, and Audiogalaxy. Digital music files are nonrivalrous: The digital code can be recopied endlessly, at almost zero cost. Therefore, it is *efficient* for this good to be provided free of charge. However, unless we want the government to run the music industry, private firms need to charge for music. Currently, music remains somewhat excludable, for two reasons: (1) it is against the law to make copyrighted music available online; and (2) many people—either because of respect for the law, fear of getting caught, lack of technical expertise, or scarce time—still prefer to buy their music from a store or online shopping service.

Public *Provision* Versus Public *Production* Don't confuse public *provision* of a good with public *production*. The government must *provide* a pure public good in order to correct the market failure problem. But it can provide it by either producing the good itself (public production) or contracting production out to private firms (private production). Many local governments, for example, pay private firms to collect trash or run prisons: private production. These services are purchased by government and *publicly provided* without charge to residents. Similarly, almost all of the *goods* that are used for national defense—tanks, radar equipment, laser-guided munitions—are produced by private firms and purchased by the federal government. However, the government chooses *public production* for the *service* of national defense itself: It hires, trains, and manages U.S. military personnel, and manages defense goods after buying them. It's the government's *provision* of national defense without charge—not the government production—that cures the market failure.

DANGEROUS CURVES

But by 2003, with an estimated 60 million people downloading music online without paying, excludablility was rapidly breaking down. The easiest solution isn't available: Years ago, the industry adopted common CD audio standards that rule out embedded copy protection. Introducing copy protection now would entail great cost, and risk public alienation, since it would require everyone to buy new stereos and handheld players to listen to the new format. The industry has tried suing the file-sharing companies, but had major success only with the first one—Napster—which it put out of business. In mid-2003, the music industry began threatening lawsuits for individual users, and lobbied for legal changes that would permit the industry to sabotage file-sharing services by flooding them with requests for downloads, redirecting users' queries to their own sites, and posting corrupted files. The music industry in the digital age is desperately looking for ways to achieve greater excludability, but has not yet found a good solution.

Nonexcludable but Rivalrous Goods. Now consider the lower left-hand corner of Figure 9, which shows nonexcludable but rivalrous goods. City streets and some important natural resources fall into this category. Economists use the term *tragedy of the commons* to describe the problem caused by many of these goods. In a traditional English village, the commons was an area freely available to all families for grazing their animals. Grazing rights are a rivalrous good: If one cow eats the grass, another can't. But the commons had no method of exclusion, so it was overgrazed, causing harm to *all* families.

Tragedy of the commons The problem of overuse when a good is rivalrous but nonexcludable.

> The *tragedy of the commons* occurs when rivalrous but nonexcludable goods are overused, to the detriment of all.

A current example of the tragedy of the commons is fishing in international waters. No one owns these areas of the ocean and no single government can tell people not to fish in them. And since no one charges for the fish removed, fishing boats use huge nets that catch just about every source of protein (most of which is ground up to be used as cattle feed). A recent study, correcting some inaccuracies in earlier research, has found that world fish landings have been declining steadily since 1980.[8] The decline would be even steeper if not for the efforts of fishers, who have been going farther offshore, fishing deeper, fishing more intensively, and going after smaller and smaller fish. But these very methods are also changing the ocean's ecosystem, threatening species of ocean life further down the food chain. Unless something is done, the decline in the world's supply of fish—and other ocean life—may accelerate, overwhelming the efforts of the fishing industry to forestall the decline in catches. Although scientists have recommended specific limits on national governments since 1987, virtually every country—concerned about the welfare of its *own* fishing industry—has chosen to ignore the recommendations. Each government is a free rider in the international community, reasoning that its own fish catch is just a "drop in the bucket," and that whatever other governments do, it is better off allowing its *own* crews to continue depleting the fish.

EFFICIENCY AND GOVERNMENT IN PERSPECTIVE

In this chapter, you've seen that an economy with *well-functioning, perfectly competitive markets* tends to be economically efficient. But notice the italicized words.

[8] Daniel Pauly and Reg Watson, "Counting the Last Fish," *Scientific American,* July 2003 (pp. 42–47).

As you've seen in this chapter, many types of government involvement are needed to ensure that markets function well and to deal with market failures. The government helps markets to function by providing a legal and regulatory infrastructure. In extreme cases of imperfect competition, government antitrust action or regulation may be needed. The government imposes taxes and subsidies and uses other methods to deal with externalities. And the government often steps in to provide goods and services that are nonrival, nonexcludable, or both.

These cases of government involvement are not without controversy. In fact, most of the controversies that pit Democrats against Republicans in the United States (or Conservatives against Labourites in Britain, or Social Democrats against Christian Democrats in Germany) relate to when, and to what extent, the government should be involved in the economy. Debates about public education, Social Security, international trade, and immigration all center on questions of the proper role for government. Some of the disagreement is over the government's role in bringing about a more fair economy, but there is also debate about the government's role in bringing about economic efficiency.

How could anyone disagree with the government's role in bringing about efficiency with a strong legal structure and corrections for market failure?

While we've been stressing how government *can* improve efficiency, it isn't always easy. First, there are information problems. Just how much damage do negative externalities from pollution cause? And how can the harm be valued in dollars? What is the dollar value of the external benefits from a college degree? These questions are not easy to answer with any accuracy, and estimates are always controversial. While government may be able to move us *closer* to efficiency, it can also fall short or overshoot based on inaccurate information.

Second, there are incentive problems for government. Government officials are the agents of the general public and are supposed to serve the public interest. But these officials may have their own incentives, such as expanding the size of their departmental budgets. Although there are checks and balances for monitoring and limiting this type of behavior, their effectiveness is sometimes limited.

Government officials can also be influenced by lobbies for special-interest groups. The benefits from a single, favorable government decision are highly concentrated on a specific firm or industry, but the *costs* of that one decision are widely dispersed among the population. Therefore, firms have great incentive to lobby for favorable policies, while the general public has little incentive to oppose them. For example, from 1997 to 2002, during a period of rapid changes in the health care system that were being shaped by legislation, the pharmaceutical industry spent an estimated $478 million directly lobbying Congress and an additional $172 million on federal campaign contributions, TV ads, and general efforts to sway public opinion.[9] Expenditures of this magnitude can tilt government decision making in favor of a specific industry—which may or may not be the efficient policy decision.

Third, in order for government to have the funds it needs to support markets and do other things, it must raise revenue through taxes. These taxes can introduce inefficiencies of their own.

Finally, there is also an inherent problem with the provision of public goods that almost guarantees *dissatisfaction* about them. With a private good, each of us—facing the market price—buys whatever quantity we choose. We may feel frustrated about the size of our income or wealth, but given those constraints, each of us is free to purchase the

---

[9] "Drug Industry Sees Increase in Lobbying," *Wall Street Journal,* June 24, 2003.

quantity of each good that brings us the most satisfaction as individuals. If one person loves Italian food and another loves rock concerts, we'd expect to see them purchasing vastly different amounts of these two goods, based on their differing preferences.

But public goods, by their nature, are provided in a politically determined quantity, and *everyone* must consume the same amount. One person can't consume a strong national defense while another consumes a weak one. So, even if the political process is working *well,* about half the population will feel we are spending too much on a specific public good, and half the population will believe we are spending too little. This does not mean the government is acting inefficiently; but it does explain some of the controversy over government involvement in the economy.

Finally, remember that there are other important roles for the government besides fostering efficiency, such as equity, fairness, justice, and more. As discussed elsewhere in this text, these are not issues over which people easily agree. Taxing gasoline to correct an externality would hit the poor harder than the rich, while taxing airline travel would do the opposite. Eliminating price supports for agricultural goods might move the economy toward efficiency, but it would cause harm to many farmers and their families. Almost every change in the tax code designed to improve either efficiency or equity will raise a firestorm of protest because of the way it might affect the other.

These controversies are so heated and so varied, that it is easy to forget how much agreement there is about the role of government. Anyone studying the role of government in the economies of the United States, Canada, Mexico, France, Germany, Britain, Japan, and the vast majority of other developed economies, is struck by one glaring fact: Most economic activity is carried out among private individuals. In all of these countries, there is widespread agreement that although government intervention is often necessary, the most powerful forces that exploit Pareto improvements and drive the economy toward efficiency are the actions of individual producers and consumers. And among these countries, there is also substantial commonality in the relatively smaller list of goods and services provided by government.

USING THE THEORY

Traffic as a Market Failure

Almost everyone in the United States has been caught in a traffic jam in some large town or city at some point in their lives. For many, it's a daily experience. Congested streets create even larger problems in some European and Asian cities, and in some developing countries, they can bring economic life to a halt for hours at a time. And the problem in most cities is getting worse.

Consider London. Traffic congestion has worsened dramatically in recent decades, especially in the historic inner city. By 2000, an average of 250,000 cars were entering this eight-square-mile area each day, and average traffic speeds had slowed to nine miles per hour—about the speed of a horse-coach a century earlier. In New York, about 250,000 cars enter central Manhattan, also about eight square miles, in just *three hours* every morning, slowing traffic to an average speed of just seven miles per hour.[10] Urban

[10] Randy Kennedy, "The Day the Traffic Disappeared," *New York Times Magazine,* April 20, 2003.

traffic congestion relates to our use of a good: *city streets*. And we can view the traffic problem as a market failure in two different ways.

First, traffic is an externality problem. When you decide to take your car onto a city street, your decision is based on the costs and benefits to *you*. But if the road is already crowded, your decision creates a negative externality as well: By adding to the traffic, you increase the delay and frustration, gasoline costs, and risk of accident for *others*. Of course, you include the effects of traffic congestion *on yourself* in making your decision to get into your car; but you don't take into account these costs for *others*.

For example, let's suppose that when 1,000 additional cars enter central Manhattan during a one-hour morning period, the result is six minutes ($\frac{1}{10}$ of an hour) of additional delay for the other 250,000 cars in the area for the next *three* hours. (Traffic congestion lasts longer than its original cause, and spreads quickly beyond its point of origin by blocking cross traffic.) Assuming just one person in each car, the total hours of delay would be $250,000 \times \frac{1}{10} = 25,000$ hours. If this time is valued at just $10 per hour—less than the average hourly wage—the cost is $250,000. Therefore, if you are just *one* of those additional 1,000 entering the area, the costs you impose on others is $250,000 / 1,000 = $250.

Would you take the additional car trip if you had to pay $250 or more? For most people entering the city, the answer would be no. But because they only bear their own direct costs—gas, wear and tear on their *own* car, and their *own* time—the result is inefficiency: People are consuming another unit of a good (the car trip) whose value to them is less than its marginal *social* cost.

Second, city streets can be viewed as a *mixed good*, in the lower left quadrant of Figure 9. At peak times, city streets are rivalrous: The space occupied by your car can't be occupied by anyone else. On the other hand, streets are not easily excludable. This is why, for the most part, governments *treat* city streets as if they are a pure public good: providing them free of charge to all who want to use them. The result—as in so many other cases of providing a rivalrous good free of charge—is a tragedy of the commons: Consumption increases until everyone is harmed.

Can the government solve the problem? From the externality perspective, the solution would require drivers to *internalize* the externality they impose on others, by making them pay the social costs of their trip. From the rivalry perspective, the solution is similar: People must pay for a rivalrous good in order to avoid the tragedy of the commons. But is this feasible?

Some cities, such as New York, do charge tolls for cars that enter via bridges or tunnels. But entry tolls are problematic, and are rarely set high enough to solve the problem of congestion at peak travel times. One reason is the difficulty of efficiently targeting the entry tolls toward those causing the externality or consuming the rivalrous good. For example, those who live *inside* the city but still contribute to the traffic don't pay the toll at all. And those entering from outside, but who plan to drive to a noncongested (nonrivalrous) area must pay the same toll as people creating more of a problem. New electronic tracking technologies could perhaps solve this problem by imposing fees on each vehicle based on their contribution to congestion. The fees could vary by time of day and the actual locations through which a vehicle travels.

But there is a bigger problem: the political damage to any elected representative who would propose a fee high enough to be efficient on a good that has traditionally been free. Such fees can create resentment among the electorate in general, and also raise serious equity issues. After all, the fee cannot be trivial: It must be high enough to dissuade at least *some* people from driving at certain hours, which is high enough to create hardship for poorer families. True, they could be promised compensation or increased government services from the revenue the fee would provide. But people might not trust the government's promise, given other priorities for city funds.

All of this conventional political wisdom may have changed since early 2003, when Ken Livingstone—the mayor of London—decided to take a chance: His administration established a 5 pound (about $8) *per day* user fee on any automobile that appeared in the eight-square-mile boundary of London's inner city. The fee had to be paid in advance, by 10 P.M. the night before travel, adding to its opportunity cost (the time and trouble of paying the fee)—especially for those who don't plan their travel well in advance. Any car that was seen parked, driving through, or in any way appeared within the eight-square-mile zone would be required to pay the fee. Violators faced fines of 80 pounds (about $130), and were almost certain to be caught: The city positioned more than 700 cameras throughout the zone to record license plate numbers and send the optical data to a central computer, which would instantly determine if the vehicle owner had paid the fee. Livingstone addressed the equity issue as well, using almost all of the additional city revenue for significant expansions in bus service.

On the first day the fee applied, traffic dropped about 25 percent: 60,000 fewer cars entered the area than on a normal day. Traffic speeds doubled to about 20 miles per hour. The political opposition turned out to be manageable. Livingstone—a far-left socialist—has even proposed expanding this market solution to other congested areas of the city. And officials in New York, Paris, Los Angeles, and other large cities around the world have been studying London's success.

Summary

A market or an economy is economically efficient when all Pareto improvements have been exploited, so there is no way to reallocate resources that makes at least one person better off without harming anyone else. The equilibrium in a well-functioning perfectly competitive market is efficient. When markets fail to achieve economic efficiency—when they leave potential Pareto improvements unexploited—government can often step in and help.

The legal system run by governments is a key element of institutional infrastructure to promote efficiency. Criminal law limits exchanges to voluntary ones. Property law contributes to enforceable property rights. Contract law helps improve the efficiency of exchange when one party must go first, while tort law affects interactions among strangers. Finally, antitrust law attempts to prevent harm to consumers from limited competition. In addition to the legal system, the government's regulatory system affects many aspects of economic life.

A market failure occurs when a market, left to itself, fails to achieve economic efficiency. Monopoly and imperfect competition, externalities, and public goods are examples of market failures. Governments have a variety of tools to correct these failures. Through antitrust action and regulation, governments can sometimes narrow the gap between price and marginal cost in imperfectly competitive markets. Externalities—unpriced by-products of economic transactions that affect outsiders—can be corrected through taxes, subsidies, regulation, or other means. And public goods—those that are nonrival and nonexcludable—can be provided by government itself. Government solutions to market failures are often imperfect and controversial. But there is widespread agreement that government action is needed to prevent the most important market failures.

Key Terms

Coase Theorem
Excludability
Externality
Free rider problem
Marginal Social Benefit (MSB)

Marginal Social Cost (MSC)
Market failure
Pareto improvement
Pure private good
Pure public good

Rivalry
Tort
Tradable Permit
Tragedy of the commons

Review Questions

1. What is the relationship between *Pareto improvements* and the concept of *economic efficiency*?

2. Which of the following actions would be a Pareto improvement? Which could become a Pareto improvement if the right side payment were included?
   a. You buy a Coke for $4.50 at an airport restaurant.
   b. You and a friend go to a movie and compromise on which one to see.
   c. An acquaintance, who values your tennis racket more than you do, borrows it, and never returns it.

3. Briefly explain why, in a perfectly competitive market with no market failure, providing *less* than the equilibrium quantity cannot be economically efficient.

4. Briefly explain why, in a perfectly competitive market with no market failure, a quantity *greater than* the equilibrium quantity cannot be economically efficient.

5. Explain how each of the following enhances economic efficiency:
   a. Criminal law
   b. Property law
   c. Contract law
   d. Tort law
   e. Antitrust law

6. What are the three major types of market failure discussed in the chapter? For each type, identify a type of government action that could, in theory, correct the failure.

7. Which type of market failure is addressed by the Coase theorem? Under what conditions does the theorem apply?

8. What role does the free rider problem play in understanding the problem posed by *negative externalities*? By *positive externalities*?

9. What is the difference between *marginal cost* and *marginal social cost*?

10. Does the Coase theorem apply to most cases of air pollution? Why or why not?

11. What is a pure public good? How is a pure public good different from a pure private good?

12. State whether the benefits from each of the following goods or services are (1) mostly excludable or mostly nonexcludable; and (2) mostly rival or mostly nonrival.
   a. Breakfast at a coffee shop
   b. Medical care to treat a highly contagious disease
   c. Efforts to maintain homeland security
   d. A movie shown in a theater with mostly empty seats
   e. Teaching young children not to steal

Problems and Exercises

1. In Figure 3, suppose that, initially, McCollum is providing the fifth guitar lesson to Zoe for a price of $16. Who would gain and who would lose from this lesson? Construct a scorecard, involving a side payment of $2 from McCollum to Zoe, showing that both of them come out ahead by agreeing *not* to provide the fifth lesson.

2. In the chapter, it was stated that a competitive market would not provide goods like chocolate-covered Brussels sprouts because their value—even to those who like them most—would be less than the cost of supplying even a small quantity. Illustrate the market for such a good with supply and demand curves.

3. Review the section of the chapter titled, "The Private Solution to a Negative Externality." Suppose that Grace gains $70,000 from building the theater, but the harm to Fernando is $100,000.
   a. Is it efficient to build the theater? Briefly, why or why not?
   b. If Fernando has the legal right to *prevent* the theater from being built, would you expect the theater to be built?

   c. If Grace has the legal right to *build* the theater, would you expect the theater to be built?

4. Last year, Pat and Chris occupied separate apartments. Each consumed 400 gallons of hot water monthly. This year, they are sharing an apartment. To their surprise, they find that they are using a total of 1,000 gallons per month between them. Why? What concept discussed in this chapter is illustrated by this example?

5. Some have argued that the music industry is by nature inefficient, because once a piece of music is produced, the firm that owns it has a monopoly and charges the monopoly price. Yet, the marginal cost of making the music available to one more member of the public (via the Internet) is zero. Draw a diagram, similar to Figure 6, to represent this situation. Identify on your diagram:
   a. the efficient level of production;
   b. the level of production a government-regulated music industry would earn if it were permitted to charge just enough for a "fair rate of return";
   c. the level of production provided by the (currently unregulated) industry.

6. In Figure 7 (b), a negative externality was corrected with a $0.50 per gallon tax on gasoline producers. Show that the total price paid by consumers, the total price received by firms, and the equilibrium quantity would have been exactly the same if the same tax had been imposed on gasoline consumers instead of producers.

7. In Figure 8 (b), a positive externality was corrected with a $30,000 subsidy paid to college students. Show that the total price paid by students, the total price received by colleges, and the equilibrium quantity of degrees would have been exactly the same if the $30,000 subsidy per student had been given to the colleges.

Challenge Questions

1. The following table shows the quantities of car alarms demanded and supplied per year in a town:

Price	Quantity Demanded	Quantity Supplied
$ 75	800	0
$100	750	150
$125	700	300
$150	650	450
$175	600	600
$200	550	750
$225	500	900
$250	450	1,050

Without drawing a graph, determine the efficient quantity in this market under each of the following assumptions:

a. Each car alarm sold creates a negative externality (noise pollution) that causes $100 in harm to the public.

b. Each car alarm creates a *positive* externality (reduced law enforcement costs) that provides $100 in benefits to the public.

 *These exercises require access to Lieberman/Hall Xtra! If Xtra! did not come with your book, visit http://liebermanxtra. swlearning.com to purchase.*

1. Use your Xtra! password at the Hall and Lieberman Web site (http://liebermanxtra.swlearning.com), select this chapter, and under Economic Applications, click on EconDebate. Choose *Microeconomics: Government and the Economy,* and scroll down to find the debate, "Should Anti-pollution Standards Be Strengthened?" The debate argues that most people agree that something must be done to reduce pollution, but are not in agreement as to how much regulation is needed. Suppose the government overregulates production that emits pollution. Show on a graph the inefficiency caused by such overregulation.

2. Use your Xtra! password at the Hall and Lieberman Web site (http://liebermanxtra.swlearning.com), select this chapter, and under Economic Applications, click on EconNews. Choose *Microeconomics: Economics and the Environment,* and scroll down to find the summary, "Reducing Airline Emissions: The Future Is the Past." Read the summary. Is this an efficient way of reducing emissions? Why or why not?

Introduction to Macroeconomics

You have no doubt seen photographs of the earth taken from satellites thousands of miles away. Viewed from that great distance, the world's vast oceans look like puddles, its continents like mounds of dirt, and its mountain ranges like wrinkles on a bedspread. In contrast to our customary view from the earth's surface—of a car, a tree, a building—this is a view of the big picture.

These two different ways of viewing the earth—from up close or from thousands of miles away—are analogous to two different ways of viewing the economy. When we look through the *microeconomic* lens—from up close—we see the behavior of *individual decision makers* and *individual markets*. When we look through the *macroeconomic* lens—from a distance—these smaller features fade away, and we see only the broad outlines of the economy.

Which view is better? That depends on what we're trying to do. If we want to know why computers are getting better and cheaper each year, or why the earnings of business professors are rising so rapidly, we need the close-up view of microeconomics. But to answer questions about the *overall* economy—about the overall level of economic activity, our standard of living, or the percentage of our potential workforce that is unemployed—we need the more comprehensive view of *macroeconomics*.

MACROECONOMIC GOALS

While there is some disagreement among economists about *how* to make the macroeconomy perform well, there is widespread agreement about the goals we are trying to achieve:

Economists—and society at large—agree on three important macroeconomic goals: economic growth, full employment, and stable prices.

Why is there such universal agreement on these three goals? Because achieving them gives us the opportunity to make *all* of our citizens better off. Let's take a closer look at each of these goals and see why they are so important.

Economic Growth

Imagine that you were a typical American worker living at the beginning of the 20th century. You would work about 60 hours every week, and your yearly salary—about $450—would buy a bit less than $8,000 would buy today. You could expect to die at the age of 47. If you fell seriously ill before then, your doctor wouldn't be able to help much: There were no X-ray machines or blood tests, and little effective medicine for the few diseases that could be diagnosed. You would probably never hear the sounds produced by the best musicians of the day, or see the performances of the best actors, dancers, or singers. And the most exotic travel you'd enjoy would likely be a trip to a nearby state.

Today, the typical worker has it considerably better. He or she works about 35 hours per week and is paid about $34,000 per year, not to mention fringe benefits such as health insurance, retirement benefits, and paid vacation. Thanks to advances in medicine, nutrition, and hygiene, the average worker can expect to live into his or her late 70s. And more of a worker's free time today is really free: There are machines to do laundry and dishes, cars to get to and from work, telephones for quick communication, and personal computers to keep track of finances, appointments, and correspondence. Finally, during their lifetimes, most Americans will have traveled—for enjoyment—to many locations in the United States or abroad.

Economic growth The increase in our production of goods and services that occurs over long periods of time.

What is responsible for these dramatic changes in economic well-being? The answer is: **economic growth**—the increase in our production of goods and services that occurs over long periods of time. In the United States, as in most developed economies, the annual output of goods and services has risen over time, and risen faster than the population. As a result, the average person can consume much more today—more food, clothing, housing, medical care, entertainment, and travel—than in the year 1900.

Economists monitor economic growth by keeping track of *real gross domestic product (real GDP)*: the total quantity of goods and services produced in a country over a year. When real GDP rises faster than the population, output per person rises, and so does the average standard of living.

Figure 1 shows real GDP in the United States from 1929 to 2002, measured in dollars of output at 1996 prices. As you can see, real GDP has increased dramatically over the greater part of the century. Part of the reason for the rise is an increase in population: More workers can produce more goods and services. But real GDP has actually increased *faster* than the population: During this period, while the U.S. population did not quite triple, the quantity of goods and services produced each year has increased more than tenfold. Hence, the remarkable rise in the average American's living standard.

But when we look more closely at the data, we discover something important: Although output has grown, the *rate* of growth has varied over the decades. From

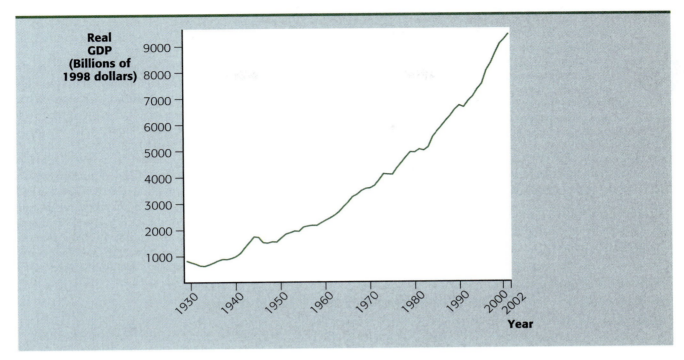

FIGURE 1

U.S. Real Gross Domestic Product, 1929–2002

Real GDP has increased dramatically over the past 73 years. In the figure, real GDP is measured in dollars of output valued at 1996 prices. (The measurement of real GDP will be discussed in more detail in the next two chapters.)

1959 to 1973, real GDP grew, on average, by 4.2 percent per year. But from 1973 to 1991, average annual growth slowed to 2.7 percent. Then, from 1991 to 2002, growth picked up again, averaging 3.7 percent per year. These may seem like slight differences. But over long periods of time, such small differences in growth rates can cause huge differences in living standards. For example, suppose that each year between 1973 and 2000, real GDP had grown by just one percentage point more than its actual rate. Then, over that entire period, the United States would have produced about $27 trillion *more* in goods and services than we *actually* produced over that period (valuing these goods and services at 1996 prices). That amounts to about $75,000 for each person in the population.

Economists and government officials are very concerned when economic growth slows down. Growth increases the size of the economic pie, so it becomes possible—at least in principle—for every citizen to have a larger slice. This is why economists agree that growth is a good thing.

But in practice, growth does *not* benefit everyone. Living standards will always rise more rapidly for some groups than for others, and some may even find their slice of the pie shrinking. For example, since the late 1980s, economic growth has improved the living standards of the highly skilled, while less-skilled workers have benefited very little. Partly, this is due to improvements in technology that have lowered the earnings of workers whose roles can be taken by computers and machines. But very few economists would advocate a halt to growth as a solution to the problems of unskilled workers. Some believe that, in the long run, everyone will indeed benefit from growth. Others see a role for the government in taxing successful people and providing benefits to those left behind by growth. But in either case, economic

DANGEROUS CURVES

Growth Rates from Graphs In Figure 1, it looks like real GDP has not only been growing over time, but growing at a faster and faster rate, since the line becomes steeper over time. But the real GDP line would get steeper even if the growth rate were *constant* over the entire period. That's because as real GDP rises from an increasingly higher and higher level, the same *percentage* growth rate causes greater and greater *absolute* increases in GDP.

For example, when real GDP is $5 trillion, 3 percent growth would cause real GDP to rise by $5 trillion × 0.03 = $0.15 trillion. But when real GDP is $10 trillion, the same 3 percent growth would be $10 trillion × 0.03 = $0.30 trillion. Since the slope of the line depends on the *absolute* rise in real GDP each year rather than its *percentage* rise, the same percentage growth rate would create a steeper line when real GDP is higher.

In fact, the line can become steeper even if the percentage growth rate *decreases* over time. As you've read, real GDP actually grew faster from 1959 to 1973 (where the line is flatter) than during any subsequent period (where the line is steeper).

growth, by increasing the size of the overall pie, is seen as an important part of the solution.

Macroeconomics helps us understand a number of issues surrounding economic growth. What makes real GDP grow in the first place? Why does it grow more rapidly in some decades than in others? Why do some countries experience very rapid growth—some much faster than the United States—while others seem unable to grow at all? Can government policy do anything to alter the growth rate? And are there any downsides to such policies?

High Employment (or Low Unemployment)

Economic growth is one of our most important goals, but not the only one. Suppose our real GDP were growing at, say, a 3 percent annual rate, but 10 percent of the workforce was unable to find work. Would the economy be performing well? Not really, for two reasons. First, unemployment affects the distribution of economic well-being among our citizens. People who cannot find jobs suffer a loss of income. And even though many of the jobless receive some unemployment benefits and other assistance from the government, the unemployed typically have lower living standards than the employed. Concern for those without jobs is one reason that consistently high employment—or consistently low *unemployment*—is an important macroeconomic goal.

But in addition to the impact on the unemployed themselves, joblessness affects *all* of us—even those who *have* jobs. A high unemployment rate means that the economy is not achieving its full economic potential: Many people who *want* to work and produce additional goods and services are not able to do so. With the same number of people—but fewer goods and services to distribute among that population—the average standard of living will be lower. This general effect on living standards gives us another reason to strive for consistently high rates of employment and low rates of unemployment.

One measure economists use to keep track of employment is the *unemployment rate*—the percentage of the workforce that is searching for a job but hasn't found one. Figure 2 shows the average unemployment rate during each of the past 80 years. Notice that the unemployment rate is never zero; there are always *some* people looking for work, even when the economy is doing well. But in some years, unemployment is unusually high. The worst example occurred during the Great Depression of the 1930s, when millions of workers lost their jobs and the unemployment rate reached 25 percent. One in four potential workers could not find a job. More recently, in 1982 and 1983, the unemployment rate averaged almost 10 percent.

The nation's commitment to high employment has twice been written into law. With the memory of the Great Depression still fresh, Congress passed the *Employment Act of 1946*, which required the federal government to "promote maximum

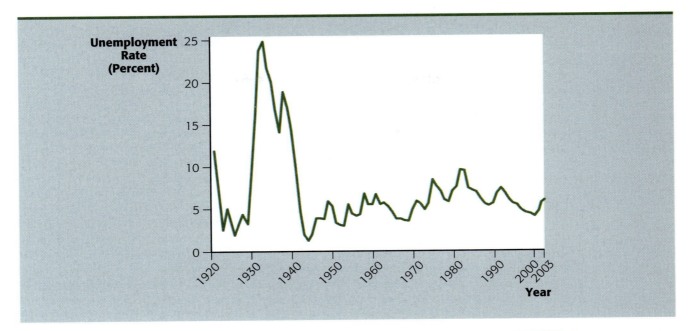

FIGURE 2
**U.S. Unemployment Rate,
1920–2003**

The unemployment rate fluctuates over time. During the Great Depression of the 1930s, unemployment was extremely high, reaching 25 percent in 1933. In the early 1980s, the rate averaged 10 percent. And during the 1990s, it fell rapidly, reaching 4 percent before turning up in the early 2000s.

employment, production, and purchasing power." It did not, however, dictate a target rate of unemployment the government should aim for. A numerical target was added in 1978, when Congress passed the *Full Employment and Balanced Growth Act,* which called for an unemployment rate of 4 percent.

A glance at Figure 2 shows how seldom we have hit this target over the last few decades. In fact, we did not hit it at all through the 1970s and 1980s. But in the 1990s, we came closer and closer and finally, in December 1999, we reached the 4 percent target for the first time since the 1960s. In 2001, the unemployment rate began to creep up again, and continued rising through the first half of 2003, when it averaged 6.0 percent.

Why has the unemployment rate been above its target so often? Why were we able to reach the target at the end of the 1990s, but not maintain it through the early 2000s? And what causes the average unemployment rate to fluctuate from year to year, as shown in Figure 2? These are all questions that your study of macroeconomics will help you answer.

Employment and the Business Cycle. When firms produce more output, they hire more workers; when they produce less output, they tend to lay off workers. We would thus expect real GDP and employment to be closely related, and indeed they are. In recent years, each 1 percent drop in output has been associated with the loss of about half a million jobs. Consistently high employment, then, requires a high, stable level of output. Unfortunately, output has *not* been very stable. If you look back at Figure 1, you will see that while real GDP has climbed upward over time, it has been a bumpy ride. The periodic fluctuations in GDP—the bumps in the figure—are called **business cycles.**

Figure 3 shows a close-up view of a hypothetical business cycle. First, notice the thin upward-sloping line. This shows the long-run upward trend of real GDP, which

Business cycles Fluctuations in real GDP around its long-term growth trend.

FIGURE 3
The Business Cycle

Over time, real GDP fluctuates around an overall upward trend. Such fluctuations are called business cycles. *When output rises, we are in the expansion phase of the cycle; when output falls, we are in a* recession.

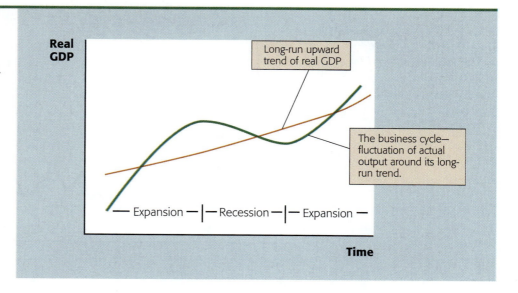

Expansion Versus Economic Growth Although the terms *expansion* and *economic growth* both refer to increases in real GDP, they are not the same. *Economic growth* refers to the long-run upward trend in output over a long period of time, usually more than a decade. It is measured as the *average* annual change in output over the entire period. An *expansion* refers to a usually shorter period of time during which output increases quarter by quarter or year by year.

Here's an example of the difference: From 1973 to 1991, output increased at an *average* rate of 2.7 percent per year over the entire period. This was the rate of economic growth during the period. But during a *part* of this long period—the early 1980s—output *fell* for several quarters. This was a contraction. During another part of this long period—the mid- and late 1980s—output *rose* every quarter. This was an expansion.

Expansion A period of increasing real GDP.

Recession A period of significant decline in real GDP.

Depression An unusually severe recession.

we refer to as *economic growth*. The thicker line shows the business cycle that occurs *around* the long-run trend. When output rises, we are in the **expansion** phase of the cycle; when output falls, we are in the *contraction* or **recession** phase. (Officially, a recession is a contraction considered significant —in terms of depth, breadth, and duration.)

Of course, real-world business cycles never look quite like the smooth, symmetrical cycle in Figure 3, but rather like the jagged, irregular cycles of Figure 1. Recessions can be severe or mild, and they can last several years or less than a single year. When a recession is particularly severe and long lasting, it is called a **depression**. In the 20th century, the United States experienced just one decline in output serious enough to be considered a depression—the worldwide *Great Depression* of the 1930s. From 1929 to 1933, the first four years of the Great Depression, U.S. output dropped by more than 25 percent.

But even during more normal times, the economy has gone through many recessions. Since 1959, we have suffered through two severe recessions (in 1974–75 and 1981–82) and several less severe ones, such as the recession from March to November of 2001.

Why are there business cycles? Is there anything we can do to prevent recessions from occurring, or at least make them milder and shorter? And why—even after a period of severe depression as in the 1930s—does the economy eventually move back toward its long-run growth trend? These are all questions that macroeconomics helps us answer.

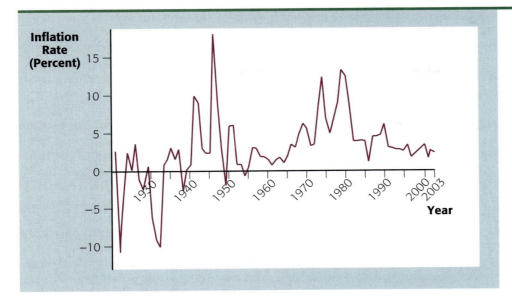

FIGURE 4

U.S. Annual Inflation Rate, 1922–2003

In most years, the inflation rate has been positive. The overall price level increased during those years.

Stable Prices

Figure 4 shows the annual inflation rate—the percentage increase in the average level of prices—from 1922 to 2003.[1] With very few exceptions, the inflation rate has been positive: On average, prices have risen in each of those years. But notice the wide variations in inflation. In 1979 and 1980, we had double-digit inflation: Prices rose by more than 12 percent in both years. During that time, polls showed that people were more concerned about inflation than any other national problem—more than unemployment, crime, poverty, pollution, or anything else. During the 1990s, the inflation rate averaged less than 3 percent per year, and it has averaged about 2½ percent during the early 2000s (through June 2003). As a result, we hardly seem to notice it at all. Pollsters no longer include "rising prices" as a category when asking about the most important problems facing the country.

Other countries have not been so lucky. In the 1980s, several Latin American nations experienced inflation rates of thousands of percent per year. In the early 1990s, some of the newly emerging nations of Central Europe and the former Soviet Union suffered annual inflation rates in the triple digits. An extreme case was the new nation of Serbia, where prices rose by 1,880 percent in the single month of August 1993. If prices had continued to rise at that rate all year, the annual inflation rate would have been 363,000,000,000,000,000 percent.

Why are stable prices—a low inflation rate—an important macroeconomic goal? Because inflation is *costly* to society. With annual inflation rates in the thousands of

---

[1] Figure 4 is based on the Consumer Price Index, the most popular measure of the price level, as well as historical estimates of what this index *would* have been in the early part of the 20th century, before the index existed. We'll discuss the Consumer Price Index and other measures of inflation in more detail in later chapters.

Two excellent print sources for news on the U.S. and world economies are The Wall Street Journal *and* The Economist, *a British magazine.*

percent, the costs are easy to see: The purchasing power of the currency declines so rapidly that people are no longer willing to hold it. This breakdown of the monetary system forces people to waste valuable time and resources bartering with each other—for example, trading plumbing services for dentistry services. With so much time spent trying to find trading partners, there is little time left for producing goods and services. As a result, the average standard of living falls.

With inflation rates of 12 or 13 percent—such as the United States experienced in the late 1970s—the costs to society are less obvious and less severe. But they are still significant. And when it comes time to bring down the inflation rate, painful corrective actions by government are sometimes required. These actions can cause output to decline and unemployment to rise. For example, in order to bring the inflation rate down from the high levels of the late 1970s (see Figure 4), government policy purposely caused a severe recession in 1981–82, reducing output and increasing unemployment.

Economists regard *some* inflation as good for the economy. In fact, during the early 2000s, policy makers began to worry that the inflation rate might be getting *too low,* and that the economy might be threatened with a harmful *deflation*—a period of *decreasing* prices. Price stabilization requires not only preventing the inflation rate from rising too high, but also preventing it from falling too *low,* where it would be dangerously close to turning negative.

The previous paragraphs may have raised a number of questions in your mind. What causes inflation or deflation? How would a *moderately* high inflation rate of 7 or 8 percent harm society? How does a recession bring down the inflation rate, and how does the government actually *create* a recession? And why might a period of decreasing prices—which sounds so wonderful—be a threat to the economy? Your study of macroeconomics will help you answer all of these questions.

THE MACROECONOMIC APPROACH

Because you have already studied *micro*economics, you will notice much that is familiar in *macro*economics. The *basic principles of economics* play an important role in both branches of the field. But the macroeconomic approach is different from the microeconomic approach in significant ways. Most importantly, in *micro*economics, we typically apply the basic principle of *markets and equilibrium* to *one market at a time*—the market for soybeans, for neurosurgeons, or for car washes. In *macro*economics, by contrast, we want to understand how the entire economy behaves. Thus, we apply the principle of markets and equilibrium to *all markets simultaneously.* This includes not only markets for goods and services, but also markets for labor and for financial assets like stocks and bonds.

How can we possibly hope to deal with all of these markets at the same time? One way would be to build a gigantic model that included every individual market in the economy. The model would have tens of thousands of supply and demand curves, which could be used to determine tens of thousands of prices and quantities. With today's fast, powerful computers, we could, in principle, build this kind of model.

But it would not be easy. We would need to gather data on every good and service in the economy, every type of labor, every type of financial asset, and so on. As you might guess, this would be a formidable task, requiring thousands of workers just to gather the data alone. And in the end, the model would not prove very useful. We would not learn much about the economy from it: With so many individual trees, we could not see the forest.

Moreover, the model's predictions would be highly suspect: With so much information and so many moving parts, high standards of accuracy would be difficult to maintain. Even the government of the former Soviet Union, which directed production throughout the economy until the 1990s, was unable to keep track of all the markets under its control. In a market economy, where production decisions are made by individual firms, the task would be even harder.

What, then, is a macroeconomist to do? The answer is a word that you will become very familiar with in the chapters to come: **aggregation**, the process of combining different things into a single category and treating them as a whole. Let's take a closer look at how aggregation is used in macroeconomics.

Aggregation The process of combining different things into a single category.

Aggregation in Macroeconomics

Aggregation is a basic tool of reasoning, one that you often use without being aware of it. If you say, "I applied for five jobs last month," you are aggregating five very different workplaces into the single category, *jobs*. Whenever you say, "I'm going out with my friends," you are combining several different people into a single category: people you consider *friends*.

Aggregation plays a key role in both micro- and macroeconomics. Microeconomists will speak of the market for automobiles, lumping Toyotas, Fords, BMWs, and other types of cars into a single category. But in macroeconomics, we take aggregation to the extreme. Because we want to consider the entire economy at once, and yet keep our model as simple as possible, we must aggregate all markets into the broadest possible categories. For example, we lump together all the goods and services that households buy—newspapers, pizza, couches, and personal computers—into the single category *consumption goods*. We combine all the different types of capital purchased by business firms—forklifts, factory buildings, office computers, and trucks—into the single category *investment goods*. Often we go even further, lumping consumption, investment, and all other

"Micro" Versus "Macro" In many English words, the prefix *macro* means "large" and *micro* means "small." As a result, you might think that in microeconomics, we study economic units in which small sums of money are involved, while in macroeconomics we study units involving greater sums. But this is not correct: The annual output of General Motors is considerably greater than the total annual output of many small countries, such as Estonia or Guatemala. Yet when we study the behavior of General Motors, we are practicing *microeconomics,* and when we study changes in the unemployment rate in Estonia, we are practicing *macroeconomics.* Why? Microeconomics is concerned with the behavior and interaction of *individual* firms and markets, even if they are very large; macroeconomics is concerned with the behavior of *entire economies,* even if they are very small.

DANGEROUS CURVES

types of goods into the single category *output* or *real GDP*. And in macroeconomics, we typically combine the thousands of different types of workers in the economy—doctors, construction workers, plumbers, college professors—into the category, *labor*. By aggregating in this way, we can create workable and reasonably accurate models that teach us a great deal about how the overall economy operates.

MACROECONOMIC CONTROVERSIES

Macroeconomics is full of disputes and disagreements. Indeed, modern macroeconomics, which began with the publication of *The General Theory of Employment, Interest, and Money* by British economist John Maynard Keynes in 1936, originated in controversy. Keynes was taking on the conventional wisdom of his time, *classical economics,* which held that the macroeconomy worked very well on its own, and the best policy for the government to follow was *laissez faire*—"leave it alone." As he was working on *The General Theory,* Keynes wrote to his friend, the playwright George Bernard Shaw, "I believe myself to be writing a book on economic theory which will largely revolutionize—not, I suppose, at once but in the course of the next ten years—the way the world thinks about economic problems."

Keynes's prediction was on the money. After the publication of his book, economists argued about its merits, but 10 years later, the majority of the profession had been won over: they had become Keynesians. This new school of thought held that the economy does *not* do well on its own (one needed only to look at the Great Depression for evidence) and requires continual guidance from an activist and well-intentioned government.

From the late 1940s until the early 1960s, events seemed to prove the Keynesians correct. Then, beginning in the 1960s, several distinguished economists began to challenge Keynesian ideas. Their counterrevolutionary views, which in many ways mirrored those of the classical economists, were strengthened by events in the 1970s, when the economy's behavior began to contradict some Keynesian ideas. Today, much of this disagreement has been resolved and a modern consensus—incorporating both Keynsian and classical ideas—has emerged. But there are still controversies.

Consider, for example, the controversy over the Bush administration's $350 billion 10-year tax cut. In May 2003, the tax cut was approved by 231 to 200 in the House of Representatives, and passed the Senate only when Vice President Cheney cast his vote to break a 50–50 tie. Within hours of passage, the following appeared on CNN's Web site:

> "*This is a great victory for the American people,*" *said Senate Majority Leader Bill Frist, R-Tennessee.* "*The wonderful thing is it really boils down to greater job security for people.*"

> "*This is a policy of debt, deficits, and decline,*" *said Sen. Kent Conrad, D-North Dakota, adding,* "*This is a scandal in the making. We're going to read there are perverse results as a result of this tax policy.*"[2]

Similar opposing views were expressed by economists associated with the Bush administration on the one hand, and those associated with the Democratic Party on the other. What are we to make of macroeconomic policy controversies like these, which occur so often on the political scene?

Remember the distinction between *positive (what is)* and *normative (what should be)*? Some of these disagreements are *positive* in nature. While economists and policy makers often agree on the broad outlines of how the macroeconomy works, they may disagree on some of the details. For example, they may disagree about the economy's current direction or momentum, or the relative effectiveness of

---

[2] "Congress Approves Tax-Cut Package," CNN.com/Inside Politics, May, 23, 2002.

different policies in altering the economy's course. Indeed, the two opposing senators quoted above were expressing a positive disagreement: a disagreement about the *impact* that tax cuts would have on the economy.

But disagreements that *sound* postive often have *normative* origins. For example in 2003, Democrats in Congress criticized the Bush tax cut as unfair, because it gave the biggest tax reduction to those with the highest incomes. Republicans in Congress countered that the tax cut was fair, because taxpayers with the highest incomes paid higher taxes to begin with. In the competitive and confrontational arena of politics—with each side trying to muster all the arguments it can—positive economics is often enlisted. In 2003, Republicans who began with the view that the Bush tax cut was fair invariably *also* argued that it was the most effective policy to spur the economy into a healthy expansion phase (see Figure 3). And they found a number of economists—who may have had similar normative views—to support that argument. Democrats who began with the view that the tax cut was *un*fair invariably *also* argued that it would cause great harm to the economy. And they found a number of economists—who may have had similar normative views—to support *that* argument.

Because of such political battles, people who follow the news often think that there is little agreement among economists about how the macroeconomy works. In fact, the profession has come to a consensus on many basic principles, and we will stress these as we go. And even when there are disagreements, there is surprising consensus on the approach that should be taken to resolve them.

You won't find this consensus expressed in a hot political debate. But you *will* find it in academic journals and conferences, and in reports issued by certain nonpartisan research organizations or government agencies. And—we hope—you will find it in the chapters to come.

Summary

Macroeconomics is the study of the economy as a whole. It deals with issues such as economic growth, unemployment, inflation, and government policies that might influence the overall level of economic activity.

Economists generally agree about the importance of three main macroeconomic goals. The first of these is economic growth. If output, real gross domestic product, grows faster than population, the average person can enjoy an improved standard of living.

High employment is another important goal. In the United States and other market economies, the main source of household incomes is labor earnings. When unemployment is high, many people are without jobs and must cut back their purchases of goods and services.

The third macroeconomic goal is stable prices. This goal is important because inflation imposes costs on society. Keeping the rate of inflation low helps to reduce these costs.

Because an economy like that of the United States is so large and complex, the models we use to analyze the economy must be highly aggregated. For example, we will lump together millions of different goods to create an aggregate called "output" and combine all their prices into a single "price index."

Key Terms

Aggregation
Business cycle

Depression
Economic growth

Expansion
Recession

Review Questions

1. Discuss the similarities and differences between macroeconomics and microeconomics.

2. What is the basic tool macroeconomists use to deal with the complexity and variety of economic markets and institutions? Give some examples of how they use this tool.

3. List the nation's macroeconomic goals and explain why each is important.

4. Consider an economy whose real GDP is growing at 4 percent per year. What else would you need to know in order to say whether the average standard of living is improving or deteriorating?

5. Explain the difference between a contraction, a recession, and a depression.

Problems and Exercises

1. In 1973, real GDP (at 1996 prices) was $4,123 billion. In 2000, it was $9,191 billion. During the same period, the U.S. population rose from 212 million to 281 million.
   a. What was the total percentage increase in real GDP from 1973 to 2000?
   b. What was the total percentage increase in the U.S. population during this period?
   c. Calculate real GDP per person in 1973 and in 2000. By what percentage did output per person grow over this period?

2. Suppose that real GDP had grown by 8 percent per year from 1973 to 2000. Using the data from Problem 1:
   a. What would real GDP have been in 2000?
   b. How much would output *per person* in 2000 have increased (compared to its actual value in 2000) if annual growth in real GDP over this period had been 8 percent?

3. a. The chapter states that the average growth rate for real GDP in the United States was 3.7 percent from 1991 to 2000. Use the information in the following table (which gives the actual GDP numbers) to calculate how much more we would have produced in 2000 if real GDP had grown by 4.7 percent over that period. [*Hint:* When real GDP grows at 4.7 percent annually, each year it will be 1.047 times its value of the year before.]

Year	Real GDP ($ Billions)
1991	$6,676.4
1992	$6,880.0
1993	$7,062.6
1994	$7,347.7
1995	$7,543.8
1996	$7,813.2
1997	$8,159.5
1998	$8,508.9
1999	$8,859.0
2000	$9,191.4

   b. Calculate, for a 2000 population of 281 million people, how much higher the average output per person would have been in 2000 if the growth rate had been 4.7 percent over this period.

4. Assume that the country of Ziponia produced real GDP equal to $5000 (in billions) in the year 2000.
   a. Calculate Ziponia's output from 2000 to 2006, assuming that it experienced a constant growth rate of 6 percent per year over this period. Use your answers to construct a graph similar to the one in Figure 1. Is the slope of this graph constant? Explain.
   b. Calculate Ziponia's output from 2000 to 2006, assuming that its growth rate was 6 percent from 2000 to 2001, and then that it fell by 1 percent each year. Plot these points onto your graph from part (a). Is the slope of this graph constant? Explain.

5. Assume that the country of Zipinia produced real GDP equal to $5000 (in billions) in the year 2000.
   a. Calculate Zipinia's output from 2000 to 2006, assuming that it experienced a constant growth rate of 10 percent per year over this period. Use your answers to construct a graph similar to the one in Figure 1. Is the slope of this graph constant? Explain.
   b. Calculate Zipinia's output from 2000 to 2006, assuming that its growth rate was 10 percent from 2000 to 2001, and then that it fell by .5 percent each year (to 9.5, 9, 8.5, etc). Plot these points onto your graph from part (a). Is the slope of this graph constant? Explain.

 **ECONOMIC** *Applications* | *These exercises require access to Lieberman/Hall Xtra! If Xtra! did not come with your book, visit http://lieberman. swlearning.com to purchase.*

1. Use your Xtra! Password at the Hall and Lieberman Web site (http://lieberman.swlearning.com), select this chapter, and under Economic Applications, click on EconDebate. Choose *Macroeconomics: Productivity and Growth,* and scroll down to find the debate, "Is More Spending on Infrastructure the Key to Economic Growth?" Read the debate and use the information to answer the following questions.

   a. In this chapter it is stated that economic growth, high employment, and stable prices are the main macroeconomic goals. Are these compatible or competing goals? Explain.

   b. What are the most common recommendations for increasing the rate of economic growth? Explain the debate on the appropriate role of government in economic growth.

2. Use your Xtra! Password at the Hall and Lieberman Web site (http://lieberman.swlearning.com), select this chapter, and under Economic Applications, click on EconNews. Choose *Macroeconomics: Productivity and Growth,* and scroll down to find "Signs of Recovery." Read the full summary.

   a. Answer the three questions posed under the full summary.

   b. Read the article "Deflation" by William Greider http://www.thenation.com/doc. mhtml?i=20030630&s=greider&c=1 and explain why both Greenspan and Greider consider deflation to be an impediment to growth.

Production, Income, and Employment

On the first Friday of every month, at 8:00 A.M., dozens of journalists mill about in a room in the Department of Labor. They are waiting for the arrival of the press officer from the government's Bureau of Labor Statistics. When she enters the room, carrying a stack of papers, the buzz of conversation stops. The papers—which she passes out to the waiting journalists—contain the monthly report on the experience of the American workforce. They summarize everything the government knows about hiring and firing at businesses across the country; about the number of people working, the hours they worked, and the incomes they earned; and about the number of people *not* working and what they did instead. But one number looms large in the journalists' minds as they scan the report and compose their stories: the percentage of the labor force that could not find jobs, or the nation's *unemployment rate*.

Every three months, a similar scene takes place at the Department of Commerce, as reporters wait for the release of the quarterly report on the nation's output of goods and services and the incomes we have earned from producing it. Once again, the report includes tremendous detail. Output is broken down by industry and by the sector that purchased it, and income is broken down into the different types of earners. And once again, the reporters' eyes will focus on a single number, a number that will dominate their stories and create headlines in newspapers across the country: the nation's *gross domestic product*.

The government knows that its reports on employment and production will have a major impact on the American political scene, and on financial markets in the United States and around the world. So it takes great pains to ensure fair and equal access to the information. For example, the Bureau of Labor Statistics allows journalists to look at the employment report at 8:00 A.M. on the day of the release (the first Friday of every month). But they must stay inside a room—appropriately called the lockup room—and cannot contact the outside world until the official release time of 8:30 A.M. At precisely 8:29 A.M., the reporters are permitted to hook up their laptop modems, and then a countdown begins. At precisely 8:30 A.M., the reporters are permitted to transmit their stories. At the same instant, the Bureau posts its report on an Internet Web site (*http://www.bls.gov*).

And the world reacts. Within seconds, wire-service headlines appear on computer screens: "Unemployment Rate up Two-Tenths of a Percent" or "Nation's Production Steady." Within minutes, financial traders, for whom these news flashes provide clues about the economy's future, make snap decisions to buy or sell, moving stock and bond prices. And within the hour, politicians and pundits will respond with sound bites, attacking or defending the administration's economic policies.

In this chapter, we will take our first look at production and employment in the economy, focusing on two key variables: *gross domestic product* and the *unemployment rate*. The purpose here is not to explain what causes these variables to rise or fall. That will come a few chapters later, when we begin to study macroeconomic models. Here, we focus on the reality behind the numbers: what the statistics tell us about the economy, how the government obtains them, and how they are sometimes misused.

PRODUCTION AND GROSS DOMESTIC PRODUCT

You have probably heard the phrase *gross domestic product*—or its more familiar abbreviation, GDP—many times. It is one of those economic terms that is frequently used by the media and by politicians. In the first half of this chapter, we take a close look at GDP.

GDP: A Definition

The U.S. government has been measuring the nation's total production since the 1930s. You might think that this is an easy number to calculate, at least in theory: Simply add up the output of every firm in the country during the year. Unfortunately, measuring total production is not so straightforward, and there are many conceptual traps and pitfalls. This is why economists have come up with a very precise definition of GDP.

> The nation's **gross domestic product (GDP)** is the total value of all final goods and services produced for the marketplace during a given period, within the nation's borders.

Gross domestic product (GDP) The total value of all final goods and services produced for the marketplace during a given year, within the nation's borders.

Quite a mouthful. But every part of this definition is absolutely necessary. To see why, let's break the definition down into pieces and look more closely at each one.

The total value . . .

An old expression tells us that "you can't add apples and oranges." But that is just what government statisticians must do when they measure our total output. In a typical day, American firms produce millions of *loaves* of bread, thousands of *pounds* of peanut butter, hundreds of *hours* of television programming, and so on.

These are *different* products, and each is measured in its own type of units. Yet, somehow, we must combine all of them into a single number. But how?

The approach of GDP is to add up the *dollar value* of every good or service—the number of dollars each product is *sold* for. As a result, GDP is measured in dollar units. For example, in 2002, the GDP of the United States was about $10,446,000,000,000—give or take a few billion dollars. (That's about $10.4 trillion.)

Using dollar values to calculate GDP has two important advantages. First, it gives us a common unit of measurement for very different things, thus allowing us to add up "apples and oranges." Second, it ensures that a good that uses more resources to produce (a computer chip) will count more in GDP than a good that uses fewer resources (a tortilla chip).

However, using the dollar prices at which goods and services actually sell also creates a problem: If prices rise, then GDP will rise, even if we are not actually *producing* more. For this reason, when tracking changes in production over time, GDP must be adjusted to take away the effects of inflation. We'll come back to this issue again a bit later in the chapter.

. . . of all final . . .

When measuring production, we do not count *every* good or service produced in the economy, but only those that are sold to their *final users*. An example will illustrate why.

Figure 1 shows a simplified version of the stages of production for a ream (500 sheets) of notebook paper: A lumber company cuts down trees and produces $1.00 worth of wood chips, which it sells to a paper mill for $1.00. The mill cooks, bleaches, and refines the wood chips, turning them into $1.50 worth of paper rolls, which it sells to an office supplies manufacturer for that price. This manufacturer cuts the paper, prints lines and margins on it, and sells its to a wholesaler for $2.25. The wholesaler sells it to a retail store for $3.50, and then, finally, it is sold to a consumer—perhaps you—for $5.00.

Should we add the value of *all* this production, and include $1.00 + $1.50 + $2.25 + $3.50 + $5.00 = $13.25 in GDP each time a ream of notebook paper is produced? No, this would clearly be a mistake, since all of this production ends up creating a good worth only $5 in the end. In fact, the $5 you pay for this good already *includes* the value of all the other production in the process.

Intermediate goods Goods used up in producing final goods.

Final good A good sold to its final user.

In our example, the goods sold by the lumber company, paper mill, office supplies manufacturer, and wholesaler are all **intermediate goods**—goods used up in the process of producing something else. But the retailer (say, your local stationery store) sells a **final good**—a product sold to its *final user* (you). If we separately added in the production of intermediate goods when calculating GDP, we would be counting them more than once, since they are already included in the value of the final good.

> To *avoid overcounting intermediate products when measuring GDP, we add up the value of final goods and services only. The value of all intermediate products is automatically included in the value of the final products they are used to create.*

. . . goods and services . . .

We all know a good when we see one: We can look at it, feel it, weigh it, and, in some cases, eat it, strum it, or swing a bat at it. Not so with a service: When you get a medical checkup, a haircut, or a car wash, the *effects* of the service may linger, but

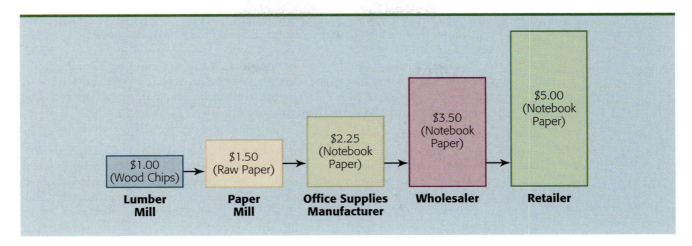

FIGURE 1
Stages of Production

the service itself is used up the moment it is produced. Nonetheless, final services count in GDP in the same way as final goods.

Services have become an increasingly important part of our total output in recent decades. The service sector has grown from about a third of U.S. output in 1950 to well over half of our output in 2002. These include the services produced by Internet providers, the health care industry, the banking industry, the educational system, and the entertainment industry.

. . . produced . . .

In order to contribute to GDP, something must be *produced*. This may sound obvious, but it is easy to forget. Every day, Americans buy billions of dollars worth of things that are *not* produced, or at least not produced during the period being considered, and so are not counted in that period's GDP. For example, people may buy land, or they may buy financial assets such as stocks or bonds. While these things cost money, they are not counted in GDP because they are not "goods and services *produced*." Land, for example, is not produced at all. Stocks and bonds represent a claim to ownership or to receive future payments, but they are not themselves goods or services.

. . . for the marketplace . . .

GDP does not include *all* final goods and services produced in the economy. Rather, it includes only the ones produced for the marketplace, that is, with the intention of being *sold*. Because of this restriction, we exclude many important goods and services from our measure. For example, when you clean your own home, you have produced a final service—housecleaning—but it is *not* counted in GDP because you are

The Services of Dealers, Brokers, and Other Sellers You've learned that GDP excludes the value of many things that are bought and sold—such as land, financial assets, and used goods—because they are not currently *produced goods and services*. But all of this buying and selling *can* contribute to GDP indirectly. How? If a dealer or broker is involved in the transaction, then that dealer or broker is producing a current service: bringing buyer and seller together. The value of this service is part of current GDP.

For example, suppose you bought a secondhand book at your college bookstore for $25. Suppose, too, that the store had bought the book from another student for $15. Then the purchase of the used book will contribute $10 to this year's GDP. Why? Because $10 is the value of the bookstore's services; it's the premium you pay to buy the book in the store, rather than going through the trouble to find the original seller yourself. The remainder of your purchase—$15—represents the value of the used book itself, and is *not* counted in GDP. The book was already counted when it was newly produced, in this or a previous year.

DANGEROUS CURVES

doing it for yourself, not for the marketplace. If you *hire* a housecleaner to clean your home, however, this final service *is* included in GDP; it has become a market transaction.

The same is true for many services produced in the economy. Taking care of your children, washing your car, mowing your lawn, walking your dog—none of these services are included in GDP if you do them for yourself, but all *are* included if you pay someone else to do them for you.

. . . *during a given period* . . .

GDP measures production during some specific period of time. Only goods produced during that period are counted. But people and businesses spend billions of dollars each year on *used* goods, such as secondhand cars, previously occupied homes, used furniture, or an old photo of Elvis talking to an extraterrestrial. These goods were all *produced,* but not necessarily in the current period. And even if they *were* produced in the current period, they would only count when sold the *first* time, as new goods; to count them again each time they are resold would lead to an overestimate of total production for the period.

What duration of time should we use for GDP? In theory, we could use any duration. In 2002, for example, the United States produced an average of $29 billion worth of output each day, $859 billion each month, and $10,446 billion for the year as a whole. Thus, we could measure daily GDP, monthly GDP, and so on. In practice, however, GDP is measured for *each quarter* and then reported as an *annual rate* for that quarter.

To understand this, look at Table 1, which shows how GDP was actually reported by the government, for six recent quarters. During 2002–I (the first quarter, January through March of 2002), the U.S. economy actually produced about $2,578.25 billion in final goods and services. But you won't see that number in the table. What you *will* see is how much we *would* have produced during an entire year if we produced at that quarter's rate for *four* full quarters (4 × $2,578.28 billion = $10,313.1 billion).[1] Once the fourth-quarter figures are in, the government also reports the official GDP figure for the entire year—what we *actually* produced during the entire year.

. . . *within the nation's borders.*

U.S. GDP measures output produced *within U.S. borders,* regardless of whether it was produced by Americans. This means we *include* output produced by foreign-owned resources and foreign citizens located in the United States, and we *exclude* output produced by Americans located in other countries. For example, when the rock star Sting, a resident of Britain, gives a concert tour in the United States, the value of his services is counted in U.S. GDP but not in British GDP. Similarly, the services of an American nurse working in an Ethiopian hospital are part of Ethiopian GDP and not U.S. GDP.

The Expenditure Approach to GDP

The Commerce Department's Bureau of Economic Analysis (BEA), the agency responsible for gathering, reporting, and analyzing movements in the nation's output, calculates GDP in several different ways. The most important of these is the

---

[1] There is one other twist to the government's reporting: Before multiplying by 4, each quarter's production is *seasonally adjusted,* raised or lowered to eliminate any changes that usually occur during that time of year.

Quarter	2002–I	2002–II	2002–III	2002–IV	2003–I	2003–II
GDP ($billions)	10,313.1	10,376.9	10,506.2	10,588.8	10,688.4	10,802.7

Source: Bureau of Economic Analysis, "National Income and Product Account Tables," accessed at *http://www.bea.gov.*

TABLE 1
GDP: Recent Quarters

expenditure approach. Because this method of measuring GDP tells us so much about the structure of our economy, we'll spend the next several pages on it.

In the expenditure approach, we divide output into four categories according to which group in the economy purchases it as the final user. The four categories are:

1. *Consumption goods and services (C),* purchased by households;
2. *Private investment goods and services (I),* purchased by businesses;
3. *Government goods and services (G),* purchased by government agencies;
4. *Net exports (NX),* purchased by foreigners.

This is an exhaustive list: Everyone who purchases a good or service included in U.S. GDP must be either a U.S. household, U.S. business, or U.S. government agency (including state and local government), or else is part of the foreign sector. Thus, when we add up the purchases of all four groups, we must get GDP:

*In the **expenditure approach** to measuring GDP, we add up the value of the goods and services purchased by each type of final user:*

$$GDP = C + I + G + NX.$$

Expenditure approach Measuring GDP by adding the value of goods and services purchased by each type of final user.

Table 2 shows the part of GDP purchased by each sector during the entire year 2002. Ignore the finer details for now and just concentrate on the last number in each column. Applying the expenditure approach to GDP in 2002 gives us GDP = C + I + G + NX = $7,304 + $1,593 + $1,973 + (−$424) = $10,446 billion.

Now let's take a closer look at each of the four components of GDP.

Consumption Spending. Consumption (C) is the largest component of GDP—making up about three-quarters of total production in recent years—and the easiest to understand:

Consumption is the part of GDP purchased by households as final users.

Consumption (C) The part of GDP purchased by households as final users.

Almost everything that households buy during the year—restaurant meals, gasoline, new clothes, doctors' visits, movies, electricity, and more—is included as part of consumption spending when we calculate GDP.

But notice the word *almost.*

Some of the things that households buy are *not* part of consumption in GDP. First, used goods or assets that households buy during the period are excluded. (Used goods were already counted when first produced, and assets are not goods or services, and therefore not part of GDP at all).

Second, *newly constructed homes*—even though part of GDP and usually purchased directly by households—are included as investment, rather than consumption. We'll discuss the reasons for this in the next section.

Consumption Purchases		Private-Investment Purchases		Government Purchases		Net Exports	
Services	$4,317	Plant, Equipment, and Sofware	$1,117	Government Consumption	$1,621	Exports	$1,015
Nondurable Goods	$2,115	New-Home Construction	$ 472	Government Investment	$ 352	Imports	$1,439
Durable Goods	$ 872	Changes in Business Inventories	$ 4				
Consumption =	$7,304	Private Investment =	$1,593	Government Purchases =	$1,973	Net Exports =	−$ 424

GDP = C + I + G + NX
   = $7,304 + $1,593 + 1,973 + (−424)
   = $10,446

Source: Bureau of Economic Analysis, "National Income and Product Account Tables," accessed at *http://www.bea.gov.*

TABLE 2
GDP in 2002: The Expenditure Approach (Billions of Dollars)

Capital stock The total value of all goods that will provide useful services in future years.

Private investment (I) The sum of business plant, equipment, and software purchases, new-home construction, and inventory changes; often referred to as just investment.

Finally, two things *are* included in consumption even though households don't actually buy them: (1) the total value of food products produced on farms that are consumed by the farmers and their families themselves; and (2) the total value of housing services provided by owner-occupied homes. The government estimates how much the food consumed on farms *could* have been sold for, and how much owner-occupied homes *could* have been rented for, and then includes these estimates as part of consumption.

Private Investment. What do oil-drilling rigs, cash registers, office telephones, and the house you grew up in all have in common? They are all examples of *capital goods*—goods that will provide useful services in future years. When we sum the value of all of the capital goods in the country, we get our **capital stock.**

Understanding the concept of capital stock helps us understand and define the concept of investment. A rough definition of **private investment** is *capital formation*—the *increase* in the nation's capital stock during the year.

More specifically,

> *private investment has three components: (1) business purchases of plant, equipment, and software; (2) new-home construction; and (3) changes in business firms' inventory stocks (changes in stocks of unsold goods).*

Each of these components requires some explanation.

Business Purchases of Plant, Equipment, and Software. This category might seem confusing at first glance. Why aren't plant, equipment, and software considered intermediate goods? After all, business firms buy these things in order to produce other things. Doesn't the value of their final goods include the value of their plant, equipment, and software as well?

Actually, no, and if you go back to the definition of intermediate goods, you will see why. Intermediate goods are *used up* in producing the current year's GDP. But a firm's plant, equipment, and software are intended to last for many years; only a small part of them is used up to make the current year's output. Thus we regard new plant, equipment, and software as final goods, and we regard the firms that buy them as the final users of those goods.

For example, suppose our paper mill—the firm that turns wood chips into raw paper—buys a new factory building that is expected to last for 50 years. Then only a small fraction of that factory building—one-fiftieth—is used up in any one year's production of raw paper, and only a small part of the factory building's value will be reflected in the value of the firm's current output. But since the entire factory is produced during the year, we must include its full value *somewhere* in our measure of production. We therefore count the whole factory building as investment in GDP.

Plant, equipment, and software purchases are always the largest component of private investment. And 2002 was no exception, as you can see in the second column of Table 2. That year, businesses purchased and installed $1,117 billion worth of plant, equipment, and software, which was about 70 percent of total private investment.

New-Home Construction. As you can see in Table 2, new-home construction made up a significant part of total private investment in 2002. But it may strike you as odd that this category is part of investment spending at all, since most new homes are purchased by households and could reasonably be considered consumption spending instead. Why is new-home construction counted as investment spending in GDP?

Largely because residential housing is an important part of the nation's *capital stock*. Just as an oil-drilling rig will continue to provide oil-drilling services for many years, so, too, a home will continue to provide housing services into the future. If we want our measure of private investment to roughly correspond to the increase in the nation's capital stock, we must include this important category of capital formation as part of private investment.

Changes in Inventories. Inventories are goods that have been produced but not yet sold. They include goods on store shelves, goods making their way through the production process in factories, and raw materials waiting to be used. We count the *change* in firms' inventories as part of investment in measuring GDP. Why? When goods are produced but not sold during the year, they end up in some firm's inventory stocks. If we did *not* count changes in inventories, we would be missing this important part of current production. Remember that GDP is designed to measure total *production*, not just the part of production that is sold during the year.

To understand this more clearly, suppose that in some year, the automobile industry produced $100 billion worth of automobiles, and that $80 billion worth was sold to consumers. Then the other $20 billion remained unsold and was added to the auto companies' inventories. If we counted consumption spending alone ($80 billion), we would underestimate automobile production in GDP. To ensure a proper measure, we must include not only the $80 billion in cars sold (consumption), but also the $20 billion *change* in inventories (private investment). In the end, the contribution to GDP is $80 billion (consumption) + $20 billion (private investment) = $100 billion, which is, indeed, the total value of automobile production during the year.

What if inventory stocks *decline* during the year, so that the change in inventories is negative? Our rule still holds: We include the change in inventories in our

© PHOTODISC/GETTY IMAGES

Unsold goods, like those pictured in this warehouse, are considered inventories. The change in these inventories is included as investment when calculating GDP.

measure of GDP. But in this case, we add a *negative* number. For example, if the automobile industry produced $100 billion worth of cars this year, but consumers bought $120 billion, then $20 billion worth must have come from inventory stocks: cars that were produced (and counted) in previous years, but that remained unsold until this year. In this case, the consumption spending of $120 billion *overestimates* automobile production during the year, so subtracting $20 billion corrects for this overcount. In the end, GDP would rise by $120 billion (consumption) − $20 billion (private investment) = $100 billion.

But why are inventory changes included in investment, rather than some other component of GDP? Because unsold goods are part of the nation's capital stock. They will provide services in the future, when they are finally sold and used. An increase in inventories represents capital formation: A decrease in inventories—negative investment—is a decrease in the nation's capital.

Inventory changes are generally the smallest component of private investment, but the most highly volatile in percentage terms. In 2002, for example, inventories rose by $4 billion; one year earlier, they fell by $60 billion, and the year before that they rose by $63 billion. Part of the reason for this volatility is that, while some inventory investment is intended, much of it is *unintended*. As the economy begins to slow, for example, businesses may be unable to sell all of the goods they have produced and had planned to sell. The unsold output is added to inventory stocks—an unintended increase in inventories. During rapid expansions, the opposite may happen: Businesses find themselves selling more than they produced—an unintended decrease in inventories.

Private Investment and the Capital Stock: Some Provisos. A few pages ago, it was pointed out that private investment corresponds only *roughly* to the increase in the nation's capital stock. Why this cautious language? Because changes in the nation's capital stock are somewhat more complicated than we are able to capture with private investment alone.

First, private investment *excludes* some production that adds to the nation's capital stock. Specifically, private investment does not include:

- *Government investment.* An important part of the nation's capital stock is owned and operated not by businesses, but by government—federal, state, and local. Courthouses, police cars, fire stations, schools, weather satellites, military aircraft, highways, and bridges are all examples of government capital. If you look at the third column of Table 2, for example, you'll see that the BEA estimated government investment to be $352 billion in 2002; that was the part of government spending that was devoted to capital formation in 2002.
- *Consumer durables.* Goods such as furniture, automobiles, washing machines, and personal computers for home use can be considered capital goods, since they will continue to provide services for many years. In 2002, households purchased $872 billion worth of consumer durables (see Table 2, first column).
- *Human capital.* Think about a surgeon's skills in performing a heart bypass operation, or a police detective's ability to find clues and solve a murder, or a Web-page designer's mastery of HTML and Java. These types of knowledge will continue to provide valuable services well into the future, just like plant and equipment or new housing. To measure the increase in the capital stock most broadly, then, we *should* include the additional skills and training acquired by the workforce during the year.

In addition to excluding some types of capital formation, private investment also errs in the other direction: It ignores depreciation—the capital that is used up during the year. Fortunately, the BEA estimates depreciation of the private and public capital stock, allowing us to calculate **net investment** (total investment minus depreciation) for these sectors. For example, for 2002, the BEA estimates that $1,164 billion of the private capital stock depreciated during the year (not shown in Table 2). So net private investment that year was only $1,593 billion − $1,164 billion = $429 billion. Similarly, the BEA estimates that $230 billion in government capital depreciated in 2002, so net government investment that year was $352 billion − $230 billion = $122 billion.

Net investment Investment minus depreciation.

Government Purchases. In 2002, the government bought $1,973 billion worth of goods and services that were part of GDP—about a fifth of the total. This component of GDP is called **government purchases**, although in recent years the Department of Commerce has begun to use the phrase *government consumption and investment purchases.* Government *investment,* as discussed earlier, refers to capital goods purchased by government agencies. The rest of government purchases is considered government *consumption:* spending on goods and services that are used up during the period. This includes the salaries of government workers and military personnel, and raw materials such as computer paper for government offices, gasoline for government vehicles, and the electricity used in government buildings.

Government purchases (G) Spending by federal, state, and local governments on goods and services.

There are a few things to keep in mind about government purchases in GDP. First, we include purchases by state and local governments as well as the federal government. In macroeconomics, it makes little difference whether the purchases are made by a local government agency like the parks department of Kalamazoo, Michigan, or a huge federal agency such as the U.S. Department of Defense.

> **Investment: Economics Versus Ordinary English** Be *extremely* careful when using the term *investment* in your economics course. In economics, investment refers to capital formation, such as the building of a new factory, home, or hospital, or the production and installation of new capital equipment, or the accumulation of inventories by business firms. In everyday language, however, *investment* has a very different meaning: a place to put your wealth. Thus, in ordinary English, you invest whenever you buy stocks or bonds or certificates of deposit or when you lend money to a friend who is starting up a business. But in the language of economics, you have not invested but merely changed the form in which you are holding your wealth (say, from checking account balances to stocks or bonds). To avoid confusion, remember that investment takes place when there is new production of capital goods—that is, when there is *capital formation.*
>
> **DANGEROUS CURVES**

Second, government purchases include *goods*—like fighter jets, police cars, school buildings, and spy satellites—and *services*—such as those performed by police, legislators, and military personnel. The government is considered to be the final purchaser of these things even if it uses them to make other goods or services. For example, if you are taking economics at a public college or university that produces educational services, then your professor is selling teaching services to a state or city government. His or her salary enters into GDP as part of government purchases.

Finally, it's important to distinguish between government *purchases*—which are counted in GDP—and government *outlays* as measured by local, state, and federal budgets and reported in the media. What's the difference? In addition to their purchases of goods and services, government agencies also disburse money for **transfer payments.** These funds are *given* to people or organizations—*not* to buy goods or services from them, but rather to fulfill some social obligation or goal. For example, Social Security payments by the federal government, unemployment insurance and welfare payments by state governments, and money disbursed to homeless shelters

Transfer payment Any payment that is not compensation for supplying goods or services.

and soup kitchens by city governments are all examples of transfer payments. The important thing to remember about transfer payments is this:

> *Transfer payments represent money redistributed from one group of citizens (taxpayers) to another (the poor, the unemployed, the elderly). While transfers are included in government budgets as outlays, they are not purchases of currently produced goods and services, and so are not included in government purchases or in GDP.*

HTTP://

The main source of information on U.S. GDP is the Bureau of Economic Analysis. Its Web page can be found at http://www.bea.doc.gov/.

Net Exports. There is one more category of buyers of output produced in the United States: *the foreign sector.* Looking back at Table 2, the fourth column tells us that in 2002, purchasers *outside* the nation bought approximately $1,015 billion of U.S. goods and services—about 10 percent of our GDP. These exports are part of U.S. production of goods and services and so are included in GDP.

However, once we recognize dealings with the rest of the world, we must correct an inaccuracy in our measure of GDP the way we've reported it so far. Americans buy many goods and services every year that were produced *outside* the United States (Chinese shoes, Japanese cars, Mexican beer, Costa Rican coffee). When we add up the final purchases of households, businesses, and government agencies, we *overcount* U.S. production because we include goods and services produced abroad. But these are *not* part of U.S. output. To correct for this overcount, we deduct all U.S. *imports* during the year, leaving us with just output produced in the United States. In 2002, these imports amounted to $1,439 billion, an amount equal to about 14 percent of our GDP.

Let's recap: To obtain an accurate measure of GDP, we must include U.S. production that is purchased by foreigners: total exports. But to correct for including goods produced abroad, we must subtract Americans' purchases of goods produced outside of the United States: total imports. In practice, we take both of these steps together by adding **net exports (NX),** which are total exports minus total imports.

Net exports (NX) Total exports minus total imports.

> *To properly account for output sold to, and bought from, foreigners, we must include net exports—the difference between exports and imports—as part of expenditure in GDP.*

In 2002, when total exports were $1,015 billion and total imports were $1,439 billion, net exports (as you can see in Table 2) were $1,015 − $1,439 = −$424 billion. The negative number indicates that the imports we're subtracting from GDP are greater than the exports we're adding.

Other Approaches to GDP

In addition to the expenditure approach, in which we calculate GDP as $C + I + G + NX$, there are other ways of measuring GDP. You may be wondering: Why bother? Why not just use one method—whichever is best—and stick to it?

Actually, there are two good reasons for measuring GDP in different ways. The first is practical. Each method of measuring GDP is subject to measurement errors. By calculating total output in several different ways and then trying to resolve the differences, the BEA gets a more accurate measure than would be possible with one method alone. The second reason is that the different ways of measuring total output give us different insights into the structure of our economy. Let's take a look at two more ways of measuring—and thinking about—GDP.

The Value-Added Approach. In the expenditure approach, we record goods and services only when they are sold to their final users—at the end of the production process. But we can also measure GDP by adding up each *firm's* contribution to the product *as it is produced.*

A firm's contribution to a product is called its *value added.* More formally,

> *a firm's **value added** is the revenue it receives for its output, minus the cost of all the intermediate goods that it buys.*

Value added The revenue a firm receives minus the cost of the intermediate goods it buys.

Look back at Figure 1, which traces the production of a ream of notebook paper. The paper mill, for example, buys $1.00 worth of wood chips (an intermediate good) from the lumber company and turns it into raw paper, which it sells for $1.50. The value added by the paper mill is $1.50 − $1.00 = $0.50. Similarly, the office supplies maker buys $1.50 worth of paper (an intermediate good) from the paper mill and sells it for $2.25, so its value added is $2.25 − $1.50 = $0.75. If we total the value added by each firm, we should get the final value of the notebook paper, as shown in Table 3. (Notice that we assume the first producer in this process—the lumber company—uses no intermediate goods.)

The total value added is $1.00 + $0.50 + $0.75 + $1.25 + $1.50 = $5.00, which is equal to the final sales price of the ream of paper. For any good or service, it will always be the case that the sum of the values added by all firms equals the final sales price. This leads to our second method of measuring GDP:

> *In the **value-added approach**, GDP is the sum of the values added by all firms in the economy.*

Value-added approach Measuring GDP by summing the value added by all firms in the economy.

The Factor Payments Approach. If a bakery sells $200,000 worth of bread during the year and buys $25,000 in intermediate goods (flour, eggs, yeast), then its value added (its revenue minus the cost of its intermediate goods) is $200,000 − $25,000 = $175,000. This is also the sum that will be *left over* from its revenue after the bakery pays for its intermediate goods.

Where does this $175,000 go? In addition to its intermediate goods, the bakery must pay for the *resources* it used during the year: the land, labor, capital, and entrepreneurship that enabled it to add value to its intermediate goods.

Payments to owners of resources are called **factor payments,** because resources are also called the factors of production. Owners of capital (the owners of the firm's buildings or machinery, or those who lend funds to the firm so that *it* can buy buildings and machinery) receive *interest payments.* Owners of land and natural resources receive *rent.* And those who provide labor to the firm receive *wages and salaries.*

Factor payments Payments to the owners of resources that are used in production

Finally, there is one additional resource used by the firm: *entrepreneurship.* In every capitalist economy, the entrepreneurs are those who visualize society's needs, mobilize and coordinate the other resources so that production can take place, and gamble that the enterprise will succeed. The people who provide this entrepreneurship (often the owners of the firms) receive a fourth type of factor payment: *profit.*

Now let's go back to our bakery, which received $200,000 in revenue during the year. We've seen that $25,000 of this went to pay for intermediate goods, leaving $175,000 in value added earned by the factors of production. Let's suppose that $110,000 went to pay the wages of the bakery's employees, $10,000 was paid out as interest on loans, and $15,000 was paid in rent for the land under the bakery.

TABLE 3
Value Added at Different Stages of Production

Firm	Cost of Intermediate Goods	Revenue	Value Added
Lumber Company	$ 0	$1.00	$1.00
Paper Mill	$1.00	$1.50	$0.50
Office Supplies Manufacturer	$1.50	$2.25	$0.75
Wholesaler	$2.25	$3.50	$1.25
Retailer	$3.50	$5.00	$1.50
			Total: $5.00

That leaves $175,000 − $110,000 − $10,000 − $15,000 = $40,000. This last sum—since it doesn't go to anyone else—stays with the owner of the bakery. It, too, is a factor payment—profit—for the entrepreneurship she provides. Thus, when all of the factor payments, including profit, are added together, the total will be $110,000 + $10,000 + $15,000 + $40,000 = $175,000—precisely equal to the value added at the bakery. More generally,

> In any year, the value added by a firm is equal to the total factor payments made by that firm.

Earlier, we learned that GDP equals the sum of all firms' value added; now we've learned that each firm's value added is equal to its factor payments. Thus, GDP must equal the total factor payments made by all firms in the economy. Since all of these factor payments are received by households in the form of wages and salaries, rent, interest, or profit, we have our *third* method of measuring GDP:

Factor payments approach
Measuring GDP by summing the factor payments earned by all households in the economy.

> In the **factor payments approach**, GDP is measured by adding up all of the income—wages and salaries, rent, interest, and profit—earned by all households in the economy.[2]

The factor payments approach to GDP gives us one of our most important insights into the marcoeconomy:

> The total output of the economy (GDP) is equal to the total income earned in the economy.

This simple idea—output equals income—follows directly from the factor payments approach to GDP. It explains why macroeconomists use the terms "output" and "income" interchangeably: They are one and the same. If output rises, income rises by the same amount; if output falls, income falls by an equal amount. We'll be using this very important insight in several chapters to come.

---

[2] Actually, this is just an approximation. Before a firm pays its factors of production, it first deducts a small amount for depreciation of its plant and equipment, and another small amount for the sales taxes it must pay to the government. Thus, GDP and total factor payments are slightly different. We ignore this difference in the text.

Measuring GDP: A Summary

You've now learned three different ways to calculate GDP:

Expenditure Approach: GDP = C + I + G + NX

Value-Added Approach: GDP = Sum of value added by all firms

Factor Payments Approach: GDP = Sum of factor payments earned by all households

= Wages and salaries + interest + rent + profit

= Total household income

We will use these three approaches to GDP again and again as we study what makes the economy tick. But for now, make sure you understand why each one of them should, in theory, give us the same number for GDP.

Real Versus Nominal GDP

Since GDP is measured in dollars, we have a serious problem when we want to track the change in output over time. The problem is that the value of the dollar—its purchasing power—is itself changing. As prices have risen over the years, the value of the dollar has steadily fallen. Trying to keep track of GDP using dollars in different years is like trying to keep track of a child's height using a ruler whose length changes each year. If we find that the child is three rulers tall in one year and four rulers tall in the next, we cannot know how much the child has grown, if at all, until we adjust for the effects of a changing ruler. The same is true for GDP and for any other economic variable measured in dollars: We usually need to adjust our measurements to reflect changes in the value of the dollar.

> *When a variable is measured over time with no adjustment for the dollar's changing value, it is called a **nominal variable**. When a variable is adjusted for the dollar's changing value, it is called a **real variable**.*

Nominal variable A variable measured without adjustment for the dollar's changing value.

Real variable A variable adjusted for changes in the dollar's value.

Most government statistics are reported in both nominal and real terms, but economists focus almost exclusively on real variables. This is because changes in nominal variables don't really tell us much. For example, from the second to the third quarter of 2001 (not shown in earlier tables), nominal GDP increased from $10,050 billion to $10,098 billion, an increase of one-half of one percent. But production as measured by *real GDP* actually *decreased* over that period. The increase in nominal GDP was due entirely to a rise in prices.

The Importance of Real Values: A Basic Principle

The distinction between nominal and real values is crucial in macroeconomics. The public, the media, and sometimes even government officials have been confused by a failure to make this distinction. Whenever we want to track significant changes in key macroeconomic variables—such as the average wage rate, wealth, income, and GDP or any of its components—we always use *real* variables.

Basic Principle #8: The Importance of Real Values
Since our economic well-being depends, in part, on the goods and services we can buy, it is important to translate nominal values (which are measured in current dollars) to real values (which adjust for the dollar's changing value).

In the next chapter, you'll learn how economists translate some important nominal variables into real variables.

How GDP Is Used

We've come a long way since 1931. In that year—as the United States plummeted into the worst depression in its history—Congress summoned economists from government agencies, from academia, and from the private sector to testify about the state of the economy. They were asked the most basic questions: How much output was the nation producing, and how much had production fallen since 1929? How much income were Americans earning, how much were they spending? How much profit were businesses earning, and what were they doing with their profits? To the surprise of the members of Congress, no one could answer any of these questions, because *no one was keeping track of our national income and output!* The most recent measurement, which was rather incomplete, had been made in 1929.

Thus began the U.S. system of national income accounts, a system whose value was instantly recognized around the world and rapidly copied by other countries. Today, the government's reports on GDP are used to steer the economy over both the short run and the long run. In the short run, sudden changes in real GDP can alert us to the onset of a recession or a too-rapid expansion that can overheat the economy. Many (but not all) economists believe that, if alerted in time, policies can be designed to help keep the economy on a more balanced course.

GDP is also used to measure the long-run growth rate of the economy's output. Indeed, we typically define the average *standard of living* as *output per capita*: real GDP divided by the population. In order for output per capita to rise, real GDP must grow faster than the population. Since the U.S. population tends to grow by about 1 percent per year, a real GDP growth rate of 1 percent per year is needed just to *maintain* our output per capita; higher growth rates are needed to increase it.

Look at Figure 2, which shows the annual percentage change in real GDP from 1960 through the second quarter of 2003. The lower horizontal line indicates the 1 percent growth needed to just maintain output per capita. You can see that, on average, real GDP has grown by more than this, so that output per capita has steadily increased over time.

Growth in real GDP is also important for another reason: to ensure that the economy is generating sufficient new *jobs* for a workforce that is not only growing in number, but in productivity. Each year, the average worker is capable of producing more output, due to advances in technology, increases in the capital stock, and the greater skills of workers themselves. But if each worker produces more output, then output must increase even *faster* than the population to create enough jobs for everyone who wants to work. If not, the unemployment rate will rise.

In practice, an average annual growth rate of about 3.3 percent—the upper line in Figure 2—seems to prevent the unemployment rate from rising. And over the long run, growth in real GDP has been sufficiently high for this purpose. But you can also see that there are periods of time when GDP growth—even though positive—is too

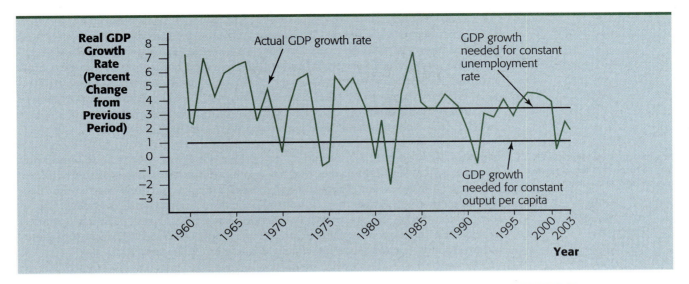

FIGURE 2
**Real GDP Growth Rate,
1960–2003**

*Although the growth rate of real
GDP has fluctuated over time,
it has rarely dipped below the 1
percent rate needed to maintain
output per capita. And although
growth has frequently fallen below the 3.3 percent rate needed
to prevent a rise in unemployment, it has met that threshold
on average.*

Source: Bureau of Economic Analysis,
National Economic Accounts, Table
5.1 (2003 data is for first half of year
only).

low to prevent a rise in the unemployment rate. During the recession of 2001 and into the first half of 2003, for example, GDP growth lagged behind the 3.3 percent re- quirement, and the unemployment rate rose. However, most economists have confi- dence that over time, real GDP growth will exceed the 3.3 percent requirement by enough to make up for the periods it has fallen behind, and that the economy will continue to generate jobs for a growing and more productive workforce, just as it has in the past. Later, you'll learn the reasons for this confidence.

To sum up: We use GDP to guide the economy in two ways. In the short run, it alerts us to recessions and give us a chance to stabilize the economy. And over long periods it tells us whether our economy is growing fast enough to raise output per capita and our standard of living, and fast enough to generate sufficient jobs for a growing population.

Problems with GDP

You have seen that GDP is an extremely useful concept. But the measurement of GDP is plagued by some serious problems.

Quality Changes. Suppose a new ballpoint pen comes out that lasts four times as long as previous versions. What *should* happen to GDP? Ideally, each new pen should count the same as four old pens, since one new pen offers the same *writing services* as four old ones. But the analysts at the Bureau of Economic Analysis (BEA) would most likely treat this new pen the same as an old pen and record an increase in GDP only if the total number of pens increased. Why? Because the BEA has a limited budget. While it does include the impact of quality changes for many goods and services (such as automobiles and computers), the BEA simply does not have the resources to esti- mate quality changes for millions of different goods and services. These include many consumer goods (such as razor blades that shave closer and last longer), medical ser- vices (increased surgery success rates and shorter recovery periods), and retail services (faster checkout times due to optical scanners). Ignoring these quality improvements causes GDP to understate the true growth in output from year to year.

The Underground Economy. Some production is hidden from government authorities, either because it is illegal (drugs, prostitution, most gambling) or because those engaged in it are avoiding taxes. Production in these hidden markets, which comprise the *underground economy,* cannot be measured accurately, so the BEA must estimate it. Many economists believe that the BEA's estimates are too low. As a result, GDP may understate total output. However, since the *relative* importance of the underground economy does not change rapidly, the BEA's estimates of *changes* in GDP from year to year should not be seriously affected.

Nonmarket production Goods and services that are produced but not sold in a market.

Nonmarket Production. With a few exceptions, GDP does not include **nonmarket production**: goods and services that are produced but not sold in the marketplace. All of the housecleaning, typing, sewing, lawn mowing, and child rearing that people do themselves, rather than hiring someone else, are excluded from GDP. Whenever a nonmarket transaction (say, cleaning your apartment) becomes a market transaction (hiring a housecleaner to do it for you), GDP will rise, even though total production (cleaning one apartment) has remained the same.

Over the last half-century, much production has shifted away from the home and to the market. Parenting, which was not counted in past years' GDP, has become day care, which *does* count—currently contributing several billion dollars annually to GDP. Similarly, home-cooked food has been replaced by takeout, talking to a friend has been replaced by therapy, and the neighbor who watches your house while you're away has been replaced by a store-bought alarm system or an increase in police protection. In all of these cases, real GDP increases, even though production has not. This can exaggerate the growth in GDP over long periods of time.

What do all these problems tell us about the value of GDP? That for certain purposes—especially interpreting *long-run* changes in GDP—we must exercise caution. For example, suppose that, over the next 20 years, the growth rate of GDP slows down. Would this mean that something is going wrong with the economy? Would it suggest a need to change course? Not necessarily. It *could* be that the underground economy or unrecorded quality changes are becoming more important. Similarly, if GDP growth accelerates, it could mean that our living standards are rising more rapidly. But it might instead mean that economic activity is shifting out of the home and into the market even more rapidly than in the past.

GDP works much better, however, as a guide to the short-run performance of the economy. Look back at the list of problems with GDP. The distortion in GDP measurement caused by each problem is likely to remain fairly constant from quarter to quarter. If GDP suddenly drops, it is extremely unlikely that the underground economy has suddenly become more important, or that there has been a sudden shift from market to nonmarket activities, or that we are suddenly missing more quality changes than usual. Rather, we can be reasonably certain that output and economic activity are slowing down.

> *Short-term changes in real GDP are fairly accurate reflections of the state of the economy. A significant quarter-to-quarter change in real GDP indicates a change in actual production, rather than a measurement problem.*

This is why policy makers, businesspeople, and the media pay such close attention to GDP as a guide to the economy from quarter to quarter.

EMPLOYMENT AND UNEMPLOYMENT

When you think of unemployment, you may have an image in your mind that goes something like this: As the economy slides into recession, an anxious employee is called into an office and handed a pink slip by a grim-faced manager. "Sorry," the manager says, "I wish there were some other way. . . ." The worker spends the next few months checking the classified ads, pounding the pavement, and sending out résumés in a desperate search for work. And perhaps, after months of trying, the laid-off worker gives up, spending days at the neighborhood bar, drinking away the shame and frustration, and sinking lower and lower into despair and inertia.

For some people, joblessness begins and ends very much like this—a human tragedy, and a needless one. On one side, we have people who want to work and support themselves by producing something; on the other side is the rest of society, which could certainly use more goods and services. Yet somehow, the system isn't working, and the jobless cannot find work. The result is often hardship for the unemployed and their families, and a loss to society in general.

But this is just one face of unemployment, and there are others. Some instances of unemployment, for example, have little to do with macroeconomic conditions. And frequently, unemployment causes a lot less suffering than in our grim story.

HTTP://
Employment-related information for the United States can be found at the Bureau of Labor Statistics Web site: **http://stats.bls.gov**.

Types of Unemployment

In the United States, people are considered unemployed if they are: (1) not working and (2) actively seeking a job. But unemployment can arise for a variety of reasons, each with its own policy implications. This is why economists have found it useful to classify unemployment into four different categories, each arising from a different cause and each having different consequences.

Frictional Unemployment. Short-term joblessness experienced by people who are between jobs or who are entering the labor market for the first time or after an absence is called **frictional unemployment**. In the real world, it takes time to find a job—time to prepare your résumé, to decide where to send it, to wait for responses, and then to investigate job offers so you can make a wise choice. It also takes time for employers to consider your skills and qualifications and to decide whether you are right for their firms. If you are not working during that time, you will be unemployed: searching for work but not working.

Because frictional unemployment is, by definition, short term, it causes little hardship to those affected by it. In most cases, people have enough savings to support themselves through a short spell of joblessness, or else they can borrow on their credit cards or from friends or family to tide them over. Moreover, this kind of unemployment has important benefits: By spending time searching rather than jumping at the first opening that comes their way, people find jobs for which they are better suited and in which they will ultimately be more productive. As a result, workers earn higher incomes, firms have more productive employees, and society has more goods and services.

Frictional unemployment Joblessness experienced by people who are between jobs or who are just entering or reentering the labor market.

Seasonal Unemployment. Joblessness related to changes in weather, tourist patterns, or other seasonal factors is called **seasonal unemployment**. For example, most

Seasonal unemployment Joblessness related to changes in weather, tourist patterns, or other seasonal factors.

ski instructors lose their jobs every April or May, and many construction workers are laid off each winter.

Seasonal unemployment, like frictional unemployment, is rather benign: It is short term and, because it is entirely predictable, workers are often compensated in advance for the unemployment they experience in the off-season. Construction workers, for example, are paid higher-than-average hourly wages, in part to compensate them for their high probability of joblessness in the winter.

However, seasonal unemployment complicates the interpretation of unemployment data. Seasonal factors push the unemployment rate up in certain months of the year and pull it down in others, even when overall conditions in the economy remain unchanged. For example, each June, unemployment rises as millions of high school and college students—who do not want to work during the school year—begin looking for summer jobs. If the government reported the actual rise in unemployment in June, it would *seem* as if labor market conditions were deteriorating, when in fact, the rise would be merely a predictable and temporary seasonal change. To prevent any misunderstandings, the government usually reports the *seasonally adjusted* rate of unemployment, a rate that reflects only those changes beyond normal for the month. For example, if the unemployment rate in June is typically one percentage point higher than during the rest of the year, then the seasonally adjusted rate for June will be the actual rate minus one percentage point.

Structural Unemployment. Sometimes, there are jobs available and workers who would be delighted to have them, but job seekers and employers are mismatched in some way. For example, in 2003, there were plenty of job openings for business professors; for nurses and nurse practitioners; for translators of strategic languages like Arabic, Persian, and Urdu; and in many other professions. Many of the unemployed, however, had been laid off from the airline and hotel industries, or from manufacturing, and did not have the skills and training to work where the jobs were going begging. This is a *skill* mismatch. The mismatch can also be *geographic,* as when construction jobs go begging in Northern California, Oregon, and Washington, but unemployed construction workers live in other states.

Structural unemployment
Joblessness arising from mismatches between workers' skills and employers' requirements or between workers' locations and employers' locations.

Unemployment that results from these kinds of mismatches is called **structural unemployment,** because it arises from *structural change* in the economy: when old, dying industries are replaced with new ones that require different skills and are located in different areas of the country. Structural unemployment is generally a stubborn, *long-term* problem, often lasting several years or more. Why? Because it can take considerable time for the structurally unemployed to find jobs—time to relocate to another part of the country or time to acquire new skills. To make matters worse, the structurally unemployed—who could benefit from financial assistance for job training or relocation—usually cannot get loans because they don't have jobs.

In recent decades, structural unemployment has been a much bigger problem in other countries, especially in Europe, than it is in the United States. Table 4 shows average unemployment rates in the United States and several European countries from 1990 to 2000 as well as in mid-2003. Unemployment rates were consistently higher in continental Europe than in the United States in the late 1990s and, in most of these countries were still high in mid-2003. And the unemployed remain jobless longer in Europe (where half of all the unemployed have been so for more than a year) than in the United States (where only 1 in 10 has been jobless for more than a year).

And within the United States, some areas have higher structural unemployment than others. For example, in June 2003 when the U.S. unemployment rate was 6.4

TABLE 4

Average Unemployment Rates
in Several Countries,
1990–2000 and 2003

Country	Average Unemployment Rate, 1990–2000	Unemployment Rate, Mid-2003
France	11.1%	9.1%
Italy	10.5%	8.7%
Greece	9.2%	9.6%
Canada	8.6%	7.8%
United Kingdom	8.0%	5.0%
Germany	7.9%	9.4%
Sweden	7.3%	5.4%
United States	5.6%	6.4%

Sources: Constance Sorrentino and Joyanna Moy, "U.S. Labor Market Performance in International Perspective," *Monthly Labor Review*, June 2002, pp. 15–35; *Standardized Unemployment Rates*, Organization for Economic Cooperation and Development, accessed July 30 at *http://www.oecd.org/dataoecd/ 41/13/2752342.pdf*. 2003 unemployment rates are for May 2003 except United Kingdom (March,) Italy (April), the United States (June), and Greece (December 2002). European unemployment rates have been adjusted by the OECD for reasonable comparability with U.S. rate.

percent, the rate in Los Angeles was 6.9 percent; in Detroit, 7.6 percent; in New York and Miami, 7.7 percent; and in Grand Rapids, Michigan, 8.0 percent.

The types of unemployment we've considered so far—frictional, structural, and seasonal—arise largely from *microeconomic* causes; that is, they are attributable to changes in specific industries and specific labor markets, rather than to the overall level of production in the country. This kind of unemployment cannot be entirely eliminated, as people will always spend some time searching for new jobs, there will always be seasonal industries in the economy, and structural changes will, from time to time, require workers to move to new locations or gain new job skills. Some amount of microeconomic unemployment is a sign of a dynamic economy. It allows workers to sort themselves into the best possible jobs, enables us to enjoy seasonal goods and services like winter skiing and summers at the beach, and permits the economy to go through structural changes when needed.

But frictional, structural, and seasonal unemployment rates are not fixed in stone, and government policy may be able to influence them. In the United States, many economists believe that we can continue to enjoy the benefits of a fast-changing and flexible economy with a lower unemployment rate. To achieve this goal, they advocate programs to help match the unemployed with employers and to help the jobless relocate and learn new skills. In Europe, by contrast, most economists believe that government labor and regulatory policies have been a *cause* of the structural unemployment problem. For example, government regulations make it costly or impossible for many European firms to lay off workers once they are hired. While that encourages firms to retain any *currently* employed workers, it also discourages new hiring, since firms regard any newly hired worker as a permanent obligation, even if future production turns down and the new worker is no longer needed. European unemployment benefits may also play a role. They are more generous than in the United States, and the benefits are given for longer durations with a greater fraction of the potential labor force eligible to receive them. While this certainly helps the unemployed deal with the hardship of job loss, it also means that European workers have less incentive to seek new work once they lose a job.

Note, however, that in both Europe and the United States, the proposed solutions for high seasonal, frictional, or structural unemployment are changes in labor or regulatory policies, rather than changes in macroeconomic policy designed to raise GDP.

Our fourth and last type of unemployment, however, has an entirely *macroeconomic* cause.

Cyclical Unemployment. When the economy goes into a recession and total output falls, the unemployment rate rises. Many previously employed workers lose their jobs and have difficulty finding new ones. At the same time, there are fewer openings, so new entrants to the labor force must spend more than the usual time searching before they are hired. This type of unemployment—because it is caused by the business cycle—is called **cyclical unemployment.**

Cyclical unemployment Joblessness arising from changes in production over the business cycle.

Look at Figure 3, which shows the unemployment rate in the United States for each quarter since 1960, and notice the rises that occurred during periods of recession (shaded). For example, in the recessions of the early 1980s, the unemployment rate rose from about 6 percent to more than 10 percent. And in the more recent recession from March to November of 2001, the unemployment rate rose from 4.2 percent to 5.8 percent; and during the very slow recovery of 2002 and the first half of 2003 the unemployment rate remained entrenched near 6 percent. These were rises in cyclical unemployment.

Since it arises from conditions in the overall economy, cyclical unemployment is a problem for *macroeconomic* policy. This is why macroeconomists focus almost exclusively on cyclical unemployment, rather than the other types of joblessness. Reflecting this emphasis, macroeconomists say we have reached **full employment** when *cyclical unemployment is reduced to zero,* even though substantial amounts of frictional, seasonal, and structural unemployment may remain:

Full employment A situation in which there is no cyclical unemployment.

> *In macroeconomics, full employment means zero cyclical unemployment. But the overall unemployment rate at full employment is greater than zero because there are still positive levels of frictional, seasonal, and structural unemployment.*

How do we tell how much of our unemployment is cyclical? Many economists believe that today, normal amounts of frictional, seasonal, and structural unemployment account for an unemployment rate of between 4.5 and 5.0 percent in the United States. Therefore, any unemployment beyond this is considered cyclical unemployment. For example, when the actual unemployment rate was 6.4 percent in June 2003, we would say that 1.4 to 1.9 percent of the labor force was cyclically unemployed.

The Costs of Unemployment

Why are we so concerned about achieving a low rate of unemployment? What are the *costs* of unemployment to our society? We can identify two different types of costs: economic costs, those that can be readily measured in dollar terms, and noneconomic costs, those that are difficult or impossible to measure in dollars, but that still affect us in important ways.

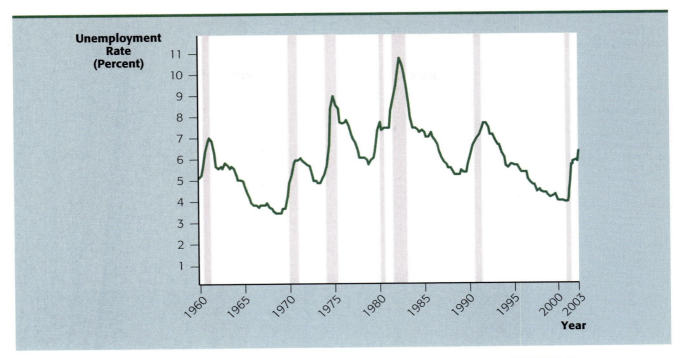

FIGURE 3
**U.S. Quarterly Unemployment
Rate, 1960–2003**

*The unemployment rate rises
during recessions (shaded) and
falls during expansions.*

Economic Costs. The chief economic cost of unemployment is the *opportunity cost* of lost output: the goods and services the jobless *would* produce if they were working but do not produce because they cannot find work. This cost is borne by our society in general, although the burden may fall more on one group than another. If, for example, the unemployed were simply left to fend for themselves, then *they* would bear most of the cost. In fact, the unemployed are often given government assistance, so that the costs are spread somewhat among citizens in general. But there is no escaping this central fact:

> *When there is cyclical unemployment, the nation produces less output, and therefore some group or groups within society must consume less output.*

One way of viewing the economic cost of cyclical unemployment is illustrated in Figure 4. The green line shows real GDP over time, while the orange line shows the path of our **potential output**—the output we *could* have produced if the economy were operating at full employment.

Notice that actual output is sometimes *above* potential output. At these times, unemployment is *below* the full-employment rate. For example, during the expansion in the late 1960s, cyclical unemployment was eliminated and the sum of frictional, seasonal, and structural unemployment dropped below 4.5 percent, its normal level for those years. At other times, real GDP is *below* potential output, most often during and following a recession. At these times, unemployment rises above the full-employment rate. In the 2001 recession, the unemployment rate rose from 4.2 percent to 5.8 percent, and stayed near or above 6 percent for the next year and a half.

Potential output The level of output the economy could produce if operating at full employment.

FIGURE 4
**Actual And Potential Real GDP,
1960–2003**

Sources: Real GDP from Bureau of
Economic Analysis, Real Gross Domestic Product, Table 1.2 (http://www.
bea.gov). Potential GDP from Congressional Budget Office, "CBO's Method
for Estimating Potential Output: An Update," August 2001 (www.cbo.gov),
Publications.

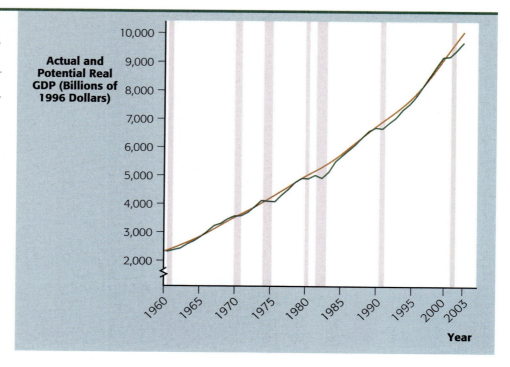

In the figure, you can see that we have spent more of the last 40 years operating *below* our potential than above it. That is, the cyclical ups and downs of the economy have, on balance, led to lower living standards than we would have had if the economy had always operated just at potential output.

Broader Costs. There are also costs of unemployment that go beyond lost output. Unemployment—especially when it lasts for many months or years—can have serious psychological and physical effects. Some studies have found that increases in unemployment cause noticeable rises in the number of heart attack deaths, suicides, and admissions to state prisons and psychiatric hospitals. The jobless are more likely to suffer a variety of health problems, including high blood pressure, heart disorders, troubled sleep, and back pain. There may be other problems—such as domestic violence, depression, and alcoholism—that are more difficult to document. And, tragically, most of those who lose their job and remain unemployed for long periods also lose their health insurance, increasing the likelihood that these problems will have serious consequences.

Unemployment also causes setbacks in achieving important social goals. For example, most of us want a fair and just society where all people have an equal chance to better themselves. But our citizens do not bear the burden of unemployment equally. In a recession, we do not all suffer a reduction in our work hours; instead, some people are laid off entirely, while others continue to work roughly the same hours.

Moreover, the burden of unemployment is not shared equally among different groups in the population, but tends to fall most heavily on minorities, especially minority youth. As a rough rule of thumb, the unemployment rate for blacks is twice that for whites; and the rate for *teenage* blacks is triple the rate for blacks overall. Table 5 shows that the unemployment rates for June 2003 are consistent with this general experience. Notice the extremely high unemployment rate for black teenagers: 39.3 percent. This contributes to a vicious cycle of poverty and discrimination: When minority youths are deprived of that all-important first job, they remain at a disadvantage in the labor market for years to come.

Group	Unemployment Rate
Whites	5.5%
Hispanics	8.4%
Blacks	11.8%
White Teenagers	16.5%
Black Teenagers	39.3%

Source: The Employment Situation: June 2003, Bureau of Labor Statistics News Release, July 3, 2003 (Tables A-2, A-3; seasonally adjusted data).

TABLE 5
Unemployment Rates for Various Groups, June 2003

How Unemployment Is Measured

In June 2003, about 150 million Americans were not employed, according to official government statistics. Were all of these people unemployed? Absolutely not. In theory, the unemployed are those who are *willing and able* to work but do not have jobs. Most of the 150 million nonworking Americans were either *unable* or *unwilling* to work. For example, the very old, the very young, and the very ill were unable to work, as were those serving prison terms. Others were able to work, but preferred not to, including millions of college students, homemakers, and retired people. Still others were in the military and are counted in the population, but not counted when calculating civilian employment statistics.

But how, in practice, can we determine who is willing and able? This is a thorny problem, and there is no perfect solution to it. In the United States, we determine whether a person is willing and able to work by his or her *behavior*. More specifically, to be counted as unemployed, you must have recently *searched* for work. But how can we tell who has, and who has not, recently searched for work?

The Census Bureau's Household Survey.
Every month, thousands of interviewers from the United States Census Bureau—acting on behalf of the U.S. Bureau of Labor Statistics (BLS)—conduct a survey of 60,000 households across America. This sample of households is carefully selected to give information about the entire population. Household members who are under 16, in the military, or currently residing in an institution like a prison or hospital are excluded from the survey. The interviewer will then ask questions about the remaining household members' activities during the *previous week*.

Figure 5 shows roughly how this works. First, the interviewer asks whether the household member has worked one or more hours for pay or profit. If the answer is yes, the person is considered employed; if no, another question is asked: Has she been *temporarily* laid off from a job from which she is waiting to be recalled? A yes means the person is unemployed whether or not the person searched for a new job; a no leads to one more question: Did the person actively *search* for work during the previous four weeks. If yes, the person is unemployed; if no, she is not in the labor force.

Figure 6 illustrates how the BLS, extrapolating from its 60,000-household sample, classified the U.S. population in July 2003. First, note that about 70 million people were ruled out from consideration because they were under 16 years of age, living in institutions, or in the military. The remaining 221 million people made up the civilian, noninstitutional population, and of these, 137.7 million were employed and 9.4 million were unemployed. Adding the employed and unemployed together gives us the **labor force,** equal to 137.7 million + 9.4 million = 147.1 million.

Labor force Those people who have a job or who are looking for one.

Finally, we come to the official **unemployment rate,** which is defined as the percentage of the labor force that is unemployed:

Unemployment rate The fraction of the labor force that is without a job.

$$\text{Unemployment rate} = \frac{\text{Unemployed}}{\text{Labor Force}} = \frac{\text{Unemployed}}{(\text{Unemployed} + \text{Employed})}$$

Using the numbers in Figure 6, the U.S. unemployment rate in June 2003 was calculated as 9.4/(9.4 + 137.7) = .064 or 6.4 percent. This was the number released to journalists at 8:00 A.M. on the first Friday of July 2003, and the number that made headlines in your local newspaper the next day.

Problems in Measuring Unemployment

The Census Bureau earns very high marks from economists for both its sample size—60,000 households—and the characteristics of its sample, which very closely match the characteristics of the U.S. population. Still, the official unemployment rate suffers from some important measurement problems.

Involuntary part-time workers Individuals who would like a full-time job, but who are working only part time.

Many economists believe that our official measure seriously underestimates the extent of unemployment in our society. There are two reasons for this belief: the treatment of *involuntary part-time workers* and the treatment of *discouraged workers.*

As you can see in Figure 5, anyone working one hour or more for pay during the survey week is treated as employed. This includes many people who would like a full-time job—and may even be searching for one—but who did some part-time work during the week. Some economists have suggested that these people, called **involuntary part-time workers,** should be regarded as partially employed and partially unemployed.

How many involuntary part-time workers are there? In June 2003, the BLS estimated that there were about 4.5 million.[3] If

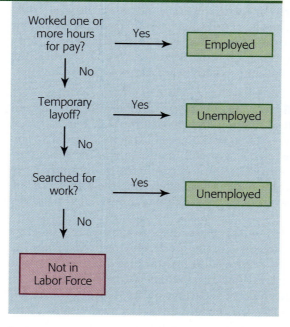

FIGURE 5
How the BLS Measures Employment Status

BLS interviewers ask a series of questions to determine whether an individual is employed, unemployed, or not in the labor force.

[3] This and other information about unemployment in June 2003 comes from *The Employment Situation: June 2003,* Bureau of Labor Statistics News Release, July 3, 2003. (All figures are seasonally adjusted except discouraged workers.)

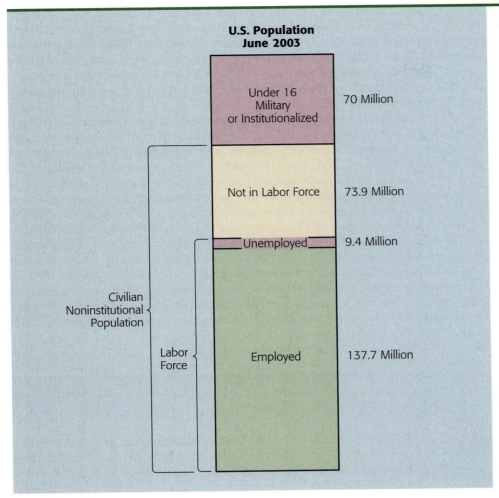

FIGURE 6
**Employment Status of the
U.S. Population—June 2003**

U.S. Population
June 2003

Under 16
Military
or Institutionalized — 70 Million

Not in Labor Force — 73.9 Million

Unemployed — 9.4 Million

Employed — 137.7 Million

Civilian Noninstitutional Population

Labor Force

each of these workers were considered half-employed and half-unemployed, the unemployment rate in that month would have been 7.9 percent, instead of the officially reported 6.4 percent.

Another problem is the treatment of **discouraged workers,** individuals who would like to work but, because they feel little hope of finding a job, have given up searching. Because they are not taking active steps to find work, they are considered "not in the labor force" (see Figure 5). Some economists feel that discouraged workers should be counted as unemployed. After all, these people are telling us that they are willing and able to work, but they are not working. It seems wrong to exclude them just because they are not actively seeking work. Others argue that counting discouraged workers as unemployed would reduce the objectivity of our unemployment measure. Talk is cheap, they believe, and people may *say* anything when asked whether they would like a job; the real test is what people *do*. Yet even the staunchest defenders of the current method of measuring employment would agree that *some* discouraged workers are, in fact, willing and able to work and should be considered unemployed. The problem, in their view, is determining which ones.

Discouraged workers Individuals who would like a job, but have given up searching for one.

How many discouraged workers are there? No one knows for sure. The BLS tries to count them, but defining who is genuinely discouraged is yet another thorny problem. Using the BLS's rather strict criteria, there were 478,000 discouraged workers in June 2003. But with a looser, unofficial definition of "discouraged worker"—people who are not working but say they want a job—the count rises to 5.1 million. Including some or all of these people among the unemployed would raise the unemployment rate significantly.

Still, the unemployment rate, as currently measured, tells us something important: the number of people who are *searching* for jobs, but have not yet found them. It is not exactly the same as the percentage of the labor force that is jobless even though willing and able to work. But if we could obtain a perfect measure of the latter, the unemployment rate, as currently measured, would be highly correlated with it.

Moreover, the unemployment rate tells us something unique about conditions in the macroeconomy. When the unemployment rate is relatively low—so that few people are actively seeking work—a firm that wants to hire more workers may be forced to lure them from other firms, by offering a higher wage rate. This puts upward pressure on wages and can lead to future inflation. A high unemployment rate, by contrast, tells us that firms can more easily expand by hiring those who are actively seeking work, without having to lure new workers from another firm and without having to offer higher wages. This suggests little inflationary danger. Later in the book, we will discuss the connection between unemployment and inflation more fully.

© ROYALTY-FREE/CORBIS

USING THE THEORY
GDP After September 11

On September 11, 2001, the United States suffered an unprecedented terrorist attack when four airliners were hijacked and three of them were used to destroy the World Trade Center in New York and a section of the Pentagon in Washington D.C., killing more than 3,000 people. The most profound dimensions of this tragedy were the human lives lost and the continuing bereavement of those left behind—a loss that stunned and disoriented the nation.

But as the nation began to find its balance, it became clear that the events of September 11 would have a significant impact in another way: on the economy. Most economists suspected that the United States was already in recession (a suspicion that was confirmed later when the beginning of the recession was dated to March 2001). But what would happen after September 11? Would the recession deepen? How badly? Could the economy actually tilt into a depression? What was the appropriate economic policy, and how should it be orchestrated? As if the shock of the attacks weren't enough, millions of Americans now began to fear for their jobs.

How an event like September 11 affects the macroeconomy, and how the government responded, are issues you will learn about in later chapters of this book. Here, we look at just one aspect of the problem: the impact of the attacks on U.S. real GDP. By taking a brief look at this now—even before you've learned much about how the macroeconomy works—you'll be able to see how an understanding of GDP and its measurement can help us gauge the effects of September 11.

It will be helpful to distinguish between the *direct* impact on GDP (the direct result of the destruction itself) and the *indirect* impact (resulting from the choices of economic decision makers in the weeks, months, and even years following the attack).

The Direct Impact on GDP

At first, it seems that the direct impact of the attacks on GDP should be huge. For example, compared to the property loss from other recent man-made disasters, September 11 was orders of magnitude more destructive. The property loss from the Los Angeles riots of 1992 amounted to about $775 million; from the first World Trade Center bombing in 1993, $510 million; and from the 1995 bombing of the Federal Building in Oklahoma City, $125 million. By contrast, on September 11, the insured property damage in New York City alone was $16 billion.

But now consider the destruction caused by some recent *natural* disasters. The 1994 earthquake centered in Northridge, California, destroyed about $15 billion in property—almost as much as the direct damage to New York City. And Hurricane Andrew in 1992 caused even more damage—about $27 billion worth—significantly more than the damage to the World Trade Center and the Pentagon combined. The direct national economic impact of both of these natural disasters hardly appeared in the national statistics. And that is not surprising, since these magnitudes amount to only a fraction of a percentage point of our GDP, and an even smaller fraction of our total capital stock.

But as may have already occurred to you, measuring destruction of property—a loss of the capital stock—is beside the point of this section. GDP measures *production,* not the value of our capital stock. So the destruction caused by September 11—while it entered into another, related measure called *net domestic product* (GDP minus depreciation of the capital stock)—had *no direct impact at all* on GDP. Put another way, GDP is not designed to measure the resources at our disposal, but rather the production we get from those resources. While the loss of property did destroy resources capable of producing things, and thus caused production to drop in future quarters, the destroyed resources themselves did *not* count in GDP. Moreover, because our resources are so vast and our production so great, the actual drop in future production from having fewer resources was virtually unnoticeable.

> *The destruction caused by the terrorist attacks of September 11 had almost no direct impact on U.S. GDP.*

Indirect Impacts on GDP

By contrast, the *indirect* losses to GDP—those that resulted from our response to the attacks—were significant. Here, it will be useful to distinguish between the short-run impact (the weeks and months following the attacks) and the long-run impact (which we'll be experiencing for several years).

The Short Run. It did not take long for the aftermath of the attacks to affect economic decision making. First came a decision by the federal government, which immediately shut down airports nationwide for more than 48 hours. Thus, for two days, the number of flights in the United States declined from 30,000 per day to zero—an immediate decrease in airline production and therefore GDP. But the more important impact was the decision made by consumers *after* airports reopened: They no longer wanted to fly. Over the next four weeks, with dramatically reduced bookings, the airlines cut the number of flights offered by more than 20 percent and laid off 80,000 workers.

But that was only the beginning. With fewer people flying, hotel occupancy rates also decreased, by about 20 percent. The hotel industry responded with thousands of layoffs. And then—since there were fewer business travelers and tourists spending money on taxis, restaurants, and amusement parks—there were layoffs in those industries as well. The problem spread further: It wasn't long before the airlines canceled orders for new aircraft and hotels and other businesses halted construction projects, some of which had already started. Thus, the problem spread to the manufacturing and raw materials sectors of the economy.

Consumers made other decisions that affected production. Retail shopping declined dramatically, at first because millions of stunned viewers spent all their free time watching events unfold on television, and then because fears of deepening recession made them worry about their incomes.

There were also instances of *increased* production. On September 11, AT&T, which normally handles 300 million calls on a Tuesday, saw the number of calls spike to 431 million. For several weeks, state and local governments, seeking to beef up security, paid overtime to hundreds of thousands of police and firefighters. And millions of people—looking for emotional escape but not wanting to leave home—created a boom in video and DVD rentals. But these increases in production were swamped by the production cuts already rippling through the economy.

GDP did a good job of capturing all of these changes in spending and production, since that is just what it is designed to do. After taking account of changes in airline flights, hotel bookings, restaurant meals, video rentals, and hundreds of thousands of other changes in production, the Bureau of Economic Analysis reported that production turned southward in the third quarter of 2001, with much of the decline occurring during the three weeks of the quarter that remained after September 11.

The Long Run. What about the long run? Look again at Figure 4. It shows us that GDP can deviate from potential output for several quarters or even several years. But it also shows that, in the long run, GDP tends to rise at about the same rate as potential output. Thus, when we ask about the long-run impact of September 11 on GDP, we are really asking about its long-run impact on *potential* GDP.

What is this long-run impact? In the weeks following the attack, it became clear that the United States was about to start on a course it would follow for many years: a huge reallocation of national resources toward fighting terrorism abroad and achieving greater security at home. These are resources that would otherwise be used to produce other things.

Some of these resources are being purchased by the government. For example, in the first three months of U.S. attacks on terrorist camps and the associated Taliban regime in Afghanistan, the Department of Defense used more than $3.8 billion of additional resources (beyond its normal expenses) for jet fuel, munitions, and additional combat pay for 50,000 troops stationed in the region. Over the next two years, the United States spent billions of additional dollars pursuing a more aggressive foreign policy, including an invasion to overthrow the regime of Saddam Hussein in Iraq, and increased aid to allies—and potential allies—in the war against terrorism. At home, the federal government hired hundreds of air marshals to protect civilian aircraft, and thousands of new airport personnel to screen passengers and luggage.

But private businesses too, have been spending more for security each year than they did before September 11. More armed security guards are stationed at corporate headquarters and manufacturing plants; more sophisticated access-pass equipment and metal detectors have been installed in office buildings; new hires are more carefully screened and investigated; deliveries are more carefully monitored; and bomb-sniffing dogs and increased security have become a routine part of rock concerts and sporting events.

All of these security expenses are slowing the growth of our potential output, and are therefore slowing the growth of real GDP over the long run. Why? Because business security services are *intermediate goods*—things that firms use as inputs to produce final goods and services for sale to others. Just as IBM must use labor, computer chips, plastic, salespeople, and buildings as inputs when it makes computers, it must also hire people to guard its office buildings, to do background checks on employees, and to monitor deliveries to its national headquarters. These are all part of the cost of doing business.

Suppose, for example, that IBM now uses $25 more in security services for each computer it produces. The computer is not faster, lighter, or better in any way than before; it still contributes the same amount to real GDP as it did before. But the additional security uses up resources—land, labor, capital, and entrepreneurship—that could otherwise have been used to produce *other* final goods, perhaps by IBM or by *other* firms in the economy. Since these other final goods are *not* being produced, our total output is lower than it would otherwise be.

To see this from another point of view, think about how technological advances normally work to increase our output of goods and services. Personal computers, the Internet, cell phones, assembly-line robots, and new medical devices have all enabled firms in various industries to produce whatever they produce using fewer resources. These freed-up resources are then used to produce other things, so potential output rises and—in the long run—so does our real GDP. But September 11 has had the *opposite* effect of a technological advance. It forces businesses to use *more* resources to produce output—resources that could have been used to make other things.

Of course, while increased security spending tends to reduce potential output, other forces are working to increase it, including technological advances, increases in the capital stock (both human and physical), increases in population. (You'll learn more about this in later chapters.) So increased security spending doesn't necessarily mean that potential output will fall, but it does create a force pulling the growth rate of potential output downward.

In the long run, as the nation shifts production away from other goods and services and toward security in the wake of September 11, the impact on our real GDP will be negative. Our potential output—and over the long run, our actual output—will grow more slowly than it otherwise would have.

Summary

This chapter discusses how some key macroeconomic aggregates are measured and reported. One important economic aggregate is *gross domestic product*—the total value of all final goods and services produced for the marketplace during a given year, within a nation's borders. GDP is a measure of an economy's total production.

In the *expenditure approach,* GDP is calculated as the sum of spending by households, businesses, government agencies, and foreigners on domestically produced goods and services. The *value-added approach* computes GDP by adding up each firm's contributions to the total product as it is being produced. Value added at each stage of production is the revenue a firm receives minus the cost of the intermediate inputs it uses. Finally, the *factor payments approach* sums the wages and salaries, rent, interest and profit earned by all resource owners. The three approaches reflect three different ways of viewing GDP.

Since nominal GDP is measured in current dollars, it changes when either production or prices change. *Real GDP* is nominal GDP adjusted for price changes; it rises only when production rises.

Real GDP is useful in the short run for giving warnings about impending recessions, and in the long run for indicating how fast the economy is growing. Unfortunately, it is plagued by important inaccuracies. It does not fully reflect quality changes or production in the underground economy, and it does not include many types of nonmarket production.

When real GDP grows, employment tends to rise and—if real GDP grows fast enough—the unemployment rate falls. In the United States, a person is considered unemployed if he or she does not have a job but is actively seeking one. Economists have found it useful to classify unemployment into four different categories. *Frictional unemployment* is short-term unemployment experienced by people between jobs or by those who are just entering the job market. *Seasonal unemployment* is related to changes in the weather, tourist patterns, or other predictable seasonal changes. *Structural unemployment* results from mismatches, in skills or location, between jobs and workers. Finally, *cyclical unemployment* occurs because of the business cycle. Unemployment, particularly the structural and cyclical forms, involves costs. From a social perspective, unemployment means lost production. From the individual viewpoint, unemployment often involves financial, psychological, and physical harm.

Key Terms

Capital stock
Consumption
Cyclical unemployment
Discouraged workers
Expenditure approach
Factor payments
Factor payments approach
Final good
Frictional unemployment
Full employment

Government purchases
Gross domestic product (GDP)
Intermediate goods
Involuntary part-time workers
Labor force
Net exports
Net investment
Nominal variable
Nonmarket production
Potential output

Private investment
Real variable
Seasonal unemployment
Structural unemployment
Transfer payment
Unemployment rate
Value added
Value-added approach

Review Questions

1. What is the difference between final goods and intermediate goods? Why is it that only the value of final goods and services is counted in GDP?

2. What is the relationship between private investment and the capital stock? What are the three components of private investment?

3. Describe the different kinds of factor payments.

4. What is the difference between nominal and real variables? What is the main problem with using nominal variables to track the economy?

5. Discuss the value and reliability of GDP statistics in both short-run and long-run analyses of the economy.

6. Real GDP (in 1996 dollars) was measured at around $8.8 trillion in 1999. Was the actual value of goods and services produced in the United States in 1999 likely to have been higher or lower than that? Why?

7. What, if anything, could the government do to reduce frictional and structural unemployment?

8. Categorize each of the following according to the type of unemployment it reflects. Justify your answers.

a. Workers are laid off when a GM factory closes due to a recession.

b. Workers selling software in a store are laid off when the store goes bankrupt due to competition from on-line software dealers.

c. Migrant farm workers' jobs end when the harvest is finished.

d. Lost jobs result from the movement of textile plants from Massachusetts to the South and overseas.

9. Can unemployment ever be good for the economy? Explain.

10. What are some of the different types of costs associated with unemployment?

11. Discuss some of the problems with the way the Bureau of Labor Statistics computes the unemployment rate. In what ways do official criteria lead to an overestimate or underestimate of the actual unemployment figure?

12. Explain this statement: "The Bureau of Economic Analysis reported a 2003 second quarter real GDP figure of $10,802.7 billion."

13. Summarize the three approaches to calculating GDP.

Problems and Exercises

1. Using the expenditure approach, which of the following would be directly counted as part of U.S. GDP in 2005? In each case, state whether the action causes an increase in C, I, G, or NX.

a. A new personal computer produced by IBM, which remained unsold at the year's end

b. A physician's services to a household

c. Produce bought by a restaurant to serve to customers

d. The purchase of 1,000 shares of Disney stock

e. The sale of 50 acres of commercial property

f. A real estate agent's commission from the sale of property

g. A transaction in which you clean your roommate's apartment in exchange for his working on your car

h. An Apple iMac computer produced in the United States, and purchased by a French citizen

i. The government's Social Security payments to retired people

2. Calculate the total change in a year's GDP for each of the following scenarios:

a. A family sells a home, without using a broker, for $150,000. They could have rented it on the open market for $700 per month. They buy a 10-year-old condominium for $200,000; the broker's fee on the transaction is 6 percent of the selling price. The condo's owner was formerly renting the unit at $500 per month.

b. General Electric uses $10 million worth of steel, glass, and plastic to produce its dishwashers. Wages and salaries in the dishwasher division are $40 million; the division's only other expense is $15 million in interest that it pays on its bonds. The division's revenue for the year is $75 million.

c. On March 31, you decide to stop throwing away $50 a month on convenience store nachos. You buy $200 worth of equipment, cornmeal, and cheese, and make your own nachos for the rest of the year.

d. You win $25,000 in your state's lottery. Ever the entrepreneur, you decide to open a Ping-Pong ball washing service, buying $15,000 worth of equipment from SpiffyBall Ltd. of Hong Kong and $10,000 from Ball-B-Kleen of Toledo, Ohio.

e. Tone-Deaf Artists, Inc. produces 100,000 new White Snake CDs that it prices at $15 apiece. Ten thousand CDs are sold abroad, but, alas, the rest remain unsold on warehouse shelves.

3. The country of Freedonia uses the same method to calculate the unemployment rate as the U.S. Bureau of Labor Statistics uses. From the data below, compute Freedonia's unemployment rate.

Population	10,000,000
Under 16	3,000,000
Over 16	
In military service	500,000
In hospitals	200,000
In prison	100,000
Worked one hour or more in previous week	4,000,000
Searched for work during previous four weeks	1,000,000

4. Toward the end of this chapter, it was stated that if half of the 4.5 million involuntary part-time workers in June 2003 were counted as unemployed, then the unemployment rate that month would have been 7.9 percent instead of 6.4 percent. Do the necessary calculations to confirm this statement, using the information in Figure 6. [*Hint:* The labor force will not be affected.]

5. Using the information given toward the end of the chapter, what would the unemployment rate have been in June 2003 if it had included among the unemployed:
   a. All officially discouraged workers?
   b. All those who were not working but said they wanted a job? [*Hint:* Don't forget about how these inclusions would affect the labor force.]

6. Ginny asks "If I buy a sweater that was produced in Malaysia, why is its purchase price subtracted from GDP?" How should you answer her question? (You may assume, for simplicity, that there was no value added to the sweater in the United States)

7. Ziponia, which uses the same method to calculate real GDP as the U.S. Bureau of Economic Analysis uses, has made the following calculations for 2004: $C = \$6,000$ million, $I = \$1,500$ million, $G = \$500$ million, and $NX = \$600$ million. Find Ziponia's real GDP for 2004 and explain how it will change for 2005 if the only difference between the two years is that Ziponia's citizens import an additional $5 million worth of DVD players in 2005. Does your answer depend on what Ziponia's firms produce? For instance, will your answer change if part of Ziponia's firms' production was $5 million worth of DVD players that they expected to sell to Ziponians, but were unable to because the Ziponians preferred imported DVD players?

8. a. The country of Ziponia uses the same method to calculate the unemployment rate as the U.S. Bureau of Labor Statistics uses. From the data below, compute Ziponia's unemployment rate.

Population	60,000
Under 16	9,000
Over 16	
In military service	600
In hospitals	60
In prison	200
Worked one hour or more in previous week	46,000
Searched for work during previous four weeks	2,140
Did not work in previous week but would have taken a job if one were offered	200

   b. How large is Ziponia's labor force?
   c. How many discouraged workers live in Ziponia?
   d. Not all of Ziponia's citizens are accounted for in part (a). How are the missing citizens classified? Give some examples of what they may be doing.
   e. How many of Ziponia's citizens are not in the labor force?

9. Refer to question 8. The 2,140 Ziponians who searched for work during the previous four weeks included: 54 ski resort employees who lost their winter jobs but expect to get them back in late fall; 200 recent high school graduates; 258 former textile workers who lost their jobs when their employers moved their operations overseas; 143 mothers and 19 fathers who had stayed at home to raise their children but who recently decided to reenter the work force; 394 high school and college students who want summer jobs; 115 people who live in West Ziponia and lost their jobs when their employers moved operations to East Ziponia, but who are not qualified for the remaining jobs in the west; 110 recent college graduates; 12 record-label designers who lost their jobs as consumers substituted CDs for records; and 32 retirees who decided to return to the workforce. The remaining job seekers lost their jobs due to a recession. Use this information to:
   a. Classify the job seekers by their type of unemployment, and calculate how many fell into each category.
   b. Find the frictional, seasonal, structural, and cyclical unemployment rates.
   c. Find how many Ziponians would be unemployed if Ziponia were to achieve full employment.

Challenge Questions

1. Suppose, in a given year, someone buys a General Motors automobile for $30,000. That same year, GM produced the car in Michigan, using $10,000 in parts imported from Japan. However, the parts imported from Japan themselves contained $3,000 in components produced in the United States.
   a. By how much does U.S. GDP rise?
   b. Using the expenditure approach, what is the change in each component (C, I, G, and NX) of U.S. GDP?
   c. What is the change in Japan's GDP and each of its components?

2. In the "Using the Theory" section of this chapter, you learned that business spending on security will work to reduce real GDP over the long run. Is the same true of government expenditures on security? Why or why not?

3. a. Federal Reserve Chairman Alan Greenspan came up with a novel (and facetious) way to measure the United States' output: by weight. Describe some of the problems inherent in measuring output by weight.
   b. What problems might arise if policy makers relied on a weight-based measure of output to determine the health of the U.S. economy?

 *These exercises require access to Lieberman/Hall Xtra! If Xtra! did not come with your book, visit http://liebermanxtra.swlearning.com to purchase.*

1. Use your Xtra! password at the Hall and Lieberman Web site (http://liebermanxtra.swlearning.com), select this chapter, and click on EconDebate. Choose *Macroeconomics: Employment, Unemployment, and Inflation* and scroll down to find the debate, "Do Technological Advances Result in Higher Unemployment?" Read the debate, and use the information to answer the following questions.
   a. How does technological change alter the composition of the demand for labor? Is the overall effect positive or negative? Why?
   b. What are the effects of technological change on productivity and growth? Explain.

2. Use your Xtra! password at the Hall and Lieberman Web site (http://liebermanxtra.swlearning.com), select this chapter, and under Economic Applications, click on EconDebate. Choose *Macroeconomics: Employment, Unemployment, and Inflation* and scroll down to find the *Real GDP*. Read the definition and click on Diagrams/Data and use the information to answer the following questions.
   a. Verify the inverse relationship between the economic growth rate and the unemployment rate. Explain this relationship.
   b. Why is there a direct relationship between real GDP and personal income?
   c. How well does the Index of Leading Economic Indicators perform in forecasting future economic conditions?

The Monetary System, Prices, and Inflation

You pull into a gas station deep in the interior of the distant nation of Chaotica. The numbers on the gas pump don't make sense to you, and you can't figure out how much to pay. Luckily, the national language of Chaotica is English, so you can ask the cashier how much the gas costs. He replies, "Here in Chaotica, we don't have any standard system for measuring quantities of gas, and we don't have any standard way to quote prices. My pump here measures in my own unit, called the slurp, and I will sell you 6 slurps of gas for that watch you are wearing, or a dozen slurps of gas for your camera." You spend the next half hour trying to determine how many slurps of gas there are in a gallon and what form of payment you can use besides your watch and camera.

Life in the imaginary nation of Chaotica would be difficult. People would spend a lot of time figuring out how to trade with each other, time that could otherwise be spent producing things or enjoying leisure activities. Fortunately, in the real world, virtually every nation has a *monetary system* that helps to organize and simplify our economic transactions.

THE MONETARY SYSTEM

A monetary system establishes two different types of standardization in the economy. First, it establishes a **unit of value**—a common unit for measuring how much something is worth. A standard unit of value permits us to compare the costs of different goods and services and to communicate these costs when we trade. The dollar is the unit of value in the United States. If a college textbook costs $100, while a round-trip airline ticket from Phoenix to Minneapolis costs $300, we know immediately that the ticket has the same value in the marketplace as three college textbooks.

Unit of value A common unit for measuring how much something is worth.

The second type of standardization concerns the **means of payment,** the things we can use as payment when we buy goods and services. In the United States, the means of payment include dollar bills, personal checks, money orders, credit cards like Visa and American Express, and, in some experimental locations, prepaid cash cards with magnetic strips.

Means of payment Anything acceptable as payment for goods and services.

These two functions of a monetary system—establishing a unit of value and a standard means of payment—are closely related, but they are not the same thing. The unit-of-value function refers to the way we *think* about and record transactions; the means-of-payment function refers to how payment is actually made.

The unit of value works in the same way as units of weight, volume, distance, and time. In fact, the same sentence in Article I of the U.S. Constitution gives Congress the power to create a unit of value along with units of weights and measures. All of these units help us determine clearly and precisely what is being traded for what. Think about buying gas in the United States; you exchange dollars for gallons. The transaction will go smoothly and quickly only if there is clarity about both the unit of fluid volume (gallons) *and* the unit of purchasing power (dollars).

The means of payment can be different from the unit of value. For example, in some countries where local currency prices change very rapidly, it is common to use the U.S. dollar as the unit of value—to specify prices in dollars—while the local currency remains the means of payment. Even in the United States, when you use a check to buy something, the unit of value is the dollar but the means of payment is a piece of paper with your signature on it.

In the United States, the dollar is the centerpiece of our monetary system. It is the unit of value in virtually every economic transaction, and dollar bills are very often the means of payment as well. How did the dollar come to play such an important role in the economy?

History of the Dollar

Prior to 1790, each colony had its own currency. It was named the "pound" in every colony, but it had a different purchasing power in each of them. In 1790, soon after the Constitution went into effect, Congress created a new unit of value called the dollar. Historical documents show that merchants and businesses switched immediately to the new dollar, thereby ending the chaos of the colonial monetary systems. Prices began to be quoted in dollars, and accounts were kept in dollars. The dollar rapidly became the standard unit of value.

But the primary means of payment in the United States until the Civil War was paper currency issued by private banks. Just as the government defined the length of the yard but did not sell yardsticks, the government defined the unit of value but let private organizations provide the means of payment.

During the Civil War, however, the government issued the first federal paper currency, the greenback. It functioned as both the unit of value and the major means of payment until 1879. Then the government got out of the business of money creation for a few decades. During that time, currency was once again issued by private banks. But in 1913, a new institution called the **Federal Reserve System** was created to be the national monetary authority in the United States. The Federal Reserve was charged with creating and regulating the nation's supply of money, and it continues to do so today.

Federal Reserve System
The central bank and national monetary authority of the United States.

Why Paper Currency Is Accepted as a Means of Payment

You may be wondering why people are willing to accept paper dollars—or the promise of paper dollars—as a means of payment. Why should a farmer give up a chicken, or a manufacturer give up a new car, just to receive a bunch of green rectangles with words printed on them? In fact, paper currency is a relatively recent development in the history of the means of payment.

The earliest means of payment were precious metals and other valuable commodities such as furs or jewels. These were called *commodity money* because they had important uses other than as a means of payment. The non-money use is what gave commodity money its ultimate value. For example, people would accept furs as payment because furs could be used to keep warm. Similarly, gold and silver had a variety of uses in industry, as religious artifacts, and for ornamentation.

Precious metals were an especially popular form of commodity money. Eventually, to make it easier to identify the value of precious metals, they were minted into coins whose weight was declared on their faces. Because gold and silver coins could be melted down into pure metal and used in other ways, they were still commodity money.

Commodity money eventually gave way to paper currency. Initially, paper currency was just a certificate representing a certain amount of gold or silver held by a bank. At any time, the holder of a certificate could go to the bank that issued it and trade the certificate for the stated amount of gold or silver. People were willing to accept paper money as a means of payment for two reasons. First, the currency could be exchanged for a valuable commodity like gold or silver. Second, the issuer—either a government or a bank—could print new money only when it acquired additional gold or silver. This put strict limits on money printing, so people had faith that their paper money would retain its value in the marketplace.

But today, paper currency is no longer backed by gold or any other physical commodity. If you have a dollar handy, put this book down and take a close look at the bill. You will not find on it any promise that you can trade your dollar for gold, silver, furs, or anything else. Yet we all accept it as a means of payment. Why?

A clue is provided by the statement in the upper left-hand corner of every bill: *This note is legal tender for all debts, public and private.* The statement affirms that the piece of paper in your hands will be accepted as a means of payment (you can "tender" it to settle any "debt, public or private") by any American because the government says so. This type of currency is called **fiat money**. *Fiat,* in Latin, means "let there be," and fiat money serves as a means of payment by government declaration.

The government need not worry about enforcing this declaration. The real force behind the dollar—and the reason that we are all willing to accept these green pieces of paper as payment—is its long-standing acceptability by *others*. As long as you have confidence that you can use your dollars to buy goods and services, you

© PHOTODISC/GETTY IMAGES

Today, dollars are not backed by gold or silver, but we accept them as payment because we know that others will accept them from us.

Fiat money Anything that serves as a means of payment by government declaration.

won't mind giving up goods and services for dollars. And because everyone else feels the same way, the circle of acceptability is completed.

But while the government can declare that paper currency is to be accepted as a means of payment, it cannot declare the terms. Whether 10 gallons of gas will cost you 1 dollar, 10 dollars, or 20 dollars is up to the marketplace. The value of the dollar—its purchasing power—does change from year to year, as reflected in the changing prices of the things we buy. In the rest of this chapter, we will discuss some of the problems created by the dollar's changing value and the difficulty economists have measuring and monitoring the changes. We postpone until later chapters the question of *why* the value of the dollar changes from year to year.

MEASURING THE PRICE LEVEL AND INFLATION

One hundred years ago, you could buy a pound of coffee for 15 cents, see a Broadway play for 40 cents, buy a new suit for $6, and attend a private college for $200 in yearly tuition.[1] Needless to say, the price of each of these items has gone up considerably since then. Microeconomic causes—changes in individual markets—can explain only a tiny fraction of these price changes. For the most part, these price rises came about because of a continually rising **price level**—the average level of dollar prices in the economy. In this section, we begin to explore how the price level is measured and how this measurement is used.

Price level The average level of prices in the economy.

Index Numbers

Most measures of the price level are reported in the form of an **index**—a series of numbers, each one representing a different period. Index numbers are meaningful only in a *relative* sense: We compare one period's index number with that of another period and can quickly see which one is larger and by what percentage. But the actual value of an index number for a particular period has no meaning in and of itself.

In general, an index number for any measure is calculated as

Index A series of numbers used to track a variable's rise or fall over time.

$$\frac{\text{Value of measure in current period}}{\text{Value of measure in base period}} \times 100.$$

Let's see how index numbers work with a simple example. Suppose we want to measure how violence on TV has changed over time, and we have data on the number of violent acts shown in each of several years. We could then construct a TV-violence index. Our first step would be to choose a *base period*—a period to be used as a benchmark. Let's choose 1996 as our base period, and suppose that there were 10,433 violent acts on television in that year. Then our violence index in any current year would be calculated as

$$\frac{\text{Number of violent acts in current year}}{10,433} \times 100.$$

In 1996, the base year, the index will have the value (10,433/10,433) × 100 = 100. Look again at the general formula for index numbers, and you will see that this is always true: *An index will always equal 100 in the base period.*

[1] Scott Derks, ed., *The Value of the Dollar: Prices and Incomes in the United States: 1860–1989* (Detroit, MI: Gale Research Inc., 1994), various pages.

Now let's calculate the value of our index in another year. If there were 14,534 violent acts in 2000, then the index that year would have the value

$$\frac{14{,}534}{10{,}433} \times 100 = 139.3.$$

Index numbers compress and simplify information so that we can see how things are changing at a glance. Our media violence index, for example, tells us at a glance that the number of violent acts in 2000 was 139.3 percent of the number in 1996. Or, more simply, TV violence grew by 39.3 percent between 1996 and 2000.

The Consumer Price Index

Consumer Price Index An index of the cost, through time, of a fixed market basket of goods purchased by a typical household in some base period.

The most widely used measure of the price level in the United States is the **Consumer Price Index (CPI)**. This index, which is designed to track the prices paid by the typical consumer, is compiled and reported by the Bureau of Labor Statistics (BLS).

Measuring the prices paid by the typical consumer is not easy. Two problems must be solved before we even begin. The first problem is to decide which goods and services we should include in our average. The CPI tracks only *consumer* prices; it excludes goods and services that are not directly purchased by consumers. More specifically, the CPI excludes goods purchased by businesses (such as capital equipment, raw materials, or wholesale goods), goods and services purchased by government agencies (such as fighter-bombers and the services of police officers), and goods and services purchased by foreigners (U.S. exports). The CPI *does* include newly produced consumer goods and services that are part of consumption spending in our GDP—things such as new clothes, new furniture, new cars, haircuts, and restaurant meals. It also includes some things that are *not* part of our GDP but that are part of the typical family's budget. For example, the CPI includes prices for *used* goods such as used cars or used books, and imports from other countries—for example, French cheese, Japanese cars, and Mexican tomatoes.

The second problem is how to combine all the different prices into an average price level. In any given month, different prices will change by different amounts. The average price of doctors' visits might rise by 1 percent, the price of blue jeans might rise by a tenth of a percent, the price of milk might fall by half a percent, and so on. When prices change at different rates, and when some are rising while others are falling, how can we track the change in the *average* price level? It would be a mistake to use a simple average of all prices, adding them up and dividing by the number of goods. A proper measure must recognize that we spend very little of our incomes on some goods—such as Tabasco sauce—and much more on others—like car repairs or rent.

The CPI's approach is to track the cost of the *CPI market basket*—the collection of goods and services that the typical consumer bought in some base period. If the market basket's cost rises by 10 percent over some period, then the price level, as reported by the CPI, will rise by 10 percent. This way, goods and services that are relatively unimportant in the typical consumer's budget will have little weight in the CPI. Tabasco sauce could triple in price and have no noticeable impact on the cost of the complete market basket. Goods that are more important—such as auto repairs or rent—will have more weight.

In recent years, the base year[2] for the CPI has been 1983, so, following our general formula for price indexes, the CPI is calculated as

$$\frac{\text{Cost of market basket in current year}}{\text{Cost of market basket in 1983}} \times 100.$$

The appendix in this chapter discusses the calculation of the CPI in more detail.

How the CPI Has Behaved

Table 1 shows the actual value of the CPI for December of selected years. Because it is reported in index number form, we can easily see how much the price level has changed over different time intervals. In December 2002, for example, the CPI had a value of 181.6, telling us that the typical market basket in that year cost 81.6 percent more than it would have cost in the July 1983 base period. In December 1970, the CPI was 39.8, so the cost of the market basket in that year was only 39.8 percent of its cost in July 1983. In July 1983 (not shown), the CPI's value was 100.

From Price Index to Inflation Rate

The Consumer Price Index is a measure of the price *level* in the economy. The **inflation rate** measures how fast the price level is changing, as a percentage rate. When the price level is rising, as it almost always is, the inflation rate is positive. When the price level is falling, as it did during the Great Depression, we have negative inflation, which is called **deflation**.

Figure 1 shows the U.S. rate of inflation, as measured by the CPI, since 1950. For each year, the inflation rate is calculated as the percentage change in the CPI from December of the previous year to December of that year. For example, the CPI in December 2000 was 174.6, and in December 2001 it was 177.3. The inflation rate for 2001 was $(177.3 - 174.6)/174.6 = 0.015$ or 1.5 percent. Notice that inflation was low in the 1950s and 1960s, was high in the 1970s and early 1980s, and has been low since then. In later chapters, you will learn what causes the inflation rate to rise and fall.

Inflation rate The percent change in the price level from one period to the next.

Deflation A *decrease* in the price level from one period to the next.

How the CPI Is Used

The CPI is the most important and widely used measure of prices in United States. It is used in three ways:

More specifically, as a Policy Target. In the introductory macroeconomics chapter, we saw that price stability—or a low

Year	Consumer Price Index (December)
1970	39.8
1975	55.6
1980	86.4
1985	109.5
1990	134.2
1995	153.9
2000	174.6
2001	177.3
2002	181.6

TABLE 1
Consumer Price Index, December, Selected Years, 1970–2002

---

[2] To be more specific: The typical consumer's market basket (used to determine the weights to apply to each good) is periodically updated. Currently, for example, the CPI uses information from its 2002 survey of consumer spending habits to determine the proper weights. But the BLS continues to use July 1983 as its official base period; that is, the value of the CPI is still set at 100 for July 1983.

FIGURE 1
The Rate of Inflation Using the Consumer Price Index, 1950–2003

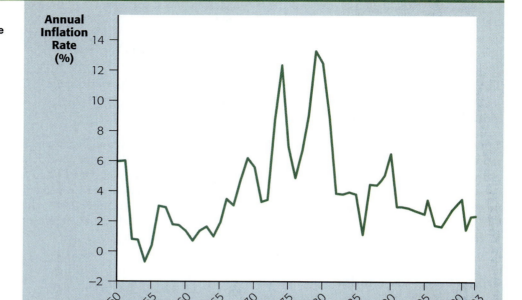

Indexation Adjusting the value of some nominal payment in proportion to a price index, in order to keep the real payment unchanged.

HTTP://

You can find the latest information on the CPI at http://www.bls.gov/bls/ newsrels.htm—the Bureau of Labor Statistics Web site.

inflation rate—is one of the nation's important macroeconomic goals. The measure most often used to gauge our success in achieving low inflation is the CPI.

To Index Payments. A payment is **indexed** when it is set by a formula so that it rises and falls proportionally with a price index. An indexed payment makes up for the loss in purchasing power that occurs when the price level rises. It raises the nominal payment by just enough to keep its purchasing power unchanged. In the United States, 52 million Social Security recipients and government retirees have their benefit payments indexed to the CPI. About one-quarter of all union members—more than 2 million workers—have labor contracts that index their wages to the CPI. Since 1985, the U.S. income tax has been indexed as well: the threshold income levels at which tax rates change automatically rise at the same rate as the CPI. And the government now sells bonds that are indexed to the CPI. The owner of an indexed bond receives a payment each year to make up for the loss of purchasing power when the CPI rises.

To Translate from Nominal to Real Values. In order to compare economic values from different periods, we must translate *nominal variables,* measured in the number of dollars, into *real variables,* which are adjusted for the change in the dollar's purchasing power. The CPI is often used for this translation. Since calculating real variables is one of the most important uses of the CPI, we devote the next section to that topic.

Real Variables and Adjustment for Inflation

Suppose that from December 2004 to December 2005, your nominal wage—what you are paid in dollars—rises from $15 to $30 per hour. Are you better off? That depends. You are earning twice as many dollars. But you should care not about how many green pieces of paper you earn, but how many goods and services you can buy with that paper. How, then, can we tell what happened to your purchasing power? By focusing not on the *nominal wage*, (the number of *dollars* you earn) but on the *real wage*, (the *purchasing power* of your wage). To track your real wage, we need to look at the number of dollars you earn *relative to the price level*.

Rising Prices Versus Rising Inflation People often confuse the statement "prices are rising" with the statement "inflation is rising," but they do not mean the same thing. Remember that the inflation rate is the *rate of change* of the price level. To have rising inflation, the price level must be rising by a greater and greater percentage each period. But we can also have rising prices and *falling* inflation. For example, from 1996 to 1998, the CPI rose each year: "Prices were rising." But they rose by a smaller percentage each year than the year before, so "inflation was falling"— from 3.4 percent in 1996 to 1.7 percent in 1997 and to 1.6 percent in 1998.

DANGEROUS CURVES

Since the "typical worker" and the "typical consumer" are pretty much the same, the CPI is usually the price index used to calculate the real wage. The real-wage formula is as follows:

$$\text{Real wage in any year} = \frac{\text{Nominal wage in that year}}{\text{CPI in that year}} \times 100.$$

To see that this formula makes sense, let's go back to our fictional example: From 2004 to 2005, your nominal wage doubles from $15 to $30. Now, suppose the price of everything that you buy doubles at the same time. It is easy to see that in this case, your purchasing power would remain unchanged. And that is just what our formula tells us: If prices double, the CPI doubles as well. With 2004 as our base year, the CPI would increase from 100 in 2004 to 200 in the year 2005. The *real* wage would be ($15/100) ×100 = $15 in 2004 and ($30/200) × 100 = $15 in 2005. The real wage would remain unchanged.

Now suppose that prices doubled between 2004 and 2005, but your nominal wage remained unchanged at $15. In this case, your purchasing power would be cut in half. You'd have the same number of dollars, but each one would buy half as much as it did before. Our formula gives us a real wage of ($15/100) × 100 = $15 in 2004 and ($15/200) × 100 = $7.50 in 2005. The real wage falls by half.

Now look at Table 2, which shows the average hourly earnings of wage earners over the past four decades. In the first two columns, you can see that the average American wage earner was paid $4.87 per hour in December 1975, and more than triple that—$15.20—in December 2002. Does this mean the average hourly worker was paid more in 2002 than in 1975? In *dollars,* the answer is clearly yes. But what about in *purchasing power*? Or, using the new terminology you've learned: What happened to the *real wage* over this period?

Let's see. We know that the *nominal wage* rose from $4.87 in 1975 to $15.20 in 2002. But, according to the table, the CPI rose from 55.6 to 181.6 over the same period. Using our formula, we find that

$$\text{Real wage in 1975} = \frac{\$4.87}{55.6} \times 100 = \$8.76.$$

$$\text{Real wage in 2002} = \frac{\$15.20}{181.6} \times 100 = \$8.37.$$

Thus, although the average worker earned more *dollars* in 2002 than in 1975, when we use the CPI as our measure of prices, her purchasing power seems to have fallen over those years. *Why* this apparent decline in purchasing power? This is an interesting and important question, and one we'll begin to answer later in the chapter. The important point to remember here is that

TABLE 2
Nominal and Real Wages (in December of Each Year)

Year	Nominal Wage, Dollars per Hour	CPI	Real Wage in 1983 Dollars per Hour
1970	3.50	39.8	8.79
1975	4.87	55.6	8.76
1980	7.12	86.4	8.24
1985	8.86	109.5	8.09
1990	10.33	134.2	7.70
1995	11.79	153.9	7.66
2000	14.26	174.6	8.17
2001	14.73	177.3	8.31
2002	15.20	181.6	8.37

Source: Bureau of Labor Statistics, Statistical Tables, *http://www.bls.gov/data/,* accessed on July 31, 2003. Wage and CPI data for December of each year. Nominal wage: average hourly earnings of production or nonsupervisory workers in nonfarm private sector CPI: CPI-All Urban Consumers.

The Importance of Real Values

when we measure changes in the macroeconomy, we usually care not about the number of dollars we are counting, but the purchasing power those dollars represent. Thus, we translate nominal values into real values using the formula

$$\text{real value} = \frac{\text{nominal value}}{\text{price index}} \times 100.$$

This formula, usually using the CPI as the price index, is how most real values in the economy are calculated. But there is one important exception: To calculate real GDP, the government uses a different procedure, to which we now turn.

Inflation and the Measurement of Real GDP

In the previous chapter, we discussed the difference between nominal GDP and real GDP. After reading this chapter, you might think that real GDP is calculated just like the real wage: dividing nominal GDP by the Consumer Price Index. But the Consumer Price Index is *not* used to calculate real GDP. Instead, a special price index—which we can call the **GDP price index**—is used.

GDP price index An index of the price level for all final goods and services included in GDP.

The most important differences between the CPI and the GDP price index are in the types of goods and services covered by each index. While the CPI tracks only the prices of goods bought by American *consumers,* the GDP price index also includes the prices of goods purchased by the government, investment goods purchased by businesses, and exports, which are purchased by foreigners.

But the GDP price index leaves out *used* goods and imports, both of which are included in the CPI. This makes sense, because while *used* goods and imports are part of the typical consumer's market basket, they do not contribute to current U.S. GDP.

We can summarize the chief difference between the CPI and the GDP price index this way:

The GDP price index measures the prices of all goods and services that are included in U.S. GDP, while the CPI measures the prices of all goods and services bought by U.S. households.[3]

THE COSTS OF INFLATION

A high rate of inflation—whether it is measured by the CPI or the GDP price index—is never welcome news. What's so bad about inflation? As we've seen, it certainly makes your task as an economics student more difficult: Rather than taking nominal variables at face value, you must do those troublesome calculations to convert them into real variables.

But inflation causes much more trouble than this. It can impose costs on society and on each of us individually. Yet when most people are asked *what* the cost of inflation is, they come up with an incorrect answer.

The Inflation Myth

Most people think that inflation, merely by making goods and services more expensive, erodes the average purchasing power of income in the economy. The reason for this belief is easy to see: The higher the price level, the fewer goods and services a given nominal income will buy. It stands to reason, then, that inflation—which raises prices—must be destroying the purchasing power of our incomes. Right?

Actually, this statement is mostly wrong.

To see why, remember that every market transaction involves *two* parties—a buyer and a seller. When a price rises, buyers of that good must pay more but sellers get more revenue when they sell it. The loss in buyers' real income is matched by the rise in sellers' real income. Inflation may *redistribute* purchasing power among the population, but it does not change the *average* purchasing power, when we include both buyers and sellers in the average.

In fact, most people in the economy participate on both sides of the market. On the one hand, they are consumers—as when they shop for food or clothing or furniture. On the other hand, they work in business firms that *sell* products, and may benefit (in the form of higher wages or higher profits) when their firms' revenues rise. Thus, when prices rise, a particular person may find that her purchasing power has either risen or fallen, depending on whether she is affected more as a seller or as a buyer. But regardless of the outcome for individuals, our conclusion remains the same:

Inflation can redistribute purchasing power from one group to another, but it does not directly decrease the average real income in the economy.

Why, then, do people continue to believe that inflation robs the average citizen of real income? Largely because real incomes sometimes do decline—for *other* reasons. Inflation—while not the *cause* of the decline—will often be the *mechanism* that brings it about. Just as we often blame the messenger for bringing bad news, so too, we often blame inflation for lowering our purchasing power when the real cause lies elsewhere.

[3] The technical name for the GDP price index is the *chain-type annual weights GDP price index*. It differs from the CPI not only in goods covered, but also in its mathematical formula.

Let's consider an example. In Table 2, notice the decline in real wages during the late 1970s. The real wage fell from $8.76 in 1975 to $8.24 in 1980, a decline of about 6 percent. During this period, not only wage earners, but also salaried workers, small-business owners, and corporate shareholders all suffered a decline in their real incomes. What caused the decline?

There were several reasons, but one of the most important was the dramatic rise in the price of imported oil—from $3 per barrel in 1973 to $34 in 1981, an increase of more than 1,000 percent. The higher price for oil meant that oil-exporting countries, like Saudi Arabia, Kuwait, and Iraq, got more goods and services for each barrel of oil they supplied to the rest of the world, including the United States. But with these countries claiming more of America's output, less remained for the typical American. That is, the typical American family had to suffer a decline in real income. As always, a rise in price shifted income from buyers to sellers. But in this case, the sellers were *foreigners,* while the buyers were Americans. Thus, the rise in the price of foreign oil caused average purchasing power in the United States to decline.

But what was the mechanism that brought about the decline? Since real income is equal to (nominal income/price index) $\times$ 100, it can decrease in one of two ways: a fall in the numerator (nominal income) or a rise in the denominator (the price index). The decline in real income in the 1970s came entirely from an increase in the denominator. (Look back at Figure 1. You can see that this period of declining real wages in the United States was also a period of unusually high inflation; at its peak in 1979, the inflation rate exceeded 13 percent.) As a result, most workers blamed *inflation* for their loss of purchasing power. But inflation was not the cause; it was just the *mechanism.* The cause was a change in the terms of trade between the United States and the oil-exporting countries—a change that resulted in higher oil prices.

To summarize, the common idea that inflation imposes a cost on society by directly decreasing average real income in the economy is incorrect. But inflation *does* impose costs on society, as the next section shows.

The Redistributive Cost of Inflation

One cost of inflation is that it often redistributes purchasing power *within* society. But because the winners and losers are chosen haphazardly—rather than by conscious social policy—the redistribution of purchasing power is not generally desirable. In some cases, the shift in purchasing power is downright perverse—harming the needy and helping those who are already well off.

How does inflation sometimes redistribute real income? An increase in the price level reduces the purchasing power of any payment that is specified in nominal terms. For example, some workers have contracts that set their nominal wage for two or three years, regardless of any future inflation. The nationally set minimum wage, too, is set for several years and specified in nominal dollars. Under these circumstances, inflation can harm ordinary workers, since it erodes the purchasing power of their prespecified nominal wage. Real income is redistributed from these workers to their employers, who benefit by paying a lower real wage.

But the effect can also work the other way: benefiting ordinary households and harming businesses. For example, many homeowners sign fixed-dollar mortgage agreements with a bank. These are promises to pay the bank the same nominal sum each month. Inflation can reduce the *real* value of these payments, thus redistributing purchasing power away from the bank and toward the average homeowner.

In general,

> *inflation can shift purchasing power away from those who are awaiting future payments specified in dollars, and toward those who are obligated to make such payments.*

But does inflation *always* redistribute income from one party in a contract to another? Actually, no; if the inflation is *expected* by both parties, it should not redistribute income. The next section explains why.

Expected Inflation Need *Not* Shift Purchasing Power. Suppose a labor union is negotiating a three-year contract with an employer, and both sides agree that each year, workers should get a 3 percent increase in their *real wage*. Labor contracts, like most other contracts, are usually specified in nominal terms: The firm will agree to give workers so many additional *dollars per hour* each year. If neither side anticipates any inflation, they should simply negotiate a 3 percent *nominal* wage hike. With an unchanged price level, the *real* wage would then also rise by the desired 3 percent.

But suppose instead that both sides anticipate 10 percent inflation each year for the next three years. Then, they must agree to *more* than a 3 percent nominal wage increase in order to raise the real wage by 3 percent. How much more?

We can answer this question with a simple mathematical rule:

> *Over any period, the percentage change in a real value (%ΔReal) is approximately equal to the percentage change in the associated nominal value (%ΔNominal) minus the rate of inflation:*
>
> $$\%\Delta\text{Real} = \%\Delta\text{Nominal} - \text{Rate of inflation.}$$

If the inflation rate is 10 percent and the real wage is to rise by 3 percent, then the change in the nominal wage must (approximately) satisfy the equation

$$3 \text{ percent} = \%\Delta\text{Nominal} - 10 \text{ percent} \Rightarrow \%\Delta\text{Nominal} = 13 \text{ percent.}$$

The required nominal wage hike is 13 percent.

You can see that as long as both sides correctly anticipate the inflation, and no one stops them from negotiating a 13 percent nominal wage hike, inflation will *not* affect either party in real terms:

> *If inflation is fully anticipated, and if both parties take it into account, then inflation will not redistribute purchasing power.*

We come to a similar conclusion about contracts between lenders and borrowers. When you lend someone money, you receive a reward—an interest payment—for letting that person use your money instead of spending it yourself. The annual *interest rate* is the interest payment divided by the amount of money you have lent. For example, if you lend someone $1,000 and receive back $1,040 one year later, then your interest is $40, and the interest *rate* on the loan is $40/$1,000 = 0.04, or 4 percent.

But there are actually *two* interest rates associated with every loan. One is the **nominal interest rate**—the percentage increase in the lender's *dollars* from making the loan. The other is the **real interest rate**—the percentage increase in the lender's

Nominal interest rate The annual percent increase in a lender's dollars from making a loan.

Real interest rate The annual percent increase in a lender's purchasing power from making a loan.

purchasing power from making the loan. It is the *real* rate—the change in purchasing power—that lenders and borrowers should care about.

In the absence of inflation, real and nominal interest rates would always be equal. A 4 percent increase in the lender's *dollars* would always imply a 4 percent increase in her purchasing power. But if there is inflation, it will reduce the purchasing power of the money paid back. Does this mean that inflation redistributes purchasing power? Not if the inflation is correctly anticipated, and if there are no restrictions on making loan contracts.

For example, suppose both parties anticipate inflation of 5 percent and want to arrange a contract whereby the lender will be paid a 4 percent *real* interest rate. What *nominal* interest rate should they choose? Since an interest rate is the *percentage change* in the lender's funds, we can use our approximation rule,

$$\%\Delta \text{Real} = \%\Delta \text{Nominal} - \text{Rate of inflation},$$

which here becomes

$$\%\Delta \text{ in Lender's purchasing power} = \%\Delta \text{ in Lender's dollars} - \text{Rate of inflation}$$

or

$$\text{Real interest rate} = \text{Nominal interest rate} - \text{Rate of inflation}.$$

In our example, where we want the real interest rate to equal 4 percent when the inflation rate is 5 percent, we must have

$$4 \text{ percent} = \text{Nominal interest rate} - 5 \text{ percent}$$

or

$$\text{Nominal interest rate} = 9 \text{ percent}.$$

Once again, we see that as long as both parties correctly anticipate the inflation rate, and face no restrictions on contracts (that is, they are free to set the nominal interest rate at 9 percent), then no one gains or loses.

When inflation is *not* correctly anticipated, however, our conclusion is very different.

Unexpected Inflation *Does* Shift Purchasing Power. Suppose that, expecting no inflation, you agree to lend money at a 4 percent nominal interest rate for one year. You and the borrower think that this will translate into a 4 percent real rate. But it turns out you are both wrong: The price level actually rises by 3 percent, so the *real* interest rate ends up being 4 percent − 3 percent = 1 percent. As a lender, you have given up the use of your money for the year, expecting to be rewarded with a 4 percent increase in purchasing power. But you get only a 1 percent increase. Your borrower was willing to pay 4 percent in purchasing power, but ends up paying only 1 percent. *Unexpected* inflation has led to a better deal for your borrower and a worse deal for you, the lender.

That will not make you happy. But it could be even worse. Suppose the inflation rate is higher—say, 6 percent. Then your real interest rate ends up at 4 percent − 6 percent = −2 percent, a negative real interest rate. You get back *less* in purchasing power than you lend out—*paying* (in purchasing power) for the privilege of lending out your money. The borrower is *rewarded* (in purchasing power) for borrowing!

Negative real interest rates like this are not just a theoretical possibility. In the late 1970s, when inflation was higher than expected for several years in a row, many borrowers ending up paying negative real interest rates to lenders.

Now, let's consider one more possibility: Expected inflation is 6 percent, so you negotiate a 10 percent nominal rate, thinking this will translate to a 4 percent real rate. But the actual inflation rate turns out to be zero, so the real interest rate is 10 percent − 0 percent = 10 percent. In this case, inflation turns out to be *less* than expected, so the *real* interest rate is higher than either of you anticipated. The borrower is harmed and you (the lender) benefit.

These examples apply, more generally, to any agreement on future payments: to a worker waiting for a wage payment and the employer who has promised to pay it; to a doctor who has sent out a bill and the patient who has not yet paid it; or to a supplier who has delivered goods and his customer who hasn't yet paid for them.

When inflationary expectations are inaccurate, purchasing power is shifted between those obliged to make future payments and those waiting to be paid. An inflation rate higher than expected harms those awaiting payment and benefits the payers; an inflation rate lower than expected harms the payers and benefits those awaiting payment.

The Resource Cost of Inflation

In addition to its possible redistribution of income, inflation imposes another cost upon society. To cope with inflation, we are forced to use up time and other resources as we go about our daily economic activities (shopping, selling, saving) that we could otherwise have devoted to productive activities. Thus, inflation imposes an *opportunity cost* on society as a whole and on each of its members:

When people must spend time and other resources coping with inflation, they pay an opportunity cost—they sacrifice the goods and services those resources could have produced instead.

 Opportunity Cost

Let's first consider the resources used up by *consumers* to cope with inflation. Suppose you shop for clothes twice a year. You've discovered that both The Gap and Banana Republic sell clothing of similar quality and have similar service, and you naturally want to shop at the one with the lower prices. If there is no inflation, your task is easy: You shop first at The Gap and then at Banana Republic; thereafter, you rely on your memory to determine which is less expensive.

With inflation, however, things are more difficult. Suppose you find that prices at Banana Republic are higher than you remember them to be at The Gap. It may be that Banana Republic is the more expensive store, or it may be that prices have risen at *both* stores. How can you tell? Only a trip back to The Gap will answer the question—a trip that will cost you extra time and trouble. If prices are rising very rapidly, you may have to visit both stores on the same day to be sure which one is cheaper. Now, multiply this time and trouble by all the different types of shopping you must do on a regular or occasional basis—for groceries, an apartment, a car, concert tickets, compact discs, restaurant meals, and more. Inflation can make you use up valuable time—time you could have spent earning income or enjoying leisure activities. True, if you shop for some of these items on the Internet, you can compare prices in less time, but not zero time. And most shopping is *not* done over the Internet.

Inflation also forces *sellers* to use up resources. First, remember that sellers of goods and services are also buyers of resources and intermediate goods. They, too, must do comparison shopping when there is inflation, which uses up hired labor time. Second, each time sellers raise prices, labor is needed to put new price tags on merchandise, to enter new prices into a computer scanning system, to update the HTML code on a Web page, or to change the prices on advertising brochures, menus, and so on.

Finally, inflation makes us all use up resources managing our financial affairs. When the inflation rate is high, we'll try to keep our funds in accounts that pay high nominal interest rates, in order to preserve our purchasing power. And we'll try to keep as little as possible in cash or in low-interest checking accounts. Of course, this means more frequent trips to the bank or the automatic teller machine, to transfer money into our checking accounts or get cash each time we need it.

All of these additional activities—inspecting prices at several stores or Web sites, changing price tags or price entries, going back and forth to the automatic teller machine—use up time and other resources. From society's point of view, these resources could have been used to produce *other* goods and services that we'd enjoy.

You may not have thought much about the resource cost of inflation, because in recent years, U.S. inflation has been so low—averaging about 3 percent during the 1990s, and about $2\frac{1}{2}$ percent in the early 2000s. Such a low rate of inflation is often called *creeping inflation;* from week to week or month to month, the price level creeps up so slowly that we hardly notice the change. The cost of coping with creeping inflation is negligible.

But it has not always been this way. Three times during the last 50 years, we have had double-digit inflation: about 14 percent during 1947–48, 12 percent in 1974, and 13 percent during 1979 and 1980. Going back farther, the annual inflation rate reached almost 20 percent during World War I and rose above 25 percent during the Civil War.

And as serious as these episodes of American inflation have been, they pale in comparison to the experiences of other countries. In Germany in the early 1920s, the inflation rate hit thousands of percent *per month*. And more recently, in the late 1980s, several South American countries experienced inflation rates in excess of 1,000 percent annually. For a few weeks in 1990, Argentina's annual inflation rate even reached 400,000 percent! Under these conditions, the monetary system breaks down almost completely. Economic life is almost as difficult as in the mythical nation of Chaotica, discussed at the very beginning of this chapter.

IS THE CPI ACCURATE?

The Bureau of Labor Statistics spends millions of dollars gathering data to ensure that its measure of inflation is accurate. To determine the market basket of the typical consumer, the BLS randomly selects thousands of households and analyzes their spending habits. In the last household survey—completed in 2002—each of about 15,000 families kept diaries of their purchases for two weeks.

But that is just the beginning. Every month, the bureau's shoppers visit 23,000 retail stores and about 50,000 housing units (rental apartments and owner-occupied homes) to record 80,000 different prices. Finally, all of the prices are combined to determine the cost of the typical consumer's market basket for the current month.

The BLS is a highly professional agency, typically headed by an economist. Billions of dollars are at stake for each 1 percent change in the CPI, and the BLS deserves high praise for keeping its measurement honest and free of political ma-

HTTP://

To learn more about the strengths and weaknesses of the CPI, read Allison Wallace and Brian Motley, "A Better CPI" (http://www.frbsf.org/econrsrch/wklyltr/wklyltr99/el99-05.html).

nipulation. Nevertheless, conceptual problems and resource limitations make the CPI fall short of the ideal measure of inflation. Economists—even those who work in the BLS—widely agree that the CPI overstates the U.S. inflation rate.

But by how much?

According to a report by an advisory committee of economists in 1996, the overall bias was at least 1.1 percent during the 1980s and early 1990s.[4] That is, in a typical year, the reported rise in the CPI was about 1 percentage point greater than the true rise in the price level. The BLS has been working hard to reduce this upward bias and—especially in the late 1990s—it made some progress. But significant bias remains.

Sources of Bias in the CPI

There are several reasons for the upward bias in the CPI.

Substitution Bias. Until recently, the CPI almost completely ignored a general principle of consumer behavior: People tend to *substitute* goods that have become relatively cheaper in place of goods that have become relatively more expensive. For example, in the seven years from 1973 to 1980, the retail price of oil-related products—like gasoline and home heating oil—increased by more than 300 percent, while the prices of most other goods and services rose by less than 100 percent. As a result, people found ways to conserve on oil products. They joined carpools, used public transportation, insulated their homes, and in many cases moved closer to their workplaces to shorten their commute. Yet throughout this period, the CPI basket—based on a survey of buying patterns in 1972–73—assumed that consumers were buying unchanged quantities of oil products.

The treatment of oil products is an example of a more general problem that has plagued the CPI for decades. Until recently, the CPI used fixed *quantities* to determine the relative importance of each item. That is, it assumed that households continued to buy each good or service in the same quantities in which they bought it during the most recent household survey—until the next household survey. Compounding the problem, the survey to determine spending patterns—and to update the market basket—was taken only about once every 10 years or so. So by the end of each 10-year period, the CPI's assumptions about spending habits could be far off the mark, as they were in the case of oil in the 1970s.

The BLS has *partially* fixed this problem, in two ways.[5] First, beginning in 2002, it began updating the market basket with a household survey every *two* years instead of every 10 years. This is widely considered an important improvement in CPI measurement.

Second, since January 1999, the CPI has no longer assumed that the typical consumer continues to buy the same *quantity* of each good that he bought in the last household "market basket" survey. Instead, the CPI now assumes that when a good's relative price rises by 10 percent, consumers buy 10 percent less of it, and switch their purchases to other goods whose prices are rising more slowly.

---

[4] See *Toward a More Accurate Measure of the Cost of Living,* Report to the Senate Finance Committee from the Advisory Commission to Study the Consumer Price Index, December 1996.
[5] For a discussion of these and other recent changes in the CPI, see "Planned Change in the Consumer Price Index Formula," Bureau of Labor Statistics, April 16, 1998 (*http://stats.bls.gov/cpigm02.htm*), and "Future Schedule for Expenditure Weight Updates in the Consumer Price Index," Bureau of Labor Statistics, December 18, 1998 (*http://stats.bls.gov/cpiupdt.htm*).

However, this is only a partial fix. The CPI still only recognizes the possibility of such substitution *within* categories of goods and *not among* them. For example, if the price of steak rises relative to the price of hamburger meat, the CPI now assumes that consumers will substitute away from steak and toward hamburger meat, since both are in the same category: *beef*. However, if the price of all beef products rises relative to chicken and pork, the CPI assumes that there is *no* substitution at all from beef toward chicken and pork. As a result, beef products still would be overweighted in the CPI until the next survey.

> *Although the BLS has partially fixed the problem, the CPI still suffers from substitution bias. That is, categories of goods whose prices are rising most rapidly tend to be given exaggerated importance in the CPI, and categories of goods whose prices are rising most slowly tend to be given too little importance in the CPI.*

New Technologies. New technologies are another source of upward bias in the CPI. One problem is that goods using new technologies are introduced into the BLS market basket only after a lag. These goods often drop rapidly in price after they are introduced, helping to balance out price rises in other goods. By excluding a category of goods whose prices are dropping, the CPI overstates the rate of inflation. For example, even though many consumers were buying and using cellular phones throughout the 1990s, they were not included in the BLS basket of goods until 1998. As a result, the CPI missed the rapid decline in the price of cell phones. Now that the market basket of the typical consumer is updated every two years instead of every 10, this source of bias has been reduced but not completely eliminated.

> *The CPI excludes new products that tend to drop in price when they first come on the market.*

TABLE 3
Goods Adjusted for Quality Changes in the CPI

Prices Adjusted for Quality Changes	Year Adjustment Began
Cars	1967
Used Cars	1987
Clothing	1991
Gasoline	1994
Personal Computers	1998
Televisions	1999
VCRs & DVD Players	2000
Refrigerators, Microwaves, Washing Machines	2000
College Textbooks	2000

Sources: "Program Report," *Monthly Labor Review,* May 2002, p. 47; and various BLS publications.

Changes in Quality. Many products are improving over time. Cars are much more reliable than they used to be and require much less routine maintenance. They have features like air bags and antilock brakes that were unknown in the early 1980s. The BLS struggles to deal with these changes. As far back as 1967, it has recognized that when the price of a car rises, some of that price hike is not really inflation but instead the result of charging more because the consumer is *getting* more. In recent years, the BLS has adopted some routine statistical procedures to automatically adjust price changes for quality improvements for a variety of goods. Table 3 lists some important examples, along with the year that the CPI began measuring and adjusting for quality improvements.

Two things stand out in the table. First, for many of the goods, quality adjustment began very late, *after* huge advances in quality had already taken place. Up until that time, the CPI treated any price hike as pure inflation, thus contributing to an overestimate of the overall inflation rate. Second, while the list of goods in the table is impressive (and growing), most goods do *not* get this special treatment. For most goods, improvements in quality are effectively ignored.

Take the Internet. Every year, it offers more information and entertainment content, a greater number of retailers from which to buy things, and faster and more intelligent search engines to help you find it all. Yet, the Internet—which was introduced into the CPI in 1998—has been treated as a service whose quality has not changed. If the price of Internet service rises, the CPI considers it inflation rather than paying more to *get* more. And if the price stays the same, the CPI ignores the *decrease* in the cost per unit of available content and treats the price as unchanged.

> *The CPI still counts as inflation many cases in which prices rise because of quality improvements. This causes the CPI to overstate the inflation rate.*

USING THE THEORY
The Use and Misuse of an Imperfect CPI

© SUSAN VAN ETTEN

The inaccuracies in measuring the Consumer Price Index discussed in the chapter, as well as an even more important conceptual issue to be discussed below, suggest that the CPI should be used and interpreted with great care. Unfortunately, the CPI is often used for purposes which it cannot handle accurately.

Indexing

Earlier in the chapter, we pointed out that more than 50 million Social Security recipients and other retirees, as well as 2 million workers, have their benefits *indexed* to the CPI: Their nominal (dollar) benefits automatically increase at the same rate as the CPI. The justification for indexing is to protect these people from any deterioration in living standards caused by inflation. But because changes in the CPI *overstate* inflation, these beneficiaries are *over*indexed. That is, their nominal benefit rises by a greater percentage than a more accurately measured price index would rise.

Let's take an example. Suppose that a Social Security recipient who retired in 1980 was promised $1,000 per month in Social Security benefits, indexed to the CPI each year. But suppose that each year from 1980 to 2002 (the period of retirement) the CPI *overstated* the annual rate of inflation by 1 percent. Then every year, the recipient receives 1 percent more in dollars than needed to maintain the *purchasing power* of the benefit, so the real benefit rises by 1 percent every year. At the end of the first year, the real payment is $1,000 \times 1.01 = \$1010$. For the second year, it's $[\$1,000 \times 1.01] \times 1.01 = \$1 \times (1.01)^2 = \$1,020.10$. And at the end of the 22nd year, it's $\$1,000 \times (1.01)^{22} = \$1,245$. Rather than just maintaining the real Social Security payment over time, indexing to the inaccurate CPI results in a continually rising *real* benefit, one that is 24 percent higher than in the initial period.

This will suit Social Security recipients just fine. And it may suit the rest of us too—when the economy is growing at a rapid pace. After all, why shouldn't retirees get a larger slice of the economic pie when the pie itself is growing rapidly and everyone else's slice is growing as well? But note that the increase in real benefits happens *automatically,* due to overindexing, *regardless* of the rate of economic growth. If the growth rate of real GDP slows down, the average Social Security recipient will *still* get a growing slice of the pie each year, even if everyone else's slice is shrinking. And because Social Security is financed by tax payments from the rest of society, any increase in real benefits shrinks the after-tax real income of nonretirees.

More generally,

> *when a payment is indexed and the price index overstates inflation, the real payment increases over time. Purchasing power is automatically shifted toward those who are indexed and away from the rest of society.*

This general principle applies whether the economy is growing rapidly or slowly, and it applies to anyone who is indexed: Social Security recipients, government pensioners, union workers with indexed wage contracts, or anyone else.

Long-Run Comparisons

If you look back at Table 2, you'll see a rather depressing story: The average hourly worker's real wage in 2002 was just a tiny bit higher than in 1980, and actually *lower* than in 1970. Has the purchasing power of the average wage really behaved this way? Not if the CPI—which was used in the table to calculate the real wage—overstates inflation.

We can get a *somewhat* more accurate view by asking the following question: What story would Table 2 tell if some of the recent improvements in the CPI measurement were applied retroactively? Fortunately, the BLS has attempted to answer this question by constructing an *unofficial* version of the CPI (called the CPI-U-RS, or the CPI for all Urban Consumers—Research Series) going back to 1978. This series is shown in Table 4. The first four columns of the data are selected rows from Table 2. They show the calculation of the wage using the *official* CPI. The fifth column shows the unofficial CPI—what the CPI *would* have been if some recent methodological improvements had been used in earlier years. Finally, the last column shows the recalculation of the real wage based on this somewhat more accurate CPI.

As you can see in the last column, the story looks a bit different. From 1980 to 2002, instead of rising from $8.24 to $8.37 (in 1983 dollars), the partially corrected real wage rose from $8.28 to $8.85. Moreover, instead of falling from 1970 to 2002, the partially corrected real wage actually rose slightly during this period. Keep in mind, too, that Columns 5 and 6 reflect only *some* of the BLS's improved measurement techniques, and these new techniques corrected only *some* of the acknowledged problems. A fuller correction would show an even greater rise in the real wage over the period.

In any case, because the BLS never alters previously published data to reflect later improvements in methodology, the official history of the real wage remains that of Column 4, not Column 6. This is the story you will see on Web sites and press reports that discuss changes in real wages over time.

(1) Year	(2) Average Nominal Wage	(3) Official CPI	(4) Official Average Real Wage (1983 dollars) [(2)/(3)] × 100	(5) Partially Corrected CPI	(6) Partially Corrected Real Wage (1983 dollars) [(2)/(5)] × 100
1970	$3.50	39.8	$8.79	(no data available)	—
1980	$7.12	86.4	$8.24	86.0	$8.28
1990	$10.33	134.2	$7.70	130.8	$7.90
2000	$14.26	174.6	$8.17	165.2	$8.63
2002	$15.20	181.6	$8.37	171.7	$8.85

Source: "The Bureau of Labor Statistics' Statement on the Use of the CPI-U-RS," at *http://www.bls.gov/cpi/cpiurstx.htm* (modified April 16, 2003). Base year of CPI-U-RS was converted from 1977 to 1983 by authors.

Because the BLS does not correct previously reported CPI numbers to reflect later methodological improvements, long-term comparisons of real variables based on the official CPI will remain inaccurate, even as CPI measurement improves.

TABLE 4
The Official and Partially Corrected Average Real Wage

The Bigger, Conceptual Problem

An even more serious problem in using the CPI has to do with the way it is typically viewed: as a measure of the *cost of living*—the cost of maintaining a fixed living standard from purchased goods and services. Indexing, after all, is usually justified as a way to prevent any deterioration in living standards. And discussions about the real wage often end with conclusions about the average worker being better or worse off. These conclusions imply that the CPI—which is used to calculate the real wage—is tracking the cost of achieving a given living standard. However, viewed as a measure of the cost of living, the CPI is even more inaccurate than our discussion so far suggests. This is because of the way it treats new goods—a problem that will not be corrected by any of the BLS's planned improvements.

When a new good comes to market, it is dropped into the CPI market basket at some point, and the CPI tracks changes in its price from that time forward. But the increase in economic well-being made possible by *introducing* the good—and the good's continued availability—is never accounted for. Even if the BLS were able to incorporate the good as soon as it came to market, and even if it accurately adjusted for subsequent quality improvements, it would still be missing the most important factor: the rise in living standards made possible by the new good's availability.

For example, we've already discussed the CPI's failure to account for quality *improvements* in the Internet after it was dropped into the basket in 1998. But in addition to this problem, the CPI has *never* recognized how the Internet has lowered the cost of achieving any given level of economic satisfaction (think of e-mail, online entertainment, online purchases, news, and more). The same is true for new medical procedures or prescription drugs that can treat or cure formerly untreatable diseases.

The CPI tracks increases in their prices *after* they appear in the basket, but ignores the impact of these new treatments on our standard of living. In this way, the CPI misses a highly relevant fact: New goods raise the living standard we can achieve at any given dollar cost or, equivalently, they lower the dollar cost of achieving any given living standard.

How serious is this problem? No one knows for sure. But some authors have suggested that the error from ignoring the effect of new goods on living standards could be substantial. This error must be *added* to the combined effects of all the other errors discussed in this chapter.[6]

How might this change the story of the hourly real wage told in Table 2 (or Table 4)? Let's suppose that the ultimate, total overstatement in the cost of living has been 2 percent each year since 1970 to 2002. This would lead the CPI in 2002 to exaggerate the cost of living by about $(1.02)^{32} = 1.88$ or 88 percent. In Table 4, the official CPI over that period rose from 39.8 to 181.6, or a percentage increase of $(181.6 - 39.8)/39.8 = 3.56$ or 356 percent. Deducting the 88 percent error would leave a *true* cost of living increase of $356 - 88 = 268$ percent. Thus, to obtain an accurate CPI in 2002, we would increase 1970's CPI by 268 percent—instead of the official 356 percent. This would give us an accurate CPI in 2002 of $39.8 + (2.68 \times 39.8) = 146.5$. Finally, using this corrected CPI would give us a 2002 hourly real wage of $[\$15.20/146.5] \times 100 = \$10.38$. Comparing with 1970, we see that the real wage would have increased substantially—from $8.79 to $10.38—rather than falling, as the official story goes.

Of course, this example arbitrarily assumed a 2 percent overstatement of the annual rise in the cost of living. The actual overstatement could be less—or considerably more. But the general point is this:

Using the CPI as an index of the cost of living *(the cost of achieving a given living standard) creates a further overstatement of inflation, because the CPI ignores the impact of new goods on living standards. Therefore, CPI-based indexing and CPI-based inferences about changes in well-being over time may be highly inaccurate.*

What the CPI Does Well

The CPI has another purpose besides indexing and making inferences about living standards: to measure inflationary tendencies in the economy. For this purpose, the CPI's interpretation as a cost-of-living index is irrelevant: The policy goal is to avoid high costs to society when the price level—however it's interpreted—changes too rapidly. The CPI is one of several useful tools to help achieve this goal.

To see why, suppose the CPI-based inflation rate (or one of its useful variants, which leaves out volatile components like food or energy prices) suddenly jumps up. Because of its measurement errors, the official inflation rate will exaggerate the true rise in prices, but it's unlikely that measurement errors alone would cause the entire increase in reported inflation. (That would require a sudden change in the relative importance of the measurement errors themselves.) Instead, a sudden spike in the CPI would tell policy makers that prices in the economy are, indeed, rising at a faster rate, and that appropriate policy measures should be considered to prevent

[6] See, for example, the suggestions of Jerry Hausman, "Sources of Bias and Solutions to Bias in the CPI," National Bureau of Economic Research, Working Paper 9298, October 2002. Much of the discussion of this subsection is based on Hausman's work.

inflation from getting out of hand. The same might apply to a rapid *decrease* in officially measured inflation to very low levels, creating a danger of deflation.

Also, in times of high inflation—as in the late 1970s—using an imperfect CPI to estimate real wages or to index retirees may be preferable to not accounting for inflation at all. With official annual inflation of 13 percent, for example, indexing Social Security benefits to an exaggerated CPI might raise the living standards of retirees by a few percentage points at the expense of the rest of society. But *not* indexing Social Security benefits at all could cause retirees' living standards to fall by 10 percent or more.

This chapter has raised many questions and left some of them unanswered. What makes the inflation rate rise and fall? Who are these *policy makers* that monitor the inflation rate and often try to alter it? How do they actually change the inflation rate? And why would they worry about an inflation rate that is too *low*? These are all questions we'll address in future chapters, after you've learned about macroeconomic models—the subject we turn to next.

Summary

Money serves two important functions. First, it serves as a *unit of value* that helps us compare the costs of different goods and services. Second, it serves as a *means of payment* by being generally acceptable in exchange for goods and services. Without money, we would be reduced to barter, a very inefficient way of carrying out transactions.

The value of money is its purchasing power, and this changes as the prices of the things we buy change. The overall trend of prices is measured using a price index. Like any index number, a price index is calculated as: (value in current period/value in base period) × 100. The most widely used price index in the United States is the *Consumer Price Index (CPI)*, which tracks the prices paid for a typical consumer's "market basket." The percent change in the CPI is the inflation rate.

The most common uses of the CPI are for indexing payments, as a policy target, and to translate from nominal to real variables. Many nominal variables, such as the nominal wage, can be corrected for price changes by dividing by the CPI and then multiplying by 100. The result is a real variable, such as the real wage, that rises and falls only when its purchasing power rises and falls. Another price index in common use is the GDP price index. It tracks prices of all final goods and services included in GDP.

Inflation, a rise over time in a price index, is costly to our society. One of inflation's costs is an arbitrary redistribution of purchasing power. Unanticipated inflation shifts purchasing power away from those awaiting future dollar payments and toward those obligated to make such payments. Another cost of inflation is the resource cost: People use valuable time and other resources trying to cope with inflation.

It is widely agreed that the CPI has overstated inflation in recent decades, probably by more than one percentage point per year. As a result, the official statistics on real variables may contain errors, and people whose incomes are indexed to the CPI have actually been overindexed, enjoying an increase in real income that is paid for by the rest of society. The Bureau of Labor Statistics has been trying to eliminate the upward bias in the CPI. Much progress has been made, but some upward bias remains. The CPI is especially inaccurate as an index of the cost of achieving a given standard of living.

Key Terms

Consumer Price Index	Index	Price level
Deflation	Indexation	Real interest rate
Federal Reserve System	Inflation rate	Unit of value
Fiat money	Means of payment	
GDP price index	Nominal interest rate	

Review Questions

1. Distinguish between the *unit-of-value* function of money and the *means-of-payment* function. Give examples of how the U.S. dollar has played each of these two roles.

2. How does the price level differ from, say, the price of a haircut or a Big Mac?

3. Explain how you might construct an index of bank deposits over time. What steps would be involved?

4. What is the CPI? What does it measure? How can it be used to calculate the inflation rate?

5. Can the inflation rate be decreasing at the same time the price level is rising? Can the inflation rate be increasing at the same time the price level is falling? Explain.

6. What are the main uses of the CPI? Give an example of each use.

7. Explain the logic of the formula that relates real values to nominal values.

8. What are the similarities between the CPI and the GDP price index? What are the differences?

9. What are the costs of inflation?

10. Under what circumstances would inflation redistribute purchasing power? How? When would it *not* redistribute purchasing power?

11. How is a nominal interest rate different from a real interest rate? Which do you think is the better measure of the rate of return on a loan?

12. Explain the common misuses of the CPI.

Problems and Exercises

1. Calculate each of the following from the data in Table 1 in this chapter.
   a. The inflation rate for the year 2002.
   b. *Total* inflation (the total percentage change in the price level) from December 1970 to December 2002.

2. Using the data in Table 2, calculate the following for the period 1995–2000.
   a. The total percentage change in the nominal wage.
   b. The total percentage change in the price level.

3. Calculate the total percentage change in the real wage from 1995 to 2000 in two ways: (a) using your answers in problems 2a and b and the rule given earlier in this chapter; and (b) using the last column of Table 2. Which method is more accurate?

4. Suppose we want to change the base period of the CPI from July 1983 to December 1995. Recalculate December's CPI for each of the years in Table 1, so that the table gives the same information about inflation, but the CPI in December 1995 is now 100 instead of 153.9.

5. Which would be more costly: a steady inflation rate of 5 percent per year, or an inflation rate that was sometimes high and sometimes low, but that averaged 5 percent per year? Justify your answer.

6. Given the following *year-end* data, calculate the inflation rate for years 2, 3, and 4. Calculate the real wage in each year:

Year	CPI	Inflation Rate	Nominal Wage	Real Wage
1	100		$10.00	____
2	110	____	$12.00	____
3	120	____	$13.00	____
4	115	____	$12.75	____

7. Your friend asks for a loan of $100 for one year and offers to pay you 5 percent real interest. Your friend expects the inflation rate over that one-year period to be 6 percent; you expect it to be 4 percent. You agree to make the loan, and the actual inflation rate turns out to be 5 percent. Who benefits and who loses?

8. If there is 5 percent inflation each year for eight years, what is the *total* amount of inflation (i.e., the total percentage rise in the price level) over the entire eight-year period? (*Hint:* The answer is *not* 40 percent.)

9. Given the following data, calculate the real interest rate for years 2, 3, and 4. (Assume that each CPI number tells us the price level at the *end* of each year.)

Year	CPI	Nominal Interest Rate	Real Interest Rate
1	100		
2	110	15%	_____
3	120	13%	_____
4	115	8%	_____

If you lent $200 to a friend at the beginning of year 2 at the prevailing nominal interest rate of 15 percent, and your friend returned the money, with the interest, at the end of year 2, did you benefit from the deal?

10. (Requires appendix) An economy has only two goods, whose prices and typical consumption quantities are as follows:

	Dec. 2005		Dec. 2006	
	Price	Quantity	Price	Quantity
Fruit (lbs)	$1.00	100	$1.00	150
Nuts (lbs)	$3.00	50	$4.00	25

a. Using December 2005 as the base period for calculations and also as the year for measuring the typical consumer's market basket, calculate the CPI in December 2005 and December 2006.
b. What is the annual inflation rate for 2006?
c. Do you think your answer in b. would understate the actual inflation rate in 2006? Briefly, why or why not?

11. a. Use Table 4. For 1990 to 2002, calculate the following:
   (i) the total percentage change in the official CPI;
   (ii) the total percentage change in the partially corrected CPI;
   (iii) the total percentage change in the official real wage; and
   (iv) the total percentage change in the partially corrected real wage.

b. Suppose a fully corrected CPI would have increased only 25 percent over this entire period. What would be the percentage change in the fully corrected real wage?
c. Suppose the CPI overstates the cost of living by 2 percent, as discussed at the end of the "Using the Theory" section of this chapter. When this assumed overstatement is corrected, by what percentage would the real wage have increased from 1990 to 2002?

12. Complete the following table. (CPI numbers are for the end of each year).

Year	CPI	Inflation Rate	Nominal Wage	Real Wage
1	37		$ 5.60	
2	48		$ 7	
3		10%	$11.26	
4		19%		$25
5	60		$15	

13. a. Jodie earned $25,000 in year 1, when the CPI was 460. If the CPI in year 2 is 504, what would Jodie have to earn in year 2 to maintain a constant real wage?
b. What would she have to earn in year 2, to obtain a 5 percent increase in her real wage? What percentage increase in the nominal wage is this?

Challenge Questions

1. During the late 19th and early 20th centuries, many U.S. farmers favored inflationary government policies. Why might this have been the case? (*Hint:* Do farmers typically pay for their land in full at the time of purchase?)

APPENDIX

CALCULATING THE CONSUMER PRICE INDEX

The Consumer Price Index (CPI) is the government's most popular measure of inflation. It tracks the cost of the collection of goods, called the *CPI market basket,* bought by a typical consumer in some *base period.* This appendix demonstrates how the Bureau of Labor Statistics (BLS) calculates the CPI. To help you follow the steps clearly, we'll do the calculations for a very simple economy with just two goods: hamburger meat and oranges (not a pleasant world, but a manageable one). Table A.1 shows prices for each good, and the quantities produced and consumed, in two different periods: December 2004 (the base period) and December 2005. The market basket (measured in the base period) is given in the third column of the table: In December 2004, the typical consumer buys 30 pounds of hamburger and 50 pounds of oranges. Our formula for the CPI in any period *t* is

CPI in period *t*

$$= \frac{\text{Cost of market basket at prices in period } t}{\text{Cost of market basket at 2004 prices}} \times 100,$$

where each year's prices are measured in December of that year.

TABLE A.1
Prices and Weekly Quantities in a Two-Good Economy

	December 2004		December 2005	
	Price (per lb.)	Quantity (lbs.)	Price (per lb.)	Quantity (lbs.)
Hamburger Meat	$5.00	30	$6.00	10
Oranges	$1.00	50	$1.10	100

Table A.2 shows the calculations we must do to determine the CPI in December 2004 and December 2005. In the table, you can see that the cost of the 2004 market basket at 2004 prices is $200. The cost of the *same* market basket at 2005's higher prices is $235.

TABLE A.2
Calculations for the CPI

	At December 2004 Prices	At December 2005 Prices
Cost of 30 lbs. of Hamburger	$5.00 × 30 = $150	$6.00 × 30 = $180
Cost of 50 lbs. of Oranges	$1.00 × 50 = $50	$1.10 × 50 = $55
Cost of Entire Market Basket	$150 + $50 = $200	$180 + $55 = $235

To determine the CPI in December 2004—the base period—we use the formula with period *t* equal to 2004, giving us

CPI in 2004

$$= \frac{\text{Cost of 2004 basket at 2004 prices}}{\text{Cost of 2004 basket at 2004 prices}} \times 100$$

$$= \frac{\$200}{\$200} \times 100 = 100.$$

That is, the CPI in December 2004—the base period—is equal to 100. (The formula, as you can see, is set up so that the CPI will always equal 100 in the base period, regardless of which base period we choose.)

Now let's apply the formula again, to get the value of the CPI in December 2005:

CPI in 2005

$$= \frac{\text{Cost of 2004 basket at 2005 prices}}{\text{Cost of 2004 basket at 2004 prices}} \times 100$$

$$= \frac{\$235}{\$200} \times 100 = 117.5.$$

From December 2004 to December 2005, the CPI rises from 100 to 117.5. The rate of inflation over the year 2005 is therefore 17.5 percent.

Notice that the CPI gives more weight to price changes of goods that are more important in the consumer's budget. In our example, the percentage rise in the CPI (17.5 percent) is closer to the percentage rise in the price of hamburger (20 percent) than it is to the percentage price rise of oranges (10 percent). This is because a greater percentage of the budget is *spent* on hamburger than on oranges, so hamburger carries more weight in the CPI.

But one of the CPI's problems, discussed in the body of the chapter, is *substitution bias*. The CPI recognizes that consumers substitute *within* categories of goods. For example, if we had a third good, steak, the CPI would recognize that consumers will buy more steak if the price of hamburger rises faster than the price of steak. But the CPI assumes there is no substitution *among* categories—between beef products and fruit, for example. No matter how much the relative price of beef products like hamburger rises, the CPI assumes that people will continue to buy the same quantity of it, rather than substitute goods in other categories like oranges. Therefore, as the price of hamburger rises, the CPI assumes that we spend a greater and greater percentage of our budgets on it; hamburger gets *increasing weight* in the CPI. In our example, spending on hamburger is assumed to rise from $150/$200 = 0.75, or 75 percent of the typical weekly budget, to $180/$235 = 0.766, or 76.6 percent. In fact, however, the rapid rise in price would cause people to substitute *away* from hamburger toward other goods whose prices are rising more slowly.

This is what occurs in our two-good example, as you can see in the last column of Table A.1. In 2005, the quantity of hamburger purchased drops to 10, and the quantity of oranges rises to 100. In an ideal measure, the decrease in the quantity of hamburger would reduce its weight in determining the overall rate of inflation. But the CPI ignores the information in the last column of Table A.1, which shows the new quantities purchased in 2005. This failure to correct for substitution bias across categories of goods is one of the reasons the CPI overstates inflation.

Economic Growth and Rising Living Standards

Economist Thomas Malthus, writing in 1798, came to a striking conclusion: "Population, when unchecked, goes on doubling itself every twenty-five years, or increases in a geometrical ratio. . . . The means of subsistence . . . could not possibly be made to increase faster than in an arithmetic ratio."[1] From this simple logic, Malthus forecast a horrible fate for the human race. There would be repeated famines and wars to keep the rapidly growing population in balance with the more slowly growing supply of food and other necessities. The prognosis was so pessimistic that it led Thomas Carlyle, one of Malthus's contemporaries, to label economics "the dismal science."

But history has proven Malthus wrong . . . at least in part. In the industrialized nations, living standards have increased beyond the wildest dreams of anyone alive in Malthus's time. Economists today are optimistic about these nations' long-run material prospects. At the same time, living standards in many of the less-developed countries have remained stubbornly close to survival level and, in some cases, have fallen below it.

What are we to make of this? Why have living standards steadily increased in some nations but not in others? And what, if anything, can governments do to speed the rise in living standards? These are questions about economic growth—the long-run increase in an economy's output of goods and services.

[1] Thomas Robert Malthus, *An Essay on the Principle of Population,* 1798.

In this chapter, you will learn what makes economies grow. And by the end of this chapter, you will know why increasing the rate of economic growth is not easy. While nations can take measures to speed growth, each measure carries an opportunity cost. More specifically,

achieving a higher rate of growth in the long run generally requires some sacrifice in the short run.

THE IMPORTANCE OF GROWTH

Why should we be concerned about economic growth? For one simple reason:

*When output grows faster than the population, GDP per capita, which we call the **average standard of living**, will rise. When output grows more slowly than the population, the average standard of living will fall.*

Average standard of living Total output (real GDP) per person.

Measuring the standard of living by GDP per capita (per person) may seem limiting. After all, as we saw two chapters ago, many important aspects of our quality of life are not captured in GDP. Leisure time, workplace safety, good health, a clean environment—we care about all of these. Yet they are not considered in GDP.

Still, many aspects of our quality of life *are* counted in GDP: food, housing, medical care, education, transportation services, and movies and video games, to name a few. It is not surprising, then, that economic growth—measured by increases in GDP—remains a vital concern in every nation.

Economic growth is especially important in countries with income levels far below those of Europe, Japan, and the United States. The average standard of living in some third-world nations is so low that many families can barely acquire the basic necessities of life, and many others perish from disease or starvation. Table 1 lists GDP per capita, infant mortality rates, life expectancies, and adult literacy rates for some of the richest and poorest countries. These statistics for poor countries are grim enough, but they capture only part of the story. Unsafe and unclean workplaces, inadequate housing, and other sources of misery are part of daily life for most people in these countries. Other than emigration, economic growth is their only hope.

Growth is a high priority in prosperous nations, too. As we know, resources are scarce, and we cannot produce enough of everything to satisfy all of our desires simultaneously. We want more and better medical care, education, housing, entertainment . . . the list is endless. When output per capita is growing, it's at least *possible* for everyone to enjoy an increase in material well-being without anyone having to cut back. We can also accomplish important social goals—helping the poor, improving education, cleaning up the environment—by asking those who are doing well to sacrifice part of the rise in their material well-being, rather than suffer a drop.

But when output per capita stagnates, material gains become a fight over a fixed pie: The more purchasing power my neighbor has, the less is left for me. With everyone struggling for a larger piece of this fixed pie, conflict replaces cooperation. Efforts to help the less fortunate, wipe out illiteracy, reduce air pollution—all are seen as threats, rather than opportunities.

In the 1950s and 1960s, economic growth in the wealthier nations seemed to be taking care of itself. Economists and policy makers focused their attention on short-run movements around full-employment output, rather than on the

TABLE 1
Some Indicators of Economic Well-Being in Rich and Poor Countries, 2003

Country	Real GDP per Capita	Infant Mortality Rate (per 1,000 Live Births)	Life Expectancy at Birth	Adult Literacy Rate
Rich Countries				
United States	$34,320	7	76.9	Greater than 99%
Japan	$25,130	3	81.3	Greater than 99%
France	$23,990	4	78.7	Greater than 99%
United Kingdom	$24,160	6	77.9	Greater than 99%
Italy	$24,670	4	78.6	98.5%
Poor Countries				
Azerbaijan	$ 3,090	74	71.8	97.0%
Ghana	$ 2,250	57	57.7	72.7%
Pakistan	$ 1,890	84	60.4	44.0%
Cambodia	$ 1,860	97	57.4	68.7%
Sierra Leone	$ 470	182	34.5	36.0%

Sources: United Nations Development Programme, *Human Development Report 2003*, pp. 237–240 and 262–265.

TABLE 2
Average Annual Growth Rate of Output per Capita

Country	1948–1972	1972–1988	1988–1995	1995–2001
United States	2.2%	1.7%	1.0%	2.7%
United Kingdom	2.4	2.1	0.9	2.4
Canada	2.9	2.6	0.6	2.3
France	4.3	2.1	1.2	2.1
Italy	4.9	2.8	1.6	1.7
West Germany	5.7	2.2	1.3	1.3
Japan	8.2	3.3	2.1	0.9

Sources: Angus Maddison, *Phases of Capitalist Development* (Oxford: Oxford University Press, 1982); U.S. Census Bureau IDB Summary Demographic Data (*http://www.census.gov/ipc/www/idbsum.html*); and *Economic Report of the President*, 2002, Table B-112, and various World Bank publications. *Note:* Data for Germany includes West Germany only through 1995, and all of Germany from 1995 to 1999.

growth of full-employment output itself. The real payoff for government seemed to be in preventing recessions and depressions—in keeping the economy operating as close to its potential as possible.

All of that changed starting in the 1970s, and economic growth became a national and international preoccupation. Like most changes in perception and thought, this one was driven by experience. Table 2 tells the story. It gives the average yearly growth rates of real GDP per capita for the United States and some of our key trading partners.

Over most of the postwar period, output in the more prosperous industrialized countries (such as the United States, the United Kingdom, and Canada) grew by 2 or 3 percent per year, while output in the less wealthy ones—those with some catching up to do—grew even faster. But beginning in the mid-1970s, all of these nations saw their growth rates slip.

In the late 1990s and early 2000s, only the United States and the United Kingdom returned to their previous high rates of growth, while the other industrialized countries continued to grow more slowly than their historical averages.

Looking at the table, you might think that this slowing in growth was rather insignificant. Do the tiny differences between the pre-1972 and the post-1972 growth rates really matter? Indeed, they do. Recall our example a few chapters ago in which an increase in the U.S. growth rate of around 1 percentage point over the past 27 years would mean $27 trillion in additional output over the entire period. Seemingly small differences in growth rates matter a great deal.

WHAT MAKES ECONOMIES GROW?

A useful way to start thinking about long-run growth is to look at what determines our potential GDP in any given period. Starting this process is very simple: We can say that real GDP depends on

- The amount of output the average worker can produce in an hour
- The number of hours the average worker spends at the job
- The fraction of the population that is working
- The size of the population

If you spend a moment considering each of these variables, you'll see that—all else equal—if any one of them increases, real GDP rises.

Before we start working with these determinants of growth, let's briefly discuss how the first three are measured. The amount of output the average worker produces in an hour is called **labor productivity**, or just **productivity**. It is measured by taking the total output (real GDP) of the economy over a period of time and dividing by the total number of hours that *everyone* worked during that period.

Labor productivity The output produced by the average worker in an hour.

$$\text{Productivity} = \text{Output per hour} = \frac{\text{Total output}}{\text{Total hours worked}}.$$

For example, if during a given month all workers in the United States spent a total of 25 billion hours at their jobs and produced $1 trillion worth of output, then on average, labor productivity would be $1 trillion / 25 billion hours = $40 per hour. Or in words, the average worker would produce $40 worth of output in an hour. As you'll see later in this chapter, increases in productivity are one of the most important contributors to economic growth.

Next, the hours of the average worker can be found by dividing the total hours worked over a period by total employment—the *number* of people who worked during the period:

$$\text{Average Hours} = \frac{\text{Total hours}}{\text{Total employment}}.$$

For example, if total employment is 200 million people and they work a total of 25 billion hours per month, then average hours per month would be 25 billion hours / 200 million workers = 125 hours per month.

Now let's turn to the fraction of the population that is working. This is often called the **employment-population ratio (EPR)**, and is found by dividing total employment by the population:[2]

Employment-population ratio (EPR)

The fraction of the population that is working.

$$\text{EPR} = \text{Total Employment} / \text{Population}$$

Now that we understand how these variables are measured, let's multiply them together:

$$\text{Productivity} \times \text{Average Hours} \times \text{EPR} \times \text{Population} = \frac{\text{Total output}}{\text{Total hours}} \times \frac{\text{Total hours}}{\text{Total employment}}$$

$$\times \frac{\text{Total employment}}{\text{Population}} \times \text{Population}$$

$$= \text{Total output}$$

where the last equality follows after cancelling terms that appear in both a numerator and a denominator. Thus, we can write our equation for total output as:

$$\text{Total output} = \text{Productivity} \times \text{Average Hours} \times \text{EPR} \times \text{Population}.$$

Next, we'll borrow a rule from mathematics that states that if two variables A and B are multiplied together, then the percentage change in their product is approximately equal to the sum of their percentage changes. In symbols:

$$\%\Delta (A \times B) = \%\Delta A + \%\Delta B.$$

Applying this rule to all four variables in the right side of our equation, as well as to total output on the left, we find that the growth rate of total output over any period of time is

$$\%\Delta \text{ Total Output} = \%\Delta \text{ Productivity} + \%\Delta \text{ Average Hours} + \%\Delta \text{ EPR} + \%\Delta \text{ Population}.$$

Table 3 shows estimates of how each of these variables have contributed to output growth during different periods of recent U.S. history, as well as a six-year future projection. For example, the first column tells us that from 1960 to 1973, real GDP grew, on average, by 4.2 percent per year. Of that growth, 1.8 percentage points were due to a growing population, and 0.2 percentage points were due to a rise in the employment-population ratio. Average hours—which decreased during the period—contributed negatively to growth, reducing it by half of a percentage point. Finally, growth in labor productivity contributed 2.7 percentage points to GDP growth during this period.

Going across the rows and moving from period to period, you can see that almost all of the growth in real GDP over the last 42 years (and projected for the near future) has come from two factors: population growth and productivity growth. Although increases in the EPR have contributed small amounts to growth during some past periods, no such contribution is expected in the near future. And average hours, rather than contributing to growth, have actually decreased, and are expected to remain constant in the near future.

---

[2] In actual practice in the United States and many other countries, the EPR is the fraction of the *civilian, noninstitutional population over the age of 16* that is employed. We'll ignore this technical definition in our analysis, and consider the EPR to be the fraction of the entire population that is working.

Annual Percentage Growth in Real GDP Due to:	1960 to 1973	1973 to 1990	1990 to 2002	2002 to 2008 (projected)
Population	1.8	1.5	1.0	1.1
EPR	0.2	0.5	0.0	0.0
Average Hours	−0.5	−0.4	−0.1	0.0
Productivity	2.7	1.3	2.0	2.0
Total	4.2	2.9	2.9	3.2

TABLE 3
Factors Contributing to Growth in Real GDP

Source: Economic Report of the President, 2003, Table 1–2, p. 66 (http://w3.access.gpo.gov/eop/), and author calculations. (The Economic Report lists nonfarm business productivity only. In Table 2, annual productivity growth has been reduced by 0.1 to 0.2 percentage points in each period to account for slightly slower output growth in the combined government and farm sectors.)

Economic Growth and Living Standards

Ultimately, growth in real GDP—by itself—does not guarantee a rising standard of living. Imagine, for example, that real GDP grew by 10 percent over some period while the population doubled. With 10 percent more output divided among twice as many people, the average standard of living would clearly decrease even though real output was growing. What matters for the standard of living is *real GDP per capita*—our total output of goods and services *per person*.

To see more clearly what causes output per person to rise, let's go back to our basic growth equation:

$$\text{Total Output} = \text{Productivity} \times \text{Average Hours} \times \text{EPR} \times \text{Population}$$

If we divide both sides of this equation by the population, we get:

$$\frac{\text{Total Output}}{\text{Population}} = \text{Productivity} \times \text{Average Hours} \times \text{EPR}$$

And, in terms of percentage growth rates:

$$\%\Delta \text{ Total Output per person} = \%\Delta \text{ Productivity} + \%\Delta \text{ Average Hours} + \%\Delta \text{ EPR}.$$

Notice that population drops out of the equation. This tells us that the only way to raise the average standard of living is to increase productivity, increase average hours, or increase the employment population ratio.

But as we saw in Table 3, average hours in the United States have decreased over the past several decades, and are projected to remain constant for several years. In continental Europe, the decrease in average hours has been even greater. This is why we'll focus our discussion on the remaining two factors in our equation: the EPR and Productivity.

> *To explain growth in output per person and living standards in the United States and other developed nations, economists look at two factors: increases in the employment-population ratio and growth in productivity.*

Now it's time to look more closely at *how* these two factors raise the average standard of living. We'll start by considering increases in the employment-population ratio.

GROWTH IN THE EMPLOYMENT-POPULATION RATIO (EPR)

Over the long run, the employment-population ratio rises only when total employment increases at a faster rate than the population. For example, if total employment is 50 million out of a population of 100 million, then the EPR is 50 million / 100 million = 0.5. If both total employment and population grow by 10 percent over some period, then the EPR will become 55 million / 110 million = 0.5, the same as before. With population growth of 10 percent, total employment would have to grow by *more* than 10 percent in order for the EPR to rise and contribute to growth in living standards. If total employment were to grow by *less* than 10 percent, the EPR would fall, contributing to a drop in living standards.

If we treat the rate of population growth as a given, then the growth rate of total employment will determine the EPR. More specifically,

> *for a given growth rate of the population, the greater the growth of total employment, the greater the rise (or the smaller the drop) in the EPR.*

But what causes employment to grow?

To answer this question, look at Figure 1, which shows how total employment is determined in the economy. Notice that the labor market depicted in the figure differs from the labor market diagrams you studied in Chapter 9. That chapter dealt with *specific* labor markets, such as the market for elementary school teachers, computer systems analysts, or factory workers. Now we are studying *macro*economics, so we lump together all the different types of labor in the economy, in all the locations in the country, into a single aggregate variable—*labor*. In so doing, we are ignoring the differences between one type of labor and another. That is why, in Figure 1, the horizontal axis is labeled *millions of workers* rather than, say, millions of teachers. Similarly, the vertical axis measures the average real hourly wage in the economy, rather than the wage rate in some specific occupation.

For now, ignore the curve labeled L_2^S and focus on the other two curves: the labor supply curve L_1^S and the labor demand curve L^D. The initial equilibrium is at point A, with a real hourly wage of $15 and total employment of 100 million workers. What would cause total employment to rise higher than 100 million workers?

One possibility is an increase in labor *supply:* a rise in the number of people who would like to work at any given wage. This is illustrated in Figure 1 by the rightward shift in the labor supply curve to L_2^S. We'll discuss *why* the labor supply curve might shift later; here, we'll concentrate on the consequences of the shift. The wage drops to $12. Business firms, finding labor cheaper to hire, increase the number of workers employed along the labor demand curve, from point A to point B. Total employment increases to 120 million workers.

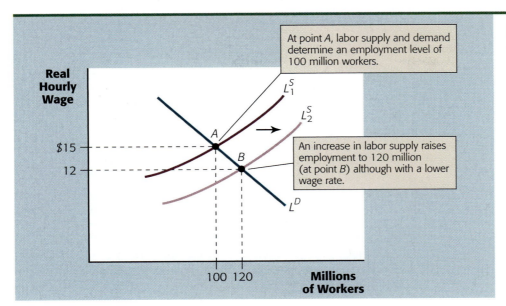

FIGURE 1
An Increase in Labor Supply

At point *A*, labor supply and demand determine an employment level of 100 million workers.

An increase in labor supply raises employment to 120 million (at point *B*) although with a lower wage rate.

But growth in employment can also arise from an increase in labor demand: a rise in the number of workers that firms would like to hire at any given wage. Once again, we'll consider the *causes* of labor demand changes momentarily; here, we focus on the *consequences*.

Graphically, an increase in labor demand is represented by a rightward shift in the labor demand curve, as in Figure 2. As the wage rate rises from $15 to its new equilibrium of $17, we move along the labor supply curve from point *A* to point *B*. More people decide they want to work as the wage rises. Equilibrium employment once again rises from 100 million to 120 million workers. Thus,

growth in employment can arise from an increase in labor supply (a rightward shift in the labor supply curve) or an increase in labor demand (a rightward shift of the labor demand curve).

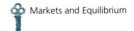 Markets and Equilibrium

You may have noticed one very important difference between the labor market outcomes in Figures 1 and 2: When labor *supply* increases, the wage rate falls (from $15 to $12 in Figure 1); when labor *demand* increases, the wage rate rises (from $15 to $17 in Figure 2). Which of the figures describes the actual experience of the U.S. labor market?

Actually, a combination of both: Over the past 50 years, for example, the U.S. labor supply curve has shifted steadily rightward, sometimes slowly, sometimes more rapidly. Why the shift in labor supply? In part, the reason has been steady population growth: The more people there are, the more will want to work at any wage. But another reason has been an important change in tastes: an increase in the desire of women (especially married women) to work.

Over the past 50 years, the labor demand curve has shifted rightward as well. Why? Throughout this period, firms have been acquiring more and better capital equipment for their employees to use. Managers and accountants now keep track of inventories and other important accounts with lightning-fast computer software

FIGURE 2
An Increase in Labor Demand

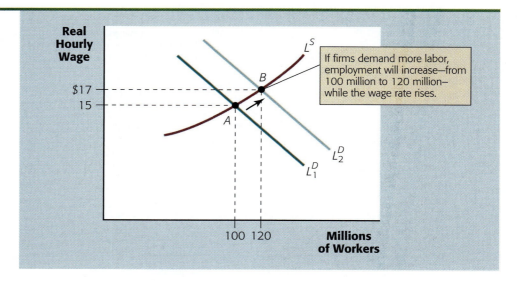

instead of account ledgers. Supermarket clerks use electronic scanners instead of hand-entry cash registers. And college professors or their research assistants now gather data by searching for a few hours on the Web instead of a few weeks in the library. At the same time, workers have become better educated and better trained. These changes have made workers more productive and more valuable to employers, so firms have wanted to hire more of them at any wage.

In fact, over time, increases in labor demand have outpaced increases in labor supply, so that, on balance, the average wage rate has risen and employment has increased. This is illustrated in Figure 3, which shows a shift in the labor supply curve from L_1^S to L_2^S, and an even greater shift in the labor demand curve from L_1^D to L_2^D.

The impact of these changes on total employment has been dramatic. Between 1948 and 2003, employment rose from 56 million to 139 million.

But what about the employment-population ratio? It did, in fact, rise—from 56 percent to 63 percent of the adult population. This tells us that employment grew *faster* than the population during this period. And as you've learned, this increase in the EPR causes not just real GDP, but real GDP *per capita*, to grow. However, most of the rise in the EPR was due to a special factor that is unlikely to be repeated: the greater labor force participation of women—especially married women—during the 1960s, 1970s, and 1980s. But in the 1990s—as female labor force participation stabilized—this source of growth disappeared.

Currently, the U.S. Bureau of Labor Statistics predicts employment growth of 1 percent per year until the year 2010—about the same as the growth rate of the population. Thus, the employment-population ratio is not expected to grow at all. Employment growth—while it will raise real GDP—will not increase real GDP per capita, and so will not contribute to a rise in living standards.

Can we do anything about this? Can we speed up the rightward shifts in the labor demand and labor supply curves over the next few years, so that employment grows faster than the 1 percent annual growth rate of the population? Yes, we can. But as you read on, keep in mind that these measures to increase employment are

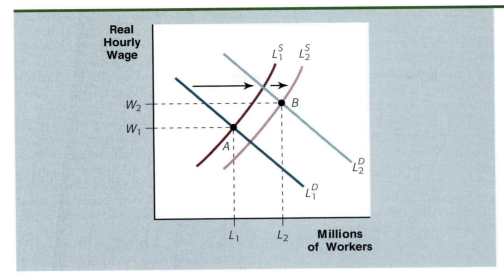

FIGURE 3
**The U.S. Labor Market
Over a Century**

*Over the past century, increases
in labor demand have outpaced
increases in supply. As a result,
both the level of employment
and the average wage have risen.*

not necessarily socially desirable. They would, most likely, accomplish the goal, but they would also have costs—costs that Americans may or may not be willing to pay. Later, we'll discuss these costs.

How to Increase Employment and the EPR

One set of policies to speed the rise in employment focuses on changing labor supply. And an often-proposed example of this type of policy is a decrease in income tax rates. Imagine that you have a professional degree in accounting, physical therapy, or some other field, and you are considering whether to take a job. Suppose the going rate for your professional services is $30 per hour. If your average tax rate is 33 percent, then one-third of your income will be taxed away, so your take-home pay would be only $20 per hour. But if your tax rate were cut to 20 percent, you would take home $24 per hour. Since you care about your take-home pay, you will respond to a tax cut in the same way you would respond to a wage increase—even if the wage your potential employer pays does not change at all. If you would be willing to take a job that offers a take-home pay of $24, but not one that offers $20, then the tax cut would be just what was needed to get you to seek work.

When we extend your reaction to the population as a whole, we can see that a cut in the income tax rate can convince more people to seek jobs at any given wage, shifting the labor supply curve rightward. This is why economists and politicians who focus on the economy's long-run growth often recommend lower taxes on labor income to encourage more rapid growth in employment. They point out that many American workers must pay combined federal, state, and local taxes of more than 40 cents out of each additional dollar they earn, and that this may be discouraging work effort in the United States.

Indeed, this was an important part of the logic behind the two tax cuts engineered by President Bush early in his administration. For example, the first tax cut, which Congress passed after much debate in June 2001, called for gradually reduced tax rates over 10 years. It reduced the cumulative tax burden on households by about $1.35 trillion over that period.

In addition to tax rate changes, some economists have advocated changes in government transfer programs to speed the growth in employment. They argue that the current structure of many government programs creates disincentives to work. For example, families receiving welfare payments, food stamps, unemployment benefits, and Social Security retirement payments all face steep losses in their benefits if they go to work or increase their work effort. Redesigning these programs might therefore stimulate growth in labor supply.

This reasoning was an important motive behind the sweeping reforms in the U.S. welfare system passed by Congress, and signed by President Clinton, in August 1996. Among other things, the reforms reduced the number of people who were eligible for benefits, cut the benefit amount for many of those still eligible, and set a maximum coverage period of five years for most welfare recipients. Later in this chapter, we'll discuss some of the *costs* of potentially growth-enhancing measures like this. Here, we only point out that changes in benefit programs have the potential to change labor supply.

> *A cut in tax rates increases the reward for working, while a cut in benefits to the needy increases the hardship of not working. Either policy can cause a greater rightward shift in the economy's labor supply curve than would otherwise occur, which can raise the employment population ratio and thereby raise output per person.*

Government policies can also affect the labor *demand* curve. In recent decades, subsidies for education and training, such as government-guaranteed loans for college students or special training programs for the unemployed, have helped to increase the skills of the labor force and made workers more valuable to potential employers. Government also subsidizes employment more directly—by contributing part of the wage when certain categories of workers are hired—the disabled, college work-study participants, and, in some experimental programs, inner-city youth. By enlarging these programs, government could increase the number of workers hired at any given wage and thus shift the labor demand curve to the right:

> *Government policies that help increase the skills of the workforce or that subsidize employment more directly can cause a greater rightward shift in the labor demand curve than would otherwise occur, which can raise the employmant-population ratio and thereby raise output per person.*

Efforts to create growth in the employment-population ratio are controversial. In recent decades, those who prefer an activist government have favored policies to increase labor *demand* through government-sponsored training programs, more aid to college students, employment subsidies to firms, and similar programs. Those who prefer a more *laissez-faire* approach have generally favored policies to increase the labor *supply* by *decreasing* government involvement—lower taxes or a less generous social safety net.

GROWTH IN PRODUCTIVITY

Our analysis of growth began with an equation explaining how total output is determined. Then—one by one—we eliminated variables that could not explain growth in total output—and living standards—over the long run. First, we ruled out population growth, based on the logic of the equation for total output per person. Second, we ruled out growth in average hours, based on the past and projected future behavior of this variable. And in the previous section, we saw that while various government policies could be used to raise the employment population ratio, significant, sustained increases in the EPR are neither projected nor likely in the near future. So only one variable remains: productivity.

If you look back at Table 3, you'll see that growth in productivity has been responsible for most of the growth in real GDP over the last 42 years. (The period from 1973 to 1990, when population growth took the lead, is the exception.) And as you've learned, population growth—while it can raise real GDP—cannot raise real GDP *per capita*. If we restrict ourselves to the three factors in Table 3 that *can* raise real GDP per capita, we see that

> over the past several decades, and into the near future, virtually all growth in the average standard of living can be attributed to growth in productivity.

Not surprisingly, when economists analyze rising living standards, they think first and foremost about growth in productivity.

Table 3 shows that productivity is expected to grow at about 2 percent during most of the 2000s. Can we do anything to make it grow even faster?

HTTP://
Paul Bauer's "Are We in a Productivity Boom?" provides a more in-depth exploration of recent U.S. productivity experience. It's available at **http://www.clev.frb.org/ research/com99/1015.htm**.

Growth in the Capital Stock

One key to productivity growth is the nation's capital stock or, more precisely, the amount of capital available for the average worker in the economy. You can dig more ditches with a shovel than with your hands, and even more with a backhoe. And the economy can produce more automobiles, medical services, and education when the average employee in these industries has more machinery, technical equipment, and computers to work with.

A rise in **capital per worker**—the total capital stock divided by the total number of workers—results in greater productivity. But capital *per worker* increases only if the nation's total capital stock grows *faster* than the workforce.

Capital per worker The total capital stock divided by total employment.

> All else equal, if the capital stock grows faster than total employment, then capital per worker will rise, and labor productivity will increase along with it. But if the capital stock grows more slowly than total employment, then capital per worker will fall, and labor productivity will fall as well.

In the United States and most other developed countries, the capital stock has grown more rapidly than employment. As a result, labor productivity has risen over time. But in some developing countries, the capital stock has grown at about the same rate as, or even more slowly than the workforce, and labor productivity has remained stagnant or fallen. We will return to this problem in the "Using the Theory" section of this chapter.

Investment and the Capital Stock

What determines how fast the capital stock rises, and whether it will rise faster than total employment? The answer is: the rate of *planned investment spending* in the economy. Investment spending and the capital stock are related to each other, but they are different *kinds* of variables. Specifically, capital is a *stock* variable while investment spending is a *flow* variable.

> A **stock variable** measures a quantity at a moment in time. A **flow variable** measures a process over a period of time.

Stock variable a variable measuring a quantity at a moment in time.

Flow variable a variable measuring a *process* over some period of time.

To use an analogy, think of a bathtub being filled with water. The water *in* the tub is a stock variable—so many gallons at any given moment. The water *flowing into* the tub is a flow variable—so many gallons *per minute* or *per hour*. You can always identify a flow variable by the addition of "per period" in its definition. Even when not explicitly stated, some period of time is always implied in a flow variable.

Now let's think about capital again. The capital stock—the total amount of plant and equipment that exists in the economy—is like the quantity of water *in* the tub. It can be measured at any given moment. Investment spending—the amount of *new* capital being installed over some time interval—is like the water flowing *into* the tub. Investment spending is defined *per period*—such as *per quarter* or *per year*. In the simplest terms, investment spending *adds* to the capital stock over time.

But there is one more flow involved in the capital-investment relationship: *depreciation*. Each period, some of the capital stock is used up. If a computer is expected to last only three years, for example, then each year the computer depreciates by about a third of its initial value. Depreciation tends to *reduce* the capital stock over time. (In our tub analogy, depreciation is like the flow of water draining *out* each period.) *As long as investment is greater than depreciation* (more water flows into the tub than drains out), *the capital stock will rise.* Moreover, for any rate of depreciation, the greater the flow of investment spending, the faster the rise in the capital stock.

Pulling all of this together leads us to an important conclusion about investment spending and the capital stock:

> For a given rate of depreciation and a given growth rate of total employment, a higher rate of investment spending causes faster growth in capital per worker and productivity, and faster growth in the average standard of living.

This is why when economists think about raising productivity via the capital stock, they focus on raising the rate of investment spending.

Can the government do anything to raise investment by business firms? Actually, it can, and it has many methods from which to choose. In order to understand how investment spending is determined and how economic policy can increase it, we must first take a detour and explore an important market in the macroeconomy: the market for loanable funds.

The Loanable Funds Market

Loanable funds market The market in which business firms obtain funds for investment.

The **loanable funds market** is where business firms obtain funds for investment. When Avis wants to add cars to its automobile rental fleet, when McDonald's wants to build a new beef-processing plant, or when the local dry cleaner wants to buy new dry-cleaning machines, it will likely raise the funds in the loanable funds market. Firms may take out bank loans, sell bonds, or sell new shares of stock. In all of these cases, they are going to the loanable funds market as *demanders* of funds. Thus, the total amount of funds demanded by firms is equal to their investment purchases.[3]

Where do the funds that business firms demand come from? Largely from household saving. When you save—that is, when you have income left over after paying taxes and buying consumption goods—you will do *something* with your surplus funds. You might put your funds in a bank, or buy bonds or shares of stock. In any of these cases, you would be a *supplier* of funds.

Our picture of the loanable funds market would be very simple if this were all there was to it. We would have firms demanding funds for investment, and households supplying them. But there is one more sector involved in this market: the government.

The government acts as a *demander* of funds when it runs a **budget deficit**—that is, when its tax revenue is not sufficient to pay for its total outlays (on final goods and services as well as transfer payments). After all, if the government cannot meet its bills with the tax revenue it has collected, it must get the funds from somewhere. By law, it has no choice: It must *borrow* the money (demand loanable funds) by issuing U.S. government bonds.[4]

We can summarize our view of the loanable funds market so far with the following two points:

> • *The supply of funds is equal to household saving.*
> • *The demand for funds is equal to the business sector's investment spending and the government sector's budget deficit (if any).*

There is just one more piece of the puzzle to discuss before we analyze the loanable funds market more formally. Those who supply funds—households, in our model—receive a reward for doing so. Those who demand funds—business firms and the government—must pay this reward. When funds are transferred from suppliers to demanders via banks or the bond market, the funds are *loaned* and the payment is called *interest*. When the funds are transferred via the stock market, the suppliers become part owners of the firm and their payment is called *dividends*. To keep our discussion simple, we'll assume that all funds transferred are loaned and that the payment is simply interest.

> • *Demanders of funds pay interest to suppliers of funds.*

The Supply of Funds Curve. Since interest is the reward for saving and supplying funds to the loanable funds market, a rise in the interest rate *increases* the quantity of funds supplied (household saving). Similarly, a drop in the interest rate should decrease it. This relationship is illustrated by the upward-sloping **supply of funds curve** in Figure 4. When the interest rate is 3 percent, households save $1.5 trillion, and if the interest rate rises to 5 percent, saving (and the supply of funds) rises to $1.75 trillion.

Budget deficit The amount by which the government's total outlays (on goods, services, and transfer payments) exceeds its total tax revenue.

Supply of funds curve Indicates the level of household saving at each interest rate.

---

[3] By making this assumption, we are ignoring investment purchases that firms make with their own funds. But with a slight reinterpretation, even this source of investment spending can be included in the demand for loanable funds. The firm that finances its investment spending with its own funds can be regarded as both supplying funds to the market and then demanding them for itself.

[4] When total tax revenue is greater than total government outlays, the difference between them is called the government's *budget surplus*. When the government runs a surplus—as it did during the late 1990s—the government becomes a *supplier* of loanable funds, along with households.

FIGURE 4
Household Supply of
Loanable Funds

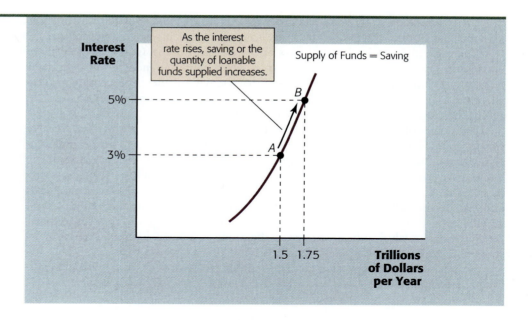

The quantity of funds supplied to the loanable funds market depends positively on the interest rate. This is why the saving, or supply of funds, curve slopes upward.

Of course, other things can affect saving besides the interest rate—tax rates, expectations about the future, and the general willingness of households to postpone consumption, to name a few. In drawing the supply of funds curve, we hold each of these variables constant. In the next section, we'll explore what happens when some of these variables change.

The Demand for Funds Curve. Like saving, investment also depends on the interest rate. This is because businesses buy plant and equipment when the expected benefits of doing so exceed the costs. Since businesses obtain the funds for their investment spending from the loanable funds market, a key cost of any investment project is the interest rate that must be paid on borrowed funds. As the interest rate rises and investment costs increase, fewer projects will look attractive, and investment spending will decline. This is the logic of the downward-sloping **business demand for funds curve** in Figure 5. At a 5-percent interest rate, firms would borrow $1 trillion and spend it on capital equipment; at an interest rate of 3 percent, business borrowing and investment spending would rise to $1.5 trillion.

Business demand for funds curve
Indicates the level of investment spending by firms at each interest rate.

When the interest rate falls, investment spending and the business borrowing needed to finance it rise. The investment demand curve slopes downward.

What about the government's demand for funds? Will it, too, be influenced by the interest rate? Probably not very much. Government seems to be cushioned from the cost–benefit considerations that haunt business decisions. Any company president who ignored interest rates in deciding how much to borrow would be quickly out of a job. U.S. presidents and legislators do so for years with little political cost.

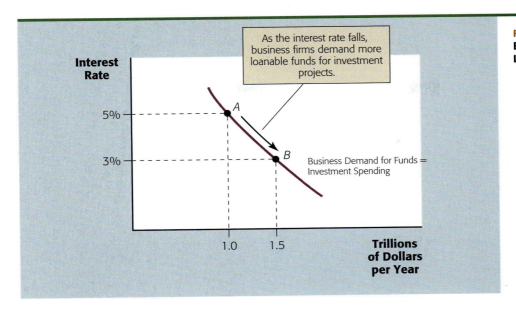

As the interest rate falls, business firms demand more loanable funds for investment projects.

Interest Rate

5% — A

3% — B

Business Demand for Funds = Investment Spending

1.0   1.5

Trillions of Dollars per Year

FIGURE 5
Business Demand for Loanable Funds

For this reason, we can treat government borrowing as independent of the interest rate: No matter what the interest rate, the government sector's deficit—and its borrowing—remain constant. This is why we have graphed the **government demand for funds curve** as a vertical line in panel (b) of Figure 6.

Government demand for funds curve Indicates the amount of governmental borrowing at each interest rate.

> *The government sector's deficit and, therefore, its demand for funds are independent of the interest rate.*

In the figure, the government deficit—and hence the government's demand for funds—is equal to $0.75 trillion at any interest rate.

In panel (c) of Figure 6, the **total demand for funds curve** is found by horizontally summing the business demand curve (panel [a]) and the government demand curve (panel [b]). For example, if the interest rate is 5 percent, firms demand $1 trillion in funds, and the government demands $0.75 trillion, so that the total quantity of loanable funds demanded is $1.75 trillion. A drop in the interest rate—to 3 percent—increases business borrowing to $1.5 trillion, while the government's borrowing remains at $0.75 trillion, so the total demand for funds rises to $2.25 trillion.

Total demand for funds curve Indicates the total amount of borrowing at each interest rate.

> *As the interest rate decreases, the quantity of funds demanded by business firms increases, while the quantity demanded by the government remains unchanged. Therefore, the total quantity of funds demanded rises.*

Equilibrium in the Loanable Funds Market. In the loanable funds market—like other markets—we can expect the price to adjust until quantity demanded and quantity supplied are equal. In this case, the price of funds—the interest rate—will rise or fall until the quantities of loanable funds supplied by households and the quantity demanded by firms and the government are equal. In Figure 7, which combines the supply and demand curves together, equilibrium occurs at point E, with an interest rate of 5 percent and total saving equal to $1.75 trillion. But notice that we can also read investment off of the graph: The investment curve (the thinner

 Markets and Equilibrium

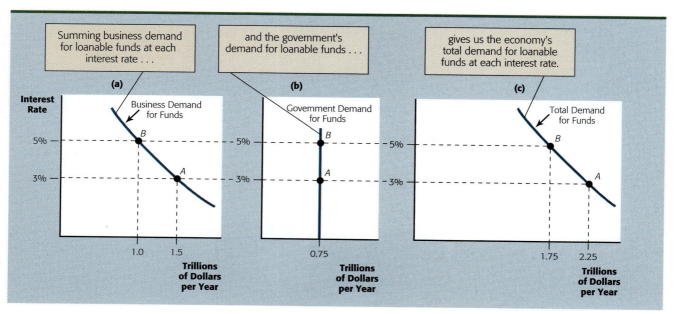

FIGURE 6
The Total Demand for Funds

FIGURE 7
Loanable Funds
Market Equilibrium

*Suppliers and demanders of
funds interact to determine the
interest rate in the loanable
funds market. The equilibrium
occurs at point E, where the
supply and demand for funds
curves intersect. The equilibrium interest rate is 5%, and
the equilibrium quantity of
funds supplied and demanded
is equal to $1.75 trillion.*

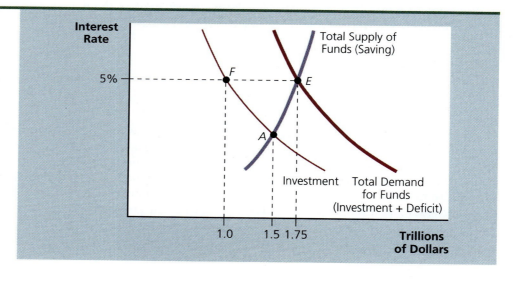

line) tells us that when the interest rate is 5%, investment spending is equal to $1.0
trillion. That is, of the total $1.75 billion saved, $1 trillion goes to business firms
for capital purchases and $0.75 trillion goes to the government to cover its deficit.

Don't be confused by point *A* in the figure. It shows us where the equilibrium in
the loanable funds market *would* be if there were no budget deficit. In that case, the
thin red line representing business borrowing would be the *total* demand for loanable funds, the interest rate would equal 3%, and investment spending would be
$1.5 trillion. But as long as the government is borrowing funds as well as firms,
point *A* is not the equilibrium. We'll come back to this idea again a bit later when
we explore the effects of the budget deficit on investment spending.

Figure 7 is important because it shows us just how the level of investment spending is determined in the loanable funds market. But it also gives us a framework for analyzing policies designed to *increase* investment, speed the growth of the capital stock, and make our living standards grow faster.

How to Increase Investment

A government seeking to spur investment has more than one weapon in its arsenal. It can direct its efforts toward businesses themselves, toward the household sector, or toward its own budget.

Targeting Businesses: Increasing the Incentive to Invest. One kind of policy to increase investment targets the business sector itself, with the goal of increasing planned investment spending. Figure 8 shows how this works. The figure shows a simplified view of the loanable funds market where—to focus on investment—we assume that there is no budget deficit, so there is no government demand for funds. The initial equilibrium in the market is at point *A*, where household saving (the supply of funds) and investment (the demand for funds) are both equal to $1.5 trillion and the interest rate is 3 percent. Now suppose that the government takes steps to make investment more profitable, so that—at any interest rate—firms will want to purchase $0.75 trillion more in capital equipment than before. Then the investment curve would shift rightward by $0.75 trillion and the interest rate would rise from 3 percent to 5 percent. Note that, as the interest rate rises, some—but not all—of the original increase in planned investment is choked off. In the end, investment rises from $1.5 trillion to $1.75 trillion, and so each year $0.25 trillion more is added to the capital stock than would otherwise be added.

These are the mechanics of a rightward shift in the investment curve. But what government measures would *cause* such a shift in the first place? That is, how could the government help to make investment spending more profitable for firms?

One such measure would be a reduction in the **corporate profits tax**, which would allow firms to keep more of the profits they earn from investment projects.

Corporate profits tax A tax on the profits earned by corporations.

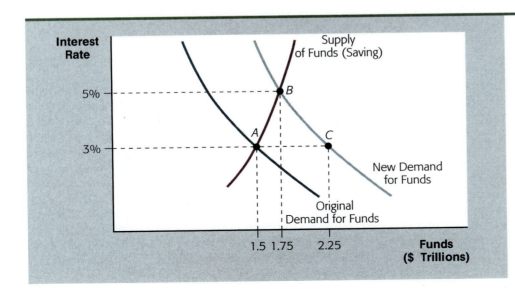

FIGURE 8
An Increase in Investment Spending

Government policies that make investment more profitable will increase investment spending at each interest rate. The resulting rightward shift of the investment demand curve leads to a higher level of investment spending, at point B.

Investment tax credit A reduction in taxes for firms that invest in new capital.

Another, even more direct, policy is an **investment tax credit,** which subsidizes corporate investment in new capital equipment.

> *Reducing business taxes or providing specific investment incentives can shift the investment curve rightward, thereby speeding growth in physical capital, and increasing the growth rate of living standards.*

Of course, the same reasoning applies in reverse: An *increase* in the corporate profits tax or the *elimination* of an investment tax credit would shift the investment curve to the left, slowing the rate of investment, the growth of the capital stock, and the rise in living standards.

Targeting Households: Increasing the Incentive to Save.

While firms purchase new capital, it is largely households that supply the funds, via personal saving. Thus, an increase in investment spending can originate in the household sector, through an increase in the desire to save. This is illustrated in Figure 9. If households decide to save more of their incomes at any given interest rate, the supply of funds curve will shift rightward. The increase in saving drives down the interest rate, from 5 percent to 3 percent, which, in turn, causes investment to increase. With a lower interest rate, NBC might decide to borrow funds to build another production studio, or the corner grocery store may decide to borrow the funds it needs for a new electronic scanner at the checkout stand. In this way, an increase in the desire to save is translated, via the loanable funds market, into an increase in investment and faster growth in the capital stock.

What might cause households to increase their saving? The answer is found in the reasons people save in the first place. And to understand these reasons, you needn't look farther than yourself or your own family. You might currently be saving for a large purchase (a car, a house, a vacation, college tuition) or to build a financial cushion in case of hard times ahead. You might even be saving to support yourself during retirement, though this is a distant thought for most college students.

Given these motives, what would make you save *more*? Several things: greater uncertainty about your economic future, an increase in your life expectancy, anticipation of an earlier retirement, a change in tastes toward big-ticket items, or even just a change in your attitude about saving. Any of these changes—if they occurred in many households simultaneously—would shift the saving curve (the supply of funds curve) to the right, as in Figure 9.

Capital gains tax A tax on profits earned when a financial asset is sold for more than its acquisition price.

But government policy can increase household saving as well. One way is to decrease the **capital gains tax.** A capital gain is the profit you earn when you sell an asset, such as a share of stock or a bond, at a higher price than you paid for it. By lowering the special tax rate for capital gains, households would be able to keep more of the capital gains they earn. As a result, stocks and bonds would become more rewarding to own, and you might decide to reduce your current spending in order to buy them. If other households react in the same way, total saving would rise, and the supply of funds to the loanable funds market would increase.

This was the logic behind a key component of the Bush administration's second tax cut, signed into law in May 2003. The tax cut included a reduction in the capital gains tax, from 20 percent to 15 percent for higher income households, and from 10 percent to 5 percent (and down to 0% in 2008) for lower income households. The lower tax rates applied only to *long-term* capital gains—gains on assets held for a year or longer—to encourage people to put their funds into stocks and other assets and keep them there, rather than engage in short-term speculation.

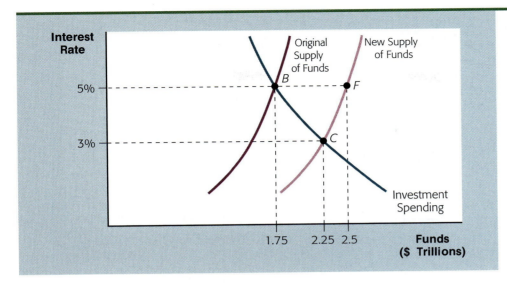

FIGURE 9
An Increase in Saving

If households decide to save more of their incomes, the supply of funds will increase. With more funds available, the interest rate will fall. Businesses will respond by increasing their borrowing, and investment will increase from $1.75 trillion to $2.25 trillion.

The 2003 tax cut on capital gains was controversial for two reasons. First, there was an equity issue: since most of the capital gains in the economy are earned by higher income households, this part of the tax cut benefited high-income households more than low-income households. Second, the government was already running a substantial budget deficit in 2003, and the tax cuts threatened to raise it further. As you'll see in the next section, higher budget deficits can work *against* economic growth.

Another frequently proposed measure is to switch from the current U.S. income tax—which taxes all income whether it is spent or saved—to a **consumption tax,** which would tax only the income that households spend. A consumption tax could work just like the current income tax, except that you would deduct your saving from your income and pay taxes on the remainder. This would increase the reward for saving. By saving, you would earn additional interest on the part of your income that would have been taxed away under an income tax. Currently, individual retirement accounts, or IRAs, allow households to deduct limited amounts of saving from their incomes before paying taxes. A general consumption tax would go much further and allow *all* saving to be deducted.

Another proposal to increase household saving is to restructure the U.S. Social Security system, which provides support for retired workers who have contributed funds to the system during their working years. Because Social Security encourages people to rely on the government for income during retirement, they have less incentive to save for retirement themselves. One proposed restructuring would link workers' Social Security benefits to their actual contributions to the system, whereas under the current system some people receive benefits worth far more than the amount they have contributed.

Consumption tax A tax on the part of their income that households spend.

Government can alter the tax and transfer system to increase incentives for saving. If successful, these policies would make more funds available for investment, speed growth in the capital stock, and speed the rise in living standards.

FIGURE 10

Deficit Reduction and Investment Spending

Eliminating the government's budget deficit will reduce government borrowing in the loanable funds market. As a result, the total demand for funds will fall, as will the interest rate. At a lower interest rate, businesses will increase their investment spending from $1 trillion (point E) to $1.5 trillion (point B).

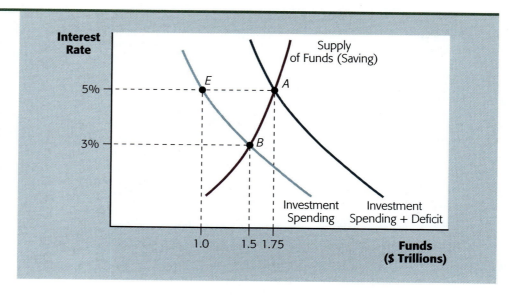

(Do any of these methods of increasing saving disturb you? Remember, we are not advocating any measures here; rather, we are merely noting that such measures would increase saving and promote economic growth. We'll discuss the *costs* of growth-promoting measures later.)

Targeting the Government's Budget Deficit. A final pro-investment measure is directed at the government sector itself. Figure 10 reintroduces the government to the loanable funds market to show how this works. Initially, the government is running a deficit of $0.75 trillion, equal to the distance *EA*. The total demand for funds is now the sum of investment and the government's budget deficit, given by the curve labeled "Investment Spending + Deficit." The demand for funds curve intersects the supply of funds curve at point *A*, creating an equilibrium interest rate of 5 percent and equilibrium saving of $1.75 trillion. At this interest rate, investment spending is only $1 trillion. The part of saving not going to finance investment spending ($1.75 trillion − $1 trillion = $0.75 trillion) is being used to finance the budget deficit.

Now consider what happens if the government eliminates the deficit—say, by reducing its purchases by $0.75 trillion. The demand for funds would consist of investment spending only. Since there would be no other borrowing, the new equilibrium would be point *B*, with an interest rate of 3 percent and investment equal to $1.5 trillion—greater than before. By balancing its budget, the government no longer needs to borrow in the loanable funds market, which frees up funds to flow to the business sector instead.

The link between the government budget, the interest rate, and investment spending is the major reason why the U.S. government, and governments around the world, try to reduce and, if possible, eliminate budget deficits. They have learned that

a shrinking deficit tends to reduce interest rates and increase investment, thus speeding the growth in the capital stock.

In the 1990s, Congress set strict limits on the growth of government spending, and the budget deficit began shrinking. The restraints on spending, and rapid economic growth during the 1990s, finally turned the federal budget from deficit to surplus in 1998, and continued surpluses were projected for more than a decade. These surpluses were viewed as positive for economic growth: They would help keep the interest rate low, which in turn would lead to greater business investment spending.

When President George W. Bush took office in 2001, the direction of growth policy shifted away from preserving budget surpluses and toward lower tax rates. The first Bush tax cut in 2001(a total of $1.35 trillion over 10 years) purposely cut into potential future surpluses in order to reduce the tax burden on American households. Shortly afterward, a series of events pushed the budget into deficit. These included a continuing recession that had begun in March 2001 and the attacks of September 11, which resulted in large increases in military and homeland security spending. And a second tax cut in 2003—amounting to $350 billion over 10 years—increased current and projected deficits further.

The tax cuts included some elements (discussed earlier) to increase investment spending, such as a lower tax rate for capital gains and tax incentives for investment by small businesses. Also, you've learned that cutting income tax rates can have some effect on employment by shifting the labor supply curve rightward. But the tax cuts—by raising current and future budget deficits—would ultimately drive the interest rate higher than it would otherwise be, which works in opposition to the growth benefits of the tax cuts.

An Important Proviso About the Government Budget. A reduction in the budget deficit—even if it stimulates private investment—is not *necessarily* a pro-growth measure. It depends on *how* the budget changes. By an increase in taxes? A cut in government spending? And if the latter, which government programs will be cut? Welfare? National defense? Highway repair? The answers can make a big difference to the impact on growth.

For example, in our discussions of the capital stock so far, we've ignored government capital—roads, communication lines, bridges, and dams. To understand the importance of government capital, just imagine what life would be like without it. How would factories obtain their raw materials or distribute their goods if no one repaired the roads? How would contracts between buyers and sellers be enforced if there were no public buildings to house courts and police departments? As you learned in Chapter 10, government capital supports private economic activity in many ways.

> *Government investment in new capital and in the maintenance of existing capital makes an important contribution to economic growth.*

This important observation complicates our view of deficit reduction. It is still true that a decrease in government spending will lower the interest rate and increase private investment. But if the budget cutting falls largely on government investment, the negative effect of smaller public investment will offset some of the positive impact of greater private investment. Shrinking the deficit will then alter the *mix* of capital—more private and less public—and the effect on growth could go either way.

A society rife with lawlessness, deteriorating roads and bridges, or an unreliable communications network might benefit from a shift toward public capital. For example, a study of public budgets in African nations—which have poor road conditions—found that each one-dollar-per-year cut in the road-maintenance budget increased vehicle operating costs by between $2 and $3 per year, and in one case, by as much as $22 per year.[5] This is an example of a cut in government spending that, even if it reduces the deficit, probably hinders growth. By contrast, in Sweden—a country with a fully developed and well-maintained public infrastructure—recent governments have decided to shift the mix away from public and toward private capital, in part because they believed this would speed growth.

> *The impact of deficit reduction on economic growth depends on which government programs are cut. Shrinking the deficit by cutting government investment will not stimulate growth as much as would cutting other types of government spending.*

Human Capital and Economic Growth

So far, the only type of capital we've discussed is physical capital—the plant and equipment workers use to produce output. But when we think of the capital stock most broadly, we include *human capital* as well. *Human capital*—the skills and knowledge possessed by workers—is as central to economic growth as is physical capital. After all, most types of physical capital—computers, CAT scanners, and even shovels—will contribute little to output unless workers know how to use them. And when more workers gain skills or improve their existing skills, output rises just as it does when workers have more physical capital:

> *An increase in human capital works like an increase in physical capital to raise productivity, and increase the average standard of living.*

College-level courses are one important way that countries increase the stock of human capital.

Human capital investments are made by business firms (when they help to train their employees), by government (through public education and subsidized training), and by households (when they pay for general education or professional training). Human capital investments have played an important role in recent U.S. economic growth. Can we do anything to increase our rate of investment in human capital?

In part, we've already answered this question: Some of the same policies that increase investment in *physical* capital also work to raise investment in human capital. For example, a decrease in the budget deficit would lower the interest rate and make it cheaper for households to borrow for college loans and training programs. A change in the tax system that increases the incentive to save would have the same impact, since this, too, would lower interest rates. And an easing of the tax burden on business firms could increase the profitability of *their* human capital investments, leading to more and better worker training programs.

But there is more: Human capital, unlike physical capital, cannot be separated from the person who provides it. If you own a building, you can rent it out to one firm and sell your labor to another. But if you have training as a doctor, your labor and your human capital must be sold together, as a package. Moreover, your wage or salary will be payment for both your labor and your human capital. This means that income tax reductions—which we discussed earlier as a means of increasing labor supply—can also increase the profitability of human capital to households, and increase their rate of investment in their own skills and training. For example, sup-

---

[5] This World Bank study was cited in *The Economist*, June 10, 1995, p. 72.

pose an accountant is considering whether to attend a course in corporate financial reporting, which would increase her professional skills. The course costs $4,000, and will increase the accountant's income by $1,000 per year for the rest of her career. With a tax rate of 40 percent, her take-home pay would increase by $600 per year, so her annual rate of return on her investment would be $600/$4,000 = 15 percent. But with a lower tax rate—say, 20 percent—her take-home pay would rise by $800 per year, so her rate of return would be $800/$4,000 = 20 percent. The lower the tax rate, the greater is the rate of return on our accountant's human capital investment, and the more likely she will be to acquire new skills. Thus,

many of the pro-growth policies discussed earlier—policies that increase employment or increase investment in physical capital—are also effective in promoting investment in human capital.

Technological Change

So far, we've discussed how economic growth arises from greater quantities of resources—more labor, more physical capital, or more human capital. But another important source of growth is **technological change**—the invention or discovery of new inputs, new outputs, or new methods of production. Indeed, it is largely because of technological change that Malthus's horrible prediction (cited at the beginning of this chapter) has not come true. In the last 60 years, for example, the inventions of synthetic fertilizers, hybrid corn, and chemical pesticides have enabled world food production to increase faster than population.

Technological change The invention or discovery of new inputs, new outputs, or new production methods.

New technology affects the economy in much the same way as does an increase in capital per worker: it raises labor productivity. In many cases, the new technology requires the acquisition of physical and human capital before it can be used. For example, a new technique for destroying kidney stones with ultrasound, rather than time-consuming surgery, can make doctors more productive—but not until they spend several thousand dollars to buy the ultrasound machine and take a course on how to use it. Similarly, the recent development of the Internet has enabled many businesses—both big and small—to order supplies and market their products using less labor time and other resources than ever before. But they can't take advantage of this technology until they purchase computer equipment and their employees learn how to master the operation of both hardware and software.

In some instances, however, a new technology can be used without any additional equipment or training, as when a factory manager discovers a more efficient way to organize workers on the factory floor. In either case, technological change will increase productivity. It follows that

the faster the rate of technological change, the greater the growth rate of productivity, and the faster the rise in living standards.

It might seem that technological change is one of those things that just happens. Thomas Edison invents electricity, or Steve Jobs and Steve Wozniak develop the first practical personal computer in their garage. But the pace of technological change is not as haphazard as it seems. The transistor was invented as part of a massive research and development effort by AT&T to improve the performance of communications electronics. Similarly, the next developments in computer technology, transportation, and more will depend on how much money is spent on research and development (R&D) by the leading technology firms:

> *The rate of technological change in the economy depends largely on firms'*
> *total spending on R&D. Policies that increase R&D spending will increase*
> *the pace of technological change.*

Patent protection A government grant of exclusive rights to use or sell a new technology.

What can the government do to increase spending on R&D? First, it can increase its own direct support for R&D by carrying out more research in its own laboratories or increasing funding for universities and tax incentives to private research labs.

Second, the government can enhance **patent protection,** which increases rewards for those who create new technology by giving them exclusive rights to use it or sell it. For example, when the DuPont Corporation discovered a unique way to manufacture Spandex, it obtained a patent to prevent other firms from copying its technique. This patent has enabled DuPont to earn millions of dollars from its invention. Without the patent, other firms would have copied the technique, competed with DuPont, and taken much of its profit away. Hundreds of thousands of new patents are issued every year in the United States: to pharmaceutical companies for new prescription drugs, to telecommunications companies for new cellular technologies, and to the producers of a variety of household goods ranging from can openers to microwave ovens.

Since patent protection increases the rewards that developers can expect from new inventions, it encourages them to spend more on R&D. By broadening patent protection—issuing patents on a wider variety of discoveries—or by lengthening patent protection—increasing the number of years during which the developer has exclusive rights to market the invention—the government could increase the expected profits from new technologies. That would increase total spending on R&D and increase the pace of technological change. Currently in the United States, patents give inventors and developers exclusive marketing rights over their products for a period of about 20 years. Increasing patent protection to 30 years would certainly increase R&D spending at many firms.

Finally, R&D spending is in many ways just like other types of investment spending: The funds are drawn from the loanable funds market, and R&D programs require firms to buy something now (laboratories, the services of research scientists, materials to build prototypes) for the uncertain prospect of profits in the future. Therefore, almost any policy that stimulates investment spending in general will also increase spending on R&D. Cutting the tax rate on capital gains or on corporate profits, or lowering interest rates by encouraging greater saving or by reducing the budget deficit, can each help to increase spending on R&D and increase the rate of technological change.

GROWTH POLICIES: A SUMMARY

In this chapter, you've learned about the forces that affect the economy's economic growth, as well as a host of government policies that can speed the economy's growth rate. If you are having trouble keeping it all straight, Table 4—which summarizes all of this information—might help.

As you look at the table, you may notice something interesting: Some of the policies that work to *increase* economic growth through one channel can simultaneously work *against* growth through another channel. For example, in the first

Source of Growth	Method		Examples of Pro-Growth Government Policies
Increase in Employment-Population Ratio	Rightward shift in labor supply curve		• Lower income tax rates • Less generous transfer payments
	Rightward shift in labor demand curve		• Subsidized college loans • Subsidized training for the unemployed • Programs that target specific types of workers (e.g., disabled, inner-city youth)
Growth in Physical Capital Stock (Productivity Growth)	Rightward shift in investment demand curve		• Investment tax credit • Lower corporate profits tax
	Lower interest rate . . .	via rightward shift in saving curve	• Tax incentives for saving • Changes in Social Security system • Lower capital gains tax
		via decrease in budget deficit (or increase in budget surplus)	• Cuts in government purchases • Cuts in transfer payments • Tax increase
Growth in Human Capital Stock (Productivity Growth)	Lower interest rate . . .	(see above)	• Any policy (above) that lowers the interest rate
	Other methods to make human capital investment more attractive		• Lower income tax rates • Subsidized student loans • Tax incentives for investment in human capital
Technological Progress (Productivity Growth)	Lower interest rate . . .	(see above)	• Any policy (above) that lowers the interest rate
	Other methods to make investment in R & D more profitable		• Investment tax credit for R&D • Lower corporate profits tax • Expansion of patent protection

TABLE 4
Factors That Influence Growth in Output per Capita

row of the table, you can see that a *decrease* in income tax rates contributes to growth by increasing employment. But farther down, you'll see that an *increase* in taxes can aid growth by shrinking a budget deficit (implying that a *decrease* in taxes would have the opposite effect and harm growth). Thus, a decrease in tax rates simultaneously helps growth through one channel and harms growth through another.

The fact that a single policy can have two competing effects on the economy helps us understand one reason for controversy in macroeconomic policy. When we cut income taxes, for example, the ultimate effect on economic growth will depend on which of the two effects is stronger, something over which economists can and do disagree. This is why the Bush tax cuts in 2001 and 2003 were seen by some observers as growth-enhancing measures (those who stressed the impact of tax cuts on employment and investment) and by others as harmful to economic growth (those who stressed the budget deficit's effect on interest rates and investment).

THE COSTS OF ECONOMIC GROWTH

So far in this chapter, we've discussed a variety of policies that could increase the rate of economic growth and speed the rise in living standards. Why don't all nations pursue these policies and push their rates of economic growth to the maximum? For example, why did the U.S. standard of living (output per capita) grow by 2.7 percent per year between 1995 and 2001? Why not 4 percent per year? Or 6 percent? Or even more?

In this section, you will see that policies to increase a nation's rate of economic growth involve trade-offs.

Policy Tradeoffs *Promoting economic growth involves unavoidable trade-offs: It requires some groups, or the nation as a whole, to give up something else that is valued. In order to decide how fast we want our economy to grow, we must consider growth's costs as well as its benefits.*

Economics is famous for making the public aware of policy trade-offs. One of the most important things you will learn in your introductory economics course is that there are no costless solutions to society's problems. Just as individuals face an opportunity cost when they take an action (they must give up something else that they value), so, too, policy makers face an opportunity cost whenever they pursue a policy: They must compromise on achieving some other social goal.

What are the costs of growth?

Budgetary Costs

If you look again at Table 4, you'll see that many of the pro-growth policies we've analyzed involve some kind of tax cut. Cutting the income tax rate may increase the employment-population ratio. Cutting taxes on capital gains or corporate profits will increase investment directly. And cutting taxes on saving will increase household saving, lower interest rates, and thus increase investment spending indirectly. Unfortunately, implementing any of these tax cuts would force the government to choose among three unpleasant alternatives: increase some other tax to regain the lost revenue, cut government spending, or permit the budget deficit to rise.

Who will bear the burden of this budgetary cost? That depends on which alternative is chosen. Under the first option—increasing some other tax—the burden falls on those who pay the other tax. For example, if income taxes are cut, real estate taxes might be increased. A family might pay lower income taxes, but higher property taxes. Whether it comes out ahead or behind will depend on how much income the family earns relative to how much property it owns.

The second option, cutting government spending, imposes the burden on those who currently benefit from government programs. These include not only those who directly benefit from a program—like welfare recipients or farmers—but also those who benefit from government spending more indirectly. Even though you may earn your income in the private sector, if government spending is cut, you may suffer from a deterioration of public roads, decreased police protection, or poorer schools for your children.

The third option—a larger budget deficit—is more complicated. Suppose a tax cut causes the government to end up with a larger deficit. Then greater government borrowing will increase the total amount of government debt outstanding—called the **national debt**—and lead to greater interest payments to be made by future generations, in the form of higher taxes.

National debt The total value of government debt outstanding as a result of financing earlier budget deficits.

But that is not all. You've learned that a rise in the budget deficit (by increasing the demand for funds) drives up the interest rate. The higher interest rate will reduce investment in physical capital by businesses, as well as investment in human capital by households, and both effects will work to decrease economic growth. It is even possible that private investment will fall so much that the tax cut, originally designed to boost economic growth, ends up slowing growth instead. At best, the growth-enhancing effects of the tax cut will be weakened. This is why advocates of high growth rates usually propose one of the other options—a rise in some other tax or a cut in government spending—as part of a pro-growth tax cut.

In sum,

while properly targeted tax cuts can increase the rate of economic growth, they often force us to either redistribute the tax burden or cut government programs.

 Policy Tradeoffs

Consumption Costs

Any pro-growth policy that works by increasing investment—in physical capital, human capital, or R&D—requires a sacrifice of current consumption spending. The land, labor, capital and entrepreneurship we use to produce new cloth-cutting machines, oil rigs, assembly lines, training facilities, college classrooms, or research laboratories could have been used instead to produce clothing, automobiles, video games, and other consumer goods. In other words, we face a trade-off: The more capital goods we produce in any given year, the fewer consumption goods we can enjoy in that year.

The role of this trade-off in economic growth can be clearly seen with a familiar tool from Chapter 2: the production possibilities frontier (PPF). Figure 11 shows the PPF for a nation with some given amount of land, labor, capital and entrepreneurship that must be allocated to the production of two types of output: capital goods and consumption goods. At point *K*, the nation is using all of its resources to produce capital goods and none to produce consumption goods. Point *C* represents the opposite extreme: all resources used to produce consumption goods and none

FIGURE 11
Consumption, Investment, and Economic Growth

In the current period, a nation can choose to produce only consumer goods (point C), or it can produce some capital goods by sacrificing some current consumption, as at point A. If investment at point A exceeds capital depreciation, the capital stock will grow, and the production possibilities frontier will shift outward. After it does, the nation can produce more consumption goods (point B), more capital goods (point D), or more of both (point E).

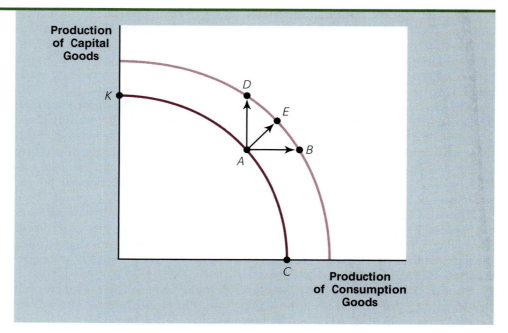

for capital goods. Ordinarily, a nation will operate at an intermediate point such as *A,* where it is producing both capital and consumption goods.

Now, as long as capital production at point *A* is greater than the depreciation of existing capital, the capital stock will grow. In future periods, the economy—with more capital—can produce more output, as shown by the outward shift of the PPF in the figure. If a nation can produce more output, then it can produce more consumption goods for the same quantity of capital goods (moving from point *A* to point *B*) or more capital goods for the same quantity of consumption goods (from point *A* to point *D*) or more of both (from point *A* to point *E*).

Let's take a closer look at how this sacrifice of current consumption goods might come about. Suppose that some change in government policy—an investment tax credit or a lengthening of the patent period for new inventions—successfully shifts the investment curve to the right. (Go back to Figure 8.) What will happen? Businesses—desiring more funds for investment—will drive up the interest rate, and households all over the country will find that saving has become more attractive. As families increase their saving, we move rightward along the economy's supply of funds curve. In this way, firms get the funds they need to purchase new capital. But a decision to *save more* is also a decision to *spend less.* As current saving rises, current consumption spending necessarily falls. By driving up the interest rate, *the increase in investment spending causes a voluntary decrease in consumption spending by households.* Resources are freed from producing consumption goods and diverted to producing capital goods instead.

Although this decrease in consumption spending is voluntary, it is still a cost that we pay. And in some cases, a painful cost: Some of the increase in the household sector's net saving results from a decrease in borrowing by households that—at higher interest rates—can no longer afford to finance purchases of homes, cars, or furniture. In sum,

Policy Tradeoffs

greater investment in physical capital, human capital, or R&D will lead to faster economic growth and higher living standards in the future, but we will have fewer consumer goods to enjoy in the present.

Opportunity Costs of Workers' Time

Living standards will also rise if a greater fraction of the population works or if those who already have jobs begin working longer hours. In either case, there will be more output to divide among the same population. But this increase in living standards comes at a cost: a decrease in time spent in nonmarket activities. For example, with a greater fraction of the population working, a smaller fraction is spending time at home. This might mean that more students have summer jobs, more elderly workers are postponing their retirement, or more previously nonworking spouses are entering the labor force. Similarly, an increase in average working hours would mean that the average worker will have less time for other activities—less time to watch television, read novels, garden, fix up the house, teach his or her children, or do volunteer work.

Thus, when economic growth comes about from increases in the employment-population ratio (or in average hours), we face a trade-off: On the one hand, we can enjoy higher incomes and more goods and services; on the other hand, we will have less time to do things other than work in the market. In a market economy, where choices are voluntary, the value of the income gained must be greater than the value of the time given up. No one forces a worker to reenter the labor force or to increase her working hours. Any worker who takes either of these actions must be better off for doing so. Still, we must recognize that *something* of value is always given up when employment increases:

Policy Tradeoffs

An increase in the fraction of the population with jobs (or a rise in working hours) will increase output and raise living standards, but also requires us to sacrifice time previously spent in nonmarket activities.

Sacrifice of Other Social Goals

Rapid economic growth is an important social goal, but it's not the only one. Some of the policies that quicken the pace of growth require us to sacrifice other goals that we care about. For example, you've seen that restructuring and even reducing Social Security benefits would increase saving, leading to more investment and faster growth. But such a move would cut the incomes of those who benefit from the current system and increase the burden on other social programs, such as welfare and food stamps. You've learned that extending patent protection would increase incentives for research and development. But it would also extend the monopoly power exercised by patent holders and force consumers to pay higher prices for drugs, electronic equipment, and even packaged foods.

Of course, the argument cuts both ways: Just as government policies to stimulate investment require us to sacrifice other goals, so, too, can the pursuit of other goals impede investment spending and economic growth. Most of us would like to see a cleaner environment and safer workplaces. But safety and environmental regulations have increased in severity, complexity, and cost over time, reducing the rate of profit on new capital and shrinking investment spending.

Does this mean that business taxes and government regulations should be reduced to the absolute minimum? Not at all. As in most matters of economic policy, we face a trade-off:

Policy Tradeoffs

> *We can achieve greater worker safety, a cleaner environment, and other social goals, but we may have to sacrifice some economic growth along the way. Alternatively, we can achieve greater economic growth, but we will have to compromise on other things we care about.*

When values differ, people will disagree on just how much we should sacrifice for economic growth or how much growth we should sacrifice for other goals.

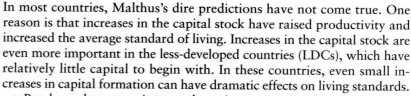

USING THE THEORY
Economic Growth in the Less-Developed Countries

In most countries, Malthus's dire predictions have not come true. One reason is that increases in the capital stock have raised productivity and increased the average standard of living. Increases in the capital stock are even more important in the less-developed countries (LDCs), which have relatively little capital to begin with. In these countries, even small increases in capital formation can have dramatic effects on living standards.

But how does a nation go about increasing its capital stock? As you've learned, there are a variety of measures, all designed to accomplish the same goal: shifting resources away from consumer-goods production toward capital-goods production. A very simple formula.

Some countries that were once LDCs—like the four Asian tigers (Hong Kong, Singapore, South Korea, and Taiwan)—have applied the formula very effectively. Output per capita in these counties has grown by an average of 6 percent per year over the past two decades. They were able to shift resources from consumption goods into capital goods in part by pursuing many of the growth-enhancing measures discussed in this chapter: large subsidies for human and physical capital investments, pro-growth tax cuts to encourage saving and investment, and the willingness to sacrifice other social goals—especially a clean environment—for growth.[6] These economies gave up large amounts of potential consumption during a period of intensive capital formation.

But other LDCs have had great difficulty raising living standards. Table 5 shows growth rates for several of them. In some cases—such as Pakistan, Bangladesh, and more recently, Ghana and Benin—slow but consistent growth has given cause for optimism. In other cases—such as Kenya—living standards have barely budged over the past few decades. In still other cases—for example, the Democratic Republic of the Congo and Sierra Leone—output per capita has been falling ever more rapidly. Why do some LDCs have such difficulty achieving economic growth?

Much of the explanation for the low growth rates of many LDCs lies with three characteristics that they share:

---

[6] The Asian tigers also had some special advantages—such as a high level of human capital to start with.

Country	Average Annual Growth Rate of Output per Capita	
	1975–2001	1990–2001
Bangladesh	2.3	3.1
Pakistan	2.7	1.2
Ghana	0.2	1.9
Benin	−0.5	1.9
Kenya	0.3	−0.6
Democratic Republic of the Congo	−5.2	−7.7
Sierra Leone	−3.3	−6.6

TABLE 5
Economic Growth in Selected Poor Countries

Source: United Nations Development Programme, *Human Development Report 2003*, pp. 279–281.

1. *Very low current output per capita.* Living standards are so low in some LDCs that they cannot take advantage of the trade-off between producing consumption goods and producing capital goods. In these countries, pulling resources out of consumption would threaten the survival of many households. In the individual household, the problem is an inability to save: Incomes are so low that households must spend all they earn on consumption.

2. *High population growth rates.* Low living standards and high population growth rates are linked together in a cruel circle of logic. On the one hand, rapid population growth by itself tends to reduce living standards; on the other hand, a low standard of living tends to increase population growth. Why? First, the poor are often uneducated in matters of family planning. Second, high mortality rates among infants and children encourage families to have many offspring, to ensure the survival of at least a few to care for parents in their old age. As a result, while the average woman in the United States will have fewer than two children in her lifetime, the average woman in Haiti will have about five children, and the average woman in Rwanda will have more than six.

3. *Poor infrastructure.* Political instability, poor law enforcement, corruption, and adverse government regulations make many LDCs unprofitable places to invest. Low rates of investment mean a smaller capital stock and lower productivity. Infrastructure problems also harm worker productivity in another way: Citizens must spend time guarding against thievery and trying to induce the government to let them operate businesses—time they could otherwise spend producing output.

These three characteristics—low current production, high population growth, and poor infrastructure—interact to create a vicious circle of continuing poverty, which we can understand with the help of the familiar PPF between capital goods and consumption goods. Look back at Figure 11, and now imagine that it applies to a poor, developing country. In this case, an outward shift of the PPF does not, in itself, guarantee an increase in the standard of living. In the LDCs, the population growth rate is often very high, and employment grows at the same rate as the population. If employment grows more rapidly than the capital stock, then even though

FIGURE 12
LDC Growth and Living Standards

In order to increase capital per worker when population is growing, yearly investment spending must exceed some minimum level N. In any year, there is a minimum level of consumption, S, needed to support the population. If output is currently at point H, capital per worker and living standards are stagnant. But movement to a point like J would require an unacceptably low level of consumption.

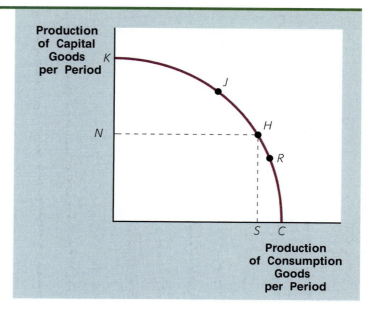

the PPF is shifting outward, capital per worker will decline. Unless some other factor—such as technological change—is raising productivity, then living standards will fall.

> *In order to have rising capital per worker—an important source of growth in productivity and living standards—a nation's stock of capital must not only grow, but grow faster than its population.*

HTTP://

The World Bank Economic Growth Project's Web site is a comprehensive source of information about economic growth (http://econ.worldbank.org/ programs/macroeconomics).

Point *N* in Figure 12 shows the minimum amount of investment needed to increase capital per worker, labor productivity, and living standards for a given rate of population growth. For example, if the population is growing at 4 percent per year, then point *N* indicates the investment needed to increase the total capital stock by 4 percent per year. If investment is just equal to *N*, then capital per worker—and living standards—remains constant. If investment exceeds *N*, then capital per worker—and living standards—will rise. Of course, the greater the growth in population, the higher point *N* will be on the vertical axis, since greater investment will be needed just to keep up with population growth. (We assume throughout this discussion that employment is rising at the same rate as the population.)

The PPF in Figure 12 has an added feature: Point *S* shows the minimum acceptable level of consumption, the amount of consumer goods the economy *must* produce in a year. For example, *S* might represent the consumption goods needed to prevent starvation among the least well off, or to prevent unacceptable social consequences, such as violent revolution.

Now we can see the problem faced by the most desperate of the less-developed economies. Output is currently at a point like *H* in Figure 12, with investment just equal to *N*. The capital stock is not growing fast enough to increase capital per worker, and so labor productivity and living standards are stagnant. In this situation, the PPF shifts outward each year, but not quickly enough to improve people's lives. It could be even worse: Convince yourself that, at a point like *R*, the average standard of living declines even though the capital stock is growing—that is, even though the PPF will shift outward in future periods.

The solution to this problem appears to be an increase in capital production beyond point *N*—a movement *along* the PPF from point *H* to a point such as *J*. As investment rises above *N*, capital per worker rises, and the PPF shifts outward rapidly enough over time to raise living standards. In a wealthy country, like the United States, such a move could be engineered by changes in taxes or other government policies. But in the LDCs depicted here, such a move would be intolerable: At point *H*, consumption is already equal to *S*, the lowest acceptable level. Moving to point *J* would require reducing consumption *below S*.

> *The poorest LDCs are too poor to take advantage of the trade-off between consumption and capital production in order to increase their living standards. Since they cannot reduce consumption below current levels, they cannot produce enough capital to keep up with their rising populations*

In recent history, countries have attempted several methods to break out of this vicious circle of poverty. During the 1930s, the dictator Joseph Stalin simply *forced* the Soviet economy from a point like *H* to one like *J*. His goal was to shift the Soviet Union's PPF outward as rapidly as possible. But, as you can see, this reduced consumption below the minimum level *S*, and Stalin resorted to brutal measures to enforce his will. Many farmers were ordered into the city to produce capital equipment. With fewer people working on farms, agricultural production declined and there was not enough food to go around. Stalin's solution was to confiscate food from the remaining farmers and give it to the urban workforce. Of course, this meant starvation for millions of farmers. Millions more who complained too loudly, or who otherwise represented a political threat, were rounded up and executed.

A less-brutal solution to the problem of the LDCs is to make the wealthy bear more of the burden of increasing growth. If the decrease in consumption can be limited to the rich, then *total* consumption can be significantly reduced—freeing up resources for investment—without threatening the survival of the poor. This, however, is not often practical, since the wealthy have the most influence with government in LDCs. Being more mobile, they can easily relocate to other countries, taking their savings with them. This is why efforts to shift the sacrifice to the wealthy are often combined with restrictions on personal liberties, such as the freedom to travel or to invest abroad. These moves often backfire in the long run, since restrictions on personal and economic freedom are remembered long after they are removed and make the public—especially foreigners—hesitant to invest in that country.

A third alternative—and the one used increasingly since the 1940s—is *foreign investment* or *foreign assistance*. If the wealthier nations—individually or through international organizations such as the World Bank or the International Monetary Fund—provide the LDCs with capital, then the capital *available* to them can increase, with *no* cutbacks in consumption. This permits an LDC to *acquire* capital goods at a point like *F* in Figure 13(a), even though its *production* remains—for the moment—at point *H*.

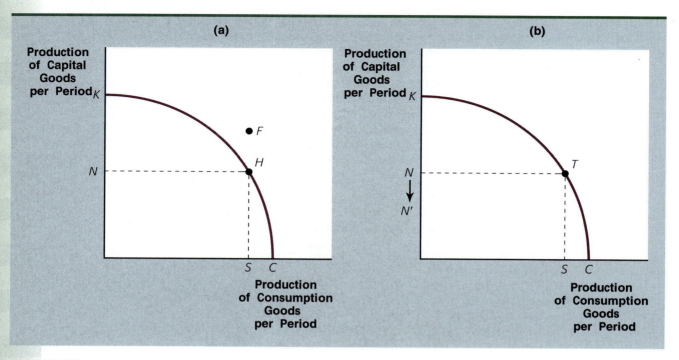

FIGURE 13
Growth Options for LDCs

Panel (a) shows an LDC producing at point H, where the available consumption goods are just sufficient to meet minimum standards (point S). If the nation can obtain goods externally, through foreign investment or foreign assistance, it can make use of capital and consumption goods at a point like F—outside of its PPF.

Panel (b) shows a case where capital production at point T is just sufficient to keep up with a rising population, but not great enough to raise capital per worker and living standards. If this nation can reduce its population growth rate, then the same rate of capital production will increase capital per worker and raise the standard of living.

A variation on this strategy is for foreign nations to provide consumer goods so that the poorer nation can shift its *own* resources out of producing them (and into capital production) without causing consumption levels to fall. Once again, if capital production exceeds point N during the year, capital per worker will grow, setting the stage for continual growth to higher standards of living.

Finally, there is a fourth alternative. Consider a nation producing at point T in Figure 13(b). Capital production is just sufficient to keep up with a rising population, so the PPF shifts outward each year, but not rapidly enough to raise living standards. If this nation can reduce its population growth rate, however, then less capital production will be needed just to keep up with population growth. In the figure, point N will move downward to N'. If production remains at point T, the PPF will continue to shift outward as before, but now—with slower population growth—productivity and living standards will rise. Slowing the growth in population has been an important (and successful) part of China's growth strategy, although it has required severe restrictions on the rights of individual families to have children. Policy trade-offs, once again.

Summary

The growth rate of real GDP is a key determinant of economic well-being. If output grows faster than the population, then output per person—and the average standard of living—will rise. But in order for output per person to rise, either average working hours, the employment-population ratio (EPR), or productivity must increase. In developed countries, average hours have been decreasing and are unlikely to rise in the near future. Therefore, higher living standards can be attributed entirely to the last two factors—higher EPR and higher productivity.

In order for the EPR to rise, employment must grow faster than the population. Employment growth arises from an increase in either labor supply or labor demand. Government tax and transfer policies can influence labor supply, and government subsidy and training programs can influence labor demand.

Productivity increases when capital per worker rises or there are advances in technology. When the flow of investment spending is greater than the flow of depreciation over some period of time, the capital stock will rise. If the capital stock rises at a faster rate than employment, then capital per worker rises, and so does productivity.

Investment can be encouraged by government policies. If the government reduces its budget deficit, the demand for loanable funds will fall, the interest rate will decline, and investment will increase. Investment can also be stimulated directly through reductions in the corporate profits tax or through subsidies to new capital. Finally, policies that encourage household saving can also lower the interest rate and contribute to capital formation.

Technological change—the application of new inputs or new methods of production—also raises productivity. The rate of technological change depends on spending on research and development, either by government or private firms. Almost any government policy that increases investment spending in general will also increase spending on research and development, and therefore increase the pace of technological change. In addition, patent protection can specifically influence research and development on new, patentable products and technologies.

Economic growth is not costless. Tax cuts that stimulate employment, capital formation, or technological progress require increases in other taxes, cuts in spending programs, or an increase in the national debt. Any increase in employment from a given population requires a sacrifice of leisure time and other nonmarket activities. More broadly, any increase in investment requires the sacrifice of consumption today.

Key Terms

Average standard of living	Employment-Population Ratio (EPR)	Patent protection
Budget deficit	Flow variable	Stock variable
Business demand for funds curve	Government demand for funds curve	Supply of funds curve
Capital gains tax	Investment tax credit	Technological change
Capital per worker	Labor productivity	Total demand for funds curve
Consumption tax	Loanable funds market	
Corporate profits tax	National debt	

Review Questions

1. How do we calculate the average standard of living? Why should economic policy makers be concerned about economic growth?

2. Discuss the three major ways a country can increase its average living standard.

3. Compare the effects on the real wage rate and output from an increase in labor demand and an increase in labor supply.

4. Who are the two major groups on the demand side of the loanable funds market? Why does each seek funds there? What is the "price" of these funds?

5. What is the source of funds supplied to the loanable funds market?

6. Explain why the supply of funds curve slopes upward, and why the curve depicting business demand for funds slopes downward.

7. How will the *slope* of the demand for funds curve be affected if the government runs a budget deficit? Why?

8. Explain how a tax cut could lead to *slower* economic growth.

9. Why did Malthus's dire prediction fail to materialize? Do you think it could still come true? Explain your reasoning.

10. "Faster economic growth can benefit everyone and need not harm anyone. That is, there is no policy trade-off when it comes to economic growth." True or false? Explain.

11. Explain the following statement: "In some LDCs, it can be said that a significant cause of continued poverty is poverty itself."

Problems and Exercises

1. Below are GDP and growth data for the United States and four other countries:

	1950 per Capita GDP (in Constant Dollars)	1990 per Capita GDP (in Constant Dollars)	Average Yearly Growth Rate
United States	$9,573	$21,558	2.0%
France	$5,221	$17,959	3.0%
Japan	$1,873	$19,425	5.7%
Kenya	$ 609	$ 1,055	1.3%
India	$ 597	$ 1,348	2.0%

Source: Angus Maddison, *Monitoring the World Economy, 1820–1992.* Paris, OECD, 1995.

a. For both years, calculate each country's per capita GDP as a percentage of U.S. per capita GDP. Which countries appeared to be catching up to the United States, and which were lagging behind?
b. If all these countries had continued to grow (from 1990 onward) at the average growth rates given, in what year would France have caught up to the United States? In what years (respectively) would India and Kenya have caught up to the United States?

2. Below are hypothetical data for the country of Barrovia:

	Population (Millions)	Employment (Millions)	Labor Productivity (Output per-Worker per-Year)	Total Yearly Output
1997	100	50	$ 9,500	____
1998	104	51	$ 9,500	____
1999	107	53	$ 9,750	____
2000	108	57	$ 9,750	____
2001	110	57	$10,000	____

a. Fill in the entries for total output in each of the five years.
b. Calculate the following for each year (except 1997):
   (1) Population growth rate (from previous year)
   (2) Growth rate of output (from previous year)
   (3) Growth rate of per capita output (from previous year)

3. State whether each of the following statements is true or false, and explain your reasoning briefly.
   a. "A permanent increase in employment from a lower to a higher level will cause an increase in real GDP, but not continued growth in real GDP."
   b. "A permanent increase in the nation's capital stock to a new, higher level will cause an increase in real GDP, but not continued growth in real GDP."
   c. "With constant population, work hours, and technology, as long as planned investment spending continues to be greater than depreciation, real GDP will continue to grow year after year."
   d. "All else equal, a permanent increase in an economy's rate of planned investment spending will cause real GDP to grow faster each year than it would at the old, lower level of investment spending."

4. Complete the table below, then find the growth rate of output from Year 1 to Year 2, from Year 2 to Year 3, and from Year 3 to Year 4, in terms of the percentage change in each of its components.

5. Using a three-panel graph similar in style to Figure 6, illustrate how the *supply* of funds curve is obtained when the government is running a budget surplus. *(Hint:* Assume that any budget surplus is held in bank accounts, where the funds are lent out just like household savings.)

6. Use graphs to depict the effect on saving, investment, and the interest rate of a *decrease* in government spending when the government is running a budget *surplus*.

	Year 1	Year 2	Year 3	Year 4
Total hours worked	192 million	200 million	285 million	368 million
Employment	1,200,000	1,400,000	1,900,000	2,100,000
Population	2,000,000	2,500,000	2,900,000	3,200,000
Productivity	$50 per hour	$52.50 per hour	$58 per hour	$60 per hour
Average hours per worker				
EPR				
Total output				

Challenge Questions

1. Economist Amartya Sen has argued that famines in underdeveloped countries are not simply the result of crop failures or natural disasters. Instead, he suggests that wars, especially civil wars, are linked to most famine episodes in recent history. Using a framework similar to Figure 13, discuss the probable effect of war on a country's PPF. Explain what would happen if the country were initially operating at or near a point like *S*, the minimum acceptable level of consumption.

2. Assume the loanable funds market is in equilibrium. Influential media pundits begin to warn about impending economic doom: recession, layoffs, and so forth. Using graphs, discuss what might happen to the equilibrium interest rate and the equilibrium quantity of loanable funds supplied and demanded. Assume that the government budget is in balance—neither a deficit nor a surplus. (*Hint:* How would these warnings separately affect household and business behavior in the loanable funds market?)

 *These exercises require access to Lieberman/Hall Xtra! If Xtra! did not come with your book, visit http://liebermanxtra.swlearning.com to purchase.*

1. Use your Xtra! password at the Hall and Lieberman Web site (http://liebermanxtra.swlearning.com), select this chapter, and under Economic Applications, click on EconDebate. Choose *Productivity Growth* and scroll down to find the debate, "Is There a New Economy?" Read the debate, and use the information to answer the following questions.
   a. List and explain the contributing factors to the GDP growth, outlined in this chapter, during the 1980s and 1990s according to the economists who argue in favor of the existence of a "new economy" and those who question it.
   b. Which of the contributing factors, listed in this chapter, are responsible for GDP growth in the manufacturing and agricultural industries? Explain.

2. Use your Xtra! password at the Hall and Lieberman Web site (http://liebermanxtra.swlearning.com), select this chapter, and under Economic Applications, click on EconData. Choose *Macroeconomics: Employment, Unemployment, and Inflation* and scroll down to find *Labor Productivity*. Read the definition and click on Diagrams/Data for information to answer the following questions.
   a. Do the diagrams confirm the existence of a "new economy"?
   b. Does the relationship between the labor productivity and real compensation per hour indicate a rising living standard for workers? Explain.

Economic Fluctuations

If you are like most college students, you will be looking for a full-time job when you graduate. As you are no doubt aware, your prospects will depend partly on the type of job you seek and your qualifications relative to others in that line of work. But it will *also* depend—importantly—on the overall level of economic activity in the country.

If the economy always operated at its potential output, with the labor force fully employed, you'd have nothing to worry about. You could be confident of getting a job within a reasonable time at the going wage for someone with your skills and characteristics. Unfortunately, this is not how the world works. *Potential* output increases every year, but *actual* output does not always grow, or grow at the same rate as potential output. Instead, as far back as we have data, the United States and similar countries have experienced *economic fluctuations*.

Look at panel (a) of Figure 1, which you've seen before in this book. The orange line shows estimated full-employment or potential output since 1960. As a result of economic growth, full-employment output rises steadily.

But now look at the green line, which shows *actual* output. You can see that actual GDP fluctuates above and below potential output. During *recessions*, which are shaded in the figure, output declines, occasionally sharply. During *expansions* (the unshaded periods) output rises quickly, usually faster than potential output is rising. Indeed, in the later stages of an expansion, output often *exceeds* potential output—a situation that economists call a **boom**.

Boom A period of time during which real GDP is above potential GDP.

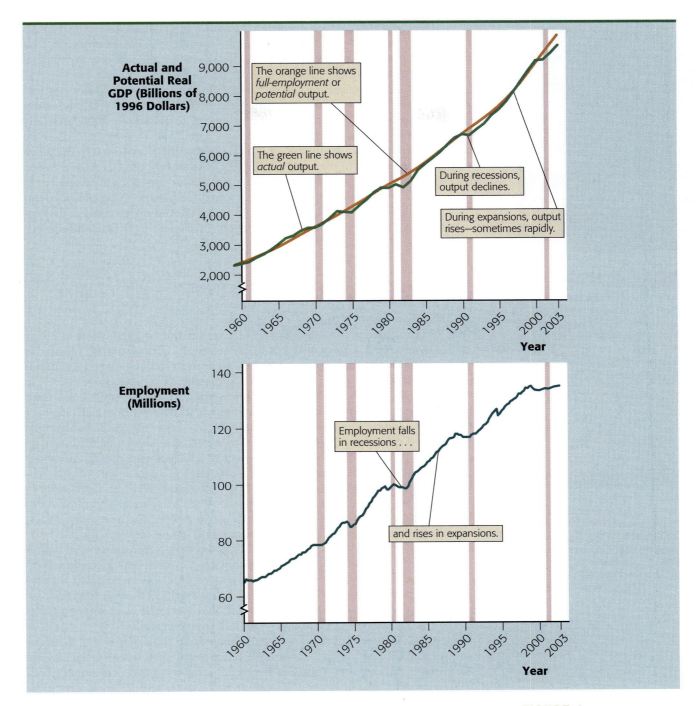

Actual and Potential Real GDP (Billions of 1996 Dollars)

The orange line shows *full-employment* or *potential* output.

The green line shows *actual* output.

During recessions, output declines.

During expansions, output rises—sometimes rapidly.

Year

Employment (Millions)

Employment falls in recessions . . .

and rises in expansions.

Year

FIGURE 1
Potential and Actual Real GDP and Employment, 1960–2003

Panel (b) shows another characteristic of expansions and recessions: fluctuations in employment. During expansions, such as the period from 1983 to 1990, employment grows rapidly. During recessions (shaded), such as 1990–91, employment declines.

Figure 1 shows us that employment and output move very closely together. But the figure doesn't tell us anything about the *causal* relationship between them.

However, we have good reason to believe that over the business cycle, it is changes in output that cause firms to change their employment levels. For example, in a recession, many business firms lay off workers. If asked why, they would answer that they are reducing employment *because* they are producing less output.

Figure 1 also shows something else: Expansions and recessions don't last forever. Indeed, sometimes they are rather brief. The recession of 1990–91, for example, ended within a year. And the recession that began in March 2001 officially ended in November of that year.

But if you look carefully at the figure, you'll see that the back-to-back recessions of the early 1980s extended over three full years. And during the Great Depression of the 1930s (not shown), it took more than a decade for the economy to return to full employment. Expansions too can last for extended periods. The expansion of the 1980s lasted about seven years, from 1983 to 1990. And the expansion that began in March 1991 turned out to be the longest expansion in U.S. economic history—a duration of 10 years.

SPENDING AND ECONOMIC FLUCTUATIONS

Why are there booms and recessions?

Much of our current understanding is based on the original work of John Maynard Keynes. In his very influential 1936 book, *The General Theory of Employment, Interest, and Money*, Keynes made two arguments: (1) a major cause of booms and recessions is fluctuations in private sector *spending*; and (2) in order to keep output close to its potential level, the government must counteract changes in private sector spending by adjusting either its own spending or taxes.

The second of these two arguments has always been controversial, but the first is accepted by most economists today. Keynes showed how shocks that initially affect spending in one sector of the economy quickly influence spending in other sectors, causing changes in total output and employment.

The basic logic of Keynes's argument is straightforward. Business firms will not continue producing output that they cannot sell. When total spending in the economy suddenly *decreases*, some firms find themselves producing more output than they are selling. They respond by reducing output and laying off workers.

But the story does not end there. The laid-off workers—even those who collect some unemployment benefits—will see their incomes decline. As a consequence, they will spend less on a variety of consumer goods. This will cause *other* firms—the ones that produce those consumer goods—to cut back on *their* production, lay off some of their workers, and so on. On a national level, the economy contracts and—if the contraction is sharp enough—we may enter a recession.

Similarly, when total spending suddenly *increases*, some firms will produce *more* output and hire additional workers (or rehire some who were previously laid off.) When these workers spend some of their additional income on consumer goods produced by other firms, the latter will begin to increase *their* production, hire more workers, and so on. The result is an economic expansion, and—if the expansion is sharp enough—a boom.

The focus of this chapter is changes in spending and their role in creating economic fluctuations.

Thinking about Spending. Before we begin our analysis of spending, we have two choices to make. The first concerns our basic approach. There are so many different types of spenders in the economy: city dwellers and suburbanites; government agencies like the Department of Defense and the local school board; and businesses of all types, ranging from the corner convenience store to a huge corporation such as AT&T. How should we organize our thinking about spending? Macro-economists have found that the most useful approach is to divide spending into four broad *aggregates:*

- Consumption spending (C)
- Planned investment spending (I^P)
- Government purchases (G)
- Net exports (NX)

These categories should seem familiar to you. They were basically the same categories we used to break down GDP in the expenditure approach. In the first part of this chapter, we'll take another look at each of these aggregates with our eye on *spending* rather than production. Then, we'll combine them to explore the behavior of total spending in the economy and, finally, look at the relationship between total spending and output.

Our second choice in analyzing spending is whether to look at *nominal* or *real* spending. (Recall that a nominal variable is measured in current dollars, while a real variable is measured in the constant dollars of some base year.) Ultimately, we care more about real variables, such as real output and real income, because they are more closely related to our economic well-being. For example, a rise in *nominal* output might mean that we are producing more goods and services, or it might just mean that prices have risen and production has remained the same or fallen. But a rise in *real* output always means that production has increased. For this reason, we will think about real variables right from the beginning. When we discuss "consumption spending," we mean "*real* consumption spending"; "investment spending" means "*real* investment spending"; and so on.

Real versus Nominal Values

CONSUMPTION SPENDING

A natural place for us to begin our look at spending is with its largest component: *consumption spending.* In all, household spending on consumer goods—groceries, restaurant meals, rent, car repairs, furniture, telephone calls, and so forth—is about two-thirds of total spending in the economy. Because we are interested in the macro-economy, we don't concern ourselves with the differences between one consumer good and another. Instead, we want to know: What determines the *total* amount of consumption spending?

Of all the factors that might influence consumption spending, the most important is **disposable income,** the income of the household sector after taxes. More formally, disposable income is defined as follows:

Disposable income The part of household income that remains after paying taxes.

$$\text{Disposable Income} = \text{Total Income} - \text{Net Taxes}$$

Notice the word "net" that modifies taxes. **Net taxes** are the taxes the government collects *minus* the transfer payments the government pays out, such as social security payments or unemployment insurance:

Net taxes The taxes the government collects minus the transfer payments the government pays out.

$$\text{Net Taxes} = \text{Tax Revenue} - \text{Transfer Payments}$$

In macroeconomics, we are interested in the tax dollars that flow from the household sector to the government. Transfer payments, however, are collected from one set of households and given to another, so we treat them as if they were never taken from the household sector at all. Thus, when we calculate disposable income, we subtract transfer payments from taxes before we subtract taxes from total income.

The Consumption Function

The relationship between consumption and disposable income is a positive one. All else equal, you'd certainly spend more on consumer goods if your *own* disposable income were $50,000 per year than if it were $20,000 per year. The same is true for the nation as a whole. A rise in aggregate disposable income causes a rise in aggregate consumption spending. (Here, as elsewhere, we are speaking about aggregate *real* variables: *real* consumption and *real* disposable income.)

Figure 2 shows the relationship between (real) consumption spending and (real) disposable income in the United States from 1985 to 2002. Each point in the diagram represents a different year. For example, the point labeled "2000" represents a disposable income in that year of $6,630 billion and consumption spending of $6,224 billion. Notice that as disposable income rises, consumption spending rises as well. Indeed, almost all of the variation in consumption spending from year to year can be explained by variations in disposable income.

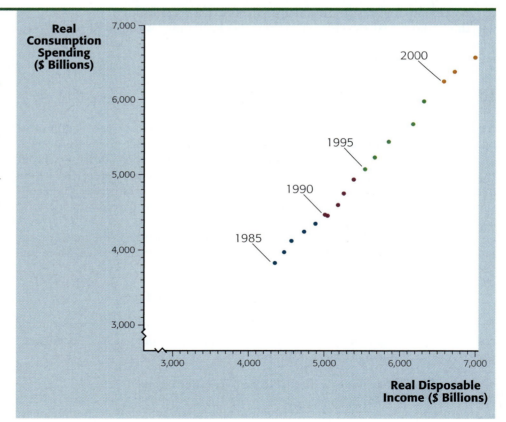

FIGURE 2
U.S. Consumption and Disposable Income, 1985–2002

When real consumption expenditure is plotted against real disposable income, the resulting relationship is almost perfectly linear: As real disposable income rises, so does real consumption spending.

Source: Bureau of Economic Analysis, National Income and Product Accounts Tables, Table 2.1.

Real Disposable Income (Billions of Dollars per Year)	Real Consumption Spending (Billions of Dollars per Year)
0	2,000
1,000	2,600
2,000	3,200
3,000	3,800
4,000	4,400
5,000	5,000
6,000	5,600
7,000	6,200
8,000	6,800

TABLE 1

Hypothetical Data on Disposable Income and Consumption

There is something even more interesting about Figure 2: The relationship between consumption and disposable income is almost perfectly *linear*—the points lie remarkably close to a straight line. This almost-linear relationship between consumption and disposable income has been observed in a wide variety of historical periods and a wide variety of nations. This is why, when we represent the relationship between disposable income and consumption with a diagram or an equation, we use a straight line.

Our discussion will be clearer if we move from the actual data in Figure 2 to the hypothetical example in Table 1. Each row in the table represents a combination of real disposable income and consumption we might observe in an economy. For example, the table shows us that if disposable income were equal to $6,000 billion in some year, consumption spending would equal $5,600 billion in that year. In Figure 3, where the data are plotted on a graph, this combination of disposable income and consumption is represented by point *A*. When all of the other points in the table are plotted in the figure, the result is a straight line. This line is called the **consumption function,** because it illustrates the functional relationship between consumption and disposable income.

Consumption function A positively sloped relationship between real consumption spending and real disposable income.

Like every straight line, the consumption function in Figure 3 has two main features: a vertical intercept and a slope. Mathematically, the intercept—in this case, $2,000 billion—tells us how much consumption spending there would be in the economy if disposable income were zero. However, the real purpose of the vertical intercept is not to identify what would actually happen at zero disposable income, but rather to help us determine which particular line represents consumption spending in the diagram. After all, there are many lines we could draw that have the same slope as the one in the figure. But only one of them has a vertical intercept of $2,000.

The vertical intercept in the figure also has a name: **autonomous consumption.** It represents the combined impact on consumption spending of all factors *other than* disposable income. We'll discuss some of these other factors a bit later.

Autonomous consumption The part of consumption spending that is independent of income; also, the vertical intercept of the consumption function.

The second important feature of Figure 3 is the slope, which shows the change along the vertical axis divided by the change along the horizontal axis as we go from one point to another on the line:

FIGURE 3
The Consumption Function

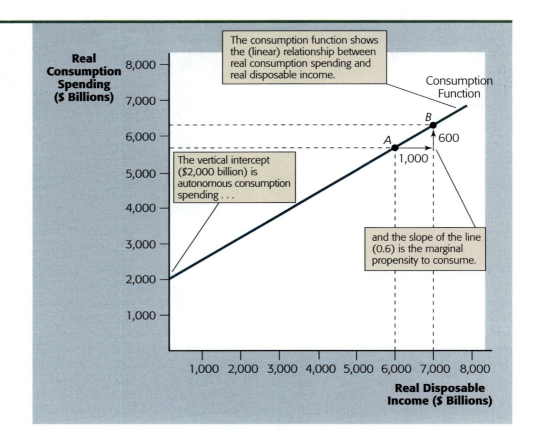

$$slope = \frac{\Delta Consumption}{\Delta Disposable\ Income}.$$

As you can see in the table, each time disposable income rises by $1,000 billion, consumption spending rises by $600 billion, so that the slope is

$$\frac{\$600\ billion}{\$1,000\ billion} = 0.6$$

The slope in Figure 3 is an important feature not just of the consumption function itself, but of the macroeconomic analysis we will build from it. This is why economists have given this slope a special name, the *marginal propensity to consume*, abbreviated *MPC*. In our example, the *MPC* is 0.6.

We can think of the *MPC* in three different ways, but each of them has the same meaning:

Marginal propensity to consume
The amount by which consumption spending rises when disposable income rises by one dollar.

*The **marginal propensity to consume (MPC)** is (1) the slope of the consumption function; (2) the change in consumption divided by the change in disposable income; and (3) the amount by which consumption spending rises when disposable income rises by one dollar.*

Logic suggests that the *MPC* should be larger than zero (when income rises, consumption spending will rise), but less than 1 (the rise in consumption will be *smaller* than the rise in disposable income). This is certainly true in our example: With an *MPC* of 0.6, a one-dollar rise in disposable income causes consumption spending to rise by 60 cents. This range of values for the *MPC* is also observed to be true in economies throughout the world. Accordingly,

we will always assume that 0 < MPC < 1.

Representing Consumption with an Equation. Sometimes, we'll want to use an equation to represent the straight-line consumption function. The most general form of the equation is

$$C = a + b \times (Disposable\ Income)$$

The term *a* is the vertical intercept of the consumption function, which you've learned is called *autonomous consumption spending*. The equation clearly shows that autonomous consumption (*a*) is the part of consumption that does *not* depend on disposable income.

The other term, *b,* is the slope of the consumption function. This is our familiar marginal propensity to consume (*MPC*), telling us how much consumption *increases* each time disposable income rises by a dollar. In our example in Figure 3, *b* is equal to 0.6.

Shifts in the Consumption Function

As you've learned, consumption spending depends positively on disposable income: If disposable income rises, consumption spending will rise with it.

In Figure 3, this change in consumption spending would be represented by a *movement along* the consumption function. For example, a rise in disposable income from $6,000 billion to $7,000 billion would cause consumption spending to increase from $5,600 billion to $6,200 billion, moving us from point A to point B along the consumption function.

But other factors besides disposable income influence consumption spending. For example, suppose your disposable income is $50,000 per year. How much of that sum will you spend, and how much will you save? Since the *interest rate* determines your reward for saving, you would probably save less at a lower interest rate like 2 percent than at a higher interest rate like 10 percent. But since you'd be saving less at a lower interest rate, you'd be spending more. The same is true for the nation as a whole:

For any given level of disposable income, we can expect a drop in the interest rate to cause an increase in consumption spending. Graphically, this is represented as an upward shift in the consumption function.

Figure 4 shows an example in which, at each level of disposable income, consumption spending rises by $800 billion.

Another determinant of consumption is *wealth*—the total value of household assets (home, stocks, bonds, bank accounts, and the like) minus total outstanding liabilities (mortgage loans, credit card debt, student loans, and so on). Even if your disposable income stayed the same, a rise in your wealth—say, because your

FIGURE 4
A Shift in the Consumption–Income Line

A variety of factors can shift the consumption function upward: a drop in the interest rate, an increase in real wealth, or optimism about the future of the economy. If the changes occur in the opposite direction (e.g., a rise in the interest rate), the consumption function will shift downward.

In this figure, the consumption function shifts upward by $800 billion. For example, at a disposable income of $6,000 billion, consumption spending increases from $5,600 billion (point A) to $6,400 billion (point D).

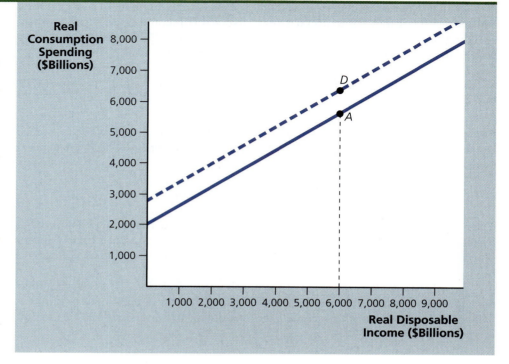

stocks or bonds became more valuable—would probably cause you to spend more. The same is true for the nation as a whole:

> *For any level of disposable income, a rise in household wealth will cause an upward shift in the consumption function.*

Expectations about the future will also affect consumption spending.

> *If households become more optimistic about their job security or expect higher future incomes, they are likely to spend more of their income now, shifting the consumption function upward.*

Similarly, increased pessimism, such as greater worries about job loss, would lead to a downward shift of the consumption function.

Notice, in Figure 4, that the new, dashed consumption function is parallel to the original. That is, after the shift, the *slope* of the consumption function—which is equal to the *MPC*—remains unchanged. Another way of saying this is that, when any of the factors we've discussed causes the consumption function to shift, it changes *autonomous consumption*—the vertical intercept of the line—represented by *a* in the consumption equation $C = a + b \times$ *(Disposable Income)*. This corresponds to what economists have observed about the real world. While autonomous consumption spending may change from year to year, the *MPC* tends to remain the same over time.

Rightward Movement along the Line	Leftward Movement along the Line	Entire Line Shifts Upward	Entire Line Shifts Downward
Disposable Income ↑	Disposable Income↓	Household wealth ↑ Interest rate ↓ Greater optimism	Household wealth ↓ Interest rate ↑ Greater pessimism

TABLE 2
Changes in Consumption Spending and the Consumption–Income Line

We can summarize our discussion of changes in consumption spending as follows:

When a change in disposable income causes consumption spending to change, we move along the consumption function. When a change in anything else besides disposable income causes consumption spending to change, the consumption function will shift.

Table 2 provides a more specific summary of how different types of changes affect consumption spending in a graph such as Figure 4. Remember that all of the changes that *shift* the line work by increasing or decreasing autonomous consumption (*a*).

GETTING TO TOTAL SPENDING

In addition to household consumption spending, there are three other types of spending on goods and services produced by American firms: investment spending, government purchases, and purchases by foreigners. Let's consider each of these types of spending in turn.

Investment Spending

In the definition of GDP, we used the term *investment* (*I*), which consists of three components: (1) business spending on plant and equipment; (2) purchases of new homes; and (3) accumulation of unsold inventories. In this chapter, we focus not on actual investment, but on **planned investment spending** (I^P)—business purchases of plant and equipment and construction of new homes. That is, planned investment does *not* include inventory changes. Why?

When we look at how spending influences the economy, we are interested in the purchases households, firms, and the government *want* to make. Inventory changes, however, are most often an *un*planned and undesired occurrence that firms try to avoid. While firms want to have some inventories on hand, sudden *changes* in inventories are not desirable; they occur when firms are producing more or less than they are selling, and usually lead to a change in production to bring it back in synch with sales. Accordingly, we exclude inventory investment when we measure spending in the economy.

Planned investment (I^P) spending Business purchases of plant and equipment and construction of new homes; also called just *investment spending.*

When analyzing total spending in the economy, we define investment spending as planned plant and equipment purchases by business firms and new home construction. Inventory investment is treated as unintentional and undesired and is therefore excluded from our definition of investment spending.

What determines the level of (planned) investment spending in a given year? In this chapter, we will regard investment spending as a *fixed value,* determined by forces outside of our analysis. This may seem a bit surprising. After all, aren't there variables that affect investment spending in predictable ways? Indeed, there are.

For example, in our discussion of long-run growth in the previous chapter, you learned that investment is likely to be affected by the interest rate. Indeed, in the real world, the investment–interest rate relationship is quite strong. Investment is also influenced by the general level of optimism or pessimism about the economy and by new technological developments. But if we introduce all of these other variables into our analysis, we would find ourselves working with a very complex framework, and much too soon. In future chapters, we'll explore some of the determinants of investment spending; but in this chapter, to keep things simple, we assume that investment spending is some given amount. We'll explore what happens when that amount changes, but we will not, in this chapter, try to explain what causes investment spending to change.

Government Purchases

Government purchases include all of the goods and services that government agencies—federal, state, and local—buy during the year. We treat government purchases in the same way as investment spending: as a given value, determined by forces outside of our analysis. Why?

The relationship between government purchases and other macroeconomic variables—particularly income—is rather weak. In recent decades, the biggest changes in government purchases have involved military spending. These changes have been based on world politics, rather than macroeconomic conditions. So when we assume that government purchases are a given value, independent of the other variables in our model, our assumption is actually realistic.

> *When analyzing total spending in the economy, government purchases are treated as a given value, determined by forces that are outside of our analysis.*

As with investment spending, we'll be exploring what happens when the "given value" of government purchases changes. But we will not try to explain what causes this value to change.

Net Exports

If we want to measure total spending on U.S. output, we must also consider the international sector. About 11 percent of American goods and services are sold to *foreign* consumers, businesses, and government. These are *exports* from the U.S. point of view, and they must be included in our measure of total spending.

But international trade in goods and services also requires us to make an adjustment to the other components of spending. A portion (about 16 percent) of the output bought by *American* consumers, firms, and government agencies is produced abroad. From the U.S. point of view, these are *imports*—spending on foreign, rather than U.S., output. These imports are included in our measures of consumption, investment spending, and government purchases, giving us an exaggerated measure of spending on *American* output. But we can easily correct for this overcount by simply deducting imported consumption goods from our measure of consumption, deducting imported investment goods from our measure of investment and imported government purchases from our measure of government purchases. Of course, this means we will be deducting total imports from our measure of total spending.

In sum, to incorporate the international sector into our measure of total spending, we must add U.S. exports and subtract U.S. imports. These two adjustments can be made together by simply including *net exports* (NX) as the foreign sector's contribution to total spending.

Net Exports = total exports – total imports

By including net exports, we simultaneously ensure that we have included U.S. output that is sold to foreigners, and excluded consumption, investment and government spending on output produced abroad.

Net exports can change for a variety of reasons: changes in tastes toward or away from a particular country's goods, changes in the price of foreign currency on world foreign exchange markets, and more. For now, to keep things simple, we assume that net exports—like investment spending and government purchases—are some given amount. We'll explore what happens when that amount changes, but we will not, in this chapter, try to explain what causes net exports to change.

Summing Up: Total Spending

We've used the phrase *total spending* several times in this chapter, and now we're ready to define it more formally.

> *Total spending is the sum of spending by households, businesses, the government, and the foreign sector on final goods and services produced in the United States.*

Total spending The sum of spending by households, businesses, the government, and the foreign sector on American final goods and services, or $C + I^P + G + NX$.

Remembering that C stands for household consumption spending, I^P for investment spending, G for government purchases, and NX for net exports, we have

$$\text{Total Spending} = C + I^P + G + NX$$

Total spending plays a key role in explaining economic fluctuations. Why? Because over several quarters or even a few years, business firms tend to respond to changes in total spending by changing their level of output. That is, a rise in total spending leads firms throughout the economy to raise their output level, while a drop in total spending causes a decrease in output throughout the economy. While these changes are temporary, they persist long enough to create the kinds of booms and recessions that you saw in Figure 1. In the next section, we'll explore just how changes in spending create these economic fluctuations.

GDP Versus Total Spending The definition of total spending looks very similar to the definition of GDP presented in the chapter entitled "Production, Income, and Employment." Does this mean that total spending and total output are always the same number? Not at all. There is a slight—but important—difference in the definitions. GDP is defined as $C + I + G + NX$. Total spending, by contrast, is defined as $C + I^P + G + NX$. The difference is that GDP adds actual investment (I), which includes business firms' inventory investment. Total spending adds just planned investment (I^P), which *excludes* inventory investment. The two numbers will not be equal unless inventory investment is zero.

DANGEROUS CURVES

TOTAL SPENDING AND EQUILIBRIUM GDP

Imagine that—after graduating from college—you go into business manufacturing cellular phones. You set up a factory, hire a dozen workers, decide on a price to charge for your phones, prepare your advertising, and begin producing.

Now suppose that, after producing phones for a few weeks or months, you notice that you aren't selling as many as you're producing. What will you do? If you are like many firms, you will decrease your output of phones and lay off some of your workers. If the problem persists, you may take other steps as well—including lowering your price. But you may hesitate to change your price, because it can be costly for you. (For example, changing prices will require you to change all of your advertising brochures, inform all of your wholesalers, etc.) Moreover, price changes can be even more costly to reverse if sales pick up again in a few months. Not only will you have to change your advertising brochures once again, but by raising prices you risk alienating customers who got used to lower prices. For these reasons, you may be hesitant to drop your price in the first place, and respond first by cutting back on production.

Now imagine the opposite scenario: After producing phones for a few weeks or months, and building up a reasonable inventory for filling orders, you begin selling *more* than you're producing. For a few days, you fill the orders by running down your inventories. But then what? Most likely, you'll *increase* your output of phones and hire some additional workers. If the situation continues for many months, you may take other steps as well—including raising your price. But, once again, price hikes can be costly and alienating to customers. You may want to wait until you are reasonably sure that your high sales will continue indefinitely before raising prices. For these reasons, your first response may be to increase production.

Under what conditions would you continue to produce an unchanged level of output? Only when your sales are equal to your production. And what is true for you is true for firms throughout the country.

Now let's consider the same line of reasoning on a macroeconomic level. Total spending in the economy is the same as total sales by all business firms. GDP is the same as total production by all business firms. We come to the following macroeconomic conclusion:

> *When total spending is less than GDP, firms in general will decrease production and GDP will drop. When total spending is greater than GDP, firms will increase production, and GDP will rise. When total spending is equal to GDP, firms will continue producing at the same rate, and GDP will remain unchanged.*

We can carry this one step further by remembering that an *equilibrium* is a situation that tends to remain unchanged, unless the underlying conditions change. In microeconomics, we are interested in the equilibrium price and quantity in individual markets—such as the market for maple syrup that we studied in Chapter 3. In macroeconomics, we use the same concept in defining equilibrium GDP.

Equilibrium GDP A level of output that is equal to total spending in the economy.

> *Equilibrium GDP is the level of GDP that tends to remain unchanged—that is, the level of GDP at which total spending and total output in the economy are equal.*

We can summarize our discussion about the relationship between GDP and total spending in this way:

$$C + I^P + G + NX > GDP \Rightarrow GDP \uparrow$$

$$C + I^P + G + NX < GDP \Rightarrow GDP \downarrow$$

$$C + I^P + G + NX = GDP \Rightarrow No \; \Delta GDP$$

Note that the economy's *equilibrium* output need not be its *potential* output. In fact, equilibrium GDP will equal potential GDP only if there is sufficient spending for firms to *sell* all the output they would produce when they are fully employing the economy's resources. But whether they will be able to sell this output or not depends on the behavior of *spenders* in the economy. Indeed, even when the economy is happily producing at potential GDP, a change in spending can throw it off course, into a boom or recession. We explore this possibility in the next section.

WHAT HAPPENS WHEN THINGS CHANGE?

Imagine that the economy is humming along at its potential output level, with the labor force fully employed. Then, there is a **spending shock**—a sudden change in one or more of the components of total spending. What will happen? To make our analysis more concrete, we'll explore a specific type of spending shock: a change in investment spending. Then, we'll generalize our results to other types of spending shocks.

Spending shock A change in spending that ultimately affects the entire economy.

A Change in Investment Spending

Suppose that business firms decide to increase yearly investment purchases by $100 billion above the original level. What will happen? First, output at firms that manufacture investment goods—firms like Dell Computer, Caterpillar, and General Electric—will increase by $100 billion. However, as you learned in Chapter 12, the economy's total output and total income are equal. Each time a dollar in output is produced, a dollar of income (factor payments) is created. Thus, the $100 billion in additional output will become $100 billion in additional income. This income will be paid out as wages, rent, interest, and profit to the households who own the resources these firms have purchased.[1]

What will households—as consumers—do with their $100 billion in additional income? How much will they spend, and how much will they save? That depends on two things: First, what happens to the taxes they must pay? To keep our discussion simple, we'll assume that household tax payments do not change at all with their additional income. (We imagine that the government wants to collect a certain amount of taxes, and—if income rises—it will lower the income tax *rate* in order to keep the total income tax payment constant.)

---

[1] Some of the sales revenue of these firms will be spent on intermediate goods, such as raw materials, electricity, and supplies. But the producers of these intermediate goods will themselves pay wages, rent, interest, and profit for *their* resources, so that household income will still rise by the full $100 billion.

FIGURE 5
The Effect of a Change in
Investment Spending

An increase in investment spending sets off a chain reaction, leading to successive rounds of increased spending and income. As shown here, a $100 billion increase in investment first causes real GDP to increase by $100 billion. Then, with higher incomes, households increase consumption spending by the MPC times the change in disposable income. In round 2, spending and GDP increase by $60 billion. In succeeding rounds, increases in income lead to further changes in spending, but in each round the increase in income is smaller than in the preceding round.

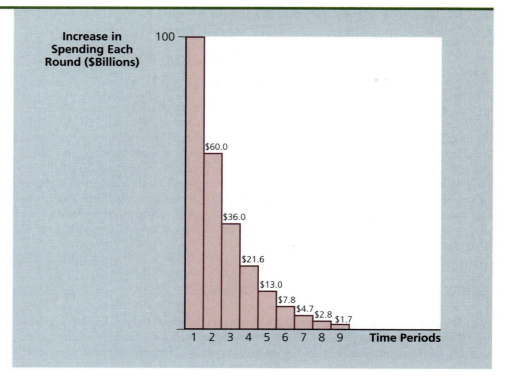

FIGURE 5
The Effect of a Change in Investment Spending

Second, what is the *marginal propensity to consume (MPC) in the economy?* Let's suppose that the *MPC* is 0.6. Then consumption spending will rise by 60 percent of the $100 billion in additional household income, or 0.6 × $100 billion = $60 billion. Households will save the remaining $40 billion.

But that is not the end of the story. When households spend an additional $60 billion, firms that produce consumption goods and services—firms such as McDonald's, Coca Cola, American Airlines, and Disney—will produce and sell an additional $60 billion in output, which, in turn, will become an equal amount of income for the households that supply resources to these firms. And when *these* households see *their* incomes rise by $60 billion, they will spend part of it as well. With an *MPC* of 0.6, consumption spending in this phase will rise by 0.6 × $60 billion = $36 billion, resulting in still more production at other firms, and so on and so on. . . .

As you can see, an increase in investment spending will set off a chain reaction, leading to successive rounds of increased spending and income. The process is illustrated in Figure 5: After the $100 billion increase in investment spending, there is a $60 billion increase in consumption, then a $36 billion increase in consumption, and on and on. Each successive round of additional spending is 60 percent of the round before. Each time spending increases, output rises to match it. These successive increases in spending and output occur quickly—the process is largely completed within a year. At the end of the process, when the economy has reached its new equilibrium, spending and output will have increased considerably. But by how much?

Round	Additional Spending in This Round (Billions of Dollars)	Additional Spending in All Rounds (Billions of Dollars)
Initial Increase in Investment spending	100	100
Round 2	60	160
Round 3	36	196
Round 4	21.6	217.6
Round 5	13	230.6
Round 6	7.8	238.4
Round 7	4.7	243.1
Round 8	2.8	245.9
Round 9	1.7	247.6
Round 10	1.0	248.6
All other rounds	Very close to 1.4	Very close to 250

TABLE 3
Cumulative Increases in Total Spending When Investment Spending Increases by $100 Billion

Table 3 gives us the answer. The second column shows us the additional spending in each round, while the third column shows the cumulative rise in spending. As you can see, the cumulative increase becomes larger and larger with each successive round, but it grows by less and less each time. Eventually, the additional spending in a given round is so small that we can safely ignore it. At this point, the cumulative increase in spending and output will be very close to $250 billion—so close that we can ignore any difference.

The Spending Multiplier

Let's go back and summarize what happened in our example: Business firms increased their investment spending by $100 billion per year, and as a result, spending and output rose by $250 billion per year. GDP increased by *more* than the initial increase in investment spending. In our example, the increase in GDP ($250 billion) was 2.5 times the initial increase in investment spending ($100 billion). As you can verify, if investment spending had increased by half as much ($50 billion), GDP would have increased by 2.5 times *that* amount ($125 billion). In fact, *whatever* the rise in investment spending, GDP would increase by a factor of 2.5, so we can write

$$\Delta GDP = 2.5 \times \Delta I^P$$

The change in investment spending must be *multiplied by* the number 2.5 in order to get the change in GDP that it causes. For this reason, 2.5 is called the *spending multiplier* in this example.

> *The **spending multiplier** is the number by which a change in spending (e.g., investment spending) must be multiplied to get the change in equilibrium GDP.*

Spending multiplier The amount by which equilibrium real GDP changes as a result of a one-dollar change in autonomous consumption, investment, government purchases, or net exports.

The value of the spending multiplier depends on the value of the MPC in the economy. If you look back at Table 3, you will see that each round of additional spending would have been larger if the MPC had been larger. For example, with an MPC of 0.9 instead of 0.6, spending in round 2 would have risen by $90 billion, in round 3 by $81 billion, and so on. The result would have been a larger cumulative change in GDP and a larger multiplier.

There is a very simple formula we can use to determine the multiplier for *any* value of the MPC. To obtain it, let's start with our numerical example in which the MPC is 0.6. When investment spending rises by $100, the change in equilibrium GDP can be written as follows:

$$\Delta GDP = \$100 \text{ billion} + \$60 \text{ billion} + \$36 \text{ billion} + \$21.6 \text{ billion} + \ldots$$

Factoring out the $100 billion change in investment, this becomes

$$\Delta GDP = \$100 \text{ billion } [1 + 0.6 + 0.36 + 0.216 + \ldots]$$

$$= \$100 \text{ billion } [1 + 0.6 + 0.6^2 + 0.6^3 + \ldots]$$

In this equation, $100 billion is the change in investment (ΔI^P), and 0.6 is the MPC. To find the change in GDP that applies to *any* ΔI^P and *any* MPC, we can write

$$\Delta GDP = \Delta I^P \times [1 + (MPC) + (MPC)^2 + (MPC)^3 + \ldots]$$

Now we can see that the term in brackets—the infinite sum $1 + MPC + (MPC)^2 + (MPC)^3 + \ldots$—is our multiplier. But what is its value?

Here, we can borrow a rule from the mathematics of sums just like this one. The rule tells us that an infinite sum

$$1 + H + H^2 + H^3 + \ldots$$

always has the value $1/(1 - H)$ as long as H is a fraction between zero and 1. When we replace H with the MPC—which is always between zero and 1—we obtain a value for the multiplier of $1/(1 - MPC)$.

For any value of the MPC, the formula for the spending multiplier is 1/(1 - MPC).

In our example, the MPC was equal to 0.6, so the spending multiplier had the value $1/(1 - 0.6) = 1/0.4 = 2.5$. If the MPC had been 0.9 instead, the spending multiplier would have been equal to $1/(1 - 0.9) = 1/0.1 = 10$. The formula $1/(1 - MPC)$ can be used to find the multiplier for any value of the MPC between zero and 1.

Using the general formula for the spending multiplier, we can restate what happens when investment spending increases:

$$\Delta GDP = \left[\frac{1}{(1 - MPC)} \right] \times \Delta I^P.$$

The multiplier effect is a rather surprising phenomenon. It tells us that an increase in investment spending ultimately affects GDP by *more* than the initial increase in investment. Moreover, the multiplier can work in the other direction, as you are about to see.

The Multiplier in Reverse

Suppose, in Table 3, that investment spending had *decreased* instead of increased. Then the initial change in spending would be –$100 billion ($\Delta I^P$ = –$100 billion). This would cause a $100 billion decrease in output at firms that produce investment goods, and they, in turn, would pay out $100 billion less in factor payments. In the next round, households—with $100 billion less in income—would spend $60 billion less on consumption goods, and so on. The final result would be a $250 billion *decrease* in equilibrium GDP.

> *Just as increases in investment spending cause GDP to rise by a multiple of the change in spending, decreases in investment spending cause GDP to fall by a multiple of the change in spending.*

The multiplier formula we've already established will work whether the initial change in spending is positive or negative.

Other Spending Shocks

Shocks to the economy can come from other sources besides investment spending. In fact, when *any* sector's spending behavior changes, it will set off a chain of events similar to that in our investment example. Let's see how an increase in government spending could set off the same chain of events as an increase in investment spending.

Suppose that government agencies increased their purchases above previous levels. For example, the Department of Defense might raise its spending on new fighter jets, or state highway departments might hire more road repair crews, or cities and towns might hire more teachers. If total government purchases rise by $100 billion, then, once again, household income will rise by $100 billion. As before, households will spend 60 percent of this increase, causing consumption—in the next round—to rise by $60 billion, and so on. The chain of events is exactly like that of Table 3, with one exception: The first line in column 1 would read, "Initial Increase in Government purchases" instead of "Initial Increase in Investment Spending." Once again, output would increase by $250 billion.

Changes in autonomous consumption (*a*), which shift the consumption function upward, or changes in net exports (*NX*), will set off the same process. In both cases, after the initial spending increase of $100 billion, we would see further increases in consumption spending of $60 billion, then $36 billion, and so forth. The first line in column 1 of Table 3 would read, "Initial Increase in Autonomous Consumption," or "Initial Increase in Net Exports," but every entry in the table would be the same.

> *Changes in investment, government purchases, autonomous consumption, or net exports lead to a multiplier effect on GDP. The spending multiplier— $1/(1 - MPC)$—is what we multiply the initial change in spending by in order to get the change in equilibrium GDP.*

The following four equations summarize how we use the spending multiplier to determine the effects of the four different types of spending shocks. Keep in mind that these formulas work whether the initial change in spending is positive or negative.

$$\Delta GDP = \left[\frac{1}{(1 - MPC)} \right] \times \Delta I^p$$

$$\Delta GDP = \left[\frac{1}{(1 - MPC)} \right] \times \Delta G$$

$$\Delta GDP = \left[\frac{1}{(1 - MPC)} \right] \times \Delta a$$

$$\Delta GDP = \left[\frac{1}{(1 - MPC)} \right] \times \Delta NX$$

Changes in Net Taxes

In addition to the spending changes we've considered so far, there is one additional factor that can change total spending and lead to a multiplier effect on output: net taxes. Suppose that the government either decreases its tax revenue or increases its transfer payments. Either of these changes will *decrease* net taxes. Since disposable income is equal to total income minus net taxes, the cut in net taxes will *raise* disposable income for any given total income.

What will happen?

With more disposable income, households will spend more, leading business firms to produce more, creating more income, and so on. Thus, a decrease in net taxes raises output in the economy by a multiple of the original tax cut. Sounds very much like all the other spending changes we've considered. There is one difference, however: The multiplier for a tax cut turns out to be *smaller* than the multiplier for other spending changes.

The Two Kinds of Spending Changes It's easy to confuse the two different types of changes in spending that occur during economic fluctuations. When spending changes for some reason *other* than a change in income, we call it a *spending* shock. Spending shocks are what set off the multiplier process. They are caused by changes in autonomous consumption, planned investment, government purchases, net exports, or taxes. But spending (specifically, consumption spending) also changes *during* the multiplier process itself. These changes in spending—because they are *caused by* changes in income—are *not* spending shocks.

DANGEROUS CURVES

To understand why, let's compare two specific changes: a $100 billion increase in government purchases versus a $100 billion tax cut. Will they have the same impact on GDP? No. When G increases, the initial change in spending—which sets off the multiplier process—is $100 billion. But when T drops, the initial change in spending will be *less* than $100 billion. That is because households—when they get the tax cut—will spend only *part* of it and save the rest. The fraction that they spend will depend on the MPC. If the MPC is 0.9, for example, then households will spend $90 billion of the tax cut, so the initial change in spending in Table 3 will be $90 billion, not $100 billion. The final result is a smaller change in GDP—and a smaller multiplier. The special multiplier for changes in tax is derived in the appendix to this chapter. Here, we can note the following important conclusion:

Changes in net taxes lead to a multiplier effect on GDP, although the multiplier for tax changes is smaller than for other spending changes. A cut in net taxes causes GDP to rise, while a rise in net taxes causes GDP to fall.

Spending Shocks in Recent History

In the real world, the economy is constantly buffeted by shocks, and they often cause full-fledged macroeconomic fluctuations. Table 4 lists some of the recessions and notable expansions of the last 50 years, along with the events and spending shocks that are thought to have caused them or at least contributed heavily. You can see that each of these shocks first affected spending and output in one or more sectors of the economy. For example, several recessions have been set off by increases in oil prices, which caused a decrease in spending on products that depend on oil and energy, such as automobiles, trucks, and new factory buildings. Other recessions were precipitated by military cutbacks. Still others came about when the Federal Reserve caused sudden increases in interest rates that led to decreased spending on new homes and other goods. (You'll learn about the Federal Reserve and its policies in the next chapter.)

Several of our recessions since the early 1950s have been caused, at least in part, by rapid rises in oil prices.

Strong expansions, on the other hand, have been caused by military buildups, by falling oil prices that stimulated spending on energy-related products, and by bursts of planned investment spending. The long expansion of the mid- and late-1990s, for example, began when the development of the Internet, and improvements in computers more generally, led to an increase in investment spending. Once the economy began expanding, it was further spurred by other factors, such as a rise in stock prices and consumer optimism, both of which led to an increase in consumption spending.

In addition to these identifiable spending shocks, the economy is buffeted by other shocks whose origins are harder to spot. For example, consumption was higher than expected in the late 1980s, contributing to the rapid expansion that occurred in those years. In the early 1990s, consumption fell back to normal, helping to cause the recession of that period. There was no obvious event that caused these changes in consumption.

And each shock has momentum. When a decrease in spending causes production cutbacks, firms will lay off workers. The laid-off workers, suffering decreases in their incomes, cut back their own spending on other products, causing further layoffs in other sectors. The economy can continue sliding downward, and remain below potential output, for a year or longer. The same process works in reverse during an expansion: Higher spending leads to greater production, higher employment, and still greater spending, possibly leading to a boom in which the economy remains overheated for some time.

Booms and recessions do not last forever, however. The economy eventually adjusts back to full-employment output. Often, a change in government macroeconomic policy helps the adjustment process along, speeding the return to full employment. Other times, a policy mistake thwarts the adjustment process, prolonging or deepening a costly recession, or exacerbating a boom and overheating the economy even more.

What brings the economy back to its potential output after a boom or a recession? And why does the process often take so long? These questions will be answered in Chapter 17, "Aggregate Demand and Aggregate Supply."

Period		Event	Spending Shock
Early 1950s	Expansion	Korean War	Defense Spending ↑
1953	Recession	End of Korean War	Defense Spending ↓
Late 1960s	Expansion	Vietnam War	Defense Spending ↑
1970	Recession	Change in Federal Reserve Policy	Spending on New Homes ↓
1974	Recession	Dramatic Increase in Oil Prices	Spending on Cars and Other Energy-using Products ↓
1980	Recession	Dramatic Increase in Oil Prices	Spending on Cars and Other Energy-using Products ↓
1981–82	Recession	Change in Federal Reserve Policy	Spending on New Homes, Cars, and Business Investment ↓
Early 1980s	Expansion	Military Buildup	Defense Spending ↑
Late 1980s	Expansion	Huge Decline in Oil Prices	Spending on Energy-using Products ↑
1990	Recession	Large Increase in Oil Prices; Collapse of Soviet Union	Spending on Cars and Other Energy-using Products ↓; Defense Spending ↓
1991–2000	Expansion	Technological Advances in Computers; Development of the Internet; High Wealth Creation	Spending on Capital Equipment ↑; Consumption ↑
2001	Recession	Investment in New Technology Slows; Technology-fueled Bubble of Optimism Bursts; Wealth Destruction	Spending on Capital Equipment ↓

TABLE 4
Expansions, Recessions, and Shocks That Caused Them

Automatic Stabilizers

In this chapter, we've analyzed an important piece of the macroeconomic puzzle: how spending shocks are transmitted throughout the economy and ultimately have a multiplier effect on total output. However, to keep our discussion as simple as possible, we've ignored many real-world factors that interfere with, and reduce the size of, the multiplier. These forces are called **automatic stabilizers** because, with a smaller multiplier, spending shocks will cause a much smaller change in GDP. As a result, booms and recessions will be milder. Or, to put it another way: if not for automatic stabilizers, the deviations away from potential output would have been greater than the ones we've actually experienced, as seen in Figure 1.

Automatic stabilizers Forces that reduce the size of the spending multiplier and diminish the impact of spending shocks.

> *Automatic stabilizers reduce the size of the multiplier and therefore reduce the impact of spending shocks on the economy. With milder booms and recessions, the economy is more stable.*

How do automatic stabilizers work? They shrink the change in spending that occurs in each round of the multiplier, and thereby reduce the final multiplier effect on equilibrium GDP. In Table 3, automatic stabilizers would reduce each of the numerical entries after the first $100 billion and lead to a final change in GDP smaller than $250 billion.

Here are some of the real-world automatic stabilizers we've ignored in our discussion.

Taxes. We've been assuming that—as the multiplier process works its way through the economy, and income rises—taxes remain constant. But some taxes (like the personal income tax) rise with income. As a result, in each round of the multiplier, the increase in disposable income will be smaller than the increase in total income. With a smaller rise in disposable income, there will be a smaller rise in consumption spending as well.

Transfer Payments. Some government transfer payments fall as income rises. For example, many laid-off workers receive unemployment benefits, which help support them for several months while they are unemployed. But when income and output rise, employment rises too, and newly hired workers must give up their unemployment benefits. As a result, a rise in income will cause a smaller rise in *disposable* income. Consumption will then rise by less in each round of the multiplier.

Interest Rates. An increase in output often leads to rising interest rates. As a result, investment spending may drop even as output expands. When the drop in investment spending is accounted for, the rise in total spending in each round of the multiplier process will be smaller. You'll learn more about this effect in the next two chapters.

Imports. Some of the additional spending in the multiplier process is on goods and services imported from abroad. This will increase the revenue of foreign firms and the incomes of foreign workers, but will not contribute to higher incomes for U.S. workers. As a result, the increase in output and spending in each round of the multiplier process will be smaller.

Forward-looking Behavior. Consumers may be *forward looking*. If they realize that recessions and booms are temporary, their consumption spending may be less sensitive to changes in their current income. Therefore, any change in income will cause a smaller change in consumption spending and lead to a smaller multiplier effect.

Remember that each of these automatic stabilizers reduces the size of the multiplier, making it smaller than the simple formulas given in this chapter. For example, the simple formula for the spending multiplier is $1/(1 - MPC)$. With an MPC of about 0.9—which is in the ballpark for the United States and many other countries—we would expect the multiplier to be about 10 . . . *if the simple formula were accurate.* In that case, every time a spending shock hit the economy, output would change by 10 times the initial shock. But after we take account of all of the automatic stabilizers, the multiplier is considerably smaller. How much smaller? Most of the forecasting models used by economists in business and government predict that the multiplier effect takes about 3 quarters of a year to work its way through the economy. At the end of the process, the multiplier has a value of about 1.5. This means that a $100 billion annual increase in, say, government purchases should cause GDP to increase by only about $150 billion per year. This is much less than the $1,000 billion increase predicted by the simple formula $1/(1 - MPC)$ when the MPC is equal to 0.9.

> *In the real world, due to automatic stabilizers, spending shocks have much weaker impacts on the economy than our simple multiplier formulas would suggest.*

Finally, there is one more automatic stabilizer you should know about, perhaps the most important of all: the *passage of time*. Why is this an automatic stabilizer? Because, as you'll see two chapters from now, the impact of spending shocks on the economy is *temporary*. A few months after a shock, corrective mechanisms begin to operate, and the economy begins to return to full employment. As time passes, the impact of a spending shock gradually disappears. And if we wait long enough—a few years or so—the effects of the shock will be gone entirely. That is, after a shock pulls us away from full-employment GDP, the economy will eventually return to full-employment GDP—right where it started. We thus conclude that

Short-Run versus Long-Run Outcomes

in the long run, our multipliers have a value of zero: No matter what the change in spending or taxes, output will return to full employment, so the change in equilibrium GDP will be zero.

COUNTERCYCLICAL FISCAL POLICY

What you've learned about the multiplier process not only helps to explain what *causes* economic fluctuations: It also suggests a method of *preventing them*. After all, if a spending shock sends output spiraling downward, the government should be able to create its *own* spending shock in the opposite direction, by changing government purchases or net taxes. Changes in the government's budget designed to affect the macro-economy are called *fiscal policy*. When the changes are specifically designed to counteract economic fluctuations, they are called *countercyclical fiscal policy*.

Countercyclical fiscal policy Any change in government purchases or net taxes designed to counteract economic fluctuations.

Countercyclical fiscal policy is any change in government purchases or net taxes designed to counteract spending shocks and keep the economy close to potential output.

Here is an example of how countercyclical fiscal policy might work. Suppose that the economy is hit by an adverse spending shock—say, a decrease in investment spending of $100 billion. Suppose, too, that the multiplier in the economy is 1.5. If the government did nothing, output would ultimately decrease by $100 billion × 1.5 = $150 billion.

If the government wanted to counteract this spending shock, it could raise its *own* spending on goods and services by $100 billion. This would tend to *increase* GDP by $100 billion × 1.5 = $150 billion—the same amount by which the adverse shock is pulling GDP down. With the countercyclical fiscal policy, the net effect of the adverse shock and the change in government purchases would be . . . no change in GDP!

In addition to changing its purchases, the government has another option: It could decrease net taxes. This could be accomplished either by cutting taxes or by increasing transfer payments. However, since the multiplier for changes in net taxes is smaller than the spending multiplier, the tax cut or the rise in transfers would have to be greater than $100 billion.

In the 1960s and early 1970s, many economists and government officials believed that countercyclical fiscal policy could be an effective tool to counteract the business cycle. Today, however, very few economists hold this position. Instead, they would leave the job of fighting the business cycle to the U.S. Federal Reserve—an institution discussed first in Chapter 13 and to which we will return in great detail in the next chapter. Indeed, the last clear use of countercyclical fiscal policy occurred in 1975, when the government gave tax rebates in the depths of a serious recession in order to stimulate consumption.

Why do economists recommend against using countercyclical fiscal policy, and why does Washington mostly follow their advice? There are several reasons.

Timing Problems. It takes many months or even longer for a fiscal change to be enacted. Consider, for example, a decision to change taxes in the United States. A tax bill originates in the House of Representatives and then goes to the Senate, where it is usually modified. Then a conference committee irons out the differences between the House and Senate versions, and the tax bill goes back to each chamber for a vote. Even if all goes smoothly—and the president does not veto the bill—this process can take many months.

But in most cases, it will *not* go smoothly: The inevitable political conflicts will cause further delays. First, there is the thorny question of distributing the cost of a tax hike, or the benefits of a tax cut, among different income groups within the country. Each party may argue for changes in the tax bill in order to please its constituents. And some senators and representatives will see the bill as an opportunity to improve the tax system in more fundamental ways, causing further political debate.

All of these problems create the danger that the tax change will take effect long after it is needed. And changes in transfer payments or government purchases would suffer from similar delays. As a result, a fiscal stimulus might take effect after the economy has recovered from a recession and is headed for a boom; or a fiscal contraction might take effect just as the economy is entering a recession. Fiscal changes would then be a *destabilizing* force in the economy—stepping on the gas when we should be hitting the brakes, and vice versa.

Even the tax cuts engineered by the Bush administration in 2001 and 2003—which helped to stimulate a weak economy—have not restored economists' faith in well-timed countercyclical fiscal policy. The first of these tax cuts was formulated in 2000, by Presidential *candidate* Bush, long before the economy was in recession or any need for fiscal stimulus could have been known. The fact that it took effect during a recession was a coincidence, rather than a purposeful timing of policy. And both tax cuts were long-term measures—applying for almost a decade—rather than short-term, temporary measures designed to fight a temporary recession.

As you will see in the next chapter, the Federal Reserve can make decisions that begin to influence the economy *on the very day it decides that the change is necessary*. While there are time lags in the *effectiveness* of the Federal Reserve's policy moves, its ability to execute its policy in short order gives it an important advantage over fiscal policy for stabilizing the economy.

Irreversibility. To be truly *countercyclical*, fiscal policy moves would have to be temporary. This is because the forces they are designed to counteract—spending shocks—are themselves temporary. If the government increases its purchases to fight an adverse shock, it must reverse course and cut its purchases as the adverse shock subsides. But reversing changes in government purchases, transfer payments or taxes can be extraordinarily difficult, for political reasons.

Spending programs that create new government departments or expand existing ones tend to become permanent, or at least difficult to terminate because those who benefit from the programs will lobby to preserve them. Many temporary tax changes become permanent as well—the public is never happy to see a tax cut reversed, and the government is often reluctant to reverse a tax hike that has provided additional revenue for government programs.

The Reaction of the Federal Reserve. Even if the government attempted to stabilize the economy with fiscal policy, it could not do so very effectively, because—to put it simply—the Fed will not allow it. As you will learn in the next chapter, the Federal Reserve sees its own goal as keeping the economy as close to potential output as possible. Its officials view any change in fiscal policy as just another spending shock threatening to create a boom or recession, to be neutralized as quickly as possible. For example, if the government cuts taxes, which tends to increase output, the Fed will typically counteract it with its own policies, designed to *decrease* output. As long as the Fed is free to set its own course, and as long as it continues to take responsibility for stabilizing the economy, there is little opportunity—and little need—for countercyclical fiscal policy.

Our discussion about countercyclical policy has probably raised several questions in your mind. What gives the Federal Reserve the audacity to claim countercylical policy for itself and to shamelessly counteract the government's fiscal policy? What policies does it use to accomplish its goals? And how do its policies affect the economy? These are important questions, and we'll address them in the next chapter.

USING THE THEORY
The Recession of 2001

Our most recent recession lasted from March 2001 to November 2001. Table 5 tells the story. Look first at the upper panel. The second column shows real GDP in 2000 dollars in each of several quarters. The figures are stated as *annual rates*. (For example, real GDP in the *second* quarter of 2001 was $9,866 billion. This means that *if* we had continued producing that quarter's GDP for an entire year, we *would* have produced a total of $9,866 billion worth of goods and services in the year 2001.) The other columns show investment spending (also at an annual rate) and the average level of employment for the quarter.

The lower panel, which is derived from the upper panel, gives a somewhat clearer picture of what happened during 2001. For each quarter, it shows the *change* in real GDP, investment spending, and average employment from the quarter before. As you can see, investment spending and real GDP—which were drifting downward before the recession—fell sharply during the second quarter of 2001 and continued to fall throughout the year. Employment mirrored this change, dropping in the second quarter and continuing to drop through the year.

(a) Real GDP, Investment, and Employment

TABLE 5
The Recession of 2001

	Quarter	Real GDP (Billions of 2000 Dollars)	Investment Spending (Billions of 2000 Dollars; excludes changes in inventories)	Average Employment (thousands)
	4th quarter, 2000	9,888	1,689	137,329
Recession Quarters	1st quarter, 2001	9,882	1,678	137,752
	2nd quarter, 2001	9,866	1,638	137,086
	3rd quarter, 2001	9,835	1,616	136,707
	4th quarter, 2001	9,884	1,571	136,218
	1st quarter, 2002	9,998	1,561	136,128

(b) Change (from previous quarter) in Real GDP, Investment, and Employment

	Quarter	Change in Real GDP (Billions of 2000 Dollars)	Change in Investment Spending (Billions of 2000 Dollars)	Change in Average Employment (thousands)
Recession Quarters	1st quarter, 2001	−6	−11	+423
	2nd quarter, 2001	−16	−40	−666
	3rd quarter, 2001	−31	−22	−379
	4th quarter, 2001	+49	−45	−489
	1st quarter, 2002	+114	−10	−90

NOTE: DATA FOR REAL GDP AND INVESTMENT FROM *WWW.BEA.GOV*, REVISED DEC 23, 2003. DATA FOR EMPLOYMENT FIGURES FROM *WWW.BLS.GOV*.

What caused this recession? And can the concepts presented in this chapter help us understand it? Indeed they can.

The decrease in investment spending was just the sort of spending shock we've discussed in this chapter. Over time, as the multiplier process takes place, a decrease in investment will bring down both GDP and employment, and that is just what happened in 2001.

But what caused these successive decreases in investment spending? In retrospect, we can see there were at least three causes.

First, during much of the late 1990s, there had been a boom in capital equipment spending as existing businesses rushed to incorporate the Internet into factories, offices, and their business practices in general. Firms like Avis, Wal-Mart, and Viacom needed servers and high-speed Internet connections, and the firms that supplied the new technology needed their own new offices, factories, and equipment. But as 2000 ended and 2001 began, firms had begun to catch up to the new technology. The rush ended and investment began to fall.

Another reason for the investment spending shock also had its roots in the 1990s. During this period, the Internet and other new technologies made the public very optimistic about the future profits of American businesses. The public became hungry to own shares of stock in almost any company that had anything to do with the Internet, and share prices rose sky high. The optimism and the high share prices that came along with it encouraged entirely new businesses to start up—businesses that used the Internet to sell pet supplies, prescription drugs, and toys, or to deliver videos, groceries, or even fresh hot pizzas. Of course, these new businesses needed their own capital equipment, warehouses, and office buildings, driving investment spending even further skyward in the late 1990s.

Unfortunately, in late 2000 and early 2001, reality set in. Competition was preventing many new firms from earning any profit at all, and many went bankrupt. Optimism shifted to pessimism. Share prices fell, and new business ventures—especially those having something to do with the Internet—came to a halt. And so did the associated investment spending.

The final reason for the investment shock—more accurately, an exacerbation of the shock already occurring—was the infamous terrorist attacks on the World Trade Center and the Pentagon on September 11, 2001. The nation was traumatized by these events. What little optimism that was left in the future of the U.S. economy turned to uncertainty and fear. Millions of potential airline passengers no longer wanted to fly, forcing the airlines to cancel flights and, of course, cancel any orders for new aircraft. Hotel vacancy rates skyrocketed, causing investment in new hotels and expansion of existing hotels to come to a halt. Similar decisions were being made in other industries, and investment spending fell sharply. (Although the table shows that investment declined only modestly in the third quarter, it is likely that most of the decrease occurred in September.)

DANGEROUS CURVES

What Makes It a Recession? Newspapers and television commentators often state that a recession occurs when real GDP declines for two consecutive quarters. But this is not correct.

Actually, when a U.S recession begins and ends is determined by a committee within the National Bureau of Economic Research, an entirely private, nonprofit research organization headquartered in Boston.[2] The committee makes its decisions by looking at a variety of factors, including employment, industrial production, sales, and personal income, all of which are reported monthly. While it is true that each of these measures tends to move closely with real GDP, the latter is measured only quarterly, and plays only a supporting role in dating recessions.

One abnormal feature of the recession of 2001 was the behavior of consumption spending. Ordinarily, as income falls in a recession, consumption declines along with it. Yet consumption spending (not shown) actually *rose* during every quarter of 2001.

Part of the reason for the upward shift was a 10-year tax cut that went into effect in June of 2001. But there were other reasons as well—which we'll look at in the next chapter. Still, the increase in consumption spending was not enough to prevent the recession. The decline in investment spending—and the multiplier process it initiated—was too powerful.

The investment spending shock, and the recession it caused, are only half of the story of the recession of 2001. The other half, entirely ignored so far, is the response of government policy makers as they tried to prevent the economic storm from becoming a hurricane. Ultimately, their actions helped to make the recession relatively short and mild by historical standards. But to understand what these policy makers did, why they did it, and why it worked reasonably well, we must learn about the banking system, the money supply, and the Federal Reserve. These are the subjects of the next chapter.

---

[2] For the past few decades, the NBER's Business Cycle Dating Committee has been chaired by Robert E. Hall, a coauthor of this textbook.

Summary

Over periods of a few years, national economies experience booms and recessions—economic fluctuations in which output rises above or falls below its long-term growth path. And when real GDP fluctuates, employment fluctuates as well.

The key to explaining booms and recessions is changes in total spending. The largest component of total spending is consumption spending (C), which depends on disposable income (total income minus net taxes). When disposable income rises by a dollar, consumption spending rises by a fraction of a dollar. The fraction is called the *marginal propensity to consume,* or MPC. The consumption function is a graph that shows how consumption spending depends on disposable income. The consumption function is a straight line, and its vertical intercept is called *autonomous consumption.* The slope of the line is the MPC.

Besides consumption, the other three components of total spending are investment spending (I^P), government purchases (G), and net exports (NX). In this chapter, these three variables are treated as given.

Deviations from the full-employment level of output are often caused by *spending shocks*—changes in autonomous consumption, investment spending, government purchases, or net exports. These initially affect one sector and then work their way through the entire economy. Negative or adverse shocks can cause recessions, while positive shocks can cause booms. Eventually, output will return to its potential, full-employment level, but it does not do so immediately.

After a spending shock, output changes by a multiple of the initial change in spending. The multiple is called the *spending multiplier.* The simple formula for the multiplier is $1/(1 - MPC)$. But this formula ignores a variety of automatic stabilizers, and in reality, the multiplier is considerably smaller than the simple formula suggests. There is also a multiplier for changes in taxes, but it is smaller than the spending multiplier.

Countercyclical fiscal policy is any change in government purchases, taxes, or transfer payments designed to stabilize the economy. Until about 25 years ago, economists believed that countercyclical fiscal policy had great promise as a stabilizing force. Today, most economists and government policy makers believe that stabilizing the economy should be the job of the Federal Reserve.

Key Terms

Automatic stabilizer
Autonomous consumption
Boom
Consumption function
Countercyclical fiscal policy

Disposable income
Equilibrium GDP
Marginal propensity to consume (MPC)
Net taxes
Planned investment (I^P) spending

Spending multiplier
Spending shock
Total spending

Review Questions

1. How does a *recession* differ from a *boom*? Describe the typical behavior of GDP and the unemployment rate during these periods?

2. Briefly describe the four main categories of spending.

3. List, and briefly explain, the main determinants of consumption spending. Indicate whether a change in each determinant causes a movement along, or a shift of, the consumption function.

4. What are the main components of investment spending? How does actual or total investment differ from planned investment?

5. Why are exports added, and imports subtracted, in measuring total spending?

6. Why are transfer payments subtracted in measuring net taxes?

7. What is the *spending multiplier*? Why does the multiplier for a change in taxes have a different value than the multiplier for a change in government purchases?

8. "Today, the business cycle is dead. The government can neutralize any spending shock with a well-timed, countercyclical change in government spending or net taxes." Comment.

9. "During the last half century economic fluctuations in the United States have been caused entirely by changes in military spending." True or false? Explain.

Problems and Exercises

1.

Disposable Income	C
7,000	6,600
8,000	7,400
9,000	8,200
10,000	9,000
11,000	9,800
12,000	10,600
13,000	11,400

a. What is the marginal propensity to consume implicit in this data?

b. What is the value of autonomous consumption spending? (Hint: if the data in the table were extrapolated, what would be the value of C when disposable income is zero?)

c. What is the numerical value of the multiplier in this economy? (Assume there are no automatic stabilizers in this economy, i.e., use the simple formula from the chapter.)

d. In this economy, if government purchases decreased by 600, what would happen to total output?

2. Using the data given in problem 1, construct a table similar to Table 3 in the chapter.

a. Show what would happen in the first five rounds following an increase in annual investment spending from 400 to 800.

b. What would be the ultimate effect of that increase in investment spending on total yearly output?

c. If consumption spending was 10,600 before the increase in investment, what would be the new value of consumption spending after the multiplier process has finished?

3. Suppose that households become more thrifty—that is, they now wish to save 500 more at any level of disposable income.

a. In the table in problem 1, which column of data would be affected? How?

b. What would be the new value of the MPC?

c. What would be the new value of autonomous consumption?

4. a. Complete the following table when autonomous consumption is $30 billion, the marginal propensity to consume is 0.85, and net taxes are $0.

Real GDP ($ Billions)	Autonomous Consumption	MPC × Disposable Income	Consumption = Autonomous Consumption + (MPC × Disposable Income)
$0			
$100			
$200			
$300			
$400			
$500			
$600			

b. Given your answers in part (a), and given that planned investment is $40 billion, government spending is $20 billion, exports are $20 billion, and imports are $35 billion, complete the following table. (See table at bottom of page.)

c. What is the equilibrium level of real GDP?

d. What will happen if the actual level of real GDP in this economy is $200 billion?

e. What will happen to equilibrium GDP if planned investment in this economy falls to $25 billion?

Real GDP ($ Billions)	Consumption Spending	Planned Investment	Government Spending	Net Exports	Total Spending
$0					
$100					
$200					
$300					
$400					
$500					
$600					

5.

Y	C	I^P	G	NX
7,000	6,100	400	1,000	500
8,000	6,900	400	1,000	500
9,000	7,700	400	1,000	500
10,000	8,500	400	1,000	500
11,000	9,300	400	1,000	500
12,000	10,100	400	1,000	500
13,000	10,900	400	1,000	500

a. What is the marginal propensity to consume implicit in these data?

b. What is the numerical value of the expenditure multiplier for this economy?

c. What is the equilibrium level of real GDP?

d. Suppose that government purchases (G) decreased from 1,000 to 400 at each level of income. What would happen to equilibrium real GDP?

6. What would be the effect on real GDP and total employment of each of the following changes?

a. As a result of restrictions on imports into the United States, net exports (NX) increase.

b. The federal government launches a new program to improve highways, bridges, and airports.

c. Banks are offering such high interest rates that consumers decide to save a larger proportion of their incomes.

d. The growth of Internet retailing leads business firms to purchase more computer hardware and software.

7. Calculate the change in real GDP that would result in each of the following cases:

a. Planned investment spending rises by $100 billion, and the MPC is 0.9.

b. Autonomous consumption spending decreases by $50 billion, and the MPC is 0.7.

c. Government purchases rise by $40 billion, while at the same time, investment spending falls by $10 billion. The MPC is 0.6.

8. Calculate the changes in real GDP that would result in each of the following cases:

a. Government purchases rise by $7,500, and the MPC is 0.95.

b. Planned investment spending falls by $300,000 and the MPC is 0.65.

c. Export spending rises by $60 billion at the same time that import spending rises by $65 billion, and the MPC is 0.75.

Challenge Questions

1. Suppose that net taxes depend on income. Specifically, each time household income increases by $100, the government's net taxes increase by $25. What is the new value for the multiplier? (Hint: Construct a table similar to Table 3, but incorporating the change in taxes. Also Note: In each round of the multiplier, the rise in disposable income will equal the rise in income *minus* any rise in taxes.)

These exercises require access to Lieberman/Hall Xtra! If Xtra! did not come with your book, visit http://liebermanxtra.swlearning.com to purchase.

1. Use your Xtra! password at the Hall and Lieberman Web site (http://liebermanxtra.swlearning.com), select this chapter, and under Economic Applications, click on EconData. Choose *Macroeconomics: Employment, Unemployment, and Inflation,* and scroll down to find *Real GDP.* Read the definition and click on Updates and use the information to answer the following questions.

a. Read the Bureau of Economic Analysis's new release http://www.bea.doc.gov/bea/newsrel/gdp402f.htm and discuss the contributions of each component of the real GDP to growth in the period considered.

b. Refer to the U.S. GDP and its Components data link http://www.economagic.com/fedstl.htm#GDP. Retrieve the data (in constant dollars), and the percent change of data for the four main components of total spending: (1) Personal Consumption Expenditures, (2) Gross Private Domestic Investment, (3) Government Purchases, and (4) Net Exports. Which is the largest component? Which is the most volatile component?

c. Refer to the U.S. GDP and its Components data link http://www.economagic.com/fedstl.htm#GDP. Retrieve the data (in constant dollars), for Personal Consumption and Disposable Income and chart Personal Consumption against Disposable Income. Draw a line to fit the trend and calculate its slope, which represents the marginal propensity to consume. Now calculate the simple multiplier. If spending increases by $1,000 billion, by how much will GDP increase?

APPENDIX

THE SPECIAL CASE OF THE TAX MULTIPLIER

You learned in this chapter how changes in autonomous consumption, investment, and government purchases affect the economy's GDP. But there is another type of change that can influence GDP: a change in net taxes. For this type of change, the formula for the multiplier is a bit different from the one presented in the chapter.

Let's suppose that net taxes (T) *decrease* by $100 billion. The immediate impact is to increase households' *disposable income* by $100 billion. As a result, consumption spending will increase. But by how much?

The answer is, by *less* than $100 billion. When households get a tax cut, they increase their spending *not* by the full amount of the cut, but only by a *part of* it. The amount by which spending initially increases depends on the *MPC*. If the *MPC* is 0.6, and disposable income rises by $100 billion, the initial change in consumption spending is just $60 billion. *This is the first change in spending that occurs after the tax cut.* Of course, once consumption spending rises, every subsequent round of the multiplier will work just as in Table 3: In the next round, consumption spending will rise by $36 billion, and then $21.6 billion, and so on.

Now let's compare what happens when net taxes are cut by $100 billion with what happens when spending rises by $100 billion. As you can see from Table 3, when investment spending rises by $100 billion, the initial change in spending is, by definition, $100 billion. But when taxes are cut by $100 billion, the initial change in spending is *not* $100 billion, but *$60 billion*. Thus, the first line of the table is missing in the case of a $100 billion tax cut. All subsequent rounds of the multiplier are the same, however. Therefore, we would expect the $100 billion tax cut to cause a $150 billion increase in equilibrium GDP—not the $250 billion increase listed in the table.

Another way to say this is: For each dollar that net taxes are cut, equilibrium GDP will increase by $1.50 rather than $2.50—the increase is one dollar less in the case of the tax cut. This observation tells us that the tax multiplier must have a numerical value *1 less than* the spending multiplier of the chapter.

Finally, there is one more difference between the spending multiplier of the chapter and the tax multiplier: While the spending multiplier is a positive number (because an increase in spending causes an increase in equilibrium GDP), the tax multiplier is a negative number, since a tax cut (a negative change in taxes) must be multiplied by a *negative* number to give us a *positive* change in GDP.

Putting all this together, we conclude that

> *the tax multiplier is 1.0 less than the spending multiplier and negative in sign.*

Thus, if the *MPC* is 0.6 (as in the chapter), so that the spending multiplier is 2.5, then the tax multiplier will have a value of $-(2.5 - 1) = -1.5$.

More generally, since the tax multiplier is 1 less than the spending multiplier and is also negative, we can write

$$\text{Tax multiplier} = -(\text{spending multiplier} - 1)$$

Because the spending multiplier is $1/(1 - MPC)$, we can substitute to get

$$\text{Tax multiplier} = -\left[\frac{1}{(1 - MPC)} - 1\right]$$
$$= -\frac{1 - (1 - MPC)}{(1 - MPC)} = \frac{-MPC}{1 - MPC}$$

Hence,

> *the general formula for the tax multiplier is*
> $$\frac{-MPC}{1 - MPC}$$

For any change in net taxes, we can use the formula to find the change in GDP as follows:

$$\Delta GDP = \left[\frac{-MPC}{(1 - MPC)}\right] \times \Delta T$$

In our example, in which net taxes were cut by $100 billion, we have $\Delta T = -\$100$ billion and $MPC = 0.6$. Plugging these values into the formula, we obtain

$$\Delta GDP = \left[\frac{-0.6}{1 - 0.6}\right] \times -\$100 \text{ billion} = \$150 \text{ billion}$$

The Banking System, the Federal Reserve, and Monetary Policy

Everyone knows that money doesn't grow on trees. But where does it actually come from? You might think that the answer is simple: The government just prints it. Right?

Sort of. It is true that much of our money supply is, indeed, paper currency printed by our national monetary authority. But most of our money supply is not paper currency at all and is not printed by anyone. Moreover, the monetary authority in the United States—the Federal Reserve System—is not technically a part of the government, but a quasi-independent agency that operates *along side* of the government.

This chapter is about money, the institutions that help create it, and how changes in the nation's money supply affect the economy. What you learn here will deepen your understanding of economic fluctuations and help you understand our policy choices in dealing with them. We will begin by taking a look at what money is and how it is measured. Then, we turn our attention to the private banking

491

system and the U.S. Federal Reserve. Next, we'll consider how the Federal Reserve works through the private banking system to change the money supply. Finally, we'll explore how the Federal Reserve uses its control over the money supply to help stabilize the economy.

WHAT IS COUNTED AS MONEY?

Money, loosely defined, is the means of payment in the economy. As you will learn in this chapter, the amount of money in circulation can affect the macro-economy. This is why governments around the world like to know how much money is available to their citizens.

In practice, the standard definition of money is *cash, checking account balances,* and *travelers' checks.*[1] What do these have in common and why are they included in the definition of money when other means of payment—such as credit cards—are not included?

First, only *assets*—things of value that people own—are regarded as money. Paper currency, travelers' checks, and funds held in checking accounts are all examples of assets. But *the right to borrow* is not considered an asset, so it is not part of the money supply. This is why the credit limit on your credit card and your ability to go into a bank and borrow money are not considered part of the money supply.

Second, only things that are widely *acceptable* as a means of payment are regarded as money. Currency, travelers' checks, and personal checks can all be used to buy things or pay bills. Other assets—such as the funds in your savings account—cannot generally be used to pay for goods and services, and so they fail the acceptability test.

The money supply is constantly changing. The Federal Reserve—the institution responsible for controlling the money supply—keeps track of the total and reports it each week. For example, on July 14, 2003, the total U.S. money supply (as reported by the Fed) was $1,266 billion.

Let's take a closer look at the different components of the money supply.

The Components of the Money Supply

Cash in the hands of the public
Currency and coins held outside of banks.

When we think about money, the first image that pops into our minds is *cash.* More specifically, we count as money **cash in the hands of the public.** Excluded are cash held by banks and cash held by the Federal Reserve itself.

The Fed has a fairly easy time keeping track of the total amount of currency in circulation, because the Fed itself has issued it. (It is also the institution that collects and destroys worn-out or damaged bills.) In July, 2003, the Fed reported that cash in the hands of the public totaled $646 billion.

---

[1] This corresponds to the official money supply measure known as M1. There are other, broader measures of the money supply as well. For example, M2 includes not only cash, checking accounts, and travelers' checks, but also savings accounts, money market funds, and small (under $100,000) certificates of deposit.

However, there is one very important detail about this number. Almost half of this cash is circulating in foreign countries.[2] Foreigners in many countries prefer to hold their wealth in U.S. dollars because the dollar's purchasing power is more stable than their own currency. Even though this cash is circulating outside our own country, it is still counted as part of the U.S. money supply.

Travelers' checks are specially printed checks that you can buy from banks or other private companies, like American Express. Travelers' checks can be easily spent at almost any hotel or store and you can often cash them at a bank. You need only show an I.D. and countersign the check. In July, 2003, the public held about $8 billion in travelers' checks.

The remaining component of the money supply is checking account balances. Most are **demand deposits**, which are checking accounts that don't pay interest held by households and business firms at commercial banks. These accounts are called "demand" deposits because when you write a check to someone, that person can go into a bank and, on demand, be paid in cash. The U.S. public held $314 billion in demand deposits in July, 2003.

Demand deposits Checking accounts that do not pay interest.

Other checkable deposits is the catchall category for several types of checking accounts that work very much like demand deposits. These include *negotiable order of withdrawal (NOW) accounts,* which are like demand deposits but pay some interest, and *automatic transfer from savings accounts (ATS accounts),* which are interest-paying savings accounts that automatically transfer funds into checking accounts when needed. In July, 2003, the U.S. public held $298 billion of these types of checkable deposits.

Adding up all of the components we've discussed gives us the total U.S. money supply:

Money Supply = cash in the hands of the public + travelers' checks + demand deposits + other checkable deposits

In July 2003, this amounted to:

Money Supply = $646 billion + $8 billion + $314 billion + $298 billion = $1,266 billion

It is important to understand that our measure of the money supply excludes many things that people use regularly as a means of payment. Credit cards, for example, are not included in any of the official measures. But for many of us, unused credit is a means of payment, to be lumped together with our cash and our checking accounts. As credit cards were issued to more and more Americans over the last several decades, the available means of payment increased considerably, much more than the increase in the money supply suggests. Technological advances—now and in the future—will continue the trend toward new and more varied ways to make payments.

---

[2] Money supply data are from the Federal Reserve Board of Governors' Web site: http://www.bog.frb.fed.us. The Fed's estimate of currency held abroad is based on Richard D. Porter, and Gretchen C. Weinbach, "Currency Ratios and U.S. Underground Economic Activity," *Federal Reserve Board Finance and Economics Discussion Series,* July 1998. They estimated cash in the hands of foreigners was $210 billion in May 1998—almost half of the total at that time.

THE BANKING SYSTEM

Think about the last time you went into a bank. Perhaps you deposited a paycheck or withdrew cash to take care of your shopping needs for the week. We make these kinds of transactions dozens of times every year without ever thinking about what a bank really is, or how our own actions at the bank—and the actions of millions of other bank customers—might contribute to a change in the money supply.

Financial Intermediaries

Financial intermediary A business firm that specializes in brokering between savers and borrowers.

Let's begin at the beginning: What are banks? They are important examples of **financial intermediaries**—business firms that specialize in accepting loanable funds from households and firms whose revenues exceed their expenditures, and channeling the funds to households, firms, and government agencies whose expenditures exceed their revenues. Financial intermediaries make the economy work much more efficiently than would be possible without them.

To understand this more clearly, imagine that Boeing, the U.S. aircraft maker, wants to borrow a billion dollars for 5 years. If there were no financial intermediaries, Boeing would have to make individual arrangements to borrow small amounts of money from thousands—perhaps millions—of households, each of which wants to lend money for, say, 3 months at a time. Every 3 months, Boeing would have to renegotiate the loans with new lenders. Borrowing money in this way would be quite cumbersome. Lenders, too, would find this arrangement troublesome. All of their funds would be lent to one firm. If that firm encountered difficulties, the funds might not be returned at the end of 3 months.

An intermediary helps to solve these problems by combining a large number of small savers' funds into custom-designed packages and then lending them to larger borrowers. The intermediary can reduce the risk to savers by spreading its loans among a number of different borrowers. If one borrower fails to repay its loan, that will have only a small effect on the intermediary and its depositors. Intermediaries also offer depositors the convenience of being able to withdraw funds whenever they want. This is possible because the intermediary can predict—from experience—the pattern of inflows and outflows of funds. On any given day, some funds may be withdrawn, and some deposited, but the overall total available for lending tends to be quite stable. In addition, intermediaries keep a certain level of funds available—called *reserves*—in case of a period of unusually high withdrawals. The reserves are held as cash, or in accounts that can be quickly and easily converted into cash. For some financial institutions, the level of reserves is even mandated by law. We'll come back to reserves—and the legal requirements to hold them—later in this chapter.

Of course, intermediaries must earn a profit for providing brokering services. They do so by charging a higher interest rate on the funds they lend than the rate they pay to depositors. But they are so efficient at brokering that both lenders and borrowers benefit. Lenders earn higher interest rates, with lower risk and greater liquidity, than if they had to deal directly with the ultimate users of funds. And borrowers end up paying lower interest rates on loans that are specially designed for their specific purposes.

The United States boasts a wide variety of financial intermediaries. Some of these intermediaries—called *depository institutions*—accept deposits from the general public and lend the deposits to borrowers. There are four types of depository institutions:

1. *Savings and loan associations (S&Ls)* obtain funds through their customers' time, savings, and checkable deposits and use them primarily to make mortgage loans.
2. *Mutual savings banks* accept deposits (called *shares*) and use them primarily to make mortgage loans. They differ from S&Ls because they are owned by their depositors, rather than outside investors.
3. *Credit unions* specialize in working with particular groups of people, such as members of a labor union or employees in a specific field of business. They acquire funds through their members' deposits and make consumer and mortgage loans to other members.
4. *Commercial banks* are the largest group of depository institutions. They obtain funds mainly by issuing checkable deposits, savings deposits, and time deposits and use the funds to make business, mortgage, and consumer loans.

Since commercial banks will play a central role in the rest of this chapter, let's take a closer look at how they operate.

Commercial Banks

A commercial bank (or just "bank" for short) is a private corporation, owned by its stockholders, that provides services to the public. For our purposes, the most important service is to provide checking accounts, which enable the bank's customers to pay bills and make purchases without holding large amounts of cash that could be lost or stolen. Checks are one of the most important means of payment in the economy. Every year, U.S. households and businesses write trillions of dollars worth of checks to pay their bills, and many wage and salary earners have their pay deposited directly into their checking accounts. If you look back at the components of the U.S. money supply, you'll see that the public holds more money in the form of demand deposits and other checking-type accounts than it holds in cash.

Banks provide checking account services in order to earn a profit. And bank profits come from *lending*. The more of its deposits a bank lends out, the higher its profits will be. But banks do not lend out *every* dollar of deposits they receive; they hold some back as reserves.

Bank Reserves and the Required Reserve Ratio

A commercial bank's **reserves** are funds that it has *not* lent out, but instead keeps in a form that is readily available to its depositors. In practice, a bank holds its reserves in two places: in its vault (as cash), or in a special *reserve account* managed by the Federal Reserve. In either case, the reserves pay no interest. Why, then, does the bank hold reserves?

There are two explanations. First, on any given day, some of the bank's customers might want to withdraw more cash than other customers are depositing. The bank must always be prepared to honor its obligations for withdrawals, so it must have some cash on hand to meet these requirements. This explains why it holds vault cash.

Second, banks are required by law to hold reserves. The amount of reserves a bank must hold are called **required reserves**. The more funds its customers hold in their checking accounts, the greater the amount of required reserves. The **required reserve ratio,** set by the Federal Reserve, tells banks the fraction of their checking accounts that they must hold as required reserves.

Reserves Vault cash plus balances held at the Fed.

Required reserves The minimum amount of reserves a bank must hold, depending upon the amount of its deposit liabilities.

Required reserve ratio The minimum fraction of checking account balances that banks must hold as reserves.

For example, suppose a bank has $100 million in demand deposits. If the required reserve ratio is 0.1, this bank's required reserves are $0.1 \times \$100$ million = $10 million in reserves. The bank must hold *at least* this amount in reserves—as the sum of its vault cash and its accounts with the Federal Reserve.

More generally, the relationship between a bank's required reserves (RR), demand deposits (DD), and the required reserve ratio (RRR) is:

$$RR = RRR \times DD$$

As you will see later in this chapter, the required reserve ratio plays a key role in the Fed's control over the money supply. But first, it's time to stop hinting around about the Federal Reserve—about what it is and what it does—and take a systematic look at this important institution.

THE FEDERAL RESERVE SYSTEM

Central bank A nation's principal monetary authority.

Every large nation controls its banking system with a **central bank.** Most of the developed countries established their central banks long ago. For example, England's central bank—the Bank of England—was created in 1694. France was one of the latest, waiting until 1800 to establish the Banque de France. But the United States was even later. Although we experimented with central banks at various times in our history, we did not get serious about a central bank until 1913, when Congress established the *Federal Reserve System.*

Why did it take the United States so long to take control of its monetary system? Part of the reason is the suspicion of central authority that has always been part of U.S. politics and culture. Another reason is the large size and extreme diversity of our country and the fear that a powerful central bank might be dominated by the interests of one region to the detriment of others. These special American characteristics help explain why our own central bank is different in form from its European counterparts.

One major difference is indicated in the very name of the institution—the Federal Reserve System. It does not have the word "central" or "bank" anywhere in its title, making it less suggestive of centralized power.

Another difference is the way the system is organized. Instead of a single central bank, the United States is divided into 12 different Federal Reserve districts, each one served by its own Federal Reserve Bank. The 12 districts and the Federal Reserve Banks that serve them are shown in Figure 1. For example, the Federal Reserve Bank of Dallas serves a district consisting of Texas and parts of New Mexico and Louisiana, while the Federal Reserve Bank of Chicago serves a district including Iowa and parts of Illinois, Indiana, Wisconsin, and Michigan.

Another interesting feature of the Federal Reserve System is its peculiar status within the government. Strictly speaking, it is not even a *part* of the government, but rather a corporation whose stockholders are the private banks that it regulates. But it is unlike other corporations in several ways. First, the *Fed* (as the system is commonly called) was created by Congress and could be eliminated by Congress if it so desired. Second, both the president and Congress exert some influence on the Fed through their appointments of key officials in the system. Finally, the Fed's mission is not to make a profit for its stockholders like an ordinary corporation, but rather to serve the general public.

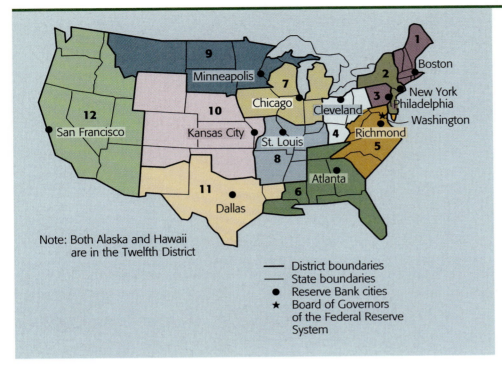

FIGURE 1
The Geography of the Federal Reserve System

The United States is divided into 12 Federal Reserve districts, each with its own Federal Reserve Bank.

The Structure of the Fed

Figure 2 shows the organizational structure of the Federal Reserve System. Near the top is the Board of Governors, consisting of seven members who are appointed by the president and confirmed by the Senate for a 14-year term. The most powerful person at the Fed is the chairman of the Board of Governors—one of the seven governors who is appointed by the president, with Senate approval, to a 4-year term as chair. In order to keep any president or Congress from having too much influence over the Fed, the 4-year term of the chair is *not* coterminous with the 4-year term of the president. As a result, every newly elected president inherits the Fed chair appointed by his predecessor, and waits several years before making an appointment of his own.

For example, the current chairman of the Board of Governors is Alan Greenspan. He was originally appointed by President Reagan in 1987 for a term lasting until 1991, well into the first George Bush's term as president. In 1991, President Bush re-appointed Greenspan to another 4-year term, which included the first 3 years of Bill Clinton's administration. In 1995 and 1999, President Clinton reappointed Greenspan twice more, and in 2003, the second President Bush announced his intention to reappoint Greenspan yet again.

Each of the 12 Federal Reserve Banks is supervised by nine directors, three of whom are appointed by the Board of Governors. The other six are elected by private commercial banks—the official stockholders of the system. The directors of each Federal Reserve Bank choose a *president* of that bank, who manages its day-to-day operations.

Notice that Figure 2 refers to "member banks." Only about 3,000 of the 9,000 or so commercial banks in the United States are members of the Federal Reserve

FIGURE 2
The Structure of the Federal Reserve System

Principal decision-making power at the Fed is vested in the Board of Governors, who are appointed by the president and confirmed by the Senate. Monetary policy is set by the Federal Open Market Committee, which consists of the seven governors plus five of the presidents of Federal Reserve Banks.

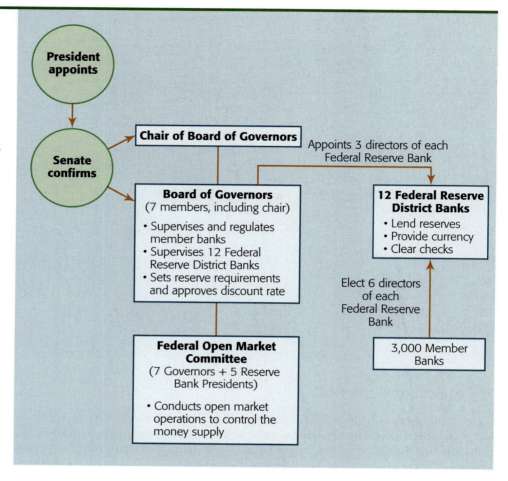

System. But they include all *national banks* (those chartered by the federal government) and some *state banks* (chartered by their state governments). All of the largest banks in the United States (e.g., Citibank, Bank of America, and Bank-Boston) are nationally chartered banks and therefore member banks as well.

The Federal Open Market Committee

Federal Open Market Committee
A committee of Federal Reserve officials that establishes U.S. monetary policy.

Finally, we come to what most economists regard as the most important part of the Fed—the **Federal Open Market Committee (FOMC).** As you can see in Figure 2, the FOMC consists of all seven governors of the Fed, along with 5 of the 12 district bank presidents.[3] The committee meets about eight times a year to discuss current trends in inflation, unemployment, output, interest rates, and international exchange rates. After determining the current state of the economy, the FOMC sets the general course for the nation's money supply.

[3] Although all Reserve Bank presidents attend FOMC meetings, only five of the 12 presidents can vote on FOMC decisions. The president of the Federal Reserve Bank of New York has a permanent vote, because New York is such an important financial center. But the remaining four votes rotate among the other district presidents.

The word "open" in the FOMC's name is ironic, since the committee's deliberations are private. Summaries of its meetings are published only after a delay of a month or more. In some cases, the committee will release a brief public statement about its decisions on the day they are made. But not even the president of the United States knows the details behind the decisions, or what the FOMC actually discussed at its meeting, until the summary of the meeting is finally released. The reason for the word "open" is that the committee controls the nation's money supply by buying and selling bonds in the public ("open") bond market. Later, we will discuss how and why the FOMC does this.

The Functions of the Federal Reserve

The Federal Reserve, as the overseer of the nation's monetary system, has a variety of important responsibilities. Some of the most important follow.

Supervising and Regulating Banks. We've already seen that the Fed sets and enforces reserve requirements, which all banks—not just Fed members—must obey. The Fed also sets standards for establishing new banks, determines what sorts of loans and investments banks are allowed to make, and closely monitors banks' financial activities.

Acting as a "Bank for Banks." Commercial banks use the Fed in much the same way that ordinary citizens use commercial banks. For example, we've already seen that banks hold some of their reserves in reserve accounts with the Fed. In addition, banks can borrow from the Fed, just as we can borrow from our local bank. The Fed charges a special interest rate, called the **discount rate,** on loans that it makes to member banks. In times of financial crisis, the Fed is prepared to act as *lender of last resort,* to make sure that banks have enough reserves to meet their obligations to depositors.

Discount rate The interest rate the Fed charges on loans to banks.

Issuing Paper Currency. The Fed doesn't actually *print* currency; that is done by the government's Bureau of Engraving and Printing. But once printed, it is shipped to the Fed (under *very* heavy guard). The Fed, in turn, puts this currency into circulation. This is why every U.S. bill carries the label *Federal Reserve Note* on the top.

Check Clearing. Suppose you write a check for $500 to pay your rent. Your building's owner will deposit the check into *his* checking account, which is probably at a different bank than yours. Somehow, the funds for your rent payment must be transferred from your bank account to your landlord's account at the other bank—a process called *check clearing*. In some cases, the services are provided by private clearinghouses. But in many other cases—especially for clearing out-of-town checks—it's done by the Federal Reserve. To clear checks, the Fed simply transfers funds from one bank's reserve account to another's.

Controlling the Money Supply. The Fed, as the nation's monetary authority, is responsible for controlling the money supply. Since this function is so important in macroeconomics, we explore it in detail in the next section.

THE FED AND THE MONEY SUPPLY

Suppose the Fed wants to change the nation's money supply. (*Why* might the Fed want to do this? We'll get to that in the next section.) There are many ways this could be done. To increase the money supply, the Fed could print up currency and give it to Fed officials, letting them spend it as they wish. Or it could hold a lottery and give all of the newly printed money to the winner. To decrease the money supply, the Fed could require that all citizens turn over a portion of their cash to Fed officials who would then feed it into paper shredders.

These and other methods would certainly work, but they hardly seem fair or orderly. In practice, the Fed uses a more organized, less haphazard method to change the money supply: *open market operations*.

Open market operations
Purchases or sales of bonds by the Federal Reserve System.

When the Fed wishes to increase or decrease the money supply, it buys or sells *government bonds in the open market*. These actions are called **open market operations**.

How the Fed Increases the Money Supply

To increase the money supply, the Fed will *buy* government bonds. This is called an *open market purchase*. To understand how an open market purchase works, let's start with a specific example. We'll assume that:

1. The Fed buys a government bond worth $1,000 from Acme Bond Dealers.
2. Acme has a checking account at First National Bank.
3. First National Bank is the only bank in its town.
4. The required reserve ratio (RRR) is 0.10.

Now, when the Fed buys the government bond, it will pay Acme Bond Dealers with a $1,000 check, which Acme will deposit into its account at First National. First National, in turn, will send the check to the Fed, which will credit First National's reserve account by $1,000.

At this point, First National's reserves have *increased* by $1,000. With more reserves, the bank can legally increase its total demand deposits. But how does a bank increase its demand deposits? By creating new loans. When a bank makes a loan, it credits the checking account of the borrower. For example, suppose the borrower is a businesswoman who wants to open a new business—Ilene's Ice Cream. When Ilene is granted a loan, First National will simply credit her checking account by the amount of the loan. Ilene is then free to spend the funds on rent, set-up costs, advertising, ingredients, and so forth.

How much can First National lend out? Remember that the required reserve ratio in our example is 0.10. That is, for each dollar of demand deposits, the bank must hold 10 cents in reserves. Or, to put it another way, for each dollar of reserves, the bank can have $10 in demand deposits. Thus, when the bank's reserves rise by $1,000, its demand deposits can rise by $10,000. Now, its demand deposits have *already* risen by $1,000 (the deposit from Acme Bond Dealers). Therefore, the bank will lend Ilene $9,000 by adding that sum to her checking account, bringing the total increase in demand deposits to $10,000.

But wait. . . . Won't Ilene spend what she borrows? And won't First National therefore *lose* its new reserves when the money is spent? For example, when Ilene writes a $500 check for advertising to the local newspaper, and the newspaper presents its check to First National, won't the bank lose $500 in reserves? The answer is no, as long as First National is the only bank in town. When Ilene pays the newspaper, the paper will just deposit her check into its *own* account at First National. Unless the newspaper wants to keep its earnings in cash, which is doubtful, all the bank must do is move funds from Ilene's account to the newspaper's account. The entire

$1,000 in reserves stays at the bank, and the total increase in demand deposits remains at $10,000.

We conclude that—*if First National is the only bank in town*— then the Fed's $1,000 open market purchase increases the money supply by $10,000. In this case, the entire increase in demand deposits occurs at First National.

Now let's be a bit more realistic. What if there are *many* banks in town? First National will know that, when Ilene spends her loan, many of those who get her checks will deposit them in other banks. For example, Ilene might use some of her loan to buy milk and sugar, and pay by writing a check to the supermarket. The supermarket, in turn, would deposit the check into its own account at another bank—let's call it SecondBank. When SecondBank submits the check to the Fed for clearing, the Fed will transfer some reserves from First National's reserve account to SecondBank's reserve account. Will this change the results of our story? Will demand deposits rise by a different amount when there are more than one bank involved?

Not at all. The total increase in demand deposits will remain the same: $10,000. How do we know? Because the Fed—with its open market purchase— has put $1,000 in new reserves into the banking system. While the Fed may transfer these reserves from one bank to another as it clears checks, this has no effect on the total amount of reserves. Each dollar of the $1,000 in new reserves ends up at *some* bank, where it enables that bank to create $10 in new demand deposits. First National itself will lend less and create less in new demand deposits when there are other banks in town. But these other banks will just do the lending *instead* of First National. The total amount of new reserves—and the total increase in demand deposits—remains the same, whether there is only one bank or many. Once again, we conclude that *when the Fed injects $1,000 in reserves into the banking system with an open market purchase, total checking accounts—and the money supply—will rise by $10,000.*

Let's go back and summarize what happened in our example. The Fed, through its open market purchase, injected $1,000 in reserves into the banking system. As a result, demand deposits rose by $10,000—10 times the injection in reserves. As you can verify, if the Fed had injected twice the amount of reserves ($2,000), demand deposits would have increased by 10 times *that* amount ($20,000). In fact, *whatever* the injection of reserves, demand deposits will increase by a factor of 10, so we can write:

$$\Delta DD = 10 \times \text{reserve injection}$$

where "DD" stands for demand deposits. The injection of reserves must be *multiplied by* the number 10 in order to get the change in demand deposits that it causes. For this reason, 10 is called the *demand deposit multiplier* in this example.

"Creating Money" Doesn't Mean "Creating Wealth" Demand deposits are a means of payment, and banks create them. This is why we say that banks "create deposits" and "create money." But don't fall into the trap of thinking that banks create *wealth*. No one gains any additional wealth as a result of money creation.

To see why, think about what happened in our story when Acme Bond Dealers deposited the $1,000 check from the Fed into its account at First National. *Acme* was no wealthier: It gave up a $1,000 check from the Fed and ended up with $1,000 more in its checking account, for a net gain of zero. Similarly, the *bank* gained no additional wealth: It had $1,000 more in cash, but it also *owed* Acme $1,000—once again, a net gain of zero.

The same conclusion holds for any other step in the money-creation process. In our simple, one-bank story, when Ilene borrows $9,000, she is no wealthier: She has $9,000 more in her checking account, but owes $9,000 to First National. And once again, the bank is no wealthier: It has $9,000 more in demand deposits—which are owed to Ilene—matched by $9,000 in loans—which Ilene owes to the bank. Always remember that when banks "create money," they do *not* create wealth.

DANGEROUS CURVES

Demand deposit multiplier The number by which a change in reserves is multiplied to determine the resulting change in demand deposits.

> *The **demand deposit multiplier** is the number by which we must multiply the injection of reserves to get the total change in demand deposits.*

The size of the demand deposit multiplier depends on the value of the required reserve ratio set by the Fed. If the *RRR* had been 0.20 instead of 0.10, then each dollar of demand deposits would require 20 cents in reserves, or each dollar of additional reserves would support an additional (1 / 0.20) = $5 in demand deposits. In that case, our formula would be

$$\Delta DD = 5 \times \text{reserve injection}$$

Generalizing, we can say that:

> *For any value of the required reserve ratio (RRR), the formula for the demand deposit multiplier is 1/RRR.*

In our example, the *RRR* was equal to 0.1, so the deposit multiplier had the value 1/0.1 = 10. If the *RRR* had been 0.2 instead, the deposit multiplier would have been equal to 1/0.2 = 5.

Using our general formula for the demand deposit multiplier, we can restate what happens when the Fed injects reserves into the banking system as follows:

$$\Delta DD = (1/RRR) \times \Delta \text{Reserves}$$

As long as all of the changes involve checking accounts (one component of the money supply), and the public does not change its holdings of cash (the other component of the money supply), then $\Delta DD = \Delta$ Money Supply. In that case, we can also write:

$$\Delta \text{Money Supply} = (1/RRR) \times \Delta \text{Reserves}$$

How the Fed Decreases the Money Supply

Just as the Fed can increase the money supply by purchasing government bonds, it can also *decrease* the money supply by *selling* government bonds—an *open market sale*.

Where does the Fed get the government bonds to sell? It has trillions of dollars worth of government bonds from open market purchases it has conducted in the past. Since, on average, the Fed tends to increase the money supply each year, it conducts more open market purchases than open market sales, and its stock of bonds keeps growing. So we needn't worry that the Fed will run out of bonds to sell.

Suppose the Fed sells a $1,000 government bond to the familiar Acme Bond Dealers, which still has its checking account at First National Bank—the only bank in town. Acme pays for the bond with a $1,000 check drawn on its account at First National. When the Fed gets Acme's check, it will present the check to First National and deduct $1,000 from First National's reserve account. In turn, First National will deduct $1,000 from Acme's checking account.

Now First National has a problem. It's reserves have decreased by $1,000. Therefore, with *RRR* = 0.10, its demand deposits must decrease by $10,000. But—

after it deducts the funds from Acme's checking account—its demand deposits *actually* decrease by only $1,000. Thus, First National must somehow reduce its demand deposits by another $9,000. How can it do this?

First National will have to *call in a loan*—that is, ask for repayment—in the amount of $9,000. In theory, the bank would tell Ilene, "You know that $9,000 in new loans we gave you? Actually, we need it back. So we're going to cancel the $9,000 credit to your checking account, and you no longer owe us the money." In this case, the bank's demand deposits would fall by a total of $10,000 after the Fed's open market sale.

Selling Bonds: the Fed vs. the Treasury In this section, you learned how the Fed sells government bonds to decrease the money supply. It's easy to confuse this with another type of government bond sale, which is done by the U.S. Treasury.

When the government runs a budget deficit, the U.S. Treasury raises the funds to cover it by issuing and selling government bonds. These are *new* government bonds, and their sale represents *new lending* to the government. By contrast, when the Fed conducts an open market sale, it does not sell *newly* issued bonds, but rather "second-hand bonds"—those already issued by the Treasury to finance past deficits. Thus, open market sales are *not* government borrowing; they are strictly an operation designed to change the money supply, and they have no direct effect on the government budget.

DANGEROUS CURVES

In reality, bank loans are for specified time periods, and a bank cannot actually demand that a loan be repaid early. Our conclusion still holds, however. Most banks have a large volume of loans outstanding, with some being repaid each day. Typically, the funds will be lent out again the very same day they are repaid. A bank that needs to reduce its total demand deposits will simply reduce its rate of new lending on that day, thereby reducing its total amount of loans outstanding. This has the same effect as "calling in a loan."

What if First National is one of *many* banks in town? Then First National will know that, as it reduces its volume of lending, some of the loans paid back will result in a transfer of reserves from other banks to First National. Thus, First National's reserves will not fall by the full $1,000, as in our simple story. Will this change the results? No. The total decrease in demand deposits will remain the same: $10,000. How do we know? Because the Fed—with its open market sale—has taken $1,000 in reserves out of the banking system. Each dollar of these reserves comes from *some* bank, where it was supporting $10 in demand deposits. Regardless of how many banks are in the system, when the Fed removes $1,000 in reserves from the banking system with an open market sale, total checking accounts—and the money supply—will fall by $10,000.

Keeping in mind that a withdrawal of reserves is a *negative change in reserves*, we can still use our demand deposit multiplier—$1/(RRR)$—and our general formula:

$$\Delta DD = (1/RRR) \times \Delta \text{Reserves}$$

Applying it to our example, we have:

$$\Delta DD = [1/0.1] \times (-\$1,000) = -\$10,000$$

In other words, the Fed's $1,000 open market sale causes a $10,000 decrease in demand deposits. As long as the public's cash holdings do not change, the money supply decreases by $10,000 as well.

Some Important Provisos about the Demand Deposit Multiplier

Although the process of money creation and destruction as we've described it illustrates the basic ideas, our formula for the demand deposit multiplier—$1/RRR$—is oversimplified. In reality, the multiplier is likely to be smaller than our formula suggests, for two reasons.

First, we've assumed that as the money supply changes, the public does *not* change its holdings of cash. But as the money supply increases, the public typically will want to hold part of the increase as demand deposits, and part of the increase as cash, where it cannot be used by banks as reserves against new demand deposits. As a result, an open market purchase of, say, $1,000, will inject *less* than $1,000 of new reserves into the banking system, and create *less* than $10,000 of new demand deposits. The demand deposit multiplier will be smaller than 1/*RRR*.

Second, we've assumed that banks are always "fully loaned up"—that is, they hold only the minimum reserves required by law and create the maximum amount of new demand deposits (the maximum amount of new loans). In reality, banks may want to hold **excess reserves**—reserves beyond those legally required. For example, they may want some flexibility to increase their loans in case interest rates—their reward for lending—rise in the near future. Or they may prefer not to lend the maximum legal amount during a recession, because borrowers are more likely to declare bankruptcy and not repay their loans. Banks end up with excess reserves when they lend out *less* than the maximum amount allowed by law, thereby creating *less* than the maximum amount of new demand deposits. In this case, the money supply will expand by less than in our simple story, and the demand deposit multiplier turns out to be smaller than 1/*RRR*.

Excess reserves Reserves in excess of required reserves.

Other Tools for Controlling the Money Supply

Open market operations are the Fed's primary means of controlling the money supply. But there are two other tools that the Fed can use to increase or decrease the money supply.

- *Changes in the Required Reserve Ratio.* In theory, the Fed can set off the process of deposit creation, similar to that described earlier, by lowering the required reserve ratio. For example, suppose the Fed lowered the required reserve ratio from 0.10 to 0.05. Suddenly, every bank in the system would find that its reserves—which used to support 10 times their value in demand deposits—can now support 20 times their value. To earn the highest profit possible, banks would increase their lending, creating new demand deposits. The money supply would increase.

  On the other side, if the Fed raised the required reserve ratio, the process would work in reverse: All banks would suddenly find that—given their reserves—their demand deposits exceed the legal maximum. They would be forced to call in loans, and the money supply would decrease.

- *Changes in the Discount Rate.* The discount rate, mentioned earlier, is the rate the Fed charges banks when it lends them reserves. In principle, a lower discount rate—enabling banks to borrow reserves from the Fed more cheaply—might encourage banks to borrow more. An increase in borrowed reserves works just like any other injection of reserves into the banking system: It increases the money supply. On the other side, a rise in the discount rate would make it more expensive for banks to borrow from the Fed and decrease the amount of borrowed reserves in the system. This withdrawal of reserves from the banking system would lead to a decrease in the money supply.

Changes in either the required reserve ratio or the discount rate *could* change the money supply by causing banks to expand or contract their lending, in much the same way outlined in this chapter. In reality, neither of these policy tools is used very often. The most recent change in the required reserve ratio was in April 1992, when the Fed lowered the ratio for most demand deposits from 12 percent to 10 percent. Changes in the discount rate are more frequent, but it is not unusual for the Fed to leave the discount rate unchanged for a year or more.

Why are these other tools used so seldom? Part of the reason is that they can have such unpredictable effects. When the required reserve ratio changes, all banks in the system are affected simultaneously. Even a tiny error in predicting how a typical bank will respond can translate into a huge difference for the money supply.

A change in the discount rate may have uncertain effects as well. In the past, many bank managers have preferred *not* to borrow reserves from the Fed, since it would put them under closer Fed scrutiny. And in the past, the Fed discouraged banks from borrowing reserves from it, unless the bank was in difficulty. Thus, a small change in the discount rate was unlikely to have much of an impact on bank borrowing of reserves, and therefore on the money supply.

In January 2003, however, the Fed changed its discount policy, and began to *encourage* banks to borrow. It established two different discount rates—one for banks in excellent financial condition and another, higher rate for banks considered more at risk. Banks in sound condition could borrow freely at the lower rate without Fed scrutiny. As a result, the discount rate may become a more effective, and more frequently used, policy tool in the future.

Still, open market operations will almost certainly remain the Fed's *principal* tool for controlling the money supply. One reason is that they can be so easily fine-tuned to any level desired. Another advantage is that they can be covert. No one knows exactly what the FOMC decided to do to the money supply at its last meeting for several weeks—unless the FOMC chooses to make an earlier announcement. And no one knows whether it is conducting more open market purchases or more open market sales on any given day (it always does a certain amount of both to keep bond traders guessing). By maintaining secrecy, the Fed can often change its policies without destabilizing financial markets, and also avoid the pressure that Congress or the president might bring to bear if its policies are not popular.

> *While other tools can affect the money supply, open market operations have two advantages over them: precision and secrecy. This is why open market operations remain the Fed's primary means of changing the money supply.*

The Fed's ability to conduct its policies in secret—and its independent status in general—is controversial. Some argue that secrecy and independence are needed so that the Fed can do what is best for the country—keeping the price level stable—without undue pressure from Congress or the president. Others argue that there is something fundamentally undemocratic about an independent Federal Reserve, whose governors are not elected and who can, to some extent, ignore the popular will. In recent years, because the Fed has been so successful in guiding the economy, the controversy has largely subsided.

THE MONEY MARKET

At this point, you may be wondering: How *does* the Fed guide the economy? Granted, the Fed can raise or lower the money supply. But so what? How does control over the money supply translate into control over the economy? These are important questions. In order to answer them, we must consider *both* sides of the market for money: not just the supply of money, which is controlled by the Fed, but also the demand for money, which depends on the behavior of the public.

The Demand for Money

Reread the title of this subsection. Does it appear strange to you? Don't people always want as much money as possible? Isn't their demand for money infinite?

Actually, no. The "demand for money" does not mean how much money people would *like* to have in the best of all possible worlds. Rather, it means *how much money people would like to hold, given the constraints that they face.* Let's first consider the demand for money by an individual, and then turn our attention to the demand for money in the entire economy.

An Individual's Demand for Money. Money is one of the ways that each of us, as individuals, can hold our *wealth.* Unfortunately, at any given moment, the total amount of wealth we have is a given; we can't just snap our fingers and have more of it. Therefore, if we want to hold more wealth in the form of money, we must hold less wealth in other forms—in savings accounts, money market funds, stocks, bonds, and so on. Indeed, individuals exchange one kind of wealth for another millions of times a day, in banks, stock markets, and bond markets. If you sell shares in the stock market, for example, you give up wealth in the form of corporate stock and acquire money. The buyer of your stock gives up money and acquires the stock.

These two facts—that wealth is given, and that you must give up one kind of wealth in order to acquire more of another—determine an individual's **wealth constraint.** Whenever we speak about the demand for money, the wealth constraint is always in the background. This is why we say:

> *An individual's demand for money is the amount of wealth that the individual chooses to hold as money, rather than as other assets.*

Why do people want to hold some of their wealth in the form of money? The most important reason is that money is a *means of payment;* you can buy things with it. Other forms of wealth, by contrast, cannot be used for purchases. (Imagine trying to pay for your groceries with stocks or bonds.) However, the other forms of wealth provide a financial return to their owners. For example, bonds and savings deposits pay interest, while stocks pay dividends. Money, by contrast, pays either very little interest (on some types of checking accounts) or none at all (cash and most checking accounts). Thus,

Wealth constraint At any point in time, wealth is fixed.

Opportunity Cost

> *when you hold money, you bear an opportunity cost—the interest or other financial return you could have earned if you held your wealth in some other form.*

Each of us must continually decide how to divide our total wealth between money and other assets. The upside to money is that it can be used as a means of payment. The more of our wealth we hold as money, the easier it is to buy things at a moment's notice, and the less often we will have to pay the costs (in time, trouble, and commissions to brokers) to change our other assets into money. The downside to money is that it pays little or no interest.

To keep our analysis as simple as possible, we'll use *bonds* as our representative nonmoney asset. Bonds have been mentioned several times in this book, but now it's time for a formal definition. A **bond** is an IOU ("I owe you") issued by a corporation or a government agency when it borrows money. The bond promises to pay back the loan either gradually (e.g., each month) or all at once at some future date. In either case, the sum the borrower pays back exceeds what was borrowed, and the difference is the *interest* on the bond.

Bond An IOU issued by a corporation or government agency when it borrows funds.

While bonds pay interest, we'll assume money pays *no interest at all*. In our discussion, therefore, people will choose between two assets that are mirror images of each other. Specifically,

> *individuals choose how to divide wealth between two assets: (1) money, which can be used as a means of payment but earns no interest; and (2) bonds, which earn interest, but cannot be used as a means of payment.*

This choice involves a clear tradeoff: The more money we hold, the less often we'll have to go through the inconvenience of changing our bonds into money . . . but the less interest we will earn.

Since interest is the opportunity cost of holding money, it follows that *the greater the interest rate, the less money an individual will want to hold.*

The Demand for Money by Businesses. Our discussion of money demand has focused on the typical individual. But some money (not a lot in comparison to what individuals hold) is held by businesses. Stores keep some currency in their cash registers, and firms generally keep funds in business checking accounts. Businesses face the same types of constraints as individuals: They have only so much wealth, and they must decide how much of it to hold in money rather than in other assets. The quantity of money demanded by businesses follows the same principles we have developed for individuals: They want to hold more money when the opportunity cost (the interest rate) is lower and less money when the interest rate is higher.

The Economy-Wide Demand for Money. When we use the term "demand for money" without the word "individual," we mean the total demand for money by all wealth holders in the economy—businesses and individuals. And just as each person and each firm in the economy has only so much wealth, so, too, there is a given amount of wealth in the economy as a whole at any given time. In our analysis, this total wealth must be held in one of two forms: money or bonds.

> *The (economy-wide) demand for money is the amount of total wealth in the economy that all households and businesses, together, choose to hold as money rather than as bonds.*

The demand for money in the economy depends on the interest rate in the same way as it does for individuals and businesses. That is,

> *a rise in the interest rate will decrease the (economy-wide) quantity of money demanded, and a drop in the interest rate will increase the quantity of money demanded.*

Money demand curve A curve indicating how much money will be willingly held at each interest rate.

The Money Demand Curve. Figure 3 shows a **money demand curve**, which tells us *the total quantity of money demanded in the economy at each interest rate.* Notice that the curve is downward sloping. As long as the other influences on money demand don't change, a drop in the interest rate—which lowers the opportunity cost of holding money—will increase the quantity of money demanded. (We'll discuss some of the other influences on money demand later in this chapter and in the next chapter.)

Point *E,* for example, shows that when the interest rate is 6 percent, the quantity of money demanded is $500 billion. If the interest rate falls to 3 percent, we move to point *F,* where the quantity demanded is $800 billion. As we move along the money demand curve, the interest rate changes, but other determinants of money demand (such as the price level and real income) are assumed to remain unchanged.

The Supply of Money

Just as we did for money demand, we would like to draw a curve showing the quantity of money *supplied* at each interest rate. Earlier in this chapter, you learned how the Fed controls the money supply: It uses open market operations to inject or withdraw reserves from the banking system and then relies on the demand deposit multiplier to do the rest. Since the Fed decides what the money supply will be, we treat it as a fixed amount. That is, the interest rate can rise or fall, but the money supply will remain constant unless and until the Fed decides to change it.

FIGURE 3
The Money Demand Curve

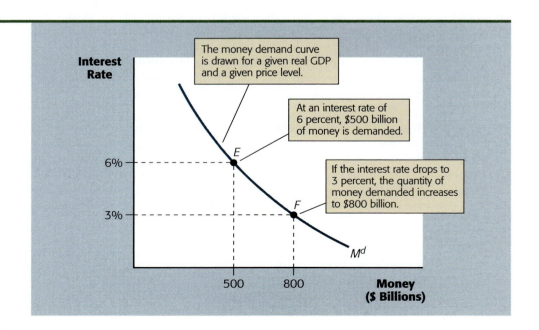

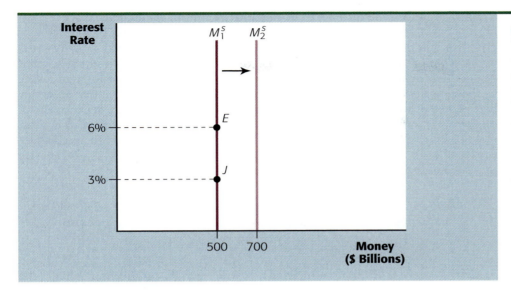

FIGURE 4
The Supply of Money

Once the Fed sets the money supply, it remains constant until the Fed changes it. The vertical supply curve labeled M$_1^S$ shows a money supply of $500 billion, regardless of the interest rate. An increase in the money supply to $700 billion is depicted as a rightward shift of the money supply curve to M$_2^S$.

Look at the vertical line labeled M_1^S in Figure 4. This is the economy's **money supply curve**, which shows the total money supply at each interest rate. The line is vertical because once the Fed sets the money supply, it remains constant until the Fed changes it. In the figure, the Fed has chosen to set the money supply at $500 billion. A rise in the interest rate from, say, 3 percent to 6 percent would move us from point *J* to point *E* along the solid money supply curve, leaving the money supply unchanged.

> **Money supply curve** A line showing the total quantity of money in the economy at each interest rate.

Now suppose the Fed, for whatever reason, were to *change* the money supply. Then there would be a *new* vertical line, showing a different quantity of money supplied at each interest rate. Recall from the previous chapter that the Fed raises the money supply by purchasing bonds in an open market operation. For example, if the demand deposit multiplier is 10, and the Fed purchases government bonds worth $20 billion, the money supply increases by 10 × $20 billion = $200 billion. In this case, the money supply curve shifts rightward, to the dashed line in the figure.

Open market purchases of bonds inject reserves into the banking system and shift the money supply curve rightward by a multiple of the reserve injection. Open market sales have the opposite effect: They withdraw reserves from the system and shift the money supply curve leftward by a multiple of the reserve withdrawal.

Equilibrium in the Money Market

Now we are ready to combine what you've learned about money demand and money supply to find the interest rate in the economy. More specifically, we want to find the *equilibrium* interest rate—the rate at which the quantity of money demanded and the quantity of money supplied are equal.

Figure 5 combines the money supply and demand curves. By now, you've seen enough economics diagrams to know that the equilibrium occurs at point *E*, where the two curves intersect. At this point, with an interest rate of 6 percent, the quantity of money demanded and the quantity supplied are both equal to $500 billion.

But before rushing through this figure, it's important to understand what equilibrium in the money market actually means. First, remember that the money supply curve tells us the quantity of money, determined by the Fed, that *actually exists* in the economy. Every dollar of this money—either in cash or in checking account balances—is held by *someone*. Thus, the money supply curve, in addition to telling us the quantity of money supplied by the Fed, also tells us the quantity of money that people *are actually holding* at any given moment. The money demand curve, on the other hand, tells us how much money people *want* to hold at each interest rate. Thus, when the quantity of money supplied and the quantity demanded are equal, all of the money in the economy is being *willingly held*. That is, people are *satisfied* holding the money that they are *actually* holding.

Markets and Equilibrium

> *Equilibrium in the money market occurs when the quantity of money people are actually holding (quantity supplied) is equal to the quantity of money they want to hold (quantity demanded).*

Can we have faith that the interest rate will reach its equilibrium value in the money market, such as 6 percent in our figure? Indeed we can. In the next section, we explore the forces that drive the money market toward its equilibrium.

How the Money Market Achieves Equilibrium. To understand how the money market reaches equilibrium, suppose that the interest rate, for some reason, were *not* at its equilibrium value. For example, suppose the interest rate in Figure 5 were 9 percent—higher than the equilibrium value of 6 percent. As you can see, at 9 percent, the quantity of money demanded would be $300 billion, while the quantity supplied would be $500 billion. Or, put another way, people would *actually* be holding $500 billion of their wealth as money, but they would *want* to hold only $300 billion as money. There would be an **excess supply of money** (the quantity of money supplied would exceed the quantity demanded) equal to $500 billion − $300 billion = $200 billion.

Excess supply of money The amount of money supplied exceeds the amount demanded at a particular interest rate.

Now comes an important point. Remember that in our analysis, money and bonds are the only two assets available. If people want to hold *less* money than they are currently holding, then, by definition, they must want to hold *more* wealth in bonds than they are currently holding—an **excess demand for bonds.**

Excess demand for bonds The amount of bonds demanded exceeds the amount supplied at a particular interest rate.

> *When there is an excess supply of money in the economy, there is also an excess demand for bonds.*

So far, we've established that if the interest rate were 9 percent, which is higher than its equilibrium value, there would be an excess supply of money and an excess demand for bonds. What would happen? The public would try to convert the undesired money into the desired bonds. That is, people would start to buy bonds. Just as there is a market for money, there is also a market for bonds. And as the public begins to demand more bonds, making them scarcer, *the price of bonds will rise*. We can illustrate the steps in our analysis so far as follows:

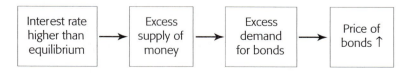

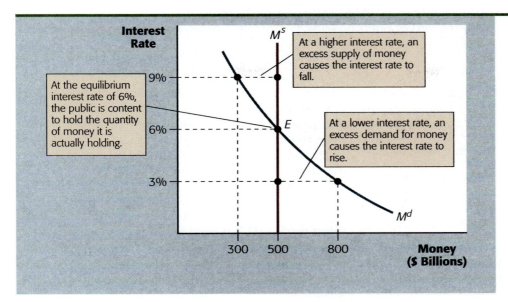

FIGURE 5
Money Market Equilibrium

We conclude that, when the interest rate is higher than its equilibrium value, the price of bonds will rise. Why is this important? In order to take our story further, we must first take a detour for a few paragraphs.

An Important Detour: Bond Prices and Interest Rates. A bond, in the simplest terms, is a promise to pay back borrowed funds at a certain date or dates in the future. There are many types of bonds. Some promise to make payments each month or each year for a certain period and then pay back a large sum at the end. Others promise to make just one payment—one, five, ten, or even more years from the date the bond is issued. When a large corporation or the government wants to borrow money, it issues a new bond and sells it in the marketplace for a price. Thus, the amount of the loan is equal to the price paid for the bond.

Let's consider a very simple example: a bond that promises to pay to its holder $1,000 in exactly one year. Suppose that you purchase this bond from the issuer—a firm or government agency—for $800. Then you are lending $800 to the issuer, and you will be paid back $1,000 in one year. What interest rate are you earning on your loan? Let's see: You will be getting back $200 more than you lent, so that is your *interest payment*. The interest *rate* is the interest payment divided by the amount of the loan, or $200/$800 = 0.25 or 25 percent.

Now, what if instead of $800, you paid a price of $900 for this very same bond. The bond still promises to pay $1,000 in one year, so your interest payment would now be $100, and your interest rate would be $100/$900 = 0.11 or 11 percent—a considerably lower interest rate. As you can see, the interest rate that you will earn on your bond depends entirely on the *price* of the bond. *The higher the price, the lower the interest rate.*

This general principle applies to virtually all types of bonds, not just the simple one-time-payment bond we've considered here. Bonds promise to pay various sums to their holders at different dates in the future. Therefore, the more you pay for any bond, the lower your overall rate of return, or interest rate, will be. Thus:

> *When the price of bonds rises, the interest rate falls; when the price of bonds falls, the interest rate rises.*[4]

Two Theories for the Interest Rate? A question may have occurred to you. Haven't we already discussed how the interest rate is determined? Indeed, we have. In Chapter 14, we used the loanable funds market—where a flow of loanable funds is offered by lenders to borrowers—to explain how the interest rate is determined. But in that chapter, we were discussing how the economy operates in the long run. Here, we are interested in how the interest rate is determined in the short run, so we must change our perspective.

Chapter 14 ignored an important idea discussed in this chapter: that the public continuously chooses how to divide its wealth between money and bonds. In the short run, the public's preferences over money and bonds can change, and this, in turn, can change the interest rate. But since these changes tend to be short-lived, when we focus on the long run, we can ignore them.

In sum: Our view of the interest rate depends on the time period we are considering. Over the long run, the interest rate is determined in the market for loanable funds, where household saving is lent to businesses and the government. In the short run, the interest rate is determined in the money market, where wealth holders adjust their wealth between money and bonds.

The relationship between bond prices and interest rates helps explain why the government, the press, and the public are so concerned about the *bond market,* where bonds issued in previous periods are bought and sold. This market is sometimes called the *secondary* market for bonds, to distinguish it from the *primary* market where newly issued bonds are bought and sold. When you hear that "the bond market rallied" on a particular day of trading, it means that prices rose in the secondary bond market. This is good news for bond holders. But it is also good news for any person or business that wants to borrow money. When prices rise in the secondary market, they immediately rise in the primary market as well, since newly issued bonds and previously issued bonds are perfect substitutes for each other. Therefore, a bond market rally not only means lower interest rates in the secondary market, it also means lower interest rates in the primary market, where firms borrow money by issuing new bonds. Sooner or later, it will also lead to a drop in the interest rate on mortgages, car loans, credit card balances, and even many student loans. This is good news for borrowers. But it is bad news for anyone wishing to lend money by buying bonds, for now they will earn less interest.

Now that you understand the relationship between bond prices and interest rates, let's return to our analysis of the money market.

Back to the Money Market. Look back at Figure 5, and let's recap what you've learned so far. If the interest rate were 9 percent, there would be an excess supply of money and an excess demand for bonds. The public would try to buy bonds, and the price of bonds would rise. Now we can complete the story. As you've just learned, a rise in the price of bonds means a *decrease* in the interest rate. The complete sequence of events is:

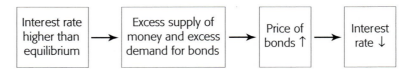

Thus, if the interest is 9 percent in our figure, it will begin to fall. Therefore, 9 percent is *not* the equilibrium interest rate.

---

[4] In macroeconomics, we refer to *the* interest rate. In the real world, there are many types of interest rates—a different one for each type of bond, and still other rates on savings accounts, time deposits, car loans, mortgages, and more. However, all of these interest rates move up and down together, even though some may lag behind a few days, weeks, or months. Thus, when bond prices rise, interest rates *generally* will fall, and vice versa.

How far will the interest rate fall? As long as there continues to be an excess supply of money and an excess demand for bonds, the public will still be trying to acquire bonds and the interest rate will continue to fall. But notice what happens in the figure as the interest rate falls: The quantity of money demanded *rises*. Finally, when the interest rate reaches 6 percent, the quantity of money demanded is finally equal to the quantity supplied. The excess supply of money, and therefore the excess demand for bonds, is eliminated. At this point, there is no reason for the interest rate to fall further. Six percent is, indeed, our equilibrium interest rate.

We can also do the same analysis from the other direction. Suppose the interest rate were *lower* than 6 percent in the figure. Then, as you can see in Figure 5, there would be an *excess demand for money* and an *excess supply of bonds*. In this case, the following would happen:

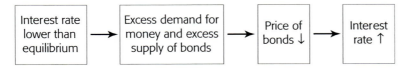

The interest rate would continue to rise until it reached its equilibrium value: 6 percent.

WHAT HAPPENS WHEN THINGS CHANGE?

In this section, we'll focus on two questions: (1) How does the Fed change the interest rate? and (2) What are the macroeconomic *consequences* of a change in the interest rate?

How the Fed Changes the Interest Rate

Suppose the Fed wants to lower the interest rate. Fed officials cannot just *declare* that the interest rate should be lower. To change the interest rate, the Fed must change the *equilibrium* interest rate in the money market, and it does this by changing the money supply.

Look at Figure 6. Initially, with a money supply of $500 billion, the money market is in equilibrium at point *E,* with an interest rate of 6 percent. To lower the interest rate, the Fed *increases* the money supply through open market purchases of bonds. In the figure, the Fed raises the money supply to $800 billion, shifting the money supply curve rightward to M_2^S. (This is a much greater shift than the Fed would engineer in practice, but it makes the graph easier to read.) At the old interest rate of 6 percent, there would be an excess supply of money and an excess demand for bonds. This will drive the interest rate down until it reaches its new equilibrium value of 3 percent, at point *F.* The process works like this:

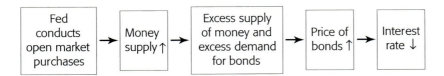

FIGURE 6
An Increase in the Money Supply

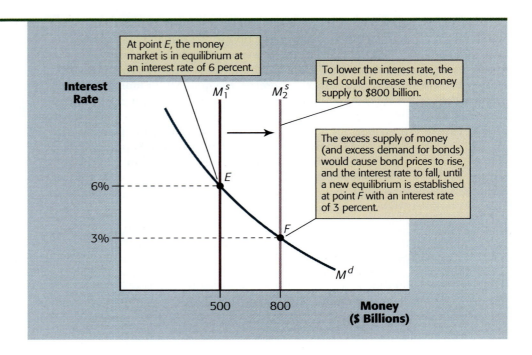

The Fed can raise the interest rate as well, through open market *sales* of bonds. In this case, the money supply curve in Figure 6 would shift leftward (not shown), setting off the following sequence of events:

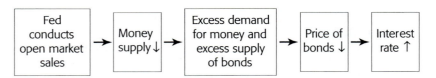

> *If the Fed increases the money supply by buying government bonds, the interest rate falls. If the Fed decreases the money supply by selling government bonds, the interest rate rises. By controlling the money supply through purchases and sales of bonds, the Fed can also control the interest rate.*

How Interest Rate Changes Affect the Economy

Suppose the Fed increases the money supply through open market purchases of bonds. The interest rate falls . . . but what then? How is the macro-economy affected? The answer is: *A drop in the interest rate will boost several different types of spending in the economy.*

How the Interest Rate Affects Spending. First, a lower interest rate stimulates business spending on plant and equipment. This idea came up a few chapters ago when we studied long-run economic growth, but we will go back over it here.

Remember that the interest rate is one of the key costs of any investment project. If a firm must borrow funds, it will have to pay for them at the going rate of interest—for example, by selling a bond at the going price. If the firm uses its *own* funds, so it doesn't have to borrow, the interest rate *still* represents a cost: Each dollar spent on plant and equipment could have been lent to someone else at the going interest rate. Thus, whether a firm has its own funds or must borrow them, the interest rate is the *opportunity cost* of funds spent on plant and equipment.

A firm deciding whether to spend on plant and equipment compares the benefits of the project—the increase in future income—with the costs (opportunity costs) of the project. With a lower interest rate, the costs of funding investment projects are lower, so more projects will get the go-ahead. Other variables can and do affect investment spending as well. But for given values of these other variables, a drop in the interest rate will cause an increase in spending on plant and equipment.

Interest rate changes also affect another kind of investment: spending on new houses and apartments that are built by developers or individuals. Most people borrow to buy houses or condominiums, and most developers borrow to build apartment buildings. The loan agreement for housing is called a *mortgage,* and mortgage interest rates move closely with other interest rates. Thus, when the Fed lowers the interest rate, families find it more affordable to buy homes, and landlords find it more profitable to build new apartments. Total investment in new housing increases.

Finally, in addition to investment spending, the interest rate affects consumption spending on "big ticket" items such as new cars, furniture, and dishwashers. Economists call these *consumer durables* because these goods usually last several years. People often borrow to buy consumer durables, and the interest rate they are charged tends to rise and fall with other interest rates in the economy. Spending on new cars, the most expensive durable that most of us buy, is especially sensitive to interest rate changes.

When the interest rate falls, consumption spending rises at *any* level of disposable income. It causes a *shift* in the consumption function, not a movement along it. Therefore, we consider this impact on consumption to be a rise in autonomous consumption spending, called *a* in our discussion of the consumption function.

We can summarize the impact of monetary policy as follows:

> *When the Fed increases the money supply, the interest rate falls and spending on three categories of goods increases: plant and equipment, new housing, and consumer durables (especially automobiles). When the Fed decreases the money supply, the interest rate rises and these categories of spending fall.*

Monetary Policy and the Economy. In the previous chapter, you learned that changes in total spending cause changes in real GDP through the multiplier process. In this chapter, you've learned that the Federal Reserve, through its control of the money supply, can change the interest rate, and therefore influence aggregate expenditure. Thus, the Fed—through its control of the money supply—has the power to influence real GDP.

When the Fed controls or manipulates the money supply in order to achieve any macroeconomic goal—such as a change in the level of real GDP—it is engaging in **monetary policy.**

Monetary policy Control or manipulation of the money supply by the Federal Reserve designed to achieve a macroeconomic goal.

FIGURE 7
**Monetary Policy
and the Economy**

Monetary policy involves an interaction between the interest rate and equilibrium real GDP. Initially, the Fed has set the money supply at $500 billion, so the interest rate is 6 percent (point E). If the Fed increases the money supply to $800 billion, money market equilibrium moves to point F, and the interest rate falls, stimulating interest-sensitive spending and driving total expenditures up. Through the multiplier process, real GDP increases.

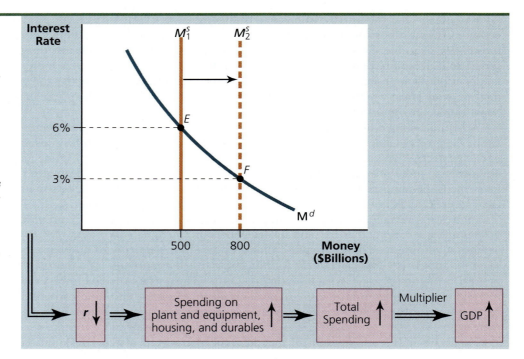

Figure 7 shows how monetary policy works. The left-hand side of the figure shows the money market, where the Fed has initially set the money supply at $500 billion. Equilibrium is at point E, with an interest rate (r) of 6 percent.

Now we suppose that the Fed increases the money supply to $800 billion. (This is an unrealistically large change in the money supply, but it makes it easier to see the change in the figure.) Equilibrium in the money market moves from point E to point F, and the interest rate drops to 3 percent. The drop in the interest rate causes spending on plant and equipment, new housing, and consumer durables (especially automobiles) to rise. That is, both investment spending (I^P) and autonomous consumption spending (*a*) will rise, setting off the multiplier effect and increasing equilibrium GDP by a multiple of the initial, interest-rate-driven rise in spending.

The new equilibrium in the money market will be at point F, with the interest rate driven down to 3 percent and total spending and GDP higher than they were initially. In the end, we see that the Fed, by increasing the money supply and lowering the interest rate, has increased output and employment.[5]

We've covered a lot of ground to reach our conclusion, so let's review the highlights of how monetary policy works. This is what happens when the Fed conducts open market purchases of bonds:

[5] There is one additional step which we are not showing here. The rise in GDP—which is also a rise in total income—will cause the money demand curve to shift rightward. This is because, as income rises, and spending rises, individuals tend to want more of their wealth in the form of money at *any* interest rate. If we include this rightward shift in money demand, the interest rate will still fall, but not by as much as it does in Figure 7.

Open market *sales* by the Fed have exactly the opposite effects. In this case, the money supply curve in Figure 7 would shift leftward (not shown), driving the interest rate up. The rise in the interest rate would cause a decrease in interest-sensitive spending (a and I^P), ultimately causing total spending to drop by a multiple of the decrease in a and I^P, and causing equilibrium GDP to drop as well.

Shifts in the Money Demand Curve

So far, we've considered changes in the interest rate engineered by the Fed. Here, we discuss an additional source of interest rate changes: a *shift in the money demand curve*.

We can imagine several causes of a spontaneous shift in money demand. For example, suppose the public began to fear that criminals would steal their credit card numbers and began to prefer making payments by cash or check. This would cause an increase in tastes for holding money, and the demand for money curve would shift rightward. On the other hand, new technology (such as electronic money cards) can lead to new substitutes for money, *decreasing* tastes for holding money and shifting the money demand curve leftward. Finally, *expectations about the future interest rate* can dramatically affect the demand for money in the present. This is the case we'll explore in detail.

Expectations and Money Demand. Why should expectations about the future interest rate affect money demand *today*? Because bond prices and interest rates are negatively related. If you expect the interest rate to rise in the future, then you also expect the price of bonds to fall in the future.

To see this more clearly, imagine (pleasantly) that you hold a bond promising to pay you $100,000 in exactly one year and that the going annual interest rate is 5 percent. The going price for your bond will be $95,238. Why? If someone bought your bond at that price, she would earn $100,000 − $95,238 = $4,762 in interest. Since the bond cost $95,238, the buyer's rate of return would be $4,762/$95,238 = 0.05, or 5 percent—the going rate of interest. If you tried to charge more than $95,238 for the bond, its rate of return would be less than 5 percent, so no one would buy it; they could always earn 5 percent by buying another bond that pays the going rate of interest.

Now suppose that you *expect* the interest rate to rise to 10 percent in the near future, say, next week. (This is an unrealistically large change in the interest rate in so short a time, but it makes the point dramatically.) Then you expect the going price for your bond to fall to about $90,909. At that price, a buyer would earn $100,000 − $90,909 = $9,091 in interest, so the buyer's rate of return would be $9,091/$90,909 = 0.10, or 10 percent. Thus, if you believe that the interest rate is about to rise from 5 to 10 percent, you also believe the price of your bond is about to fall from $95,238 to $90,909.

What would you do?

Logically, you would want to sell your bond *now*, before the price drops. If you still want to hold this type of bond later, you can always buy it back next week at the lower price and gain from the transaction. Thus, if you expect the interest rate to rise in the future, you will want to exchange your bonds for money *today.* Your demand for money will increase.

Of course, if *you* expect the interest rate to rise (and the price of bonds to drop), and your expectation is reasonable, others will probably feel the same way. They, too, will want to trade in their bonds for money. Thus, if the expectation is widespread, there will be an increase in the demand for money economy-wide.

> *A general expectation that interest rates will rise (bond prices will fall) in the future will cause the money demand curve to shift rightward in the present.*

Notice that when people expect the interest rate to rise, we *shift* the money demand curve, rather than move along it. People will want to hold more money at any *current* interest rate.

Figure 8 shows what will happen in the money market when people expect the interest rate to rise. Initially, with the money supply equal to $500 billion, the equilibrium is at point *E* and the interest rate is 5 percent. But the expected rise in the interest rate shifts the money demand curve rightward. After the shift, there is an excess demand for money and an excess supply of bonds at the original interest rate of 5 percent. The price of bonds will fall, which means the interest rate will rise.

How far will the interest rate rise? That depends. Imagine a simple case where *everyone* in the economy expected the interest rate to rise to 10 percent next week. Then no one would want to hold bonds at any *current* interest rate less than 10 percent. For example, if the interest rate rose to 9 percent, people would still expect it to rise further (and the price of bonds to fall further), so they would still want to sell their bonds. Therefore, to return the money market to equilibrium, the interest rate would rise to exactly the level that people expected. This is the case we've illustrated in Figure 8, where the money demand curve shifts rightward by just enough to raise the interest rate to 10 percent. More generally:

> *When the public as a whole expects the interest rate to rise in the future, they will drive up the interest rate in the present.*

When information comes along that makes people believe that interest rates will rise and bond prices fall in the near future, the result is an immediate rise in the interest rate and a fall in bond prices. This principle operates even if the information is false and there is ultimately no reason for the interest rate to rise. Thus, a general expectation that interest rates will rise can be a *self-fulfilling prophecy:* Because people believe it, it actually happens. Their expectation alone is enough to drive up the interest rate.

This immediate response to information about the future—and the possibility of a self-fulfilling prophecy—works in the opposite direction as well:

> *When the public expects the interest rate to drop in the future, they will drive down the interest rate in the present.*

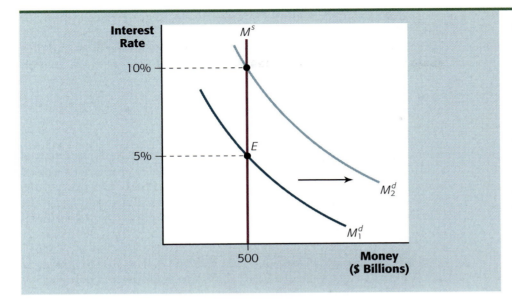

FIGURE 8
Interest Rate Expectations

If households and firms expect the interest rate to rise in the future, their demand for money will increase today. Starting from equilibrium at point E, an expected increase in the interest rate from 5 percent to 10 percent will increase money demand to M_2^d. The result is a self-fulfilling prophecy: The interest rate increases to 10 percent today.

In this case, the public expects bond prices to rise, so they try to shift their wealth from money to bonds. In Figure 8, the money demand curve would shift leftward (not shown). The price of bonds would rise, and the interest rate would fall, just as was originally expected.

Expectations and the Fed. Changes in interest rates due to changes in expectations can have important consequences. Fortunes can be won and lost depending on how people bet on the future. For example, suppose you believe the interest rate is about to drop, so you buy bonds, thinking that bond prices are about to rise. But suppose you are wrong, the interest rate actually *rises* instead, and bond prices *drop*. Then your bonds will be worth less than what you paid for them. In fact, it is not unusual for major bondholders—such as pension funds or money market mutual funds—to gain or lose millions of dollars in a single day based on a good or a bad bet.

Another consequence of changes in expectations is the effect on the overall economy. When a change in expectations becomes a self-fulfilling prophecy, it causes *current* interest rates to change. As you've learned, this will affect total spending and output. Fortunately, the Fed can counteract these changes with open market purchases or sales of bonds, as needed, and we'll discuss this a bit later.

Still, the public's ever-changing expectations about future interest rates make the Fed's job more difficult. Expectations can change interest rates, and changes in interest rates can affect individual fortunes as well as the economy as a whole. This observation helps explain some seemingly mysterious Fed behavior. Public policy statements made by the Fed's chair (currently Alan Greenspan) or by other Fed officials are remarkably tentative and sometimes downright confusing. You can read them again and again and still have no idea what the Fed intends to do about interest rates in the future. But from the Fed's point of view, the obfuscation is understandable. If the officials of the FOMC give strong hints about their thinking, the money and bond markets might go into overdrive, as people rush to buy or sell bonds in order to profit (or avoid loss) from the Fed's action. On rare occasions, Fed officials—by speaking clearly—have given unintentional hints and then had to quickly undo the damage with further statements or open market operations.

FEDERAL RESERVE POLICY IN PRACTICE

The Fed's overall guidelines have changed over the years. In the past, it has followed a policy of stabilizing the interest rate at a low level in order to enable the business and government sectors to borrow cheaply. At other times, it has set targets for the growth rate of the money supply and tried to stick to them. But beginning in the 1990s, under Chairman Alan Greenspan, the Fed switched its focus toward real GDP.

> *The Fed's goal over the past 15 years has been to keep GDP as close to potential GDP as possible and to prevent short-run fluctuations around potential GDP. When the economy seems in danger of expanding beyond potential (a boom), the Fed uses monetary policy to decrease total spending and reign the economy in. When the economy is in danger of slipping into recession, the Fed uses monetary policy to increase total spending and expand the economy.*

Why is the Fed so intent on keeping the economy at its potential output—no more and no less? Because it is very costly for the economy to deviate in either direction. The economic and human costs of recessions were outlined earlier, in Chapter 12. But a boom, too, imposes significant costs on society. In the next chapter, you will see how booms—if allowed to continue—inevitably lead to inflation. And inflation, as you learned in Chapter 13, creates economic inefficiencies and redistributes purchasing power rather haphazardly among the population.

Here, we'll consider how the Fed tries to keep the economy on track in the face of two different types of challenges: shifts in the money demand curve and spending shocks.

The Fed's Response to Changes in Money Demand

Earlier in the chapter, you saw that changes in the expected future interest rate can shift the money demand curve. Changes in tastes for holding money and other assets, or changes in technology, can also shift the money demand curve. For example, the increasing use of substitutes for money—such as credit cards or, in the future, electronic money cards—can decrease the demand for money.

Money demand shifts—if ignored—would create problems for the economy. A look back at Figure 8 shows why. In that figure, the money supply is $500 billion and the money market is initially in equilibrium at point *E*, with an interest rate of 5 percent. Then, the money demand curve shifts rightward. If the Fed does nothing, the interest rate will rise—to 10 percent in the figure.

But if the Fed's goal is to stabilize real GDP, it cannot sit by while these events occur. For if the Fed does nothing, the rise in the interest rate will *decrease* investment and interest-sensitive consumption spending, thereby decreasing total spend-

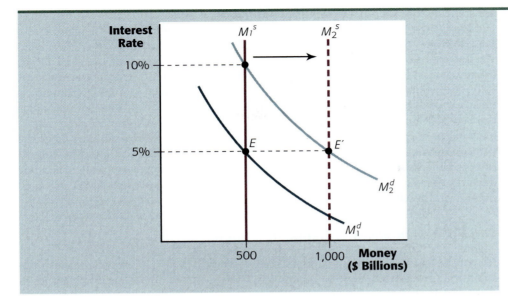

FIGURE 9
The Fed's Response to Changes in Money Demand

A spontaneous increase in money demand would disturb the equilibrium at point E. In the absence of a Fed response, the interest rate would increase to 10 percent. The Fed can off-set this increase in the interest rate by raising the money supply (from $500 billion to $1,000 billion). At E', the interest rate is the same as it was originally.

ing. Real GDP will decrease. What can the Fed do to keep real GDP constant? It must *neutralize* the change in the interest rate.

Figure 9 illustrates how the Fed—by increasing the money supply—can neutralize a rightward shift of the money demand curve. In this case, a money supply of $1,000 billion will do the trick. (As in all of our examples, this is an unrealistically huge change in the money supply, but it makes the graph easier to read.) With the equilibrium interest rate back at 5 percent, there is no reason for total spending to drop, and a recession is avoided.

> *To stabilize real GDP when money demand changes on its own (not in response to a spending shock), the Fed must change the money supply. Specifically, it must increase the money supply in response to an increase in money demand, and decrease the money supply in response to a decrease in money demand.*

Notice an interesting (and pleasant) by-product of this policy. In order to stabilize real GDP, the Fed must also stabilize the interest rate. This gives it an easy guideline to follow when disturbances to the economy arise from changes in money demand:

> *To prevent changes in money demand from affecting real GDP, the Fed should set a target for the interest rate, and adjust the money supply as necessary to maintain that target.*

In normal times, when there are no significant spending shocks to the economy, the Fed can concentrate its efforts on maintaining its interest rate target. This was the Fed's main activity during the mid 1990s. In practice, keeping the interest rate

constant during such periods is straightforward. When the interest rate rises, the Fed knows the money demand curve has shifted to the right. When the interest rate falls, it knows the money demand curve has shifted leftward.

The Fed does not even need to know the precise amount of the shift in the money demand curve in order to stabilize the interest rate. It can operate successfully with educated guesses. A mistake that it makes one day can be fixed the next day, because the mistake will show up in the interest rate. (For example, suppose the Fed had increased the money supply to $800 billion in Figure 9. What would have happened to the interest rate? How would the Fed have responded?) Since the Fed conducts open market operations each day, it is able to use continuous feedback to keep the interest rate relatively constant. While small changes occur between one day and the next, the changes largely disappear when the interest rate is averaged over several weeks.

The Fed's Response to Spending Shocks

As you've learned, shifts in total spending—due to changes in autonomous consumption, investment spending, taxes, or government purchases—cause changes in real GDP. How can the Fed keep real GDP close to potential output when there are direct spending shocks like these?

Figure 10 provides the answer. Initially, the money market is in equilibrium at point *E*, with a money supply of $500 billion and an interest rate of 5 percent. Now suppose a positive spending shock hits the economy, say, an increase in government purchases. If the Fed does nothing, the economy will head into a boom, so real GDP would still rise. To prevent this, the Fed will have to *raise* its interest rate target. The idea is to decrease interest-sensitive spending by the same amount that spending increased due to the shock—in the case, a government purchases shock.

The Fed can hit its new, higher interest rate target by *decreasing* the money supply. In Figure 10, we assume that an interest rate target of 7.5 percent will do the trick, so that the Fed must decrease the money supply from $500 billion to $300 billion. With the new, lower money supply, the equilibrium interest rate is the required 7.5 percent (point *H*).

What if there were a *negative* spending shock to the economy, say, a decrease in government purchases? Then the Fed—to keep real GDP constant—would follow the opposite policy. It would *lower* its interest rate target and *increase* the money supply to hit it. In this way, it could prevent any decrease in total spending and thereby prevent a recession.

> *To stabilize real GDP, the Fed must change its interest rate target in response to a spending shock, and change the money supply to hit its new target. Specifically, it must raise its interest rate target (decrease the money supply) in response to a positive spending shock and lower the interest rate target (increase the money supply) in response to a negative spending shock.*

Notice that the Fed's policy of stabilizing real GDP comes at a price: fluctuations in the interest rate. In Figure 10, in response to a positive spending shock, the Fed raises the interest rate all the way to 7.5 percent. When the shock is a decrease in spending the Fed must decrease its interest rate target.

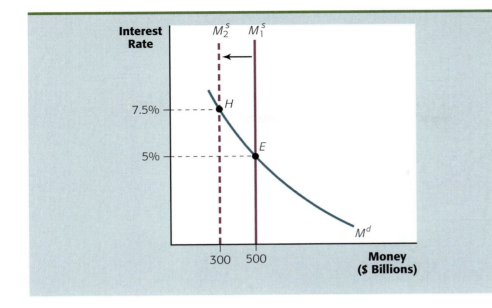

FIGURE 10

The Fed's Response to Spending Shocks

Initially, the Fed is maintaining an interest rate target of 5 percent. When a spending shock threatens to cause a boom, the Fed can neutralize it by raising its interest rate target and decreasing the money supply to hit the new, higher target. Interest-sensitive spending will decrease, preventing GDP from rising above potential output.

Fluctuations in the interest rate are costly in some ways. They make it more difficult for households and businesses to plan, and they increase the risks to bondholders (remember that changes in interest rates translate into changes in bond prices). They can also cause problems for the interest-sensitive sectors of the economy, especially housing construction and automobiles. Nevertheless, fluctuations in real GDP are costly too, and the Fed—especially in recent decades—has concluded that it is a good idea to adjust its interest rate targets aggressively when necessary to stabilize real GDP. An example is the Fed's behavior in 2001, explored in the "Using the Theory" section that follows.

USING THE THEORY

The Fed and the Recession of 2001

In the previous chapter, we began an analysis of our most recent recession, which officially lasted from March to November of 2001. We saw that an investment spending shock caused a decrease in total spending, which in turn caused equilibrium GDP and employment to drop. But we left two questions unanswered: (1) What did policy makers do to try to prevent the recession, and to deal with it once it started? and (2) Why did consumption spending behave abnormally, rising as income fell and preventing the recession from becoming a more serious downturn? Now that you've learned about monetary policy, we can begin to answer these questions.

Starting in January 2001—three months before the official start of the recession—the Fed began to worry. Although the economy was operating at its potential output (the unemployment rate the previous month was

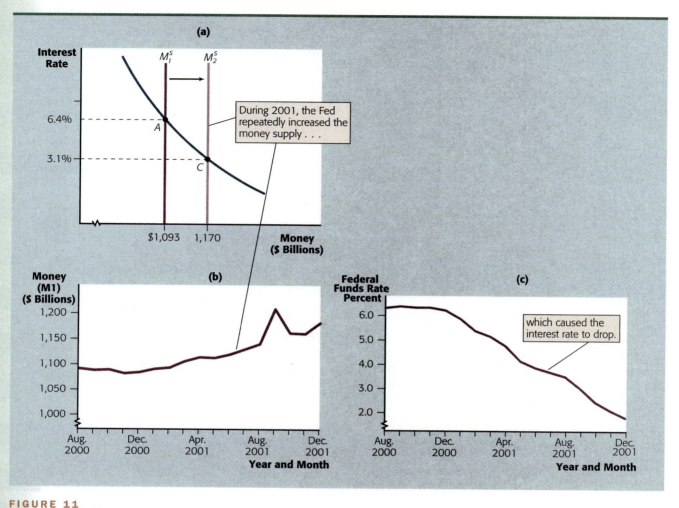

FIGURE 11
The Fed in Action: 2001

3.9 percent), there was danger on the horizon: Investment spending had already decreased for two quarters in a row. The decrease in investment spending had started a negative multiplier effect, which was working its way through the economy and could ultimately cause a recession. Other factors made the Fed worry that investment spending could decrease further. And a sharp decrease in stock prices over the previous year—which had destroyed billions of dollars in household wealth—suggested that consumption spending might begin to fall as well.

The Fed feared that if it did nothing, the investment slowdown would lead, through the multiplier, to a significant drop in real GDP.

The Fed decided to take action, indicated by panels (b) and (c) of Figure 11. Panel (b) tracks the money supply (monthly) from the period before and after January 2001. It shows that beginning in January, the Fed began increasing the money supply rapidly. Panel (c) shows changes in the *federal funds rate*—the interest rate that the Fed watches most closely when it conducts monetary policy. The **federal funds rate** is the interest rate that banks with excess reserves charge for lending reserves to other banks. Although it is just an interest rate for lending among banks, many other interest rates in the economy vary with it closely, so it gives us a good

Federal funds rate The interest rate charged for loans of reserves among banks.

idea of how interest rates in general ("the interest rate" in our highly aggregated view) were changing during this period. As you can see, the federal funds rate fell continually and dramatically during the year, from 6.4 percent down to 1.75 percent. In September of 2001, during which real GDP probably hit bottom, the federal funds rate averaged about 3.1 percent.

Now look at Panel (a), which shows the effect of the Fed policy in the money market. In January 2001, the money market was in equilibrium at point A, with the money supply at $1,093 billion and the federal funds rate at 6.4 percent. As the money supply increased to an average of about $1,170 during the third quarter of 2001, the money supply curve shifted rightward and the interest rate fell.

Although the Fed's policy did not completely prevent the recession, it no doubt saved the economy from a more severe and longer-lasting one. The lower interest rate was especially helpful in maintaining new-home construction, a category of investment spending that is especially sensitive to the interest rate.

The Fed's policy also helps us understand the other question we raised about the 2001 recession: the continued rise in consumption spending throughout the period. Lower interest rates, as you've now learned, stimulate consumption spending on consumer durables, especially automobiles. Indeed, helped by lower interest rates, auto sales rose in every quarter of 2001.

Moreover, when interest rates drop dramatically and rapidly—as they did in 2001—a frenzy of *home mortgage refinancing* can occur: Households rush to exchange their existing, higher-interest-rate mortgages for new mortgages at a lower interest rate. After a refinance, monthly mortgage payments are reduced, freeing up disposable income to be spent on goods and services. But many households go further, taking advantage of the refinancing to borrow even more than they owed on their original mortgage. This provides them with a one-time burst of cash to spend. Home refinancing and additional borrowing on homes seemed to play a major role in boosting consumption spending during the recession of 2001.

Summary

In the United States, the standard measure of the money supply consists of cash in the hands of the public, checking account balances, and travelers' checks. Each of these assets is widely acceptable as a means of payment.

The amount of money in the economy is controlled by the Federal Reserve, operating through the banking system. Banks and other financial intermediaries are profit-seeking firms that collect loanable funds from households and businesses, then repackage them to make loans to other households, businesses, and governmental agencies.

The Federal Reserve injects money into the economy mostly through open market operations. When the Fed wants to increase the money supply, it buys bonds in the open market and pays for them with a check. This is called an *open market purchase*. When the Fed's check is deposited in a bank, the bank obtains reserves and can create new loans. The reserves may move from one bank to another, as borrowers spend what they borrow and the proceeds are deposited into different banks. But eventually, demand deposits, and the money supply,

increase by some multiple of the original injection of reserves by the Fed. The *demand deposit multiplier*—the inverse of the required reserve ratio—gives us that multiple.

The Fed can decrease the money supply by selling government bonds—an open market sale—causing demand deposits to shrink by a multiple of the initial reduction in reserves. The Fed can also change the money supply by changing either the required reserve ratio or the discount rate it charges when it lends reserves to banks.

In the short run, the supply and demand for money interact to determine the interest rate. On one side of the market is the demand for money. An individual's demand for money indicates the part of wealth that person wishes to hold in the form of money, for different interest rates. Money is useful as a means of payment, but holding money means sacrificing the interest that could be earned by holding bonds instead. The higher the interest rate, the larger the fraction of their wealth people will hold in the form of bonds, and the smaller the fraction they will hold as money.

The money supply is under the control of the Fed and is independent of the interest rate. Equilibrium in the money market occurs at the intersection of the downward-sloping money demand curve and the vertical money supply curve. The interest rate will adjust so that the quantity of money demanded by households and firms just equals the quantity of money supplied by the Fed and the banking system.

Conditions in the money market mirror conditions in the bond market. If the interest rate is above equilibrium in the money market, there will be an excess supply of money there. People *want to* hold less money than they actually *do* hold, which means that they wish to hold more bonds than they do hold. An excess supply of money means an excess demand for bonds. As people try to obtain more bonds, the price of bonds rises and the interest rate falls. Thus an excess supply of money will cause the interest rate to fall. Similarly, an excess demand for money will cause the interest rate to rise.

The Fed, by changing the money supply, can change the interest rate. An increase in the money stock creates an ex-

cess supply of money. Very quickly, the interest rate will fall so that the public is willing to hold the now-higher money supply. A decrease in the money stock will drive up the interest rate.

Changes in the interest rate affect interest-sensitive forms of spending—firms' spending on plant and equipment, new housing constructions, and households' purchases of "big ticket" consumer durables. By lowering the interest rate, the Fed can stimulate aggregate expenditures and increase GDP through the multiplier process.

For the past decade, the Fed has used monetary policy to counteract booms and recessions. In normal times—when the only disturbances to the economy are shifts in money demand—the Fed will adjust the money supply to maintain an unchanged interest rate target. By preventing changes in the interest rate, the Fed prevents shifts in money demand from affecting the economy. But to deal with spending shocks, the Fed *changes* its interest rate target, and changes the money supply to meet its new target.

Key Terms

Bond
Cash in the hands of the
    public
Central bank
Demand deposits
Demand deposit multiplier
Discount rate
Excess demand for bonds

Excess reserves
Excess supply of money
Federal funds rate
Federal Open Market
    Committee
Financial intermediary
Monetary policy

Money demand curve
Money supply curve
Open market operations
Required reserve ratio
Required reserves
Reserves
Wealth constraint

Review Questions

1. Describe the main characteristics of money. What purpose does money serve in present-day economies?

2. Which of the following is considered part of the U.S. money supply?
   a. A $10 bill you carry in your wallet
   b. A $100 travelers' check you bought but did not use
   c. The $325.43 balance in your checking account
   d. A share of General Motors stock worth $40

3. What is a financial intermediary?

4. What are the main functions of the Federal Reserve System?

5. Explain how the Federal Reserve can use open market operations to change the level of bank reserves. How does a change in reserves affect the money supply? (Give answers for both an increase and a decrease in the money supply.)

6. Suppose that the money supply is $1 trillion. Decision makers at the Federal Reserve decide that they wish to re-

duce the money supply by $100 billion, or by 10 percent. If the required reserve ratio is 0.05, what does the Fed need to do to carry out the planned reduction?

7. Why do individuals choose to hold some of their wealth in the form of money? Besides individual tastes, what factors help determine how much money an individual holds?

8. Why is the money demand curve downward sloping? Why does a change in the expected interest rate cause the money demand curve to shift?

9. Why is the economy's money supply curve vertical? What causes the money supply curve to shift?

10. What sequence of events brings the money market to equilibrium if there is an excess supply of money? An excess demand for money?

11. The text mentions that starting in January, 2001 the Fed began purchasing government bonds, and as a result, the

interest rate fell to a little over 3 percent. Explain how the Fed's purchase of bonds led to a lower interest rate.

12. Describe how an increase in the interest rate affects spending on the following:
    a. plant and equipment
    b. new housing
    c. consumer durables

13. In the face of increased government spending, what could the Fed do to maintain a stable level of real GDP? In the case of a decrease in government spending, how can the Fed maintain a stable level of real GDP?

Problems and Exercises

1. Suppose the required reserve ratio is 0.2. If an extra $20 billion in reserves is injected into the banking system through an open market purchase of bonds, by how much can demand deposits increase? Would your answer be different if the required reserve ratio were 0.1?

2. Suppose total bank reserves are $100 billion, the required reserve ratio is 0.2, and banks are "fully loaned up" (that is, banks hold no excess reserves). What is the total amount of demand deposits in the economy? Now suppose that the required reserve ratio is lowered to 0.1 and that banks once again become fully "loaned up" with no excess reserves. What is the new level of demand deposits?

3. For each of the following situations, determine whether the money supply will increase, decrease, or stay the same.
    a. Depositors become concerned about the safety of depository institutions and begin withdrawing cash.
    b. The Fed lowers the required reserve ratio.
    c. The economy enters a recession and banks have a hard time finding credit-worthy borrowers.
    d. The Fed sells $100 million of bonds to First National Bank of Ames, Iowa.

4. A bond promises to pay $500 one year from now. For the following prices, find the corresponding interest payments and interest rates that the bond offers.

Price	Amt. Paid in One Year	Interest Payment	Interest Rate
$375	$500	_____	_____
$425	$500	_____	_____
$450	$500	_____	_____
$500	$500	_____	_____

As the price of the bond rises, what happens to the bond's interest rate?

5. "A general expectation that the interest rate will fall can be a self-fulfilling prophecy." Explain what this means.

6. Suppose that the money demand curve shifts leftward, instead of rightward as in Figure 9.
    a. If the Fed did nothing, would the economy be in danger of a boom or a recession?
    b. Illustrate graphically, using a diagram similar to Figure 9, how the Fed can prevent the money demand shift from affecting the economy.
    c. Which would cause the money demand curve to shift leftward: an *increase* or a *decrease* in the expected interest rate? Why?

7. The government, thinking the economy is below potential GDP, decides to raise GDP, so it cuts taxes. The Fed, believing the economy was *already* at potential GDP, wants to neutralize the impact of the tax cut on the economy. What should the Fed do? Illustrate on a graph.

8. Assume that the Fed's goal is to stabilize GDP. How would it respond to the following changes in money demand? How will the interest rate and GDP be affected in each case? Illustrate each case with a diagram.
    a. People believe the interest rate will fall in the near future, so money demand falls.
    b. Many credible financial advisors recommend buying bonds, and consequently the demand for bonds increases.
    c. Tired of credit card debt, the general public begins to use credit cards less frequently and money more frequently.

9. A bond promises to pay $20,000 one year from now.
    a. Complete the following chart.

Price	Amount Paid in One Year	Interest Payment	Interest Rate	Quantity of Money Demanded
	$2000			$2300 billion
	$1500			$2600 billion
	$1000			$2900 billion
	$500			$3200 billion
	$0			$3500 billion

b. Draw a graph of the money market, assuming that it is currently in equilibrium at an interest rate of 5.26 percent. What is the price of this bond? How large is the money supply?

10. A fellow student in your economics class stops you in the hallway and says: "An increase in the demand for money causes the interest rate to rise. But a rise in the interest rate causes people to demand *less* money. Therefore, in-creases in money demand largely cancel themselves out, and have very little effect on the interest rate." Is this correct? Why or why not? (*Hint:* Draw a graph.)

11. Figure 10 (c) shows a spike in money growth during September 2001. Using what you know about bonds versus money and the money demand curve, explain why this spike might have occurred.

Challenge Questions

1. Sometimes banks wish to hold reserves in excess of the legal minimum. Suppose that banks initially hold no excess reserves and the required reserve ratio is 0.1. Then the Fed makes an open market purchase of $100,000 in government bonds, and each bank decides to hold excess reserves equal to 5 percent of its deposits.
   a. Derive the demand deposit multiplier in this case. Is it larger or smaller than when banks hold no excess reserves?
   b. What is the ultimate change in demand deposits in the entire banking system?

2. A fellow student in your economics class is confused again: "Economics makes no sense. On the one hand, we're told that if everyone expects the interest rate to rise, then everyone will sell bonds, and that will cause the price of bonds to fall (and the interest rate to rise). Fair enough. But in the real world, no one can sell a bond unless someone else buys it. And if everyone expects the price of bonds to fall, no one will buy them. Therefore, no one can *sell* them either, and, therefore, there will be no change in the price of bonds or the interest rate." Can you resolve your friend's confusion

These exercises require access to Lieberman/Hall Xtra! If Xtra! did not come with your book, visit http://liebermanxtra.swlearning.com to purchase.

1. Use your Xtra! password at the Hall and Lieberman Web site (http://liebermanxtra.swlearning.com), select this chapter, and under Economic Applications, click on EconDebate. Choose *Macroeconomics: Money and the Financial System,* and scroll down to find the debate, "Should U.S. financial markets be deregulated?" Read the debate, and use the information to answer the following questions.
   a. Explain how the Federal Deposit Insurance Corporation (FDIC) increases the moral hazard problem.
   b. Do you expect the deregulation of U.S. financial markets to increase financial fragility and failures or not? Explain. Can you support your answer with an example from current events?

2. Use your Xtra! password at the Hall and Lieberman Web site (http://liebermanxtra.swlearning.com), select this chapter, and under Economic Applications, click on

EconData. Choose *Macroeconomics: Money and the Financial System,* and scroll down to find *Stock Prices S&P 500.* Read the definition and click on Updates and use the information to answer the following questions.
   a. Click on the "review the latest S&P 500 Total Return data," and scroll down to see the percent change from last year for the year 2000 and onward. Describe the trend, and what might have contributed to it.
   b. Scroll down to the article "The Stock Market: Beyond Risk Lies Uncertainty." Read the article. In absence of regulations separating commercial from investment banking, how should the Federal Reserve System intervene to stabilize the financial system? Would Fed intervention exacerbate the moral hazard problem and lead to more instability or alternatively lead to long-term stability of financial markets? Explain.

Aggregate Demand and Aggregate Supply

Booms and recessions are a fact of life. If you need a reminder, look back at Figure 1 in Chapter 15. There you can see that while potential GDP rises steadily year after year—due to economic growth—*actual* GDP tends to fluctuate around its potential.

But Figure 1 also reveals another important fact about the economy: Booms and recessions don't last forever. When output dips below or rises above potential, the economy always returns to potential output after a few quarters or years. True, in some of these episodes, government policy—either fiscal or monetary—helped the economy return to full employment more quickly. But even without corrective policies—such as during long parts of the Great Depression of the 1930s—the economy shows a remarkable tendency to begin moving back toward potential output. Why? And what is the mechanism that brings us back to our potential when we have strayed from it? These are the questions we will address in this chapter. We'll do this by studying the behavior of a variable that we've put aside for several chapters: the price level.

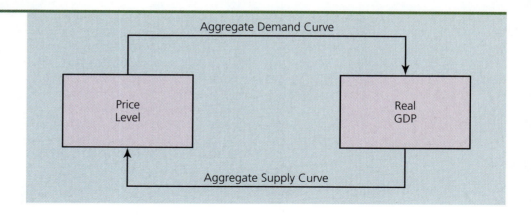

FIGURE 1

The Two-Way Relationship between Output and the Price Level

The chapter begins by exploring the relationship between the price level and output. This is a two-way relationship, as you can see in Figure 1. On the one hand, changes in the price level cause changes in real GDP. This causal relationship is captured in the *aggregate demand curve,* which we will discuss shortly. On the other hand, changes in real GDP cause changes in the price level. This relationship is summarized by the *aggregate supply curve,* to which we will turn later.

Once we've developed the aggregate demand and supply curves, we'll be able to use them to understand how changes in the price level—sometimes gently, other times more harshly—steer the economy back toward potential output.

THE AGGREGATE DEMAND CURVE

In this section, we'll focus on how changes in the price level affect real GDP. We'll postpone till later the question of *why* the price level might change.

The Price Level and the Money Market

The first effect of a change in the price level occurs in the money market. When the price level rises, the money demand curve shifts rightward. Why? Remember the money demand curve tells us how much of their wealth people want to hold as money (as opposed to bonds) at each interest rate. People hold bonds because of the interest they pay; people hold money because of its convenience. Each day, as we make purchases, we need cash or funds in our checking account to cover them. If the price level rises, and the average purchase becomes more expensive, we'll need to hold more of our wealth as money just to achieve the same level of convenience. Thus, at any given interest rate, the demand for money increases, and the money demand curve shifts rightward.

> *A rise in the price level—because it makes purchases more expensive—increases the demand for money and shifts the money demand curve rightward. Conversely, a drop in the price level makes purchases cheaper, decreases the demand for money, and shifts the money demand curve leftward.*

Now, its time for a bit of review. Look back at Figure 8 in the previous chapter. There you saw that, when the money demand curve shifts rightward, the interest rate rises. You also learned that a rise in the interest rate reduces interest-sensitive spending—on plant and equipment, new housing, and consumer durables. Finally, you learned that a decrease in spending causes a (multiplied) decrease in equilibrium GDP. Putting all of this together:

> *A rise in the price level causes the interest rate to rise and interest-sensitive spending to fall. Equilibrium GDP decreases by a multiple of the decrease in interest-sensitive spending.*

The Price Level and Net Exports

The second effect of a higher price level brings in the foreign sector. When the U.S. price level rises, American goods become more expensive to foreigners, so U.S. exports decrease. At the same time, foreign goods become *relatively* cheaper to Americans, so U.S. imports increase. The decrease in U.S. exports, and the increase in U.S. imports, each contributes to a decrease in *net exports*—one of the components of total spending. When total spending drops, so does equilibrium GDP.

> *A rise in the price level causes net exports to drop and equilibrium GDP to decrease by a multiple of the drop in net exports.*

Deriving the Aggregate Demand (*AD*) Curve

Now let's combine these insights about the price level and output in a graph. Figure 2 plots the price level on the vertical axis and the economy's real GDP on the horizontal axis. We'll assume that initally, the price level is 100, and equilibrium GDP is $10 trillion, represented by point *J*. Then—for some reason that we will not yet identify—the price level rises to 140. As you've just learned, the rise in the price level will raise the interest rate and raise the price of U.S. goods relative to foreign goods. Both of these will contribute to a drop in total spending and a (multiplied) drop in equilibrium GDP. In Figure 2, we assume that equilibrium GDP decreases to $6 trillion, so the economy moves to point *K*.

If we continued to change the price level to other values—raising it further to 150, lowering it to 85, and so on—we would find that each different price level results in a different equilibrium GDP. This is illustrated by the downward-sloping curve in the figure, which we call the *aggregate demand curve*.

> *The **aggregate demand** (AD) **curve** tells us the equilibrium real GDP at any price level.*

Aggregate demand (*AD*) curve A curve indicating equilibrium GDP at each price level.

Movements along the *AD* Curve

As you will see later in this chapter, a variety of events can cause the price level to change, and move us along the *AD* curve. It's important to understand what happens in the economy as we make such a move.

FIGURE 2
Deriving the Aggregate Demand Curve

With a price level of 100, equilibrium GDP is $10 trillion, so the economy is at point J. As the price level rises to 140, output decreases to $6 trillion, at point K. Output falls because the rise in the price level: (1) increases money demand, raises the interest rate, and reduces interest sensitive spending; and (2) makes U.S. goods more expensive relative to foreign goods and decreases U.S. net exports. Connecting points like J and K yields the downward-sloping aggregate demand (AD) curve.

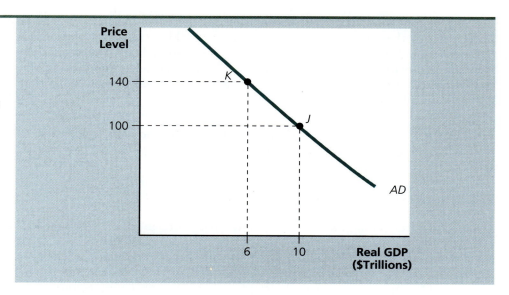

Look again at the *AD* curve in Figure 2. Suppose the price level rises, and we move from point *J* to point *K* along this curve. Then the following sequence of events occurs: The rise in the price level increases the demand for money, raises the interest rate, decreases autonomous consumption (*a*) and investment spending (I^P), and works through the multiplier to decrease equilibrium GDP. At the same time, the rise in the price level raises the price of U.S. goods, decreases U.S. exports, and raises U.S. imports, which also works through the multiplier to decrease equilibrium GDP. The process can be summarized as follows:

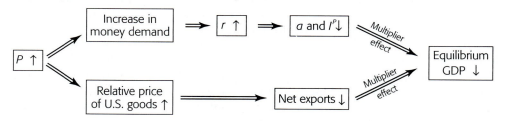

The opposite sequence of events will occur if the price level falls, moving us rightward along the *AD* curve:

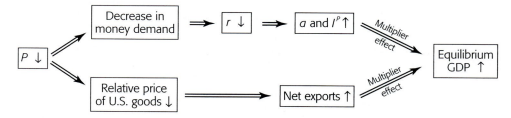

Shifts of the *AD* Curve

When we move along the *AD* curve in Figure 2, we assume that the price level changes, but that other influences on equilibrium GDP remain constant. When any of these other influences on GDP changes, the *AD* curve will shift. The distinction between movements along the *AD* curve and shifts of the curve itself is very important. Always keep the following rule in mind:

When a change in the price level causes equilibrium GDP to change, we move along the AD *curve. Whenever anything other than the price level causes equilibrium GDP to change, the* AD *curve itself shifts.*

What are these other influences on GDP? They are the very same changes you learned about in previous chapters. Specifically, equilibrium GDP will change whenever there is a change in any of the following:

- government spending
- taxes
- autonomous consumption spending
- investment spending
- the money supply curve
- the money demand curve

Let's consider some examples and see how each causes the *AD* curve to shift.

Spending Shocks. Spending shocks initially affect the economy by changing total spending and then changing output by a multiple of that original change in spending. For example, a positive spending shock—say, an increase in government purchases—causes an increase in total spending and an increase in equilibrium GDP. But now that we've introduced the price level into our analysis, we can be more precise: A positive spending shock raises equilibrium GDP *at any given price level.* Thus, a positive spending shock *shifts* the *AD* curve rightward.

Figure 3 illustrates a rightward shift in the *AD* curve. We assume that the economy begins at a price level of 100, with equilibrium GDP at $10 trillion—point *J* on *AD*₁.

Now let's increase government purchases by $2 trillion and ask what happens if the price level remains at 100. Let's suppose that the multiplier is 2.5. Then equilibrium GDP rises by $5 trillion to $15 trillion—point *N*. This point lies to the right of our original curve *AD*₁. Point *N*, therefore, must lie on a *new AD* curve—a curve that tells us equilibrium GDP at any price level *after the increase in government spending.* The new *AD* curve is the one labeled, *AD*₂, which goes through point *N*. What about the other points on *AD*₂? They tell us that, if we had started at any *other* price level, an increase in government spending would have increased equilibrium GDP at that price level, too. We conclude that *an increase in government purchases shifts the entire AD curve rightward.*

Other spending shocks can shift the *AD* curve rightward just as in Figure 3. More specifically,

the AD *curve shifts rightward when government purchases, investment spending, autonomous consumption spending, or net exports increase, or when taxes decrease.*

Our analysis also applies in the other direction. For example, at any given price level, a *decrease* in government spending decreases total spending and, decreases equilibrium GDP. This in turn shifts the *AD* curve leftward.

More generally,

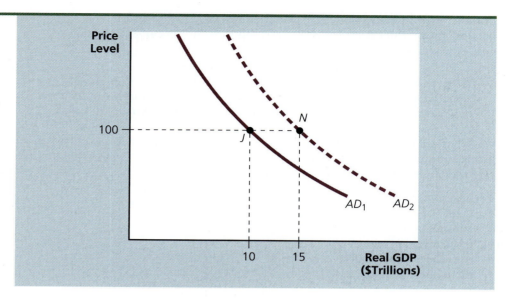

the AD *curve shifts leftward when government purchases, investment spending, autonomous consumption spending, or net exports decrease, or when
taxes increase.*

Changes in the Money Market. Changes that originate in the money market will
also shift the aggregate demand curve. To see why, imagine once again that the
economy begins at point *J* in Figure 3.

Now suppose the Fed conducts an open market purchase of bonds, thereby increasing the money supply. As you learned in the last chapter, this will shift the
money supply curve rightward. (If you need to refresh your memory, flip back to
Figure 7 in the previous chapter.) As the interest rate drops, total spending rises, increasing equilibrium GDP *at any given price level*. In Figure 3, at the initial price
level P = 100, equilibrium GDP rises from $10 trillion to $15 trillion, so the economy moves—once again—from point *J* to point *N*. As you can see, the *AD* curve
has *shifted* from AD_1 to AD_2.

A decrease in the money supply would have the opposite effect in Figure 3: The
money supply curve would shift leftward. As a result, the interest rate would rise,
total spending would fall, and *equilibrium GDP at any price level would fall*. We
conclude that

an increase in the money supply shifts the AD *curve rightward. A decrease
in the money supply shifts the* AD *curve leftward.*

Shifts versus Movements along
the *AD* Curve: A Summary

Figure 4 summarizes how different events in the economy cause a movement along,
or a shift in, the *AD* curve.

Notice that the figure tells us how a variety of events affect the *AD* curve, but
not how they affect *real* GDP. The reason is that, even if we know which *AD* curve
the economy is on, we don't know the level of GDP until we know *where* on that *AD*

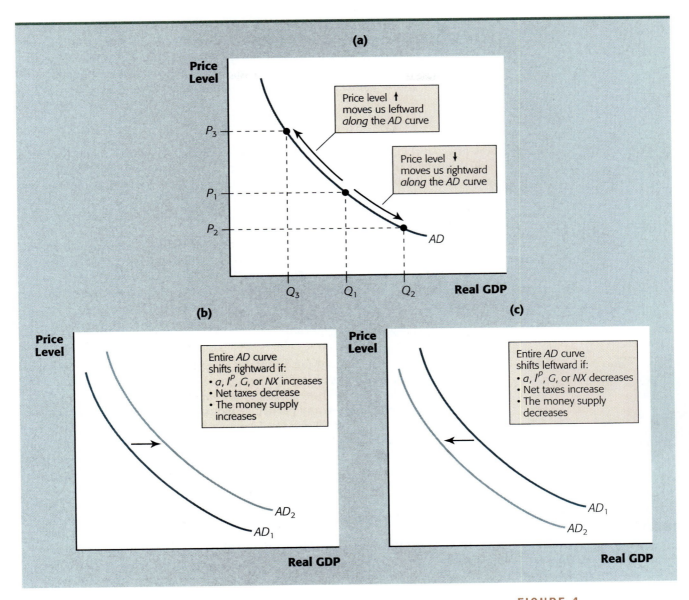

(a)

Price Level

Price level ↑ moves us leftward *along* the AD curve

Price level ↓ moves us rightward *along* the AD curve

P_3

P_1

P_2

AD

Q_3 Q_1 Q_2 **Real GDP**

(b)

Price Level

Entire AD curve shifts rightward if:
• a, I^P, G, or NX increases
• Net taxes decrease
• The money supply increases

AD_2

AD_1

Real GDP

(c)

Price Level

Entire AD curve shifts leftward if:
• a, I^P, G, or NX decreases
• Net taxes increase
• The money supply decreases

AD_1

AD_2

Real GDP

FIGURE 4
Effects of Key Changes on the Aggregate Demand Curve

curve we are operating. And that, in turn, depends on the value of the price level. But how is the price level determined? Our first step in answering that question is to understand the other side of the relationship between GDP and the price level.

THE AGGREGATE SUPPLY CURVE

Look back at Figure 1, which illustrates the *two-way* relationship between the price level and output. On the one hand, changes in the price level affect output. This is the relationship, summarized by the *AD* curve, that we've just explored in the previous section. On the other hand, changes in output affect the price level. This relationship—summarized by the *aggregate supply curve*—is the focus of this section.

The effect of changes in output on the price level is complex, involving a variety of forces. Current research is helping economists get a clearer picture of this relationship. Here, we will present a simple model of the aggregate supply curve that focuses on the link between prices and costs. Toward the end of the chapter, we'll discuss some additional ideas about the aggregate supply curve.

Costs and Prices

The price *level* in the economy results from the pricing behavior of millions of individual business firms. In any given year, some of these firms will raise their prices, and some will lower them. For example, during the 1990s, personal computers and long-distance telephone calls came down in price, while college tuition and the prices of movies rose. These types of price changes are subjects for *microeconomic* analysis, because they involve individual markets.

But often, all firms in the economy are affected by the same *macroeconomic* event, causing prices to rise or fall throughout the economy. This change in the price *level* is what interests us in macroeconomics.

To understand how macroeconomic events affect the price level, we begin with a very simple assumption:

> *A firm sets the price of its products as a markup over cost per unit.*

For example, if it costs Burger King $2.00, on average, to produce a Whopper (cost per unit is $2.00), and Burger King's percentage markup is 10 percent, then it will charge $2.00 + (0.10 × $2.00) = $2.20 per Whopper.[1]

The percentage markup in any particular industry will depend on the degree of competition there. If there are many firms competing for customers in a market, all producing very similar products, then we can expect the markup to be relatively small. Thus, we expect a relatively low markup on fast-food burgers or personal computers. In industries where there is less competition—such as daily newspapers or jet aircraft—we would expect higher percentage markups.

In macroeconomics, we are not concerned with how the markup differs in different industries, but rather with the *average percentage markup* in the economy:

> *The average percentage markup in the economy is determined by competitive conditions in the economy. The competitive structure of the economy changes very slowly, so the average percentage markup should be somewhat stable from year to year.*

But a stable markup does not necessarily mean a stable price level, because unit costs can change. For example, if Burger King's markup remains at 10 percent, but the unit cost of a Whopper rises from $2.00 to $3.00, then the price of a Whopper will rise to $3.00 + (0.10 × $3.00) = $3.30. Extending this example to all firms in the economy, we can say:

Fast-food restaurants, like other firms in the economy, charge a markup over cost per unit. The average markup in the economy is determined by competitive conditions, and tends to change slowly over time.

© SUSAN VAN ETTEN

---

[1] In the microeconomic chapters of this book, you learned a more sophisticated theory of how prices are determined. In competitive markets, prices are determined by the intersection of supply and demand curves. In imperfectly competitive or monopoly markets, each firm sets its price using marginal analysis. But the simple markup model in this chapter captures a central conclusion of those theories: that an increase in costs will result in higher prices.

In the short run, the price level rises when there is an economy-wide increase in unit costs, and the price level falls when there is an economy-wide decrease in unit costs.

GDP, Costs, and the Price Level

Our primary concern in this chapter is the impact of *total output or real GDP* on unit costs and, therefore, on the price level. Why should a change in output affect unit costs and the price level? We'll focus on three key reasons.

As total output increases:

Greater amounts of inputs may be needed to produce a unit of output. As output increases, firms hire new, untrained workers who may be less productive than existing workers. Firms also begin using capital and land that are less well suited to their industry. As a result, greater amounts of labor, capital, land, and raw materials are needed to produce each unit of output. Even if the prices of these inputs remain the same, unit costs will rise.

For example, imagine that Intel increases its output of computer chips. Then it will have to be less picky about the workers it employs, hiring some who are less well suited to chip production than those already working there. Thus, more labor hours will be needed to produce each chip. Intel may also have to begin using older, less-efficient production facilities, which require more silicon and other raw materials per chip. Even if the prices of all of these inputs remain unchanged, unit costs will rise.

The prices of nonlabor inputs rise. In addition to needing greater quantities of inputs, firms will also have to pay a higher price for them. This is especially true of inputs like land and natural resources, which may be available only in limited quantities in the short run. An increase in the output of final goods raises the demand for these inputs, causing their prices to rise. Firms that produce final goods experience an increase in unit costs, and raise their own prices accordingly.

The nominal wage rate rises. Greater output means higher employment, leaving fewer unemployed workers looking for jobs. As firms compete to hire increasingly scarce workers, they must offer higher nominal wage rates to attract them. Higher nominal wages increase unit costs, and therefore result in a higher price level. Notice that we use the nominal wage, rather than the real wage we've emphasized elsewhere in this book. That's because we are interested in explaining how firms' prices are determined. Since price is a nominal variable, it will be marked up over *nominal* costs.

A decrease in output affects unit costs through the same three forces, but with the opposite result. As output falls, firms can be more selective in hiring the best, most efficient workers and in choosing other inputs, decreasing their input requirements per unit of output. Decreases in demand for land and natural resources will cause their prices to drop. And as unemployment rises, wages will fall as workers compete for jobs. All of these contribute to a drop in unit costs, and a decrease in the price level.

The Short Run. All three of our reasons are important in explaining why a change in output affects the price level. However, they operate within different time frames. When total output increases, new, less productive workers will be hired rather quickly. Similarly, the prices of certain key inputs—such as lumber, land, oil, and wheat—may rise within a few weeks or months.

But our third explanation—changes in the nominal wage rate—is a different story. While wages in some lines of work might respond very rapidly, we can expect wages in many industries to change very little or not at all for a year or more after a change in output.

> *For a year or so after a change in output, changes in the average nominal wage are less important than other forces that change unit costs.*

Here are some of the more important reasons why wages in many industries respond so slowly to changes in output:

- Many firms have union contracts that specify wages for up to three years. While wage increases are often built into these contracts, a rise in output will not affect the wage increase. When output rises or falls, these firms continue to abide by the contract.
- Wages in many large corporations are set by slow-moving bureaucracies.
- Wage changes in either direction can be costly to firms. Higher wages to attract new workers must be widely publicized in order to raise the number of job applicants at the firm. Lower wages can reduce the morale of workers—and their productivity. Thus, many firms are reluctant to change wages until they are reasonably sure that any change in their output will be long lasting.
- Firms may benefit from developing reputations for paying stable wages. A firm that raises wages when output is high and labor is scarce may have to lower wages when output is low and labor is plentiful. Such a firm would develop a reputation for paying unstable wages, and have difficulty attracting new workers.

In this section, we focus exclusively on the short run—a time horizon of a year or so after a change in output. Since the average nominal wage rate changes very little over the short run, we'll make the following simplifying assumption: *The nominal wage rate is fixed in the short run.* More specifically,

> *we assume that changes in output have no effect on the nominal wage rate in the short run.*

Keep in mind, though, that our assumption of a constant wage holds only in the *short run.* As you will see later, wage changes play a very important role in the economy's adjustment over the long run.

Since we assume a constant nominal wage in the short run, a change in output will affect unit costs through the other two factors we mentioned earlier. Specifically, in the short run, a rise in real GDP raises firms' unit costs because (1) input requirements per unit of output rise, and (2) the prices of nonlabor inputs rise. With a constant percentage markup, the rise in unit costs translates into a rise in the price level. Thus,

> *in the short run, a rise in real GDP, by causing unit costs to increase, will also cause a rise in the price level.*

In the other direction, a *drop* in real GDP lowers unit costs because (1) input requirements per unit of output fall, and (2) the prices of nonlabor inputs fall. With a constant percentage markup, the drop in unit costs translates into a drop in the price level.

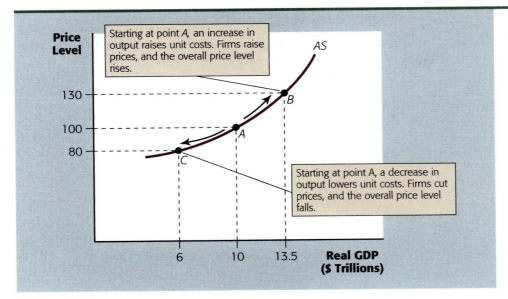

FIGURE 5
The Aggregate Supply Curve

In the short run, a fall in real GDP, by causing unit costs to decrease, will also cause a decrease in the price level.

Deriving the Aggregate Supply Curve

Figure 5 summarizes our discussion about the effect of output on the price level in the short run. Suppose the economy begins at point *A*, with output at $10 trillion and the price level at 100. Now suppose that output rises to $13.5 trillion. What will happen in the short run? Even though wages are assumed to remain constant, the price level will rise because of the other forces we've discussed. In the figure, the price level rises to 130, indicated by point *B*. If, instead, output *fell* to $6 trillion, the price level would fall—to 80 in the figure, indicated by point *C*.

As you can see, each time we change the level of output, there will be a new price level in the short run, giving us another point on the figure. If we connect all of these points, we obtain the economy's *aggregate supply curve:*

The aggregate supply curve (or AS curve) tells us the price level consistent with firms' unit costs and their percentage markups at any level of output over the short run.

Aggregate supply (AS) curve A curve indicating the price level consistent with firms' unit costs and markups for any level of output over the short run.

A more accurate name for the *AS* curve would be the "short-run-price-level-at-each-output-level" curve, but that is more than a mouthful. The *AS* curve gets its name because it *resembles* a microeconomic market supply curve. Like the supply curve for maple syrup we discussed in Chapter 3, the *AS* curve is upward sloping, and it has a price variable (the price level) on the vertical axis and a quantity variable (total output) on the horizontal axis. But there, the similarity ends.

Movements Along the *AS* Curve

When a change in output causes the price level to change, we *move along* the economy's *AS* curve. But what happens in the economy as we make such a move?

Look again at the *AS* curve in Figure 5. Suppose we move from point *A* to point *B* along this curve in the short run. The increase in output raises the prices of raw materials and other (nonlabor) inputs and also raises input requirements per unit of output at many firms. Both of these changes increase costs per unit. As long as the markup remains somewhat stable, the rise in unit costs will lead firms to raise their prices, and the price level will increase. Thus, as we move upward along the *AS* curve, we can represent what happens as follows:

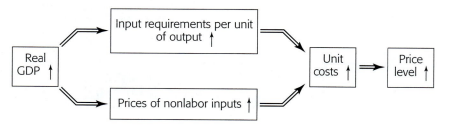

The opposite sequence of events occurs when real GDP falls, moving us downward along the *AS* curve:

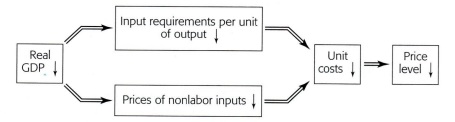

Shifts of the *AS* Curve

When we drew the *AS* curve in Figure 5, we assumed that a number of important variables remained unchanged. In particular, we assumed that the only changes in unit costs were those caused by a change in output. But in the real world, unit costs sometimes change for reasons *other* than a change in output. When this occurs, unit costs—and the price level—will change at *any* level of output, so the *AS* curve will shift.

In general, we distinguish between a movement along the *AS* curve, and a shift of the curve itself, as follows:

> *When a change in real GDP causes the price level to change, we move along the AS curve. When anything other than a change in real GDP causes the price level to change, the AS curve itself shifts.*

Figure 6 illustrates the logic of a shift in the *AS* curve. Suppose the economy's initial *AS* curve is AS_1. Now suppose that some economic event *other* than a change in output—for the moment, we'll leave the event unnamed—causes firms to raise their prices. Then the price level will be higher at *any* level of output we might imagine, so the *AS* curve must shift *upward*—for example, to AS_2 in the figure. At an

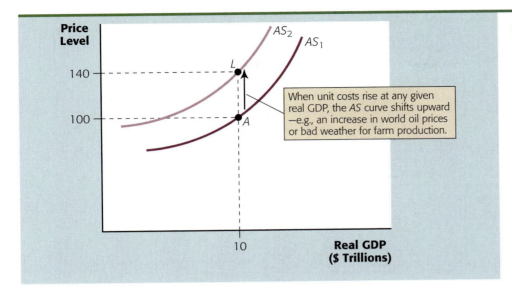

FIGURE 6
Shifts of the Aggregate Supply Curve

When unit costs rise at any given real GDP, the *AS* curve shifts upward —e.g., an increase in world oil prices or bad weather for farm production.

output level of $10 trillion, the price level would rise from 100 to 140. At any other output level, the price level would also rise.

What can cause unit costs to change at any given level of output? The following are some important examples:

- *Changes in world oil prices.* Oil is traded on a world market, where prices can fluctuate even while output in the United States does not. And changes in world oil prices have caused major shifts in the *AS* curve. Three events over the past few decades—an oil embargo by Arab oil-producing nations in 1973–74, the Iranian revolution in 1978–79, and Iraq's invasion of Kuwait in 1990—all caused large jumps in the price of oil. Each time, costs per unit rose for firms across the country, and they responded by charging higher prices than before for *any* output level they might produce. As in Figure 6, the *AS* curve shifted upward. Conversely, oil prices fell sharply during 1997 and 1998. This caused unit costs to decrease at many firms, shifting the *AS* curve downward.

- *Changes in the weather.* Good crop-growing weather increases farmers' yields for any given amounts of land, labor, capital, and other inputs used. This decreases farms' unit costs, and the price of agricultural goods falls. Since many of these goods are final goods (such as fresh fruit and vegetables), the price drop will contribute directly to a drop in the price level and a downward shift of the *AS* curve. Additionally, agricultural products are important inputs in the production of many other goods. (For example, corn is an input in beef production.) Good weather thus leads to a drop in input prices for many other firms in the economy, causing their unit costs, and their prices, to decrease. For these reasons, we can expect good weather to shift the *AS* curve downward. Bad weather, which decreases crop yields, increases unit costs at any level of output and shifts the *AS* curve upward.

- *Technological change.* New technologies can enable firms to produce any given level of output at lower unit costs. In recent years, for example, we've seen revolutions in telecommunications, information processing, and medicine. The result has been steady downward shifts of the *AS* curve.

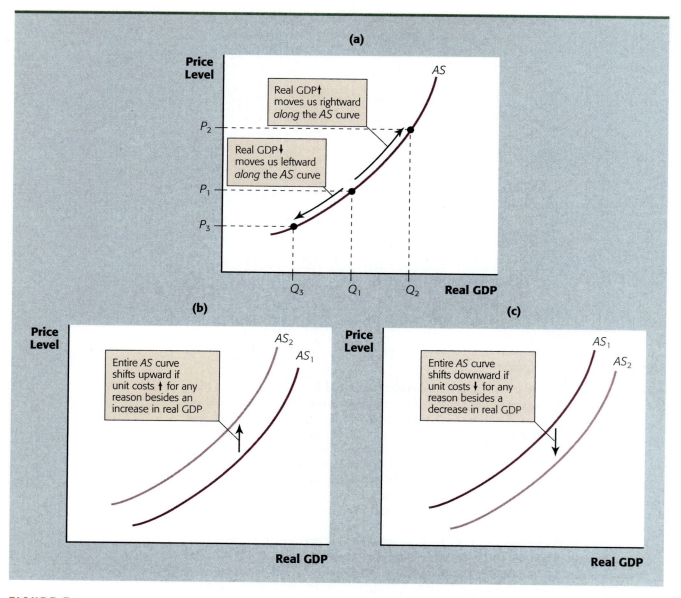

FIGURE 7
Effects of Key Changes on the Aggregate Supply Curve

• *The Nominal Wage.* Remember that in our short-run analysis we're assuming the nominal wage rate does *not* change. As we move along the *AS* curve, we hold the nominal wage rate constant. But later in the chapter—when we extend our time horizon beyond a year or so—you'll see that changes in the nominal wage are an important part of the economy's long-run adjustment process. Here we just point out that, *if* the nominal wage were to increase for any reason, it would raise unit costs for firms at any level of output and therefore *shift* the *AS* curve *upward*. Similarly, *if* the nominal wage rate were to fall for any reason, it would *decrease* unit costs at any level of output and shift the *AS* curve downward. We'll come back to this important fact later.

Figure 7 summarizes how different events in the economy cause a movement along, or a shift in, the *AS* curve. But the *AS* curve tells only half of the economy's

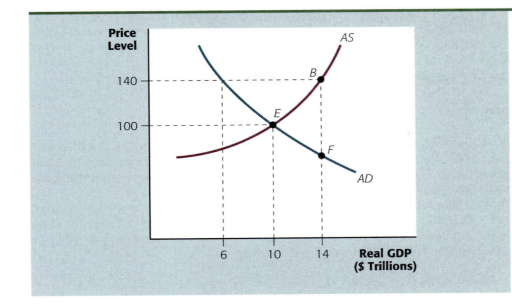

FIGURE 8
Short-Run Macroeconomic Equilibrium

Short-run equilibrium occurs where the AD *and* AS *curves intersect. At point E, the price level of 100 is consistent with an output of $10 trillion along the* AD *curve. The output level of $10 trillion is consistent with a price level of 100 along the* AS *curve. At any other combination of price level and output, such as point F or point B, at least one condition for equilibrium will not be satisfied.*

story: It shows us the price level *if* we know the level of output. The *AD* curve tells the other half of the story: It shows us the level of output *if* we know the economy's price level. In the next section, we finally put the two halves of the story together, allowing us to determine both the price level and output.

AD AND *AS* TOGETHER: SHORT-RUN EQUILIBRIUM

Where will the economy settle in the short run? That is, where is our **short-run macroeconomic equilibrium?** Figure 8 shows how to answer that question, using both the *AS* curve and the *AD* curve. If you suspect that the equilibrium is at point *E*, the intersection of these two curves, you are correct. At that point, the price level is 100 and output is $10 trillion. But it's worth thinking about *why* point *E*—and only point *E*—is our short-run equilibrium.

First, we know that in equilibrium, the economy must be at some point on the *AD* curve. For example, suppose the economy were at point *B*, which lies to the right of the *AD* curve. At this point, the price level is 140 and output is $14 trillion. But the *AD* curve tells us that with a price level of 140, *equilibrium* output is $6 trillion. Thus, at point *B*, real GDP would be greater than its equilibrium value. As you learned several chapters ago, this situation cannot persist for long, since firms—unable to sell all that they're producing—would be forced to cut back their output. Thus, point *B* cannot be our short-run equilibrium.

Second, short-run equilibrium requires that the economy be operating on its *AS* curve. Otherwise, firms would not be charging the prices dictated by their unit costs and the average percentage markup in the economy. For example, point *F* lies *below* the *AS* curve. But the *AS* curve tells us that if output is $14 trillion, based on the average percentage markup and unit costs, the price level should be 140 (point *B*), not something lower. That is, the price level at point *F* is *too low* for equilibrium. This situation will not last long either, since firms will want to raise prices, causing the overall price level to rise.

Short-run macroeconomic equilibrium A combination of price level and GDP consistent with both the *AD* and *AS* curves.

We could make a similar argument for any other point that is off the *AS* curve, off the *AD* curve, or off of both curves. Our conclusion is always the same: Unless the economy is on *both* the *AS* and the *AD* curves, the price level and the level of output will change. Only when the economy is at point *E*—on *both* curves—can we have a sustainable level of real GDP and the price level.

WHAT HAPPENS WHEN THINGS CHANGE?

Now that we know how the short-run equilibrium is determined, and armed with our knowledge of the *AD* and *AS* curves, we are ready to put the model through its paces. In this section, we'll explore how different types of events cause the short-run equilibrium to change.

Our short-run equilibrium will change when either the *AD* curve, the *AS* curve, or both, *shift*. Since the consequences for the economy are very different for shifts in the *AD* curve as opposed to shifts in the *AS* curve, economists have developed a shorthand language to distinguish between them:

> *An event that causes the* AD *curve to shift is called a **demand shock***. *An event that causes the* AS *curve to shift is called a **supply shock***.

In earlier chapters, we've used the phrase *spending shock*: a change in spending by one or more sectors that ultimately affects the entire economy. As you're about to see, shifts in the aggregate demand curve or the aggregate supply curve both create changes in total spending, although in different ways. So *demand shocks* and *supply shocks* are just two *different ways for spending shocks to originate*.

In this section, we'll first explore the effects of demand shocks, both in the short run and during the adjustment process to the long run. Then, we'll take up the issue of supply shocks.

Demand Shocks in the Short Run

Figure 4, which lists the causes of a shift in the *AD* curve, also serves as a list of demand shocks to the economy. Let's consider some examples.

An Increase in Government Purchases. You've learned that an increase in government purchases shifts the *AD* curve rightward. Now we can see how it affects the economy in the short run. Figure 9 shows the initial equilibrium at point *E*, with the price level equal to 100 and output at $10 trillion. Now, suppose that government purchases rise by $2 trillion. Figure 4(b) tells us that the *AD* curve will shift rightward. What will happen to equilibrium GDP?

Let's suppose that the *MPC* is 0.6, so that the multiplier is $1/(1 - 0.6) = 2.5$. Also, let's suppose that the price level remains unchanged. Then a $2 trillion rise in government purchases would increase output by $5 trillion to $15 trillion. The *AD* curve would shift, and the economy would move from point *E* to point *J* in Figure 9. Would we stay there? Absolutely not. Point *J* lies below the *AS* curve, telling us that when GDP is $15 trillion, the price level consistent with firms' average costs and average markup is 130, not 100. Firms would soon raise prices, and this would cause a movement leftward along AD_2. The price level would keep rising and output would keep falling, until we reached point *H*. At that point, with out-

Demand shock Any event that causes the *AD* curve to shift.

Supply shock Any event that causes the *AS* curve to shift.

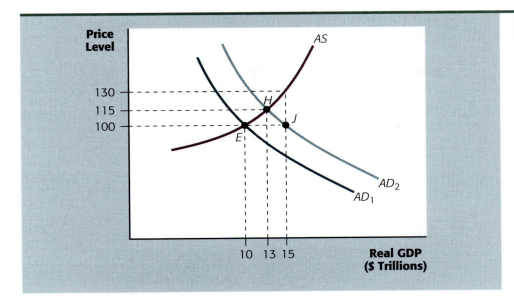

FIGURE 9
The Effect of a Demand Shock

Starting at point E, an increase in government purchases would shift the AD curve rightward to AD₂. Point J illustrates where the economy would move if the price level remained constant. But as output increases, the price level rises. Thus, the economy moves along the AS curve from point E to point H.

put at $13 trillion, we would be on both the *AS* and *AD* curves, so there would be no reason for a further rise in the price level and no reason for a further fall in output.

However, the process we've just described is not entirely realistic. It assumes that when government purchases rise, *first* output increases (the move to point *J*) and *then* the price level rises (the move to point *H*). In reality, output and the price level tend to rise *together*. Thus, the economy would likely *slide along* the *AS* curve from point *E* to point *H*. As we move along the *AS* curve, output rises, increasing unit costs and the price level. At the same time, the rise in the price level *reduces equilibrium GDP* (the level of output toward which the economy is heading on the *AD* curve) from point *J* to point *H*.

We can summarize the impact of a rise in government purchases this way:

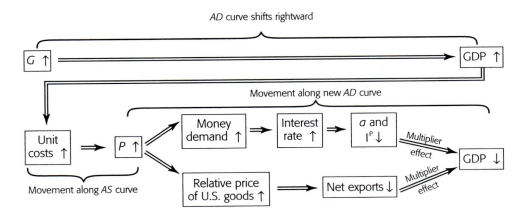

Net Effect: GDP ↑, but by less due to effect of P ↑

Let's step back a minute and get some perspective on this example of fiscal policy. This is the second time in this text that we've considered fiscal policy in the short run. Here, our discussion is more realistic, because we're incorporating changes in the price level—and we've seen that the effect of fiscal policy becomes weaker. More specifically, a rise in government purchases *increases* the price level. The rise in the price level causes the other components of total spending—consumption, investment, and net exports—to drop. The result is: Real GDP rises by less than the simple multiplier suggests. (In our example, a $2 trillion increase in government purchases increases equilibrium GDP by $3 trillion, so the multiplier would be 1.5.) Or, to put it another way, the multiplier is not really as large as our simple formula—$1/(1 - MPC)$—would suggest. However, as you can see in Figure 9, a rise in government purchases—even when we include the rise in the price level—still raises GDP in the short run.

We can summarize the impact of price-level changes this way:

> *When government purchases increase, the horizontal shift of the AD curve measures how much real GDP would increase if the price level remained constant. But because the price level rises, real GDP rises by less than the shift in the AD curve.*

Now let's switch gears into reverse: How would we illustrate the effects of a *decrease* in government purchases? In this case, the *AD* curve would shift *leftward*, causing the following to happen:

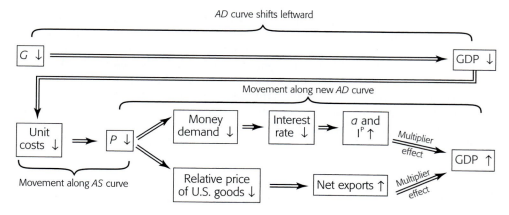

Net Effect: GDP ↓, but by less due to effect of P ↓

As you can see, the same sequence of events occurs in the same order, but each variable moves in the opposite direction. A decrease in government purchases decreases equilibrium GDP, but the multiplier effect is smaller because the price level falls.

An Increase in the Money Supply. Monetary policy stimulates the economy through a different channel than fiscal policy. But once we arrive at the *AD* and *AS* diagram, the two kinds of policy look very much alike. For example, an increase in the money supply, which reduces the interest rate, will stimulate interest-sensitive consumption and investment spending. Real GDP then increases, and the *AD* curve shifts rightward, just as in Figure 7. Once output begins to rise, we have the same sequence of events as in fiscal policy: The price level rises, so the increase in GDP will be smaller. We can represent the situation as follows:

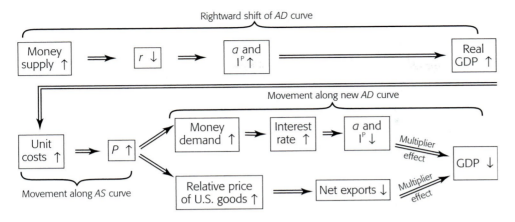

Net Effect: GDP ↑, but by less due to effect of P ↑

Other Demand Shocks. You may want to go through the other demand shocks in Figure 4 on your own and explain the sequence of events in each case that causes output and the price level to change. This will help you verify the following general conclusion about demand shocks:

A positive demand shock—one that shifts the AD *curve rightward—increases both real GDP and the price level in the short run. A negative demand shock—one that shifts the* AD *curve leftward—decreases both real GDP and the price level in the short run.*

An Example: The Great Depression. The U.S. economy collapsed far more seriously during 1929 through 1933—the onset of the Great Depression—than it did at any other time in the country's history. Because the price level fell during the contraction, we know that the contraction was caused by an adverse demand shock. An adverse supply shock would have caused the price level to *rise* as GDP fell.

What specific demand shock caused the depression? This question has been debated by economists almost continuously in the 70 years since the contraction began. The candidates are numerous, and it appears that a combination of bad developments was responsible. The 1920s were a period of optimism—with high levels of investment by businesses and spending by families on houses and cars. The stock market soared. But in the fall of 1929, the bubble of optimism burst. The stock market crashed, and investment and consumption spending plummeted. Similar events occurred in other countries, and the demand for products exported by the United States fell. The Fed—then only 16 years old—reacted by cutting the money supply sharply, which added an adverse monetary shock to all of the cutbacks in spending. Each of these events contributed to a leftward shift of the *AD* curve, causing both output and the price level to fall.

Demand Shocks: Adjusting to the Long Run

In Figure 9, point *H* shows the new equilibrium after a positive demand shock *in the short run*—a year or so after the shock. But point *H* is not necessarily where the economy will end up in the long run. For example, suppose full-employment output is $10 trillion, and point *H*—representing an output of $13 trillion—is

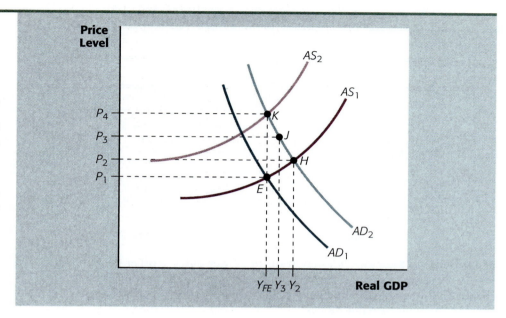

FIGURE 10
The Long-Run Adjustment Process

Beginning at point E, a positive demand shock would shift the aggregate demand curve to AD₂, raising both output and the price level. At point H, output is above the full-employment level, Y_FE. Firms will compete to hire scarce workers, thereby driving up the wage rate. The higher wage rate will shift the AS curve to AS₂. Only when the economy returns to full-employment output at point K will there be no further shifts in AS.

above full-employment output. Then—with employment unusually high and unemployment unusually low—business firms will have to compete to hire scarce workers, driving up the wage rate. It might take a year or more for the wage rate to rise significantly—recall our earlier list of reasons that wages adjust only slowly. But when we extend our horizon to several years or more, we must recognize that if output is beyond its potential, the wage rate will rise. Since the *AS* curve is drawn for a *given wage,* a rise in the wage rate will *shift* the curve upward, changing our equilibrium.

Alternatively, we could imagine a situation in which short-run equilibrium GDP was *below* its potential. In this case, with abnormally high unemployment, workers would compete to get scarce jobs, and eventually the wage rate would fall. Then the *AS* curve would shift downward, once again changing our equilibrium GDP.

Short-Run versus Long-Run Outcomes

In the short run, we treat the wage rate as given. But in the long run, the wage rate can change. When output is above full employment, the wage rate will rise, shifting the AS curve upward. When output is below full employment, the wage rate will fall, shifting the AS curve downward.

Now we are ready to explore what happens over the long run in the aftermath of a demand shock. Figure 10 shows an economy in equilibrium at point *E*. We assume that the initial equilibrium is at full-employment output (Y_{FE}), since—as you are about to see—this is where the economy always ends up after the long-run adjustment process is complete. To make our results as general as possible, we'll use symbols, rather than numbers, to represent output and price levels.

Now suppose the *AD* curve shifts rightward, say, due to an increase in government purchases. In the short run, the equilibrium moves to point *H*, with a higher price level (P_2) and a higher level of output (Y_2). Point *H* tells us where the economy will be about a year after the increase in government purchases, before the wage rate has a chance to adjust. (Remember, along any given AS curve, the wage rate is assumed to be constant.)

But now let's extend our analysis beyond a year. Notice that Y_2 is greater than Y_{FE}. The wage will begin to rise, raising average costs at any given output level and causing firms to raise prices. In the figure, the AS curve would begin shifting upward. The new aggregate supply curve, AS_2, shows where the economy might be 2 years after the shock, after the long-run adjustment process has begun. With this AS curve, the economy would be at point J, with output at Y_3. The rise in the price level has moved us along the new aggregate demand curve, AD_2.

Is point J our final, long-run equilibrium? No, it cannot be. At Y_3, output is *still* greater than Y_{FE}, so the wage rate will continue to rise, and the AS curve will continue to shift upward. At point J, the long-run adjustment process is not yet complete. When will the process end? Only when the wage rate stops rising—that is, only when output has returned to Y_{FE}. This occurs when the AS curve has shifted all the way to AS_3, moving the economy to point K—our new, long-run equilibrium.

As you can see, the increase in government purchases has no effect on equilibrium GDP in the long run: The economy returns to full employment, which is just where it started. This is why the long-run adjustment process is often called the economy's **self-correcting mechanism**. And this mechanism applies to any demand shock, not just an increase in government purchases:

Self-correcting mechanism The adjustment process through which price and wage changes return the economy to full-employment output in the long run.

> If a demand shock pulls the economy away from full employment, changes in the wage rate and the price level will eventually cause the economy to correct itself and return to full-employment output.

For a positive demand shock that shifts the AD curve rightward, the self-correcting mechanism works like this:

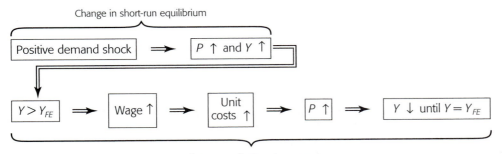

Figure 11 illustrates the case of a negative demand shock, in which the AD curve shifts leftward. In this case, the short-run equilibrium GDP is *below* Y_{FE}. Over the long run, unusually high unemployment drives the wage rate down, shifting the AS curve down as well. The price level decreases, causing equilibrium GDP to rise along the AD_2 curve. The process comes to a halt only when output returns to Y_{FE}. Thus, in the long run, the economy moves from point E to point M, and the negative demand shock causes no change in equilibrium GDP. The complete sequence of events after a negative demand shock looks like this:

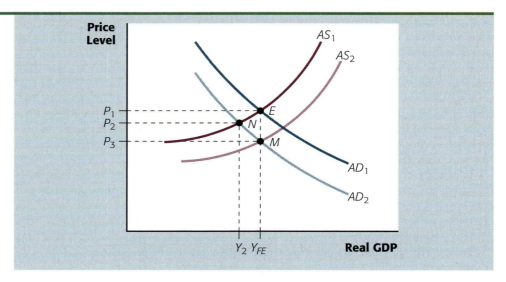

Long-Run Adjustment After a Negative Demand Shock

Starting from point E, *a negative demand shock shifts the* AD *curve to* AD$_2$, *lowering GDP and the price level. At point* N, *output is below the full-employment level. With unemployed labor available, wages will fall, enabling firms to lower their prices. The* AS *curve shifts downward until full employment is regained at point* M, *with a lower price level.*

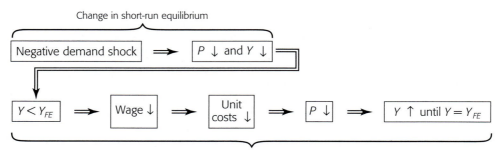

Pulling all of our observations together, we can summarize the economy's self-correcting mechanism as follows:

> *Whenever a demand shock pulls the economy away from full employment, the self-correcting mechanism will eventually bring it back. When output exceeds its full-employment level, wages will eventually rise, causing a rise in the price level and a drop in GDP until full employment is restored. When output is less than its full-employment level, wages will eventually fall, causing a drop in the price level and a rise in GDP until full employment is restored.*

The Long-Run Aggregate Supply Curve

The self-correcting mechanism provides an important link between the economy's long-run and short-run behavior. It helps us understand why booms and recessions don't last forever. Often, however, we are primarily interested in the long-run effects of a demand shock. In these cases, we may want to skip over the self-correcting mechanism and go straight to its end result. A new version of the *AS* curve helps us do this.

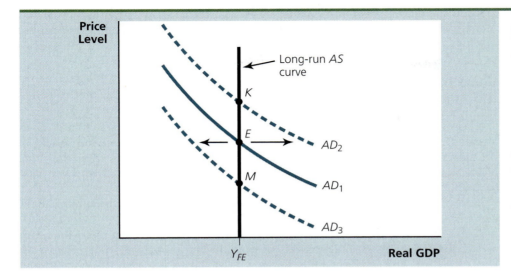

FIGURE 12

The Long-Run Aggregate Supply Curve

In the long run, GDP will be at its full-employment level regardless of the position of the AD curve. A positive demand shock would shift AD rightward to AD_2, moving the economy from point E to point K with a higher price level. A negative shock would shift AD to AD_3, leading to a lower price level at point M. The long-run AS curve is vertical at full-employment output.

Figure labels: Price Level; Long-run AS curve; K; E; M; AD_2; AD_1; AD_3; Y_{FE}; Real GDP

Look again at Figure 10, which illustrates the impact of a positive demand shock. The economy begins at full employment at point *E*, then moves to point *H* in the short run (before the wage rate rises), and then goes to point *K* in the long run (after the rise in wages). If we skip over the short-run equilibrium, we find that the positive demand shock has moved the economy from *E* to *K*, which is vertically above *E*. That is, in the long run, the price level rises, but output remains unchanged.

Now look at Figure 12, which shows another way of illustrating this long-run result. In the figure, the vertical line is the economy's **long-run aggregate supply curve**. It summarizes all possible output and price-level combinations at which the economy could end up in the long run. It is vertical because, in the long run, GDP will be the same—full-employment output—*regardless* of the position of the *AD* curve. The price level, however, will depend on the position of the *AD* curve. In the figure, a positive demand shock would shift the *AD* curve rightward, moving the economy from *E* to *K*: a higher price level, but the same level of output. A negative demand shock would shift the *AD* curve leftward, moving the economy from *E* to *M*: a lower price level with the same level of output.[2]

Figure 12 tells us something very important about the economy: In the long run, after the self-correcting mechanism has done its job, *neither fiscal nor monetary policy has any influence on the level of output or employment.* In the long run, these policies shift the *AD* curve along a vertical *AS* curve, changing the price level, but without affecting real GDP.

But notice the words "long run" in the previous statement. It can take several years before the economy returns to full employment after a demand shock. This is why governments around the world are reluctant to rely on the self-correcting

Long-run aggregate supply curve
A vertical line indicating all possible output and price-level combinations at which the economy could end up in the long run.

---

[2] Of course, full-employment output can increase from year to year, as you learned in the chapter on economic growth. When the economy is growing, the long-run *AS* curve will shift rightward. In that case, the level of output at which the economy will eventually settle increases from year to year.

mechanism alone to keep the economy on track. Instead, they often use fiscal and monetary policy in an attempt to return the economy to full employment more quickly.

Some Important Provisos about the Adjustment Process

The upward-sloping aggregate supply curve we've presented in this chapter gives a realistic picture of how the economy actually behaves after a demand shock. In the short run, positive demand shocks that increase output also raise the price level. Negative demand shocks that decrease output generally put downward pressure on prices.

However, the story we have told about what happens as we move along the *AS* curve is somewhat incomplete.

First, we made the assumption that prices are completely flexible—that they can change freely over short periods of time. In fact, however, some prices take time to adjust, just as wages take time to adjust. Firms print catalogs containing prices that are good for, say, 6 months. The regulatory commission in your state generally sets the prices of electricity, gas, water, and basic telephone service in advance for a year or more.

Second, we assumed that wages are completely *inflexible* in the short run. But in *some* industries, wages respond quickly. For example, in the construction industry, contractors hire workers for projects lasting a few months. When they can't find the workers they want, they immediately offer higher wages—they don't wait for a year.

Third, there is more to the process of recovering from a shock than the adjustment of prices and wages. During a recession, many workers lose their jobs at the same time. It takes time for those workers to become re-established in new jobs. As time passes, and job losers become job finders, the economy tends to recover. This process, in addition to the changes in wages and prices we've discussed, is part of the long-run adjustment process and helps to bring the economy back to full employment after a demand shock.

Supply Shocks

In recent decades, supply shocks have been important sources of economic fluctuations. The most dramatic supply shocks have resulted from sudden changes in world oil prices. As you are about to see, supply shocks affect the economy differently than demand shocks.

Short-Run Effects of Supply Shocks. Figure 13 shows an example of a supply shock: an increase in world oil prices that shifts the aggregate supply curve upward, from AS_1 to AS_2. As rising oil prices increase average costs, firms will begin raising prices, and the price level will increase. The rise in the price level decreases equilibrium GDP along the *AD* curve. In the short run, the price level will continue to rise, and the economy will continue to slide leftward along its *AD* curve, until we reach the AS_2 curve at point R. At this point, the price level is consistent with firms' average costs and average markup (we are on the *AS* curve), and total output is equal to total spending (we are on the *AD* curve). As you can see, the short-run impact of

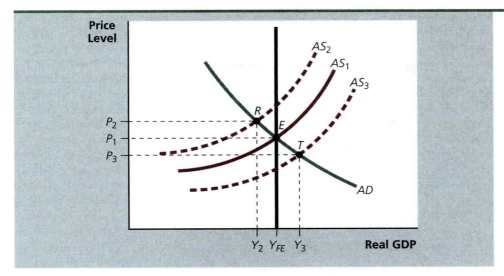

FIGURE 13
The Effect of Supply Shocks

An adverse supply shock would shift the AS curve upward from AS_1 to AS_2. In the short-run equilibrium at point R, the price level is higher and output is below Y_{FE}. Eventually, wages will fall, causing average costs to fall, and the AS curve will shift back to its original position. A positive supply shock would have just the opposite effect.

higher oil prices is a rise in the price level and a fall in output. We call this a *negative* supply shock, because of the negative effect on output.

> *In the short run, a negative supply shock shifts the AS curve upward, decreasing output and increasing the price level.*

Notice the sharp contrast between the effects of negative supply shocks and negative demand shocks in the short run. After a negative demand shock (see, for example, Figure 11), both output and the price level fall. After a negative supply shock, output falls, but the price level rises. Economists and journalists have coined the term **stagflation** to describe a *stag*nating economy experiencing in*flation*.

Stagflation The combination of falling output and rising prices.

> *A negative supply shock causes stagflation in the short run.*

Stagflation caused by increases in oil prices is not just a theoretical possibility. Three of our recessions in the last quarter century—in 1973–1974, 1978–1979, and 1990–1991—followed increases in world oil prices. And each of these three recession also saw jumps in the price level.

Positive supply shocks increase output by shifting the *AS* curve downward, as in the shift from AS_1 to AS_3 in Figure 13. As you can see in the figure,

> *a positive supply shock shifts the AS curve downward, increasing output and decreasing the price level.*

Unusually good weather or a drop in oil prices are examples of positive supply shocks. In addition, a positive supply shock can sometimes be caused by government policy. A few chapters ago, we discussed how the government could use tax incentives and other policies to increase the rate of economic growth. These policies work by shifting the *AS* curve downward, thus increasing output while tending to decrease the price level.

Long-Run Effects of Supply Shocks. What about the effects of supply shocks in the long run? In some cases, we need not concern ourselves with this question, because some supply shocks are temporary. For example, except in unusual cases, periods of rising oil prices are followed by periods of falling oil prices. Similarly, supply shocks caused by unusually good or bad weather, or by natural disasters, are always short lived. A temporary supply shock causes only a temporary shift in the *AS* curve; over the long run, the curve simply returns to its initial position, and the economy returns to full employment. In Figure 13, the *AS* curve would shift back from AS_2 to AS_1, and the economy would move from point *R* back to point *E*.

In other cases, however, a supply shock can last for an extended period. One example was the rise in oil prices during the 1970s, which persisted for several years. In cases like this, is there a self-correcting mechanism that brings the economy back to full employment after a long-lasting supply shock? Indeed, there is, and it is the same mechanism that brings the economy back to full employment after a demand shock.

Look again at Figure 13. At point *R*, output is below full-employment output. In the long run, as workers compete for scarce jobs, the wage rate will decline. This will cause the *AS* curve to shift *downward*. The wage will continue to fall until the economy returns to full employment; that is, until we are back at point *E*.

Short-Run versus
Long-Run Outcomes

In the long run, the economy self-corrects after a supply shock, just as it does after a demand shock. When output differs from its full-employment level, the wage rate changes, and the AS curve shifts until full employment is restored.

© CHRIS HONDROS/GETTY IMAGES/LIAISON

USING THE THEORY
The Story of Two Recessions and "Jobless" Expansions

The aggregate demand and aggregate supply curves are more than just abstract graphs; they're tools to help us understand important economic events. For example, they can help us understand why the economy suffered its two most recent recessions, and also how and why these recessions differed from one another.

The Recession of 1990–91

The story of the 1990–91 recession begins in mid-1990, when Iraq invaded Kuwait, a major oil producer. During this conflict, Kuwait's oil was taken off the world market, and so was Iraq's. The reduction in oil supplies resulted in a rapid and substantial increase in the price of oil, a key input to many industries. From the second to the fourth quarter of 1990, oil prices rose from $14 to $27 per barrel.

The left-hand panel of Figure 14 shows our *AS–AD* analysis of the shock. Initially, the economy was on both AD_{1990} and AS_{1990}. Equilibrium was at point *E*, and output was at the full-employment level. Then, the oil price shock shifted the *AS* curve upward, to AS_{1991}, while leaving the *AD* curve more or less unchanged. As the short-run equilibrium moved to point *R*, real GDP fell and the price level *rose*. Now look at the left side of the next figure (Figure 15). The upper panel shows the

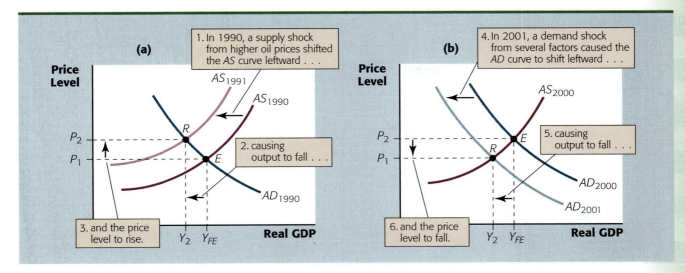

FIGURE 14
An AD and AS Analysis of Two Recessions

behavior of GDP during the period leading up to, and during, the recession. As you can see, consistent with our AS–AD analysis, real GDP fell—from a high of $6.73 trillion in the second quarter of 1990 to a low of $6.63 trillion in the first quarter of 1991 (a decrease of 1.5 percent). The lower panel shows the behavior of the Consumer Price Index (CPI). While the CPI was rising modestly before the recession began, it rose more rapidly during the second half of 1990, as the recession took hold. Once again, this is consistent with what our AS–AD analysis predicts for a negative supply shock, such as the rise in oil prices in 1990.

The Recession of 2001

The story of the 2001 recession was quite different. This time, there was no spike in oil prices and no other significant supply shock to plague the economy. Rather, there was a demand shock, and a Federal Reserve policy during the year before the recession that might have made it a bit worse.

In earlier chapters, you learned that the major cause of the recession was a decrease in investment spending. To review: In the years leading up to 2001, businesses rushed to acquire and develop new equipment needed to exploit new technologies, such as the Internet and wireless communication. By 2001, many firms had sufficiently "caught up" and the flow of investment spending—while still positive and high—began to decrease relative to previous years. This decrease in investment spending was a demand shock to the economy: In 2001, the AD curve shifted leftward.

Now we can introduce another force that may have contributed to the recession of 2001: the policy of the Fed. During the late 1990s, the Fed had become concerned that the investment boom and consumer optimism were shifting the AD curve rightward too rapidly, creating a danger that we would overshoot potential GDP and set off higher inflation. The Fed responded by tightening up on the money supply and raising the interest rate. From mid-1999 to mid-2000, the Fed raised the federal funds rate six times—a total of almost two full percentage points in less than a year. The Fed then held the rate at a relatively high 6.50 percent for another six months until early 2001. In retrospect, the Fed may have continued raising and holding the rate high a bit too long, even after the AD curve stopped moving rightward. And the

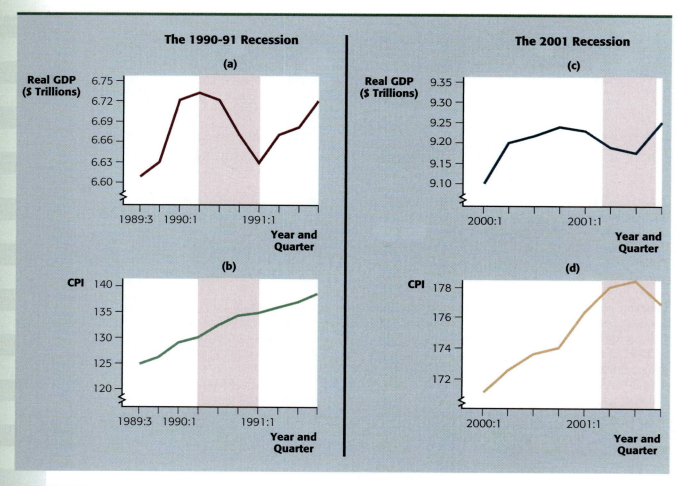

FIGURE 15
GDP and the Price Level
in Two Recessions

effects of this policy may have continued into early 2001, exacerbating the decrease in investment that was occurring for other reasons. In this way, the rate hikes themselves may have contributed to a further leftward shift of the *AD* curve.

The right-hand panel of Figure 14 shows our *AS–AD* analysis of this period. Initially, the economy was on both AD_{2000} and AS_{2000}, with equilibrium at point *E* and output roughly at the full employment level. Then, the decrease in investment spending—helped along by the Fed—shifted the *AD* curve leftward, to AD_{2001}, while leaving the *AS* curve more or less unchanged. As the short-run equilibrium moved to point *R*, real GDP fell. This is mirrored in Figure 15, where the upper right-hand panel shows the behavior of GDP during the period leading up to, and during, the 2001 recession. As you can see, consistent with our *AS–AD* analysis, real GDP first slowed and then fell slightly—from a high of $9.24 trillion in the first quarter of 2001 to $9.18 trillion in the third quarter of that year.

But what about the price level? Here, we need to recognize that there is a slight difference between what our *AS–AD* analysis predicts and what actually happened. In the right panel of Figure 14, the price level falls. And indeed, in the lower right panel of Figure 15, you can see that the price level eventually fell—in the fourth quarter of 2001. But for much of the recession, instead of the price

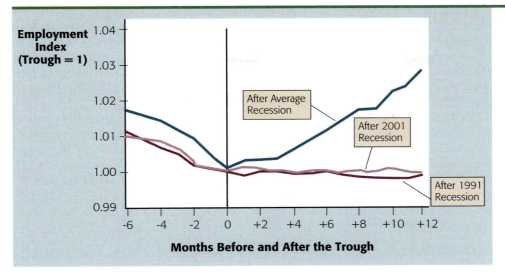

FIGURE 16
The Average Expansion Versus Two Recent Jobless Expansions

Sources: "A Closer Look at Jobless Recoveries," *Economic Review,* Second Quarter 2003, Federal Reserve Bank of Kansas City, p. 48.

level falling we can see that it was rising, but more slowly as 2001 continued. That's because inflation often has some momentum: When it's been rising at a certain rate for some time, then—left alone—it will continue to rise at that rate. The leftward shift in the *AD* curve meant that inflation was *not* left alone in early 2001, so while prices continued to rise, they rose more slowly due to the *AD* shift. And, as you can see, the *AD* shift's downward pressure on prices eventually overcame the inflationary momentum, causing a drop in the price level toward the end of 2001. This is just what we'd expect from our *AS–AD* analysis.

Jobless Expansions

After a recession, the economy enters the expansion phase of the business cycle. Typically, because real GDP is starting from such a low level, it grows rapidly in the first year or so of the expansion, as the economy catches back up to potential output. Employment usually grows rapidly during this period as well.

But in our two most recent recessions, the economy experienced abnormal, prolonged periods during which employment did not grow at all. These are *jobless expansions* (often called *jobless recoveries*).

Figure 16 illustrates the behavior of employment during our two most recent recessions, and the average of the six previous recessions. There is a lot going on in the figure, so let's go through it carefully.[3]

The horizontal axis measures the months before and after the *bottom* (or **trough**) of any given recession. For example, the month marked −2 is two months *before* the trough, when we were still in the *contraction* phase of the cycle. The month marked +6 is six months *after* the trough—six months into the expansion phase.

Trough The bottom point of a recession, when a contraction ends and an expansion begins.

---

[3] Analysis for this section is based on Stacey L. Schreft and Aarti Singh, "A Closer Look at Jobless Recoveries," *Economic Review,* Federal Reserve Bank of Kansas City, Second Quarter, 2003; Mark Schweitzer, "Another Jobless Recovery," *Economic Commentary,* Federal Reserve Bank of Cleveland, March 1, 2003; and "The NBER's Business Cycle Dating Procedure," July 17, 2003 (*http://www.nber.org/cycles/recessions.html*). Additional data on employment, hours, and real GDP from several tables at the Bureau of Economic Analysis (*http://www.bea.gov*) and the Bureau of Labor Statistics (*http://www.bls.gov*).

The vertical axis shows an employment index: employment *divided by* employment at the trough. For each recession, the employment index during any month will be higher or lower than 1.0, depending on whether employment is higher than or lower than it was at the trough. For example, an index number of 1.035 in some month would tell us that employment was 3.5 percent higher that month than during the trough of the recession, while an index number of .99 would tell us that employment was 1 percent lower.

Now, look at the blue line, which shows the average of the employment indices for the six business cycles *before* 1990–91. The blue line shows that employment falls during the contraction phase of the average cycle (the months up to 0), and rises rapidly during the first year of the expansion phase (from months 0 to +12). But the red and pink lines show what happened in the first year of our two most recent expansions—during 1992 and 2002. In both cases, employment drifted slightly *downward,* telling us that the total number of jobs *decreased* during the year. These were jobless expansions. Why?

Explaining Jobless Expansions. Since the story is similar for both of the jobless expansions, we'll focus on the most recent case: the expansion after the recession of 2001. We can start by going back to the equation breaking down output into its different components, as we did several chapters ago ("Economic Growth and Rising Living Standards"):

$$\text{Total output } = \text{productivity} \times \text{average hours} \times \text{EPR} \times \text{population}$$

where EPR stands for the employment-population ratio—the fraction of the population that is working. Note that multiplying the last two terms (EPR × population) gives us total employment, so we can write:

$$\text{Total output } = \text{productivity} \times \text{average hours} \times \text{total employment}$$

Next, we'll convert this equation into percentage changes (using the same method as in the earlier economic growth chapter):

$$\%\Delta \text{ Real GDP} = \%\,\Delta \text{ productivity} + \%\Delta \text{ average hours} + \%\Delta \text{ employment}$$

Since average work hours did not change during the first year of our most recent expansion, we'll set %Δ average hours equal to zero, leaving us with

$$\%\Delta \text{ real GDP} = \%\Delta \text{ productivity} + \%\Delta \text{ employment}.$$

Finally, rearranging, we end up with:

$$\%\Delta \text{ employment} = \%\Delta \text{ real GDP} - \%\Delta \text{ productivity}$$

$$(-0.3\%) \qquad\qquad\qquad (2.9\%) \qquad (3.2\%)$$

We'll get to the numbers in parenthesis in a moment. But notice what this equation tells us: in periods with no significant changes in average hours, the percentage change in total employment is equal to the rate of output growth minus the rate of productivity growth. If output grows faster than productivity, then %Δ employment will be positive: the number of jobs increases. If output grows slower than productivity, then %Δ employment will be negative: the total number of jobs decreases.

Now to the numbers in parenthesis under the last equation: these show the *actual* percentage changes in the first year of the expansion after the 2001 recession. And they show us why that expansion was jobless: *growth in real GDP did not keep up with growth in productivity.* Specifically, real GDP grew at 2.9%, while productivity rose by 3.2 percent. Employment therefore *fell* by 0.3 percent.

But *why* didn't growth in real GDP keep up with productivity growth?

First, because growth in real GDP was unusually low. In the first year of an expansion, output typically grows about 6 percent, but during 2002 it grew by 2.9 percent—less than half its usual rate. Business investment spending gets most of the blame: It usually rises during the first year of an expansion, but in 2002 business investment *decreased*. The reasons for this may include continuing global uncertainty after September 11, 2001, which was followed by the war in Afghanistan and the buildup to war in Iraq. It may also be due to the high levels of investment in information technology and other capital equipment during the 1990s: Once firms caught up with the amount of capital they desired, they had no reason to maintain or return to those previously high rates of annual investment spending.

The second reason for the jobless recovery is productivity, which grew at about the *same* rate as in the average expansion, in spite of the low growth in output. Ordinarily, increases in the capital stock are a major source of productivity growth, but since business investment in new capital *decreased* during 2002, we might expect that productivity growth would slow down that year. But another factor was maintaining high productivity growth: firms' behavior in the labor market. Throughout the first year of the expansion, firms were reluctant to hire full-time, permanent workers, perhaps because the international instability discussed above created uncertainty about the strength and duration of the expansion. Instead, businesses expanded output by hiring part-time and temporary workers.

Why would this boost productivity? Because it enabled firms to adjust their workforce more easily to fluctuations in production. When firms hire regular, full-time employees, they tend to keep them employed at full-time hours even when production dips. But with temporary or part-time workers, firms can adjust employment or hours as production fluctuates. As a result, any given level of output can be produced, on average, with fewer total hours of employed labor. This increases productivity. Firms behaved similarly during the 1990s: Productivity growth exceeded output growth, largely because in 1992—as in 2002—firms relied more heavily on temporary and part-time workers than during a typical expansion.

It might seem odd to think of productivity growth as something harmful. After all, productivity growth is a good thing, the major reason that living standards grow . . . *in the long run.* But in the *short run,* as you've seen, if productivity grows faster than output, it threatens jobs. Keep in mind, though, that the phrase "jobless expansion" refers to just *part* of the expansion phase. Eventually, employment catches up, even to the higher levels of output made possible by productivity growth.

However, the problem can persist for some time. In the early 1990s, even after the expansion finally began to create new jobs after about a year, job creation was so slow that we remained significantly below full employment for another few years, into the mid-1990s. And in mid-2003, a full eighteen months after the trough of the recession, employment was still lower than it was at the trough. Job creation had not yet begun.

It's too early to say if jobless expansions will become the norm in the first year of so after future recessions. Expansions are more likely to be jobless if the early phases of output growth are low—due to uncertainty, abnormally high investment in prior periods, or any other cause. And they are more likely if firms remain wary of hiring regular, full-time workers until the expansion is well under way. But jobless expansions are painful. They leave hundreds of thousands of additional workers without jobs even as the economy expands, and also raise the average *duration* of unemployment. Their mere possibility raises the stakes for the Fed and other government policy makers in trying to prevent future recessions.

Summary

The model of aggregate supply and demand explains how the price level and output are determined in the short run—a period of a year or so following a change in the economy—and how the economy adjusts over longer time periods as well.

The aggregate demand (*AD*) curve shows how changes in the price level affect equilibrium real GDP. A change in the price level has two effects on output. First, it shifts the money demand curve and alters the interest rate in the money market. The change in the interest rate, in turn, affects interest-sensitive forms of spending, triggers the multiplier process, and leads to a new level of equilibrium real GDP. The second effect works through the foreign sector: A change in the price level changes the price of U.S. goods relative to foreign goods, which causes a change in net exports. The change in net exports, in turn, triggers the multiplier process and leads to a new level of equilibrium GDP.

A lower price level means a higher equilibrium real GDP, and a higher price level means lower GDP. The downward-sloping *AD* curve is drawn for given values of government spending, taxes, autonomous consumption spending, investment spending, the money supply, and the public's preferences for holding money and bonds. Changes in any of those factors will cause the *AD* curve to shift.

The aggregate supply (*AS*) curve summarizes the way changes in output affect the price level. To draw the *AS* curve, we assume that firms set the price of individual products as a markup over their average cost, and that the economy's average markup is determined by competitive conditions. We also assume that the nominal wage rate is fixed in the short run. As we move upward along the *AS* curve, a rise in real GDP—by raising average costs—causes the price level to increase. When anything other than a change in real GDP causes the price level to change, the entire *AS* curve shifts.

AD and *AS* together determine real GDP and the price level. The economy must be on the *AD* curve or real GDP would not be at its equilibrium level. It must be on the *AS* curve or firms would not be charging prices dictated by their average costs and markups. Both conditions are satisfied at the intersection of the two curves.

The *AD*–*AS* equilibrium can be disturbed by a demand shock. An increase in government purchases, for example, shifts the *AD* curve rightward. As a result, the price level rises, and so does real GDP. In the long run, if GDP is above potential, wages will rise. This causes average costs to rise and shifts the *AS* curve upward. Eventually, GDP will return to potential and the only long-run result of the demand shock is a higher price level. This implies that the economy's long-run aggregate supply curve is vertical at potential output.

The short-run *AD*–*AS* equilibrium can also be disturbed by a supply shock, such as an increase in world oil prices. With average costs higher at each level of output, the *AS* curve shifts upward, decreasing real GDP and increasing the price level. Eventually, the shock will be self-correcting: With output below potential, the wage rate will fall, average costs will decrease, and the *AS* curve will shift back downward until full employment is restored.

Key Terms

Aggregate demand (*AD*) curve

Aggregate supply (*AS*) curve

Demand shock

Long-run aggregate supply curve

Self-correcting mechanism

Short-run macroeconomic equilibrium

Stagflation

Supply shock

Trough

Review Questions

1. What causal relationship does the aggregate demand curve describe? Why is the *AD* curve downward sloping?

2. "Only changes in spending shift the aggregate demand curve." True or false? Explain.

3. List two reasons why a change in output affects average costs and subsequently the price level.

4. What causal relationship does the aggregate supply curve describe? Why is the *AS* curve upward sloping?

5. Why does equilibrium occur only where the *AD* and *AS* curves intersect?

6. What is meant by the economy's *self-correcting mechanism* after a demand shock?

7. What is the long-run aggregate supply curve? Why is it vertical?

8. How does an economy recover from a negative supply shock?

9. Explain why real GDP growth did not keep up with productivity in 2002.

Problems and Exercises

1. Suppose firms become pessimistic about the future and consequently investment spending falls. With an *AD* and *AS* graph, describe the short-run effects on real GDP and the price level. If the price level were constant, how would your answer change?

2. With an *AD* and *AS* diagram, explain the short-run effect of a decrease in the money supply on real GDP and the price level. What is the effect in the long run? Assume the economy begins at full employment.

3. Use an *AD* and *AS* graph to explain the short-run and long-run effects on real GDP and the price level of an increase in autonomous consumption spending. Assume the economy begins at full employment.

4. A new government policy successfully lowers firms' unit costs. What are the short-run and the long-run effects of such a policy? (Assume that full-employment output does not change.)

5. Make two copies of Figure 14(a) on a sheet of paper. Add curves to illustrate your answer to (a) on one copy and (b) on the other:
   a. What *would* have happened in the years after 1991 if the Fed had done nothing and the economy had relied solely on the self-correcting mechanism to return to full employment?
   b. What *did* happen as a result of the Fed bringing down the interest rate to end the recession?
   c. Is there a difference in the behavior of the price level during the recovery in these two cases? Explain.

6. Make two copies of Figure 14(b) on a sheet of paper. Add curves to illustrate the impacts of Fed policy for (a) on one copy and (b) on the other:
   a. What *would* have happened in the years following 2001 if the Fed had done nothing and the economy had relied solely on the self-correcting mechanism to return to full employment?

   b. What did happen as a result of the Fed's actual policy in 2001 (successive cuts in the interest rate throughout the year)?
   c. Is there a difference in the behavior of the price level during the recovery in these two cases? Explain.

7. Suppose that aggressive antitrust action by the U.S. Justice Department were to successfully increase the degree of competition in many U.S. industries. Use *AS* and *AD* curves to illustrate the short-run impact on the economy if, at the same time,
   a. The Fed does nothing.
   b. The Fed pursues a policy that successfully achieves the highest possible level of GDP with no rise in the price level.

8. (a) Use an *AD* and *AS* graph to show the effects of a decrease in net exports, assuming that the Fed intervenes to keep the economy at full employment. Assume the economy begins at full employment. (b) What would be the short-run and long-run effects if the Fed does not intervene?

9. a. Graphically show the effects of a temporary decrease in nonlabor input prices.
   b. How will your results change if this decrease lasts for an extended period?
   c. How would your results differ if the Fed intervened to keep the economy at full employment?

10. What will happen if real GDP grows by 4 percent while productivity grows by 4.6 percent?

Challenge Questions

1. Suppose that wages are slow to adjust downward but rapidly adjust upward. What would the *AS* curve look like? How would this affect the economy's adjustment to demand shocks (compared to the analysis given in the chapter)?

2. During the 1990s, because of technological change, the *AS* curve was shifting downward, but—except for a few months—the price level did not fall. Why not? (*Hint:* What was the Fed doing?)

 *These exercises require access to Lieberman/Hall Xtra! If Xtra! did not come with your book, visit http://liebermanxtra. swlearning.com to purchase.*

1. Use your Xtra! password at the Hall and Lieberman Web site (http://liebermanxtra.swlearning.com), select this chapter, and under Economic Applications, click on EconDebate. Choose *Monetary Policy,* and scroll down to find the debate, "Will the European Monetary Union Succeed?" Read the debate, and use the information to answer the following questions.

   a. This debate emphasizes the relationship between monetary and fiscal policy. Use the AD–AS framework to explain what would happen to the output and inflation rate of a country at full employment, if the European Central Bank engages in expansionary monetary policy and reduces interest rates.

   b. Use the AD–AS framework to explain what would happen to the output and inflation rate of a country

in recession, if another (larger) country increases government borrowing to finance fiscal expenditures, and in the process raises the interest rates in all participating countries.

2. Use your Xtra! password at the Hall and Lieberman Web site (http://liebermanxtra.swlearning.com), select this chapter, and under Economic Applications, click on EconData. Choose *Monetary Policy,* and scroll down to find *Civilian Unemployment Rate.* Read the definition, then click on Diagrams/Data. The CPI Inflation Rate and the Unemployment Rate diagram illustrates the pattern of inflation and unemployment during the business cycle. Confirm that during recessions inflation rates fall while unemployment rates rise.

Comparative Advantage and the Gains from International Trade

Consumers love bargains. And the rest of the world offers U.S. consumers bargains galore: cars from Japan, computer memory chips from Korea, shoes from China, tomatoes from Mexico, lumber from Canada, and sugar from the Caribbean. But Americans' purchases of foreign-made goods have always been a controversial subject. Should we let these bargain goods into the country? Consumers certainly benefit when we do so. But don't cheap foreign goods threaten the jobs of American workers and the profits of American producers? How do we balance the interests of specific workers and producers on the one hand with the interests of consumers in general? These questions are important not just in the United States, but in every country of the world.

Over the post–World War II period, there has been a worldwide movement toward a policy of *free trade*—the unhindered movement of goods and services across national boundaries. An example of this movement was the creation—in 1995—of a new international body: the World Trade Organization (WTO). The WTO's goal is to help resolve trade disputes among its members, and to reduce obstacles to free trade around the world. And to some extent it has succeeded: Import taxes, import limitations, and all kinds of crafty regulations designed to keep out imports are gradually falling away. By mid-2003, 146 countries had joined the WTO, including China, which was admitted in December 2001. And some 26 other countries, including Russia, Saudi Arabia, and Vietnam, were eager to join the free-trade group.

But while many barriers have come down, others are being put up. Asian governments have been dragging their feet on allowing U.S. firms to sell telecommunications and financial services there. The United States has renewed its long-standing quota on sugar imports and—in 2002—took serious steps to reduce imports of steel from China, Russia, Europe, and Japan. Europeans have restricted the sale of American satellite communications services and American beef. Canada has interfered with the sale of American magazines and television programs within its borders. Poor countries have imposed tariffs on computers, semiconductors, and software exported by rich countries. Rich countries have announced their intention to maintain, at least through the year 2005, existing quotas on textiles and clothing sold by poor countries.

Looking at the contradictory mix of trade policies that exist in the world, we are left to wonder: Is free international trade a good thing that makes us better off, or is it bad for us and something that should be kept in check? In this chapter, you'll learn to apply the tools of economics to issues surrounding international trade. Most important, you'll see how we can extend economic analysis to a global context, in which markets extend across international borders, and the decision makers are households, firms, and government agencies in different nations.

THE LOGIC OF FREE TRADE

Many of us like the idea of being self-reliant. A very few even prefer to live by themselves in a remote region of Alaska or the backcountry of Montana. But consider the defects of self-sufficiency: If you lived all by yourself, you would be poor. You could not *export* or sell to others any part of your own production, nor could you *import* or buy from others anything they have produced. You would be limited to consuming the goods and services that you produced. Undoubtedly, the food, clothing, and housing you would manage to produce by yourself would be small in quantity and poor in quality—nothing like the items you currently enjoy. And there would be many things you could not get at all—electricity, television, cars, airplane trips, or the penicillin that could save your life.

The defects of self-sufficiency explain why most people do not choose it. Rather, people prefer to specialize and trade with each other. In Chapter 2, you learned that specialization and exchange enable us to enjoy greater production and higher living standards than would otherwise be possible.

This principle applies not just to individuals, but also to *groups* of individuals, such as those living within the boundaries that define cities, counties, states, or nations. That is, just as we all benefit when *individuals* specialize and exchange with each other, so, too, we can benefit when *groups* of individuals specialize in producing different goods and services, and exchange them with other *groups*.

Imagine what would happen if the residents of your state switched from a policy of open trading with other states to one of self-sufficiency, refusing to import anything from "foreign states" or to export anything to them. Such an arrangement would be preferable to individual self-sufficiency; at least there would be specialization and trade *within* the state. But the elimination of trading between states would surely result in many sacrifices. Lacking the necessary inputs for their production, for instance, your state might have to do without bananas, cotton, or tires. And the goods that *were* made in your state would likely be produced inefficiently. For example, while residents of Vermont *could* drill for oil, and Texans *could* produce maple syrup, they could do so only at great cost of resources.

Thus, it would make no sense to insist on the economic self-sufficiency of each of the 50 states. And the founders of the United States knew this. They placed prohibitions against tariffs, quotas, and other barriers to interstate commerce right in the U.S. Constitution. The people of Vermont and Texas are vastly better off under free trade among the states than they would be if each state were self-sufficient.

What is true for states is also true for entire nations. The members of the WTO have carried the argument to its ultimate conclusion: National specialization and exchange can expand world living standards through free *international* trade. Such trade involves the movement of goods and services across national boundaries. Goods and services produced domestically, but sold abroad, are called **exports;** those produced abroad, but consumed domestically, are called **imports.** The long-term goal of the WTO is to remove all barriers to exports and imports in order to encourage among nations the specialization and trade that have been so successful within nations.

Exports Goods and services produced domestically, but sold abroad.

Imports Goods and services produced abroad, but consumed domestically.

THE THEORY OF COMPARATIVE ADVANTAGE

Economists who first considered the benefits of international trade focused on a country's *absolute advantage*.

> A country has an ***absolute advantage*** in a good when it can produce it using fewer resources *than another country.*

Absolute advantage The ability to produce a good or service, using fewer resources than other producers use.

As the early economists saw it, the citizens of every nation could improve their economic welfare by specializing in the production of goods in which they had an absolute advantage and exporting them to other countries. In turn, they would import goods from countries that had an absolute advantage in those goods.

Way back in 1817, however, the British economist David Ricardo disagreed. Absolute advantage, he argued, was not a necessary ingredient for mutually beneficial international trade. The key was *comparative advantage:*

> A nation has a ***comparative advantage*** in producing a good if it can produce it at a lower opportunity cost *than some other country.*

Comparative advantage The ability to produce a good or service at a lower opportunity cost than other producers.

Notice the difference between the definitions of absolute advantage and comparative advantage. While absolute advantage in a good is defined by the resources used to produce it, comparative advantage is based on the *opportunity cost* of producing it. And we measure the opportunity cost of producing a good not by the resources used to produce it, but rather by the *other goods* that these resources *could* have produced instead.

TABLE 1	Labor Requirements per:	China	United States
Labor Requirements per Unit	**Suit**	125 hours	50 hours
	Computer	625 hours	100 hours

Ricardo argued that a potential trading partner could be absolutely inferior in the production of every single good—requiring more resources per unit of each good than any other country—and still have a comparative advantage in some good. The comparative advantage would arise because the country was *less* inferior at producing some goods than others. Likewise, a country that had an absolute advantage in producing everything could—contrary to common opinion—still benefit from trade. It would have a comparative advantage only in some, but not all, goods.

Opportunity Cost

> *Mutually beneficial trade between any two countries is possible whenever one country is relatively better at producing a good than the other country is. Being relatively better means having the ability to produce a good at a lower opportunity cost—that is, at a lower sacrifice of other goods foregone.*

Opportunity Cost and Comparative Advantage

To illustrate Ricardo's insight, let's consider a hypothetical world of two countries, China and the United States. Both are producing only two goods, men's suits and computers. Could they better themselves by trading with one another? Ricardo would have us look at opportunity costs. But how do we determine the opportunity cost of a computer or a suit?

Let's start out as simply as possible. We'll imagine there is only one resource in each country—labor—and that it takes a constant number of hours to make one computer or one suit no matter how many units of these goods are produced. Table 1 lists the labor hours required. For example, the entry of 125 in the upper left corner tells us that it takes 125 hours of labor to make one suit in China, no matter how many suits are produced there. The upper right corner tells us that it takes 50 hours to make a suit in the United States.

This is all the information we'll need to find the opportunity cost of a computer or a suit in China or the United States.

First, suppose China were to produce one additional computer. Then it would have to divert 625 hours of labor from the suit industry. This, in turn, would require China to produce fewer suits. How many fewer? Since each suit uses up 125 hours of labor, then using 625 hours for one computer would require producing 625/125 = 5 fewer suits. Thus, the opportunity cost of a computer in China is *5 suits*. This opportunity cost is recorded in Table 2; check the table and make sure you can find this entry.

In the United States, producing an additional computer requires diverting 100 hours of labor from suit making. Since each suit requires 50 hours, this means a sac-

Opportunity Costs per:	China	United States	TABLE 2
Suit	$\frac{1}{5}$ computer	$\frac{1}{2}$ computer	**Opportunity Costs**
Computer	5 suits	2 suits	

rifice of 2 suits. Thus, in the United States, the opportunity cost of one computer is 2 suits, which can also be found in Table 2.

Summing up, we see that in China, the opportunity cost of a computer is 5 suits; in the United States, it is 2 suits. Therefore, the United States—with the lower opportunity cost of producing computers—*has a comparative advantage in making computers.*

Notice that in Table 2, we do similar calculations for the opportunity cost of making a suit, measuring the opportunity cost in terms of *computers foregone.* These computations are summarized in the first row of the table. Make sure you can use these numbers to verify that China has a comparative advantage in producing suits.

Now we can use our conclusions about comparative advantage to show how both countries can gain from trade. The explanation comes in two steps. First, we show that if China could be persuaded to produce more suits and the United States more computers, the world's total production of goods will increase. Second, we show how each country can come out ahead by trading with the other.

Specialization and World Production

Using the numbers in Table 2, if China produced, say, 10 more suits, it would have to sacrifice the production of 2 computers as resources were shifted between the two industries. If the United States, simultaneously, produced 4 extra computers, it would have to sacrifice 8 suits—again because resources would have to be moved. But note: As a result of even this small change, the world's production of suits increases by 2, and its production of computers also rises by 2—despite the fact that no more labor is used than before. Table 3 summarizes the changes.

The additional production of suits and computers in this example represents the gain from specializing according to comparative advantage—a gain, as the next section will show, that the two trading partners will share. It is also the kind of gain that, multiplied a million times, lies behind the substantial benefits countries enjoy from free trade.

The particular example given here is not the only one that can be derived from our table of opportunity costs. For example, if China produced 20 more suits and, therefore, produced 4 fewer computers, while the United States changed as in Table 3, then world output of suits would increase by 12, while computer production would remain unchanged. And we could come up with other examples in which the world output of computers rises, but suits remain the same. (As an exercise, try to create such an example on your own.)

	China	United States	World
TABLE 3 **A Small Change in Production**			
Suit Production	+10	−8	+2
Computer Production	−2	+4	+2

In all cases, however, the key insight remains the same:

Specialization and
Exchange

> *If countries specialize according to comparative advantage, a more efficient use of given resources occurs. That is, with the same resources, the world can produce more of at least one good, without decreasing production of any other good.*

How Each Nation Gains from International Trade

Now we proceed to the second step in Ricardo's case, showing that *both* countries can gain from trade. As you've seen (Table 3), when the two countries shift labor hours toward their comparative advantage good, they produce more of that good but less of the other. For example, China produces more suits but fewer computers. However, by *trading* some of its comparative advantage good for the other good, each country can consume more of *both* goods.

Table 4 shows just one example of trading that benefits both countries. The first row of numbers shows the changes in production in each country. These numbers have been taken from Table 3. For example, the first two entries in the first row tell us that when China produces 10 more suits (+10), it sacrifices 2 computers (−2).

The second row shows an example of China's trade with the United States. In this example, China—which has increased suit production by 10—trades 9 of those suits for 3 computers. The entry "−9" means China is giving up or *exporting* 9 suits, and the entry "+3" means it is getting or *importing* 3 computers in exchange for them. The result of these changes in production, as well as exports and imports, is shown in the third row. Since China increases suit production by 10, but exports 9, it is able to consume 1 more suit (+1) than it could before trade. At the same time, since China produces 2 fewer computers but imports 3, it is able to consume 1 more computer (+1) than before trade.

Continuing to the last two columns of the table, we see the numbers for the United States. Because we are dealing with only two countries, China's exports of suits must be the same as U.S. imports of suits, so in the second row, we show +9 for U.S. suit imports. And if China imports 3 computers from the United States, the United States must be exporting them to China, so the table shows −3 to represent U.S. computer exports. In the third row, we see that the United States—like China— gains from trade by being able to consume more of both goods. It produces 4 more computers, but exports only 3, so it gains 1 computer (+1). And it produces 8 fewer suits, but imports 9, so it gains 1 suit (+1).

Let's take a step back and consider what we've discovered. First, look back at Table 1. Note that based on the required labor hours, the United States has an *absolute advantage* in both goods: It can produce both suits and computers using

	China		United States	
	Suits	Computers	Suits	Computers
Change in Production	+10	−2	−8	+4
Exports (−) or Imports (+)	−9	+3	+9	−3
Net Gain	+1	+1	+1	+1

TABLE 4
The Gains from Specialization and Trade

fewer hours of labor than can China. But in Table 2, we saw that the United States has a *comparative advantage* in only *one* of these goods—computers—and China has a comparative advantage in the other—suits. This is because the *opportunity costs* of each good differ in the two countries. Then, in Table 3, we saw how world production of both goods increases when each country shifts its resources toward its comparative advantage good. Finally, in the last row of Table 4, we saw that *international trade* can enable *each* country to end up with more of *both* goods.

Of course, we've only been looking at a *small* change in production toward comparative advantage. But as long as such benefits continue, a country can gain even greater benefits by shifting more and more of its resources toward its comparative advantage good. In our example, China should *specialize* in suit production, and the United States should *specialize* in making computers.

> *As long as opportunity costs differ, specialization and trade can be beneficial to all involved. This remains true regardless of whether the parties are different nations, different states, different counties, or different individuals. It remains true even if one party has an all-round absolute advantage or disadvantage.*

 Specialization and Exchange

The Terms of Trade

In our ongoing example, China exports 9 suits in exchange for 3 computers. This exchange ratio (9 suits for 3 computers, or 3 suits per computer) is known as the **terms of trade**—the quantity of one good that is exchanged for a unit of the other.

The terms of trade determine how the gains from international trade are *distributed* among countries. Our particular choice of 3 suits to 1 computer for the terms of trade happened to apportion the gains equally between the two countries: Both China and the United States each gain one suit and one computer every time they make the trade shown in Table 4. With *different* terms of trade, however, the benefits would have been distributed differently. For example, an end-of-chapter problem will ask you to calculate the gains for each country when the terms of trade (suits per computer) are 4 to 1 instead of 3 to 1. In that case, while both countries will still gain, the United States gains more than China.

But notice that the terms of trade were not even *used* in our example until we arrived at Table 4. The gains from trade for the *world as a whole* were demonstrated

Terms of trade The ratio at which a country can trade domestically produced products for foreign-produced products.

in Table 3, and were based entirely on the increase in world production when countries specialize according to comparative advantage.

> *For the world as a whole, the gains from international trade are due to increased production as nations specialize according to comparative advantage.* How *those world gains are distributed among specific countries depends on the terms of trade.*

We won't consider here precisely *how* the terms of trade are determined (it's a matter of supply and demand). But we *will* establish the limits within which the terms of trade must fall.

Look again at Table 2. China would never give up *more than* 5 suits to import 1 computer. Why not? Because it could always get 1 computer for 5 suits *domestically,* by shifting resources into computer production.

Similarly, the United States would never export a computer for *fewer than* 2 suits, since it can substitute 1 computer for 2 suits domestically (again, by switching resources between the industries). Therefore, the equilibrium terms of trade must lie *between* 5 suits for 1 computer and 2 suits for 1 computer. Outside of that range, one of the two countries would refuse to trade. Note that in our example, we assume terms of trade of 3 suits for 1 computer—well within the acceptable range.

HOW POTENTIAL GAINS TURN INTO ACTUAL GAINS

So far in this chapter, we have discussed the *potential* advantages of specialization and trade among nations, but one major question remains: How is that potential realized? Who or what causes a country to shift resources from some industries into others and then to trade in the world market?

Do foreign trade ministers at WTO meetings decide who should produce and trade each product? Does some group of omniscient and benevolent people in Washington and other world capitals make all the necessary arrangements? Not at all. Within the framework of the WTO, government officials are supposed to create the environment for free trade, but they do not decide who has a comparative advantage in what, or what should be produced in this or that country. In today's market economies around the world, it is individual consumers and firms who decide to buy things, at home or abroad. By their joint actions, they determine where things are produced and who trades with whom. That is, the promise of Ricardo's theory is achieved through markets. People only have to do what comes naturally: buy products at the lowest price. Without their knowing it, they are promoting Ricardo's vision.

In order to see how this works, we'll have to translate from the labor *hours* required to produce a good into labor *costs.* This is done in Table 5. Because Chinese firms keep books in Chinese yuan (CNY) and American firms in U.S. dollars, our cost data are expressed accordingly.

Going across the first row of the table, we see that one suit requires 125 hours of labor in China (just as it did before, in Table 1). The second column shows the

Countries gain when they shift production toward their comparative advantage goods (such as athletic shoes in China), and trade them for other goods from other countries.

HTTP://

The World Trade Organization's Web page (http://www.wto.org/) is a good source for all kinds of information on international trade.

	China			United States		
	(1) Labor Hours per Unit	**(2)** Wage Rate	**(3)** Cost per Unit (1) × (2)	**(4)** Labor Hours per Unit	**(5)** Wage Rate	**(6)** Cost per Unit (4) × (5)
Suits	125 hours	16 CNY per hour	**2,000 CNY**	50 hours	$10 per hour	**$500**
Computers	625 hours	16 CNY per hour	**10,000 CNY**	100 hours	$10 per hour	**$1,000**

TABLE 5
Costs of Production

wage rate in China (assumed to be 16 CNY per hour), so the total labor cost for one suit in China is 125 hours × 16 CNY per hour = 2,000 CNY. In the United States, a suit requires 50 hours of labor, which—at a wage rate of $10 per hour—implies a total labor cost of $500 per suit. The second row shows the same calculations for a computer, which has costs of 10,000 CNY in China, and $1,000 in the United States.

We can use the cost per unit of each good to determine *opportunity cost*. For example, suppose China wants to produce another computer. Then it will have to shift 10,000 CNY worth of resources (labor hours) out of suit production. This will require a sacrifice of 10,000 CNY / 2,000 CNY = 5 suits. So in China, the opportunity cost of one computer is 5 suits—just as it was earlier, in Table 2, before we translated from labor *hours* to labor *cost*. In fact, expressing resource requirements as *costs*, rather than hours, leads to the same opportunity cost numbers, and the same conclusions derived from them. That is, once again, China has a comparative advantage in suits, and the United States in computers.

Now, back to our question: What *makes* China shift resources into its comparative advantage good, suits, and away from computers? And what *makes* the United States shift resources in the other direction? The answer is: *prices*. In the absence of trade, the *price* of a good within a country will generally reflect the cost of the resources needed to produce another unit of that good. That is, if a suit requires 2,000 CNY worth of resources in China, then before trade, the price of a suit in China will be about 2,000 CNY. For the same reason, before trade, the price of a suit will be about $500 in the United States, because that's what it costs to make one there.

Now suppose we allow trade to open up between the two countries. Consider the decision of a U.S. consumer who can choose to purchase computers or suits in either country. To buy goods from Chinese producers (who want to be paid in their own currency) Americans must obtain yuan. Americans can get the needed yuan by going to the *foreign exchange market*, trading their dollars for yuan at the going **exchange rate**—the rate at which one currency can be exchanged for another. Using the exchange rate, we can calculate the *dollar* cost of a suit from China—what it would cost an American. Similarly, we can calculate the dollar

Exchange rate The amount of one currency that is traded for one unit of another currency.

	China	United States
TABLE 6 **Prices in China and the United States With an Exchange Rate of 8 CNY for $1**		
Per Suit	**2,000 CNY** ($250)	**$500** (4,000 CNY)
Per Computer	**10,000 CNY** ($1,250)	**$1,000** (8,000 CNY)

cost of a computer made in China, or the yuan cost of either good made in the United States.

This is done in Table 6. The bold numbers show the price of each good in each country in *local currency*. The numbers in parentheses show how these numbers translate to the *other country's currency* based on an exchange rate of 8 CNY per dollar.

It's not a big table, but there is a lot going on in it, so let's step carefully through it. Start with the entry in the upper left-hand corner. First, the entry tells us that the price of a suit in China is 2,000 CNY. If an American wants to buy this suit, he can do so—by exchanging dollars for yuan and then buying the suit. With an exchange rate of 8 CNY per dollar, it would take $250 to get 2,000 CNY, since $250 \times 8 = 2,000$. Thus, to the American, the dollar price of a Chinese suit is $250, which appears in parentheses next to the price in yuan. Similarly, the dollar price of a 10,000 CNY Chinese computer is $1,250—also in parentheses.

Looking at Table 6, you can see that, to an American, suits from China at $250 are cheaper than U.S. suits at $500, so *Americans will prefer to buy suits from China*. But when it comes to computers, we reach the opposite conclusion: A U.S. computer at $1,000 is cheaper than a Chinese computer at $1,250, so *Americans will prefer to buy computers in the United States*.

Now take the viewpoint of a Chinese consumer who can buy U.S. or Chinese goods. To buy U.S. goods, China's consumers will need dollars, which they can obtain at the going exchange rate: 8 CNY for $1. The last column of the table shows the prices of U.S. goods in yuan (in parentheses). To a Chinese buyer, Chinese suits at 2,000 CNY are cheaper than U.S. suits at 4,000 CNY, while U.S. computers at 8,000 CNY are cheaper than Chinese computers at 10,000 CNY. Thus, *a Chinese, just like an American, will prefer to buy computers from the United States and suits from China*.

Now suppose that trade in suits and computers had previously been prohibited, but is now opened up. Everyone would buy suits in China and computers in the United States, and the process of specialization according to comparative advantage would begin. Chinese suit makers would expand their production, while Chinese computer makers would suffer losses, lay off workers, and even exit the industry. Unemployed computer workers in China would find jobs in the suit industry. Analogous changes would occur in the United States, as production of computers expanded there. These changes in production patterns would continue until China specialized in suit production and the United States specialized in computer production—that is, until each country produced according to its comparative advantage.

Our example illustrates a general conclusion:

> *When consumers are free to buy at the lowest prices, they will naturally buy a good from the country that has a comparative advantage in producing it. That country's industries respond by producing more of that good and less of other goods. In this way, countries naturally move toward specializing in those goods in which they have a comparative advantage.*[1]

This conclusion applies even beyond the simple example we've been considering. It applies when there are many countries and many goods. And it applies when countries use a *variety* of resources to produce goods, rather than just labor. For example, the prices in Table 6 could come from the cost of *all* resources needed to make a unit of each good in each country—labor, capital equipment, land, and entrepreneurship. The opportunity costs would still be as given in Table 2, and the entire story we've told about the gains from trade, and how they come about, would be the same.

Some Important Provisos

Look back at Tables 3 and 4. There you saw how a small change in production—with China shifting toward suits and the United States shifting toward computers—caused world production of both goods to rise. But if this can happen once, why not again? And again? And again? In fact, our simple example seems to suggest that countries should specialize *completely,* producing *only* the goods in which they have a comparative advantage. In our example, it seems that China should get out of computer production *entirely,* and the United States should get out of suit production *entirely.*

The real world, however, is more complicated than our simplified examples might suggest. Despite divergent opportunity costs, sometimes it does *not* make sense for two countries to trade with each other, or it might make sense to trade, but *not* completely specialize. Following are some real-world considerations that can lead to reduced trade or incomplete specialization.

Costs of Trading. If there are high transportation costs or high costs of making deals across national boundaries, trade may be reduced and even become prohibitively expensive. High transportation costs are especially important for perishable goods, such as ice cream, which must be shipped frozen, and most personal services, such as haircuts, eye exams, and restaurant meals. These goods are less subject to trade according to comparative advantage. (Imagine the travel cost for a U.S. resident to see an optometrist in China, where eye exams are less expensive.)

---

[1] Something may be bothering you about the way we reached this conclusion: We merely *asserted* that the exchange rate was 8 yuan per dollar. What if we had chosen another exchange rate? With a little work, you can verify that at any exchange rate between 4 yuan per dollar and 10 yuan per dollar, our conclusion will still hold: Countries will automatically produce according to their comparative advantage. Further, you can verify that if the exchange rate went *beyond* those bounds, the residents of both countries would want to buy both goods from just one country. This would change the demand for yuan or dollars, and force the exchange rate back between 8 yuan per dollar and 4 yuan per dollar.

The costs of making deals are generally higher for international trade than for trade within domestic borders. For one thing, different laws must be dealt with. In addition, there are different business and marketing customs to be mastered. High transportation costs and high costs of making deals help explain why nations continue to produce some goods in which they do not have a comparative advantage and why there is less than complete specialization in the world.

One final cost of international trade arises from the need to exchange domestic for foreign currency. In international trade, either importers or exporters typically take some risk that the exchange rate might change. For example, suppose a U.S. importer of suits from China agrees in advance to pay 100,000 CNY for a shipment of suits. At the time the agreement is made, the exchange rate is 8 CNY per dollar, so the importer figures the shipment will cost him $12,500. But suppose that, before he pays, the exchange rate changes to 5 CNY per dollar. Then the suit shipment—for which the importer must still pay 100,000 CNY—will cost him $20,000. The rise in costs could cause him to lose money on the shipment.

It is interesting to note that countries can work to reduce the cost of trading. Indeed, this was the primary reason behind the creation of a new, single currency—the *euro*—to be shared by 12 European countries, including France, Germany, Holland, and Italy. The euro was introduced into commerce in early 1999. In 2002, the French franc, the Italian lira, the German mark, and several other national currencies became relics of the past. The move to a single currency has eliminated the costs and risks of foreign exchange transactions from intra-European trade. This should enable these European countries to specialize more completely according to their comparative advantage, and increase the gains from trade even further.

Sizes of Countries. Our earlier example featured two large economies capable of fully satisfying each other's demands. But sometimes a very large country, such as the United States, trades with a very small one, such as the Pacific island nation of Tonga. If the smaller country specialized completely, its output would be insufficient to fully meet the demand of the larger one. While the smaller country would specialize *completely,* the large country would not. Instead, it would continue to produce both goods and would specialize only in the sense of producing *more* of its comparative advantage good after trade than it did before trade. This helps to explain why the United States continues to produce bananas, even though we do so at a much higher opportunity cost than many small Latin American nations.

Increasing Opportunity Cost. In all of our tables, we have assumed that opportunity cost remains constant as production changes. For example, in Table 2, the opportunity cost of a suit in China is ⅕ of a computer, regardless of how many suits or computers China makes. But more typically, the opportunity cost of a good rises as more of it is produced. (Why? You may want to review the law of increasing opportunity cost in Chapter 2.) In that case, each step on the road to specialization would change the opportunity cost. A point might be reached—before complete specialization—in which opportunity costs became *equal* in the two countries, and there would be no further mutual gains from trading. (Remember: Opportunity costs must *differ* between the two countries in order for trade to be mutually beneficial.) In the end, while trading will occur, there will not be complete specialization. Instead, each country will produce both goods, just as China and the United States each produce suits *and* computers in the real world.

Government Barriers to Trade. Governments can enact barriers to trading. In some cases, these barriers increase trading costs; in other cases, they make trade impossible. Since this is such an important topic, we'll consider government-imposed barriers to trade in a separate section, later in the chapter.

THE SOURCES OF COMPARATIVE ADVANTAGE

We've just seen how nations can benefit from specialization and trade when they have comparative advantages. But what determines comparative advantage in the first place?

In many cases, the answer is the *resources* a country has at its disposal.

> *A country that has relatively large amounts of a particular resource at its disposal will tend to have a comparative advantage in goods that make heavy use of that resource.*

This is most easy to see when the relevant resources are *gifts of nature*, such as a specific natural resource or a climate especially suited to a particular product.

The top part of Table 7 contains some examples. Saudi Arabia has a comparative advantage in the production of oil because it has oil fields with billions of barrels of oil that can be extracted at low cost. Canada is a major exporter of timber because its climate and geography make its land more suitable for growing trees than other crops. Canada is a good example of comparative advantage without absolute advantage: It grows a lot of timber, not because it can do so using fewer resources than other countries, but because its land is even more poorly suited to growing other things.

But now look at the bottom half of Table 7. It shows examples of international specialization that arise from some cause *other* than natural resources. Japan has a huge comparative advantage in making automobiles: More than 40 percent of the world's automobiles are made there. And that number would be even larger, except for laws that limit the import of Japanese cars into Europe. Yet none of the *natural* resources needed to make cars are available in Japan; the iron ore, coal, and oil needed to produce cars are all imported.

What explains the cases of comparative advantage in the bottom half of Table 7? In part, it is due to resources *other* than natural resources or climate. The United States is rich in both physical capital and human capital. As a result, the United States tends to have a comparative advantage in goods and services that make heavy use of computers, tractors, and satellite technology, as well as goods that require highly skilled labor. This, in part, explains the U.S. comparative advantage in the design and production of aircraft, a good that makes heavy use of physical capital (such as computer-based design systems) and human capital (highly trained engineers).

In less-developed countries, by contrast, capital and skilled labor are relatively scarce, but less-skilled labor is plentiful. Accordingly, these countries tend to have a

TABLE 7
Examples of National Specialties in International Trade

Country	Specialization Resulting from Natural Resources or Climate
Saudi Arabia	Oil
Canada	Timber
United States	Grain
Spain	Olive oil
Mexico	Tomatoes
Jamaica	Aluminum ore
Italy	Wine
Israel	Citrus fruit

Country	Specialization *Not* Based on Natural Resources or Climate
Japan	Cars, consumer electronics
United States	Software, movies, music, aircraft
Switzerland	Watches
Korea	Steel, ships
Hong Kong	Textiles
Great Britain	Financial services
Pakistan	Textiles

comparative advantage in products that make heavy use of less-skilled labor, such as textiles and light manufacturing. Note, however, that as a country develops—and acquires more physical and human capital—its pattern of comparative advantage can change. Japan, Korea, and Singapore, after a few decades of very rapid development, acquired a comparative advantage in several goods that, at one time, were specialties of the United States and Europe—including automobiles, steel, and sophisticated consumer electronics.

But another aspect of the bottom half of Table 7 is harder to explain: Why do specific countries develop a *particular* specialty? For example, if you think you know why Japan dominates the world market for VCRs and other consumer electronics—say, some unique capacity to mass-produce precision products—be sure you can explain why Japan is a distant second in computer printers. The company that dominates the market for printers—Hewlett Packard—is a U.S. firm.

Similarly, we take the worldwide dominance of American movies for granted. But if you try to explain it based on the availability of resources like physical capital or highly skilled labor, or cultural traditions that encouraged artists, writers, or actors, then why not Britain or France? At the time the film industry developed in the United States, these two countries had similar endowments of physical and human capital, and much older and stronger theatrical traditions than the United States. Yet their film industries—in spite of massive government subsidies—are a very distant second and third compared to that of the United States.

In even the most remote corner of the world, the cars, cameras, and VCRs will be Japanese, the movies and music American, the clothing from Hong Kong or China, and the bankers from Britain. These specialties are certainly *consistent* with the capital and other resources each nation has at its disposal, but explaining why each *specific* case of comparative advantage arose in the first place is not easy.

We can, however, explain why a country retains its comparative advantage once it gets started. Japan today enjoys a huge comparative advantage in cars and consumer electronics in large part because it has accumulated a capital stock—both physical capital and human capital—well suited to producing those goods. The physical capital stock includes the many manufacturing plants and design facilities that the Japanese have built over the years. But Japan's human capital is no less important. Japanese managers know how to anticipate the features that tomorrow's buyers of cars and electronic products will want around the world. And Japanese workers have developed skills adapted for producing these products. The stocks of physical and human capital in Japan sustain its comparative advantage just as stocks of natural resources lead to comparative advantages in other countries. More likely than not, Japan will continue to have a comparative advantage in cars and electronics, just as the United States will continue to have a comparative advantage in making movies.

> *Countries often develop strong comparative advantages in the goods they have produced in the past, regardless of why they began producing those goods in the first place.*

HTTP://

The International Trade Administration maintains a Web page that is full of information on U.S. international trade. Find it at **http://www.ita.doc.gov/**.

WHY SOME PEOPLE OBJECT TO FREE TRADE

Given the clear benefits that nations can derive by specializing and trading, why would anyone ever *object* to free international trade? Why do the same governments that join the WTO turn around and create roadblocks to unhindered trade? The answer is not too difficult to find: Despite the benefit to the nation as a whole, some groups within the country, in the short run, are likely to lose from free trade, even while others gain a great deal more. Unfortunately, instead of finding ways to compensate the losers—to make them better off as well—we often allow them to block free-trade policies. The simple model of supply and demand helps illustrate this story.

In our earlier example, after trade opens up, China exports suits and the United States imports them. Figure 1 illustrates the impact on the market for suits in the two countries. To keep things simple, we'll convert the price of suits in China into dollars, so that we can measure dollar prices on the vertical axis of both panels.

Before trade opens up, the Chinese suit market is in equilibrium at point *E*, with a price of $250 and quantity of 200,000 suits per month. The U.S. suit market is in equilibrium at point *F*, with price $500 and quantity 250,000. Notice that before trade opens up, the price is lower in China—the country with a comparative advantage in suits.

Now, when trade opens up, Americans will begin to buy Chinese suits, driving their price upward. As the price in China rises from $250 to $350, Chinese

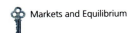
Markets and Equilibrium

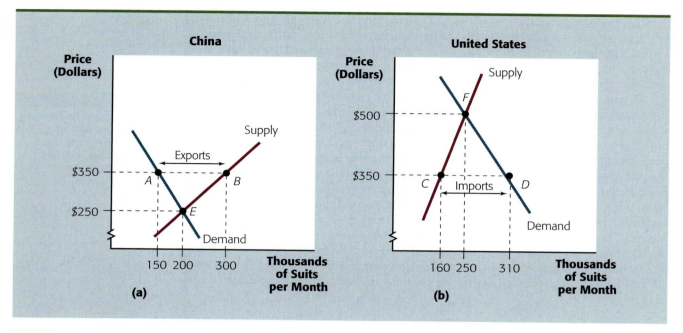

FIGURE 1
The Impact of Trade

Before trade, the Chinese suit market is in equilibrium at point E, and the U.S. market is in equilibrium at point F. When trade begins, Americans buy the cheaper Chinese suits, driving up their price. In response, Chinese manufacturers increase output, and Chinese consumers decrease their purchases. At the world equilibrium price, $350 per suit, Americans buy 150,000 Chinese suits each month (distance CD). China produces 300,000 suits, but Chinese consumers buy only 150,000, with the rest (distance AB) being exported to the United States.

producers increase their output to 300,000, moving from *E* to *B* along the supply curve, and Chinese consumers decrease their purchases to 150,000, moving from *E* to *A* along the demand curve. This seems to create an "excess supply" of suits in China, equal to distance *AB* or 300,000 − 150,000 = 150,000. But it is not *really* an excess supply, because that is precisely the number of suits that are exported to the United States. So, China's entire output of suits, 300,000, is purchased by either Chinese or Americans.

Now let's consider the effects in the United States. There, consumers are switching from suits made in the United States to suits made in China. With less demand for U.S. suits, their price will fall. With free trade, the United States must be able to buy Chinese suits at the same price as the Chinese (ignoring transportation costs), so the price of suits in the United States must fall to $350. As the price falls, U.S. suit producers will decrease their output to 160,000, moving from *F* to *C* along the supply curve, and U.S. consumers will increase their purchases to 310,000 moving from *F* to *D* along the demand curve. This seems to create a shortage of suits in the United States, equal to 310,000 − 160,000 = 150,000, but it is not a shortage: That is precisely the number of suits imported from China.

Now let's see how different groups are affected by the opening up of trade.

The Impact of Trade in the Exporting Country

When trade opens up in suits, China is the exporting country. How are different groups affected there?

- *Chinese suit producers and workers are better off.* Before international trade, producers sold 200,000 suits at $250 each, but with trade, they sell a larger quantity of 300,000 at a higher price of $350. The industry's workers are equally delighted because they undoubtedly share in the bonanza as the number of workers demanded rises along with the level of production. Both management and labor in the Chinese suit industry benefit from free trade.
- *Chinese suit buyers are worse off.* Why? Before trade, they bought 200,000 suits at price $250, and now they must pay the higher price, $350, and consume the smaller quantity 150,000.

When the opening of trade results in increased exports of a good, the producers of the good are made better off. Consumers of the good in the exporting country will be made worse off.

The Impact of Trade in the Importing Country

Now let's consider the impact of free trade in suits on the United States, the importing country. Once again, it is easy to figure out who is happy and who is unhappy with the new arrangement.

- *U.S. suit producers and workers are worse off.* They formerly sold 250,000 at $500 each, but now they sell the lower quantity of 160,000 at the lower price, $350. The industry's workers suffer, too, because the number of workers demanded falls with the level of production.
- *U.S. suit buyers are better off.* They used to buy 250,000 at $500 each, but now they pay the lower price, $350, and consume the larger quantity, 310,000.

When the opening of trade results in increased imports of a product, the domestic producers of the product are made worse off. Consumers of the good in the importing country are better off.

Attitudes and Influence on Trade Policy

In our examples, we've been discussing the impact of free trade in suits. We could tell the same story about free trade in computers. In this case, the United States has the role of exporter and China is the importer. But our conclusions about the impacts on different groups in exporting and importing countries would remain the same. These impacts are summarized in Table 8.

Each group in the table forms a natural constituency for government policies that encourage or discourage free trade. Notice, however, that one of the entries is italicized: producers of a good (and their employees) who would suffer from cheap imports. This group is emphasized because it typically has more influence on trade policy than the others in the table.

An example can help explain why. Imagine that a bill comes before Congress to permit completely free trade in apparel, allowing cheap clothing to enter the United States from Jordan, Pakistan, and several other less-developed countries.

TABLE 8
The Impact of Free Trade

	In Export Sectors That Enjoy Comparative Advantage	In Import Sectors That Suffer from Comparative Disadvantage
Gains from Trade	Owners of firms, workers	Consumers
Harm from Trade	Consumers	*Owners of firms, workers*

The benefits to the United States as a whole would be huge, enjoyed mostly by American consumers of clothing—basically, the entire U.S. population. But because the benefits would be spread so widely, the gains for each *individual* consumer would be small. For example, if the benefits to *all* U.S. consumers amounted to $20 billion per year, the annual benefits to any single consumer would be less than $100. As a result, no single consumer has a strong incentive to lobby Congress, or to join a dues-paying organization that would act on his or her behalf.

By contrast, the harm that free trade would do to the owners and employees of domestic apparel firms would be highly concentrated on a much smaller group of people. An individual owner might lose millions of dollars competing with cheap imports, and a worker would face a substantially higher risk of being permanently laid off. These individuals have a powerful incentive to lobby against free trade. Not surprisingly, when it comes to trade policy, the voices raised *against imports* are loud and clear, while those *for imports* are often nonexistent. Since a country has the power to restrict imports from other countries, the lobbying can—and often does—lead to a restriction on free trade. The United States, for example, continues to keep out imports of cheap clothing from low-cost producers, largely due to powerful lobbying by the U.S. textile industry.

What about the export side? Here, as Table 8 suggests, it's the reverse: Individuals involved in the export sector who benefit from trade have the incentive to lobby, while individual consumers who would be harmed by higher prices have little incentive to act. Indeed, in the United States, farmers and cattle ranchers have been active advocates of free-trade policies so they can export corn, rye, soybeans, and beef. This suggests that the forces mounted for and against free trade might be evenly balanced. But notice in Table 8 that this group—firms and workers who benefit from exports—has not been emphasized. Why not?

The Antitrade Bias. While exporters have the incentive to lobby—and do—their effectiveness is limited. After all, it's not the U.S. government that is preventing them from exporting their products; it's some *foreign* government responding to pressure from its *own* producers who would be harmed by U.S. exports. The United States does not have the legal right to *force* another country to import American products. Indeed, European governments have for years used trade barriers to tightly restrict imports of American corn and American beef (officially attributed to environmental and health claims). Despite heavy lobbying from U.S. producers, the U.S. government has been unable to change European policy. Moreover, because the United States has so often given in to pressure from its own producers to restrict imports, it lacks the moral high ground.

> *The distribution of gains and losses creates a policy bias against free trade. Those who benefit from trade in a specific product either have little incentive to lobby for it (consumers of imports) or have limited power to influence policy (producers of exports). But one constituency harmed by trade—domestic producers threatened by imports—has both a powerful incentive to lobby and the ability to influence policy.*

There are, however, three antidotes to this policy bias.

Multilateral Agreements. In a bilateral or multilateral trade agreement, two or more countries agree to trade freely in many goods—or even *all* goods—simultaneously. Producers threatened by imports will lobby against such agreements in each country. But producers of potential exports will lobby just as strongly *for* the agreement. If the agreement is structured as an all-or-nothing proposition, a balance of influence is created that can enable governments to resist antitrade lobbying. An example was the North American Free Trade Agreement (NAFTA) between the United States, Canada, and Mexico, which went into effect in 1994, and, in phases, will eventually apply to virtually all the products produced by the three nations. NAFTA was hotly opposed by many producers and some labor unions in all three countries who stood to lose from imports, but was just as hotly favored by producers and workers that stood to gain from exports. (The biggest gainers—consumers in the three countries—were hardly involved in the debate, for reasons we've discussed.)

The World Trade Organization. Another antidote is the World Trade Organization (WTO). By setting standards for acceptable and unacceptable trade restrictions, and making rulings in specific cases, the WTO has some power to influence nations' trade policies. But its influence is limited because the WTO has no enforcement power. For example, the WTO has ruled several times against European trade barriers against U.S. corn and beef, with little effect. Still, a negative WTO ruling does put some public relations pressure on a country, and it allows a nation harmed by restrictions on its exports to retaliate, in good conscience, with its own trade barriers.

Industries as Consumers. Whenever we use the word *consumer*, we naturally think of a household buying products for its own enjoyment. But the term can apply to *any* buyer of a product, including a firm that uses it as an *input*. If these firms are among the consumers in Table 8 who benefit from cheaper imports, and if the good is an important part of these firms' costs, they have an incentive to lobby for free trade in the good. Moreover, because the issue at stake—import restrictions—is under the control of the *domestic* government, lobbying by industrial consumers can influence policy. For example, in 2001, the steel industry lobbied the Bush administration to restrict imports of steel from Russia, Japan, Korea, and several other countries. But steel *consumers*—including U.S. automobile companies and U.S. appliance manufacturers—lobbied just as strongly *against* the restrictions. While the steel consumers lost the battle, their influence helped to weaken the restrictions on imported steel.

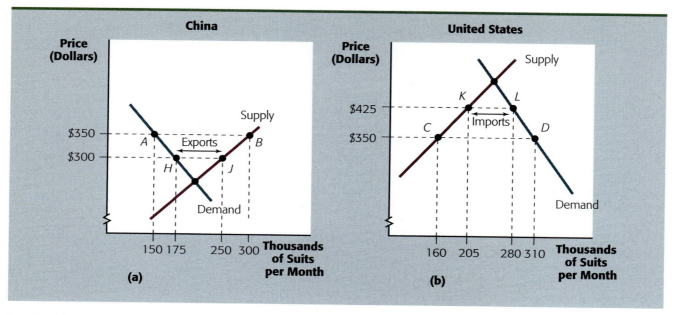

FIGURE 2

The Effects of a Tariff on Suits

A U.S. tariff of $125 on imported Chinese suits raises their price in the United States and reduces U.S. imports. It also lowers the price in China and reduces China's exports. In the new equilibrium, the price is $425 in the United States and $300 in China, the prices at which China's exports (distance HJ) are equal to U.S. imports (distance KL). The difference in the two prices—$125—is equal to the U.S. tariff on each imported suit.

Tariff A tax on imports.

HOW FREE TRADE IS RESTRICTED

So far in this chapter, you've learned that specialization and trade according to comparative advantage can dramatically improve the well-being of entire nations. This is why governments generally favor free trade. Yet international trade can, in the short run, hurt particular groups of people. These groups often lobby their government to restrict free trade.

When governments decide to accommodate the opponents of free trade, they are apt to use one of two devices to restrict trade: tariffs or quotas.

Tariffs

A **tariff** is a tax on imported goods. It can be a fixed dollar amount per physical unit, or it can be a percentage of the good's value. In either case, the effect in the tariff-imposing country is similar.

Figure 2 illustrates the effects of a U.S. government tariff on Chinese suits. Initially, before the tariff is imposed, the price of suits in both countries is $350, and China exports 150,000, given by the distance *AB*, while the United States imports the same number (represented by the distance *CD* in the U.S. market). Now, suppose the United States imposes a tariff of $125 on each suit imported from China. Since it is more costly for Chinese suit makers to sell suits in the United States than before, they will shift some of their output back to the home market in China. In the United States, at the old price of $350, this decrease in the supply of suits *would* create a shortage, but—as we know—shortages force the price up. In our diagram, the United States price rises to $425. As the price rises, the quantity of suits supplied domestically increases, and the quantity demanded domestically decreases. U.S. imports are accordingly cut back to *KL,* or 75,000 per month. In China, the sale of suits formerly exported drives the price there down to $300. Notice that—in the final equilibrium with U.S. price equal to $425 and the price in China equal to $300—U.S. imports (*KL*) and Chinese exports (*HJ*) are equal at 75,000. That is, every Chinese suit that is *not* bought by a Chinese consumer is bought by an American consumer. As you can see, American consumers are worse off: They pay a higher price for fewer suits. U.S. producers, on the other hand, are much better off: They sell more suits at a higher price. In China, the impact is the opposite: The price of suits falls, so Chinese producers lose and Chinese consumers gain.

But we also know this: Since the volume of trade has decreased, the gains from trade according to comparative advantage have been reduced as well. Both countries, as a whole, are worse off as a result of the tariff:

> *Tariffs reduce the volume of trade and raise the domestic prices of imported goods. In the country that imposes the tariff, producers gain and consumers lose. But the world as a whole loses, because tariffs decrease the volume of trade and therefore decrease the gains from trade.*

 Policy Tradeoffs

Quotas

A **quota** is a government decree that limits the imports of a good to a specified maximum physical quantity, such as 75,000 Chinese suits per month. Because the goal is to restrict imports, a quota is set below the level of imports that would occur under free trade. Its general effects are very similar to the effects of a tariff.

Quota A limit on the physical volume of imports.

Figure 2, which we used to illustrate tariffs, can also be used to analyze the impact of a quota. In this case, we suppose that the U.S. government simply decrees that it will allow only 75,000 suits from China into the United States (the distance *KL*), and that it is able to enforce this quota. Once again, the U.S. market price in our example will rise to $425. (Why? Because at any price lower than $425, total imports of 75,000, plus the domestic quantity supplied of 205,000—given by the supply curve—would be smaller than quantity demanded. This would cause the price to rise.) And once again, the decrease in U.S. imports translates into a shrinkage in Chinese exports, down to 75,000, or the distance *HJ*. Both countries' suit markets end up in exactly the same place as if the United States had imposed a tariff that raised the U.S. price to $425.

The previous discussion seems to suggest that tariffs and quotas are pretty much the same. But even though prices in the two countries may end up at the same level with a tariff or a quota, there is one important difference between these two trade-restricting policies. A tariff, after all, is a *tax* on imported goods. Therefore, when a government imposes a tariff, it collects some revenue every time a good is imported. Even though the world loses from a tariff, the country that imposes it loses a bit less (compared to a quota) because at least it collects some revenue from the tariff. This revenue can be used to fund government programs or reduce other taxes, to the benefit of the country as a whole. When a government imposes a quota, however, it typically gains no revenue at all.

> *Quotas have effects similar to tariffs: They reduce the quantity of imports and raise domestic prices. While both measures help domestic producers, they reduce the benefits of trade to the nation as a whole. However, a tariff has one saving grace: increased government revenue.*

Economists, who generally oppose measures such as quotas and tariffs to restrict trade, argue that, if one of these devices must be used, tariffs are the better choice. While both policies reduce the gains that countries can enjoy from specializing and trading with each other, the tariff provides some compensation in the form of additional government revenue.

PROTECTIONISM

Protectionism The belief that a nation's industries should be protected from foreign competition.

This chapter has outlined the *gains* that arise from international trade, but it has also outlined some of the *pain* trade can cause to different groups within a country. While the country as a whole benefits, some citizens in both the exporting and importing countries are harmed. The groups who suffer from trade with other nations have developed a number of arguments against free trade. Together, these arguments form a position known as **protectionism**—the belief that a nation's industries should be *protected* from free trade with other nations.

Myths About International Trade

Some protectionist arguments are rather sophisticated and require careful consideration. We'll consider some of these a bit later. But antitrade groups have also promulgated a number of myths to support their protectionist beliefs. Let's consider some of these myths.

Myth #1: "A HIGH-WAGE COUNTRY CANNOT AFFORD FREE TRADE WITH A LOW-WAGE COUNTRY. THE HIGH-WAGE COUNTRY WILL EITHER BE UNDERSOLD IN EVERYTHING AND LOSE ALL OF ITS INDUSTRIES, OR ELSE ITS WORKERS WILL HAVE TO ACCEPT EQUALLY LOW WAGES AND EQUALLY LOW LIVING STANDARDS."

It's true that some countries have much higher wages than others. Here are 2001 figures for average hourly wages of manufacturing workers, including benefits such as holiday pay and health insurance: Germany, $22.86; United States, $20.32; Japan, $19.59; Italy, $13.76; Korea, $8.09; Singapore, $7.77; Brazil, $3.02; Mexico, $2.34; and less than a dollar in China, India, and Bangladesh. This leads to the fear that the poorer countries will be able to charge lower prices for their goods, putting American workers out of jobs unless they, too, agree to work for low wages.

But this argument is incorrect, for two reasons. First, it is true that American workers are paid more than Chinese workers, but this is because the average American worker is more *productive* than his or her Chinese counterpart. After all, the American workforce is more highly educated, and American firms provide their workers with more sophisticated machinery than do Chinese firms. If an American could produce 25 times as much output as a Chinese worker in an hour, then even though wage rates in the United States may be about 20 times greater, cost *per unit* produced would still be lower in the United States. This is reflected in our example in Tables 5 and 6. If you look closely, you'll see that even though American workers are paid more than their Chinese counterparts, we've assumed that American workers can produce a computer with so much less labor input that labor costs per computer are actually lower in the United States.

But suppose the cost per unit *were* lower in China. Then there is still another, more basic argument against the fear of a general job loss or falling wages in the United States: comparative advantage. Let's take an extreme case. Suppose that labor productivity were the same in the United States and China, so that China—with lower wages—could produce *everything* more cheaply than the United States could. Both countries would still gain if China specialized in products in which its cost advantage was relatively large and the United States specialized in goods in which China's cost advantage was relatively small. That is, even though China would have an absolute advantage in everything, the United States would still have a comparative advantage in some things. The mutual gains from trade arise not from absolute advantage, but from comparative advantage.

Myth #2 "A LOW-PRODUCTIVITY COUNTRY CANNOT AFFORD FREE TRADE WITH A HIGH-PRODUCTIVITY COUNTRY. THE FORMER WILL BE CLOBBERED BY THE LATTER AND LOSE ALL OF ITS INDUSTRIES."

This argument is the flip side of the first myth. Here, it is the poorer, less-developed country that is supposedly harmed by trade with a richer country. But this myth, like the first one, confuses absolute advantage with comparative advantage. Suppose the high-productivity country (say, the United States) could produce *every* good with fewer resources than the low-productivity country (say, China). Once again, the low-productivity country would *still* have a comparative advantage in *some* goods. It would then gain by producing those goods and trading with the high-productivity country. This is the case in our example, where a glance at Table 1 or Table 5 reminds us that that the United States has an absolute advantage in both goods, yet—as we've seen—trade still benefits both countries.

To make the point even clearer, let's bring it closer to home. Suppose there is a small, poor town in the United States where workers are relatively uneducated and work with little capital equipment, so their productivity is very low. Would the residents of this town be better off sealing their borders and not trading with the rest of the United States, which has higher productivity? Before you answer, think what this would mean: The residents of the poor town would have to produce everything on their own: grow their own food, make their own cars and television sets, and even provide their own entertainment. Clearly, they would be worse off in isolation. And what is true *within* a country is also true *between* different countries: Closing off trade will make a nation, as a whole, worse off, regardless of its level of wages or productivity. Even a low-productivity country is made better off by trading with other nations.

Myth #3: "IN RECENT TIMES, AMERICA'S UNSKILLED WORKERS HAVE SUFFERED BECAUSE OF EVER-EXPANDING TRADE BETWEEN THE UNITED STATES AND OTHER COUNTRIES."

True enough, unskilled workers lost ground in the 1980s and 1990s, for *some* reason. College graduates have enjoyed growing purchasing power from their earnings, while those with only a grade school education have lost purchasing power. Rising trade with low-wage countries has been blamed for this adverse trend.

But before we jump to conclusions, let's take a closer look. Our discussion earlier in this chapter tells us where to look for effects that come through trade. If the opening of trade has harmed low-skilled workers in the United States, it would have done so by lowering the prices of products that employ large numbers of those workers. For example, if the United States has been flooded recently with cheap clothes, then we should see a relative decline in U.S. clothing prices and reductions in earnings among clothing workers, who are mostly unskilled. A study taking this approach found almost no change in the relative prices of products in the United States that employ large numbers of unskilled workers. Studies that take other approaches have found only modest effects. In general, economists who have looked at the relation between changes in trade patterns and the depressed earnings of unskilled American workers have concluded that foreign trade is a small contributor.[2]

Sophisticated Arguments for Protection

While most of the protectionist arguments we read in the media are based on a misunderstanding of comparative advantage, some more recent arguments for protecting domestic industries are based on a more sophisticated understanding of how markets work. These arguments have become collectively known as *strategic trade policy*. According to its proponents, a nation can gain in some circumstances by assisting certain *strategic industries* that benefit society as a whole, but that may not thrive in an environment of free trade.

Strategic trade policy is most effective in situations where a market is dominated by a few large firms. With few firms, the forces of competition—which ordinarily reduce profits in an industry to very low levels—will not operate. Therefore, each firm in the industry may earn high profits. These profits benefit not only the owners of the firm, but also the nation more generally, since the government will be able to capture some of the profit with the corporate profits tax. When a government helps an industry compete internationally, it increases the likelihood that high profits—and the resulting general benefits—will be shifted from a foreign country to its own country. Thus, interfering with free trade—through quotas, tariffs, or even a direct subsidy to domestic firms—might actually benefit the country as a whole.

Infant industry argument The argument that a new industry in which a country has a comparative advantage might need protection from foreign competition in order to flourish.

An argument related to strategic trade policy is the **infant industry argument**. This argument begins with a simple observation: In order to enjoy the full benefits of trade, markets must allocate resources toward those goods in which a nation has

[2] The studies include Robert Z. Lawrence and Matthew J. Slaughter, "Trade and U.S. Wages: Giant Sucking Sound or Small Hiccup?" *Brookings Papers on Economic Activity: Microeconomics,* 2:1993, pp. 161–210; Jeffrey D. Sachs and Howard J. Shatz, "Trade and Jobs in U.S. Manufacturing," *Brookings Papers on Economic Activity,* 1:1994, pp. 1–84; and Gary Burtless, Robert Lawrence, Robert Litan, and Robert Shapiro, *Globaphobia: Confronting Fears About Free Trade* (1998), The Brookings Institution Press (Washington, DC).

a comparative advantage. This includes not only markets for resources such as labor and land, but also *financial markets,* where firms obtain funds for new products. But in some countries—especially developing countries—financial markets do not work very well. Poor legal systems or incomplete information about firms and products may prevent a new industry from obtaining financing, even though the country would have a comparative advantage in that industry once it was formed. In this case, protecting the infant industry from foreign competition may be warranted until the industry can stand on its own feet.

Strategic trade policy and support for infant industries are controversial. Opponents of these ideas stress three problems:

1. Once the principle of government assistance to an industry is accepted, special-interest groups of all kinds will lobby to get the assistance, whether it benefits the general public or not.
2. When one country provides assistance to an industry by keeping out foreign goods, other nations may respond in kind. If they respond with tariffs and quotas of their own, the result is a shrinking volume of world trade and falling living standards. If subsidies are used to support a strategic industry, and another country responds with its own subsidies, then both governments lose revenue, and neither gains the sought-after profits.
3. Strategic trade policy assumes that the government has the information to determine which industries, infant or otherwise, are truly strategic and which are not.

Still, the arguments related to strategic trade policy suggest that government protection or assistance *may* be warranted in some circumstances, even if putting this support into practice proves difficult. Moreover, the arguments help to remind us of the conditions under which free trade is most beneficial to a nation:

> *Production is most likely to reflect the principle of comparative advantage when firms can obtain funds for investment projects and when they can freely enter industries that are profitable. Thus, free trade, without government intervention, works best when markets are working well.*

This may explain, in part, why the United States, where markets function relatively well, has for decades been among the strongest supporters of the free trade ideal.

Protectionism in the United States

Americans can enjoy the benefits of importing many of the products listed in Table 7: olive oil from Spain, watches from Switzerland, tomatoes from Mexico, cars and VCRs from Japan. But on the other side of the ledger, U.S. consumers have suffered and U.S. producers have gained, from some persistent barriers to trade. Table 9 lists ten examples of American protectionism—through tariffs, quotas, or similar policies—that have continued for years.

As you can see, protection is costly. Quotas and tariffs on apparel and textiles, the most costly U.S. trade barrier, force American consumers to pay $33.6 billion more for clothes each year. And while protection saves an estimated 168,786

TABLE 9
Some Examples of
U.S. Protectionism[3]

Protected Industry	Annual Cost to Consumers	Number of Jobs Saved	Annual Cost per Job Saved
Apparel and Textiles	$33,629 million	168,786	$ 199,241
Maritime Services	$ 2,522 million	4,411	$ 571,668
Sugar	$ 1,868 million	2,261	$ 826,104
Dairy Products	$ 1,630 million	2,378	$ 685,323
Softwood Lumber	$ 632 million	605	$1,044,271
Women's Nonathletic Footwear	$ 518 million	3,702	$ 139,800
Glassware	$ 366 million	1,477	$ 247,889
Luggage	$ 290 million	226	$1,285,078
Peanuts	$ 74 million	397	$ 187,223

workers in this industry from having to make the painful adjustment of finding other work, it does so at an annual cost of $199,241 per worker. Both workers and consumers could be made better off if textile workers were paid any amount up to $199,241 *not* to work and consumers were allowed to buy inexpensive textiles from abroad.

In some cases, the cost per job saved is staggering. The table shows that trade barriers preventing Americans from buying inexpensive luggage save just a couple of hundred jobs, at a yearly cost of more than $1 million each. Trade barriers on sugar are almost as bad: While 2,261 jobs are saved, the annual cost per job is $826,104.

In addition to the dozens of industries in the United States permanently protected from foreign competition, dozens more each year are granted temporary protection when the U.S. government finds a foreign producer or industry guilty of *dumping*—selling their products in the United States at "unfairly" low prices that harm a U.S. industry. Most economists believe that these low prices are most often the result of comparative advantage, and that the United States as a whole would gain from importing the good. Vietnam, for example, has a clear comparative advantage in producing catfish. But based on a complaint by the Catfish Farmers of America, the U.S. government has imposed tariffs of 35 to 65 percent on Vietnamese catfish, starting in August 2003.

In the "Using the Theory" section that follows, we take a closer look at one of the longest-running examples of protectionism in the United States.

---

[3] *The Fruits of Free Trade*, Federal Reserve Bank of Dallas, Annual Report, 2002, Exhibit 11.

USING THE THEORY
The U.S. Sugar Quota[4]

The United States has protected U.S. sugar producers from foreign competition since the 1930s. Since the 1980s, the protection has been provided in the form of a price guarantee. Essentially, the government has promised U.S. sugar beet and sugar cane producers and processors that they can sell their sugar at a predetermined price—22 cents a pound—regardless of the world price of sugar. The promise is backed by a guarantee: If U.S. sugar prices fall *below* 22 cents, the government will buy the sugar at that price itself.

This may not sound like a high price for sugar. But in the rest of the world, people and businesses can buy sugar for a lot less. Over the last 20 years, the world price of sugar has averaged about 11 cents a pound, while Americans have continued to pay 22 cents. Even in 1985, when the world price of sugar plunged to just 4 cents a pound—a bonanza for sugar buyers around the word—American buyers were not invited to the party: The United States price remained at 22 cents.

Because the world price of sugar is so consistently below the U.S. price, the government cannot keep its promise to support sugar prices while simultaneously allowing free trade in sugar. With free trade, the price of sugar in the United States would plummet and the government would have to spend billions of dollars each year making good on its guarantee to buy the sugar itself. The government's solution is a sugar quota. More accurately, the government decides how much foreign sugar it will allow into the United States each year, free of any tariff; all sugar beyond the allowed amount is hit with a heavy tariff of about 16 cents a pound. Since the tariff is so high, no country exports sugar to the United States beyond the allowed amount. So, in effect, the United States has a sugar quota.

The *primary* effects of the sugar quota are on sugar producers and sugar consumers. As you've learned, an import quota raises the domestic price of sugar (the quota's purpose). Sugar producers benefit. Sugar consumers are hurt.

And the harm is substantial. Table 9 shows that American consumers pay almost $2 billion more each year for sugar and products containing sugar due to the sugar quota. But spread widely over the U.S. population, this amounts to less than $15 per person per year. This probably explains why you haven't bothered to lobby for free trade in sugar.

---

[4] Information in this section is based on: Mark A. Groombridge "America's Bittersweet Sugar Policy," *Trade Briefing Paper No. 13*, Cato Institute, December 4, 2001; John C. Beghin, Barbara El Osta, Jar Y. Cherlow, and Samarendu Mohanty, "The Cost of the U.S. Sugar Program Revisited," *Working Paper 01-WP-273*, March 2001, Center for Agricultural and Rural Development, Iowa State University; Lance Gay, "Soured on Sugar Prices, Candy Makers Leave the U.S." *Scripps Howard News Service*, June 18, 2003; "Closing the 'Stuffed Molasses' Loophole," *White Paper*, United States Sugar Corporation (*http://www.ussugar.com/pressroom/white_papers/stuffed_molasses.html*).

But the costs of the sugar quota go beyond ordinary consumers. Industrial sugar users—such as the ice cream industry—are affected by the higher price too, not all of which can be passed on to consumers. So they try to avoid the quota's harm in other ways. One way is to waste resources buying sugar abroad disguised as other products. In the late 1990s and early 2000s, U.S. firms bought about 125,000 tons of sugar each year mixed with molasses, which was not restricted by the sugar quota. The sugar was then reseparated from the molasses. Even with these additional (and wasteful) processing costs, it was still a better deal to buy the disguised sugar abroad than to buy it through regular channels in the United States.

And sometimes a firm decides it's just not worth it anymore. In June 2003, Lifesavers was added to the list of other candy and baked-goods manufacturers who simply gave up trying to buy sugar in the United States, and moved their production facilities to Canada. In Canada, which doesn't have a quota, sugar can be purchased at the lower, world price.

Taxpayers, too, pay a cost for the sugar quota, because as part of its price support program, the U.S. government must occasionally buy excess sugar from producers. In 2000, the U.S. government was storing about 793,000 tons of sugar at a cost of about $1.6 million per month. The government must also hire special agents to detect and prevent sugar from entering the country illegally.

But perhaps the most significant cost of the sugar quota is indicated by Figure 2 in this chapter. There we saw that a U.S. tariff or quota on Chinese suits raised their price in the United States, but lowered their price in China, the exporting country. The sugar quota has a similar effect: The price in the exporting "country" (in this case, the *rest of the world*) decreases. And since the United States is such a large potential importer of sugar, the quota—by keeping sugar out—causes greater quantities of sugar to be dumped onto the world market, depressing its price. This hurts the poorest countries in the world that rely on sugar as an important source of export revenue. The sugar quota's harm to these countries has been estimated at about $1.5 billion per year.

Why do we bear all of these costs? Because of lobbying by groups who enjoy highly concentrated benefits. There are about 13,000 sugar farms in the United States. When the $2 billion in additional spending by U.S. consumers is spread among this small number of farms, the additional revenue averages out to more than $150,000 per farm per year. Those benefits are sizable enough to mobilize sugar producers each time their protection is threatened.

But there is another group that receives concentrated benefits: producers of high-fructose corn syrup, the closest substitute for sugar. Because of the sugar quota, high-fructose corn syrup can be sold at a substantially higher price.

Not surprisingly, the largest producer of high-fructose corn syrup in the U.S. market—the Archer Daniels Midland (ADM) company—has funded organizations that lobby Congress and try to sway public opinion in the United States. Occasionally, you may see a full-page newspaper advertisement paid for by one of these groups, arguing that sugar in the United States is cheap. And it is . . . until you find out what the country next door is paying.

Summary

International specialization and trade enable people throughout the world to enjoy greater production and higher living standards than would otherwise be possible. The benefits of unrestrained international trade can be traced back to the idea of comparative advantage. Mutually beneficial trade is possible whenever one country can produce a good at a lower opportunity cost than its trading partner can. Whenever opportunity costs differ, countries can specialize according to their comparative advantage, trade with each other, and end up consuming more.

Despite the net benefits to each nation as a whole, some groups within each country lose, while others gain. When trade leads to increased exports, domestic producers gain and domestic consumers are harmed. When imports increase as a result of trade, domestic producers suffer and domestic consumers gain. The losers often encourage government to block or reduce trade through the use of tariffs (taxes on imported goods) and quotas (limits on the volume of imports).

A variety of arguments have been proposed in support of protectionism. Some are clearly invalid and fail to recognize the principle that both sides gain when countries trade according to their comparative advantage. More sophisticated arguments for restricting trade may have merit in certain circumstances. These include strategic trade policy—the notion that governments should assist certain strategic industries—and the idea of protecting "infant" industries when financial markets are imperfect.

Key Terms

Absolute advantage
Comparative advantage
Exchange rate
Exports

Imports
Infant industry argument
Protectionism
Quota

Tariff
Terms of trade

Review Questions

1. Describe the theory of comparative advantage.

2. What is the difference between absolute advantage and comparative advantage?

3. What are the terms of trade and why are they important?

4. What are the sources of comparative advantage?

5. What makes a country shift resources into its comparative advantage good?

6. Briefly describe the antidotes to the antitrade bias.

7. What is a tariff? What are its main economic effects? How does a quota differ from a tariff?

8. What arguments have been made in support of protectionism? Which of them may be valid, and under what circumstances?

9. List the ways in which a quota on imported coffee would harm the nation that imposes it

Problems and Exercises

1. Suppose that the costs of production of winter hats and wheat in two countries are as follows:

	United States	Russia
Per Winter Hat	$10	5,000 rubles
Per Bushel of Wheat	$1	2,500 rubles

a. What is the opportunity cost of producing one more winter hat in the United States? In Russia?

b. What is the opportunity cost of producing one more bushel of wheat in the United States? In Russia?

c. Which country has a comparative advantage in winter hats? In wheat?

d. Construct a table similar to Table 3 that illustrates how a change in production in each country would increase world production.

e. If the exchange rate were 1,000 rubles per dollar, would mutually beneficial trade occur? If yes, explain what mechanism would induce producers to export according to their country's comparative advantage. If no, explain why not, and explain in which direction the exchange rate would change. (*Hint:* Construct a table similar to Table 6.)

f. Answer the same questions for an exchange rate of 100 rubles per dollar.

2. The following table gives information about the supply and demand for beef in Paraguay and Uruguay. (You may wish to draw the supply and demand curves for each country to help you visualize what is happening.)

	Paraguay			Uruguay	
Price	Quantity Supplied	Quantity Demanded	Price	Quantity Supplied	Quantity Demanded
0	0	1,200	0	0	1,800
5	200	1,000	5	0	1,600
10	400	800	10	0	1,400
15	600	600	15	0	1,200
20	800	400	20	200	1,000
25	1,000	200	25	400	800
30	1,200	0	30	600	600
35	1,400	0	35	800	400
40	1,600	0	40	1,000	200
45	1,800	0	45	1,200	0

a. In the absence of trade, what is the equilibrium price and quantity in Paraguay? In Uruguay?

b. If the two countries begin to trade, what will happen to the price of beef? How many sides of beef will be purchased in Paraguay and how many in Uruguay at that price?

c. How many sides of beef will be produced in Paraguay and how many in Uruguay? Why is there a difference between quantity purchased and quantity produced in each country?

d. Who benefits and who loses from the opening of trade between these two countries?

3. Use the data on supply and demand given in Question 2 to answer the following questions:

a. Suppose that Uruguay imposed a tariff that raised the price of beef imported from Paraguay to $25 per side. What would happen to beef consumption in Uruguay? To beef production there? How much beef would be imported from Paraguay?

b. How would the tariff affect Paraguay? Specifically, what would happen to the price of beef there after Uruguay imposed its tariff? How would Paraguay's production and consumption be affected?

4. Use the data on supply and demand given in Question 2 to answer the following questions:

a. Suppose that Uruguay imposed a quota on the import of beef from Paraguay—only 200 sides of beef can be imported each year. What would happen to the price of beef in Uruguay? What would happen to beef consumption in Uruguay? To beef production there?

b. How would the quota affect Paraguay? Specifically, what would happen to the price of beef there after Uruguay imposed its quota? How would Paraguay's production and consumption be affected?

5. Refer to Table 4 in the chapter. Calculate the gains for each country when the terms of trade (suits per computer) are 2 to 1, instead of 3 to 1. This time, assume that China increases suit production by 25 suits and exports 20, while the U.S. decreases suit production by 20. Which country gains more under these terms of trade?

6. Refer to Table 4 in the chapter. Calculate the gains for each country when the terms of trade (suits per computer) are 4 to 1, instead of 3 to 1. This time, assume that China increases suit production by 15 suits and exports 12, while the United States increases computer production by 4 computers. Which country gains more under these terms of trade?

7. The following table shows the hypothetical labor requirements per ton of wool and per hand-knotted rug, for New Zealand and for India.

Labor Requirements per Unit

	New Zealand	India
Per Ton of Wool	10 hours	20 hours
Per Hand-Knotted Rug	70 hours	100 hours

a. Use this information to calculate the opportunity cost in each country for each of the two products. Which country has a comparative advantage in each product?

b. Use this information to construct a table similar to Table 3 in the text, showing the overall gain in production if each country produces one unit less of the product for which it does not have a comparative advantage.

c. If India produces one more rug and exports it to New Zealand, what is the lowest price (measured in tons of wool) that it would accept? What is the highest price that New Zealand would pay? Where will the equilibrium terms of trade lie?

8. In Table 6 of this chapter, it was assumed that the exchange rate was 8 yuan per dollar. Recalculate the entries in parentheses in the table assuming that the exchange rate is 6 yuan per dollar. Will trade still take place? Explain briefly.

Challenge Questions

1. Suppose that the Marshall Islands does not trade with the outside world. It has a competitive domestic market for VCRs. The market supply and demand curves are reflected in this table:

Price ($/VCR)	Quantity Demanded	Quantity Supplied
500	0	500
400	100	400
300	200	300
200	300	200
100	400	100
0	500	0

a. Plot the supply and demand curves and determine the domestic equilibrium price and quantity.

b. Suddenly, the islanders discover the virtues of free exchange and begin trading with the outside world. The Marshall Islands is a very small country, and so its trading has no effect on the price established in the world market. It can import as many VCRs as it wishes at the world price of $100 per VCR. In this situation, how many VCRs will be purchased in the Marshall Islands? How many will be produced there? How many will be imported?

c. After protests from domestic producers, the government decides to impose a tariff of $100 per imported VCR. Now how many VCRs will be purchased in the Marshall Islands? How many will be produced there? How many will be imported?

d. What is the government's revenue from the tariff described in part (c)?

e. Compare the effect of the tariff described in part (c) with a quota that limits imports to 100 VCRs per year.

2. a. Use the information in the following table to plot supply and demand curves and determine the domestic equilibrium price and quantity for these two countries.

	Country A			Country B	
Price per Unit of Good X (measured in dollars)	Quantity Demanded of Good X	Quantity Supplied of Good X	Price per Unit of Good X (measured in dollars)	Quantity Demanded of Good X	Quantity Supplied of Good X
$10	1	25	$10	5	13
9	2	22	9	6	10
8	3	19	8	7	7
7	4	16	7	8	4
6	5	13	6	9	2
5	6	10	5	10	½
4	7	7	4	11	¼
3	8	4	3	12	⅛

b. Show graphically what will happen if these two countries begin to trade. What will happen to the price of Good X in each country? What will happen to consumption in each country? What will happen to production in each country? Which country has the competitive advantage in the production of Good X? Which country will export Good X? How many units will it export?

 **Applications** | *These exercises require access to Lieberman/Hall Xtra! If Xtra! did not come with your book, visit http://liebermanxtra. swlearning.com to purchase.*

1. Use your Xtra! password at the Hall and Lieberman Web site (http://liebermanxtra.swlearning.com), select this chapter, and under Economic Applications, click on EconDebate. Choose *World Economy: International Trade,* and scroll down to find the debate, "Does the United States economy benefit from the WTO?" Read the debate.

   a. What is the role of the WTO?

   b. Is free trade, as envisioned by the WTO, inconsistent with national sovereignty? That is, will WTO regulations require that nations give up some authority over their own environment, workplace rules, etc, in the name of free trade? Does that really matter? Explain your answer carefully.

2. Use your Xtra! password at the Hall and Lieberman Web site (http://liebermanxtra.swlearning.com), select this chapter, and under Economic Applications, click on EconDebate. Choose *World Economy: International Trade,* and scroll down to find the debate, "Does the anti-sweatshop movement help or harm workers in low-wage countries?" Read the debate, and write a short essay explaining how the anti-sweatshop movement works in concert with, or in opposition to, the theory of comparative advantage.

Glossary

A

Absolute advantage The ability to produce a good or service, using fewer resources than other producers use.

Accounting profit Total revenue minus accounting costs.

Aggregate demand (*AD*) curve A curve indicating equilibrium GDP at each price level.

Aggregate supply (*AS*) curve A curve indicating the price level consistent with firms' unit costs and markups for any level of output over the short run.

Aggregation The process of combining different things into a single category.

Alternate goods Other goods that a firm could produce, using some of the same types of inputs as the good in question.

Automatic stabilizers Forces that reduce the size of the expenditure multiplier and diminish the impact of spending shocks.

Autonomous consumption The part of consumption spending that is independent of income; also, the vertical intercept of the consumption function.

Average fixed cost Total fixed cost divided by the quantity of output produced.

Average standard of living Total output (real GDP) per person.

Average total cost Total cost divided by the quantity of output produced.

Average variable cost Total variable cost divided by the quantity of output produced.

B

Basic Principles of Economics A small set of methods and conclusions that appear repeatedly in analyzing economic problems. They form the foundation of economic theory.

Behavioral economics A subfield of economics focusing on behavior that deviates from the standard assumptions of economic models.

Bond An IOU issued by a corporation or government agency when it borrows funds.

Boom A period of time during which real GDP is above potential GDP.

Budget constraint The different combinations of goods a consumer can afford with a limited budget, at given prices.

Budget deficit The amount by which the government's total outlays (on goods, services, and transfer payments) exceeds its total tax revenue.

Budget line The graphical representation of a budget constraint, showing the maximum affordable quantity of one good for given amounts of another good.

Business cycles Fluctuations in real GDP around its long-term growth trend.

Business demand for funds curve Indicates the level of investment spending by firms at each interest rate.

Business firm An organization, owned and operated by private individuals, that specializes in production.

C

Capital Something produced that is long-lasting and used to produce other goods.

Capital gains tax A tax on profits earned when a financial asset is sold for more than its acquisition price.

Capital per worker The total capital stock divided by total employment.

Capital stock The total amount of capital in a nation that is productively useful at a particular point in time.

Capitalism A type of economic system in which most resources are owned privately.

Cartel A group of firms that selects a common price that maximizes total industry profits.

Cash in the hands of the public Currency and coins held outside of banks.

Central bank A nation's principal monetary authority.

Change in demand A shift of a demand curve in response to a change in some variable other than price.

Change in quantity demanded A movement along a demand curve in response to a change in price.

Change in quantity supplied A movement along a supply curve in response to a change in price.

Change in supply A shift of a supply curve in response to some variable other than price.

Coase theorem When a side payment can be arranged without cost, the market will solve an externality problem—and create the efficient outcome—on its own.

Command or centrally planned economy An economic system in which resources are allocated according to explicit instructions from a central authority.

Communism A type of economic system in which most resources are owned in common.

Comparative advantage The ability to produce a good or service at a lower opportunity cost than other producers.

Compensating wage differential A difference in wages that makes two jobs equally attractive to a worker.

Complement A good that is used *together with* some other good.

Constant cost industry An industry in which the long-run supply curve is horizontal because each firm's *ATC* curve is unaffected by changes in industry output.

Constant returns to scale Long-run average total cost is unchanged as output increases.

Consumer Price Index An index of the cost, through time, of a fixed market basket of goods purchased by a typical household in some base period.

Consumption (C) The part of GDP purchased by households as final users.

Consumption function A positively sloped relationship between real consumption spending and real disposable income.

Consumption tax A tax on the part of their income that households spend.

Consumption-income line A line showing aggregate consumption spending at each level of income or GDP.

Copyright A grant of exclusive rights to sell a literary, musical, or artistic work.

Corporate profits tax A tax on the profits earned by corporations.

Corporation A firm owned and ultimately controlled by all those who buy shares of stock in the firm, who may receive part of the firm's profit as dividend payments.

Countercyclical fiscal policy Any change in government purchases or net taxes designed to counteract economic fluctuations.

Critical assumption Any assumption that affects the conclusions of a model in an important way.

Cyclical unemployment Joblessness arising from changes in production over the business cycle.

D

Decreasing cost industry An industry in which the long-run supply curve slopes downward because each firm's *ATC* curve shifts downward as industry output increases.

Deflation A *decrease* in the price level from one period to the next.

Demand curve facing the firm A curve that indicates, for different prices, the quantity of output that customers will purchase from a particular firm.

Demand deposit multiplier The number by which a change in reserves is multiplied to determine the resulting change in demand deposits.

Demand deposits Checking accounts that do not pay interest.

Demand schedule A list showing the quantities of a good that consumers would choose to purchase at different prices, with all other variables held constant.

Demand shock Any event that causes the *AD* curve to shift.

Depression An unusually severe recession.

Diminishing marginal returns to labor The marginal product of labor decreases as more labor is hired.

Discount rate The interest rate the Fed charges on loans to banks.

Discouraged workers Individuals who would like a job, but have given up searching for one.

Discrimination When a group of people have different opportunities because of personal characteristics that have nothing to do with their abilities.

Diseconomies of scale Long-run average total cost increases as output increases.

Disposable income The part of household income that remains after paying taxes.

Dominant Strategy A strategy that is best for a firm no matter what strategy its competitor chooses.

Duopoly An oligopoly market with only two sellers.

E

Economic growth The increase in our production of goods and services that occurs over long periods of time.

Economic profit Total revenue minus all costs of production, explicit and implicit.

Economic system A system of resource allocation and resource ownership.

Economics The study of choice under conditions of scarcity.

Economies of scale Long-run average total cost decreases as output increases.

Employment-popuation ratio (EPR) The fraction of the population that is working.

Entrepreneurship The ability and willingness to combine the *other* resources—labor, capital, and natural resources—into a productive enterprise.

Equilibrium GDP In the short run, the level of output at which output and aggregate expenditure are equal.

Equilibrium price The market price that, once achieved, remains constant until either the demand curve or supply curve shifts.

Equilibrium quantity The market quantity bought and sold per period that, once achieved, remains constant until either the demand curve or supply curve shifts.

Excess demand At a given price, the excess of quantity demanded over quantity supplied.

Excess demand for bonds The amount of bonds demanded exceeds the amount supplied at a particular interest rate.

Excess reserves Reserves in excess of required reserves.

Excess supply At a given price, the excess of quantity supplied over quantity demanded.

Excess supply of money The amount of money supplied exceeds the amount demanded at a particular interest rate.

Exchange The act of trading with others to obtain what we desire.

Exchange rate The amount of one currency that is traded for one unit of another currency.

Excludability The ability to exclude those who do not pay for a good from consuming it.

Exit A permanent cessation of production when a firm leaves an industry.

Expansion A period of increasing real GDP.

Expenditure approach Measuring GDP by adding the value of goods and services purchased by each type of final user.

Expenditure multiplier The amount by which equilibrium real GDP changes as a result of a one-dollar change in autonomous consumption, investment spending, government purchases, or net exports.

Explicit collusion Cooperation involving direct communication between competing firms about setting prices.

Explicit cost The dollars sacrificed—and actually paid out—for a choice.

Exports Goods and services produced domestically, but sold abroad.

Externality A by-product of a good or activity that affects someone not immediately involved in the transaction.

F

Factor payments Payments to the owners of resources that are used in production

Factor payments approach Measuring GDP by summing the factor payments earned by all households in the economy.

Federal funds rate The interest rate charged for loans of reserves among banks.

Federal Open Market Committee A committee of Federal Reserve officials that establishes U.S. monetary policy.

Federal Reserve System The central bank and national monetary authority of the United States.

Fiat money Anything that serves as a means of payment by government declaration.

Final good A good sold to its final user.

Financial intermediary A business firm that specializes in brokering between savers and borrowers.

Firm's quantity supplied The specific amount a firm would choose to sell over some time period, given (1) a particular price for the good; (2) all other constraints on the firm.

Firm's supply curve A curve that shows the quantity of output a competitive firm will produce at different prices.

Fixed costs Costs of fixed inputs.

Fixed input An input whose quantity must remain constant, regardless of how much output is produced.

Flow variable a variable measuring a *process* over some period of time.

Free rider problem When the efficient outcome requires a side payment but individual gainers will not contribute.

Frictional unemployment Joblessness experienced by people who are between jobs or who are just entering or reentering the labor market.

Full employment A situation in which there is no cyclical unemployment.

G

Game theory An approach to modeling the strategic interaction of oligopolists in terms of moves and countermoves.

GDP price index An index of the price level for all final goods and services included in GDP.

Government demand for funds curve Indicates the amount of governmental borrowing at each interest rate.

Government franchise A government-granted right to be the sole seller of a product or service.

Government purchases (G) Spending by federal, state, and local governments on goods and services.

Gross domestic product (GDP) The total value of all final goods and services produced for the marketplace during a given year, within the nation's borders.

H

Household's quantity demanded The specific amount a household would choose to buy over some time period, given (1) a particular price, (2) all other constraints on the household.

Human capital The skills and training of the labor force.

I

Imperfect Competition A market structure with more than one firm, but in which one or more of the requirements of perfect competition are violated.

Imperfectly competitive market A market in which a single buyer or seller has the power to influence the price of the product.

Implicit cost The value of something sacrificed when no direct payment is made.

Imports Goods and services produced abroad, but consumed domestically.

Income The amount that a person or firm earns over a particular period.

Income effect As the price of a good decreases, the consumer's purchasing power increases, causing a change in quantity demanded for the good.

Increasing cost industry An industry in which the long-run supply curve slopes upward because each firm's ATC curve shifts upward as industry output increases.

Increasing marginal returns to labor The marginal product of labor increases as more labor is hired.

Index A series of numbers used to track a variable's rise or fall over time.

Indexation Adjusting the value of some nominal payment in proportion to a price index, in order to keep the real payment unchanged.

Individual demand curve A curve showing the quantity of a good or service demanded by a particular individual at each different price.

Infant industry argument The argument that a new industry in which a country has a comparative advantage might need protection from foreign competition in order to flourish.

Inferior good A good that people demand less of as their income rises.

Inflation rate The percent change in the price level from one period to the next.

Input Anything (including a resource) used to produce a good or service.

Intermediate goods Goods used up in producing final goods.

Investment tax credit A reduction in taxes for firms that invest in new capital.

Involuntary part-time workers Individuals who would like a full-time job, but who are working only part time.

L

Labor The time human beings spend producing goods and services.

Labor force Those people who have a job or who are looking for one.

Labor productivity The output produced by the average worker in an hour.

Land The physical space on which production takes place, as well as the naturally occurring materials that come with it.

Law of demand As the price of a good increases, the quantity demanded decreases.

Law of diminishing marginal returns As more and more of any input is added to a fixed amount of other inputs, its marginal product will eventually decline.

Law of diminishing marginal utility As consumption of a good or service increases, marginal utility decreases.

Law of increasing opportunity cost The more of something that is produced, the greater the opportunity cost of producing one more unit.

Law of supply As the price of a good increases, the quantity supplied increases.

Loanable funds market The market in which business firms obtain funds for investment.

Long run A time horizon long enough for a firm to vary all of its inputs.

Long-run aggregate supply curve A vertical line indicating all possible output and price-level combinations at which the economy could end up in the long run.

Long-run average total cost The cost per unit of producing each quantity of output in the long run, when all inputs are variable.

Long-run supply curve A curve indicating the quantity of output that all sellers in a market will produce at different prices, after all long-run adjustments have taken place.

Long-run total cost The cost of producing each quantity of output when all inputs are variable and the least-cost input mix is chosen.

Loss The difference between total cost (TC) and total revenue (TR), when $TC > TR$.

Lumpy input An input whose quantity cannot be increased gradually as output increases, but must instead be adjusted in large jumps.

M

Macroeconomics The study of the behavior of the overall economy.

Marginal approach to profit A firm maximizes its profit by taking any action that adds more to its revenue than to its cost.

Marginal cost The increase in total cost from producing one more unit of output.

Marginal product of labor The additional output produced when one more worker is hired.

Marginal propensity to consume The amount by which consumption spending rises when disposable income rises by one dollar.

Marginal revenue The change in total revenue from producing one more unit of output.

Marginal social benefit (MSB) The full benefit of producing another unit of a good, including the benefit to the consumer and any benefits enjoyed by third parties.

Marginal social cost (MSC) The full cost of producing another unit of a good, including the marginal cost to the producer *and* any harm caused to third parties.

Marginal utility The change in total utility an individual obtains from consuming an additional unit of a good or service.

Market A group of buyers and sellers with the potential to trade with each other.

Market demand curve The graphical depiction of a demand schedule; a curve showing the quantity of a good or service demanded at various prices, with all other variables held constant.

Market economy An economic system in which resources are allocated through individual decision making.

Market failure A market that fails to take advantage of every Pareto improvement.

Market quantity demanded The specific amount of a good that *all* buyers in the market would choose to buy over some time period, given (1) a particular price, (2) all other constraints they face.

Market quantity supplied The specific amount of a good that *all* sellers in the market would choose to sell over some time period, given (1) a particular price for the good; (2) all other constraints on firms.

Market signals Price changes that cause changes in production to match changes in consumer demand.

Market structure The characteristics of a market that influence how trading takes place.

Market supply curve A curve indicating the quantity of output that all sellers in a market will produce at different prices.

Means of payment Anything acceptable as payment for goods and services.

Microeconomics The study of the behavior of individual households, firms, and governments; the choices they make; and their interaction in specific markets.

Minimum efficient scale The lowest output level at which the firm's *LRATC* curve hits bottom.

Model An abstract representation of reality.

Monetary policy Control or manipulation of the money supply by the Federal Reserve designed to achieve a macroeconomic goal.

Money demand curve A curve indicating how much money will be willingly held at each interest rate.

Money supply curve A line showing the total quantity of money in the economy at each interest rate.

Monopolistic Competition A market structure in which there are many firms selling products that are differentiated, yet are still close substitutes, and in which there is free entry and exit.

Monopoly firm The only seller of a good or service that has no close substitutes.

Monopoly market The market in which a monopoly firm operates.

N

National debt The total value of government debt outstanding as a result of financing earlier budget deficits.

Natural monopoly A market in which a single firm's production is characterized by economies of scale, even when its output expands to serve the entire market.

Natural oligopoly A market that tends naturally toward oligopoly because the minimum efficient scale of the typical firm is a large fraction of the market.

Net exports (*NX*) Total exports minus total imports.

Net investment Investment minus depreciation.

Net taxes The taxes the government collects minus the transfer payments the government pays out.

Network externalities A situation in which the value of a good or service to each user increases as more people use it.

Nominal interest rate The annual percent increase in a lender's dollars from making a loan.

Nominal variable A variable measured without adjustment for the dollar's changing value.

Nonmarket production Goods and services that are produced but not sold in a market.

Nonmonetary job characteristic Any aspect of a job—other than the wage—that matters to a potential or current employee.

Nonprice competition Any action a firm takes to increase the demand for its product, other than cutting its price.

Normal good A good that people demand more of as their income rises.

Normal profit Another name for zero economic profit.

Normative economics The study of what *should be*; it is used to make value judgments, identify problems, and prescribe solutions.

O

Oligopoly A market structure in which a small number of firms are strategically interdependent.

Open market operations Purchases or sales of bonds by the Federal Reserve System.

Opportunity cost is given up when taking an action or making a choice.

P

Pareto improvement An action that makes at least one person better off, and harms no one.

Partnership A firm owned by two or more people, who receive all of the firm's profit as household income.

Patent A temporary grant of monopoly rights over a new product or scientific discovery.

Patent protection A government grant of exclusive rights to use or sell a new technology.

Payoff Matrix A table showing the payoffs to each of two firms for each pair of strategies they choose.

Perfect competition A market structure in which there are many buyers and sellers, the product is standardized, and sellers can easily enter or exit the market.

Perfect price discrimination Charging each customer the most he or she would be willing to pay for each unit purchased.

Perfectly competitive labor market Market with many indistinguishable sellers of labor and many buyers, and with easy entry and exit of workers.

Perfectly competitive market A market in which no buyer or seller has the power to influence the price.

Physical capital The part of the capital stock consisting of physical goods, such as machinery, equipment, and factories.

Planned investment spending (I^P) Business purchases of plant and equipment and construction of new homes; also called just *investment spending*.

Positive economics The study of how the economy works.

Potential output The level of output the economy could produce if operating at full employment.

Price The amount of money that must be paid to a seller to obtain a good or service.

Price discrimination Charging different prices to different customers for reasons other than differences in cost.

Price leadership A form of tacit collusion in which one firm sets a price that other firms copy.

Price level The average level of prices in the economy.

Price taker Any firm that treats the price of its product as given and beyond its control.

Principle of Opportunity Cost All economic decisions made by individuals or society are costly. The correct way to measure the cost of a choice is its opportunity cost—that which is given up to make the choice.

Private investment (*I*) The sum of business plant, equipment, and software purchases, new-home construction, and inventory changes; often referred to as just *investment*.

Production function A function that indicates the maximum amount of output a firm can produce over some period of time from each combination of inputs.

Production possibilities frontier (PPF) A curve showing all combinations of two goods that can be produced with the resources and technology currently available.

Productive inefficiency A situation in which more of at least one good can be produced without sacrificing the production of any other good.

Profit Total revenue minus total cost.

Protectionism The belief that a nation's industries should be protected from foreign competition.

Pure private good A good that is both rivalrous and excludable.

Pure public good A good that is both nonrivalrous and nonexcludable.

Q

Quota A limit on the physical volume of imports.

R

Rational preferences Preferences that satisfy two conditions: (1) Any two alternatives can be compared, and one is preferred or else the two are valued equally, and (2) the comparisons are logically consistent or transitive.

Real interest rate The annual percent increase in a lender's purchasing power from making a loan.

Real variable A variable adjusted for changes in the dollar's value.

Recession A period of significant decline in real GDP.

Relative price The price of one good relative to the price of another.

Rent-seeking activity Any costly action a firm undertakes to establish or maintain its monopoly status.

Repeated play A situation in which strategically interdependent

Required reserve ratio The minimum fraction of checking account balances that banks must hold as reserves.

Required reserves The minimum amount of reserves a bank must hold, depending upon the amount of its deposit liabilities.

Reserves Vault cash plus balances held at the Fed.

Resource allocation A method of determining which goods and services will be produced, how they will be produced, and who will get them.

Resource Markets Markets in which households sell resources—land, labor, and natural resources—to firms.

Resources The labor, capital, land and natural resources, and entrepreneurship that are used to produce goods and services.

Rivalry A situation in which one person's consumption of a good or service means that no one else can consume it.

S

Scarcity A situation in which the amount of something available is insufficient to satisfy the desire for it.

Seasonal unemployment Joblessness related to changes in weather, tourist patterns, or other seasonal factors.

Self-correcting mechanism The adjustment process through which price and wage changes return the economy to full-employment output in the long run.

Short run A time horizon during which at least one of the firm's inputs cannot be varied.

Short-run macroeconomic equilibrium A combination of price level and GDP consistent with both the AD and AS curves.

Shutdown price The price at which a firm is indifferent between producing and shutting down.

Shutdown rule In the short run, the firm should continue to produce if total revenue exceeds total variable costs; otherwise, it should shut down.

Simplifying assumption Any assumption that makes a model simpler without affecting any of its important conclusions.

Single-price monopoly A monopoly firm that is limited to charging the same price for each unit of output sold.

Socialism A type of economic system in which most resources are owned by the state.

Sole proprietorship A firm owned by a single individual, who receives all of the firm's profit as household income.

Specialization A method of production in which each person concentrates on a limited number of activities.

Spending multiplier The amount by which equilibrium real GDP changes as a result of a one-dollar change in autonomous consumption, investment, government purchases, or net exports.

Spending shock A change in spending that ultimately affects the entire economy.

Stagflation The combination of falling output and rising prices.

Statistical discrimination When individuals are excluded from an activity based on the statistical probability of behavior in their group, rather than their personal characteristics.

Stock variable a variable measuring a quantity at a moment in time.

Structural unemployment Joblessness arising from mismatches between workers' skills and employers' requirements or between workers' locations and employers' locations.

Substitute A good that can be used in place of some other good and that fulfills more or less the same purpose.

Substitution effect As the price of a good falls, the consumer substitutes that good in place of other goods whose prices have not changed.

Sunk cost A cost that has been paid or must be paid, regardless of any future action being considered.

Supply curve A graphical depiction of a supply schedule; a curve showing the quantity of a good or service supplied at various prices, with all other variables held constant.

Supply of funds curve Indicates the level of household saving at each interest rate.

Supply schedule A list showing the quantities of a good or service that firms would choose to produce and sell at different prices, with all other variables held constant.

Supply shock Any event that causes the AS curve to shift.

T

Tacit collusion Any form of oligopolistic cooperation that does not involve an explicit agreement.

Tariff A tax on imports.

Technological change The invention or discovery of new inputs, new outputs, or new production methods.

Technology A method by which inputs are combined to produce a good or service.

Terms of trade The ratio at which a country can trade domestically produced products for foreign-produced products.

Tit-for-tat A game-theoretic strategy of doing to another player this period what he has done to you in the previous period.

Tort A wrongful act that harms someone.

Total cost The costs of all inputs—fixed and variable.

Total demand for funds curve Indicates the total amount of borrowing at each interest rate.

Total fixed cost The cost of all inputs that are fixed in the short run.

Total product The maximum quantity of output that can be produced from a given combination of inputs.

Total revenue The total inflow of receipts from selling a given amount of output.

Total spending The sum of spending by households, businesses, the government, and the foreign sector on American final goods and services, or $C + IP + G + NX$.

Total variable cost The cost of all variable inputs used in producing a particular level of output.

Tradable Permit A license that allows a company to release a unit of pollution into the environment over some period of time.

Traditional economy An economy in which resources are allocated according to long-lived practices from the past.

Tragedy of the commons The problem of overuse when a good is rival but nonexcludable.

Transfer payment Any payment that is not compensation for supplying goods or services.

Trough The bottom point of a recession, when a contraction ends and an expansion begins.

U

Unemployment rate The fraction of the labor force that is without a job.

Unit of value A common unit for measuring how much something is worth.

Utility A quantitative measure of pleasure or satisfaction obtained from consuming goods and services.

V

Value added The revenue a firm receives minus the cost of the intermediate goods it buys.

Value-added approach Measuring GDP by summing the value added by all firms in the economy.

Variable costs Costs of variable inputs.

Variable input An input whose usage can change as the level of output changes.

W

Wealth constraint At any point in time, wealth is fixed.

Wealth The total value of everything a person or firm owns, at a point in time, minus the total value of everything owed.

Index